CIPM® PROGRAM LEVEL II VOLUME 2

CFA Institute

2024

ISBN 978-1-953337-89-4

September 2023

CONTENTS

◘ indicates an optional segment

◘ indicates an optional segment

How to Use the CIPM Program Curriculum

Welcome to the Level II of the Certificate in Investment Performance Measurement (CIPM®) Program. This exciting and rewarding program of study reflects your desire to become a serious portfolio evaluation professional. You are pursuing a program noted for its high ethical standards and the depth of knowledge, skills, and abilities it develops. Your commitment to the CIPM Program should be educationally and professionally rewarding. CIPM certificants are dedicated to life-long learning and maintaining currency with the ever-changing dynamics of a challenging profession. The CIPM Program represents the first step towards a career-long commitment to professional education.

To begin your study:

1 Schedule your examination.

2 Access the CIPM Learning Ecosystem and access your study materials.

EXAM SCHEDULING

Examinations are provided online by our testing partner, Pearson VUE. We suggest you schedule your exam appointment with them as soon as possible, because appointments are first-come, first-served. With 24 hours notice, Pearson VUE allows you to reschedule your exam to another available time and place within the same exam window. Rescheduling your exam appointment must be completed within the exam scheduling window. When you schedule or reschedule your exam appointment with Pearson VUE, you will receive an e-mail confirmation. Contact Pearson VUE www.pearsonvue.com/contact/ if you do not receive a confirmation of your appointment.

CIPM LEARNING ECOSYSTEM

The Learning Ecosystem is a customized learning program that makes studying for the CIPM Exam enjoyable, efficient, and effective. The Learning Ecosystem is an online portal that adapts to your needs, strengths, and weaknesses, serving you the right material at the right time and focusing on the areas you need to focus on the most. It helps you stay focused, engaged, and on track while you study.

TIP

Everything you need is in one place. We provide an eBook version of the curriculum for your convenience should that be your preferred method of study. The Learning Ecosystem contains the exact same content. There is no need to do both. If you elect to use the eBook, you may still log into the Learning Ecosystem to take advantage of study tools, such as flashcards, practice tests, and the mock exam.

FEATURES OVERVIEW

The Learning Ecosystem is web-based and accessible through all common browsers.

- The Learning Ecosystem is designed to work well on whatever device is convenient at the moment, whether your desktop, tablet, or smartphone.
- Your progress through the course is automatically recorded so you can seamlessly switch between devices.

TIP

If you are accessing the Learning Ecosystem on a mobile device, it is possible to preload some content for times when you will not have continuous internet access. While you still have Internet access, log in to the Learning Ecosystem and launch your next study activity. This content will remain available when internet access is cut off, for example if you are on mass transit.

Home: Dashboard

Here you will find a summary of your progress through the material and a summary of your strengths and weaknesses with the content.

Study Plans

There are two kinds of study plans from which to choose: structured and adaptive.

- The structured plan will help you keep track of the time remaining before your exam and will suggest the number of activities to complete each day to stay on track. The structured plan will take you through the content in the same order as it appears in the eBook.
- The adaptive plan will begin with a short pre-test to establish a baseline for your existing knowledge. From that point forward, the system will track and adapt to your strengths and weaknesses with the content each time you interact with it. For example, it may adjust your pace through the material to spend less time on content where you are strong and more time on content where you comparatively weaker.

TIP

You are not stuck with your choice of study plan. You can switch back and forth between the structured and adaptive plans. When you switch from one study plan to the other your progress is not lost, and you do not need to start again at the beginning.

TIP

Whichever study plan you choose, studying consistently is the key to success.

Study Tasks

Whichever study plan you are using, the Learning Ecosystem will always let you know which study task is next. Study tasks can include reading a lesson, completing practice questions, completing chapter review questions, reviewing flashcards, or taking a mock exam.

- Lessons are composed of the same content found in the eBook.
- Practiced questions help you review and make sure you understood what you have learned.
- Flashcards test your understanding and recall of important terms and definitions.
- The mock exam is of similar length and weight as the live examination and can help gauge your overall readiness for the live exam.

TIP

As you work through lessons, practice problems, and flashcards, the Learning Ecosystem will frequently ask you to assess your confidence in knowing the material being covered. This information is tracked and presented to you in your Learning History. In the case of the adaptive plan, this information may supplement the system's understanding of your relative strengths and weaknesses.

TIP

If you are studying primarily from the eBook, you can still access the study tools in the Learning Ecosystem without working through a study plan. All of the study tools are accessible directly through the tabs within the menu bar on the left side of the Learning Ecosystem screen.

Other Study Resources

The Learning Ecosystem provides resources that supplement your study tasks.

- The Game Center makes reviewing your flashcards more enjoyable by presenting them within the context of a game in which you may compete with fellow candidates.
- Discussion boards are a place where you can confer with fellow candidates when you need a little extra help or a motivational nudge.

TIP

Discussion boards are **not** actively monitored or moderated by CFA Institute; please use them with that caution in mind. Our vendor monitors the boards for vulgarity and inflammatory language; to speak with a CFA Institute representative please contact us at info@cfainstitute.org.

> **TIP**
>
> For technical support assistance or to give us feedback on the Learning Ecosystem or course of study, you may also use the messaging feature.

- The Learning History tab reports trends in your performance over time with tracking on how you have done on practice tests and the mock exam. Additionally, the learning history summarizes your confidence in the topics within the program.

CURRICULUM DEVELOPMENT

The CIPM Program curriculum is grounded in the practice of the portfolio evaluation profession. CFA Institute performs a continuous practice analysis with investment professionals around the world to determine the knowledge, skills, and abilities that are relevant to the profession. Regional expert panels and targeted surveys are conducted to verify and reinforce the insights from practice analysis. The practice analysis process ultimately defines the CIPM Candidate Body of Knowledge (CBOK™).

The examinations are written by practicing certificants and are designed to allow you to demonstrate your mastery of the CBOK as set forth in the CIPM Program curriculum. As you structure your personal study program, you should emphasize mastery of the CBOK and the practical application of that knowledge. For more information on the practice analysis, CBOK, and development of the CIPM Program curriculum, please visit www.cfainstitute.org/programs/cipm/courseofstudy/Pages/index.aspx.

ORGANIZATION OF THE CURRICULUM

The reading assignments are the basis for all examination questions, and are selected or developed specifically to teach the CBOK. These readings are drawn from CIPM Program-commissioned content, textbook chapters, and professional journal articles. Learning outcome statements are listed with each lesson. These LOS indicate what you should be able to accomplish after studying the lesson. We encourage you to review how to properly use LOS, and the descriptions of commonly used LOS "command words," at http://www.cfainstitute.org/programs/cipm/courseofstudy/Pages/cipm_learning_outcome_statements.aspx. The command words signal the depth of learning you are expected to achieve from the reading. You should use the LOS to guide and focus your study, as each examination question is based on an assigned lesson and one or more LOS. However, the lessons provide context for the LOS and enable you to apply a principle or concept in a variety of scenarios. *Candidates are responsible for the entirety of all required material in the curriculum.*

CANDIDATE RESOURCES

CFA Institute provides a web page that contains numerous resources to help in your successful completion of the CIPM Program. On this page you will find links to testing policies (calculator policy, ID policy, and others); exam details and logistics; testing accommodations; curriculum errata; and a detailed glossary of terms. You should visit this site often to obtain current information: www.cfainstitute.org/programs/cipm/Pages/index.aspx.

FEEDBACK

At CFA Institute, we are committed to delivering a comprehensive and rigorous curriculum for the development of competent, ethically grounded investment professionals. We rely on candidate and member feedback as we work to incorporate content, design, and packaging improvements. You can be assured that we will continue to listen to your suggestions. Please send any comments or feedback—or perceived errors—to info@cfainstitute.org. Ongoing improvements in the curriculum will help you prepare for success on the upcoming examinations, and for a lifetime of learning as a serious investment professional.

Performance Evaluation

Measurement, Attribution, and Appraisal

STUDY SESSIONS

Study Session 2	Performance Measurement
Study Session 3	Performance Attribution
Study Session 4	Performance Appraisal
Study Session 5	Manager Selection

TOPIC LEVEL LEARNING OUTCOME

The candidate should be able to explain and apply methodologies for calculating returns of portfolios that contain futures and options and returns of multicurrency portfolios; explain the factors that enter benchmark selection decisions; calculate and evaluate commonly used performance appraisal risk measures; conduct performance attribution analyses of equity and fixed-income portfolios and interpret the results; and explain performance appraisal and manager selection processes.

PERFORMANCE EVALUATION

STUDY SESSION 4

Performance Appraisal

Recognizing that distinguishing between skill and luck is problematic, performance appraisal and manager selection address questions such as how to measure investment skill and whether a fund sponsor should hire, retain, or fire an investment manager.

The first reading presents various performance appraisal approaches and techniques that will help the evaluator materially improve the assessment of investment performance and presents a mini case to reinforce many of the reading's core ideas.

The second reading presents an approach to equity style analysis; equity style is often a major consideration in active equity manager selection.

READING ASSIGNMENTS

8 Topics in Performance Appraisal
by Mark M. Carhart, PhD, CFA, and Russ Wermers, PhD

9 Equity Style Analysis: Beyond Performance Measurement
by George Degroot, CFA, and Paul Greenwood, CFA

READING

8

Topics in Performance Appraisal

by Mark M. Carhart, PhD, CFA, and Russ Wermers, PhD

Mark M. Carhart, PhD, CFA, is at Kepos Capital LP (USA). Russ Wermers, PhD, is at the University of Maryland (USA).

LEARNING OUTCOMES

Mastery	The candidate should be able to
☐	a. Describe considerations in distinguishing investment skill from luck in an investment record;
☐	b. analyze mistakes in performance appraisal;
☐	c. demonstrate the use of quality control charts in performance appraisal;
☐	d. evaluate how benchmark and factor selection affect performance appraisal and the consequences of selecting an incorrect benchmark;
☐	e. evaluate how cash holdings can affect performance appraisal;
☐	f. describe limitations of relying on historical performance data in performance appraisal;
☐	g. describe characteristics of superior active managers;
☐	h. justify the selection of one or more appraisal measures;
☐	i. describe techniques for evaluating strategies with non-linear returns;
☐	j. analyze the skill of an active manager.

INTRODUCTION

1

Professional performance evaluators face many challenges in fairly assessing past performance. Foremost among these is the amount of "noise" (randomness) in investment returns. Although this issue cannot be eliminated, various performance appraisal approaches and techniques will help the evaluator materially improve the assessment of investment performance.

This module begins by exploring methods for distinguishing investment skill from luck. We then consider various limitations and mistakes in performance appraisal, with the aim of giving the evaluator the knowledge to apply performance appraisal techniques in many different investment contexts. We will explore some of these mistakes and limitations in more detail. We also examine the challenges of dealing with historical data, as well as how to select among multiple performance appraisal measures. Approaches for dealing with non-linear return distributions, such as those often present with option-like securities and tactical asset allocation strategies, are then addressed before the module concludes with a mini case to reinforce many of the reading's core ideas.

2 DISTINGUISHING LUCK FROM SKILL

Randomness (luck, either good or bad) is a part of life, and it plays a very large role in investment management. Therefore, in assessing an investment manager, it is important to separate the relative effects of luck and skill in order to identify superior managers and to properly incentivize and reward portfolio managers.

Because we observe only the joint combination of skill and luck, perfect measurement of true skill is unattainable. Instead, we must look at the statistical evidence in a given period and assess the *probability* that any outperformance resulted from skill. We will show how to apply statistical approaches to better measure skill.

Consider a categorization of managers according to their skill:

1 "Negative alpha" (unskilled) managers—investment managers whose skill in selecting investments is insufficient to overcome fees and trading costs.

   Example: On a risk-adjusted basis, a manager outperforms her benchmark by 2% per year over a five-year period before any costs. But the manager's expense ratio is 1.5% per year, and trading costs are 1% per year. Her 0.5% per year underperformance, if relatively consistent through the five-year period, is evidence that the manager lacks sufficient skill to overcome costs.

2 "Zero-alpha" managers—investment managers with skills sufficient only to offset fees and trading costs.

   Example: An active US stock manager matches the risk-adjusted returns of his benchmark, net of fees and trading costs, over a 10-year period. This manager can be considered a zero-alpha manager: He has skills sufficient to compensate for the higher costs of active management.

3 "Positive alpha" or skilled managers—investment managers with skills sufficient to beat fees and trading costs.

   Example: An active US bond fund manager generates risk-adjusted returns, net of fees and trading costs, that exceed her benchmark over a five-year period. This manager can be considered a skilled manager.

A literal implication of these definitions is that a manager who lowers fees increases his "skill" and vice versa. In general, we prefer to undertake statistical analysis of the net alpha of a given investment account. Asset owners with sufficient scale, however, often can negotiate more-favorable fees, and a gross-of-fee analysis may also be useful—and provide insights as to the level of fees one might be willing to pay.

Because our estimates of skill will be based on a subset (or sample) of the manager's entire return stream, past and future, we should consider each of these three labels as being probabilistic (it is *likely* that the manager has no skill), not deterministic (a definitive conclusion that the manager has no skill). The labels are merely our perception of the manager's true skills, given the data available. Our inference about a manager's skill can (and should) change if further evidence arrives (e.g., more return data on the manager) that differs substantially from the original evidence.

2.1 Determining the Probability That Observed Skill Is True Skill

Distinguishing luck from skill is both the most important and the most difficult task in evaluating and selecting investment managers. Managing a portfolio of stocks, for example, exposes the manager to total stock market risk, industry risk, style risk, idiosyncratic risks of firms, and liquidity risk. The variability of a portfolio's return can be quite high from any combination of these sources of risk.

2.1.1 *Statistical methods of determining the probability a manager is skilled.*

Various statistical measures can be applied to determine the probability that a manager is skilled. A commonly used measure is the t-statistic. In performance appraisal, the analyst derives an estimate of the manager's alpha by running a regression of the manager's returns minus the risk-free rate against the chosen benchmark returns minus the risk-free rate. The estimated intercept in this regression is the estimated alpha. The t-statistic—the ratio of the estimated intercept to its standard error—is used to check the statistical significance of an estimated regression coefficient (the manager's estimated alpha).

It is important to remember that, when evaluating a manager's returns, we are looking at only a subset of her entire track record—*a sample.* The statistical methods we use when evaluating the manager's track record will be *sample* statistics, not *population* statistics. Assuming that the underlying population from which we draw a sample is at least approximately normally distributed, the mean of the sample divided by the standard deviation of the mean of the sample (the standard error) is t-distributed, and we can use readily available statistical tables to assess the probability that the sample mean represents the population mean. (The issue of non-normal return distributions is discussed later in the reading.)

We begin with the null hypothesis that the manager is not skilled, in which case we would find that the manager has a low t-statistic. How do we assess the reliability of this estimate? If the sample is drawn from a normally distributed population, we use the P-value of the t-statistic, available from any widely used statistics software. The P-value is the probability of observing the t-statistic by random chance if the null hypothesis is true. A high P-value indicates a high probability that the null hypothesis is true (i.e., the manager's alpha is zero) and that the manager is unskilled. We typically reject the null hypothesis when the P-value is low. The cutoffs most often used to determine if the P-value is low are 0.10, 0.05, or 0.01 (10%, 5%, or 1%).

An equivalent method of deciding whether to reject the null hypothesis is to compare the calculated t-statistic mentioned earlier with a t-value from a table. This t-value is usually referred to as the critical t-value.[1] The greater the difference between the calculated t-statistic and the critical t-value, the more likely we would be to reject the null hypothesis. In addition to testing a manager's mean return, the t-statistic and P-value can be applied to tests of risk-adjusted performance ratios (e.g., Sharpe ratio) and regression coefficients (i.e., slope coefficients). We will illustrate this application later.

Generally, we consider two-tailed tests of the null hypothesis, which means that a calculated t-statistic that is either unusually high or unusually low will result in a rejection of the null hypothesis. With a very large sample of returns, we would reject the null hypothesis that the manager has no skill if the calculated t-statistic is greater than +1.96 or less than −1.96. The 1.96 critical value corresponds to 2.5% probability in each tail of the distribution. For example, a t-statistic greater than 1.96 implies that

1 Each critical t-value corresponds to a particular desired P-value.

there is less than a 2.5% chance a manager's true alpha is zero. Given this evidence, we would likely conclude that the manager is skilled. The critical value varies slightly with the degrees of freedom, but as a rule of thumb we often use a critical t-value of 2.[2]

To illustrate, suppose that an investment manager generates an alpha of 0.1% per month over a 24-month period. If the sample standard deviation of the manager's returns is 0.32% per month, is this manager skilled?

The t-statistic for the alpha is computed by dividing the alpha by the standard error. (The standard error is the sample standard deviation, s, divided by the square root of the number of observations, n):

$$t = \frac{\alpha}{s/\sqrt{n}} = \frac{0.001}{0.0032/\sqrt{24}} = 1.53 \quad (1)$$

Because 1.53 is less than the critical t-value rule of thumb of 2, we would conclude that this manager likely has no skill.

Suppose, alternatively, that this mean alpha of 0.1% a month, with a standard deviation of 0.32% a month, is observed over a 48-month period. Then, the t-statistic equals

$$t = \frac{0.001}{0.0032/\sqrt{48}} = 2.17$$

In this case, because 2.17 is greater than 2, we would conclude that the manager likely possesses skill. Our inference about this manager's skill changes because this longer sample, with the same distribution, allows us to be more confident in our conclusion.

Recall that a Type I error is the probability of falsely rejecting the null hypothesis—that is, concluding that the manager has skill when in fact he does not—and a Type II error is the probability of failing to reject the null hypothesis—that is, concluding that the manager does not have skill when in fact he does. If we increase our required critical t-value from 2 to 3, we would reject the null less frequently. This change would reduce the occurrence of Type I error but increase the occurrence of Type II error, because the use of a critical t-value of 3 sets a much higher hurdle to reject the null of no skill. Although we would end up with fewer instances of falsely concluding that a manager has skill, with a higher critical t-value we run the risk of ending up with more instances of falsely concluding that a manager lacks skill.

Thus, changing the required critical t-value is always a tradeoff between a Type I error and a Type II error. If an evaluator is strongly averse to incorrectly classifying skilled managers as unskilled—for example, because it may result in frequent costly manager changes—then it makes sense to decrease the required critical t-value to minimize Type II errors (at the expense of making Type I errors more likely).

Assuming that the econometric model is correct, simultaneously reducing both Type I and Type II errors is possible only by using more data.[3] This situation creates a dilemma for the performance appraiser—using more time-series data is preferred, but there is an implicit assumption that the return distribution is the same across all periods. If a manager's skill, team, fees, and transaction costs change, or if the market environment changes dramatically, the characteristics of a manager's return stream may be quite different at different points in time.

Many performance appraisal measures are means divided by standard deviations that can be easily converted to t-statistics to determine their statistical significance. Consider the annualized ex post (or realized or historical) Sharpe ratio, which is the (arithmetically) annualized return minus the risk-free return divided by the annualized standard deviation.

2 Critical t-values converge against the z-value of 1.96 as the sample size/degrees of freedom increase.

3 If the econometric model used to measure performance is flawed, because of either model misspecification or the use of inappropriate factors in the model, then Type I and Type II error may be simultaneously reduced through an improvement in the model without requiring more data.

Using historical returns, the Sharpe ratio is:

$$SR = \frac{\bar{r}_p - \bar{r}_F}{\sigma_p} \quad (2)$$

where

$\bar{r}_p$ = the mean portfolio return;

σ_p = the standard deviation of the returns; and
$\bar{r}_F$ = the mean risk-free rate.

Both the *t*-statistic and Sharpe ratio are measures of return divided by return variability. The *t*-statistic uses the standard error of the mean in the denominator, however, whereas the Sharpe ratio uses the standard deviation of the distribution. (Recall that the standard error is the standard deviation divided by the square root of the number of observations.)

2.1.2 *Essential fundamental principles in performance appraisal*

A performance appraiser must follow three fundamental principles in the quest to determine whether a manager's returns resulted from skill or luck:

1 Choose an appropriate benchmark

The role of a benchmark is to provide an economically justified (fair) "opportunity cost" of selecting an investment. It should answer the question, "If you had not selected a particular manager during the past 10 years, what would be the most closely risk-matched alternative?" If a manager chooses stocks from the S&P 500 Index, this index would be a good starting point for a proper benchmark choice.

2 Select an appropriate estimation model

An estimation model is used to make adjustments to the benchmark(s) to more appropriately reflect the manager's risk exposures. Such a model is useful when we are supplied with manager returns but not full information on portfolio holdings; or when we have incomplete information about the strategies used (e.g., we know that the manager is a small-cap growth manager but do not know specifically how she defines her universe of stocks). This scenario is most likely the case when one is evaluating the returns of a mutual fund or a hedge fund. The performance analyst or investment consultant working in an institutional setting often has sufficient information to select an appropriate benchmark without the need to make these adjustments.

To illustrate, suppose we know that a manager's universe is limited to the stocks in the S&P 500, but we find that the volatility of the manager's returns is persistently less than that of the index. We review the fund prospectus and quarterly letters and find no indication that the manager is pursuing a strategy that would account for this lower volatility. We could use Jensen's model, which is based on the CAPM, to risk-adjust the benchmark. By regressing the portfolio's periodic excess returns (those returns in excess of the risk-free rate) on the excess returns of a broad market cap–weighted portfolio, we can estimate a portfolio's systematic risk (beta). If the regression indicates a beta to the benchmark of 0.90, we might use a benchmark composed of 90% S&P 500 Index and 10% Treasury bills.

3 Validate the model fit (analysis of regression residuals)

After choosing appropriate benchmarks and applying an estimation model—which together we call the "performance model"—we have three time-series of returns: the manager's original returns, the estimation model's returns, and the difference between these two return series. We refer to this last time series as the residuals.

Each period's residual measures the amount by which the manager outperformed (or underperformed) the risk-adjusted benchmark. The average of these residuals is the intercept in the regression, otherwise referred to as alpha. If returns are measured monthly, this calculation is the monthly alpha. We can create a final time series of model errors by subtracting the average residual from the time series of residuals. The errors represent variation not explained by the model. This time series of errors has a mean of zero, and we use this time series to evaluate model fit.

If the residuals conform to a known statistical distribution, the performance evaluator can use the properties of that distribution to compute the likelihood that a manager has skill. If we assume a normal distribution for the residuals, we can calculate the *t*-statistic by dividing the observed alpha by the standard error. The *t*-statistic can then be compared with a critical *t*-statistic table to determine the likelihood that the null hypothesis (zero skill) holds.

Exhibit 1 illustrates the validation of a model fit using the Fidelity Contrafund and the Fama–French market factor as the "model."

Exhibit 1 Performance Appraisal Illustration

The Fidelity Contrafund (CTFAX) is a diversified US equity mutual fund. Assume that we choose the Fama–French market factor (RMRF) as an appropriate benchmark and apply a linear regression as the estimation method. Using monthly excess returns for the Fidelity Contrafund from November 1990 to August 2016, we estimate a market beta of 0.83. We can see each month's residual by subtracting the estimated market-beta-multiplied RMRF from Contrafund's excess return. Here is a visual representation of these data over a small sample (one year) of the total period:

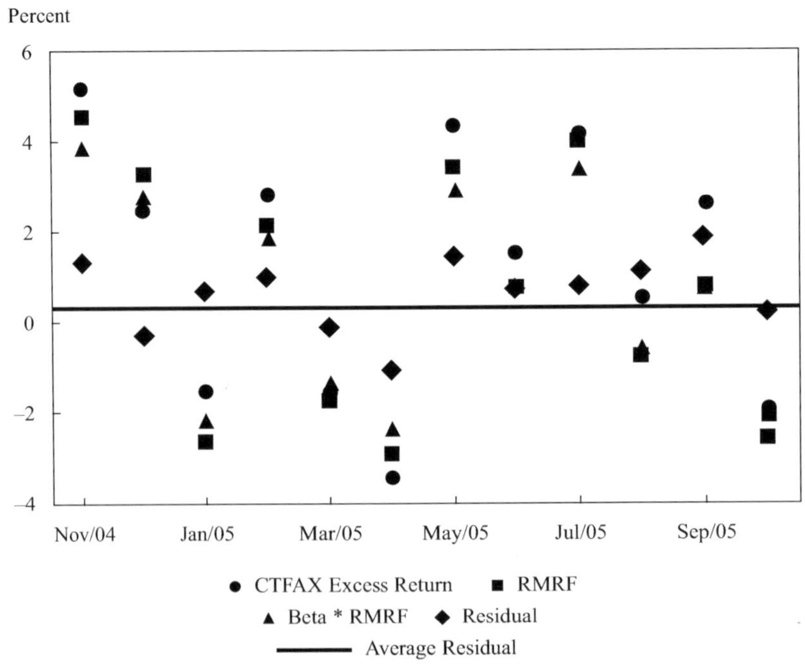

Exhibit 1 (Continued)

The average residual for the full period under evaluation—also known as the intercept in the regression—is 0.315% a month, or 3.78% a year. This is the manager's alpha. The standard deviation in the residuals is 1.66% a month. The standard error in the average residual is 0.095% (1.66% divided by the square root of number of observations; $1.66\%/\sqrt{308} = 0.095\%$). The t-statistic for the hypothesis that the Fidelity Contrafund's alpha is zero is 3.32 (0.315%/0.095%). Assuming the residuals are normal, this statistic is drawn from the Student's t-distribution with 308 degrees of freedom, resulting in a probability value (P-value) of 0.1%. This low P-value indicates we should reject the null hypothesis of no skill.

It is important to understand that statistical tests only improve our *guess* as to whether a manager is truly skilled. The appraiser should therefore never rely solely on statistics when selecting investment managers. Other considerations relevant to the analysis of a manager's track record include the following:

- Has the manager chosen to show a particular portfolio's results and not others that he also manages, or to limit the analysis to specific periods that might not be representative of his full track record? If so, it's likely that our conclusions will be biased.
- If the observed skill was generated during a certain macroeconomic climate, what are the implications for future performance?
- How much did the manager's assets under management (AUM) change during the evaluation period, how much might they grow in the future, and how much do we believe changes in AUM affect performance?
- Is the investment strategy articulated by the manager evident in the historical results? What changes in the management team and the investment process occurred during the period under evaluation, and what does that information imply for replication of past performance?

These questions—and others like them—attempt to transform a manager's observed historical performance into a prediction of future performance. Each of these issues must be considered to best distinguish luck from skill and to make relevant investment decisions.

EXAMPLE 1

Distinguishing Luck from Skill

1 Given the null hypothesis that the manager has no skill, a P-value for a test of manager alpha of 4% indicates a:

   A 4% probability that the manager's true alpha is zero.

   B 96% probability that the manager's true alpha is zero.

   C 4% probability that the manager's true alpha is nonzero.

2 The t-statistic for a test of whether a Sharpe ratio is equal to zero is calculated as:

   A geometric mean return divided by the standard error.

   B money-weighted return multiplied by the standard error.

   C Sharpe ratio multiplied by the square root of the number of observations.

Solution to 1:

A is correct. If the *P*-value for a test of manager performance is 4%, there is a 4% chance that the manager's true alpha is zero.

Solution to 2:

C is correct. The Sharpe ratio is similar to the *t*-statistic, except that the standard deviation is not adjusted by the number of observations. Therefore, to convert a Sharpe ratio to a *t*-statistic, we multiply the Sharpe ratio by the square root of the number of observations. Only the arithmetic mean return should be used in the Sharpe ratio, not the geometric mean return or the money-weighted return.

3 MISTAKES IN AND LIMITATIONS OF PERFORMANCE APPRAISAL

Performance evaluators face many choices as they conduct their analysis. In some cases, these choices are relatively straightforward, while in others, substantial judgment is required. Performance evaluation processes should be designed to avoid common mistakes. We discuss here 14 pitfalls common in performance appraisal and suggest methods of mitigating their effects. The key issues are as follows:

1 Not recognizing noise or chance in past performance statistics;
2 Overreliance on historical return data:
3 Use of incorrect benchmarks or factors;
4 Selection of an inappropriate performance appraisal measure;
5 Failure to consider the scalability of risk;
6 Not properly accounting for synthesized index exposure;
7 Not considering the effect of total AUM;
8 Not recognizing investment strategy constraints;
9 Not incorporating the risk-free or benchmark returns in appraisal measures;
10 Not considering the investor's complete portfolio or utility;
11 Not considering the convexity or tactical asset allocation of investment strategies;
12 Imposing limitations on the estimation window;
13 Not correcting for autocorrelation in standardized measures; and
14 Ignoring selection biases.

3.1 Not Recognizing Noise or Chance in Past Performance Statistics

Calculating statistics using past performance data should be an objective exercise—using the same data, different evaluators should calculate the same values for each performance measure. In reality, we must recognize the imprecision inherent in performance appraisal measures and acknowledge the estimation errors when reporting the measures.

If we calculate that a manager realized an alpha of 2.3% per year, 2.3% is our best estimate of that manager's skill. But models never perfectly explain the variation in a manager's returns, and there is an estimation error that we can also calculate.

One method for visualizing the estimation error uses a quality control chart. This chart shows the statistic of interest along with an expected range of its value, called the **confidence interval**. A confidence interval uses the standard error to estimate the boundaries and is determined by a specified probability. For example, if the null hypothesis for the manager's alpha is a mean of zero with a monthly standard error of 1%, a 68% confidence interval would span −1 to +1 standard error, or −1% to +1%. Over time, a zero-alpha manager's random gains will be offset by losses, such that the manager's alpha tends toward zero. A quality control chart plots the manager's cumulative alpha over time in an attempt to determine if the manager's true alpha is significantly different from zero.

Quality control charts can be used for any statistic. For example, suppose you are evaluating a manager who claims to be able to deliver a Sharpe ratio of at least 1.0. Your null hypothesis is that the manager's realized Sharpe ratio is 1. You calculate the manager's since-inception Sharpe ratio and standard error as of each quarter-end over the manager's history. Exhibit 2 shows a quality control chart of the manager's since-inception Sharpe ratio.

Exhibit 2 Quality Control Chart for Sharpe Ratio

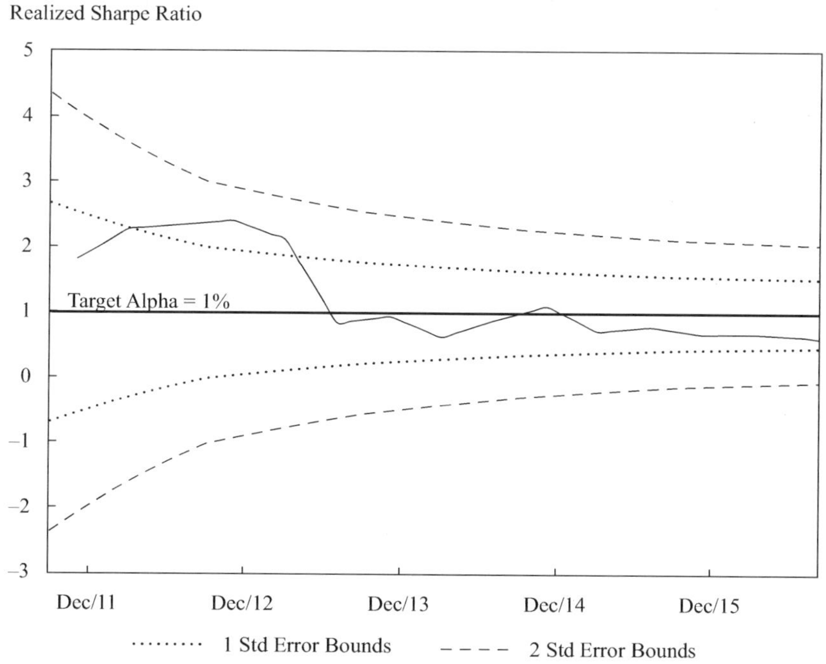

The solid line represents the realized since-inception Sharpe ratio on a quarterly basis. The null-hypothesis level of 1.0 is shown as the horizontal target line. The probability boundaries are represented by the dotted lines that exponentially shrink toward the target Sharpe ratio of 1.0.

As the manager's track record lengthens (and we have more data points), the since-inception Sharpe ratio estimate changes and the standard error of the Sharpe ratio estimate declines.

In this chart, both a 68% probability window (one standard error) and a 95% probability window (two standard errors) are shown by the dotted lines. As we know from statistics, if the null hypothesis is true—in this case, that the manager's true Sharpe ratio is 1—then the manager's realized Sharpe ratio should lie within the one-standard-error confidence interval 68% of the time and within the two-standard-error confidence interval 95% of the time.

In this example, we see that the Sharpe ratio exceeds the 68% confidence interval in three quarters (March 2012, September 2012, March 2013), although it is never outside of the 95% band. Further, the Sharpe ratio has oscillated around the expected value, spending roughly equal time above and below the target. This quality control chart shows that the manager's realized performance, despite not achieving the 1.0 target Sharpe ratio at each measurement point, has remained statistically very close to its target for its full history. From the chart, then, we can reasonably conclude that the manager's true Sharpe ratio might be 1. The use of the quality control chart helps us refine our guess as to whether a manager can generate superior performance.

3.2 Over-reliance on Past Performance

Past returns, even properly adjusted for risk, contain a good deal of statistical estimation error and cannot be regarded as a reliable indicator of future performance. Simply put, a manager may exhibit a positive and consistent alpha over a period of a few months or even a few years by luck alone!

Accordingly, it is important to conduct a holistic assessment of a manager, evaluating not only the performance, but the firm itself, the investment process used, and the investment (and operational) staff responsible for the management of the portfolio. This more broad-based assessment is likely to provide a well-informed opinion as to a manager's ability to replicate past success.

3.3 Use of Incorrect Benchmarks or Factors

To best assess a manager's skill, performance appraisal requires careful benchmarking. In an institutional investment setting, benchmark specification is a carefully considered exercise. Both the asset owner and the investment manager have a strong incentive to agree on what is being measured. Even when a tailored benchmark has been agreed upon, however, the manager is also likely to be evaluated relative to a broader asset class benchmark. As an example, consider a manager who invests in cyclical stocks for which there is a perceived catalyst for accelerating earnings. He is cap-size agnostic but requires that a stock meet a certain minimum liquidity threshold to be included in the portfolio. The benchmark that represents his investment process would include the same liquidity filter, but the asset owner is also likely to measure the manager's performance against the Russell 3000 Value Index.

When evaluating a mutual fund, the benchmark specified in the fund's documents is most often a broad benchmark that is merely *representative* of the manager's investment universe. To assess whether the manager of that mutual fund is skilled, a more precise benchmark, representative of her investment process, is necessary.

An incomplete or incorrect benchmark results in a misestimation of manager alpha. Let us look at a rather extreme example, in which we have only the return stream and cannot identify the manager's investment universe. We can run a single-factor regression (Jensen model), regressing a manager's excess returns against two different benchmarks: the S&P 500 and the Russell 2000 Index. (Although the two benchmarks represent different cap-size sectors of the market, they are highly correlated with one another and illustrate our point regarding benchmark mis-specification.)

Our regression gives us a beta estimate with respect to the S&P 500 Index of 1.4 and a beta estimate with respect to the Russell 2000 Index of 1.2.

Assume that the average return of the S&P 500, minus the risk-free return, is 12% and that the same measure is 18% for the Russell 2000.

We can now look at the effect of benchmark selection on our alpha estimate for this manager.

With the S&P 500 as our benchmark, we derive an expected excess return of 16.8%:

$1.4 \times 12\% = 16.8\%.$

Using the Russell 2000 as our benchmark, we derive an expected excess return of 21.6%:

$1.2 \times 18\% = 21.6\%$

Suppose the manager generated an excess return of 20% over the measurement period. She would have a positive alpha relative to the S&P 500 but a negative alpha relative to the Russell 2000. If the manager's equity holdings more closely match the Russell 2000, the alpha estimate using the S&P 500 will lead the appraiser to overestimate the manager's skill.

Common benchmark and factor model misspecification errors include the following:

- Poor benchmark selection—the benchmark or factor model omits relevant risk factors and/or securities;
- Invalid factor selection—the factors are not investable, sufficiently comprehensive, reflective of systematic risks, or specified in advance; or they do not reflect implementation costs;
- Improper treatment of cash holdings; and
- Failure to consider the effects of non-linear relationships between returns and factors arising from returns with option-like characteristics or tactical asset allocation decisions.

3.4 Selection of an Inappropriate Performance Appraisal Measure

A performance appraisal measure is appropriate when it correctly ranks investment options in the relevant context. Is the manager being evaluated on a *standalone* basis, or is the objective to evaluate a manager under consideration for the *total* portfolio? Or, are we looking to evaluate the manager for just a *portion* of the investor's portfolio?

It is also essential to consider an appraisal measure that can adapt to the character of the manager's returns. If the manager has returns with option-like characteristics or pursues tactical asset allocation strategies, a simple linear model is not appropriate. We address ways to deal with non-linear strategies later.

3.5 Failure to Consider the Scalability of Risk

Some investment approaches are not readily scalable up or down, and depending on the investor's risk appetite, it may not be optimal to choose strategies with the highest appraisal measures.

For example, an investor might be evaluating two managers, each benchmarked against the S&P 500. Assume Manager A has a higher information ratio (and lower tracking error) than Manager B and that Manager B beats the benchmark by a wider margin than Manager A. If the goal is to generate the highest return within the confines of the mandate, and no leverage or portfolio engineering is allowed, the investor should choose Manager B. However, if the investor has a tracking error budget that is larger than Manager A's tracking error, and he is allowed to use S&P 500 futures for portfolio engineering, then he could scale up the size of an investment with Manager A to reach his tracking error target, and he could hedge the excess dollar amount by holding short positions in S&P 500 futures. By doing so, the investor maximizes portfolio returns within his tracking error budget.

3.6 Not Properly Accounting for Leverage Achieved through Synthesized Exposure

Synthetic positions in an index, sector, or individual security are sometimes used to deploy capital more efficiently. The synthetic exposure is often through the use of futures contracts, although swaps, forwards, and margined exchange-traded funds (ETFs) can also be used. Earlier in the curriculum, we discussed the importance of measuring the performance of portfolios that hold derivatives using their notional market value.

Derivatives might also be used to leverage exposure. In the simplest case, a manager funded with \$1 million to invest in the S&P 500 might buy S&P index futures with a notional exposure of \$2 million. A factor analysis would expose the leverage—it would be reflected in a beta coefficient of approximately 2. But she might also take off-benchmark risk, investing the cash not held as margin in risky bonds (e.g., the Bloomberg Barclays Aggregate Bond Index) or to overweight exposure to a particular sector (e.g., a purchase of E-mini Technology Select Sector Futures). A factor analysis here would also reveal the off-benchmark risk taken by the manager. We should compute a performance measure that adds a penalty for this off-benchmark risk, which can be done using the information ratio.

Factor Models in Performance Appraisal

A factor is a variable or a characteristic with which individual asset returns are correlated. Factor models are designed to capture systematic risks in markets. The "factors" in factor-based models are portfolios of securities designed to mimic a risk or return component common in security returns. For example, the Fama–French (Fama and French,1993) Small Minus Big (SMB) factor is a portfolio that is long small-capitalization stocks and short large-capitalization stocks to capture the return associated with small-cap stock risk. Investable factors can be created for any risk. For example, an inflation factor could be defined as a portfolio that is long stocks whose returns are highly positively related to inflation and short stocks whose returns are not. Because this factor does not actually measure inflation, it is common to refer to it as a "factor-mimicking portfolio." In performance appraisal, factor benchmarks must consist of investable securities. (Factor models that incorporate transactions costs are typically preferred in performance evaluation.) We will use the more common generic term "factor" to refer to factor portfolios.

A valid factor must explain some common variation in returns. For example, the SMB factor explains variation in the performance of small-cap stocks relative to large-cap stocks beyond that attributable to movements in the broad stock market. The SMB factor has high volatility, indicating that small-cap stocks do not strongly correlate with large-cap stocks. Contrast this factor with a hypothetical factor that is long stocks whose companies start with vowels and short stocks whose companies start with consonants. Stocks show no common variation according to the first letter in their names, so a Vowel Minus Consonant (VMC) factor would not explain much variation in stock returns that is not already explained by the broad market.

There is no universal set of accepted factors but rather many different factors created by various researchers over time. An ongoing academic debate questions whether some factors are "legitimately priced"—that is, is there an intuitive reason why these factors have earned a return premium over time? Most practitioners use one of the more widely accepted factor models.

The most common factor model is the CAPM (capital asset pricing model), in which the global market cap–weighted portfolio is the factor. The three-factor model of Fama and French (1992) and the four-factor model of Carhart (1997) are also widely used to evaluate equity portfolios. All factors consist of stocks and are expressed in excess returns (net of the risk-free return). The Carhart four factors are as follows:

- RMRF: the risk premium for the cap-weighted market proxy portfolio—that is, the return on the market minus the risk-free return—the Market factor;
- SMB: the return on small-cap stocks minus the return on large-cap stocks—the Size factor;
- HML: the return on high book-to-market stocks (value stocks) minus that for low book-to-market stocks (growth stocks)—the Value factor; and
- WML: one-year momentum in stock returns, calculated as the return on winner stocks minus the return on loser stocks—the Momentum factor.

Additional factors such as Quality (a persistent return to high-quality stocks), Liquidity (a persistent return to less liquid stocks), and Volatility (a persistent return to volatile stocks) have been identified and are often incorporated in factor-based analyses.

3.7 Not Considering the Effect of Total AUM

Growth in AUM can lead to an increase in market impact costs or cause a portfolio manager to avoid low-liquidity securities or low-capitalization markets, either of which might reduce expected returns. The performance evaluator must assess the effect of asset growth on the manager's excess returns. It is important to consider not only the AUM of the particular fund being evaluated but also the AUM of the strategy as a whole—the manager may offer multiple products following a substantially similar strategy, or more managers may crowd into a strategy that has been successful, reducing the opportunity for excess returns across the board.

Looking at the Fidelity Contrafund mutual fund, we can explore the possible relationship between AUM and alphas. Exhibit 3 summarizes the fund's average total assets, three-factor exposures, and three-factor alphas over three-year rolling periods from 2004 to 2016.

Exhibit 3 Assets, Factor Exposures, and Alpha for Fidelity Contrafund

1	2	3	4	5	6
Three Years Ending	**Total Fund Assets**	**RMRF Exposure**	**SMB Exposure**	**HML Exposure**	**Annualized Alpha**
2004	36,077	0.50	0.33	0.25	2.9%
2005	46,877	0.72	0.29	−0.01	4.0%
2006	57,714	0.78	0.34	−0.07	3.7%
2007	69,841	0.86	0.16	−0.30	6.4%
2008	65,967	0.92	−0.01	−0.51	1.4%
2009	64,410	0.94	−0.12	−0.39	0.9%
2010	62,627	0.92	−0.03	−0.38	−1.2%
2011	70,805	0.89	0.00	−0.30	−0.3%
2012	77,686	0.91	−0.03	−0.39	0.9%
2013	89,545	0.94	−0.14	−0.38	1.5%

(continued)

Exhibit 3 (Continued)

1	2	3	4	5	6
Three Years Ending	Total Fund Assets	RMRF Exposure	SMB Exposure	HML Exposure	Annualized Alpha
2014	101,824	0.95	−0.07	−0.39	1.1%
2015	110,189	0.91	−0.01	−0.43	1.4%
2016	108,445	0.90	−0.02	−0.38	1.0%

Has asset growth affected the investment strategy and/or its alpha? Although the numbers alone cannot tell us the whole story, some apparent relationships are worth noting. First, as the fund's assets increased, its small-cap bias—as measured in its SMB coefficient in column 4—declined. This dynamic is fairly intuitive; it is more difficult to gain small-cap stock exposure with AUM of $108 billion than with AUM of $36 billion. We also see evidence in the rising RMRF coefficient (column 3) that Contrafund's equity beta increased. In column 5, we can see that the fund's early value bias (2004) migrated to a decided growth bias by 2007. In column 6, we can see that the fund's trailing three-year alpha has a modest negative relationship with fund assets—average annual alphas are smaller in later periods as the fund grows. This may result, in part, from the difficult task of locating underpriced stocks in the highly efficient large-cap market, although other factors, such as market volatility, could also affect the fund's ability to achieve alpha.

The performance evaluator should use this analysis in conjunction with other quantitative and qualitative analyses to reach a conclusion regarding the effect of AUM growth on the manager's ability to add alpha in the future.

3.8 Not Recognizing Investment Strategy Constraints

When seeking to draw conclusions regarding a fund's performance relative to other products offered by that same manager, or relative to competing products from other managers, it is important to consider the differences in constraints among the products. Do all products define their investment universe similarly? For example, consider the following:

- Some constituents in a universe of global equity managers may define their universe as MSCI All-Country World, while others constrain themselves to non-US markets and thus would be more appropriately benchmarked against the MSCI All Country World ex-US.
- Some constituents in a universe of small-cap managers may use the same minimum market cap size when defining the universe of eligible securities, while others may be willing to buy even the smallest small-cap stocks.
- Some of the manager's portfolios may contain an environmental, social, and governance (ESG) mandate, whereas others do not.
- An institutional or hedge fund manager moves to offer the flagship strategy in a mutual fund or UCITS[4] format. The legal and operational constraints are restrictive in these vehicles, and it is unlikely that the two would be expected to generate the same risk-adjusted return.

4 Undertakings for the Collective Investment of Transferable Securities, a regulatory framework for the management and sale of mutual funds throughout Europe.

Strategy constraints must be considered when selecting a peer group or factor model to use in manager evaluation. For instance, a US small-cap growth peer group universe may include managers that benchmark against the Russell 2000 as well as managers that invest more narrowly in technology stocks. A typical factor model, such as the Jensen model or the four-factor model, would not correct for the strong loading on technology, and the manager's alpha will be mis-stated. Thus, the analyst must carefully evaluate the meaning of the alpha in such a situation or consider adding a factor that captures the constraint—in this case, a technology factor.

3.9 Not Incorporating the Risk-Free or Benchmark Return Performance Measures

A common mistake evaluators make is to look at average total returns divided by a measure of risk without subtracting a benchmark return or the risk-free rate. In Exhibit 4, we compare the rankings of three managers over a multi-year period. The return/volatility ratio does adjust for the level of risk-taking (volatility), but it does not account for the level of the risk-free rate. The Sharpe ratio deducts the risk-free return from the mean return in the numerator, and then adjusts for the level of risk-taking.

Why did the rankings shift from the first to the second ratio? The Sharpe ratio implicitly recognizes the risk-free rate as an opportunity cost for an investment in each fund—the investor could have invested in T-bills with zero risk instead of the actual investment in the risky fund—whereas the return/volatility ratio does not. Under a 4.1% annual risk-free rate regime, Manager 1 does not exceed the hurdle of the risk-free asset, so the fact that his volatility is lower than the volatility of Managers 2 and 3 becomes irrelevant.

Exhibit 4 Performance Statistics for Three Managers

	Arithmetic Mean Yearly Manager Return (rank)	Yearly Volatility	Return/ Volatility (rank)	Sharpe Ratio* (rank)
Manager 1	4.0% (3)	10%	0.40 (1)	−0.010 (3)
Manager 2	8.5% (1)	30%	0.28 (3)	0.147 (2)
Manager 3	8.0% (2)	25%	0.32 (2)	0.156 (1)

* Risk-free rate = 4.1%

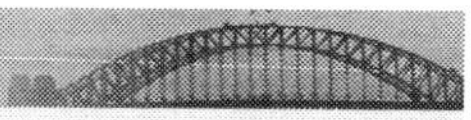

Arithmetic vs. Geometric Returns in Risk-Scaled Performance Measures

It is common in performance appraisal to use the geometric mean return in all appraisal measures. In appraisal measures that compare return to risk, however, this approach results in a form of double jeopardy: The manager is penalized for risk-taking in both the numerator *and* the denominator.

Consider the math of the geometric (or compound annual) return: high return volatility dampens the compound annual return. If Manager A delivers 10% in year 1 and year 2 and Manager B delivers +30% in year 1 and −10% in year 2, both will have the same arithmetic average return of 10%. But Manager A's compound annualized return is 10%, whereas Manager B's compound annualized return is 8.17%.

Although in most instances, using the geometric return in risk-scaled performance measures will not make a meaningful difference in the manager rankings, the analyst should be aware of the technical inaccuracy and explore the implications when the managers under consideration have high and/or materially different volatilities.

3.10 Not Considering the Investor's Complete Portfolio or Utility

It is common practice to look at performance appraisal statistics on a standalone basis. In most applications, however, the evaluator is making manager selection/retention decisions in the context of a larger portfolio. Under these circumstances, a more appropriate analysis would examine the effect a manager might have on the total portfolio's Sharpe ratio and expected return.

Assume your client's current portfolio is invested passively as 60% MSCI All Country World Index (ACWI) and 40% Bloomberg Barclay's Global Aggregate Bond Index (BGA). The client wants to explore diversification options and is considering a relative value hedge fund (HFRI) and a systematic trend-following fund. From June 20X0 through September 20X1, you estimate the statistics shown in Exhibit 5:

Exhibit 5 Performance Statistics for Index, Hedge Funds, and Risk-Free Return

Portfolio, Strategy, or Index	Annual Mean Return	Annual Volatility	Sharpe Ratio
60% ACWI/40% BGA	5.6%	9.7%	0.42
HFRI relative value (RV) manager	6.2%	4.2%	1.10
Systematic trend–following manager	13.7%	17.3%	0.70
Risk-free return	1.6%		

Your client tells you that she wants to allocate no more than 15% of her total assets to the new manager and that total portfolio volatility cannot rise. Given the client's objectives and constraints, which manager is the better choice?

On the surface, the relative value fund appears to be the best option, given its lower volatility and higher Sharpe ratio. To confirm that idea, you create pro forma simulations and derive the portfolio statistics shown in Exhibit 6:

Exhibit 6 Performance Statistics for Portfolio and Two Hedge Funds

Portfolio, Strategy, or Index	Annual Mean Return	Annual Volatility	Sharpe Ratio
85% 60/40 + 15% HFRI RV manager	5.71%	8.51%	0.49
85% 60/40 + 15% Trend-following manager	6.84%	7.48%	0.71

Despite its higher risk and lower Sharpe ratio, the trend-following strategy offers a superior portfolio profile—higher return, lower risk, and a higher Sharpe ratio.

These results are driven by the relative correlations of the two funds—the relative value fund exhibits a correlation of 0.41 with the 60/40 stock/bond portfolio, whereas the systematic trend-following fund exhibits a correlation of −0.43. The trend-following fund provides better diversification than the relative value fund. This scenario illustrates the hazard of relying only on the Sharpe ratio to compare the relative merits of managers that will be part of a broader portfolio.

To determine the marginal benefit of a new manager, an evaluator might also calculate an appraisal ratio (alpha divided by residual risk): By regressing the new manager's return on the existing portfolio's return, one can derive an estimate of the alpha and residual risk contributed by the new manager. If that alpha is positive, the strategy adds orthogonal (i.e., statistically unique) value to the portfolio. The appraisal ratio then indicates how much orthogonal mean return the strategy delivers for each unit of orthogonal risk. The manager with the highest appraisal ratio delivers the highest marginal return per unit of residual risk and would thus be the best selection.

3.11 Not Considering the Convexity or Tactical Asset Allocation of Investment Strategies

A common issue in performance appraisal is shifting exposure to factors. This situation may arise when a portfolio contains option-like securities, if the manager uses tactical asset allocation strategies in which the portfolio sensitivity to certain underlying markets varies over time, or in "opportunistic" strategies whereby the manager moves among sectors or styles within an asset class to achieve alpha. A factor analysis implicitly assumes a constant exposure over the estimation window, but the estimated average exposure can be deceiving.

As an extreme example, imagine a manager that simply sells far-out-of-the money S&P 500 put options every month. In a period of low market volatility, the strategy will have a low exposure to the market because the fund earns stable returns from collecting put option premiums by shorting. In a period of high market volatility, the manager should be able to collect relatively high levels of put premiums. However, the manager will also have a higher true exposure to market risk—it is more likely in a high-volatility scenario that the short put strategy will lose money in tandem with a negative market return. If relying solely on fund returns in the analysis, the performance evaluator may be unable to detect that the manager's exposure to systematic risk has increased unless a large downturn in the high-volatility state occurred during the evaluation period.

Convex or option-like payoffs are actually very common in many active strategies, especially among hedge funds. Even when positions are observable, a periodic snapshot might not reveal whether the manager is pursuing an option replication strategy.[5] If a strategy's convexity results from a successful tactical asset allocation strategy, it is important to measure the manager's success in that dimension. Models have been developed to address these situations.

5 A call-option replication strategy can be created through a leveraged investment in equities plus downside protection with a long put option position. Such a replication strategy should be easy to detect using periodic holdings. It is also possible to replicate an option through a dynamic position in shares of the stock and cash. A short put option position can be replicated by buying the stock while borrowing money (a leveraged position in the stock). The amount of stock bought (and money borrowed) must be adjusted frequently as the stock price moves. This strategy is impossible to observe using coarsely reported periodic holdings information.

3.12 Imposing Limitations on the Estimation Window

Investment performance is very noisy, and certainty requires a lot of data. As an example, an often-cited work from Fama and French (2002) tells us that the excess return on US equities from 1872 through 2000 was 5.57%, with a realized annual standard deviation of 18.51%. This *129-year* sample yields a statistically significant Sharpe ratio of 0.30 with a t-statistic of 3.41. If the sample were only 25 years, however—still quite a long period—the t-statistic for a null hypothesis that the excess return is equal to 0% would be 1.50 and not significant at the usual levels.

For purposes of statistical inference, we want to use as long a time span of data as possible. An analyst is typically working with manager track records that are significantly shorter than a 129- or 25-year sample, making it more difficult to find significance in the estimation of a manager's alpha. Further, when comparing multiple managers, one or more manager's track records will often be truncated in order to facilitate an analysis over a common period. In doing so, valuable information contained in that longer track record is lost. Although it is necessary to compare managers over a common timeframe, it is important to retain the insights that can be gathered from a manager's longer-term track record.

3.13 Not Correcting for Autocorrelation in Standardized Measures

We generally report risk and return measures standardized to annual periods. Annualizing the standard deviation often assumes independence of returns over time, an assumption that does not always hold. When might returns not be independent? As an example, when markets drop a lot in a day, more often than not they drop again the next day—a dynamic that might result from some investors deciding to sell some of their positions after their prices decline. This phenomenon is an example of positive **serial correlation**, or **autocorrelation** in market returns. Positive feedback in investor trading such as this can explain several time-series return patterns, including price momentum and market panics. As another important example, fund managers may "smooth" their returns, either purposely (to fool investors by reducing apparent exposure to systematic risk factors) or because their pricing models for illiquid assets fail to adjust prices quickly enough in changing market conditions (Getmansky, Lo, and Makarov, 2004). Smoothing is frequently evident in real estate, private equity, and hedge fund returns.

3.14 Ignoring Selection Biases

It is not uncommon for investors to learn about or focus on a manager or strategy only after that manager or strategy generates strong performance—"glittery" performance attracts attention from everyone, including the media, consultants, and fund sponsors. When an appraiser compares the performance of an incumbent manager with that of other managers, the resulting analysis can be biased. For example, imagine an investor who hired Manager A 10 years ago. The investor is now considering Managers B, C, and D as possible replacements for Manager A. It is quite likely that Managers B, C, and D all had better performance than Manager A over the past 10 years (it would be unlikely for B, C, and D to be considered as replacements for Manager A if they had weaker performance). Further, the universe of managers from which these competitors was selected is biased upward—it excludes managers that closed and/or failed in the 10-year period. Thus, the analysis of Manager A's skill relative to Managers B, C, and D is biased.[6]

A very similar bias exists in self-reporting databases (such as most hedge fund databases), whereby managers start reporting only after they have achieved good performance, then backfill the database with their good returns. When analyzing a group of managers using self-reported data, it is critical to remove the backfilled history because managers are likely to backfill good performance and not backfill poor performance. Fortunately, most good database vendors keep track of the date that the manager first started reporting, permitting the evaluator to eliminate backfilled history from the analysis.

As an example, an investor is looking at the performance of his existing manager over the past five years. He is comparing that performance with the average of the manager's peer group for that same five-year period. The investor finds that his manager ranks at the peer group median, meaning that if the peer group universe contains 50 managers, 25 of them have better performance over the same five years. Should he replace his existing manager with one of these 25?

The answer will depend on many factors, but consider the selection bias inherent in this example. There may be many more managers with at least a five-year track record who could have been included in this universe—assume 100 managers in total. But only 50 of them have chosen to report their past five-year performance. It is highly likely that the other 50 managers had less-impressive track records and chose not to be included in the database. Thus, the five-year peer group median return is significantly upward-biased. Perhaps the existing manager is actually much better than the median manager!

EXAMPLE 2

Mistakes in Performance Appraisal

1 Which of the following statements is true of a quality control chart?

 A The standard deviation bands widen over time.

 B One-standard-deviation bands correspond to a 68% confidence interval.

 C An alpha that plots within the standard deviation bands indicates a positive alpha.

2 Your client is considering terminating the manager whose alpha is depicted in the following quality control chart. What is the *best* response to the client?

6 Note that the disappearance of some competitor funds is unknown when the investment in the existing manager was made. Yet, the investment could have been made in one of these now-defunct funds. Therefore, comparing an existing manager only with funds that still exist and that also existed at the historical point-in-time of the investment selection does not assess with perfect accuracy the success in choosing the existing manager and whether the manager should be retained.

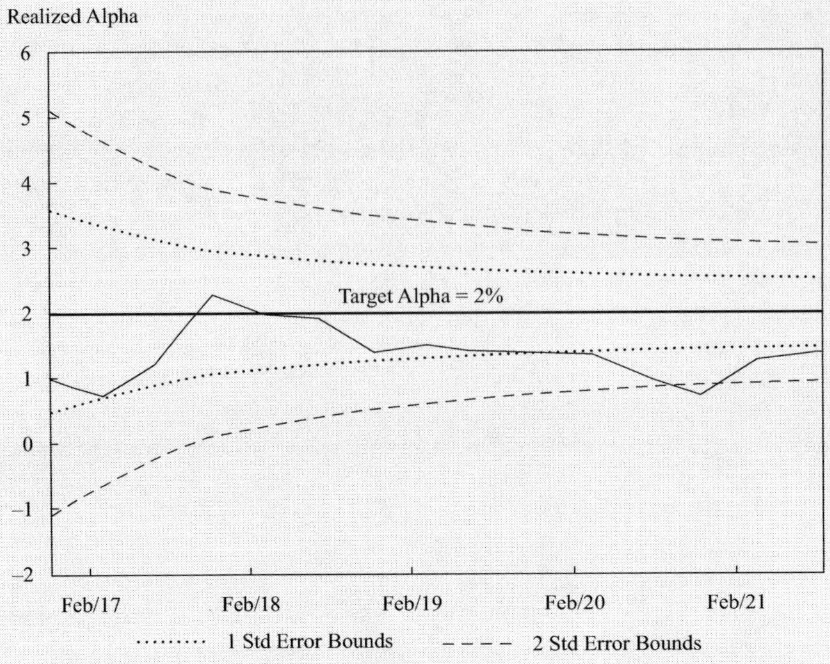

A Yes, terminate the manager. Her cumulative alpha falls persistently below the 2% alpha expectation.

B Yes, terminate the manager. Her realized alpha violated the two-standard-deviation band.

C No, do not terminate the manager. Her realized alpha has largely remained within the designated confidence intervals.

3 A US-based endowment fund has hired a global equity manager whose base currency is the euro. The manager does not manage currency exposure. He is benchmarked to the MSCI ACWI. The following table provides data for benchmark returns and the manager's beta.

	MSCI ACWI in US$	MSCI ACWI in €
Benchmark return	12.00%	10.00%
Manager's beta relative to index	0.95	1.05
Risk-free rate	3.00%	

You are appraising the manager's performance. Based on this information, the manager's alpha is *closest to*:

A 7.35%.

B 8.55%.

C 10.50%.

4 You are constructing a peer group for core Asia-Pacific equity managers. Which of the following three funds is *least likely* to belong to the peer group?

Fund A invests in dividend-paying equity securities of companies located in the Asia-Pacific region. It may also invest in convertible debt and equity securities of any maturity and in those that are unrated, or would be below investment grade if rated, of companies located in Asia. The fund's objective is total return with an emphasis on providing current income. Fund A conducts both top-down and bottom-up research to identify companies that exhibit attractive dividend yields and the propensity to pay increasing dividends. The manager expects that such companies typically will be of medium or large size, but the fund may invest in companies of any size.

Fund B invests in equity securities of companies in the Asia-Pacific region with the potential for above-average sales and earnings growth, overall financial strength, competitive advantages, and capable management. The investment approach includes both a top-down strategy, which considers overall economic and market trends in each country, and a bottom-up strategy, which uses fundamental research for security selection. The manager constructs the portfolio by seeking both growth and value opportunities in stocks of any market capitalization.

Fund C invests in equity securities of companies in the Asia-Pacific region. The manager seeks securities of issuers believed to have potential for earnings or revenue growth. The fund may invest in the securities of issuers of all capitalization sizes and may invest a significant amount of its net assets in the securities of small- and mid-cap issuers. The investment process combines a disciplined bottom-up and top-down multifactor analysis. The country weightings within the fund reflect both bottom-up opportunities and top-down country preferences.

A Fund A

B Fund B

C Fund C

Solution to 1:

B is correct. A 68% confidence interval would span −1 to +1 standard deviation. The standard deviation bands narrow over time as more data are collected. An alpha within the standard deviation bands may be either positive or negative.

Solution to 2:

C is correct. If the null hypothesis is true—in this case, that the manager's true alpha is 2—then the manager's realized alpha should lie within the one-standard-error confidence interval 68% of the time and within the two-standard-error confidence interval 95% of the time.

Solution to 3:

A is correct. The manager's base currency is the euro, and thus the correct benchmark is the MSCI ACWI in euros. The manager's alpha is calculated as its beta multiplied by the excess returns of the benchmarks: (10.00% − 3%) × 1.05 = 7.35%.

Solution to 4:

A is correct. Although all three managers invest in the same geographic region, include securities of all capitalization sizes, and use a combination of top-down and bottom-up investment processes, Manager A explicitly emphasizes dividend yield, which indicates the universe of securities from which she selects is narrower than that of the others.

4 BENCHMARK SELECTION AND MANAGER APPRAISAL ISSUES

Although we cannot completely remove noise from investment performance data, we can avoid some of it by removing the return correlated with appropriate benchmarks. By choosing appropriate benchmarks, we remove the performance variation that results not from manager skill but rather from other factors, such as the manager's style and the characteristics of the universe of securities from which he chooses (e.g., liquidity, value, momentum, and other such characteristics).

Consider the case in which your client has hired a manager who is running a strategy based on the MSCI World Index (excluding emerging markets stocks) to fill a portion of her equity allocation. The equity allocation is benchmarked against the MSCI All-Country World Index, but this manager is just one portion of the overall equity allocation. The benchmark selection should reflect the goal of the manager appraisal exercise. Irrespective of the total-equity benchmark selected, it is known in advance that this manager's universe is more appropriately defined by the MSCI World Index. If the purpose of the evaluation exercise is to evaluate the manager's execution of her investment strategy—both her skill and her adherence to the stated strategy—then the Total Equity MSCI All-Country World benchmark is irrelevant.

Every benchmark has advantages and disadvantages, with most benchmarks failing to meet one or more of the properties of a valid benchmark. Here we discuss the use of broad market indexes, peer groups, style indexes, and factor-model-based benchmarks.

4.1 Consequences of Poor Benchmark Selection

We previously noted that the most direct consequence of choosing a poor benchmark is a poor estimate of manager skill. We demonstrated that measuring a manager's performance relative to an S&P 500 benchmark when his true universe may be closer to the Russell 2000 universe led to an overestimation of the manager's true security selection skill. Other consequences of choosing a poor benchmark include:

- a poor understanding of the factors that drive that manager's returns;
- the selected manager being ill-suited to fill the desired role in the investor's portfolio, creating gaps between the investor's actual and target portfolios;
- the investor being compelled to spend limited staff resources managing turnover in his managers;
- the investor incurring the hard costs associated with terminating one manager and transitioning to the replacement manager; and
- the investor incurring opportunity costs arising from a mismatch between the desired portfolio profile and the manager's actual portfolio profile.

Generally, the performance evaluator can identify a good benchmark fit by considering key facets of the investment strategy and benchmark:

- Does the universe of securities in the benchmark generally match that of the manager?
- Does the manager exhibit any biases in holdings or strategy that relate to common factors or styles? For example, if a manager tends to hold mostly the larger-cap names within the universe, a cap-weighted index would be a better fit than an equal-weighted index. Another example might be a manager who

pursues a momentum strategy of buying recent winners and selling recent losers, which might be better mimicked by a momentum strategy index for that manager's investment universe.

- Is the manager held to any constraints that would limit her ability to fairly track a given benchmark? Managers who are restricted from holding "sin stocks," for example, might be better compared with a benchmark that reflects this restriction. Similarly, a manager required to hold a certain amount in cash, or who is managing an account with frequent inflows and outflows, might not be fairly compared with a fully invested benchmark.

When a good benchmark is unavailable, an evaluator might use a custom benchmark. Custom benchmarks require a clear definition of the appropriate universe, rebalancing strategy, and weighting scheme. The construction of custom benchmarks—and calculation of their returns—is typically outsourced to an independent benchmarking firm. The advantage of a custom benchmark is a clear fit to the manager's strategy. The costs of maintaining a custom benchmark are not trivial, however, and because the benchmark composition differs from traditional benchmarks, accounts measured relative to custom benchmarks are not readily compared with peers.

4.2 Peer Group Comparisons: Uses and Limitations

Although peer group comparisons are quite common in manager evaluation, these comparisons suffer from two very significant weaknesses.

- Although managers within the peer group may all nominally be classified as "large-cap value" or "small-cap growth," they may not truly be substitutable one for another. Some managers in the universe may have tilts that create an investment product very different from the one offered by the manager being evaluated. Some may have ESG-related constraints. Some may be institutional accounts, whereas others are retail mutual funds. Some may have a substantial asset base that constrains their investment approach, whereas others may be newer, smaller managers with limited track records.
- A manager's ranking within the peer group might change considerably with very small changes in performance, often in response to factors outside of the manager's control. A change in the ranking may be driven not by something he did but by the actions of others in the peer group (e.g., other managers in the peer group may have chosen to overweight a "hot" sector, whereas the target manager's investment discipline constrains them from making a similar bet). Peer group rankings can be especially noisy when there are relatively few members in the group. This issue often arises in niche strategies, which may have too few managers to form a robust peer group.

There are circumstances in which a peer group comparison does provide useful insights. If, for example, benchmark performance is dominated by a handful of highly weighted, strong-performing securities, most managers would underperform the benchmark unless they happened to be overweight these few securities. In this case, relative performance between managers might provide insights about their broader investment skill.

Peer group analyses also enable the investor to put a manager's performance into context. Underperforming the benchmark by 2% does not seem so bad if that level of performance is the median among all managers in the peer group. In contrast, if 90% of managers in a peer group outperformed the benchmark over a given window when the manager being evaluated slightly underperformed the benchmark, a performance appraiser would question the manager's skill more diligently (considering the point made earlier regarding selection biases in peer group analyses, of course).

4.3 Factor-Based Benchmarks

Factor-based benchmarks offer the appraiser the opportunity to closely identify a manager's unique skills. Some aspects of what had previously been attributed to manager skill are now known to result from static factor exposures that today can be obtained more cheaply than through active management (in most, though not all, instances). A factor based-benchmark allows the appraiser to more narrowly describe a manager's alpha.

4.3.1 *Factor-based equity benchmarks*

To perform a factor analysis of a given investment strategy using the four-factor model, we run a regression of a manager's excess returns (portfolio returns of $r_{p,t}$ minus the risk-free return, $r_{F,t}$) after trading costs, r_t, against the four factors:

$$r_{p,t} - r_{F,t} = \alpha + \beta \times RMRF_t + \beta_{smb} \times SMB_t + \beta_{hml} \times HML_t + \beta_{wml} \times WML_t + \varepsilon_t\varepsilon_t\varepsilon_t \quad (3)$$

In this regression, the coefficients or "betas" on each of the four factors reflect the investment strategy's estimated exposure to the systematic risks implied by the factors. The intercept or "alpha" is the return not attributable to systematic risk. If the factor model is a good fit for the investment strategy, it should explain a large portion of strategy's variation of returns and will exhibit a high R-squared.

Assume, for example, that a large-cap strategy has a persistent bias toward smaller-cap stocks. It can be expected to have a positive beta to SMB. If small-cap stocks had higher returns than large-cap stocks over the evaluation period, the positive beta multiplied by the positive SMB return creates a return attributable to that small-cap bias—that component of the manager's return should not be attributed to alpha.

The manager's alpha is the return left over after considering the return explained by factor exposures. Alpha could be generated from either security selection or factor timing, both of which we interpret as skill. The relevance of this analysis, however, depends primarily on the factor selected. If the factors do not reflect the manager's risk exposures, then the alpha will not accurately measure the manager's skill.

As an example of factor-based performance analysis, assume you are tasked with an evaluation of the Fidelity Contrafund. After obtaining the fund's monthly total returns since November 1990, you subtract the monthly risk-free return to find the fund's monthly excess returns, and then you run an ordinary least squares linear regression on various factor models using Excel. You first estimate a single-factor model using only the RMRF factor, which results in the Excel output shown in Exhibit 7.

Exhibit 7 Performance Evaluation Using a One-Factor Model

Regression Statistics

R-squared	82.0%
Adjusted R-squared	82.0%
Standard error	1.66%
Observations	310

	Coefficients	Standard Error	*t*-Statistic	*P*-Value
Intercept	0.31%	0.10%	3.29	0.11%
RMRF	0.83	0.02	37.47	0.00%

The R-squared of 82% means that 82% of the total variance in monthly returns can be explained by variation in the monthly returns of RMRF. The RMRF coefficient—commonly referred to as the "beta" or "equity beta"—is 0.83. It is estimated very precisely, with a standard error of only 0.02.

The intercept coefficient of 0.31% means that the monthly abnormal return above the market model is 31 bps. To annualize, we multiply by 12, yielding a Jensen's alpha estimate of 3.72% per year, which is unusually high. This fact is confirmed by the t-statistic of 3.29, which means that the estimated alpha is 3.29 standard errors above zero. The P-value of 0.11% indicates the probability that the null hypothesis is true (the alpha is equal to zero) is only 0.11%, or only about one-tenth of 1%.

The market model, however, adjusts only for the market factor, not any other risk exposures. Therefore, you decide to run the analysis using the Carhart four-factor model. Exhibit 8 shows the key outputs from that regression:

Exhibit 8 Performance Evaluation Using a Four-Factor Model

Regression Statistics

R-squared	88.4%
Adjusted R-squared	88.3%
Standard error	1.34%
Observations	310

	Coefficients	Standard Error	t-Statistic	P-Value
Intercept	0.15%	0.08%	1.88	6.08%
RMRF	0.87	0.02	45.08	0.00%
SMB	0.05	0.03	1.81	7.11%
HML	0.06	0.03	2.45	1.47%
WML	0.21	0.02	12.23	0.00%

The four-factor model explains a larger proportion (88.4%) of Contrafund's variation of returns. The coefficient on the momentum factor (WML) is highly significant. The positive t-statistic of 12.23 indicates that the Contrafund's investment strategy has a significant momentum component. The positive t-statistics of 1.81 and 2.45 for the SMB and HML factors indicate that the fund also has modest tilts toward small-cap and value stocks.

Perhaps most interesting, the alpha is now 0.15% per month, or 1.80% per year. With a t-statistic of 1.88, the alpha is now only marginally significantly different from zero.

These examples illustrate that, if the performance appraiser chooses the wrong benchmark (in this case, an incomplete factor model), then inferences about the manager's risk exposures and skills will likely be flawed. Given that many factor exposures are available via inexpensive, liquid index funds and ETFs, the evaluator should understand whether an active manager is adding value relative to these alternate investment vehicles.

4.3.2 *Factor-based fixed-income benchmarks*

Elton and Gruber (Elton, Gruber, and Blake, 1995) suggest the following factor model for analyzing bond portfolios:

$$r_{p,t} - r_{F,t} = \alpha + \beta \times RMRF_t + \beta_{firf} \times FIRF_t + \beta_{term} \times TERM_t + \beta_{default} \times DEFAULT_t + \beta_{option} \times OPTION_t + \varepsilon_t \quad (4)$$

where

- *FIRF* is the excess return of the Bloomberg Barclays Aggregate Bond Index Total Return,
- *TERM* is the bond market maturity premium (10-year Treasury yield minus 30-day T-bill yield),
- *DEFAULT* is the default risk premium (Baa bond yield minus 10-year Treasury yield), and
- *OPTION* captures bond optionality features (e.g., the holding of mortgage securities) and is constructed as the difference in return between the Bloomberg Barclays GNMA index and intermediate government bonds with the same duration.

A stock factor (as in RMRF above) can be added to the bond factors to capture residual equity risk not captured by the other factors.

4.3.3 *Considerations in selecting a factor-based benchmark*

When constructing a factor model for any asset, the factors in the model should meet the following requirements:

1 Investable
2 Comprehensive
3 Proxies for systematic risk
4 Specified in advance

Investable: All the factors should be investable and reflect transactions costs. It is not reasonable to compare a manager with a factor that is not attainable and does not reflect transactions costs.

Comprehensive: All relevant systematic factors for the manager's strategy must be included. Omitting relevant factors would invalidate a factor model and result in mismeasurement of a manager's true skill and risk. For instance, comparing a high-yield bond strategy with a factor model consisting only of a government bond factor will lead to an overestimation of the manager's alpha, because it does not incorporate the systematic risk contributed by the credit premium from investing in credit risky securities.

Proxies for systematic risk: The choice of true "risk" factors requires a careful balance of finding explanatory variables that have historical variation in return but also make economic sense. There are many examples of factors that explain return but not risk, and many are simply spurious. A classic case is a finding that butter production in Bangladesh provided good explanatory power for the level of the S&P 500 return.[7] Clearly, this idea is silly, and the Bangladeshi Butter Production factor should *not* be used to evaluate a manager.

Factor-based benchmarks are not without their own idiosyncrasies. Each index provider has its own definition of "Quality," "Value," and "Momentum" and establishes its own protocols for rebalancing. It is likely that a manager who espouses a quality,

7 See Leinweber (2009).

value, or momentum tilt defines that exposure with her own unique twist. In some cases, factor index rebalancing can lead to a large shift in the underlying holdings. In one instance of its semi-annual rebalancing, the MSCI Quality Index experienced a 64% shift from North America to the rest of world during a single rebalance.

The performance appraiser should be aware that sometimes researchers explore many different factor specifications and then report only the single best factor, often with an ex post story created to give it credibility (an example of data mining). Factors substantiated in rigorous peer-reviewed academic research are less likely to be derived from biased samples or lead to spurious correlations.

Take the Fidelity Contrafund as an example. This fund invests almost exclusively in US stocks. We conducted regressions on about 150 possible factors and found statistically significant coefficients on a number of seemingly spurious factors (t-statistics in parentheses): investment-grade credit default risk (5.5), global dividend futures (2.1), short commodity volatility (2.0), long interest rate volatility (2.0), large-cap Australian stocks (2.8), short EU ex-UK earnings momentum stocks (4.0), long Japanese growth stocks (4.8), and short UK quality stocks (5.7). It seems unlikely that this fund holds short commodity index variance swaps or shorts in UK quality stocks, yet a naïve statistical analysis suggests this would be the case. This example illustrates the importance of judgment as well as statistics in choosing an appropriate factor model.

Specified in advance: Best practice tells us that managers should be advised in advance of the benchmarks that will be used to evaluate them. The factor "universe" continues to evolve, however. For example, the Quality factor (QMJ) reflects the recent finding that "high quality" stocks outperform junk stocks after controlling for market capitalization (Asness et al. 2013).[8] The historical average return on this factor is quite high. But before this article was published, it was not generally recognized that a systematic return to Quality existed. A manager that uncovered and began exploiting this effect 20 years ago should be credited with *alpha* for the excess return contributed by the factor. Although a regression of the manager's full historical track record using a factor model that includes QMJ would be technically valid, it would be more reasonable to measure the manager's historical skill as the sum of the alpha *and* the return resulting from the Quality factor exposure. If the Quality factor exposure is accessible more cheaply through an ETF or mutual fund, however, this information should be incorporated into the evaluation going forward—it might alter an estimate of the manager's future value added.

4.3.4 *After-cost factor returns*

To reflect the investability of the factors and evaluate the manager fairly, the performance appraiser should reduce a factor return by the costs required to implement the factor on a passive basis. In the previous four-factor analysis on the Fidelity Contrafund, we estimated a monthly alpha of 0.15% using manager returns after trading and management costs. How would we adjust the alpha estimates if we knew the trading costs for implementing each of the four factors?

Trading costs are small relative to the volatility in returns and should not materially alter the regression results. Exhibit 9 shows one estimate of trading costs along with the gross and net mean monthly returns on each factor over the Contrafund's history.

8 See Asness, Frazzini, and Pedersen (2013).

Exhibit 9 Monthly Average Factor Trading Costs and Gross and Net Factor Returns

Monthly Averages	RMRF	SMB	HML	WML
Trading costs	0.00%	0.06%	0.05%	0.48%
Mean gross returns	0.70%	0.14%	0.23%	0.58%
Mean net returns	0.70%	0.08%	0.18%	0.10%

Source: Novy-Marx and Velikov (2016).

Over Contrafund's full history, the average monthly return is 0.90%. Using gross factor returns and the factor betas from Exhibit 8, the monthly alpha is 0.1484%:

$= 0.90\% - (0.87 \times 0.70\% + 0.05 \times 0.14\% + 0.06 \times 0.23\% + 0.21 \times 0.58\%)$

$= 0.90\% - 0.7516\% = 0.1484\%$ per month, or 1.78% per year.

If we adjust for trading costs using the mean net factor returns, the monthly alpha estimate rises to 0.2552%:

$= 0.90\% - (0.87 \times 0.70\% + 0.05 \times 0.08\% + 0.06 \times 0.18\% + 0.21 \times 0.10\%)$

$= 0.90\% - 0.6448\% = 0.2552\%$ per month, or 3.06% per year.

Our estimate of manager skill is higher after adjusting for the factors' trading costs, demonstrating that using an incorrect benchmark (in this case, factors not adjusted for trading costs) can lead to an incorrect appraisal of manager performance.

4.3.5 *Limitations of the factor-based approach*

Factor analysis is subject to estimation issues, creating noise in the assessment of risk and of skill. For example:

1. With a limited number of observations, you might estimate a beta that is different from zero merely as a result of sampling error.
2. The underlying assets in the factor portfolios may include securities that are not in the fund's benchmark. One approach to this issue is to perform the same factor model regression on the benchmark and examine the differences in alphas and coefficients between the fund and benchmark regressions.
3. Factor-based models assume that, in equilibrium, the fund's returns are linearly related to the factor returns—a simplifying and not always accurate assumption.

In the example that follows, we illustrate some of the limitations of a factor-based approach.

Let us evaluate the performance of the Vanguard 500 Index Fund Admiral Shares (VFIAX), which typically invests in stocks in the S&P 500. A standard benchmark analysis produces the results shown in Exhibit 10:

Exhibit 10 Benchmark Analysis for Vanguard 500 Index Fund Admiral Shares

	VFIAX		S&P 500
Compound annual return	6.22%		6.24%
Annualized volatility	14.65%		14.65%
Tracking error		0.05%	

The fund tracked the index very closely, with an annualized tracking error of only 0.05%, and it (very slightly) underperformed the benchmark by 0.02% a year.[9] These numbers are *after* the deduction of the fund's operational expenses and management fees, totaling about 0.10%. Thus, we can conclude that the fund performed in line with its benchmark.

A factor analysis using the Fama–French three-factor model produces the results shown in Exhibit 11:

Exhibit 11 Factor Analysis for Vanguard 500 Index Fund Admiral Shares

Regression Statistics			Coefficients	Standard Error	*t*-Statistic	*P*-Value
R-squared	99.3%	Intercept	0.09%	0.03%	3.45	0.07%
Adjusted *R*-squared	99.3%	RMRF	0.99	0.01	151.08	0.00%
Standard error	0.36%	SMB	−0.18	0.01	−14.60	0.00%
Observations	185	HML	−0.01	0.01	−0.79	43.32%

- The three-factor model explains 99.3% of the fund's monthly variation of returns, indicating that it is a good model of the fund's returns.
- The large *t*-statistic on the RMRF coefficient indicates a strong relationship with the broad market, and the negative SMB coefficient accurately reflects the fund's large-cap tilt.
- The insignificance of the HML coefficient indicates that the fund is not tilted to value or growth.
- When viewed though this factor lens, the fund earned a positive alpha of 1.08% per year (12 months multiplied by the intercept of 0.09%) with a *t*-statistic of 3.45, indicating that its alpha was statistically different from zero.
- The monthly residual risk derived from the factor model—as represented in the regression standard error—is 0.36% a month, or 1.25% a year ($0.36\% \times \sqrt{12}$). This result is significantly greater than the tracking error of 0.05% we derived through the simple benchmark analysis.

The alpha and residual risk estimates arise from differences in the composition of the factors relative to the fund's benchmark. Given the clarity of the benchmark (this is an S&P 500 Index fund) and the unusually low tracking error relative to the benchmark, a benchmark analysis provides a clear, simple, and accurate performance assessment. When a strategy does contain factor tilts, however, a factor model approach allows the analyst to delve deeper to determine whether the factor exposures add or detract from value.

Now let's evaluate the Vanguard Small Cap Index Fund (VSMAX), which tracks a specified small-cap index. The specified benchmark changed during the period under evaluation, however. For most of its history, the fund's benchmark was the Russell 2000, but since 2013, it has been benchmarked to the CRSP (Center for Research in Security Prices) US Small Cap Index. This change complicates our analysis. Comparing the fund with the longest-used Russell 2000 benchmark results in the statistics shown in Exhibit 12:

9 Note that the annualized volatility of the VFIAX and the S&P 500 can be the same, but the tracking error can be non-zero—in this case, 0.05% per year.

Exhibit 12 Analysis for Vanguard Small Cap Index Fund

	VSMAX	Russell 2000
Compound annual return	9.33%	8.24%
Annualized volatility/tracking error	19.02%	19.36%
Tracking error	2.28%	

This index fund appears to have generated significant alpha (9.33% – 8.24% = 1.09% a year) with a tracking error of 2.28% a year, significantly higher than would be expected from an index fund. What additional insights might be gathered using a factor model? Using the Fama–French three-factor model yields the results shown in Exhibit 13:

Exhibit 13 Analysis for Vanguard Small Cap Index Fund Using a Three-Factor Model

Regression Statistics			Coefficient	Standard Error	*t*-Statistic	*P*-Value
R-squared	97.7%	Intercept	0.15%	0.06%	2.44	1.55%
Adjusted *R*-squared	97.7%	RMRF	1.01	0.02	65.84	0.00%
Standard error	0.84%	SMB	0.78	0.03	27.20	0.00%
Observations	185	HML	0.19	0.03	7.27	0.00%

The three-factor model explains 97.7% of monthly returns. The significantly positive SMB coefficient accurately reflects the fund's small-cap tilt. The significantly positive coefficient on HML reflects a value bias that was not apparent from the simple benchmark analysis using the Russell 2000.

The alpha estimate from the factor analysis is 0.15% per month, or 1.80% per year. This estimate is higher than the alpha of 1.09% per year implied from the benchmark analysis. The regression standard error of 0.84% gives an estimated annual tracking error of 2.91%, slightly higher than the tracking error of 2.28% relative to the benchmark.

These results do not differ meaningfully from those we derived using the benchmark analysis, but we do see a value bias that was not apparent in the simple benchmark analysis. The factor analysis confirms what we know about the fund's strategy.

When a manager has a clearly defined and investable benchmark and does not hold cash or target a different level of risk—as is typical in index funds—a traditional benchmark approach is often more sensible than a factor analysis. When there is some ambiguity in the benchmark, a factor-based analysis might yield additional insights.

4.4 Performance Appraisal with Cash Holdings

Even the most seemingly straightforward performance evaluation issues can be complicated by a number of issues. Consider, for example, a low tracking error investment strategy benchmarked to the S&P 500. It will most likely have an estimated beta near 1 in a regression on the S&P 500. If, however, the fund permits daily inflows and outflows, it likely holds a cash buffer for potential redemptions. This cash drag will result in underperformance when the equity market rises and outperformance when it falls.

A factor analysis using the benchmark as the factor (rather than simply comparing the portfolio's return with the benchmark's return) can be helpful. As an example, a fund that holds securities that, in aggregate, have a beta of 1 but always holds 5% in cash will exhibit a total fund beta of approximately 0.95. To more accurately assess the manager's skill, the performance evaluator can create a custom benchmark composed of a 95% market factor weight and a 5% short-term cash weight.

There are many different situations in which cash holdings can complicate the performance evaluator's task—some managers may choose to hold a portfolio of stocks with a beta greater than 1 to offset the cash drag; other managers may experience unpredictable investor flows that temporarily push them away from their target cash position. Or, investors in the funds may put more money in the fund during a bull market and/or take money out of the fund during a bear market, inducing a "negative market-timing" effect if the manager cannot immediately offset the effect on cash holdings. An even more complex situation arises when evaluating a manager who uses tactical asset allocation (TAA), changing the weights of equity and cash depending on the market forecast. For instance, the Columbia Thermostat mutual fund uses TAA to decide how much of its total portfolio value to hold in cash. Without knowing a fund's strategy, how can an evaluator gauge whether its manager has engaged in significant market timing?

One approach would be to look at the fund's historical rolling equity beta. Using a rolling 18-month window, Exhibit 14 shows the fund's equity beta from 2004 through 2016:

Exhibit 14 Historical Equity Beta over Time

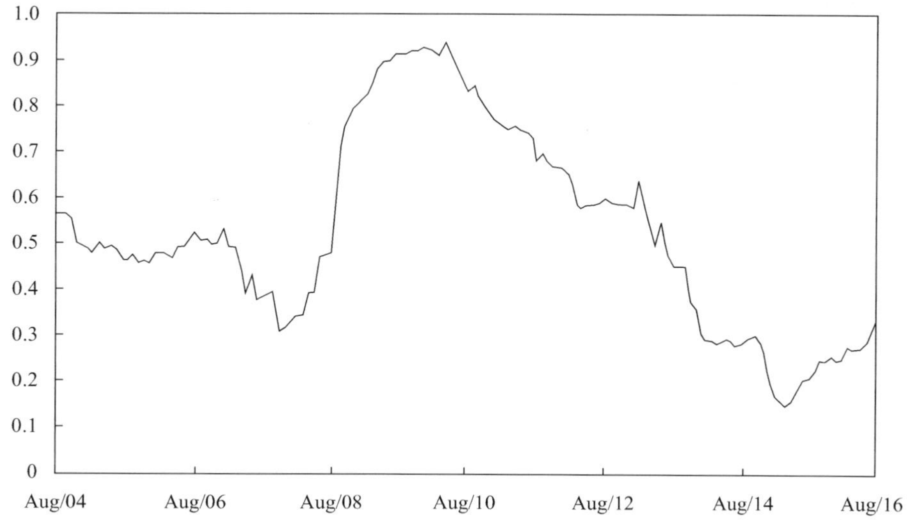

Clearly, the fund's beta has varied significantly over its history, indicating the likelihood of market timing. Later, we discuss the factor analysis adjustments necessary when evaluating a strategy that uses TAA.

4.5 Benchmark and Factor Analysis When Portfolio Risk Differs from the Benchmark's

A related issue is the possibility of different risk levels between the benchmark and the investment strategy. We have discussed the simple case in which cash holdings push the fund away from a beta of 1 from a regression model. In this case, we can use the regression coefficient on the single factor to adjust for the mismatch.

More-complicated mismatches can occur, however, that are not easily detected (or corrected) using a single-factor model. For example, suppose that a particular US government bond strategy tracks its benchmark, although it persistently targets a 10% higher duration. A simple benchmark comparison would likely find that the manager outperforms when interest rates fall and underperforms when interest rates rise. But this performance difference results purely from luck in taking a systematic risk that is higher than the benchmark. Thus, the simple benchmark comparison would lead to an incorrect appraisal of the manager's skill. If the duration bias is known in advance, a custom benchmark could be defined that reflects the manager's duration bias, such as a higher-duration government bond benchmark.

Without specific knowledge of the manager's positions, however, this exposure bias can be difficult to determine. A regression analysis can be designed to expose this type of bias. One commonly used approach is to include a general bond benchmark (with a standard duration level) as well as a second benchmark that captures the difference in returns (e.g., monthly) between a 10-year government bond index and T-bills. The coefficient on this second factor, if positive (and statistically significant), would indicate that the manager is taking a longer-duration bet than the general benchmark. This result could be confirmed using a robust fixed-income attribution model that specifically analyzes duration contribution. The regression would estimate the appropriate scaling factor to be applied to the benchmark to ensure that the benchmark's risk level is comparable to the manager's risk level.

EXAMPLE 3

Benchmark and Factor Selection in Manager Appraisal

1 In a factor model for a small-cap value manager, the coefficient on the SMB factor should be:

   A positive, and the coefficient on the HML factor should be positive.

   B negative, and the coefficient on the HML factor should be positive.

   C positive, and the coefficient on the HML factor should be negative.

2 In which of the following situations would a traditional benchmark be *most likely* preferred over factor analysis for performance evaluation?

   A The portfolio's benchmark has changed over time.

   B The regression analysis is subject to large estimation error.

   C The manager experienced significant portfolio cash inflows.

Solution to 1:

A is correct. The SMB factor is the return on small-cap stocks minus the return on large-cap stocks, and the HML factor is the return on high book-to-market stocks (value stocks) minus the return on low book-to-market stocks (growth stocks). Therefore, the coefficient on each factor should be positive.

Solution to 2:

B is correct. Traditional benchmarking is less subject to estimation issues, relative to factor analysis, in which regression parameters will be estimated with error. Factor analysis reflects changes in the portfolio benchmark over time or when the manager holds substantial cash.

LIMITATIONS OF HISTORICAL DATA

5

Although historical return data are the least subjective data we have on which to base our assessment of manager skill, using them has many limitations. For example, a manager's process or philosophy may have evolved over time, as a result either of new insights or of asset growth that restricted the manager's ability to implement the initial investment process. Or, the manager may be an "opportunistic" manager whose investment process might vary with the market environment. Or, shifts in the market environment could bias our assessment. If the market characteristics were relatively homogeneous throughout the assessment period (i.e., correlations were stable, volatility was uniformly low, and there were no large drawdowns), our analysis will be helpful only if that same environment prevails in the future. Some strategies might depend on market trends that occur episodically. In some cases, sub-period analysis might yield additional insights, although at the expense of statistical significance. For all of these reasons, a simple statistical analysis on historical data may fail to accurately assess a manager's ability. Even absent these considerations, a "simple statistical analysis" is not so straightforward.

5.1 Statistical Challenges in Analyzing Return Data

When we draw a sample of a manager's returns for performance analysis, the typical assumption is that the sample provides an unbiased representation of the manager's true return distribution and can be used to assess his true skills.[10] That is, we assume (hope) that statistics that are computed for the sample, such as the mean, variance, or intercept from a regression of the sample returns on some factors, are unbiased estimates of the true population statistics. We then use formal statistical tests to infer the likelihood (probability) that the manager is, in fact, skilled.

Much can be learned from analyzing the residuals from a fitted model of performance using returns, such as a multi-factor regression analysis. The residuals in a multi-factor regression are the period-by-period variation in the manager's returns that are not explained by the benchmarks or factors used in the regression. These residuals are used to test for evidence of manager skill.

If the historical data do not correspond to assumptions in traditional statistical inference tests, however, the *P*-values from inference tests can be incorrect, and the corresponding conclusions from the use of flawed *P*-values can be incorrect. The three primary assumptions of the statistical techniques are that

- residuals are normally distributed;
- residuals are independent over time; and
- residuals are identically distributed.

Let us start with the first assumption. The use of standard deviation and other appraisal measures that build on the residual's standard deviation (e.g., the information and appraisal ratios or the *t*-statistic of a Jensen regression alpha) assumes that each residual from the regression output is drawn from a normal distribution. But there are many reasons why the residuals might deviate substantially from the normality

10 The "population of returns" for a particular manager during a certain period can be viewed as the distribution of his returns over a very large number of repeated "tries" of that manager over similar periods (but with potentially different randomness in outcomes).

assumption. Two frequently occurring situations are when the returns to the risk factors used in the model are themselves non-normally distributed and when the manager's strategy causes portfolio characteristics to change over time.[11]

The performance evaluator needs to determine how well the historical data conform with the normality assumption. Consider the histogram of residuals in Exhibit 15, obtained from a Jensen model applied to a hypothetical manager's monthly returns. Does this histogram conform to the expectation of a normally distributed sample? We might apply some formal statistical tests to answer that question,[12] but an experienced evaluator can often subjectively judge whether the distribution satisfies the necessary assumptions. Given the histogram's non-symmetrical nature, it is apparent that the residuals might not conform to the symmetric normal distribution. If we believe that these residual returns are *not* independent, then we must adjust either the traditional statistical measures or the corresponding *P*-values of such measures to improve the reliability of our inferences.

Exhibit 15 Histogram of Model Monthly Return Residuals

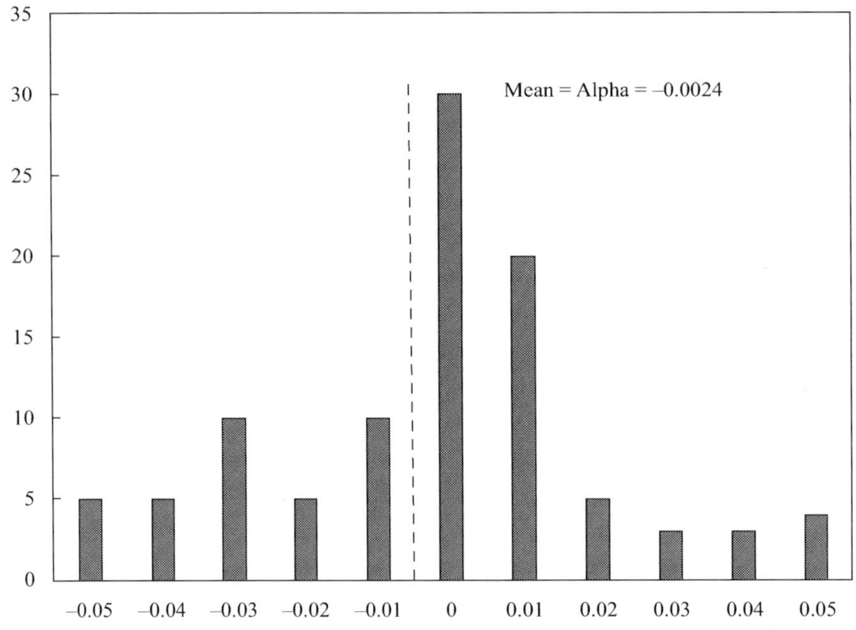

The presence of materially non-normal return residuals might indicate that the underlying portfolio securities exhibit non-normality themselves (such as securities that have option-like payoffs) or that the investment manager is implementing a non-linear strategy (such as a dynamic tactical asset allocation strategy). In the former case, a "bootstrapping analysis" can be used to improve the precision of the test's statistical inference.[13] In the latter case, the evaluator might incorporate additional factors into a regression model to account for the strategy.

11 See Fischer and Wermers (2012), Chapter 6, for a detailed discussion of several possible causes of non-normal return residuals from a regression of manager returns on factor returns.

12 Examples include a Jarque–Bera test and a chi-squared test.

13 Bootstrapping involves randomly choosing a sample of residuals (with replacement) from the actual model residuals for a given investment manager, repeating this random sample thousands of times, then determining the fraction of the random samples that have an average residual level that is higher than the alpha from the original model. This fraction is then used as the *P*-value, rather than using the *P*-value from a standard Student's *t* table. See Fischer and Wermers (2012), Chapter 6 for further details on bootstrapping performance measures.

The deviation from normality can be significant, especially for fund managers who take larger risks than the median fund. (Top-decile US domestic equity mutual fund managers, ranked by their four-factor alpha over a given five-year period between 1975 and 2002, exhibit alphas with a distribution that deviates substantially from normality.[14])

When data fulfill the second and third assumptions listed above, they are said to be **independent and identically distributed (IID)**. Independence means that the data in any one period are not influenced by the data in any other period. For example, flips of a fair coin are independent, because the result of any given coin flip does not depend on any of the prior results. Returns are identically distributed if, for example, the return drawn from a particular five-year period in the manager's history has the same mean and standard deviation (and other sample statistics) as the return drawn from another five-year period in the manager's history. We sometimes refer to IID distributions as "stationary," meaning that draws in one period come from the same distribution as that of any other period.

When monthly returns are independent, we can annualize the Sharpe ratio as follows:

$$\text{Sharpe ratio} = \frac{\text{Monthly average excess return}}{\text{Standard deviation of monthly returns}}$$

$$\text{Annualized Sharpe ratio} = \frac{\text{Monthly average excess return} \times 12}{\text{Standard deviation of monthly returns} \times \sqrt{12}}$$

The (arithmetic) mean return is annualized by multiplying by 12. The standard deviation is annualized by multiplying by $\sqrt{12}$.[15] Simplifying, the Sharpe ratio is annualized by multiplying it by $\sqrt{12}$. For equity mutual funds, returns are generally assumed to be independent and identically distributed over time, and if so, this annualization is appropriate.

If there is serial correlation in monthly returns, however, then the simple $\sqrt{12}$ annualization scaling term is incorrect and results in biased estimates of annualized risk—and therefore a biased estimate of any risk-scaled performance measure, including the Sharpe ratio.

When might returns appear to be non-independent? If our regression model omits a risk factor that significantly influences the investment fund's returns, we may find spurious serial correlation in the manager's returns. As an example, if we measure the performance of a small-cap equity manager using the simple Jensen one-factor model, the resulting alpha and residuals from the model fail to account for the risk-premium for investing in less-liquid stocks. Because liquidity differences of small-cap stocks tend to persist over several-month periods, this analysis may mislead us into thinking that the residuals in the manager's returns exhibit serial correlation.

Serial correlation in residuals can also arise from infrequent pricing of portfolio holdings, either because the holdings are illiquid, making repricing difficult, or because the investment manager purposely smooths prices to reduce her perceived return volatility. Serial correlation is frequently found in the returns of alternative investment portfolios, where many underlying positions may be illiquid or infrequently priced.

Consider the monthly risk-adjusted return in Exhibit 16.[16] It seems clear that the level of return residual in one month helps to predict that of the next month (i.e., positive values are mostly followed by additional positive values, and negative values are mostly followed by additional negative values), which implies a serial correlation

14 Fischer and Wermers (2012), Chapter 6.

15 These calculations assume that the random variable (the monthly return) is independent and identically distributed over time (over all months).

16 The risk-adjusted return in a given month is the intercept (alpha) plus that month's model residual.

in residuals. One way to test this idea is by regressing this series on its one-month lagged series. This regression yields a coefficient of 0.22 with a P-value of 0.9%[17]—we can reject the null hypothesis that these residuals are uncorrelated over time at the 99.1% confidence level.

Exhibit 16 Alpha Plus Monthly Model Residual

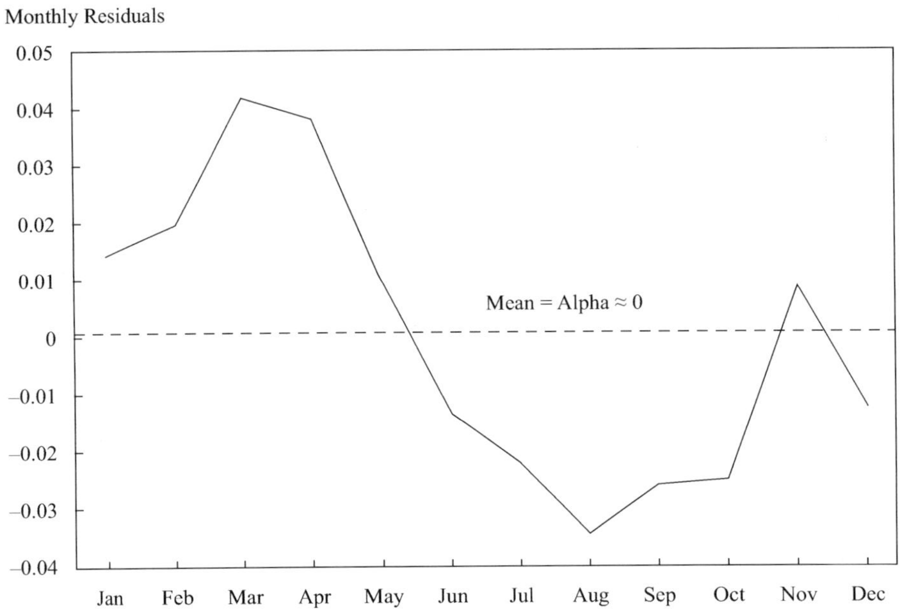

The performance evaluator should investigate the source of any suspected time-series dependencies. If on further investigation, for instance, it is found that a particular investment manager marks illiquid securities to market only at quarter ends (e.g., he prices using an approximation model at other points in time), then we should use a modeling approach to adjust that manager's stated monthly returns to correct for infrequent repricing. Alternatively, we could use a quarterly return model rather than monthly.

When might returns not be identically distributed? There are many examples. For instance, volatility in markets is persistent but mean reverting. Thus, after a shock and a large market return, the distribution from which future returns are drawn will have a higher standard deviation than before the shock, but this higher level of risk gradually decays back to the original risk level.[18]

When returns are not identically distributed, we can make corrections to the statistical tests to adjust for this issue. For example, in a linear regression in which the residuals exhibit heteroskedasticity (heteroskedasticity means that the volatility is not the same in each period),[19] we need to use a regression model that accounts for this issue, or our assessment of manager skill may be incorrect.

17 This is an AR(1) autoregressive model, which measures the correlation of a variable with its prior-period value.

18 We describe this type of behavior as a generalized autoregressive conditional heteroskedasticity (GARCH) process.

19 Ordinary least-squares regression statistics typically assume that the error terms of the model are drawn from a population with constant-variance errors. When this "homoskedastic" assumption is violated, the distribution of model errors is "heteroskedastic." A heteroskedastic distribution will lead to downward-biased estimates of variance (upward-biased t-statistics). An adjustment must be made to correct such biased estimates.

EXAMPLE 4

Limitations of Historical Data

1 Which of the following data characteristics would most likely allow a performance analyst to use unadjusted traditional statistical tests?

A Smoothing of returns by the manager

B Asymmetrical distribution of residuals

C Independent and identically distributed data

2 The Sharpe ratio is:

A understated when returns are smoothed.

B overstated when returns are positively correlated.

C not applicable when managers can borrow and invest at the risk-free rate.

3 In evaluating Fund F, you are trying to determine the reliability of the calculated Sharpe ratio. You ran a regression of the fund's returns on a one-month lagged series of the fund's own returns to test for serial correlation, the results of which appear in the following table. A description of the fund's investment strategy is also provided. Which of the statements regarding Fund F is *most* correct? The Sharpe ratio:

A is likely to be reliable given the *t*-statistic.

B is reliable given the low *P*-value of the regression.

C is likely to be biased given the fund's investment in illiquid securities.

Regression Statistics	Fund F	Fund Statistics	
Multiple *R*	0.4305	Monthly mean return	0.4510
R-squared	0.1854	Standard deviation	0.5176
Adjusted *R*-squared	0.1563	Monthly risk-free rate	0.0025
Standard error	0.4798	Monthly Sharpe	0.8664
Observations	30	Annualized Sharpe	1.7328
Intercept	0.2456		
t-Statistic	2.1092		
P-Value	0.0440		

Monthly Excess Returns for Fund F and its Benchmark

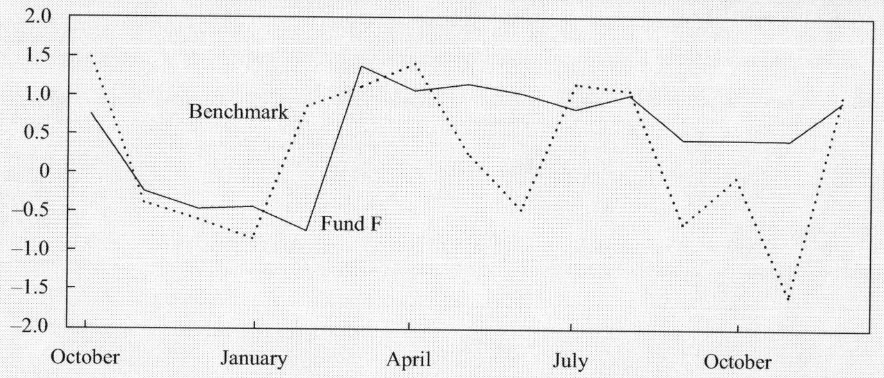

Investment Strategy: Fund F allocates its assets across multiple non-traditional or "alternative" strategies in the fixed-income and credit areas, taking long and/or short positions in corporate bonds; mortgage-backed securities and asset-backed securities; US government and agency securities; collateralized debt and loan obligations; non-US government and supranational debt securities; loans and loan participations; and derivatives with similar economic characteristics. Up to 15% of the fund's net assets may be invested in illiquid investments. Fund F invests in debt securities of any credit quality or rating. The fund uses derivatives to obtain net long or short exposures to select instruments, currencies, interest rates, countries, durations, or credit risks. The fund's use of derivatives may result in economic leverage.

Solution to 1:

C is correct. If the data are IID, then traditional statistical tests can be used. If, however, the data are asymmetric (hence non-normal) or smoothed (thus likely having serially correlated residuals), statistical tests must be adjusted for these issues.

Solution to 2:

B is correct. Positive serial correlation in returns (e.g., smoothed valuations) results in an upward bias in risk-scaled performance measures. If the investor cannot borrow or invest at the risk-free rate, then the Sharpe ratio is not an appropriate measure when managers have different risk levels.

Solution to 3:

C is correct. The fund's investment in illiquid securities indicates the potential for serial correlation in monthly returns. When such serial correlation arises, the simple $\sqrt{12}$ annualization scaling term is incorrect and results in biased estimates of annualized risk—and therefore a biased estimate of any risk-scaled performance measure, including the Sharpe ratio. The regression's high t-statistic indicated the likelihood of serial correlation in the fund's returns, and the low P-value indicates a low probability that the t-statistic resulted from random chance.

6 CHARACTERISTICS OF SUPERIOR ACTIVE MANAGERS

Much research has been conducted in an attempt to identify the qualitative characteristics of funds, portfolio managers, or fund management companies that are correlated with superior future performance. The characteristics with the strongest empirical support include the following:

- *Experience (tenure)*. At least among large funds, experienced managers outperform less experienced managers by 92 bps a year.[20] (The opposite is often true for small funds, where the management company typically controls the board, which in turn oversees hiring and firing the management company. Thus, a manager of a small fund can build tenure while continuing to underperform his peers.)

20 Ding and Wermers (2009).

- *Social connections.* Managers who have social connections with their portfolio companies (e.g., the officers or board members attended the same college as the fund manager) tend to outperform those without such connections.[21] This dynamic may occur because connected managers have better access to private information or can better assess the quality of the company's management.
- *Academic background.* Managers with high SAT scores and/or high-quality MBA degrees tend to outperform those without these credentials; managers with a CFA designation tend to take lower tracking-error risks while pursuing performance.[22,23]
- *Lower expense ratios, lower load fees, and lower turnover.* Managers whose funds have these qualities tend to outperform their peers[24] (and those with higher cash holdings and higher expenses tend to underperform their peers).[25]
- *Contrarian investment process.* Contrarian managers generally outperform herding managers, by supplying liquidity to the herd and/or from superior analysis and superior information collection.[26]
- *Positive return gap.* A positive gap in returns between the fund's performance and the performance of its publicly disclosed holdings is another characteristic of a superior manager. A large negative return gap may indicate sloppy trading or a manager who is trying to hide bad trades (e.g., "window dressing" at the end of a reporting period when holdings are published).[27]
- *Stable risk profile.* By comparing a fund's realized volatility with the volatility estimated using its most recently reported holdings, it is possible to identify "risk shifting" funds. Such funds tend to underperform funds that maintain a stable risk profile. This phenomenon has been attributed to agency problems, because these fund managers may be either cutting risk to "lock in" gains to protect their fees or increasing risk ("doubling down") in an attempt to catch up to other funds.[28]
- *High active share.* Equity fund managers who take bigger active positions away from their "best-fit benchmark" and also have low levels of portfolio turnover outperform the average mutual fund manager.[29]

It is important to remember that the conclusions from these studies are *generalizations* and must be applied with caution.

EXAMPLE 5

Superior Manager Characteristics

1 Which of the following *best* describes the evidence regarding the predictability of investment performance?

---

21 Cohen, Frazzini, and Malloy (2008).

22 Chevalier and Ellison (1999), Gottesman and Morey (2006), and Dincer, Gregory-Allen, and Shawky (2010).

23 Those who have earned the right to use the Chartered Financial Analyst designation may not misrepresent or exaggerate the meaning or implications of the designation. A charterholder may claim that "completion of the CFA Program has enhanced my portfolio management skills" but may not claim that "CFA charterholders achieve better performance results."

24 Carhart (1997).

25 Edelen (1999) and Kinnel (2017).

26 Wei, Wermers, and Yao (2015).

27 Kasperczyk, Sialm, and Zheng (2008).

28 Huang, Sialm, and Zhang (2011).

29 Cremers and Pareek (2016).

A Experienced managers of small funds tend to outperform their peers.

B Contrarian managers generally outperform herding managers.

C Managers with MBA degrees generally outperform their peers.

Solution to 1:

B is correct. Contrarian managers generally outperform herding managers. The research supports a claim that managers with *high-quality* MBA degrees and experienced managers of *large* funds tend to outperform their peers.

7 CHOOSING APPROPRIATE PERFORMANCE APPRAISAL MEASURES

The goal of performance appraisal is to make manager allocation decisions that result in the best *future* performance. Of course, however, we can observe only the manager's historical record. Although we can measure and decompose past performance in very detailed or statistically precise ways, that analysis may not improve our performance forecasts. All performance statistics are noisy measures of true skill. The evaluator should recognize this noise when deciding which statistics are most relevant. The most relevant measures will generally depend on the investor objectives, the information available, the context of the analysis, and perhaps other factors.

Manager evaluation may be done on a standalone basis or in the context of adding to an existing portfolio. In the following sections, we summarize some of the performance appraisal measures the analyst has in her toolbox and explore how the selection of an appropriate measure depends on the context of the performance evaluation exercise.

7.1 Appraisal Measures and Techniques

7.1.1 *Information ratio*

The information ratio (IR) is a simple measure that allows the evaluator to assess performance relative to the benchmark—*scaled by risk.* The implicit assumption is that the chosen benchmark is well matched to the risk of the investment strategy. IR is the annualized average active return (return in excess of the benchmark) $(\bar{r}_p - \bar{r}_B)$ divided by the annualized active risk (tracking error), $\hat{\sigma}(r_p - r_B)$.

$$IR_p = \frac{\bar{r}_p - \bar{r}_B}{\hat{\sigma}(r_p - r_B)} \quad (5)$$

With excess return scaled by risk, the evaluator can more equitably compare performance across managers.

7.1.2 *Appraisal ratio*

The appraisal ratio (AR) is a returns-based measure similar to the IR. It is the annualized alpha divided by the annualized residual risk. Think of it as a "signal-to-noise" ratio. The numerator, α, is the non-benchmark-related return of a manager, and σ_ε is the noise in the manager's alpha over the same period. Both the alpha and the residual risk are computed from a factor regression. (The AR can be computed using any factor model appropriate for the portfolio.) For example, suppose that a single-factor regression model is used, whereby the manager's return in excess of the risk-free rate $(r_{p,t} - r_{F,t})$ is regressed against the benchmark return in excess of the risk-free rate, $(r_{B,t} - r_{F,t})$. Equation 6 is the regression model used to derive the alpha.

$$r_{p,t} - r_{F,t} = \alpha + \beta \times \left(r_{B,t} - r_{F,t}\right) + \varepsilon_t \quad (6)$$

The appraisal ratio is

$$\text{AR} = \frac{\alpha}{\sigma_\varepsilon} \quad (7)$$

where σ_ε equals the standard deviation of ε_t, which is readily available from the output of commonly used statistical software (commonly denoted as the "standard error of regression").

7.1.3 *Sharpe ratio*

The Sharpe ratio is the average return in excess of the risk-free return per unit of total volatility:

$$\text{Sharpe ratio} = \frac{\overline{R}_P - R_F}{\sigma_P} \quad (8)$$

where $\overline{R}_P$ is the average return on the portfolio, R_F is the risk-free return, and σ_P is the standard deviation of portfolio return.

For the Sharpe ratio, the information ratio and the appraisal ratio, the t-statistic is equal to the respective ratio multiplied by the square root of the number of years of data. This t-statistic can be compared across managers with different history lengths.

The Sharpe ratio is extremely easy to compute, requiring only the historical periodic portfolio returns. A Sharpe ratio does not require an explicit benchmark. Although the Sharpe ratio has a well-established theoretical foundation, some key assumptions from capital market theory must be used for the Sharpe ratio to be an appropriate summary statistic:

1 The portfolio is the entire portfolio held by an investor, not just a portion.

2 The investor is risk averse and cares only about the mean return and standard deviation of his portfolio.

3 The investor is making decisions for only one period at a time.

4 The investor may borrow or lend (invest) at the risk-free interest rate.

The Sharpe ratio provides a very intuitive reward to risk trade-off, also called the "price of risk" of a particular portfolio. For instance, all else being equal, any risk-averse mean–variance investor would rather hold a portfolio with a Sharpe ratio of 2 than a portfolio with a Sharpe ratio of 1—each unit of risk is rewarded with double the excess return of the lower Sharpe ratio portfolio.

The Sharpe ratio uses only the mean and standard deviation—it does not consider other dimensions of risk. If returns are normally distributed, the standard deviation will completely describe the risk to the investor. If returns are non-normally distributed, the portfolio standard deviation will not reflect some risk investors might care about—such as skewness, drawdown, or semi-variance, which are used to evaluate asymmetric distributions. An alternative approach is to use logarithmic returns, which are typically normally distributed.

A one-period Sharpe ratio can result in poor investment choices if the manager's strategy entails actively shifting risk exposure. For example, suppose that returns are expected to be lower than average (but positive) this year and higher than average next year. Given a long-term risk objective, a good strategy would be to take less risk this year and more risk next year. The full-period Sharpe ratio cannot accurately measure the reward-to-risk ratio of this multi-period strategy.

Using the Sharpe ratio, an investor (who can borrow or lend at the risk-free rate, as per Sharpe's fourth assumption) with a risk appetite larger than that implied by the volatility of the highest Sharpe ratio manager can lever an investment in that manager to deliver a higher risk and return portfolio. The return and risk *levels* of a given manager are inconsequential; only the *ratio* of return to risk matters. Consider the case in which an investor desires an annualized volatility of 10% but the highest Sharpe ratio strategy has an annualized volatility of 5%. If the investor can borrow 100% of her portfolio value at the risk-free rate and then invest twice her portfolio value in that strategy, she will achieve her desired 10% volatility at the same Sharpe ratio. If the investor's borrowing rate is above the risk-free rate, then a second strategy with 10% volatility but a slightly lower Sharpe ratio might be the optimal choice. This scenario would occur if the cost of borrowing lowered the effective Sharpe ratio on the first strategy to below that of the second strategy.

7.1.4 *Factor analysis*

A factor analysis decomposes returns into components driven by factors and their residuals (the alpha). Factor analysis may help the evaluator to better understand a manager's return drivers. In its simplest form—a single-factor regression against a market benchmark—a factor analysis might reveal that a manager delivered any excess performance entirely through a higher beta relative to the benchmark. A deeper factor analysis might reveal that a manager's excess performance can be attributed in part to intentional tilts toward systematic risk factors such as size, value, or momentum. These insights are necessarily neither good nor bad—the analysis adds depth to the evaluator's understanding of a manager's return drivers and allows him to assess a manager's fit with the balance of the portfolio, or whether the particular combination of factor exposures is sufficient justification for active management fees. Note that a factor analysis can be conducted using portfolio holdings, but portfolio holdings information is often available only at discrete time intervals (quarterly or monthly).

7.1.5 *Peer group comparisons*

Peer group analysis permits an investor to see how a particular fund ranks over various periods compared with funds using similar investment strategies. A peer group comparison can serve as a quick and easy reference point—what would performance have been if the investor had been able to allocate to the average or the median manager?[30] It may also be useful when there are investment strategy constraints that are not reflected in a currently available index. As an example, a midcap portfolio managed under an ESG constraint that prohibits investment in alcohol, gaming, tobacco, and weapons manufacturers cannot be adequately evaluated relative to an unconstrained midcap benchmark. When there are multiple investors with similar constraints, and multiple products managed under those same constraints, a peer group comparison provides the evaluator with perspective on the performance of other accounts and products managed with similar constraints.

Peer group analysis can be performed using any of the various manager statistics—return, drawdown, Sortino ratio, Sharpe ratio, etc.

30 Answering this question violates one of the required properties of a valid benchmark—a peer group median manager is not investable ex ante because the median manager's identity and holdings are not specified in advance.

7.1.6 *Holdings-based vs. returns-based analysis*

All of the measures can be applied when the analyst is working with historical return streams. An analyst with access to portfolio holdings can perform a more detailed analysis at every point for which holdings are observed. Here are some of the advantages of holdings-based analysis over returns-based analysis:

1 Portfolio holdings can be used to estimate the factor exposure of each security in the portfolio at a given point in time, and then the manager-level exposure can be computed as the portfolio-weighted security exposure.

2 Following the information in each period's factor exposures, the manager's dynamic tilts toward and away from each factor can be computed from the time-period manager factor exposures. These explicit observations of dynamics in factor exposure are not available in returns-based approaches.

3 Using the history of factor exposures from holdings data, the manager's shift in factor exposures can be used to carefully compute the attribution of manager returns to factor timing. This approach allows a more precise estimate of market timing skills than returns-based methods offer.

7.2 Contexts for Performance Evaluation

There are various contexts in which the performance evaluator must choose one or more performance appraisal measures or techniques. Let us review the primary situations and lay out the considerations for analysis:

- Evaluating investment managers with unambiguous benchmarks;
- Evaluating investment managers with uncertain benchmarks;
- Evaluating standalone investment strategies; and
- Evaluating investment strategies for addition to the investor's current portfolio.

7.2.1 *Unambiguous benchmark*

An unambiguous benchmark is among the most common applications of performance measurement, and it results from the typical governance structure in institutions, whereby boards or investment committees make high-level asset allocation and benchmarking decisions and staff make specific manager and product allocation decisions. The benchmarks have been pre-determined by the board, so the staff's decision is limited to choosing among options. (It is important to ensure that the chosen benchmark is relevant to each of the options under consideration; for instance, a large-cap manager whose universe is the S&P 500 is not fairly evaluated relative to a Russell 1000 Index benchmark.)

Frequently, the peer group of managers being considered will typically have track records with very similar active risk budgets. In this case, simple comparison of average active return could be used to assess relative performance. To the extent that there is some variation in risk across managers, an information ratio would appropriately adjust performance for realized active risk taken. (Separately, it may also be important to know whether the active risk observed for each manager is consistent with its ex ante targeted active risk. This information can indicate the effectiveness of the manager's risk management processes.)

7.2.2 *Uncertain benchmarks and factor exposures*

If comparing performance across managers with uncertain benchmarks, a factor-based analysis generally is required. The factor analysis will allow you to gauge the differences in the factor exposures across the managers under consideration. It will also provide an estimate of each manager's alpha and the level of active risk each has taken. The appraisal ratio is the appropriate performance appraisal metric in this case, supplemented with additional insights from the factor analysis.

7.2.3 *Evaluating standalone investment strategies*

Many evaluation exercises begin by assessing manager skill independent of its potential role in an investor's portfolio. The full range of measures can be applied to build a multi-dimensional picture of the manager's risk and reward.

Benchmark-relative measures such as the information ratio provide a simple way to rank managers with the same benchmark on the basis of reward per unit of risk.

Peer group comparisons can add context to the information ratio, especially in market segments that are experiencing difficulty in successfully implementing active management. Suppose you are considering a manager who delivered an information ratio of 0.25. On its own, the information ratio might imply that the manager is not particularly skilled, but if that manager's return falls into the top decile of all similar managers over the same horizon, our perspective on the manager's skill might be quite different.[31]

The appraisal ratio provides a more nuanced perspective on reward per unit of risk. The alpha estimated from a multi-factor regression isolates a manager's alpha from the excess returns that can be obtained more cheaply, and the appraisal ratio scales that alpha by its volatility.

Absolute risk-adjusted measures such as the Sharpe ratio can be used to compare managers' risk-adjusted returns, irrespective of their benchmark.

Factor analysis or holdings-based attribution analysis may also be useful to add additional perspective on a manager's strategy and risk exposures.

7.2.4 *Evaluating investment strategies as an addition to the investor's current portfolio*

The Sharpe ratio of a standalone strategy does not indicate how beneficial it is to an investor's overall portfolio unless the evaluator also knows its correlation with that portfolio. A manager with a low Sharpe ratio may still improve the investor's total portfolio Sharpe ratio if its correlation to the balance of the investor's portfolio is low enough (the strategy might provide protection if the stock market decreases).

For example, suppose you currently hold a portfolio that is 67% in global equities and 33% in cash. The global equity portfolio has a Sharpe ratio of 0.20 and a volatility of 12%. You are evaluating the two choices shown in Exhibit 17 to invest the cash.

Exhibit 17 Descriptive Statistics for Two Hedge Funds

	Sharpe Ratio	Volatility	Correlation with Current Global Equity Portfolio
Equity long–short fund	0.25	10%	0.5
Macro fund	0.15	15%	−0.2

Which choice results in the highest portfolio Sharpe ratio?

First, calculate each manager's excess returns by reverse-engineering the Sharpe ratio, as shown in Exhibit 18.

31 Alternatively, it may be that low information ratios for all funds in a universe or period indicate that the value of active management in general is low.

Exhibit 18 Performance Statistics for Two Hedge Funds

	Sharpe Ratio	×	Volatility	=	Excess Return
Global equity portfolio	0.20	×	12%	=	2.40%
Equity long–short fund	0.25	×	10%	=	2.50%
Macro fund	0.15	×	15%	=	2.25%

Next, calculate the expected excess return and volatility of the total portfolio. The excess return for each combination is the weighted average of the excess return of the component parts. For the portfolio that would be 67% Global Equity + 33% Equity Long–Short, the expected excess return is [(0.67)(0.0240) + (0.33)(0.0250)] = 2.43%. For the portfolio that would be 67% Global Equity + 33% Macro, the expected excess return is [(0.67)(0.0240) + (0.33)(0.0225)] = 2.35%.

Calculating portfolio volatility uses the weights of the portfolio assets, their individual standard deviations, and their correlations. Because the assets are less than perfectly correlated, the portfolio volatility will be lower than the weighted average of the standard deviations of the individual investments. The formula for calculating the volatility of a two-asset portfolio is

$$\sigma_p = \sqrt{w_1^2\sigma_1^2 + w_2^2\sigma_2^2 + 2w_1w_2\rho_{1,2}\sigma_1\sigma_2} \tag{9}$$

For the 67% Global Equity + 33% Equity Long–Short portfolio, the expected portfolio standard deviation is 10.10%:

$$\sigma_p = \sqrt{\left(0.67^2 \times 0.12^2\right) + \left(0.33^2 \times 0.10^2\right) + \left(2 \times 0.67 \times 0.33 \times 0.50 \times 0.12 \times 0.10\right)}$$
$$= 0.101027 = 10.10\%$$

For the 67% Global Equity + 33% Macro portfolio, the expected portfolio standard deviation is 8.56%:

$$\sigma_p = \sqrt{\left(0.67^2 \times 0.12^2\right) + \left(0.33^2 \times 0.15^2\right) + \left(2 \times 0.67 \times 0.33 \times -0.20 \times 0.12 \times 0.15\right)}$$
$$= 0.085572 = 8.56\%$$

Using these volatilities, we can calculate each portfolio's expected Sharpe ratio as shown in Exhibit 19.

Exhibit 19 Expected Portfolio Sharpe Ratios

Portfolio Statistics if Excess Cash Is Invested in:	Excess Return	÷	Volatility	=	Sharpe Ratio
Equity long–short fund	2.43%	÷	10.10%	=	0.24
Macro fund	2.35%	÷	8.56%	=	0.27

Despite its lower standalone Sharpe ratio, the macro fund looks to be the better choice.

When multiple active managers are under consideration, particularly when multiple benchmarks are involved, a better measure to use is the appraisal ratio. The AR considers the impact of each manager on the investor's "risk budget" through the ratio of that manager's alpha to residual risk. In the absence of any constraints, and for a given risk allocation to the new strategy, choosing the strategy with the highest AR relative to the investor's current portfolio will yield the largest improvement in that investor's overall Sharpe ratio.[32]

To calculate the AR, we need the alpha from the regression. The alpha is given by

$$\alpha = r_{new} - \beta_{new}\left(r_p\right) \quad \textbf{(10)}$$

We can back into the alpha using information already at hand (Exhibits 17 and 18). The beta of each new investment (*new*) to the current portfolio (*p*) can be estimated using the covariance (cov) between them and the volatility of the current portfolio:

$$\beta_{new} = \frac{\text{cov}_{new,p}}{\sigma_p^2} = \rho\frac{\sigma_{new}}{\sigma_p} \quad \textbf{(11)}$$

The volatility of the current portfolio is derived from the volatility of its two component parts—global equities (67%) and cash (33%). Because the global equity portfolio and cash are uncorrelated, the current portfolio's volatility equals the global equity volatility multiplied by its weight in the portfolio: (0.67 × 12%) = 8.04%.

Now, using Equation 11, calculate the beta of the equity long–short fund to the current portfolio:

$$\beta_{l/s} = \frac{\text{cov}_{l/s,p}}{\sigma_p^2} = \rho\frac{\sigma_{l/s}}{\sigma_p} = 0.50\frac{0.1010}{0.0804} = 0.62$$

The beta of the macro fund to the current portfolio is −0.37:

$$\beta_{macro} = \frac{\text{cov}_{macro,p}}{\sigma_p^2} = \rho\frac{\sigma_{macro}}{\sigma_p} = -0.20\frac{0.15}{0.0804} = -0.37$$

We need one last component to estimate the alphas for the equity long–short fund and the macro fund: the expected excess return on the current portfolio. This calculation is derived from the excess return of its two component parts—global equities (67%) and cash (33%):

$$(0.67 \times 2.40\%) + (0.33 \times 0\%) = 1.61\%$$

Using Equation 10, the betas we have just calculated, and the expected excess returns for each fund (Exhibit 18), the alpha for the equity long–short fund is 1.50%:

$$\alpha_{l/s} = 2.5\% - (0.62 \times 1.61\%) = 1.50\%$$

and the alpha for the macro fund is 2.85%:

$$\alpha_{macro} = 2.25\% - (-0.37 \times 1.61\%) = 2.85\%$$

We now need to calculate the denominator of the AR, the residual variance.

The variance of the new fund under consideration, σ_{new}^2, measures total risk and has two components: (1) systematic risk, measured using the current portfolio as the benchmark, and (2) non-systematic risk of the fund under consideration. The systematic component is $\beta^2\sigma_p^2$, and the residual (non-systematic) component is $\sigma_{\varepsilon,new}^2$. Thus, the residual variance for each fund is calculated by subtracting the fund's systematic variance from its total variance.

$$\sigma_{\varepsilon,new}^2 = \sigma_{new}^2 - \beta^2\sigma_p^2 \quad \textbf{(12)}$$

Using Equation 12, the residual variance of the equity long–short fund is

$$0.10^2 - (0.62)^2(0.0804)^2 = 0.0075,$$

32 See Hecht (2014).

and the residual variance of the macro fund is

$$0.15^2 - (-0.37)^2(0.0804)^2 = 0.0216.$$

Taking the square root of the residual variance to arrive at the standard deviation terms, the residual risks for the two funds are 8.67% and 14.70%, respectively.

We can now calculate the ARs. The AR for the equity long–short fund is 0.17 (1.50%/8.67%). The AR for the macro fund is 0.19 (2.85%/14.70%). Adding the macro fund to the current portfolio will result in a larger improvement in the portfolio's Sharpe ratio.

7.3 Other Considerations for Selecting Performance Measures

Several other considerations may influence your selection of appraisal measures:

1 What is the longest period available, and are there specific sub-periods common across managers that should be evaluated?

2 Will the analysis be conducted in a traditional benchmark-relative framework, or will a factor lens be applied?

7.3.1 *Time period*

It is common practice to evaluate managers using the longest common period in which all managers have a track record. Often this is a standardized period such as 3, 5, 7, or 10 years or a rolling 3-, 5-, 7-, or 10-year window. The benefit of using identical periods to compare managers is that they all navigated the same market conditions. Shorter periods contain greater noise, however, limiting the usefulness of the analysis.

When the managers being evaluated have track records of differing lengths, one approach to consider is to compare the *t*-statistics of each manager's mean outperformance using the longest period available for each manager.[33] We can calculate the *t*-statistics for the information ratios in the same way that we calculated the *t*-statistic for the Sharpe ratio earlier. Because the standard error in an estimated mean is the standard deviation divided by the square root of the number of observations, the *t*-statistic can be approximated by multiplying the annualized information ratio by the square root of the number of years in the sample.

Consider a manager with realized annual excess returns of 2.5% a year and realized tracking error of 6% a year. That manager's information ratio is 0.42 (0.417, rounded). If the manager's track record is nine years, then the standard error in the annual excess return is approximately $6\%/\sqrt{9} = 2\%$. The *t*-statistic for the hypothesis that the manager's mean return equals zero is approximately 2.5%/2% = 1.25. We can arrive at the same number simply by multiplying the information ratio of 0.42 by $\sqrt{9}$, which is also 1.25. If that manager had a 25-year track record, the *t*-statistic would be 2.1.

As an example, assume a pension plan you advise has decided to allocate 10% of total assets to non-US equity that is benchmarked to the MSCI EAFE Index. The client has assigned a tracking error budget of 5% relative to the benchmark. You have been asked to recommend a single manager for this allocation from a universe of managers that are benchmarked to the MSCI EAFE index. You are further told that the MSCI EAFE index is a good fit for all of the managers—all have betas of approximately 1.0 with the index. Exhibit 20 provides summary statistics for the managers:

33 Technically, the evaluator should compare the *P*-value, not the *t*-statistic, because the degrees of freedom will differ for track records of different length. In practice for long evaluation periods, however, the difference in Student's *t*-distributions is very small.

Exhibit 20 Summary Data for Three Managers

	Data Length	Annualized Outperformance	Annualized Tracking Error
Manager 1	10 years	+1.13%	2.15%
Manager 2	24 years	+0.95%	2.81%
Manager 3	12 years	+2.23%	4.89%

Let us calculate the information ratios and *t*-statistics for each manager. The calculations for Manager 1 are as follows:

IR = 1.13/2.15 = 0.5256

t-Statistic = $0.5256 \times 10^{1/2} = 1.66$

Exhibit 21 shows the results for all three managers:

Exhibit 21 Analysis Using the Information Ratio

	IR	*t*-Statistic
Manager 1	+0.5256	1.66
Manager 2	+0.3381	1.66
Manager 3	+0.4560	1.58

Which manager do you recommend? All three managers have similar *t*-statistics, meaning that they have statistically similar levels of skill. Manager 1 has the highest IR, but given her lower tracking error, she has delivered only 1.13% of outperformance per year. In contrast, Manager 3 targets higher active risk with a realized tracking error of 4.89%. Despite a modestly lower information ratio than that of Manager 1, Manager 3's outperformance has been about twice as high, at 2.23% per year.

An important point here is that any performance statistic is estimated with error. When one compares across managers with the same history length, their *t*-statistics—which measure statistical confidence in each manager's track record—are proportional to their IRs, eliminating the need to make any adjustments before comparing. When their histories differ in length, simply comparing the IRs might mislead an evaluator to select a manager with a higher point estimate but with a lot more uncertainty in that estimate. Another important variable to consider when comparing managers with different length track records is the differences in the market environment that prevailed during the course of compiling the track record.

7.3.2 *Traditional benchmark vs. factor lens*

Let us extend our earlier example, moving beyond the traditional benchmark-relative analysis to perform a factor analysis. Here we use a version of the Fama–French three-factor model based on the MSCI EAFE universe of stocks to evaluate three managers who invest relative to the EAFE index. Assume that, for all three manager histories, the three factors RMRF, SMB, and HML earned positive premiums. Exhibit 22 shows the results of the factor analysis.

Exhibit 22 Analysis Using Three-Factor Model

	Alpha	Factor Beta RMRF	Factor Beta SMB	Factor Beta HML	Residual Risk	AR
Manager 1	0.93% (1.75)	1.0 (6.5)	0.1 (0.5)	−0.1 (−0.3)	1.95%	+0.48
Manager 2	1.35% (3.21)	1.0 (13.1)	−0.3 (−1.2)	−0.5 (−2.1)	2.13%	+0.63
Manager 3	−0.15% (−0.23)	1.0 (8.1)	0.5 (1.9)	0.8 (2.7)	1.25%	−0.12

Note: *t*-Statistics are in parentheses.

What do we learn from this analysis? First, because RMRF is a cap-weighted portfolio of EAFE stocks, it should track the EAFE benchmark very closely. All three managers appear to have an RMRF beta near 1. Manager 1's outperformance (0.93% per year) is not explained by the other two factors, because SMB and HML betas are near zero and the annualized alpha is very similar to the benchmark-relative outperformance shown in Exhibit 20.

For Manager 2, the analysis suggests that its alpha is actually higher than the benchmark outperformance in Exhibit 20. The negative exposures to the size and value factors (−0.3 and −0.5, respectively) indicate a modest tilt toward larger-cap stocks and a more significant tilt toward growth stocks. Based on the alpha *t*-statistic of 3.21, this manager demonstrates the most statistically significant skill.

In this three-factor analysis, Manager 3 shows no statistically significant skill—and alpha of −0.15% with a *t*-statistic of −0.23 as compared with outperformance of +2.23% in Exhibit 20. His performance is almost entirely explained by positive loadings on the size (0.5) and value (0.8) factors, indicating tilts toward small-cap and high book-to-market stocks.

The AR summarizes each manager's idiosyncratic skill. By this measure, Manager 2 is the most skilled manager.

Would you choose Manager 2 based on the stronger evidence of skill? Or would you choose Manager 3 based on the absolute level of outperformance driven by exposure to small-cap and value factors? The answer to this question depends on the investor's goals and constraints. If the emphasis is on maximizing return, you would probably choose Manager 3. The investor should explore whether these factor exposures can be accessed more cheaply, however—for example, through a separate allocation to low-cost passively managed funds or ETFs. If the goal is to generate alpha through skill, you might prefer Manager 2. In practice, the "right" answer must consider costs, leverage, and investor willingness to explore more-complex portfolio solutions.

In summary, there are various performance appraisal metrics, contexts, and considerations when undertaking a performance evaluation. Although it is unrealistic to give a simple protocol for an analysis, Exhibit 23 attempts to list which measures are generally appropriate in the contexts discussed in this section. In the real world, the evaluator must consider the information available, the objective of the analysis, and any other considerations that might affect her choice of metrics and techniques.

Exhibit 23 Which Appraisal Measure?

Facts and Circumstances of the Appraisal	Excess Return	Information Ratio	Appraisal Ratio	Sharpe Ratio	Peer Group Comparison	Factor Analysis
Returns information	X	X	X	X	X	X
Holdings information	X				X	X
Unambiguous benchmark	X	X			X	

(continued)

Exhibit 23 (Continued)

Facts and Circumstances of the Appraisal	Excess Return	Information Ratio	Appraisal Ratio	Sharpe Ratio	Peer Group Comparison	Factor Analysis
Uncertain benchmark			X			X
Lengthy, common track record	X	X	X	X	X	X
Track records of varying lengths		X *t*-statistic	X *t*-statistic	X *t*-statistic		X
Standalone investment				X		
As part of a portfolio			X			X

EXAMPLE 6

Selecting the Appropriate Performance Appraisal Measure

1 When choosing among multiple managers, which of the following *best* allows the analyst to solve for the optimal combination of managers?

  A Peer group comparison

  B The appraisal ratio

  C Holdings-based attribution analysis

2 The Sharpe ratio is the *most* appropriate measure of a manager's performance when the:

  A investor is risk neutral.

  B portfolio returns are skewed.

  C portfolio is the entire portfolio held by an investor.

3 Using the appraisal ratio, which of the following managers would be the best to add to the investor's current portfolio?

	Manager 1	Manager 2	Manager 3
Standard deviation	14.00%	12.00%	16.00%
Expected excess return	3.20%	2.90%	2.80%
Beta with current portfolio	1.10	0.60	−0.40
Current portfolio excess return	2.00%	2.00%	2.00%
Current portfolio standard deviation	12.00%	12.00%	12.00%

  A Portfolio 1

  B Portfolio 2

  C Portfolio 3

Solution to 1:

B is correct. The appraisal ratio is useful when multiple active managers are considered because it makes it possible to analytically solve for the optimal combination of managers that maximize improvement in the portfolio's Sharpe ratio.

Solution to 2:

C is correct. The Sharpe ratio is an appropriate measure of manager performance when considering a single manager to manage the investor's complete portfolio. The Sharpe ratio assumes that an investor is risk averse and does not consider risk other than the standard deviation.

Solution to 3:

C is correct. For Manager 3, alpha is the expected excess return minus the beta multiplied by the current portfolio excess return: 2.80% – (–0.40 × 2.00%) = 3.60%. The residual variance is found by subtracting the fund's systematic variance from its total variance; $0.16^2 - (-0.40)^2 \times (0.12^2) = 0.0233$. In standard deviation terms, the residual risk is $\sqrt{0.0233} = 15.26\%$. The appraisal ratio is then 3.60%/15.26% = 0.24.

Using the same steps, for Manager 1, the appraisal ratio is 1.00%/4.66% = 0.21. For Manager 2, it is 1.70%/9.60% = 0.18. Thus, even though Manager 3 had the lowest excess return and highest standard deviation, it would be the best manager to add to the current portfolio given its higher appraisal ratio (resulting in part from its negative beta with the current portfolio).

PERFORMANCE APPRAISAL OF NON-LINEAR STRATEGIES

8

When analyzing a manager who engages in market timing (including factor timing) or whose strategy makes extensive use of securities with non-linear payoffs, such as options, the standard approach to performance appraisal can significantly misestimate manager skill. Suppose that a manager successfully times the market portfolio by constructing a high-beta portfolio when the market is expected to perform above average and a low-beta portfolio when the market is expected to perform below average. An evaluator who does not know that the manager is implementing timing would estimate a beta according to the slope of the solid line labeled "Estimated Portfolio" in Exhibit 24.

Exhibit 24 Potential Bias in the Alpha Estimate for Market Timing Managers

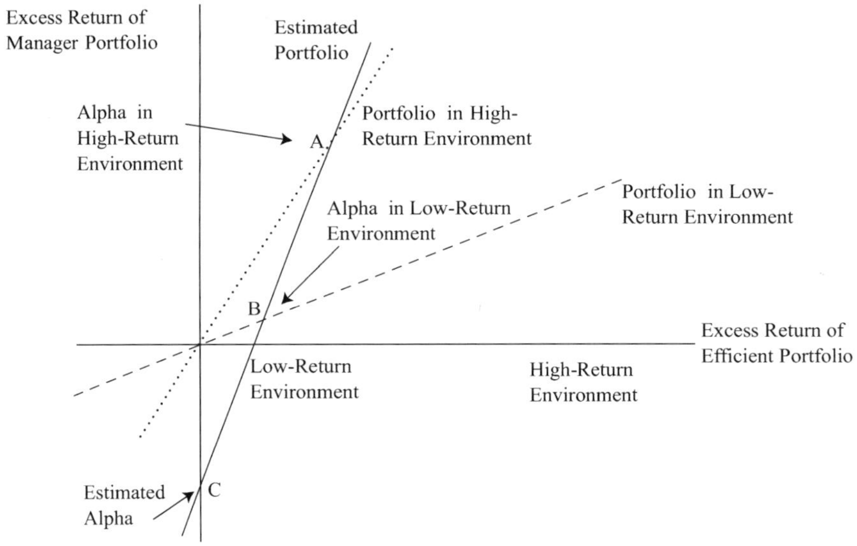

Although the estimated beta is technically correct, it results in a negative alpha, as indicated by the negative intercept (point C), which is clearly not representative of this manager's skill. This outcome results from estimating a simple linear model when the correct model would be non-linear, using different betas depending on the market state. In this section, we consider several different sources of non-linearity that require specific models to correctly appraise performance.

In some situations, we may suspect that the manager's portfolio holdings contain either explicit or implicit option-like payoffs. For example, an equity portfolio manager who holds options on the S&P 500 will have an explicit option return for this component of his portfolio. Or, a bond manager holding mortgages will have implicit option-like returns because of the issuer's right to prepay mortgages. In these cases, the portfolio returns will not be normally distributed and standard statistical techniques will not suffice. How do we adjust our performance evaluation approach when we expect option-like payoffs?

Option-like securities generate skewness in returns. As examples, a hedge fund that sells out-of-the-money put options on the S&P 500 has negatively skewed returns (frequent small gains and a few large losses), and a fund that buys at-the-money call options on the S&P 500 has positively skewed returns (frequent small losses and a few large gains). The presence of skewed returns indicates the need to include a performance model factor that captures skewness. Investors value positive skewness and tend to avoid negative skewness, so any such factor needs to adequately capture the premium (discount) paid for positive (negative) skewness as well as the distribution of (skewed) returns that the risk presents (because skewness can take many distributional forms).

There are a few approaches to use when evaluating a portfolio with skewed returns. In general, these approaches introduce a factor or a benchmark with the same conditionally skewed return distribution in order to capture the managed portfolio's skewness risks. To have the same conditional skewness, this factor or benchmark needs to have large returns of the same sign (i.e., positive or negative) and at the same time (e.g., when the S&P 500 crashes) as the positions held by the manager. Ideally, this factor should also mimic the degree of moneyness (the difference between the asset price and the exercise price) in the manager's positions. The factor measures the manager's effective use of non-linear strategies—the coefficient multiplied by the average factor return will be positive if the manager is effective, and the alpha will correctly measure the manager's independent stock-picking skill.

We present two examples for modeling optionality using factors; they differ in the precision with which they model option-like returns.

8.1 A Single-Factor/Benchmark Approach

Sometimes simplicity is more important than precision—perhaps because the holdings of securities with option-like returns are insignificant. In such a case, the evaluator may choose to simply add a single risk factor to a model or to create a custom benchmark in a traditional benchmarking analysis that helps to capture the returns on similar broad security portfolios having option-like payoffs.[34]

For instance, to evaluate a bond manager who is known to overweight mortgages but the extent of this overweighting is not known, one can simply add a factor that captures the difference between mortgage-backed securities (MBS) and government bonds to a standard bond factor model.[35] This factor will exhibit negative conditional skewness in returns, because upside returns are substantially reduced by the prepayment of mortgages when interest rates drop. If the extent of the overweight *is* known, the evaluator could construct a custom (blended) benchmark using, for example, the Barclays Aggregate Bond Index and a time-series of MBS returns. The blending proportions should match the policy proportions used by the bond manager.

In a more general case, we may not know the intended target holding of securities with optionality, and the manager may hold several different types of securities that exhibit optionality in returns. As an example, suppose we wish to evaluate the performance of a bond manager who holds a mixture of US bonds—government, corporate, and convertible corporate bonds. Assume that the corporate bonds are non-callable. Also, assume that the convertible bonds are a small part of portfolio value. Thus, it is reasonable to add a single factor to capture optionality.

We can use the Elton–Gruber (1995) model:

$$\begin{aligned} r_{p,t} - r_{F,t} &= \alpha + \beta \times RMRF_t + b \times FIRF_t + m \times TERM_t \\ &\quad + d \times DEFAULT_t + o \times OPTION_t + \varepsilon_t \end{aligned} \qquad (13)$$

Note that this model has an *OPTION* factor to incorporate the convertible's optionality.

8.2 A More Structured Factor Approach

If non-linear payoffs are a significant component of portfolio returns, we can use more-complex "strategy-based" factors to more precisely model these non-linearities. It may be infeasible (or undesirable) to create a custom blended benchmark, because the optionality of the manager's fund may change quickly over time as the market portfolio moves up or down in value. A blended benchmark would require an analysis at each point in time of the manager's intended next-period exposure to optionality—a daunting task.

When non-linear payoffs are significant, it is often more efficient to use a multi-factor model containing factors that mimic the changing non-linearity of the fund's returns over time. A flexible model that accounts for different moneyness of option-like holdings (potentially both calls and puts) would add multiple factors to a standard

34 As motivation for such a simple approach, recall that adding too many factors of any kind can result in "overfitting," which leads to erroneous inference about a manager's abilities.

35 Elton, Gruber, and Blake (1995) compute such a factor using the difference in monthly returns between the Lehman Brothers GNMA and a blend of two more-general Lehman Brothers government bond indexes that results in the same duration as the GNMA index. The simplicity in this approach is that the factor is constructed from a portfolio of numerous bonds having different durations and skewness, rather than constructing a precise factor return having a targeted level and shape of skewness.

performance evaluation model. Given that the managed portfolio may contain several different distributional types of skewness, we need multiple factors, each with different regression coefficients (i.e., weights), to more precisely "span" these different types.

For example, consider a model that adds two call option factors and two put option factors to a standard Jensen regression:

$$r_{p,t} - r_{F,t} = \alpha + \beta_1 RMRF_t + \beta_2 C(k_1) + \beta_3 C(k_2) + \beta_4 P(k_1) + \beta_5 P(k_2) + \varepsilon_t \quad (14)$$

where $C(k)$ and $P(k)$ represent the returns on one-month call and put options with exercise price of k.

The second and third factors are periodic (e.g., monthly) returns to calls on the stock market with strike prices of k_1 and k_2, respectively, and the fourth and fifth factors are payoffs to puts with strike prices of k_1 and k_2, respectively. The returns on the option factors are computed as follows: On the first trading day in January, buy an at-the-money (ATM) call option on the S&P 500 that expires in February. On the first trading day in February, sell the option bought a month ago (i.e., at the beginning of January) and buy another ATM call option on the S&P 500 that expires in March. Repeating this trading pattern every month provides the time-series of returns on buying an ATM call option.[36] A similar procedure provides the time-series of returns on other moneyness call and put positions.

More-complicated non-linear strategies can also be represented in an augmented factor model. The most widely used model for equity hedge fund returns is the Fung and Hsieh (2004) seven-factor model:[37]

$$\begin{aligned} r_{p,t} - r_{F,t} &= \alpha + \beta \times RMRF_t + s \times SMB_t + g \times TREAS10YR_t \\ &+ c \times CREDIT_t + b \times BONDPTFS_t + d \times CURRPTFS_t \\ &+ e \times COMMPTFS_t + \varepsilon_t \end{aligned} \quad (15)$$

where the factors not previously defined are the monthly change in the 10-year Treasury constant maturity yield (*TREAS10YR*), the change in the Moody's Baa yield less 10-year Treasury constant maturity yield (*CREDIT*), and three primitive trend-following strategies—derived from bond markets (*BONDPTFS*), currency markets (*CURRPTFS*), and commodities markets (*COMMPTFS*).[38] The last three factors are explicitly designed to mimic the trend-following strategies used by many equity hedge funds. As such, these "strategy-based factors" create skewness in their factor returns that, by design, should mimic the skewed returns of many hedge funds.

The performance appraiser could also suspect that some of the non-linearity in portfolio returns results from a tactical asset allocation strategy of "timing" risk-factors, such as the return on the stock market. If so, the use of specific timing factors can provide further precision in the performance evaluation. We explore this idea next.

8.3 Non-linearity Resulting from Tactical Asset Allocation Skills

Tactical asset allocation (TAA) skills refers to an active manager's ability to overweight (underweight) a sector or asset class at the right time—that is, prior to an abnormally high (low) period of performance. A Brinson–Fachler attribution analysis will reveal the extent to which a manager uses tactical allocation, as well as the extent to which the approach contributed to investment performance. There are also returns-based

36 The model and computational procedure are from Agarwal and Naik (2004).

37 Fung and Hsieh (2004). The authors have since added an eighth factor to capture emerging market equity exposure (EM).

38 These trend-following factors are constructed from lookback option straddle strategies, as described in Fung and Hsieh (2001, 2004).

solutions to estimating TAA skill. Although they are not widely used in practice, we provide a brief introduction to them here. Readers interested in more detailed discussion of these models should consult the referenced articles.

The Treynor–Mazuy (Treynor and Mazuy, 1966) model is an adaptation of the Jensen model. It assumes that a manager is a "proportional timer"—uses the forecasted return on the market factor, RMRF, and assumes that the manager adjusts the portfolio beta to be proportional to his forecast of the market. Equation 16 shows how the Jensen model is modified to accommodate market timing:

$$r_{p,t} - r_{F,t} = \alpha + \beta \times RMRF_t + \gamma \times \left(RMRF_t\right)^2 + \varepsilon_t \quad (16)$$

Security selection skill is measured by $\hat{\alpha}$, and TAA skill is captured by $\hat{\gamma} \times \widehat{\text{Var}}\left(RMRF_t\right)$. $\widehat{\text{Var}}\left(RMRF_t\right)$ is the variance of the RMRF factor over the measurement period.

Exhibit 25 illustrates a hypothetical relationship between a long-only manager's excess returns and market excess returns (RMRF, proxied by the CRSP value-weighted US stock return index). The curved line shows the actual manager returns as a function of market returns. The straight line shows the manager's full-sample beta as a function of the market's return:[39]

Exhibit 25 Excess Returns and Beta for a Manager with Timing Skills

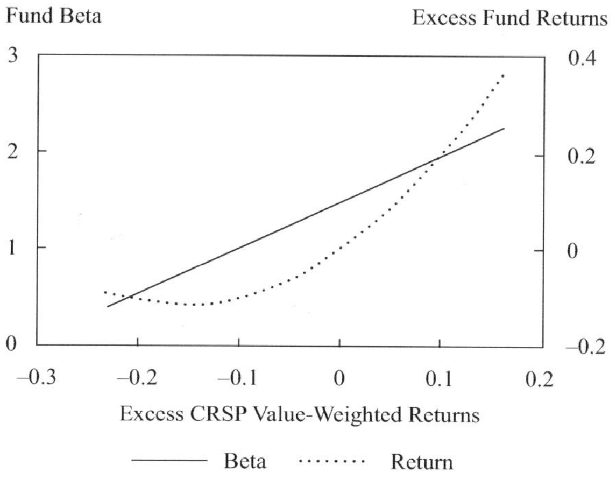

This manager's beta is always positive, but her market exposure is proportional to market return. The relationship between fund beta and excess market return indicates that this manager increases his beta in proportion to his expectation of the market excess return. Here, we might use the Treynor–Mazuy model to quantify the manager's TAA skill adding a factor, $RMRF_t^2$, to capture the manager's potential market timing.

The Henriksson–Merton (Henriksson and Merton, 1981) model assumes that a manager chooses from only two values of beta—a high beta if the market excess returns are expected to be positive, and a low beta if the expected returns are not positive:

$$r_{p,t} - r_{F,t} = \alpha + \beta \times RMRF_t + \gamma \times \left(RMRF_t\right)^+ + \varepsilon_t \quad (17)$$

39 This graph is idealized—it assumes no randomness in markets. The manager's beta perfectly forecasts the excess market return, and the excess fund return is perfectly captured by the non-linear relation between it and the market excess return. In the real world, we would observe a noisy relation between beta and market excess returns, as well as between fund and market excess returns.

where α is the measure of selection for the managed portfolio, controlling for any market-timing abilities (under certain assumptions), and $(RMRF_t)^+ = \max(0, RMRF_t)$.

Selection skill is measured by $\hat{\alpha}$. TAA skill is captured by $\hat{\gamma}$ multiplied by the value of an at-the-money call option on the excess market return ($C[RMRF,T]$, where T is the length of the performance evaluation period).

Exhibit 26 illustrates another hypothetical relationship between manager (excess) returns and market (excess) returns. The continuous line shows the actual manager returns as a function of market returns. The irregular line shows the manager's beta as a function of the market's return:

Exhibit 26 Excess Returns and Discrete Beta for a Manager with Timing Skills

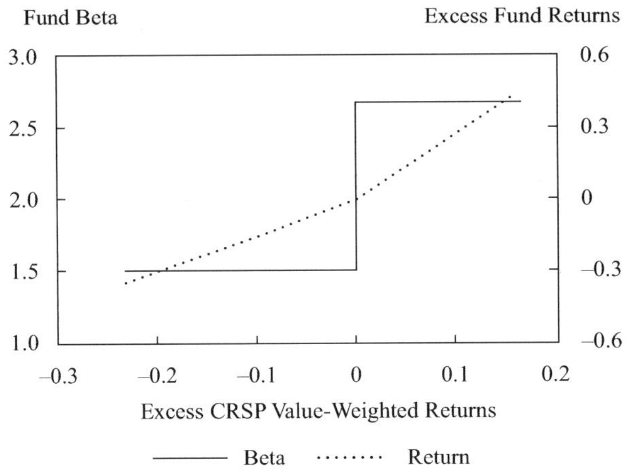

Here, it is clear that the manager is engaging in a binary strategy that discretely changes portfolio beta to either 1.5 or 2.7, depending on forecasted market conditions. Observing this relationship (i.e., that the manager is simply choosing between beta values, not adjusting his beta proportionately to his market forecast), we might use the Henriksson–Merton model to quantify the manager's TAA skill.

EXAMPLE 7

Incorporating Optionality and Timing Skills into Performance Evaluation

1 Which of the following *best* describes a structured factor approach to evaluating portfolios with options?

A The holdings of option-like securities are assumed to be limited.

B The returns of peers with option-like returns are incorporated into an evaluation model.

C An evaluation model is augmented with factors that account for the option-like holdings.

2 A manager holds a balanced portfolio of stocks and bonds. The manager has a very low level of turnover and holds a small proportion of callable bonds. Which of the following models should *most likely* be used to evaluate portfolio performance?

A The Treynor–Mazuy model

B The Henriksson–Merton model

C The Elton–Gruber model augmented with the factors SMB, HML, and WML

3 A long-only manager successfully times market movements by setting a beta equal to 0.5 or 1.5 depending on market conditions. Which of the following models should *most likely* be used to evaluate portfolio performance?

A The Jensen model

B The Treynor–Mazuy model

C The Henriksson–Merton model

Solution to 1:

C is correct. A structured factor approach adds multiple option-like factors to a standard performance evaluation model. If the holdings of option-like securities are limited, a simple one-factor model is more likely to be used. A peer-based approach uses the returns of the manager's peers.

Solution to 2:

C is correct. We would use the Elton–Gruber (1995) model that incorporates bond risk factors as well as an *OPTION* factor to incorporate the optionality of the callable bonds. The factors SMB, HML, and WML would capture equity risk. A and B are incorrect because with low turnover, the manager is likely not using tactical asset allocation.

Solution to 3:

C is correct. If the manager makes binary choices in its beta depending on market conditions, the Henriksson–Merton model would best fit its returns. The Jensen model does not account for non-linearity in returns, and the Treynor–Mazuy model assumes more-linear changes in beta.

EVALUATING AND RANKING ACTIVE INVESTMENT MANAGERS: A MINI CASE 9

A robust process of analyzing an active investment manager's skill requires a number of measures and statistical tests. Each test of risk-adjusted performance provides a different perspective on the inferred abilities of an active manager, and no test can by itself provide a summary measure of active manager skill. This case study provides examples of manager appraisal to illustrate key themes from this reading.

You are tasked with assessing several investment strategies, most of which hold long US equity positions. Some also allocate to US fixed-income securities, and all hold a buffer of cash for investor outflows. The return data are net of management fees and expenses and cover an 18-year period. For the purposes of this analysis, we make the simplifying assumption that past performance is representative of future performance. This assumption allows the evaluator to make fund recommendations based on past performance. Exhibit 27 presents the arithmetic and geometric monthly mean return, rank, and annualized standard deviation for each fund.

Exhibit 27 Performance Statistics for Funds[40]

Fund	Arithmetic Mean Monthly Return	Geometric Mean Monthly Return	Arithmetic Mean Return Rank	Geometric Mean Return Rank	Annualized Standard Deviation
Dreyfus	1.15%	1.07%	8	8	13.42%
Fidelity Equity	1.25%	1.16%	6	6	14.81%
Fidelity Puritan	1.26%	1.21%	5	4	10.67%
Founders Growth	1.32%	1.19%	3	5	17.29%
Franklin Growth	1.09%	1.00%	11	12	15.30%
Franklin Income	1.19%	1.15%	7	7	10.44%
Putnam	1.07%	1.01%	12	11	11.85%
Investment Company	1.31%	1.23%	4	3	14.00%
MFS	1.12%	1.07%	9	9	10.60%
Pioneer Growth	1.04%	0.91%	14	14	17.29%
Pioneer Income	0.88%	0.86%	15	15	7.64%
Steadman	0.47%	0.37%	16	16	15.38%
T. Rowe Price Growth	1.05%	0.93%	13	13	16.30%
Value Line	1.47%	1.30%	2	2	19.83%
Vanguard Wellington	1.10%	1.05%	10	10	11.16%
Vanguard Windsor	1.50%	1.41%	1	1	15.19%

1 ***From the foregoing table, you note that three funds rank higher using geometric-average returns than arithmetic-average returns. Explain why this situation might occur.***

The more volatile a fund's returns, the greater the difference between its arithmetic mean returns and the geometric mean returns. Funds with higher standard deviations will see a larger diminution of their geometric mean return relative to their arithmetic mean return than will funds with lower volatility. Therefore, funds that are less variable move up when ranked by geometric mean returns. For example, the Franklin Growth is ranked 11th by arithmetic mean return, ahead of Putnam at 12th. If the geometric mean return is used, however, the rankings reverse, with the lower-volatility Putnam now ranked at 11th.

2 ***If the average monthly risk-free return over this period was 0.59%, what are the realized annualized Sharpe ratios for each of these funds?***

To annualize the monthly arithmetic mean returns for consistency with the annual standard deviation, we multiply the monthly arithmetic mean return by 12. This calculation is used in the numerator of the Sharpe ratio calculation. For example, for Dreyfus, it is

$$[(1.15\% - 0.59\%) \times 12]/13.42\% = 0.50.$$

Applying this calculation to the other funds results in the Sharpe ratios shown in Exhibit 28.

40 This and subsequent exhibits present values rounded to two significant digits. Subsequent calculations, however, use inputs of greater precision that are recalled from a calculator's memory. Therefore, your calculated values may differ slightly from those presented.

Exhibit 28 Fund Sharpe Ratios

Fund	Sharpe Ratio
Dreyfus	0.50
Fidelity Equity	0.54
Fidelity Puritan	0.75
Founders Growth	0.51
Franklin Growth	0.40
Franklin Income	0.69
Putnam	0.49
Investment Company	0.62
MFS	0.60
Pioneer Growth	0.31
Pioneer Income	0.46
Steadman	−0.09
T. Rowe Price Growth	0.34
Value Line	0.53
Vanguard Wellington	0.55
Vanguard Windsor	0.72

You then calculate the return and tracking error relative to the S&P 500 and estimate the funds' alphas using a one-factor CAPM. Exhibit 29 shows the results of the analysis.

Exhibit 29 Performance Statistics for Funds

Fund	Annual Excess Return vs. S&P 500	Annualized Tracking Error to S&P 500	CAPM Beta	Annualized Jensen's Alpha	*R*-Squared	Annualized Residual Risk
Dreyfus	−1.09%	5.51%	0.83	0.24%	87%	4.88%
Fidelity Equity	0.15%	3.95%	0.95	0.55%	93%	3.88%
Fidelity Puritan	0.21%	6.88%	0.65	2.96%	83%	4.37%
Founders Growth	0.92%	7.41%	1.04	0.64%	82%	7.41%
Franklin Growth	−1.75%	7.28%	0.90	−0.98%	79%	7.14%
Franklin Income	−0.58%	12.01%	0.42	3.91%	38%	8.30%
Putnam	−2.01%	6.01%	0.73	0.10%	86%	4.42%
Investment Company	0.85%	4.15%	0.89	1.67%	93%	3.84%
MFS	−1.49%	6.70%	0.65	1.25%	85%	4.12%
Pioneer Growth	−2.38%	9.23%	0.97	−2.16%	72%	9.24%
Pioneer Income	−4.29%	10.16%	0.40	0.37%	63%	4.67%
Steadman	−9.24%	10.04%	0.80	−7.68%	61%	9.59%
T. Rowe Price Growth	−2.33%	5.16%	1.03	−2.56%	90%	5.15%
Value Line	2.73%	10.10%	1.14	1.63%	75%	9.89%

(continued)

Exhibit 29 (Continued)

Fund	Annual Excess Return vs. S&P 500	Annualized Tracking Error to S&P 500	CAPM Beta	Annualized Jensen's Alpha	*R*-Squared	Annualized Residual Risk
Vanguard Wellington	−1.68%	5.31%	0.71	0.57%	93%	3.07%
Vanguard Windsor	3.17%	7.13%	0.90	3.97%	79%	6.98%

3 ***Using data from Exhibits 27, 28, and 29, make a recommendation for each of the following situations:***

A *Your client can borrow or invest at the risk-free rate, and she is seeking a single manager for her entire portfolio.*

i. *Identify an appropriate appraisal metric, calculate the relevant statistic, and recommend the best fund.*

The Sharpe ratio is the most relevant statistic when a single manager will manage the entire portfolio. This ratio can be replicated at any risk level to achieve the target volatility. With a Sharpe ratio of 0.75, the Fidelity Puritan Fund is the best fund.

ii. *If your client is willing to take 20% annualized volatility, what will her portfolio look like?*

Because the Fidelity Puritan Fund has a realized standard deviation of 10.67%, you will need to lever the portfolio to achieve risk of 20%. To do this, you invest 20%/10.67% = 187% of the client's assets in the Fidelity Puritan Fund and borrow to fund that amount of leverage.

iii. *What if your client is willing to take only 10% annualized volatility?*

The target volatility of 10%, divided by the 10.67% standard deviation of the Puritan Fund, is 94%. So, 94% of the client's assets would be invested in the Fidelity Puritan Fund, and the remaining 6% would be held in cash.

B *Your client cannot borrow, is seeking a single manager for the entire portfolio, and is willing to take only 15% annualized volatility. Identify an appropriate appraisal metric, calculate the relevant statistic, and recommend an appropriate fund.*

The Sharpe ratio is again the best metric. Because your client cannot borrow, however, you need to find a combination of cash and a single manager that delivers the highest return at the target level of volatility (15%). To estimate the expected annual excess return, multiply the Sharpe ratio by the standard deviation of returns.

If you simply choose the highest Sharpe ratio fund, your client will hold 100% in Fidelity Puritan and have an expected annual excess return of 0.75 × 10.67% = 8%. The more appropriate approach is to look at each fund and determine what proportion of the client's assets can be invested in that fund without exceeding the target volatility level of 15%.

For example, if you choose the second-highest Sharpe ratio fund, the Vanguard Windsor fund, with a Sharpe ratio of 0.72, your client will hold 99% (15%/15.19%) of her assets in this fund and 1% in cash. The expected annual excess return will be

$$(0.99 \times 15.19\% \times 0.72) = (15\% \times 0.72) = 10.8\%.$$

The Vanguard Windsor fund is the best single fund choice for this client's total portfolio.

C *Your client is seeking a single manager benchmarked to the S&P 500 and wants to limit tracking error to the S&P 500 Index. Identify an appropriate appraisal metric, calculate the relevant statistic, and recommend the best fund.*

The information ratio is the best appraisal metric in this case: the arithmetic-average excess return over the S&P 500 divided by the tracking error to the S&P 500.

The IRs for each fund are shown in Exhibit 30. For example, we calculate the IR for Dreyfus as follows: −1.09%/5.51% = −0.20.

Exhibit 30 Information Ratios for Funds

Fund	IR
Dreyfus	−0.20
Fidelity Equity	0.04
Fidelity Puritan	0.03
Founders Growth	0.12
Franklin Growth	−0.24
Franklin Income	−0.05
Putnam	−0.33
Investment Company	0.20
MFS	−0.22
Pioneer Growth	−0.26
Pioneer Income	−0.42
Steadman	−0.92
T. Rowe Price Growth	−0.45
Value Line	0.27
Vanguard Wellington	−0.32
Vanguard Windsor	0.44

Based on the information ratio, the Vanguard Windsor fund would again be the best choice.

D *Your client is seeking a single manager for its US equity allocation that is benchmarked to the S&P 500. The client wants to limit tracking error but is able to use futures to adjust the portfolio's beta. Identify an appropriate appraisal metric, calculate the relevant statistic, and recommend the best fund.*

Now we need to know the beta and alpha of each fund to the S&P 500, which we obtain from the CAPM results in Exhibit 29. The fund with the highest CAPM appraisal ratio (Jensen's alpha divided by the residual risk) will be the best choice. For Dreyfus, it is 0.24%/4.88% = 0.05. The CAPM appraisal ratios for each fund are shown in Exhibit 31.

Exhibit 31 CAPM Appraisal Ratios for Funds

Fund	CAPM Appraisal Ratio
Dreyfus	0.05
Fidelity Equity	0.14
Fidelity Puritan	0.68
Founders Growth	0.09
Franklin Growth	−0.14
Franklin Income	0.47
Putnam	0.02
Investment Company	0.44
MFS	0.30
Pioneer Growth	−0.23
Pioneer Income	0.08
Steadman	−0.80
T. Rowe Price Growth	−0.50
Value Line	0.16
Vanguard Wellington	0.18
Vanguard Windsor	0.57

The Fidelity Puritan strategy has the highest CAPM appraisal ratio and is the best choice. It may be surprising that Fidelity Puritan would yield the highest CAPM appraisal ratio, given its low active return. This result comes from this strategy's unusually low CAPM beta of 0.65. Because your client can use futures to scale up the beta (and expected return) of the strategy, the portfolio of futures plus Fidelity Puritan would deliver the highest appraisal ratio while also maintaining a beta of 1.0 with the S&P 500 benchmark. Assuming that futures contracts require no initial margin, the portfolio held would be 100% in Fidelity Puritan plus an S&P 500 futures position equal to 35% of portfolio capital. The beta of this portfolio is 0.65 from Fidelity Puritan plus 0.35 from the futures overlay, for a total beta of 1.0.

If your client could use futures and was not averse to tracking error, then the Vanguard Windsor Fund—with the largest Jensen's alpha of 3.97% per year—would be the best choice. In this case, the portfolio held would be 100% in the Vanguard Windsor Fund (beta of 0.90) plus an S&P 500 futures position of 10% of this holding.

4 ***What do we learn about the strategies of funds based on the changes in their relative performance when comparing average returns to Jensen's alphas?***

Funds with a lower level of "beta" or systematic risk will often rise in the rankings when using the Jensen model. For example, the Franklin Income rises substantially, which is not surprising because it has an objective of mixed stocks and fixed income—leading to a lower exposure to stock market risk. On the other hand, the Value Line has a higher beta exposure to the stock market than the Investment Company, which results in a lower appraisal ratio for Value Line than Investment Company, despite Value Line having higher mean returns than Investment Company.

5 ***From the funds' names, as well as a quick scan of the funds' portfolio holdings, it appears that a growth/value style tilt may explain some of the relative performance. To account for this dynamic, as well as potential small-cap or momentum tilts, you next decide to implement the basic four-factor equity model:***

$$r_{p,t} - r_{F,t} = \alpha + \beta \times RMRF_t + \beta_{smb} \times SMB_t + \beta_{hml} \times HML_t + \beta_{wml} \times WML_t + \varepsilon_t \quad (18)$$

Over this period, the returns on all factors are positive. Exhibit 32 shows the results from this analysis.

Exhibit 32 Performance Statistics for Funds

Fund	Annualized Four-Factor Alpha	Annualized Residual Risk	Coefficients				*t*-Statistics				
			RMRF	SMB	HML	WML	RMRF	SMB	HML	WML	*R*-Sq
Dreyfus	−0.13%	4.33%	0.83	0.03	0.03	0.02	40.7	0.8	1.0	0.6	89.8%
Fidelity Equity	0.34%	3.47%	0.93	−0.01	−0.02	0.06	56.9	−0.4	−0.8	2.8	94.6%
Fidelity Puritan	1.99%	3.28%	0.70	0.01	0.26	−0.08	45.6	0.3	10.0	−4.1	90.8%
Founders Growth	−0.09%	5.68%	0.94	0.15	−0.24	0.23	35.3	3.3	−5.4	6.6	89.4%
Franklin Growth	0.89%	6.91%	0.85	0.03	−0.19	−0.05	26.2	0.5	−3.5	−1.1	80.1%
Franklin Income	0.70%	7.10%	0.49	0.17	0.40	−0.01	14.7	3.1	7.1	−0.2	54.9%
Putnam	−0.27%	4.21%	0.77	−0.13	0.15	−0.01	38.7	−3.9	4.4	−0.6	87.7%
Investment Company	1.72%	3.84%	0.90	−0.09	0.06	0.00	49.9	−2.9	1.8	0.1	92.6%
MFS	0.73%	3.75%	0.69	−0.08	0.16	−0.03	39.0	−2.6	5.5	−1.3	87.8%
Pioneer Growth	−1.06%	8.07%	0.87	0.21	−0.34	0.08	22.8	3.4	−5.4	1.7	78.7%
Pioneer Income	−0.07%	4.38%	0.44	−0.06	0.16	−0.05	21.6	−1.7	4.7	−1.9	67.9%
Steadman	−9.52%	9.29%	0.77	0.12	0.04	0.15	17.5	1.7	0.5	2.6	64.3%
T. Rowe Price Growth	−0.15%	4.68%	0.98	−0.04	−0.24	−0.05	44.4	−1.1	−6.6	−1.6	92.0%
Value Line	−2.52%	7.42%	1.07	0.42	0.03	0.30	30.6	7.4	0.6	6.6	86.3%
Vanguard Wellington	0.51%	2.61%	0.76	−0.21	0.17	−0.03	62.0	−10.3	8.0	−2.1	94.6%
Vanguard Windsor	2.97%	4.77%	0.99	0.04	0.43	−0.21	44.3	1.2	11.3	−7.3	90.4%

A *Which funds indicate significant small-cap, value, or momentum exposure?*

Founders Growth, Franklin Income, Pioneer Growth, and Value Line all demonstrate statistically significant positive exposure to small-cap stocks as indicated by their SMB *t*-statistics above 2. Putnam, Investment Company, MFS, and Vanguard Wellington demonstrate statistically significant negative exposure to small caps (i.e., positive exposure to large caps) because they have *t*-statistics below −2.

Fidelity Puritan, Franklin Income, Putnam, MFS, Pioneer Income, Vanguard Wellington, and Vanguard Windsor all demonstrate statistically significant positive exposure to value stocks based on their HML *t*-statistics above 2.

On the other hand, Founders Growth, Franklin Growth, Pioneer Growth, and T. Rowe Price Growth all demonstrate statistically significant exposure to growth stocks as indicated by HML *t*-statistics below –2.

Fidelity Equity, Founders Growth, Steadman, and Value Line all demonstrate statistically significant positive momentum exposure based on their WML *t*-statistics greater than 2. However, Fidelity Puritan, Vanguard Wellington, and Vanguard Windsor exhibit an anti-momentum or contrarian exposure of selling winners and buying losers, as evidenced by WML *t*-statistics less than –2.

B *If your client wants to allocate part of its portfolio to the manager with the highest skill per unit of risk relative to the four-factor model, which performance appraisal metric is most appropriate? Based on this measure, which fund do you recommend?*

The four-factor appraisal ratio is the four-factor alpha divided by the residual risk. For example, for Dreyfus it is –0.13%/4.33% = –0.03. Exhibit 33 shows the four-factor appraisal ratios for the other funds.

Exhibit 33 Four-Factor Appraisal Ratios for Funds

Fund	Four-Factor Appraisal Ratio
Dreyfus	–0.03
Fidelity Equity	0.10
Fidelity Puritan	0.60
Founders Growth	–0.02
Franklin Growth	0.13
Franklin Income	0.10
Putnam	–0.06
Investment Company	0.45
MFS	0.19
Pioneer Growth	–0.13
Pioneer Income	–0.02
Steadman	–1.02
T. Rowe Price Growth	–0.03
Value Line	–0.34
Vanguard Wellington	0.19
Vanguard Windsor	0.62

The best fund by this criterion is Vanguard Windsor, which may have investment selection skills not obtainable from low-cost passive investments. Exposure to the four factors can be obtained cheaply through index funds, and thus funds with negative or low appraisal ratios are not attractive.

C *Based on your new four-factor model results, relative to the CAPM results, which fund shows the largest increase in skill per unit of risk and why? Which fund shows the largest decrease and why?*

The differences between the four-factor and CAPM appraisal ratios are shown in Exhibit 34.

Exhibit 34 Differences between Four-Factor and CAPM Appraisal Ratios for Funds

Fund	Difference in Appraisal Ratio
Dreyfus	−0.08
Fidelity Equity	−0.04
Fidelity Puritan	−0.07
Founders Growth	−0.10
Franklin Growth	0.27
Franklin Income	−0.37
Putnam	−0.09
Investment Company	0.01
MFS	−0.11
Pioneer Growth	0.10
Pioneer Income	−0.10
Steadman	−0.22
T. Rowe Price Growth	0.47
Value Line	−0.50
Vanguard Wellington	0.01
Vanguard Windsor	0.05

T. Rowe Price Growth and Franklin Growth see the largest increases in appraisal ratio when moving from the CAPM to the four-factor model. T. Rowe Price Growth exhibits negative exposures to the SMB, HML, and WML factors (Exhibit 32). These negative factor exposures lower its predicted four-factor model return relative to the CAPM, which excludes these factors. Similarly, Franklin Growth demonstrates negative exposures to both HML and WML, lowering its predicted return and increasing its alpha relative to the CAPM.

Value Line and Franklin Income see the largest decreases in appraisal ratio. Value Line shows the largest exposures of any fund to the SMB and WML factors, which raises its predicted return, thereby lowering its alpha.

D *Calculate the* t-*statistic (approximately) for the four-factor alpha of each of the funds. Which managers have statistically significant positive skill at the 95% confidence level?*

The *t*-statistic is calculated as the appraisal ratio multiplied by the square root of the number of years in the track record. Because these are all 18-year period records, we multiply each fund's four-factor appraisal ratio by the square root of 18 (4.24). Each fund's *t*-statistic is shown in Exhibit 35.

Exhibit 35 Four-Factor Appraisal Ratio *t*-Statistics for Funds

Fund	*t*-Statistic
Dreyfus	−0.13
Fidelity Equity	0.42
Fidelity Puritan	2.57
Founders Growth	−0.06

(continued)

Exhibit 35 (Continued)

Fund	t-Statistic
Franklin Growth	0.54
Franklin Income	0.42
Putnam	−0.28
Investment Company	1.90
MFS	0.83
Pioneer Growth	−0.56
Pioneer Income	−0.07
Steadman	−4.35
T. Rowe Price Growth	−0.13
Value Line	−1.44
Vanguard Wellington	0.82
Vanguard Windsor	2.64

Only the Fidelity Puritan and Vanguard Windsor strategies demonstrate statistically significant positive skill relative to the four-factor model over this 18-year period as implied by the *t*-statistics in Exhibit 35 (the only two funds with *t*-statistics above 2). This result provides further evidence that the managers of the Fidelity Puritan and Vanguard Windsor funds appear to have investment skills not obtainable through passive factor exposures. On the other hand, the Steadman strategy demonstrates statistically significant negative skill over this period, with a *t*-statistic of −4.35.

6 ***You note that some funds have an income orientation and may have bond holdings. The majority of the bond positions are corporate and government bonds; very little is allocated to option-like securities, such as convertible bonds or mortgages.[41] Thus, you decide to control for equity style tilts as well as fixed-income risk factors using a six-factor model that adds a bond term premium factor (TERM) and a corporate bond default risk factor (DEFAULT) to the four-factor model[42]:***

$$\begin{aligned} r_{p,t} - r_{F,t} &= \alpha + \beta \times RMRF_t + \beta_{smb} \times SMB_t + \beta_{hml} \times HML_t \\ &+ \beta_{wml} \times WML_t + \beta_{term} \times TERM_t \\ &+ \beta_{default} \times DEFAULT_t + \varepsilon_t \end{aligned} \tag{16}$$

Exhibit 36 shows the six-factor alphas, residual risks, the additional two bond factor coefficients and *t*-statistics, and the *R*-squared from these regressions.

41 In general, if a set of funds is to be compared with each other, the same model should be applied to each fund in the set. This approach ensures that, for example, a fund does not become highly rated simply because it took a particular type of systematic risk that was unexpected (such as a fund that holds a high allocation to small stocks, even though its investment objective and prospectus benchmark do not reflect this strategy).

42 Because the bond factors are constructed to be uncorrelated with the other factors, adding the bond factors does not affect the coefficients on the equity factors.

Exhibit 36 Performance Statistics for Funds

Fund	Annualized Six-Factor Alpha	Annualized Residual Risk	Coefficients		t-Statistics		R-Sq
			TERM	DEF	TERM	DEF	
Dreyfus	−0.16%	4.30%	0.08	−0.01	1.05	−0.14	90.1%
Fidelity Equity	0.28%	3.46%	−0.01	0.07	−0.18	0.85	94.7%
Fidelity Puritan	1.74%	2.89%	−0.05	0.28	−1.02	4.05	92.9%
Founders Growth	0.06%	5.60%	0.28	−0.31	2.85	−2.32	89.8%
Franklin Growth	0.76%	6.91%	−0.05	0.16	−0.43	0.95	80.3%
Franklin Income	0.01%	5.75%	−0.20	0.81	−2.03	5.97	70.6%
Putnam	−0.60%	3.27%	0.04	0.30	0.76	3.93	92.6%
Investment Company	1.79%	3.81%	0.14	−0.15	2.16	−1.65	92.8%
MFS	0.37%	2.53%	0.02	0.36	0.35	5.92	94.5%
Pioneer Growth	−0.85%	8.05%	0.23	−0.34	1.61	−1.78	79.0%
Pioneer Income	−0.51%	2.95%	−0.01	0.45	−0.20	6.48	85.6%
Steadman	−9.54%	9.20%	0.23	−0.12	1.46	−0.54	65.4%
T. Rowe Price Growth	−0.15%	4.70%	0.00	0.00	−0.03	0.03	92.0%
Value Line	−2.19%	7.25%	0.46	−0.60	3.63	−3.48	87.0%
Vanguard Wellington	0.32%	2.02%	0.06	0.15	1.60	3.21	96.8%
Vanguard Windsor	3.07%	4.66%	0.25	−0.25	3.11	−2.26	90.9%

A *Which funds indicate significant exposure to the TERM and DEFAULT risk factors?*

Founders Growth, Investment Company, Value Line, and Vanguard Windsor show significant positive exposure to TERM; Franklin Income shows significant negative exposure to TERM. Fidelity Puritan, Franklin Income, Putnam, MFS, Pioneer Income, and Vanguard Wellington show significant positive exposure to DEFAULT; and Founders Growth, Value Line, and Vanguard Windsor show significant negative exposure to DEFAULT.

B *Calculate the six-factor appraisal ratios for each fund and identify which funds have the highest and lowest values.*

The six-factor appraisal ratio is the six-factor alpha divided by the residual risk. For example, for Dreyfus it is −0.16%/4.30% = −0.04. The six-factor appraisal ratios for the other funds are shown in Exhibit 37:

Exhibit 37 Six-Factor Appraisal Ratios for Funds

Fund	Six-Factor Appraisal Ratio
Dreyfus	−0.04
Fidelity Equity	0.08
Fidelity Puritan	0.60
Founders Growth	0.01
Franklin Growth	0.11
Franklin Income	0.00
Putnam	−0.18
Investment Company	0.47

(continued)

Exhibit 37 (Continued)

Fund	Six-Factor Appraisal Ratio
MFS	0.15
Pioneer Growth	−0.11
Pioneer Income	−0.17
Steadman	−1.04
T. Rowe Price Growth	−0.03
Value Line	−0.30
Vanguard Wellington	0.16
Vanguard Windsor	0.66

Vanguard Windsor and Fidelity Puritan have the highest six-factor appraisal ratios, and Steadman continues to have the lowest appraisal ratio.

C *Explain why the six-factor alpha for Vanguard Windsor is higher than its four-factor model.*

Vanguard Windsor has offsetting coefficients of +0.25 for TERM and −0.25 for DEF. In order for this fund's alpha to increase when adding these two factors, the net return predicted by these two factors for Vanguard Windsor must be negative. Because we are told that all the factors earned positive returns over the evaluation period, it must be the case that DEF earned a higher average return than TERM over this period. The higher return for DEF and Vanguard Windsor's negative exposure reduces its expected six-factor return, thereby increasing its six-factor alpha.

D *Based on all of the data and results, how helpful to your analysis were the additional two bond factors?*

It was interesting how several funds demonstrated statistically significant exposures to the two additional bond factors. This information seems to indicate that the additional factors were very important to understanding the fund's strategy.

When looking at the skill measures, however—whether alpha or appraisal ratio—the benefit of the additional two factors seems small. Exhibit 38 shows the six-factor and four-factor results and ranks side by side.

Exhibit 38 Appraisal Ratios for Funds

Fund	Six-Factor Appraisal Ratio	Four-Factor Appraisal Ratio	Six-Factor Appraisal Rank	Four-Factor Appraisal Rank
Dreyfus	−0.04	−0.03	11	11
Fidelity Equity	0.08	0.10	7	7
Fidelity Puritan	0.60	0.60	2	2
Founders Growth	0.01	−0.02	8	9
Franklin Growth	0.11	0.13	6	6
Franklin Income	0.00	0.10	9	8
Putnam	−0.18	−0.06	14	13
Investment Company	0.47	0.45	3	3

Exhibit 38 (Continued)

Fund	Six-Factor Appraisal Ratio	Four-Factor Appraisal Ratio	Six-Factor Appraisal Rank	Four-Factor Appraisal Rank
MFS	0.15	0.19	5	4
Pioneer Growth	−0.11	−0.13	12	14
Pioneer Income	−0.17	−0.02	13	10
Steadman	−1.04	−1.02	16	16
T. Rowe Price Growth	−0.03	−0.03	10	12
Value Line	−0.30	−0.34	15	15
Vanguard Wellington	0.16	0.19	4	5
Vanguard Windsor	0.66	0.62	1	1

Although most of the appraisal ratio estimates change—and one (Founders Growth) even changes sign—the rank order of funds remains quite similar, with the top and bottom funds unchanged in the rankings.

7 ***Your client's portfolio has an (arithmetic) expected return of 10% per year and annualized standard deviation of 15%. If your client intends to invest 25% into only one of these funds and the objective is to maximize the Sharpe ratio of the combined portfolio, which fund do you recommend, and what is the resulting Sharpe ratio?***

You estimate the correlation of the funds' returns with your client's portfolio. Under the assumptions of 75% in the current portfolio and 25% in one of the other funds, the resulting expected excess portfolio returns and standard deviations are calculated and shown in Exhibit 39.

Exhibit 39 Performance Statistics for Funds

Fund	Correlation with Client Portfolio	Portfolio Expected Excess Return	Portfolio Standard Deviation	Total Portfolio Sharpe Ratio	Rank
Dreyfus	−0.25	3.89%	10.91%	0.36	3
Fidelity Equity	0.35	4.20%	13.02%	0.32	8
Fidelity Puritan	0.20	4.21%	12.07%	0.35	4
Founders Growth	0.70	4.39%	14.61%	0.30	9
Franklin Growth	0.65	3.72%	14.04%	0.27	12
Franklin Income	0.25	4.02%	12.17%	0.33	6
Putnam	−0.60	3.66%	9.76%	0.37	2
Investment Company	0.55	4.37%	13.50%	0.32	7
MFS	0.60	3.79%	13.01%	0.29	10
Pioneer Growth	0.75	3.57%	14.77%	0.24	15
Pioneer Income	0.25	3.09%	11.87%	0.26	13
Steadman	−0.75	1.85%	8.74%	0.21	16
T. Rowe Price Growth	0.60	3.58%	14.08%	0.25	14
Value Line	0.10	4.84%	12.74%	0.38	1

(continued)

Exhibit 39 (Continued)

Fund	Correlation with Client Portfolio	Portfolio Expected Excess Return	Portfolio Standard Deviation	Total Portfolio Sharpe Ratio	Rank
Vanguard Wellington	0.50	3.74%	12.87%	0.29	11
Vanguard Windsor	0.80	4.95%	14.47%	0.34	5

The Value Line strategy maximizes the portfolio Sharpe ratio at 0.38. That strategy benefits from a low correlation of 0.1 with the existing portfolio. Dreyfus, Putnam, and Steadman all have even lower correlations but not by enough to offset their relatively lower returns.

It is somewhat surprising, given their attractiveness using previous criteria, that Vanguard Windsor and Fidelity Puritan are not as attractive here. Although Vanguard Windsor had the highest return, its relatively high correlation of 0.80 with the current portfolio makes it slightly less attractive than the Value Line strategy in this analysis. Likewise, although Fidelity Puritan had a relatively low correlation of 0.20 with the current portfolio, its relatively lower return reduces its attractiveness relative to Value Line.

8 ***Considering the characteristics that have been shown to be correlated with future returns, which fund do you predict will have the best future performance, and why?***

There are several possible perspectives here. If you interpret the question to mean "Which fund will likely have the best six-factor alpha," the academic evidence suggests that past skill has value for forecasting future skill. In this case, you could either choose the fund with the highest six-factor alpha or, perhaps better, the fund with the highest six-factor appraisal ratio, which in our case will be proportional to the *t*-statistic for the test of whether the six-factor alpha is zero. The fund with the highest six-factor alpha and the highest six-factor appraisal ratio is Vanguard Windsor.

Another possible interpretation is "Which fund is likely to have the highest total return?" In this case, you need to assess not only the skill-based or alpha return but also the factor-based return. In general, you want funds with high exposures to factors with high premia *plus* high alphas. Identifying such a fund requires predicting both the future factor loadings of the funds and the future factor returns. If you assume that past factor exposures and past mean factor returns will be the same in the future, and also that past skill return is the best predictor of future skill return, then the best predictor of future excess return is past excess return. Alternatively, you can make some assumptions about expected factor returns, assume factor loadings stay the same, and then do the calculation fund by fund.

Looking at the funds' factor coefficients, it seems that Value Line has the highest overall set of factor sensitivity. This is because it has the highest RMRF, SMB, WML and TERM coefficients of any fund and is also positive on HML, albeit with a material negative coefficient on DEF. However, Value Line has one of the lowest six-factor alphas. Another interesting fund, Vanguard Windsor, has the second-highest RMRF, the highest HML loading, and the third-highest TERM loading, with small negative loadings on WML and DEF. Coupled with the highest overall six-factor alpha, it is reasonable to surmise that Vanguard

Windsor would have one of the highest expected total returns looking forward. Ideally, the analysis should be updated through time as the return history expands.

REFERENCES

Agarwal, Vikas, and Narayan Y. Naik. 2004. "Risks and Portfolio Decisions Involving Hedge Funds." *Review of Financial Studies* 17 (1): 63–98.

Asness, Clifford, Andrea Frazzini, and Lasse Pedersen. 2013. "*Quality Minus Junk.*" AQR Capital Management working paper.

Carhart, Mark M. 1997. "On Persistence in Mutual Fund Performance." *Journal of Finance* 52 (1): 57–82.

Chevalier, Judith, and Glenn Ellison. 1999. "Are Some Mutual Fund Managers Better than Others? Cross-Sectional Patterns in Behavior and Performance." *Journal of Finance* 54 (3): 875–99.

Cohen, Lauren, Andrea Frazzini, and Christopher Malloy. 2008. "The Small World of Investing: Board Connections and Mutual Fund Returns." *Journal of Political Economy* 116 (5): 951–79.

Cremers, Martijn, and Ankur Pareek. 2016. "Patient Capital Outperformance: The Investment Skill of High Active Share Managers Who Trade Infrequently." *Journal of Financial Economics* 122 (2): 288–306.

Dincer, Oguzhan, Russell Gregory-Allen, and Hany Shawky. 2010. "*Are You Smarter than a CFA'er?*" SSRN Working Paper.

Ding, Bill, and Russ Wermers. 2009. "*Mutual Fund Performance and Governance Structure: The Role of Portfolio Managers and Boards of Directors.*" University of Maryland working paper.

Edelen, Roger. 1999. "Investor flows and the assessed performance of open-end mutual funds." *Journal of Financial Economics* 53 (3): 439–66.

Elton, E. J., M. J. Gruber, and C. R. Blake. 1995. "Fundamental Economic Variables, Expected Returns, and Bond Fund Performance." *Journal of Finance* 50 (4): 1229–56.

Fama, Eugene F., and Kenneth R. French. 1992. "The Cross-Section of Expected Stock Returns." *Journal of Finance* 47 (2): 427–65.

———. 1993. "Common Risk Factors in the Returns on Stocks and Bonds." *Journal of Financial Economics* 33 (1): 3–56.

———. 2002. "The Equity Premium." *Journal of Finance* 57 (2): 637–59.

Fischer, Bernd, and Russ Wermers. 2012. *Performance Evaluation and Attribution of Security Portfolios*. Oxford, UK: Elsevier.

Fung, William, and David A. Hsieh. 2001. "The Risk in Hedge Fund Strategies: Theory and Evidence from Trend Followers." *Review of Financial Studies* 14 (2): 313–41.

———. 2004. "Hedge Fund Benchmarks: A Risk-Based Approach." *Financial Analysts Journal* 60 (5): 65–80.

Fung, William, David A. Hsieh, Narayan Y. Naik, and Tarun Ramadorai. 2008. "Hedge Funds: Performance, Risk, and Capital Formation." *Journal of Finance* 63 (4): 1777–803.

Getmansky, Mila, Andrew Lo, and Igor Makarov. 2004. "An Econometric Model of Serial Correlation and Illiquidity in Hedge Fund Returns." *Journal of Financial Economics* 74 (3): 529–609.

Gottesman, Aron, and Matthew R. Morey. 2006. "Manager Education and Mutual Fund Performance." *Journal of Empirical Finance* 13 (2): 145–82.

Hecht, Peter. 2014. "*How to Evaluate Hedge Funds or Any New Investment: Alphas, Sharpe Ratios, and the Underutilized—but Most Important—Appraisal Ratio.*" Evanston Capital white paper (October).

Henriksson, Roy D., and Robert Merton. 1981. "On Market Timing and Investment Performance. II. Statistical Procedures for Evaluating Forecasting Skills." *Journal of Business* 54 (4): 513–33.

Huang, Jennifer, Clemens Sialm, and Hanjiang Zhang. 2011. "Risk Shifting and Mutual Fund Performance." *Review of Financial Studies* 24 (8): 2575–616.

Kasperczyk, Marcin, Clemens Sialm, and Lu Zheng. 2008. "Unobserved Actions of Mutual Funds." *Review of Financial Studies* 21 (6): 2379–416.

Kinnel, Russel. 2017. "*How Expense Ratios and Star Ratings Predict Success.*" Morningstar Advisor (10 August).

Leinweber, David. 2009. *Nerds on Wall Street*. Hoboken, NJ: Wiley.

Novy-Marx, Robert, and Mihail Velikov. 2016. "A Taxonomy of Anomalies and their Trading Costs." *Review of Financial Studies* 29 (1): 104–47.

Treynor, Jack L., and K. K. Mazuy. 1966. "Can Mutual Funds Outguess the Market?" *Harvard Business Review* 44 (4): 131–36.

Wei, Kelsey, Russ Wermers, and Tong Yao. 2015. "Uncommon Value: The Investment Performance of Contrarian Funds." *Management Science* (October): 2394–414.

PRACTICE PROBLEMS

The following information relates to Questions 1–6

The Ming Education Foundation (the Foundation) plans to invest $10 million in large-cap stocks. Kevin Handley, the chief investment officer of the Foundation, notices that the D&T Fund (the Fund) has generated significant alpha in the past five years (2013–2017). Handley shares this information with Eric Jolley, the performance analyst of the Foundation. Handley makes two comments about Fund manager appraisal:

Comment 1 Past returns properly adjusted for risk are a reliable indicator of a manager's future performance.

Comment 2 Conducting a holistic assessment provides a more informed opinion about a manager's ability to replicate past successes.

After reviewing the Fund's history of top 10 holdings, Jolley suspects the Fund may have overweighted value stocks relative to its benchmark (the S&P 500 Index) over the past five years. To investigate, Jolley runs a regression of the Fund's excess returns against the excess returns of the S&P 500 and the S&P 500 Value indexes in two separate benchmark analyses. The results are shown in Exhibit 1. The average annual excess return (over the risk-free rate) was 13.14% for the S&P 500 Index and was 14.78% for the S&P 500 Value Index. Based on the regression results, Jolley asserts that the S&P 500 Value Index is a more appropriate benchmark for the Fund.

Exhibit 1 Betas and Tracking Errors of D&T Fund (2013–2017)

Index	Fund Beta	Tracking Error
S&P 500	1.35	2.27%
S&P 500 Value	1.25	1.02%

Handley wants to investigate further whether the Fund's manager has skill. He asks Jolley to use the Carhart four-factor model to study the Fund's risk exposures. Jolley makes the following two statements regarding this approach:

Statement 1 If the fund manager truly has a persistent bias toward value stocks, beta on the HML (high-minus-low) factor is expected to be negative.

Statement 2 If the factors in the Carhart model do not reflect the manager's risk exposures, the alpha calculated from the factor benchmark will not be an accurate measure of the manager's skill.

Jolley runs a regression on the Fund's monthly excess returns for 2013–2017 using the Carhart four-factor model. He calculates the coefficients of the four factors of the Carhart model as well as the mean monthly gross returns and the trading costs of the four factors over the five-year period. A summary of the results is displayed in Exhibit 2. Handley asks Jolley to adjust the alpha estimate of the Carhart model with the known trading costs.

Exhibit 2 Factor Coefficients, Mean Gross Monthly Returns, and Trading Costs (2013–2017)

Factor	Coefficient	*t*-Statistic	Mean Monthly Gross Return	Trading Cost
RMRF	0.88	50.23	0.80%	0.00%
SMB	0.02	1.17	0.33%	0.06%
HML	0.36	15.89	0.13%	0.05%
WML	0.01	1.71	0.65%	0.48%

* The Fund has an average monthly return of 1.50% from 2013 to 2017.

Handley asks why the regression standard error derived from the Carhart four-factor model, 1.43%, is significantly different from the tracking error derived from the benchmark analysis using the S&P 500 Value Index. Jolley provides an explanation.

1 Which of the comments by Handley regarding manager appraisal is *most* accurate?

A Only Comment 1

B Only Comment 2

C Both Comment 1 and Comment 2

2 Evaluating the Fund manager's performance against the S&P 500 Index instead of against the S&P 500 Value Index will *most likely*:

A understate the manager's skill.

B accurately assess the manager's skill.

C overstate the manager's skill.

3 Which of the statements made by Jolley regarding the Carhart four-factor model are correct?

A Only Statement 1

B Only Statement 2

C Both Statement 1 and Statement 2

4 Based on the results of the Carhart four-factor model given in Exhibit 2, which additional factor *most significantly* contributes to the reduction in the model's Market factor beta from its estimate of 1.35 in the single-factor market model?

A The Size factor

B The Value factor

C The Momentum factor

5 Based on Exhibit 2, the Fund's annual alpha adjusted for trading costs is *closest* to:

A 8.83%.

B 9.12%.

C 15.84%.

6 Which of the following is the *most likely* explanation provided by Jolley regarding the regression results?

A The Fund has a significant tilt toward large-cap stocks.

B The underlying assets in the factor portfolios may include securities that are not in the Fund's benchmark.

C The regression standard error in the four-factor model should be lower than the tracking error in the single-factor model.

The following information relates to Questions 7–12

A pension plan is considering adding the Gimel Fund (the Fund), an actively managed equity growth fund, to its investment allocation. However, the pension manager is concerned that the Fund's cash management policy is too restrictive: The Fund seeks to minimize cash holdings by limiting investor contributions and withdrawals to month end. The pension manager requests that the Fund consider adjusting its policy to allow for daily contributions and redemptions, while holding a cash reserve. The Fund's investment policy allows for the purchase of option contracts on the S&P 500 Index.

The pension manager requested the analyst prepare a performance summary to check the Fund's most recent 10-year performance, even though the analyst recommended using the 25-year return history that was available for both the Fund and the benchmark. Select performance data are provided in Exhibit 1.

Exhibit 1 Most Recent 10-Year Manager Fund Performance Statistics

	Annual Mean Return	Annual Volatility	Sharpe Ratio	Beta	Alpha *t*-Statistic
Gimel Fund	5.56%	3.62%	0.91	0.34	2.70

* All returns are net of fees

The analyst suspects the Fund's low beta may result from the use of derivative instruments. The analyst modifies the standard Jensen model to account for option-like return payoffs. The following model is proposed to the pension manager:

$$r_{p,t} - r_{F,}t = \alpha + \beta_1 RMRF_t + \beta_2 C(k_1) + \beta_3 C(k_2) + \beta_4 P(k_1) + \beta_5 P(k_2) + \varepsilon_t$$

$C(k)$ represents the return on one-month call options with an exercise price of k, and $P(k)$ represents the return on one-month put options with an exercise price of k.

The pension manager suggests that the 10-year Sharpe ratio be recalculated using the geometric mean instead of the arithmetic mean in the numerator. The pension manager indicates that the geometric mean return takes into account the impact of compounding.

7 The alpha *t*-statistic in Exhibit 1 *most likely* indicates that the portfolio manager is a:

A negative-alpha manager.

B zero-alpha manager.

C positive-alpha manager.

8 The *t*-statistic to determine whether the Fund's 10-year Sharpe ratio equals zero is *closest* to:

A 1.54.

B 2.88.

C 9.10.

9 The pension manager's suggested method to recalculate the 10-year Sharpe ratio would *most likely*:

A create a distorted appraisal metric.

B reflect risk only in the denominator.

C use the appropriate measure of return.

10 The time frame requested by the pension manager for the performance summary, in contrast to the analyst's recommended time frame, *most likely* increases the likelihood that the:

A estimated alpha will be statistically insignificant.

B manager's performance cannot be compared with peer performance.

C noise affecting investment performance evaluation will be reduced.

11 The factors added to the Jensen model in Equation 1 are used to:

A model trend-following strategies.

B more precisely model non-linearities.

C control for one distributional type of skewness.

12 The pension manager's requested change to the Fund's cash management policy, if implemented without offsetting leverage adjustments, would *most likely* result in:

A a lower tracking error.

B an increase in the portfolio beta.

C improved performance when the market falls.

The following information relates to Questions 13–17

Kim Lee is an investor with a goal to lower the volatility of her portfolio. She is considering allocating a portion of her assets to Fund A, which holds Indian equities and has outperformed its benchmark significantly over the last 10 years. Fund A is actively managed and uses equity index futures to maintain consistent leverage in the portfolio. Lee notices that the average market capitalization of the Fund's investments is materially smaller than the average for the Indian equity peer group.

Lee runs a traditional benchmark-relative analysis on Fund A's last 10 years of returns, using the MSCI India Index to represent the market. The annualized alpha calculated in this analysis is −2.2, with a *t*-statistic of −3.6. The beta is 1.5, with a *t*-statistic of 24.7. Lee assesses the results and draws the following conclusions:

Conclusion 1 The alpha calculated for Fund A includes the impact of futures mispricing.

Conclusion 2 The alpha calculated for Fund A captures the component of the stock returns not attributable to systematic risk.

Lee also considers an investment in Fund X, Fund Y, or Fund Z, all of which have market betas near 1. She compares the performance statistics for her current portfolio and the four funds as shown in Exhibit 1. The appraisal ratios are calculated using her current portfolio as the benchmark. Based on her analysis, Lee decides to calculate the standard deviation for a new portfolio consisting of 90% in the current portfolio and 10% allocated to Fund Z. She will compare results across allocations to Funds X, Y, and Z based on that target level of risk.

Exhibit 1 Annualized 10-Year Performance Statistics

	Annual Standard Deviation	Sharpe Ratio	Correlation with Portfolio	Appraisal Ratio
Portfolio	6.75%	0.74		
Fund A	15.11%	0.86	0.60	
Fund X	8.63%	0.89	0.65	0.54
Fund Y	6.97%	1.04	0.54	0.77
Fund Z	6.91%	1.06	0.69	0.76

13 Which performance appraisal technique would be *most appropriate* for assessing the skill of Fund A's manager?

A Factor analysis

B Peer group comparison

C Excess return comparison

14 Based on Lee's benchmark-relative analysis and Exhibit 1, Fund A's portfolio manager has:

A demonstrated skill.

B generated a return below the risk-free rate.

C underperformed the market after adjusting for leveraged market exposure.

15 Which of Lee's conclusions about Fund A's alpha is correct?

A Only Conclusion 1

B Only Conclusion 2

C Both Conclusion 1 and Conclusion 2

16 Which of the following fund statistics is *most appropriate* for Lee to use in selecting a fund that will help achieve her stated goal?

A The fund's Sharpe ratio

B The fund's information ratio

C The fund's correlation with her current portfolio

17 Assuming no constraints on investment allocations, the addition of which fund to the current portfolio will yield the largest improvement in the Sharpe ratio?

A Fund X

B Fund Y

C Fund Z

The following information relates to questions 18–23

Amanda Harrison, an analyst for a registered investment adviser, is assessing the performance of the GT Small-Cap Fund. The fund's benchmark is the Russell 2000 Index. The fund's manager, Karl Janacek, claims the ability to deliver an excess risk-adjusted return of 1.8% annually. Harrison decides to test the accuracy of Janacek's claim by creating a quality control chart. She compares the realized monthly alpha calculated cumulatively over the most recent 10-year period with its expected value as well as with one- and two-standard-error confidence intervals.

Harrison discovers that investors in the fund tend to increase their investment during rising markets and increase their withdrawals during declining markets. She is concerned about the potential impact on the fund's performance from this tendency and makes the following two statements to Janacek:

Statement 1	The cash flows will be a drag on the fund's performance if you cannot offset the effect on cash holdings immediately.
Statement 2	The effect on cash holdings of negative market timing can be determined by looking at the fund's historical alpha on a rolling basis.

Harrison examines how well the fund's historical data conform to the assumptions in statistical inference tests. She reviews a graph of the Fama–French three-factor model residuals relative to the fund's alpha and finds that positive values are mostly followed by additional positive values and negative values are mostly followed by additional negative values. Harrison then calculates the fund's Sharpe ratio, annualizing the value by multiplying it by the square root of twelve (3.464).

Since the fund is actively managed, Harrison is concerned about potential agency problems and performs the following three checks. First, she compares the fund's realized volatility with the volatility estimated using the fund's most recently reported holdings and discovers that the fund has experienced increased volatility recently. Second, Harrison examines the fund's holdings and notes that Janacek takes bigger active positions away from the benchmark than similar fund managers do and also has low portfolio turnover. And third, she finds a positive gap in returns between the fund's performance and the performance of its publicly disclosed holdings.

The fund's most recent prospectus removed the prohibition against investing in derivatives. Janacek now invests up to 20% of the fund in at-the-money call options. Examining the fund's subsequent performance, Harrison notices frequent small losses and a few large gains. As a result, she considers developing a new performance evaluation model.

Harrison finds that non-linear payoffs have become a significant component of the fund's total returns. She realizes that because of changes in the distribution of the fund's returns, the new model must deliver more precision than the current version does.

18 For Harrison to reasonably conclude that Janacek's true alpha is as claimed, the actual values should lie within the one- and two-standard-error bounds of her quality control chart for:

A 75 and 120 months, respectively.

B 90 and 116 months, respectively.

C 95 and 110 months, respectively.

19 Which of Harrison's statements regarding the effect on cash holdings is correct?

A Statement 1

B Statement 2

C Both Statement 1 and Statement 2

20 The annualized Sharpe ratio calculated by Harrison *most likely* is biased because the:

A return distribution is stationary.

B model omits the small-cap risk premium.

C model's residuals exhibit serial correlation.

21 Which potential agency problem has Harrison's three checks uncovered?

A Doubling down

B High active share

C Window dressing

22 Any factors added to the performance evaluation model by Harrison must:

A capture the discount received for negative skewness.

B track the changes in the price of the at-the-money call options' underlying assets.

C have large returns of the same sign and at the same time as the positions held by the fund.

23 Harrison's requirement for the new performance model will *most likely* be satisfied by:

A including "strategy-based" factors.

B creating a custom blended benchmark.

C adding a factor to measure different types of skewness.

The following information relates to questions 24–29

Ling Chen, an analyst at the White Foundation, is conducting a year-end review of the foundation's UK large-cap equity fund. Kelvin Graham, the fund's portfolio manager, claims to be able to deliver an annualized Sharpe ratio of at least 1.5. To evaluate Graham's claim, Chen creates a quality control chart covering the manager's performance record with probability windows set at one and two standard errors, respectively.

In conducting her review, Chen discovers that the fund has a tendency to outperform when the equity market falls and underperform when the equity market rises. She reviews a graph of the fund's rolling 12-month beta and finds a relatively straight horizontal line at the level of the fund's beta target. Chen notes that the fund permits daily inflows and outflows. Graham informs Chen that the state of the equity market has had very little impact on the level of inflows and outflows to and from the fund.

Chen asks Graham to describe the qualitative characteristics he believes most strongly correlate with superior performance of actively managed equity portfolios. Graham makes the following two statements to Chen:

Statement 1 Managers who take bigger active positions away from their benchmarks and also have low portfolio turnover tend to outperform the average manager.

Statement 2 Contrarian managers generally outperform herding managers, in part by superior information collection.

Next, Chen runs a multi-factor performance evaluation model with the MSCI United Kingdom Index as the market factor. She examines a histogram of the model's monthly return residuals and notices that the distribution is asymmetric. Chen verifies with Graham that the fund's investment policy is to hold only UK large-cap stocks. Graham mentions that he adjusts the fund's price-to-earnings and price-to-book ratios on the basis of his quarterly market forecast while maintaining the fund's beta at 0.85.

A change in the fund's investment guidelines now allows its manager to invest in equity options. Graham begins buying options on constituents of the MSCI UK Large Cap Index to a significant degree. Graham believes the existing performance evaluation model is inadequate given the changing nature of the fund's holdings and asks Chen to consider revising the model.

24 Assuming Graham's claim is true, the realized Sharpe ratio displayed in Chen's quality control chart *most likely* will:

- **A** fall within the larger-probability window at least 90% of the time.
- **B** fall outside the smaller-probability window a maximum of 32% of the time.
- **C** exceed two standard errors above the target ratio a maximum of 5% of the time.

25 Which of the following is the *most accurate* statement about Chen's quality control chart?

- **A** The Sharpe ratio estimate is a constant value provided by Graham.
- **B** The null hypothesis level of zero is shown as a horizontal target line on the chart.
- **C** The standard error of the Sharpe ratio estimate diminishes as the performance record lengthens.

26 The fund's tendency to experience smaller gains and smaller losses than the large-cap segment of the UK equity market is *most likely* caused by:

- **A** market timing by the fund manager.
- **B** negative market timing by fund investors.
- **C** holding a cash buffer for potential redemptions.

27 Based on empirical evidence, which of the following statements by Graham regarding superior active managers is correct?

- **A** Statement 1 only
- **B** Statement 2 only
- **C** Both Statement 1 and Statement 2

28 Which statement *best* explains the return residuals observed by Chen prior to the change in investment guidelines?

- **A** The returns to the risk factors used in the model are stationary.
- **B** Graham's strategy causes fund characteristics to change over time.
- **C** Graham is taking much higher risks than the median UK large-cap fund.

29 Chen's revision to the performance evaluation model will *most likely* involve adding:

- **A** a factor to capture the discount received for positive skewness.
- **B** factors that mimic the changing non-linearity of the fund's returns over time.
- **C** equally weighted factors for each of the distributional types of skewness contained in the fund.

SOLUTIONS

1 B is correct. Comment 2 is correct. It is important to conduct a holistic assessment of a manager, evaluating not only the performance but also the firm itself, the investment process used, and the investment (and operational) staff responsible for the management of the portfolio. This more broad-based assessment is likely to provide a more informed opinion on a manager's ability to replicate past success.

Comment 1 is incorrect because past returns, even properly adjusted for risk, contain a good deal of statistical estimation error and cannot be regarded as a reliable indicator of future performance.

2 C is correct. Using the S&P 500 Value Index as the Fund's benchmark, an expected excess return is derived as 1.25 × 14.78% = 18.48%. With the S&P 500 as the Fund's benchmark, an expected excess return is derived as 1.35 × 13.14% = 17.74%. In Jensen's model, the alpha estimated with the S&P 500 Index is larger than the alpha estimated with the S&P 500 Value Index, which is the proper index for the Fund. Therefore, the Fund manager's skill measured by S&P 500 Index is overstated.

3 B is correct. Statement 2 is correct. The manager's alpha is the return left over after considering the return explained by factor exposures. The relevance of the factor analysis depends primarily on the factors selected. If the factors do not reflect the manager's risk exposures, then the alpha will not be an accurate measure for the manager's skill.

Statement 1 is incorrect. If the fund manager has a persistent bias toward value stocks, a positive beta will be calculated for HML, the Value factor. When value stocks outperform growth stocks, the manager's bias will provide a positive contribution to returns of the fund.

4 B is correct. In the Carhart four-factor model, the beta coefficient of the Market factor is 0.88, which is less than the beta (1.35) in the market model. This reduction in the beta is primarily caused by the introduction of another significant factor, HML, called the Value factor, which has a coefficient of 0.36 and a t-statistic of 15.89. This result indicates that the Fund has a significant tilt to value stocks.

5 B is correct. Based on Exhibit 2, the mean monthly net returns of the four factors are calculated as follows:

RMRF: 0.80% – 0.00% = 0.80%.

SMB: 0.33% – 0.06% = 0.27%.

HML: 0.13% – 0.05% = 0.08%.

WML: 0.65% – 0.48% = 0.17%.

The monthly after-trading-cost alpha estimate is 1.50% – [(0.88 × 0.80%) + (0.02 × 0.27%) + (0.36 × 0.08%) + (0.01 × 0.17%)] = 1.50 – 0.74% = 0.76%. The annual after-cost alpha estimate is 0.76% × 12 = 9.12%.

6 B is correct. The tracking error of a single-factor benchmark model is the regression standard error, making Handley's comparison relevant. The low tracking error (1.02%) relative to the S&P 500 Value Index suggests that it is the proper benchmark for the Fund. Factor portfolios in the Carhart model may include securities that are not in the S&P 500 Value Index, creating noise that remains in the error terms.

7 C is correct. The calculated t-statistic for the 10-year time period is 2.70. The null hypothesis that the manager has no skill (mean residual return equals zero) should be rejected if the calculated t-statistic is greater than the critical t-value of 2. Because $2.70 > 2$, the null hypothesis can be rejected and the alpha is positive, which indicates that this is a positive-alpha manager who likely has skill.

8 B is correct. The Sharpe ratio t-statistic can be calculated by multiplying the Sharpe ratio by the square root of the number of observations: $0.91 \times \sqrt{10} = 0.91 \times 3.16 = 2.88$.

9 A is correct. The pension manager proposes to use the geometric mean return in the numerator instead of the arithmetic mean in the calculation of the Sharpe ratio. Using the geometric mean return distorts the appraisal metric because risk is reflected in both the numerator and the denominator.

10 A is correct. The pension manager decided to limit the estimation window to 10 years, even though a 25-year history is available. The likelihood of calculating a statistically significant alpha (rejecting the null hypothesis) tends to increase with the length of data record used. For example, the manager may be "opportunistic" or have a strategy that relies on trends that occur episodically. Thus, using a shorter time period may come at the expense of statistical significance.

11 B is correct. The analyst suspects that the portfolio manager uses alternative strategies with option-like payoffs and includes strategy-based factors in the Jensen model. The additional factors—$C(k_1)$, $C(k_2)$, $P(k_1)$, and $P(k_2)$—would be expected to measure the strategy decisions made by the manager, thus controlling for them in the model.

12 C is correct. The impact of allowing daily contributions to and redemptions from the Fund would create a cash drag that would cause negative market-timing effects, or underperformance when the equity market rises and outperformance when it falls.

13 A is correct. Factor analysis will adjust for the leveraged exposure to the market gained through the use of futures and can accommodate the small cap bias Lee has identified.

B is incorrect because Fund A's market capitalization is significantly different from the typical fund in the peer group, which will impair the peer group comparison results. Peer group comparisons suffer from significant weaknesses: The managers/products in the peer group may not be truly substitutable, which is the case if market capitalizations differ significantly. C is incorrect because an excess return comparison will not account for leverage or for the small cap bias. Returns from additional market exposure will not be distinct from true alpha. "If there is little variation in risk budget across managers, the use of simple excess return comparison is appropriate."

14 C is correct. The negative alpha from the factor analysis, −2.2, indicates that Fund A underperformed the market after adjusting for the elevated systematic (market) risk, as measured by the beta of 1.5, which in this case was gained through the use of futures to add leverage.

15 C is correct. Both conclusions are correct. Any deviation in returns between the futures contracts and the underlying cash index is considered cash mispricing and will show up as alpha, as will the active management results that are not related to market exposure.

16 C is correct. The correlation between an additional investment and the current portfolio affects the risk and return of the combined portfolio. Lee has indicated that her goal is to lower portfolio volatility, and a lower correlation will provide better risk reduction benefits.

17 B is correct. In the absence of any constraints, choosing the fund with the highest appraisal ratio relative to an investor's current portfolio will yield the largest improvement in that investor's overall Sharpe ratio. Fund Y had the highest appraisal ratio, 0.77.

18 B is correct. At a minimum, the manager's realized alpha should fall within a one-standard-error confidence interval 68% of the time and within a two-standard-error confidence interval 95% of the time. For the 10-year (120-month) period examined, the manager's realized alpha fell within the one-standard-error confidence interval 75% (90/120) of the time and within the two-standard-error confidence interval 96.7% (116/120) of the time. Therefore, it is reasonable to conclude that Janacek's claimed alpha might equal the true value.

19 A is correct. Investors in the fund tend to put more money in during rising markets and take more money out during declining markets. This situation will induce a "negative market-timing" effect (i.e., buying "high" and selling "low") if the manager cannot immediately offset the impact on cash holdings.

20 C is correct. Regarding the Fama–French three-factor model's residuals, Harrison finds that positive values are mostly followed by positive values and negative values are mostly followed by negative values, with the implication being there is serial correlation in the fund's monthly returns. Consequently, using the square root of 12 as the annualization scaling term is incorrect and results in a biased estimate of annualized risk. Therefore, risk-scaled performance measures, such as the Sharpe ratio, will be biased.

21 A is correct. Increasing fund volatility is a potential agency problem because the fund manager may be increasing risk ("doubling down") in an attempt to catch up to other funds. In her first check, Harrison discovers that the fund has experienced increased volatility recently.

22 C is correct. Capturing the fund's skewness risks requires a factor with the same conditionally skewed return distribution. To have the same conditional skewness, the factor needs to have large returns of the same sign and at the same time as the positions held by the fund.

A is incorrect. Investors value positive skewness and tend to avoid negative skewness, so the new factors need to capture the premium paid for positive skewness and the discount received for negative skewness. However, since the fund has frequent small losses and a few large gains, its return distribution exhibits positive skewness. In this scenario, the factors need to capture the premium paid for positive skewness.

B is incorrect. The factors should mimic the degree of moneyness (the difference between the asset price and the exercise price) in the manager's positions. Tracking the changes in the price of the call option's underlying asset is not the same as tracking the degree of moneyness in the manager's positions.

23 A is correct. Because options are contributing significant returns to the fund (based on the skewed return distribution), more-complex strategy-based factors are needed to precisely model non-linearities.

B is incorrect. It may be infeasible (or undesirable) to create a custom blended benchmark because the optionality of the manager's fund may change quickly over time as the market portfolio moves up or down in value.

C is incorrect. Given that the portfolio may contain several different distributional types of skewness, we need *multiple* factors—each with different regression coefficients—to more precisely span these different types.

24 B is correct. If the null hypothesis is true (i.e., that Graham's "true" Sharpe ratio is 1.5), then the realized Sharpe ratio should fall within the one-standard-error boundary 68% of the time. Consequently, the realized Sharpe ratio may fall outside the smaller-probability window (one standard error) a maximum of 32% of the time.

25 C is correct. As the manager's track record lengthens (and we have more data points), the standard error of the Sharpe ratio estimate declines.

26 C is correct. Chen notes that the fund permits daily inflows and outflows, making it likely that the fund holds a cash buffer for potential redemptions. This cash drag will result in underperformance when the equity market rises and outperformance when it falls.

A is incorrect. A fund beta that varies significantly over its history would be an indication of market timing. However, the graph examined by Chen of the fund's rolling 12-month beta showed a relatively straight horizontal line at the level of Graham's beta target.

C is incorrect because (according to Graham) the state of the equity market has had little impact on the level of inflows and outflows to and from the fund. The fund's investors, therefore, were not inducing a negative market timing effect by putting more money in the fund during bull markets or taking money out of the fund during bear markets.

27 C is correct. Statement 1 is correct because equity fund managers who take bigger active positions away from their "best-fit benchmark" and also have low levels of portfolio turnover outperform the average mutual fund manager. Statement 2 is correct because contrarian managers generally outperform herding managers, by supplying liquidity to the herd and/or from superior analysis and superior information collection.

28 B is correct. One of the reasons why the return residuals might deviate substantially from the normality assumption is if the manager's strategy causes portfolio characteristics to change over time. In this case, the fund's price-to-earnings and price-to-book ratios change over time, on the basis of Graham's market forecast.

A is incorrect. Data are sometimes referred to as "stationary" when they are independent and identically distributed (IID). However, having IID data does not account for why the return residuals are non-normally distributed.

C is incorrect. Although the deviation from normality can be significant for fund managers who take larger risks than the median fund takes, Graham maintains a fund beta of 0.85, an average to below-average risk profile.

29 B is correct. When non-linear payoffs are significant, it is often more efficient to use a multi-factor model containing factors that mimic the changing non-linearity of the fund's returns over time than it is to use a custom blended benchmark.

A is incorrect because investors value positive skewness and tend to avoid negative skewness, so any such factor needs to capture the premium paid for positive skewness and the discount received for negative skewness.

C is incorrect because portfolios holding options may contain several different distributional types of skewness. As a consequence, multiple factors with different regression coefficients (i.e., weights) are needed to more precisely span each of these different types.

READING

9

Equity Style Analysis
Beyond Performance Measurement

by George Degroot, CFA, and Paul Greenwood, CFA

George Degroot, CFA (USA). Paul Greenwood, CFA (USA).

LEARNING OUTCOME STATEMENTS

Mastery	*The candidate should be able to:*
☐	a. describe how characteristic-based analysis provides a deeper understanding of a manager's strategy;
☐	b. explain how characteristic-based analysis can be used to evaluate a manager's investment philosophy and risk tolerance;
☐	c. explain how characteristic-based analysis can be used to compare the performance of large cap growth managers;
☐	d. explain how characteristic-based analysis can be used to assess how a manager's strategy will perform in different market environments;
☐	e. describe how characteristic-based analysis can be used to assess how a manager performed across multiple time periods.

CHALLENGES FACING INSTITUTIONAL INVESTORS IN MANAGER SELECTION

Institutional investors face a number of challenges when it comes to the selection and evaluation of investment managers. When institutional investors are working with existing managers, they will continuously question the performance, approach, and understanding of their portfolios:

1 How did my manager perform relative to peers?

2 Has their investment process changed?

3 How is the portfolio structured relative to other investment approaches?

4 Are the portfolio characteristics consistent with my understanding of the investment process?

The authors would like to acknowledge Darin Padur, Tom White and Michelle Pierce for their contributions to this article.

For a prospective manager, institutional investors need to know if the manager's style/exposure complement or overlap their existing managers. With new market realities challenging institutional investors daily, the ability to compare portfolios quickly and concisely is more important than ever.

Reliance on Historical Performance

Past performance is no guarantee of future results, yet the temptation to conduct performance-only comparisons is ever-present and difficult to resist. Past performance information is easy to obtain. Managers are willing to share their performance results, particularly when they've had periods of superior results. An institutional investor runs the risk of being drawn to strong recent performance that may not be indicative of the returns they are likely to experience going forward. Additionally, past performance is easy to compare: How did the manager perform relative to the index? To peers? These are straight-forward, easy-to-answer questions.

Institutional investors are under ever-increasing pressure to generate additional value in their investment portfolios relative to their benchmarks, so it is tempting to hire investment managers who have generated excellent historical returns.

While historical performance is an important part of any analysis, it is only one part of the review that should be conducted when evaluating managers. Characteristic analysis combined with returns and compared with a universe of relevant peers provides a deeper understanding of a manager's strategy than merely evaluating it on performance-based results alone.

Portfolio Diversification

Many institutional investors want to effectively diversify assets across investment styles and sub-styles. They are aware of the benefits achieved through diversification and know that investment styles rotate in and out of favor. The challenge, however, is to confirm that investment managers are adhering to the style/sub-style they claim to inhabit, or were hired to invest in. Investment managers can be subject to style drift as a result of asset growth, diminishing attractiveness of their current stock universe, or simply due to their style being out of favor. These factors can undermine an institutional investor's diversification objective.

There are several ways of monitoring a portfolio or composite's style diversification. One way to see if a portfolio has drifted over time is to plot it in a characteristic universe and compare its position in quarters or years. When reviewing the positioning of the portfolio versus the index, universe mean, or median, the institutional investor might see changing trends that could lead to better questions for manager discussions. Correlation and other returns-based characteristics can help identify portfolios that exhibit unintended performance over different time periods as well. Diversification of assets is important for any institutional investor, but rendered largely irrelevant if the assets are highly correlated with one another.

Investment Philosophy and Risk Tolerance

Institutional investors have different risk tolerances. Some take more risk in hopes of generating higher returns; others have relatively conservative views and structure their portfolios accordingly. Given an institutional investor's current spending policies or future funding needs, either approach may be prudent.

Portfolio concentration is one such measure of risk. An institutional investor can determine how highly concentrated the manager is relative to peers and determine the level of comfort that strategy provides. Additionally, over time an institutional investor can track the level of concentration and whether the investment manager is behaving consistently with, or deviating from, their stated approach. In other words, is the manager's portfolio constructed in a way that's consistent with their stated investment process?

In their evaluation of a manager, an institutional investor can measure the manager's adherence to a style by looking at their investment in terms of one or several key characteristics of that style. For example, a manager that advertises its style as large cap growth would be expected to have both a high weighted market capitalization and a relatively high expected earnings growth rate. Alternatively, a value manager's portfolio would be expected to have relatively low price-to-book and price-to-earnings ratios. The institutional investor will quickly be able to detect if style drift has occurred and therefore will be able to make informed decisions regarding manager selection and/or retention. While not universal, these challenges are common and can prove difficult to manage without effective tools to analyze the myriad of individual investments that make up a particular investment manager's portfolio.

CASE STUDY

In the exhibits that follow, a manager selection/evaluation process will be reviewed from an institutional investor's perspective. This case study approach will use actual investment manager performance and portfolio characteristic data to illustrate how this data can assist in the manager selection and evaluation process.

The case study is structured from the perspective of a large institutional investor responsible for managing tax-exempt institutional assets. The institutional investor is evaluating three large cap growth managers to fulfill a mandate, using equity characteristics to look beyond the managers' historical performance. Large cap developed market stocks tend to provide a maximum level of data for analysis purposes. The caveat for any analysis is that the results will only be as informative as the data supporting it is complete.

The analysis is provided in terms of combinations of characteristics which are designed to expose an element of the manager's strategy or the degree of success achieved. The analysis uses actual manager holdings and performance results as of September 30, 2008.

The managers under analysis were selected from Russell Investment Group's Growth Equity universe. The universe is defined as follows:

> Managers in this style try to identify large cap companies with above-average earnings growth prospects. In general, two basic categories of securities are owned: Companies with consistent above-average historical and prospective profitability and growth; and those expected to generate above-average near-term earnings momentum based upon company, industry, or economic factors. In this category, securities may not have exhibited above-average historical growth but are expected to do so over the near future.
>
> These managers are willing to pay above-market multiples for the superior growth rate/profitability they anticipate. Other typical characteristics of this style include selection of higher quality companies; emphasis on consumer service, health care, and technology stocks; and light weightings in deep cyclical and defensive stocks. The focus is on earnings growth and/or profitability, either above average or accelerating. In addition, dividend yield is frequently well below market averages, valuation statistics are typically above market averages, the volatility of returns is above that of the market, and beta is frequently above 1.00.

The managers being evaluated:

1 **Manager ABC:** Manager ABC's investment philosophy is to purchase stocks poised for strong growth due to catalysts such as rapidly expanding markets or the introduction of new and innovative products into existing markets. Manager ABC also looks for companies undergoing promising change such as new management, technologies, or products.
2 **Manager XYZ:** Manager XYZ is a bottom up, growth-oriented equity manager looking to acquire stocks likely to produce positive earnings surprises. Similarly, Manager XYZ looks to sell or avoid purchasing stocks falling short of earnings expectations.
3 **Manager DEF:** Manager DEF's investment philosophy is to purchase high quality growth companies trading at substantial discounts. The firm employs a research intensive process, holding a very concentrated portfolio with relatively low portfolio turnover.

Looking initially at portfolio performance results in Figure 1, the institutional investor might be inclined to select Manager ABC, since it is top quartile or better in four of five time periods. However, as the case study will illustrate, a thorough analysis of these managers based on fundamental equity characteristics can yield further insight which may very well alter the investor's ultimate decision.

Figure 1 Manager Performance

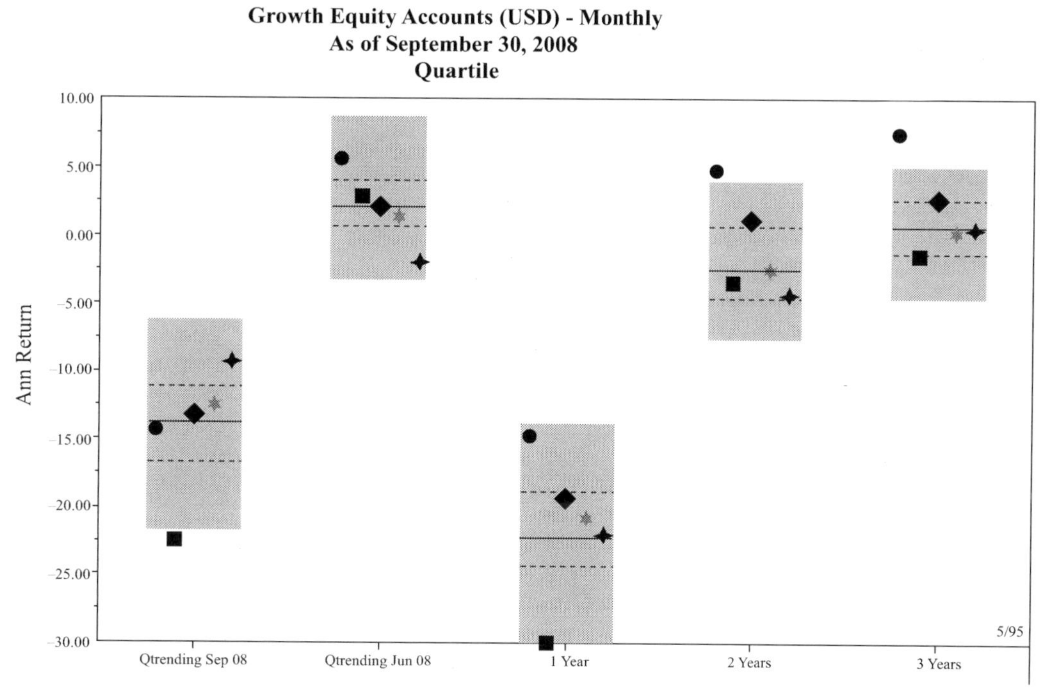

	Value	% Tile	Rank	Value	% Tile	Rank	Value	% Tile	Rank	Value	% Tile	Rank	Value	% Tile	Rank
5th Percentile	−6.33			8.66			−14.06			3.82			4.74		
25th Percentile	−11.22			3.95			−18.94			0.49			2.43		
Median Percentile	−13.82			2.18			−22.32			−2.59			0.39		
75th Percentile	−16.71			0.58			−24.44			−4.72			−1.57		
95th Percentile	−21.85			−3.39			−29.86			−7.76			−4.72		
# of portfolios	128			128			125			113			105		
● Manager ABC	−14.21	54	69	5.55	17	21	−14.85	8	9	4.55	4	4	7.30	2	2
■ Manager XYZ	−22.64	96	124	2.82	35	45	−29.99	96	121	−3.63	63	71	−1.65	77	81
◆ Manager DEF	−13.29	45	58	2.02	53	68	−19.45	31	39	−1.04	18	20	2.46	25	26
✱ Russell 1000 Growth Index	−12.33	33	42	1.25	66	85	−20.88	41	52	−2.82	52	59	0.04	58	62
✦ Russell 1000 Index	−9.35	12	15	−1.89	90	117	−22.10	50	63	−4.57	74	84	0.13	54	57

Source: Russell Investment Group; Universe Status: Final, Calculated

The following questions can be quite useful when looking for additional insights into large cap equity growth managers, and will be explored in further detail.

Questions for Large Cap Growth Managers:

1 Does the manager buy traditional growth stocks or are they attempting to capitalize on cyclical opportunities?

2 How adept is the manager at capturing strong earnings growth while avoiding negative earnings surprise?

3 Do the portfolio's earnings justify the price paid?

4 What is the earnings quality of the manager's portfolio?

5 Is the portfolio's growth rate likely to be accompanied by a high level of performance volatility?

Other Questions for Characteristic-based Analysis:

6. How does your manager's strategy fare in different market environments?
7. Does analysis of the interaction of multiple portfolio characteristics provide additional insight?
8. Do managers exhibit consistent relative characteristics across multiple time periods?

Analysis

Question 1: Does the manager buy traditional growth stocks or are they attempting to capitalize on cyclical opportunities?

A growth manager buys securities with the assumption that the earnings of the companies whose stock it buys will increase faster than the average stock. A manager is usually willing to pay more for these stocks than for those with lower forecasted growth. If earnings increase as anticipated, the manager should expect to be compensated with higher portfolio returns. However, since the manager is forced to pay a premium for these higher-growth securities, if the actual performance falls short of the forecast, the manager will have overpaid for an underperforming stock and the portfolio performance will suffer accordingly.

A combination of forward- and backward-looking equity characteristics can be used to help the investor evaluate the manager in this context:

Long Term Growth IBES Means vs. EPS Growth – 5 Years

The EPS Growth statistic measures the earnings growth rate the portfolio has achieved over the prior five years, while the Long Term Growth statistic is a forward-looking estimate of earnings. If a portfolio reflects high historic earnings growth coupled with high forecasted earnings, it usually indicates the manager is buying high secular growth type companies that generally exhibit greater earnings consistency. If long term forecasted growth is high and historical growth is low, it is likely the manager is more focused on expected changes in earnings. It could also be the case that this type of manager is more likely to invest in highly cyclical companies and thus will tend to have more economically sensitive performance.

Observations

In Figure 2, Manager ABC appears to focus on the highest growth securities at the exclusion of others. For the five years ended September 30, 2008, they have achieved nearly the highest level of growth relative to the universe of growth equity accounts (black dots plotted). However, it is clear from their location on the growth forecast axis that their strategy involves buying many stocks with high growth forecasts. A fair assumption would be that they are buying stocks at a premium, since high growth rates tend to command high prices. Further analysis should involve the P/E ratio of the portfolio and the incidence of disappointing earnings results, since given the premium they are likely paying, negative earnings surprises could be devastating to their performance. Careful attention should be paid to the research process for Manager ABC and also to their sell discipline for securities that under-perform. It would also be prudent to consider their sector exposure as their focus on high growth may be a symptom of extreme sector concentration that the institutional investor may find excessively risky.

Figure 2 Long Term Growth IBES Means vs. EPS Growth 5 Years

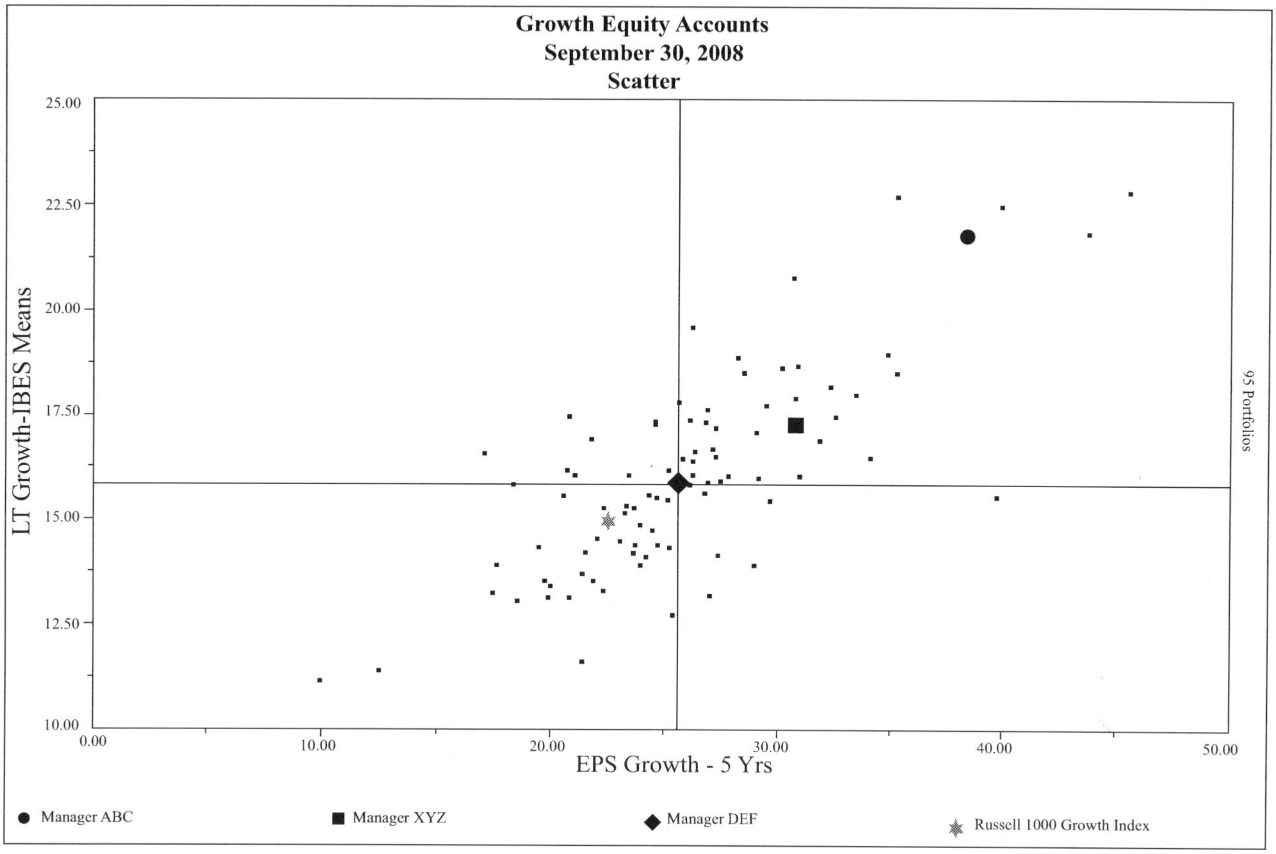

Source: Russell Investment Group; Universe Status: Final

In Figure 2, Manager XYZ appears to be more moderate in its growth purchases relative to Manager ABC. They are above the median for both forward- and backward-looking earnings but not to the degree of Manager ABC. Manager DEF is near the median large cap growth portfolio for both statistics, looking rather conservative in comparison. This implies that they place a greater emphasis on the price that they pay for the stocks in their portfolio and are not willing to pay a premium for the highest possible growth projections.

Question 2: How adept is the manager at capturing strong earnings growth while avoiding negative earnings surprise?

A successful growth manager requires the knowledge to forecast a company's future earnings growth better than other investors. If reported earnings are lower than analysts' expectations, the manager faces the risk of a steep stock price drop. Two statistics that can help evaluate the manager's strength in this capacity are:

Long Term Growth IBES Means vs. Negative Earnings Surprise

The Negative Earnings Surprise statistic reflects the percentage of a portfolio's holdings with earnings that fall below estimates; the fewer there are, the better the manager is at estimating future growth. For a portfolio with high forecasted growth, a high incidence rate of negative earnings can be disastrous since the forecast of elevated growth likely commands a significant premium in the market. If the securities don't produce the high earnings they are supposed to, the stocks in the portfolio will decline and overall performance will suffer. Correspondingly, stocks with lower earnings forecasts tend to weather Negative Earnings Surprise better. The general rule is that going extreme on high forecasted growth not only increases the likelihood of exposure to Negative Earnings Surprise but also amplifies the negative effects on portfolio performance when the Negative Earnings Surprise occurs.

Observations

In Figure 3, Manager ABC has a forecasted level of EPS Growth significantly higher than its peers, with a level of Negative Earnings Surprise slightly above the median. However, as in Figure 2, Manager ABC is focused heavily on stocks that have the highest possible growth forecasts, which are likely to trade at high premiums. When the earnings for these securities are reported at lower levels than expected, the result for their portfolio returns can be amplified relative to a more conservative manager.

Figure 3 LT Growth IBES Means vs. Negative Earnings Surprises

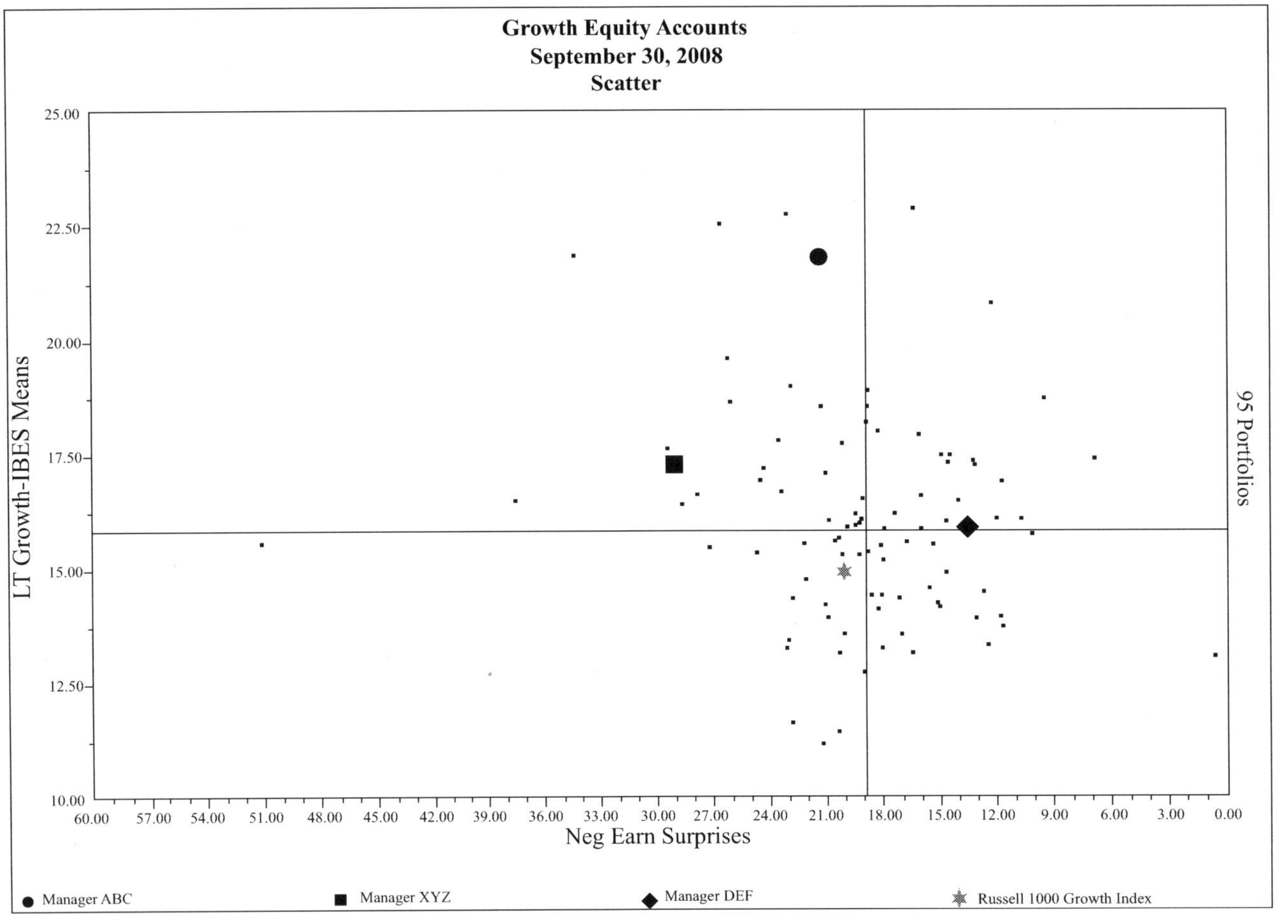

Source: Russell Investment Group; Universe Status: Final

Although the level of Negative Earnings Surprise is higher than the median growth manager in absolute terms for Manager XYZ, the fact that Manager XYZ is less aggressive in their growth targets means that the impact on their portfolio is less extreme. Manager DEF, while only approximating the universe median in terms of forecast growth, has a level of Negative Earnings Surprise that is among the best in the universe. As a result, Manager DEF has a lower risk of negative earnings, causing poor performance relative to its peers.

Question 3: Do the portfolio's earnings justify the price paid?

For investment styles focused on near term earnings, a valuable measure of how well a manager may be at selecting stocks is to compare whether the companies purchased meet their earnings estimates. A manager exhibiting a high percentage of Negative Earnings Surprises at a given level of P/E ratio indicates the manager may be a poor judge at forecasting earnings. This is a problem because it implies that they are overpaying for the performance they receive. Conversely, selecting stocks that beat their earnings estimates can lead to the opposite conclusion namely that the manager is a superior forecaster of earnings, and their stock selection is generating value. In Figure 5, these two characteristics have been selected to demonstrate the managers' effectiveness:

P/E (Excluding Negative Earnings)

Positive Earnings Surprise

For this time period, the index (Russell 1000 Growth) is near the median of the universe's two characteristics. In Figure 4, of the universe of managers, Manager ABC has among the highest P/E Excluding Negative Earnings; however they have a somewhat sub-median Positive Earnings Surprise. Manager DEF is above the peer median for both characteristics, while Manager XYZ exhibits below median rankings for both characteristics. No clear linear relationship between these characteristics exists, but investors prefer a manager that exhibits greater success at selecting companies with earnings that exceed analysts' expectations for a given valuation (*i.e.*, P/E, P/B, etc.) level.

Figure 4 Positive Earnings Surprise vs. P/E Excluding Negative Earnings

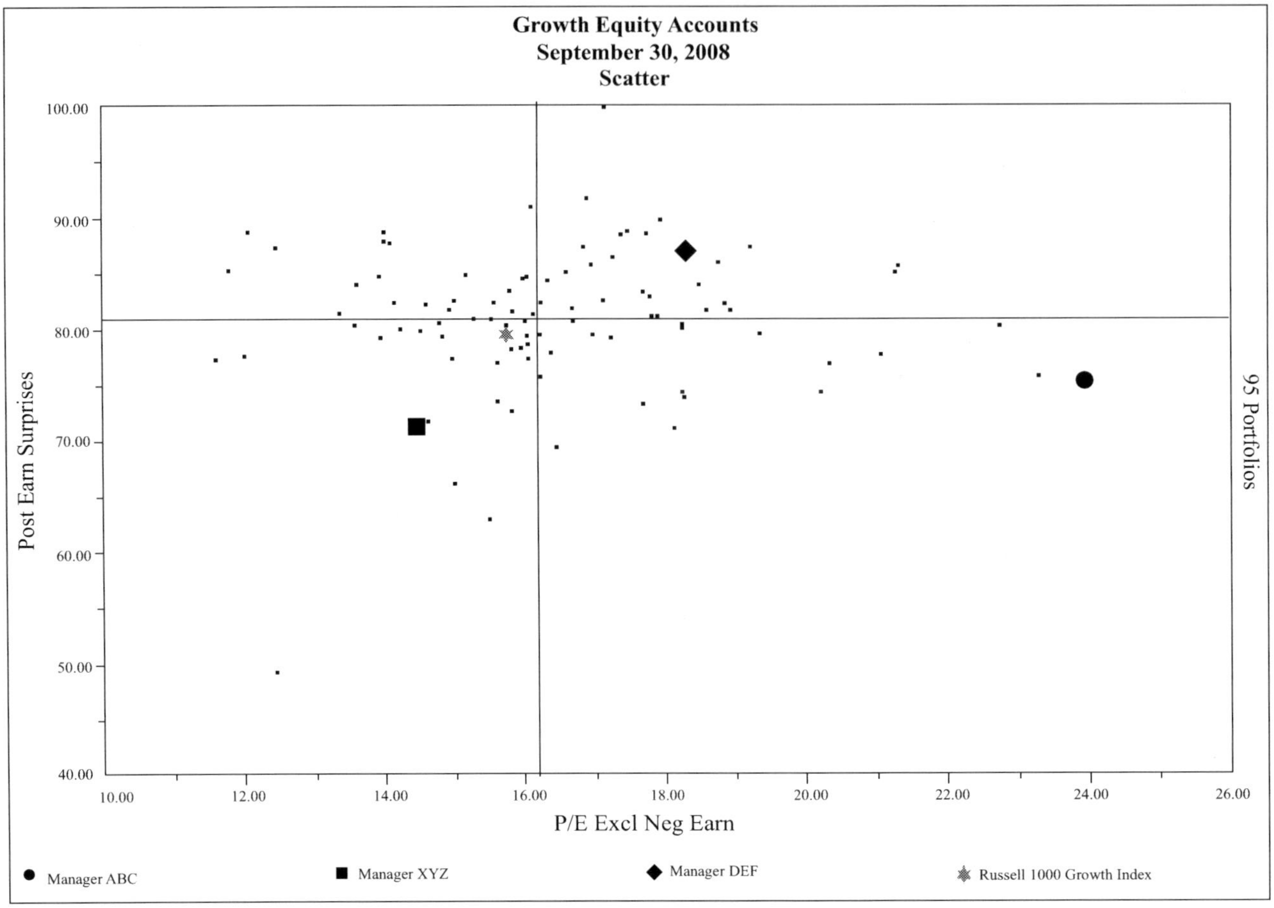

Source: Russell Investment Group; Universe Status: Final

Figure 5 Cash Flow Growth – 5 Years vs. EPS Growth – 5 Years

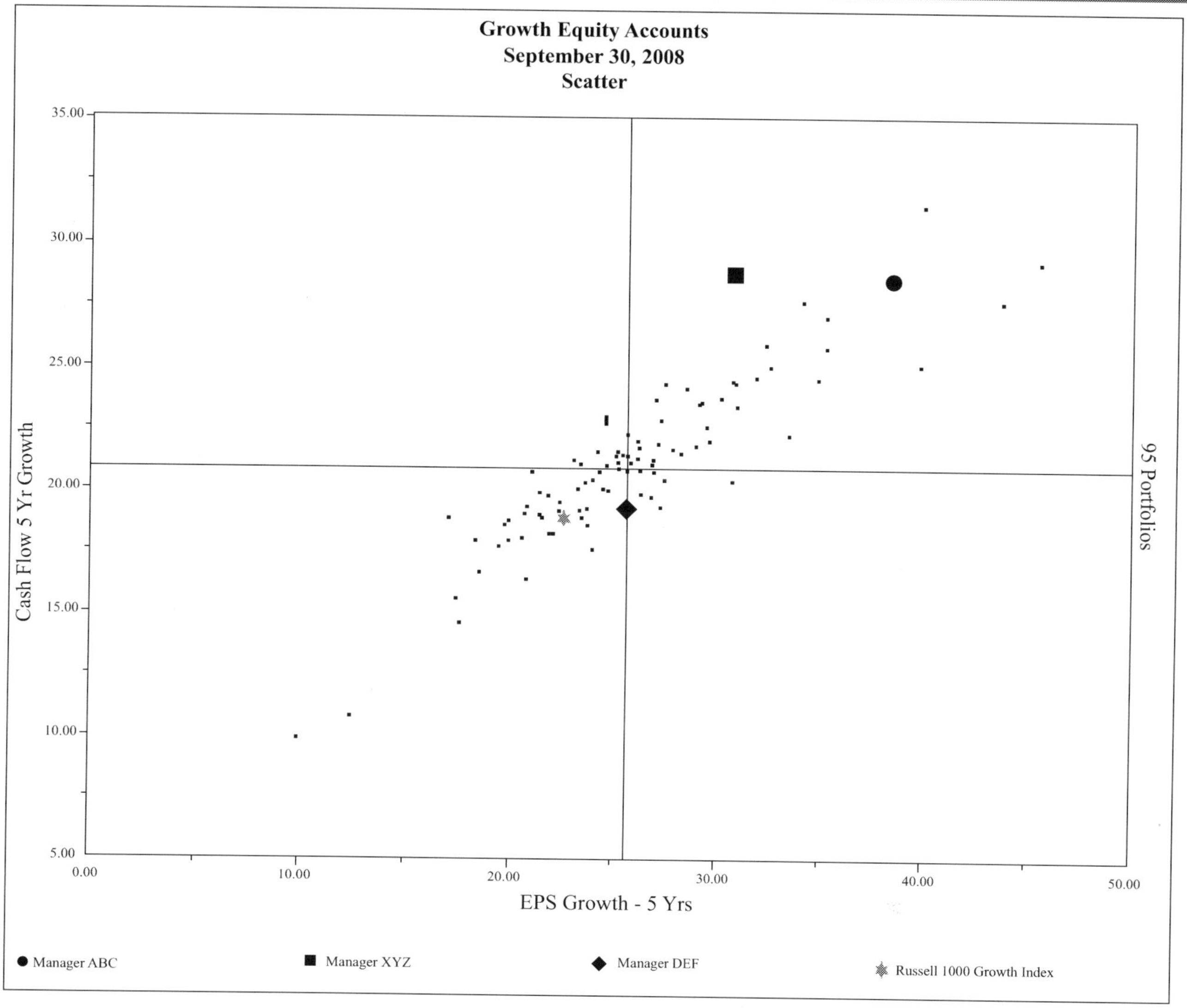

Source: Russell Investment Group; Universe Status: Final

Observations

As was the case with Negative Earnings Surprise, the Positive Earnings Surprise characteristic suggests that Manager ABC may be in for a volatile investing experience. Given that their P/E is the highest of any manager in the universe, there is a high likelihood their picks must have earnings that meet or exceed the expectations of analysts in order to have success. If that does not happen, the premium paid for their aggregate P/E ratio, which in Figure 4 is approximately 24, becomes unjustified. In that environment, the investor can expect performance to suffer.

Manager XYZ has a portfolio with below median Positive Earnings Surprise, lower than Manager ABC, and one might expect that their performance would suffer accordingly. However, based on the relative positions of these two characteristics allows an institutional investor to conclude that they are not overpaying for the Positive Earnings Surprise to the degree that Manager ABC is. Since they are not paying the premium for the highest possible growth as Manager ABC must pay, their performance is not likely to be as impacted by sub-median Positive Earnings Surprise. These two managers have clearly different approaches to growth investing. Manager DEF does deserve some attention since they are above the universe median in Positive Earnings Surprise to balance their above median aggregate P/E ratio.

Question 4: What is the earnings quality of the manager's portfolio?

Investors are interested in knowing the quality of earnings of the underlying companies in a portfolio since companies with more sustainable earnings are typically more stable, long-term investments. Similarly to Sales per Share Growth, a portfolio's Cash Flow Growth should be close to, or above, it's EPS Growth. Investors gain insight into the sustainability of an underlying portfolio's earnings by comparing the following two characteristics:

Cash Flow 5 Yr Growth

EPS Growth – 5 Yrs

Cash Flow 5 Yr Growth is indicative of the overall business growth and financial stability of companies held in the portfolio (even if the growth is not flowing through to the bottom line). It is a useful alternative measure of growth for companies that either do not have earnings, have weak earnings, or their book values do not reflect intangible assets (*e.g.*, service companies or high technology companies). EPS Growth – 5 Yrs measures the earnings per share growth of a portfolio's holdings over the prior five years. Strong growth in EPS is an indicator of a healthy company. Without ample liquidity, a company may have to temper its plans for growth, which demonstrates why the Cash Flow measure is so important.

Observations

In Figure 5, only Manager XYZ's Cash Flow Growth is on par with its EPS Growth. Both Manager ABC and Manager DEF reflect EPS Growth exceeding Cash Flow; sustained EPS Growth higher than Cash Flow Growth is not a positive indicator of sustainable future growth rates for these portfolios.

Question 5: Is the portfolio's growth rate likely to be accompanied by a high level of performance volatility?

The historical earnings growth rate of a portfolio, when observed for an extended period of time, can help illustrate a great deal about the profile of securities a manager is likely to select. However, when the results over the period of time are condensed into a single number, a significant portion of the story can be obscured. For example, if a manager attains a growth rate of 25 percent each year for five years, the compound annual growth rate of the portfolio will be 25 percent. However, a portfolio which has yearly growth rates of 5%, 37%, 12%, 58% and 20% will also yield a five year annual growth rate of approximately 25 percent. When looking at the single metric of five-year growth, these two portfolios would appear identical, but clearly investing in the second portfolio will produce much more variability in earnings. To better understand these results, an institutional investor should look at a comparison between the following two characteristics:

EPS Growth – 5 Years

EPS Variability – 5 Years

The characteristics provided in Figure 6 allow the institutional investor to determine how much variability was experienced while realizing the portfolio's historical earnings growth, and in turn whether or not the portfolio is a good fit with stated investment goals and objectives.

Figure 6 EPS Growth – 5 Years vs. EPS Variability – 5 Years

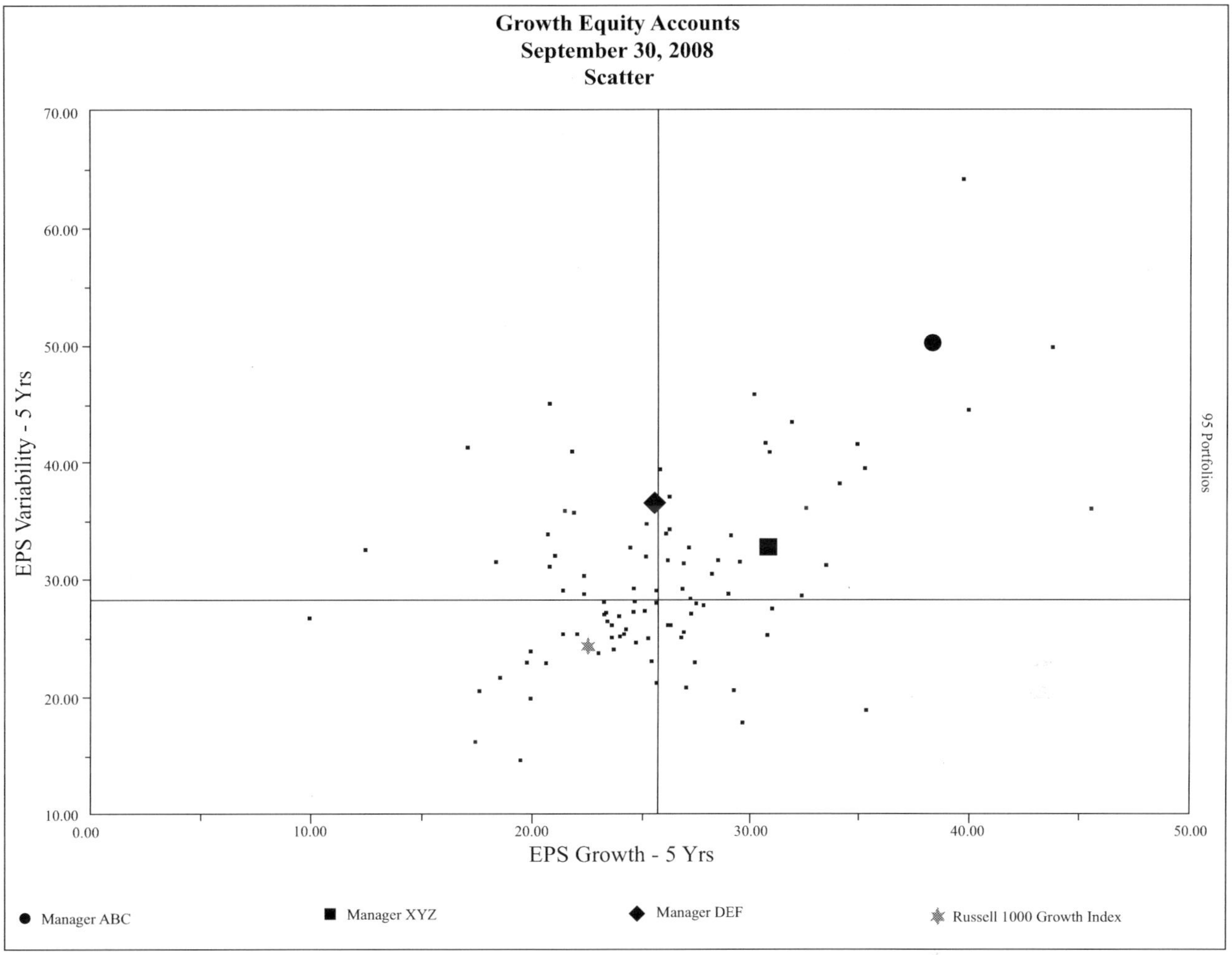

Source: Russell Investment Group; Universe Status: Final

Consistent with the earlier analyses, Manager ABC experienced the highest levels of both earnings growth and earnings variability. Their earnings growth ranks in the upper range for the universe, approaching 40% per annum over the previous five years. Accompanying this high growth rate are significantly higher levels of variability relative to peers. Manager XYZ delivered an annualized growth rate just over 30%, which is significantly above the universe median but with far less variability than Manager ABC. Manager DEF generated a growth rate that approximates the universe median, with slightly more variability than Manager XYZ.

Observations

A high level of EPS Variability within a portfolio is not necessarily a negative but likely suggests that performance will be highly correlated with general economic performance. When economic conditions are favorable, their bets can pay off big, but when conditions turn negative these same investments can significantly underperform. A high level of EPS Variability also suggests that the portfolio is focused on and sensitive to earnings changes. In this situation, the manager may need to be more sensitive to short-term progress of companies such as reported earnings relative to analyst expectations.

Question 6: How does your manager's strategy fare in different market environments?

When evaluating a manager, a common tendency is to look at the manager's performance relative to peers over standard time periods. However, this practice in isolation can cause an institutional investor to overlook other informative factors. For example, an institutional investor should consider what was happening in the overall market during the period in question. In the case of large cap growth managers, performance would tend to suffer during periods that strongly favor value strategies. At first glance, that may lead an institutional investor to write off a potentially strong manager for having disappointing returns compared to its peers. An institutional investor can isolate the performance of a manager specifically in terms of periods when the market was rising and falling by reviewing the historical performance for portfolios, composites, and universes for time periods identified as rising and falling markets. This can contextualize a positive or negative return and, through universe comparison, rate a manager's performance against their peers.

Observations

Based on the results in Figure 7, all three managers are top performers relative to the index and peers in the rising market period. Even in the falling market period, all three outperformed the index. Manager XYZ continued to be a top quartile performer, with Manager ABC slipping into the second quartile and Manager DEF dropped into the third quartile. From this exhibit, an institutional investor can see that all three managers outperformed in the market environment favorable to their style, while both Manager XYZ and Manager ABC's strategies were more resilient in the falling markets period.

Figure 7 Market Cycles

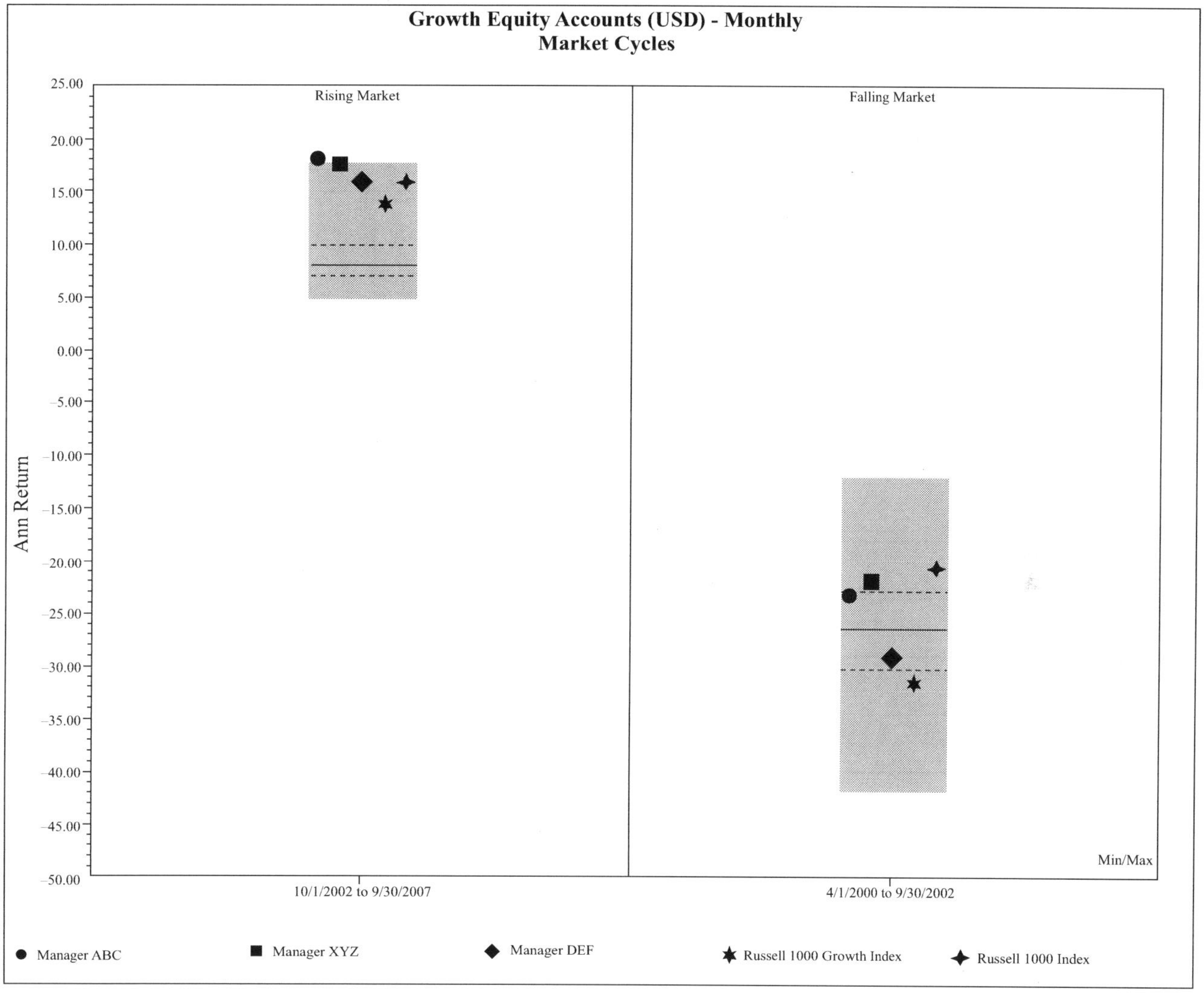

Source: Russell Investment Group; Universe Status: Final

Question 7: Does analysis of the interaction of multiple portfolio characteristics provide additional insight?

Using Portfolio Rankings, institutional investors can compare a manager against peers across multiple characteristics at a time. In the exhibit below, the three large cap growth portfolios are ranked against peers in terms of the following characteristics:

EPS Growth – 5 Yrs

Cash Flow 5 Yr Growth

Sales Per Share Growth 5 Yrs

Long Term Growth IBES Means

In Figure 8, Manager ABC exhibits the strongest mix of characteristics, consistently in the top quartile of its peer group for each of the metrics selected. Manager XYZ is close behind, actually exceeding Manager ABC in the Cash Flow Growth statistic. Manager DEF tends to be close to the median of the peer group, almost falling out of the third quartile in terms of Cash Flow Growth.

Figure 8 Portfolio Rankings – Growth Characteristics

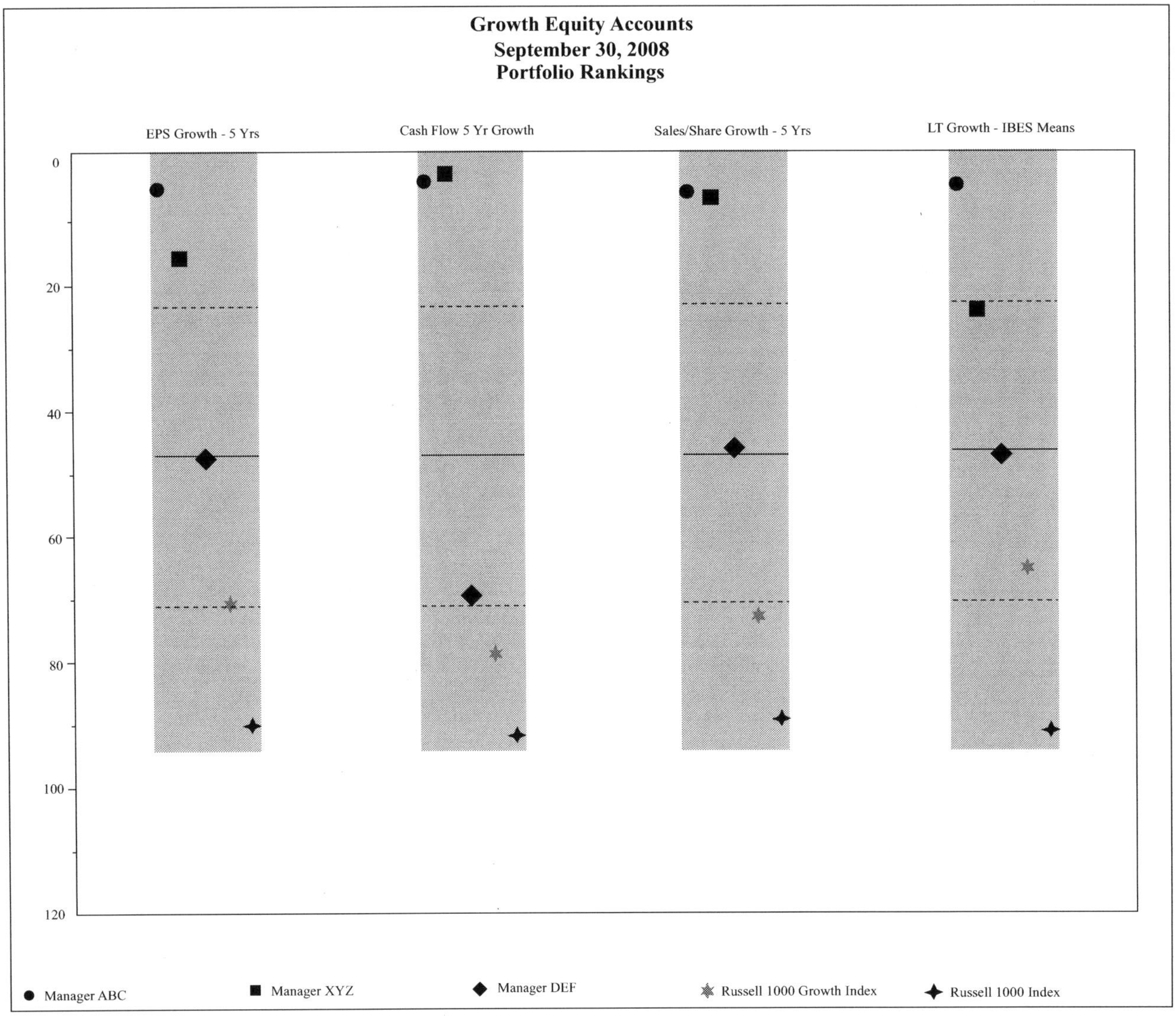

Source: Russell Investment Group; Universe Status: Final

Observations

When reviewing Figure 8, one can conclude that Manager ABC, with its peer-leading growth statistics, may fare best during investment climates that favor high growth companies. However, in periods of underperformance for growth strategies, its performance may suffer more than Manager XYZ or Manager DEF. These are some potential outcomes that an institutional investor should consider before making manager selection and retention decisions.

Question 8: Do managers exhibit consistent relative characteristics across multiple time periods?

In addition to comparing return information across time or multiple characteristics across managers for a single time period, institutional investors can evaluate consistency by comparing managers and their peers over multiple time periods for a single characteristic. In Figure 9, the three managers are ranked against each other and the Growth Equity Accounts universe for the previous four quarters. The statistic they are measured by is:

Sales Per Share Growth – 5 Years

As shown in Figure 9, Manager ABC exhibited the highest Sales Per Share Growth of the three during each time period, consistently in the top quartile of its peer group. Manager XYZ also tended to rank high on this statistic, although its ranking was less consistent than either Manager ABC or Manager DEF. Manager DEF placed consistently in the second quartile relative to peers.

Observations

Figure 9 is useful as it illustrates where a manager stands compared to peers, as well as demonstrating whether that ranking is consistent over time. Manager XYZ appears to be the least consistent of the three managers; it may be a reflection of a more volatile investment approach or that their strategy changed over time. These are questions an institutional investor may pursue further with the manager. Overall, Manager ABC shows itself to be consistently among the most aggressive managers in the peer group, with Manager XYZ a close second, and Manager DEF tending toward the median in its Sales per Share Growth measure.

SUMMARY COMMENTS

The often quoted statement: "a picture is worth a thousand words" or in this case, a thousand numbers is certainly true when it comes to investment analysis. Graphical displays of performance and analytics data can transform a page of numbers into a more accessible and easier-to-interpret representation of investment information. By incorporating peer and index comparisons, time dimensions and a visual representation of the data, a story that might be missed in a tabular view is uncovered.

The three managers reviewed share a common broad investment style but have very different implementations to their approach. While an institutional investor may be attracted to the top tier returns of Manager ABC, upon closer examination, the underlying risk profile may prove more than their risk budget will allow. On the other hand, a large institutional investor with multiple managers in the large cap growth category may be comfortable adding such a manager to their line-up; the higher risk may complement more traditional players already in the fund. While Manager XYZ posted solid returns, its less consistent results across some of the characteristics may be the impetus for further conversations. Manager DEF stands out as potentially the best fit for an institutional investor seeking a more conservative growth manager profile.

For further analysis, one could review these managers using performance attribution versus a relevant benchmark to assess asset allocation and stock selection decisions. This could help explain the source or potential bias of a manager's performance compared to the benchmark. If a manager's performance results are unexpected, this more detailed analysis can provide insight into the portfolio and help prepare an institutional investor for an in-depth conversation with their manager.

The graphical nature of the results within this case study in combination with the equity characteristic analysis allows the investor to quickly assess key pieces of information across multiple managers on a consistent basis, which can yield valuable insight into a manager's underlying investment approach and philosophy.

Figure 9 Portfolio Ranking – Sales per Share Growth

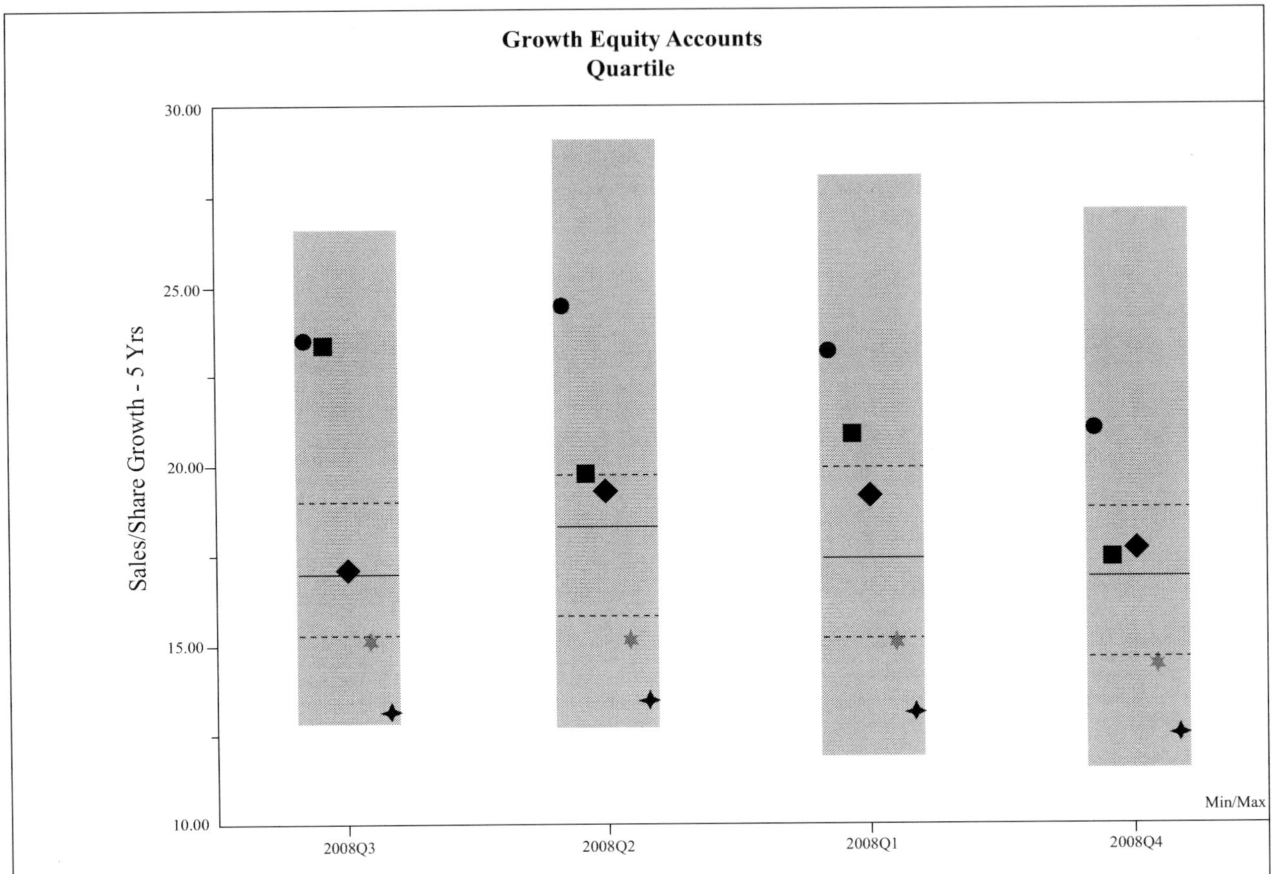

	Value	%Tile	Rank	Value	% Tile	Rank	Value	% Tile	Rank	Value	% Tile	Rank
Maximum	26.59			29.10			28.08			27.08		
25th Percentile	18.99			19.71			19.91			18.78		
Median Percentile	17.02			18.27			17.39			16.82		
75th Percentile	15.27			15.79			15.16			14.60		
Minimum	12.58			12.65			11.90			11.53		
# of portfolios	95			108			101			96		
● Manager ABC	23.49	7	6	24.37	5	5	23.14	7	7	20.98	9	8
■ Manager XYZ	23.29	8	7	19.72	25	27	20.84	16	16	17.31	44	43
◆ Manager DEF	17.09	50	47	19.28	34	36	19.10	31	31	17.63	40	38
✳ Russell 1000 Growth Index	15.09	77	73	15.19	82	89	15.04	77	79	14.40	79	76
✦ Russell 1000 Index	13.11	95	90	13.35	97	105	13.03	98	100	12.56	96	93

Source: Russell Investment Group; Universe Status: Final

PRACTICE PROBLEMS

The following information relates to Questions 1–3

The investment committee of CEH Industries' pension fund has recently hired Sarah Smith, an investment consultant, to analyze the performance of its large-cap growth equity portfolio. The portfolio has three investment managers—A, B, and C—all of whom share the same growth equity benchmark. The investment committee is concerned that the managers may be deviating from their stated mandate. The strategy implementation description for each manager is as follows:

Manager A	Uses a bottom-up approach and strives to hold companies with consistent earnings per share growth and minimal negative earnings surprise without overpaying for growth prospects.
Manager B	Uses proprietary analytics to screen stocks from the entire large-cap equity universe to find the top quartile of expected future growth. The results of these screens are then analyzed for earnings quality and weighted by their long-term growth potential.
Manager C	Focuses on high-quality companies with reasonably predictable earnings with higher sales-per-share growth compared with the growth equity benchmark. The strategy targets a low tracking error with the growth equity benchmark.

Smith compiles forward- and backward-looking growth characteristics of the three managers along with a peer group of growth equity managers. Using the long-term growth I/B/E/S mean estimates as the forward-looking growth measure and the earnings per share (EPS) growth over the past five years as the backward-looking measure, Smith compiles the chart shown in Exhibit 1.

Exhibit 1 Long-Term Growth I/B/E/S Mean Estimates vs. EPS Growth over Past Five Years

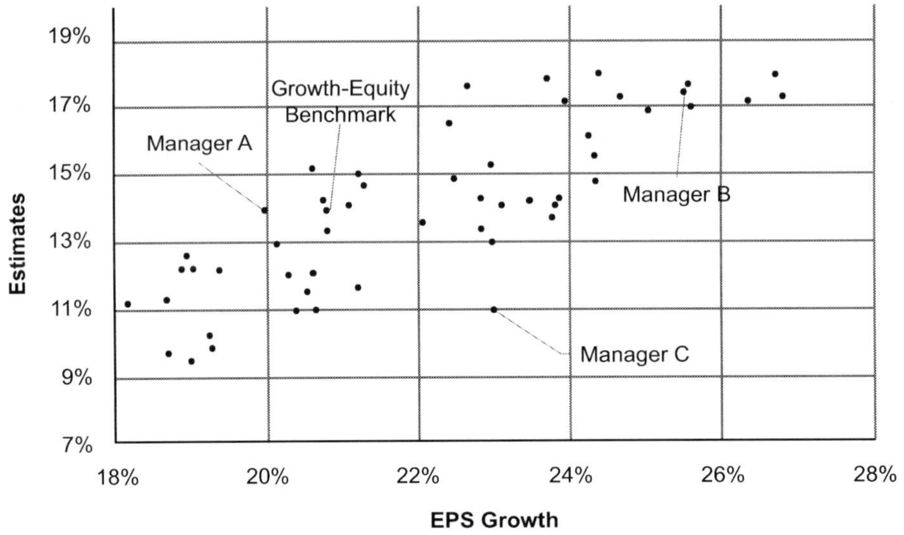

The investment committee is also concerned with the volatility of the current market environment and wonders how that will affect the growth equity managers. Smith compiles the data shown in Exhibit 2 for her analysis.

Exhibit 2 Manager Characteristics Comparison

	Positive Earnings Surprise, Last Quarter (%)	Current P/E	EPS Variability, Five Years (%)	EPS Growth, Five Years (%)
Manager A	81.4	16.8	27.5	20.0
Manager B	79.5	25.3	36.1	25.5
Manager C	78.5	12.2	30.1	23.0
Growth equity peer group median	75.6	17.2	28.6	20.7

Note: Positive earnings surprise represents the percentage of a portfolio's holdings for which earnings are greater than the I/B/E/S consensus estimates.

1 Based on the strategy implementation descriptions and Exhibit 1, which manager *most likely* displays style drift?

A Manager A

B Manager B

C Manager C

2 Based on the EPS variability and EPS growth over the past five years, as shown in Exhibit 2, the manager who is *most likely* to be sensitive to general economic performance is:

A Manager A.

B Manager B.

C Manager C.

3 Based on the positive earnings surprise and P/E in Exhibit 2, which of the following *best* describes a greater risk to Manager B relative to the other managers?

A Exhibiting style drift that indicates a value equity style

B Underperforming if earnings are less than expectations

C Underperforming in favorable growth markets environments

SOLUTIONS

1 C is correct. Based on the peer group for growth equity managers, Manager C has an average backward-looking growth rate of 23%; however, the forward-looking growth rate of 11% is significantly less than the growth equity benchmark of 14%. These results could indicate that Manager C has moved away from its stated growth mandate.

2 B is correct. Manager B has significantly higher EPS variability than the other managers, suggesting that performance will be more highly correlated with general economic performance.

3 B is correct. All three managers have similar positive earnings surprise ratios and all are greater than the peer group, consistent with the three managers having similar ability to correctly identify stocks that will exceed analysts' earnings expectations. But Manager B's P/E of 25.3 is significantly higher than Manager A and Manager C (16.8 and 12.2, respectively) and the peer group (17.2). To the extent that Manager B commands a valuation premium over the other managers for its ability to select holdings that have positive earnings surprises, its performance is more likely to be harmed if earnings are less than expectations.

PERFORMANCE EVALUATION

STUDY SESSION

5

Manager Selection

This study session addresses important topics in investment manager selection. The first reading provides a framework that introduces and describes the important elements of the manager selection process. The second reading explores important principles of investment manager selection including distinctive due diligence concerns for investment managers of traditional and alternative investments, the manager interview process, considerations in forming a portfolio of managers, and manager monitoring and continuance. The third reading in the sequence illustrates many of these principles via a series of case studies. The fourth reading takes a generally quantitative approach to determining allocations to passive and active managers.

The final reading in this study session examines various foundational issues in manager selection, arguing the importance of using measures of active return and active risk purged of any systematic risk influences. The reading also describes considerations in constructing an optimal portfolio of managers.

READING ASSIGNMENTS

10 Investment Manager Selection: An Introduction
by Jeffrey C. Heisler, PhD, CFA, and Donald W. Lindsey, CFA

11 Topics in Investment Manager Selection
by Jeffrey C. Heisler, PhD, CFA, Jeffrey R. Nipp, CAIA, CFA, Morgan Webber, Ross Morrison, and Steven G. Bloom, CFA

12 Cases in Investment Manager Selection
by Jeffrey C. Heisler, PhD, CFA, Jeffry R. Nipp, CAIA, CFA, Morgan Webber, Ross Morrison, and Steven G. Bloom, CFA

13 Setting Weights for Active and Index Managers

READING

10

Investment Manager Selection: An Introduction

by Jeffrey C. Heisler, PhD, CFA, and Donald W. Lindsey, CFA

Jeffrey C. Heisler, PhD, CFA, is at TwinFocus Capital Partners (USA). Donald W. Lindsey, CFA (USA).

LEARNING OUTCOMES

Mastery	*The candidate should be able to:*
☐	a. describe how investment manager selection takes place in the context of the client's investment policy statement;
☐	b. describe qualitative considerations in evaluating investment managers;
☐	c. describe the components of a manager selection process, including due diligence;
☐	d. contrast Type I and Type II errors in manager hiring and continuation decisions;
☐	e. describe uses of style analysis in investment manager selection;
☐	f. compare returns-based and holdings-based style analysis, including the advantages and disadvantages of each;
☐	g. describe uses of the upside capture ratio, downside capture ratio, maximum drawdown, drawdown duration, and up/down capture in evaluating managers;
☐	h. describe uses of the "batting average" in evaluating managers;
☐	i. evaluate a manager's investment philosophy and investment decision-making process;
☐	j. evaluate the costs and benefits of pooled investment vehicles and separate accounts;
☐	k. compare types of investment manager contracts, including their major provisions and advantages and disadvantages;
☐	l. describe the three basic forms of performance-based fees;
☐	m. analyze and interpret a sample performance-based fee schedule.
☐	n. evaluate a manager's adherence to a stated investment philosophy and investment decision-making process.

1 INTRODUCTION

Most investors do not hold securities directly but rather invest using intermediaries. Whether the intermediary is a separately managed account or a pooled investment vehicle, such as mutual funds in the United States, unit trusts in the United Kingdom, Undertakings for the Collective Investment of Transferable Securities (UCITS) in the European Union, hedge funds, private equity funds, or exchange-traded funds (ETFs), a professional investment manager is being entrusted with helping investors achieve their investment objectives. In all of these cases, the selection of appropriate investment managers is a challenge with important financial consequences.

Evaluating an investment manager is a complex and detailed process that encompasses a great deal more than analyzing investment returns. The investigation and analysis in support of an investment action, decision, or recommendation is called **due diligence**. In conducting investment manager due diligence, the focus is on understanding how the investment results were achieved and on assessing the likelihood that the investment process that generated these returns will produce superior or at least satisfactory investment results going forward. Due diligence also entails an evaluation of a firm's integrity, operations, and personnel. As such, due diligence involves both quantitative and qualitative analysis.

This reading provides a framework that introduces and describes the important elements of the manager selection process. Although it is important to have a well-defined methodology, this reading is not intended to be a rigid checklist, a step-by-step guide, or an in-depth analysis but rather to present a structure from which the reader can develop their own approach.

We assume that the investment policy statement (IPS) has been drafted, the asset allocation determined, and the decision to use an outside adviser has been made. As a result, the focus is on determining which manager offers the "best" means to implement or express those decisions. The discussion has three broad topics:

- Placing manager selection in the context of the investment policy statement (Section 2).
- Outlining a framework for identifying, evaluating, and ultimately selecting investment managers (Section 3).
- Quantitative (Section 4) and qualitative considerations (Section 5) in manager selection.

The reading concludes with a summary of selected important points.

2 MANAGER SELECTION AND THE INVESTMENT POLICY STATEMENT

In selecting a manager, an investor is attempting to find the "best" manager for expressing a particular portfolio need. This entails a broader set of considerations than whether the manager appears to display skill. The manager must also be suitable for the investor's needs, as expressed by the IPS, as well as the investor's views on active and passive management.

Each investor has particular assumptions about, expectations for, and biases surrounding their investments. The **investment policy statement** frames the manager selection process by capturing all of this information in addition to investor constraints (liquidity, time horizon, tax concerns, legal and regulatory factors, and unique circumstances).

The IPS's sections concerning objectives and constraints will determine the universe of managers that is suitable for the investor and which therefore should be considered. It is important to identify the appropriate universe from which to search and select managers: Managers that display skill but are not suited for the role the investor seeks to fill will not be a good fit.

The first consideration in screening managers is to determine the appropriate benchmark for the allocation (e.g., to equities or fixed income) being considered. This process naturally incorporates the return requirements and some aspects of the risk tolerance specified in the IPS.

The following investment objectives and constraints are generally specified in the IPS:

- **Risk tolerance:** What is the investor's willingness and ability to bear risk? The IPS may place limitations, stated in absolute or relative terms, on risk.
- **Investment objectives:** Absolute and/or benchmark relative return objectives may be stated. For some investors, an important goal is to fund the payment of a set of long-term liabilities. The objective in such cases may be stated relation to the liabilities.
- **Investment disciplines (investment philosophy):** The IPS often provides guidance on how the investor's assets are to be managed. It may indicate a preference for, or place a constraint on, the use of active and/or passive managers. This preference or constraint can be based on investor or asset allocator assumptions about market efficiency in general or for particular segments of the market. A liability-relative investment approach may be relevant if funding the payment of liabilities is an investment objective.
- **Liquidity:** The portfolio's liquidity must be fitting with the investor's demands. An investor with shorter-term liquidity needs typically does not hold long-term assets, such as private equity or real estate.
- **Time horizon:** In addition to liquidity needs, the investment horizon relates to the tolerance for risk. An investor closer to retirement has less time to recover from losses, which places more emphasis on absolute measures of risk, such as capture ratio and drawdown. It is appropriate for investors with a long-term horizon to take on more risk to ensure that the purchasing power of the portfolio is maintained.
- **Taxes:** Taxes may be an important consideration for some investors, in which case lower-turnover, more tax efficient strategies are preferred. In addition, separately managed accounts may be preferable to pooled investment vehicles to customize the strategy in a way that minimizes tax liabilities.
- **Regulatory:** Individual investors may have trust and estate considerations, and institutional investors may face legal and regulatory issues.
- **Unique circumstances (investment preferences):** The IPS may state any unique considerations or concerns that need to be observed. Examples include restrictions on allowable investments dictated by religious or other beliefs, or a requirement to maintain voting control of a family-owned portfolio investment. Such considerations might make a separately managed account preferable.

Exhibit 1 lists some of the key features of an IPS that are particularly important to the manager selection process as well as their potential implications for the process. Although the specifics may vary significantly across investors based on their views, investment horizons, size of assets, and past investment experience, every IPS should include these key features regardless of the investor's individual circumstances and characteristics.

Exhibit 1 Various IPS Features and Their Implications for Manager Selection

IPS Feature	Potential Implications for Manager Selection
Objectives	
Philosophy	Compatibility of investment philosophy and process.
Asset size considerations	Investment vehicle compatibility; capacity of market to support execution of the strategy for given asset amount.
Return objectives	
■ Total vs. relative	Manager ability to generate a specific absolute return, or return in excess of a specified benchmark.
■ Real vs. nominal	Level and type of net risk exposures; inflation hedging characteristics of the portfolio.
■ Net vs. gross	Level and structure of fees and expenses, portfolio turnover.
Risk tolerance	Level and type of net risk exposures. Acceptable level of portfolio volatility, either in absolute terms or relative to a benchmark. Level of downside risk.
Constraints	
Liquidity	Fund terms regarding withdrawals and redemptions. Investor types and concentrations.
Horizon	Drawdown risk over investor's horizon.
Taxes	Tax management ability.
Legal and regulatory	Allowable investments, manager diversification, short sales.
Unique circumstances	Allowable investments, level, and type of net risk exposures
Other considerations	
Asset class selection	Level and type of net risk exposures, manager investment style.
Rebalancing frequency	Portfolio and market liquidity.
Review and reporting frequency	Transparency.

Source: Based on Stewart 2013.

EXAMPLE 1

Investment Manager Selection and the IPS

1 Which of the following sections of an IPS *most likely* relates to the feasibility of adding a distressed debt investment manager as part of an institution's diversified investment portfolio?

A Risk tolerance

B Return objectives

C Legal and regulatory constraints

2 Which of the following IPS constraints might suggest the use of a separately managed account rather than a pooled vehicle?

A Taxes and preferences

B Liquidity and transparency
C Regulatory and time horizon

Solution to 1:

C is correct. Within a diversified portfolio, distressed debt may have a role for various levels of risk tolerance and investment objectives. Regulatory and legal constraints, however, may rule out distressed debt investment.

Solution to 2:

A is correct. Separately managed accounts allow for customization, which may be preferable to pooled investment vehicles if minimizing tax liabilities or if the IPS includes any special considerations or concerns that need to be expressed.

A FRAMEWORK FOR INVESTMENT MANAGER SEARCH AND SELECTION

3

An underlying assumption of investment manager due diligence is that a consistent, robust investment process will generate a similar return distribution relative to risk factors through time, assuming the underlying dynamics of the market have not dramatically changed. One important goal of manager due diligence is to understand whether the manager's investment process, people, and portfolio construction satisfy this assumption—that is, will the investment process generate the expected return from the expected sources? The manager search and selection process has three broad components: the universe, a quantitative analysis of the manager's performance track record, and a qualitative analysis of the manager's investment process. The qualitative analysis consists of investment due diligence, which evaluates the manager's investment process, and operational due diligence, which evaluates the manager's infrastructure and firm. Exhibit 2 details these components.

Exhibit 2 Manager Selection Process Overview

Key aspects	Key Question
Universe	
Defining the universe	What is the feasible set of managers that fit the portfolio need?
■ Suitability	Which managers are suitable for the IPS?
■ Style	Which have the appropriate style?
■ Active vs. passive	Which fit the active versus passive decision?
Quantitative Analysis	
Investment due diligence	Which manager "best" fits the portfolio need?
Quantitative	What has been the manager's return distribution?
■ Attribution and Appraisal	Has the manager displayed skill?
■ Capture ratio	How does the manager perform in "up" markets versus "down" markets?
■ Drawdown	Does the return distribution exhibit large drawdowns?
Qualitative Analysis	

(continued)

Exhibit 2 (Continued)

Key aspects	Key Question
Investment due diligence	Which manager "best" fits the portfolio need?
Qualitative	Is the manager expected to continue to generate this return distribution?
■ Philosophy	What market inefficiency does the manager seek to exploit?
■ Process	Is the investment process capable of exploiting this inefficiency?
■ People	Do the investment personnel possess the expertise and experience necessary to effectively implement the investment process?
■ Portfolio	Is portfolio construction consistent with the stated investment philosophy and process?
Operational due diligence	Is the manager's track record accurate, and does it fully reflect risks?
■ Process and procedure	Is the back office strong, safeguarding assets and able to issue accurate reports in a timely manner?
■ Firm	Is the firm profitable, with a healthy culture, and likely to remain in business? Is the firm committed to delivering performance over gathering assets?
■ Investment vehicle	Is the vehicle suitable for the portfolio need?
■ Terms	Are the terms acceptable and appropriate for the strategy and vehicle?
Monitoring	Does the manager continue to be the "best" fit for the portfolio need?

EXAMPLE 2

Components of the Manager Selection Process

1 Qualitative analysis of the manager selection process includes:

- **A** attribution.
- **B** defining the universe.
- **C** investment and operational due diligence.

2 Which of the following is considered a key aspect of operational due diligence?

- **A** People
- **B** Philosophy
- **C** Procedures

Solution to 1:

C is correct. Qualitative analysis consists of investment due diligence, which evaluates the manager's investment process, and operational due diligence, which evaluates the manager's infrastructure and firm.

Solution to 2:

C is correct. Process and procedures are key aspects of operational due diligence, whereas people and philosophy are key aspects of investment due diligence.

3.1 Defining the Manager Universe

The manager selection process begins by defining the universe of feasible managers, those managers that potentially satisfy the identified portfolio need. The objective is to reduce the manager universe to a manageable size relative to the resources and time available to evaluate it. This process also involves balancing the risks of too narrow a search, which potentially excludes interesting managers, and too broad a search, which leads to little gain in reducing the list of potential managers. Like many interesting problems, this step is a combination of art and science. In the initial screening process, the search parameters can be narrowed and widened to determine which managers enter and exit and to evaluate whether these additions or deletions improve the universe.

The IPS and the reason for the manager search largely determine the universe of managers considered and the benchmark against which they are compared. A new search based on a strategic or tactical view, such as adding a new strategy or risk exposure, will examine a broad universe of comparable managers and look to select the best within the universe. Adding a manager to increase capacity or diversification within a strategy already held will look for a complement to current holdings. Replacing a single manager in a particular strategy will look for the best manager within the strategy universe. The IPS in part determines what the relative terms "best," "complement," and "cost/benefit" mean.

Typically, a search starts with a benchmark that represents the manager's role within the portfolio. The benchmark also provides a reference for performance attribution and appraisal. There are several approaches to assigning a manager to a benchmark:

- **Third-party categorization:** Database or software providers and consultants typically assign managers to a strategy sector. This categorization provides an easy and efficient way to define the universe. The risk is that the provider's definition may differ from the desired portfolio role. As such, it is important to understand the criteria used by the provider.
- **Returns-based style analysis:** The risk exposures derived from the manager's actual return series has the advantage of being objective. The disadvantage is additional computational effort and the limitations of returns-based analysis.
- **Holdings-based style analysis:** This approach allows for the estimation of current factor exposures but adds to computational effort and depends on timing and amount of transparency.
- **Manager experience:** The assignment can be based on an evaluation of the manager and observations of portfolios and returns over time.

Not surprisingly, a hybrid strategy that combines elements of each approach is recommended. Using third-party categorizations is an efficient way to build an initial universe that can then be complemented and refined with quantitative methods and experience. The screening should avoid using performance at this point. The focus should be on understanding the manager's risk profile and identifying candidates to fill the desired role in the portfolio. Lastly, the universe of potential managers is not static—it will evolve through time not only as manager strategies evolve but also as a result of the entry and exit of managers.

3.2 Type I and Type II Errors in Manager Selection

Certain concepts from the area of inferential statistics known as hypothesis testing can be relevant to the decision to hire an investment manager or to retain or dismiss a manager previously hired.

The determination of whether a manager is skillful typically starts with the null hypothesis (the hypothesis assumed to be true until demonstrated otherwise) that the manager is not skillful. As a result, there are two types of potential error:

- Type I: Hiring or retaining a manager who subsequently underperforms expectations. Rejecting the null hypothesis of no skill when it is correct.
- Type II: Not hiring or firing a manager who subsequently outperforms, or performs in line with, expectations. Not rejecting the null hypothesis when it is incorrect.

Exhibit 3 Type I and Type II Errors

		Realization	
		Below expectations (no skill)	At or above expectations (skill)
Decision	Hire/Retain	Type I	Correct
	Not Hire/Fire	Correct	Type II

Type I and Type II errors can occur anytime a decision is made regarding the hiring or firing of a manager. The decision maker must determine which error is preferred based on the expected benefits and costs of changing managers.

3.2.1 *Qualitative considerations in Type I and Type II errors*

Decision makers appear predisposed to worry more about Type I errors than Type II errors. Potential reasons for this focus on Type I errors are as follows:

- Psychologically, people seek to avoid feelings of regret. Type I errors result in using an underperforming manager, an error of commission, whereas Type II errors result in not using an overperforming manager, an error of omission. As a result, Type I errors create explicit costs, whereas Type II errors create opportunity costs. Because individuals appear to put less weight on opportunity costs, Type I errors are psychologically more painful than Type II errors.
- Type I errors are relatively straightforward to measure and are often directly linked to the decision maker's compensation. Portfolio holdings are regularly monitored, and managers' out- and underperformance expectations are clearly identified. Type II errors are less likely to be measured—what is the performance impact of not having selected a particular manager? As such, the link between compensation and Type II errors is less clear.
- Similarly, Type I errors are more transparent to investors, so they entail not only the regret of an incorrect decision but the pain of having to explain this decision to the investor. Type II errors, firing (or not hiring) a manager with skill, are less transparent to investors, unless the investor tracks fired managers or evaluates the universe themselves.

Although Type I errors are likely more familiar and more of a concern to most decision makers, a consistent pattern of Type II errors can highlight weaknesses in the manager selection process. One approach to examine this issue is to monitor not only managers currently held but also managers that were evaluated and not hired as well as managers that were fired. The goal of monitoring is to determine the following:

- Are there identifiable factors that differentiate managers hired and managers not hired?
- Are these factors consistent with the investment philosophy and process of the decision maker?
- Are there identifiable factors driving the decision to retain or fire managers?
- Are these factors consistent with the investment philosophy and process of the decision maker?
- What is the added value of the decision to retain or fire managers?

The objective is to avoid making decisions based on short-term performance (trend following) and to identify any evidence of behavioral biases (regret, loss aversion) in the evaluation of managers during the selection process.

3.2.2 *Performance implications of Type I and Type II errors*

The cost of Type I errors is holding a manager without skill, as opposed to the cost of Type II errors, which is not holding managers with skill. The cost is driven by the size, shape, mean, and dispersion of the return distributions of the skilled and unskilled managers within the universe. The smaller the difference in sample size and distribution mean and the wider the dispersion of the distributions, the smaller the expected cost of the Type I or Type II error. More-efficient markets are likely to exhibit smaller differences in the distributions of skilled and unskilled managers, indicating a lower opportunity cost of retaining and the lower the cost of hiring an unskilled manager.

The extent to which markets are mean-reverting also has a bearing on the cost of Type I and Type II errors. If performance is mean reverting, hiring or retaining a strong performer only to see a reversion in performance results in a Type I error. A Type II error would be firing poor performers and avoiding hiring managers with weaker short-term track records, which can be costly if their performance reverts to the mean. One study found that individual investors significantly underperformed the average mutual fund because of poor timing and fund selection decisions (DALBAR 2005). A study of institutional plan sponsor allocation decisions found that investment products receiving contributions subsequently underperformed products experiencing withdrawals. The study estimated that more than $170 billion was lost during the period examined (Stewart, Neumann, Knittel, and Heisler 2009).

EXAMPLE 3

Type I and Type II Errors

1 A Type I error is:

A hiring or retaining a manager that subsequently underperforms expectations.

B hiring or retaining a manager that subsequently outperforms, or performs in line with, expectations.

C not hiring or firing a manager who subsequently outperforms, or performs in line with, expectations.

2 A Type II error is:

A hiring or retaining a manager that subsequently underperforms expectations.

B hiring or retaining a manager that subsequently outperforms, or performs in line with, expectations.

C not hiring or firing a manager who subsequently outperforms, or performs in line with, expectations.

3 The difference in expected cost between Type I and Type II errors is *most likely*:

A higher the smaller the perceived difference between the distribution of skilled and unskilled managers.

B lower the smaller the perceived difference between the distribution of skilled and unskilled managers.

C the expected cost difference of Type I and Type II error is zero, because they reflect different aspects of the same issue.

Solution to 1:

A is correct. The error consists of rejecting the null hypothesis (no skill) when it is correct.

Solution to 2:

C is correct. The error consists of not rejecting the null hypothesis (no skill) when it is incorrect.

Solution to 3:

B is correct. The less distinct the distribution of skilled managers from unskilled managers, the lower the opportunity cost of retaining and cost of hiring an unskilled manager. That is, the smaller the perceived difference between the distribution of skilled and unskilled managers, the lower the cost and incentive to fire a manager.

4 QUANTITATIVE ELEMENTS OF MANAGER SEARCH AND SELECTION

Performance appraisal captures most aspects of quantitative analysis, evaluating a manager's strengths and weaknesses as measured by that manager's ability to add value to a stated benchmark. Although the determination of whether the manager possesses skill is important, it is equally important to understand the manager's risk profile. The manager has likely been selected to fill a particular role in the portfolio. As such, although it is important to select a skillful manager, the "best" manager may be one that delivers the desired exposures and is suitable for the investor's assumptions, expectations, and biases.

4.1 Style Analysis

An important component of performance appraisal and manager selection is understanding the manager's risk exposures relative to the benchmark and how they evolve over time. This understanding helps define the universe of potential managers and the monitoring of selected managers. The process is referred to as style analysis.

A manager's self-reported risk exposures, such as portfolio concentration, industry exposure, capitalization exposure, and other quantitative measures, are the starting point in style analysis. They provide a means to classify managers by style for defining the selection process, a point of reference for evaluating the returns-based and holdings-based style analysis, and an interesting operational check on the manager.

The results of the returns-based style analysis (RBSA) and the holdings-based style analysis (HBSA) should be consistent with the manager's philosophy and the investment process. If not, the process might not be repeatable or might be implemented inconsistently. It is essential to look at all portfolio construction and risk management issues.

The results of the returns-based style analysis and the holdings-based style analysis should be tracked over time in order to ascertain if the risk trends or exposures are out of line with expectations or the manager's stated style. Deviations may signal that issues, such as style drift, are developing.

Returns-based and holdings-based style analyses provide a means to determine the risks and sources of return for a particular strategy. To be useful, style analysis must be:

- *Meaningful:* The risks reported must represent the important sources of performance return and risk.
- *Accurate:* The reported values must reflect the manager's actual risk exposures.
- *Consistent:* The methodology must allow for comparison over time and across multiple managers.
- *Timely:* The report must be available in a timely manner so that it is useful for making informed investment decisions.

Style analysis is most useful with strategies that hold publicly-traded securities where pricing is frequent. It can be applied to other strategies (hedge funds and private equity, for example), but the insights drawn from a style analysis of such strategies are more likely to be used for designing additional lines of inquiry in the course of due diligence rather than for confirmation of the investment process.

Returns-based style analysis (RBSA) is a top-down approach that involves estimating a portfolio's sensitivities to security market indexes representing a range of distinct factors. Although RBSA adds the additional analytical step of estimating the risk factors, as opposed to using a third-party or self-reported style categorization, the analysis is straightforward and typically does not require a large amount of additional, or difficult to acquire, data. RBSA should identify the important drivers of return and risk factors for the period analyzed and can be estimated even for complicated strategies. In addition, the process is comparable across managers and through time, and the use of returns data provides an objective style check that is not subject to window dressing. The analysis can be run immediately after the data is available, particularly in the case of publicly traded securities. As such, RBSA has many of the attributes of effective risk reporting.

The disadvantage is that RBSA is an imprecise tool. Although the additional computational effort required is not onerous, accuracy may be compromised, because RBSA effectively attributes performance to an unchanging average portfolio during the period. This attribution limits the ability to identify the impact of dynamic investment decisions and may distort the decomposition across sources of added value. Furthermore, the portfolio being analyzed might not reflect the current or future portfolio exposures. If the portfolio contains illiquid securities, stale prices may understate the risk exposure of the strategy. This is a particular problem for private equity (PE) and venture capital (VC) managers that hold illiquid or non-traded securities. VC and PE firms report performance based on the internal rate of return of cash distributions and appraisals of ongoing projects. As a result, reported performance can understate the volatility of return for shorter horizons or time periods with limited liquidity events. Longer periods generally provide more-accurate estimates of the manager's underlying standard deviation of return. The timeliness of any analysis depends on the securities that take the longest to price, which can be challenging for illiquid or non-traded securities.

Holdings-based style analysis (HBSA) is a bottom-up approach that estimates the risk exposures from the actual securities held in the portfolio at a point in time. This approach allows for estimation of current risk factors and offers several advantages. Similar to RBSA, HBSA should identify all important drivers of return and risk factors; be comparable across managers and through time; provide an accurate view of the manager's risk exposures, although potentially subject to window dressing; and be estimated immediately after the data become available.

Exhibit 4 presents a typical holdings-based style map. The manager being evaluated, along with the other managers in the universe, is placed along the size (y-axis) and style (x-axis) dimensions. The portfolio holdings of the manager being evaluated exhibit a large-cap value bias in what is otherwise a rather diverse universe.

Exhibit 4 Example of Holdings-Based Style Analysis

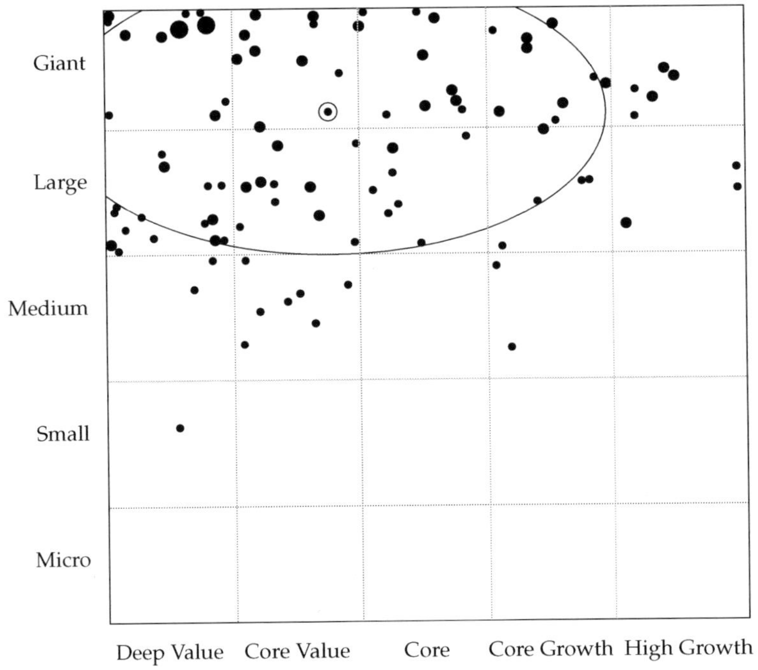

Source: Morningstar Direct, The Mutual Fund Research Center.

As with RBSA, HBSA has some disadvantages. The computational effort increases with the complexity of the strategy and depends on the timing and degree of the transparency provided by the manager. This extra effort can be challenging for hedge fund, private equity, and venture capital managers that may be averse to or unable to provide position-level pricing. Even with mutual funds, the necessary transparency may come with a time lag. The usefulness of the analysis may be compromised, because the portfolio reflects a snapshot in time and might not reflect the portfolio going forward, particularly for high-turnover strategies. Some factors may be difficult to estimate if the strategy is complex because HBSA requires an understanding of the underlying strategy. In general, HBSA is typically easier with equity strategies. If the portfolio has illiquid securities, stale pricing may underestimate the risk exposure of the strategy. The report's timeliness depends on the securities that take the longest to price, which can be challenging for illiquid or non-traded securities.

EXAMPLE 4

Style Analysis

1 Which of the following is an advantage of RBSA?

A It is a more precise tool than HBSA.

B It does not require potentially difficult to acquire data.

C It is more accurate than HBSA when the portfolio contains illiquid securities.

2 Which of the following is an advantage of HBSA?

A It works well for high-turnover strategies.

B It can identify important drivers of return and risk factors and is comparable across managers and through time.

C It effectively attributes performance to a snapshot of the portfolio at a particular time and thus is not subject to window dressing.

Solution to 1:

B is correct. The data needed for RBSA are usually easier to obtain than the data required for HBSA. RBSA is not a precise tool, and it is not more accurate than HBSA when the portfolio holds illiquid securities.

Solution to 2:

B is correct. Although HBSA allows for estimation of current risk factors and is comparable across managers and through time, the necessary computational effort increases with the strategy's complexity and depends on the timing and degree of the transparency provided by the manager. Some factors may be difficult to estimate if the strategy is complex because this approach requires an understanding of the underlying strategy. In general, HBSA is typically easier for equity strategies. If the portfolio has illiquid securities, stale pricing may underestimate the risk exposure of the strategy. Window dressing and high turnover can compromise the results because the results are attributed to a snapshot of the portfolio.

4.2 Capture Ratios and Drawdowns

Because large losses require proportionally greater gains to reverse or offset, drawdowns and capture ratios can be important factors in investment manager evaluation. A manager that experiences larger drawdowns may be less suitable for an investor closer to the end of their investment horizon. Capture ratios help assess manager suitability relative to the investor's IPS, especially in relation to the investor's time horizon and risk tolerance. This section reviews capture ratios and drawdowns, their implications for performance, and their use in evaluating manager performance and suitability.

4.2.1 *Capture Ratios*

Capture ratios measure the manager's participation in up and down markets—that is, the manager's percentage return relative to that of the benchmark. The **upside capture ratio**, or upside capture (UC) for short, measures capture when the benchmark return is positive. The **downside capture ratio**, or downside capture (DC), measures capture when the benchmark return is negative. Upside capture greater (less) than 100% generally suggests out- (under-) performance relative to the benchmark, and downside capture less (greater) than 100% generally suggests out- (under-) performance relative to the benchmark. One problem is that when the manager and benchmark returns are of the opposite sign, the ratio will be negative—for example, a manager with a 1% return when the market is down 1% will have a downside capture ratio of −100%. The expressions for upside capture and downside capture are

$$\mathrm{UC}(m,B,t) = \mathrm{R}(m,t)/\mathrm{R}(B,t) \text{ if } \mathrm{R}(B,t) \geq 0, \text{ and}$$

$$\mathrm{DC}(m,B,t) = \mathrm{R}(m,t)/\mathrm{R}(B,t) \text{ if } \mathrm{R}(B,t) < 0$$

where

$\mathrm{UC}(m,B,t)$ = up capture for manager m relative to benchmark B for time t
$\mathrm{DC}(m,B,t)$ = down capture for manager m relative to benchmark B for time t
$\mathrm{R}(m,t)$ = return of manager m for time t
$\mathrm{R}(B,t)$ = return of benchmark B for time t

The up/down capture, or simply the **capture ratio** (CR), is the upside capture divided by downside capture. It measures the asymmetry of return. A capture ratio greater than 1 indicates positive asymmetry—the manager captures more of the benchmark's upside and/or less of the benchmark's downside. A capture ratio less than 1 indicates negative asymmetry—the manager captures less of the benchmark's upside and/or more of the benchmark's downside.

Consider the following return series for the manager, R(m), and the benchmark, R(B), shown in Exhibit 5 The upside columns calculate the cumulative return for the manager, Cum R(m), and the benchmark, Cum R(B), for those periods when the benchmark return is positive. The downside columns calculate the cumulative returns when the benchmark return is negative.

Exhibit 5 Capture Ratio

			Upside Return				Downside Return			
t	R(*m*)	R(*B*)	R(*m*)	R(*B*)	Cum R(*m*)	Cum R(*B*)	R(*m*)	R(*B*)	Cum R(*m*)	Cum R(*B*)
1	0.6%	1.0%	0.6%	1.0%	0.60%	1.00%			0.00%	0.00%
2	−0.3%	−0.5%			0.60%	1.00%	−0.3%	−0.5%	−0.30%	−0.50%
3	1.0%	1.5%	1.0%	1.5%	1.61%	2.52%			−0.30%	−0.50%
4	0.1%	0.2%	0.1%	0.2%	1.71%	2.72%			−0.30%	−0.50%
5	−1.0%	−2.0%			1.71%	2.72%	−1.0%	−2.0%	−1.30%	−2.49%
6	0.5%	0.6%	0.5%	0.6%	2.22%	3.34%			−1.30%	−2.49%
7	0.2%	0.1%	0.2%	0.1%	2.42%	3.44%			−1.30%	−2.49%
8	−0.8%	−1.0%			2.42%	3.44%	−0.8%	−1.0%	−2.09%	−3.47%
9	0.8%	1.0%	0.8%	1.0%	3.24%	4.47%			−2.09%	−3.47%
10	0.4%	0.5%	0.4%	0.5%	3.65%	5.00%			−2.09%	−3.47%
Geometric average			0.51%	0.70%			−0.70%	−1.17%		
Upside capture				0.51%/0.70% = 72.8%			Downside capture		−0.70%/−1.17% = 59.8%	
Capture ratio				72.8%/59.8% = 121.7%						

During up markets, the geometric average return is 0.51% for the manager and 0.70% for the benchmark, giving an upside capture of 72.8%. During down markets, the geometric average return is −0.70% for the manager and −1.17% for the benchmark, giving a downside capture of 59.8%. The manager's capture ratio is 1.217, or 121.7%. Exhibit 6 shows a graph the cumulative upside and downside returns.

Exhibit 6 Cumulative Upside and Downside Returns

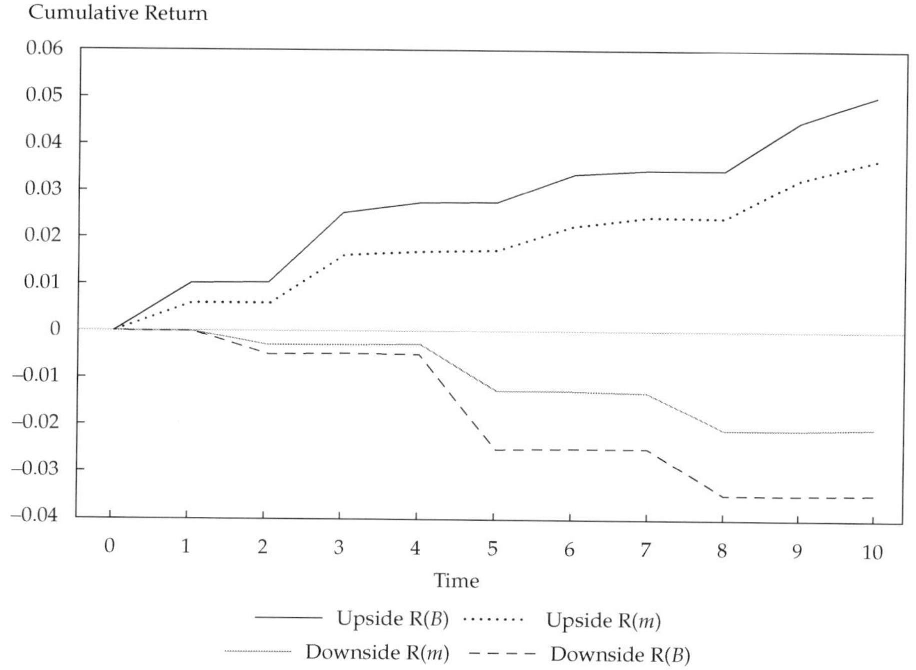

4.2.2 *Drawdown*

Drawdown measures were introduced in earlier material on risk measurement and risk attribution. Drawdown is the cumulative peak-to-trough loss during a particular continuous period. Drawdown duration is the total time from the start of the drawdown until the cumulative drawdown recovers to zero, which can be segmented into the drawdown phase (start to trough) and recovery phase (trough-to-zero cumulative return).

Consider the return on the S&P 500 Index from January 2011 to February 2012, shown in Exhibit 7A and 7B. The drawdown is 0% until May 2011, when the return is –1.13% and the drawdown continues to grow, reaching a maximum of –16.26% in September 2011. The strong returns from October 2011 to February 2012 reverse the drawdown. The total duration of the drawdown was 10 months, with a 5-month recovery period.

Exhibit 7A Drawdown

Month	R(*m*)	Cumulative R(*m*)	Drawdown	Cumulative Drawdown	
January 2011	2.37%	2.37%		0.00%	
February 2011	3.43%	5.88%		0.00%	
March 2011	0.04%	5.92%		0.00%	
April 2011	2.96%	9.06%		0.00%	
May 2011	–1.13%	7.83%	–1.13%	–1.13%	Drawdown begins
June 2011	–1.67%	6.03%	–1.67%	–2.78%	
July 2011	–2.03%	3.87%	–2.03%	–4.75%	
August 2011	–5.43%	–1.77%	–5.43%	–9.93%	

(continued)

Exhibit 7A (Continued)

Month	R(*m*)	Cumulative R(*m*)	Drawdown	Cumulative Drawdown	
September 2011	−7.03%	−8.67%	−7.03%	−16.26%	Maximum drawdown
October 2011	10.93%	1.31%		−7.11%	Recovery begins
November 2011	−0.22%	1.09%	−0.22%	−7.31%	
December 2011	1.02%	2.12%		−6.36%	
January 2012	4.48%	6.69%		−2.17%	
February 2012	4.32%	11.30%		0.00%	Drawdown recovered

Exhibit 7B Drawdown

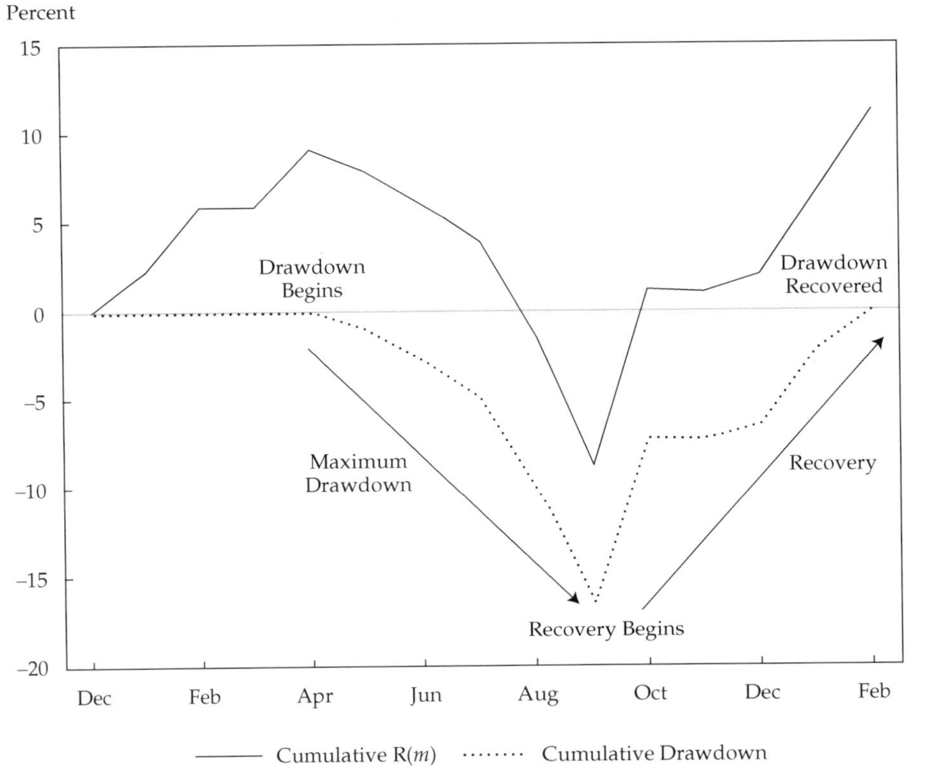

An asymmetrical return profile or avoiding large drawdowns, particularly during periods when the market is not trending strongly upward, can result in higher risk-adjusted returns.

4.2.3 *Capture Ratio and Drawdown in Manager Evaluation*

Let's illustrate the use of capture ratios in the analysis of manager returns. Consider the four stylized return profiles in Exhibit 8. These stylized return profiles are designed to illustrate the potential of the capture ratio and drawdown in evaluating investment performance.

Exhibit 8 Return Profile Summary

Profile	Upside Capture	Downside Capture	Ratio
Long only	100%	100%	1.0
Positive asymmetry	75%	25%	3.0
Low beta	50%	50%	1.0
Negative asymmetry	25%	75%	0.3

Each strategy's allocation to the S&P 500 Total Return (TR) Index and to 90-day T-bills (assuming monthly rebalancing to simplify the calculations) is based on the realized monthly return from January 2000 to December 2013. (This time period encompasses two significant drawdowns: the "tech bubble burst" of the early 2000s and the extreme drawdown of the Global Financial Crisis in 2008–2009.)

- The long-only profile is 100% allocated to the S&P 500 throughout the period.
- The low-beta profile is allocated 50% to the S&P 500 throughout the period.
- The positive asymmetry profile is allocated 75% to the S&P 500 for months when the S&P 500 return is positive and 25% when the S&P 500 return is negative.
- The negative asymmetry profile is allocated 25% to the S&P 500 for months when the S&P 500 return is positive and 75% when the S&P 500 return is negative.

The remainder for all profiles is allocated to 90-day T-bills. Exhibit 9 shows each profile's cumulative monthly return for the period.

Exhibit 9 Each Profile's Cumulative Monthly Return, January 2000–December 2013

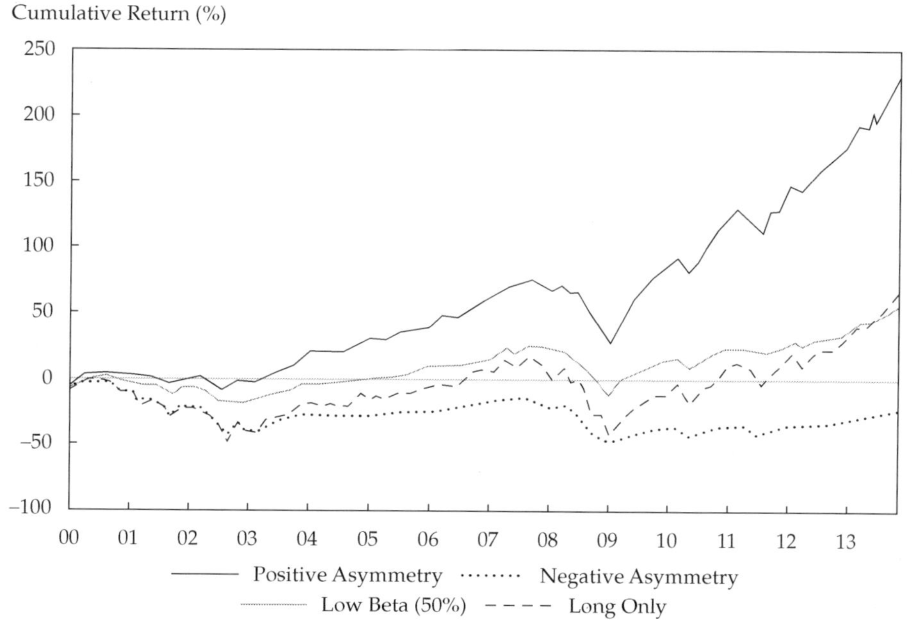

Exhibit 10 provides summary statistics for each profile based on monthly returns from January 2000 to December 2013. Although the long-only profile outperformed the low-beta profile over the full period, this outperformance resulted from the strong up market of 2013—the long-only profile lagged the low-beta profile for most of the period. The low beta profile achieved higher risk-adjusted returns and only half the volatility for the full period. The low-beta profile declined only 18.8% from January 2000 to September 2002, compared with the long-only decline of 42.5%. As a result, the low-beta profile had higher cumulative performance from January 2000 to October 2007 despite markedly lagging the long-only profile (56.0% to 108.4%) from October 2002 to October 2007.

Although a low-beta approach may sacrifice performance, it shows that limiting drawdowns can result in better absolute and risk-adjusted returns in certain markets.

Not surprisingly, positive asymmetry results in better performance relative to long only, low beta, and negative asymmetry. Although the positive asymmetry profile lags in up markets, this lag is more than offset by the lower participation in down markets. Not surprisingly, the negative asymmetry profile lags.

Exhibit 10 Summary Statistics for Each Profile, January 2000–December 2013

Strategy	Long Only	Low Beta	Positive Asymmetry	Negative Asymmetry
Cumulative return	64.0%	54.2%	228.1%	–24.4%
Annualized return	3.60%	3.14%	8.86%	–1.98%
Annualized standard deviation	15.64%	7.79%	9.61%	10.01%
Sharpe ratio	0.10	0.14	0.71	–0.40
Beta	1.00	0.50	0.61	0.64
Drawdown (maximum)	–50.9%	–28.3%	–26.9%	–48.9%

We've shown that positive asymmetry is a desirable trait. When evaluating a manager that exhibits positive asymmetry in its returns, we need to understand whether the strategy is inherently convex or whether the profile is a result of manager skill. For example, a hedging strategy implemented by rolling forward out-of-the-money put options will typically return many small losses because more options expire worthless than are compensated for by the occasional large gain during a large market downturn. A manager employing this strategy will likely exhibit consistent positive asymmetry in his returns, but the positive asymmetry is likely a due to the nature of the strategy rather than on investment skill.

Capture ratios can be useful in evaluating the consistency between the stated investment process and reported investment performance. When markets are driven by rising betas, a bottom-up, value-oriented active manager can be expected to have lower upside capture than a momentum-driven manager. A high-beta manager can be expected to have higher up capture *and* higher down capture.

Let's consider now the use of drawdowns in the analysis of manager returns. Drawdowns are stress-tests of the investment process and provide a natural point to evaluate and improve processes; they can expose potentially flawed or inconsistently implemented investment processes, inadequate risk controls, or operational issues. Did the manager implement the stated investment process consistently? If yes, what lessons were learned and how might the investment process have been adapted as a result? If the drawdown resulted from a deviation from the stated investment process, why? During a large or long drawdown, a manager could start to worry more about business risk than investment risk and act in their own best interest rather than that of their investors. How a manager responds to a large drawdown as it occurs, and what lessons are learned, provide evidence of the robustness and repeatability of the investment, portfolio construction, and risk management processes, as well as insight into the people implementing the processes. The allocator must determine whether any resulting changes in the investment process are consistent with the investment philosophy and correctly and completely address the weakness in the process.

Events of August 2007

Starting on 7 August 2007, many quantitative equity long–short strategies began to experience large drawdowns. Many managers had never experienced such losses or market conditions and started to sell positions as stop-loss and risk management policies were triggered (Khandani and Lo 2011). This activity added to additional selling pressure, and the S&P 500 declined 13.4% by 8 August. Those managers that sold ended up locking in large losses because the underperforming stocks and market subsequently recovered, with the S&P 500 down only 5.7% for the month. In many cases, those funds that sold experienced redemptions or ended up closing.

As August 2007 demonstrated, distinguishing prudent risk management from a misalignment of interests is not always straightforward. Should a manager continue to actively trade a portfolio if the market environment no longer reflects their investment philosophy? In addition, traders will claim that it is better to cut losses because losses can signal that something has changed or that the timing of the trade is not right. Conversely, selling into a down market raises the risk of crystallizing losses and missing any subsequent reversal. The decision maker must assess whether the manager's behavior was a disciplined application of the investment process, reflected a misalignment of interests, or simply resulted from panic or overreaction by the manager.

One aspect of suitability for the IPS is the investment horizon and its relationship to risk capacity. An investor closer to retirement, with less time to recover from losses, places more emphasis on absolute measures of risk. If there has been no change to investment policy and no change in the view that the manager remains suitable, the temptation to exit should be resisted to avoid exiting at an inauspicious time. Investors with shorter horizons, with lower risk capacity, or prone to overreact to losses may be better served by allocating to managers with shallower and shorter expected drawdowns.

EXAMPLE 5

Capture Ratios

t	R(*m*)	R(*B*)
1	−3.06%	−3.60%
2	6.32%	3.10%
3	6.00%	6.03%
4	3.21%	1.58%
5	−9.05%	−7.99%
6	−4.09%	−5.23%
7	4.34%	7.01%
8	−5.72%	−4.51%
9	12.76%	8.92%

(continued)

t	R(*m*)	R(*B*)
10	5.38%	3.81%
11	0.33%	0.01%
12	5.68%	6.68%

Using the return information in the table, what is the manager's downside capture ratio?

A 103%

B 115%

C 118%

Solution:

A is correct.

			Upside Return				Downside Return			
t	R(*m*)	R(*B*)	R(*m*)	R(*B*)	Cum R(*m*)	Cum R(*B*)	R(*m*)	R(*B*)	Cum R(*m*)	Cum R(*B*)
1	−3.06%	−3.60%			0.00%	0.00%	−3.06%	−3.60%	−3.06%	−3.60%
2	6.32%	3.10%	6.32%	3.10%	6.32%	3.10%			−3.06%	−3.60%
3	6.00%	6.03%	6.00%	6.03%	12.70%	9.32%			−3.06%	−3.60%
4	3.21%	1.58%	3.21%	1.58%	16.32%	11.04%			−3.06%	−3.60%
5	−9.05%	−7.99%			16.32%	11.04%	−9.05%	−7.99%	−11.83%	−11.30%
6	−4.09%	−5.23%			16.32%	11.04%	−4.09%	−5.23%	−15.44%	−15.94%
7	4.34%	7.01%	4.34%	7.01%	21.36%	18.83%			−15.44%	−15.94%
8	−5.72%	−4.51%			21.36%	18.83%	−5.72%	−4.51%	−20.28%	−19.73
9	12.76%	8.92%	12.76%	8.92%	36.85%	29.43%			−20.28%	−19.73%
10	5.38%	3.81%	5.38%	3.81%	44.21%	34.36%			−20.28%	−19.73%
11	0.33%	0.01%	0.33%	0.01%	44.69%	34.37%			−20.28%	−19.73%
12	5.68%	6.68%	5.68%	6.68%	52.91%	43.35%			−20.28%	−19.73%
Geometric average			5.45%	4.60%			−5.51%	−5.35%		
Upside capture			5.45%/4.60% = 118%				**Downside capture**		**−5.51%/−5.35% = 103%**	
Capture ratio			118%/103% = 115%							

4.3 Batting Average

One goal of manager selection is to determine whether the investment process is repeatable and consistently implemented to provide some sense that past performance provides guidance for expected future performance. Inconsistent performance might signal a lack of skill. One measure of performance consistency is batting average. **Batting average** measures the frequency of positive outcomes that can alternatively be defined as

- the number of investment decisions that result in a profit divided by the total number of investment decisions, or
- the number of positive return periods relative to the benchmark or peers divided by the total number of return periods.

The first definition, which we can call "absolute" batting average, highlights the importance of trade frequency in performance appraisal and allows different strategies to be distinguished by the frequency of trades. The number of investment decisions can be used as a measure for the frequency with which the manager creates implementable investment ideas (Constable and Armitage 2006). Higher trade frequency can be desirable because less frequent trading requires higher batting averages to produce the same level of risk-adjusted return. This effect is accentuated if the returns from negative trades are larger than those from positive trades. The greater the number of independent positive value-added trades, the higher the probability that the portfolio will outperform during a given period (Stewart 1998).

The second definition, which we can call "relative" batting average, captures the intuition that a higher batting average might improve performance by limiting losses. What better way to limit drawdowns than consistent positive returns as reflected by a high batting average? The problem is that batting average does not measure the magnitude of returns. Consider a strategy characterized by many small gains with the occasional large loss—that is, the approach of "picking up nickels in front of a steamroller" implemented by "arbitrage" strategies, such as Long Term Capital Management. Such a strategy has a high batting average, but the distribution of returns is negatively skewed. This return distribution is in fact less attractive to investors looking to limit large drawdowns. Alternatively, a strategy with many small losses that are compensated for by the occasional large gain, such as long volatility strategies, exhibits positive skew and provides a useful hedge but has a lower batting average. As such, although batting average does provide a measure of consistency, it is best used in combination with other measures.

EXAMPLE 6

Batting Average

t	R(*m*)	R(*B*)
1	–3.06%	–3.59%
2	6.31%	3.09%
3	6.00%	6.03%
4	3.20%	1.57%
5	–9.05%	–7.98%
6	–4.08%	–5.23%
7	4.33%	7.00%
8	–5.71%	–4.51%
9	12.75%	8.92%
10	5.37%	3.80%
11	0.33%	0.01%
12	5.68%	6.68%

1 Using the return information in the table, what is the manager's batting average relative to the benchmark?

A 42%

B 58%

C 67%

2 A limitation of batting average is that it does **not**:

A measure the magnitude of returns.

B measure the frequency of positive outcomes.

C allow different strategies to be distinguished by the frequency of trades.

Solution to 1:

B is correct. The manager outperformed the benchmark in 7 out of the 12 periods (t = 1, 2, 4, 6, 9, 10, and 11).

Solution to 2:

A is correct. The batting average does not measure the magnitude of returns. Strategies characterized by many small gains with the occasional large loss will have high batting averages, but the distribution of returns will be negatively skewed. This return distribution is in fact less attractive to investors that want to limit large drawdowns.

The Concept of Active Share

Active share measures the difference in portfolio holdings relative to the benchmark. A manager that precisely replicates the benchmark will have an active share of zero; a manager with no holdings in common with the benchmark will have an active share of one.

Given a strategy with N securities (i = 1, 2, …, N), active share is calculated as

$$\text{Active Share} = \frac{1}{2}\sum_{i=1}^{N}\left|\text{Strategy Weight}_i - \text{BenchmarkWeight}_i\right|$$

Typically, managers are somewhere along the spectrum. The categorization of active share and tracking risk in Exhibit 11 has been suggested for active managers. It is clear that full replication will appear as a closet indexer. A manager that uses sampling techniques to build the portfolio may, however, appear as a diversified stock picker depending on the universe under consideration and the dispersion of active share of the constituents. Tracking risk will be low, but active share might not be because only a subset of constituents is held. One reason is that high and low are relative to the universe being examined and the category definitions used. As such, it is important to examine risk factors and portfolio construction techniques of both active and passive managers.

Exhibit 11 Active Share vs. Tracking Risk

		Active Share	
		Low	High
Tracking risk	High	Sector rotation	Concentrated stock pickers
	Low	Closet indexer	Diversified stock pickers

QUALITATIVE ELEMENTS OF MANAGER DUE DILIGENCE

5

The goal of manager due diligence is to weigh the potential risks that may arise from entering into an investment management relationship and entrusting assets to a firm. Although it is impossible to eliminate all potential risks, the allocator must assess how the firm will manage the broad range of risks it is likely to face in the future. This section outlines the general aspects of manager due diligence and the particular questions the investor needs to answer.

Investment due diligence examines and evaluates the qualitative considerations that illustrate that the manager's investment process is repeatable and consistently implemented. The objective is to understand whether the investment philosophy, process, people, and portfolio construction satisfy the assumption that past performance provides some guidance for expected future performance. In other words, are the conclusions drawn from performance measurement, attribution, and appraisal reliable selection criteria? In addition, it is important to remember that investment managers are businesses. Regardless of the strength of the investment process or historical performance, investment management firms must be operated as successful businesses to ensure sustainability. Operational due diligence examines and evaluates the firm's policies and procedures, to identify potential risks that might not be captured in historical performance and to assess the firm's sustainability.

5.1 Investment Philosophy

The investment philosophy is the foundation of the investment process. Every investment strategy is based on a set of assumptions about the factors that drive performance and the manager's beliefs about their ability to successfully exploit these sources of return. The investment manager should have a clear and concise investment philosophy.

First, every manager makes assumptions about market efficiency, including the degree and the time frame. Passive strategies assume markets are sufficiently efficient and that active management cannot add value after transaction costs and fees. As a result, passive strategies seek to earn risk premiums. A **risk premium** is the expected return in excess of a minimal-risk ("risk-free") rate of return that accrues to bearing a risk that is not easily diversified away—so-called systematic risk.

Passive strategies seek to capture return through exposure to systematic risk premiums, such as equity risk, duration risk, or credit risk. These strategies can also look to capture alternative risk premiums. such as liquidity risk, natural disaster risk (e.g., insurance-linked securities, such as catastrophe bonds and quota shares), volatility risk, or some combination of these premiums (e.g., distressed strategies seek to capture credit and liquidity risk premiums).

In contrast, active strategies assume markets are sufficiently inefficient that security mispricings can be identified and exploited. These opportunities typically arise when market behavior deviates from the manager's fundamental assumptions. Generally speaking, inefficiencies can be categorized as behavioral or structural.

- *Behavioral inefficiencies* are perceived mispricings created by the actions of other market participants, usually associated with biases, such as trend following or loss aversion. These inefficiencies are temporary, lasting long enough for the manager to identify and exploit them before the market price and perceived intrinsic value converge.
- *Structural inefficiencies* are perceived mispricings created by external or internal rules and regulations. These inefficiencies can be long lived and assume a continuation of the rules and regulations rather than a convergence.

Active strategies also typically make assumptions about the dynamics and structures of the market, such as the following: The correlation structure of the market is sufficiently stable over the investment horizon to make diversification useful for risk management; prices eventually converge to intrinsic value, which can be estimated by using a discounted cash flow model; or market prices are driven by predictable macroeconomic trends.

It is important to evaluate these assumptions and the role they play in the investment process to understand how the strategy will behave through time and across market environments.

- Can the manager clearly and consistently articulate their investment philosophy? It is hard to have confidence in the repeatability and efficacy of an investment process if the manager, and investment personnel, cannot explain the assumptions that underpin the process. This clarity also provides a consistency check that the investment process and personnel are appropriate for the stated philosophy.
- Are the assumptions credible and consistent? That is, does the decision maker agree with the assumptions underlying the strategy, and are these assumptions consistent with the investment process? A decision maker who believes a market is efficient would likely not find the assumptions of an active manager in that market credible. In the decision maker's judgment, the assumptions must support a repeatable and robust investment process.
- How has the philosophy developed over time? Ideally, the philosophy is unchanged through time, suggesting a repeatable process. If philosophy has evolved, it is preferred that changes are judged to be reasonable responses to changing market conditions rather than a series of ad hoc reactions to performance or investor flows. Such changes suggest a lack of repeatability and robustness.
- Are the return sources linked to credible and consistent inefficiencies? The decision maker must judge whether the investment philosophy is based on an inefficiency that is based on an informational advantage, likely a behavioral inefficiency by interpreting information better than other market participants, or a structural inefficiency that suggests the investment process is repeatable.

If the source of return is linked to a credible inefficiency, there is the additional issue of capacity. Capacity has several related aspects, such as the level of assets the strategy or opportunity can absorb without a dilution of returns, the number of opportunities or securities available, and the ability to transact in a timely manner at or near the market price—that is, liquidity. Overall, capacity is the level, repeatability, and sustainability of returns that the inefficiency is expected to support in the future.

- Does the inefficiency provide a sufficient frequency of opportunity and level of return to cover transaction costs and fees? If so, does this require leverage?
- Does the inefficiency provide a repeatable source of return? That is, can the opportunity be captured by a repeatable process, or is each opportunity unique, requiring a different process of skill set to exploit?
- Is the inefficiency sustainable? That is, at what asset level would the realized return from the inefficiency be unacceptably low? Sustainability will be a function of the market's depth and liquidity, as well as how much capital is allocated, either by the manager or competitors, to the inefficiency.

Uncommon Ways of Passing the Investment Philosophy Test

1 Managers that measure the success of the steps of the process and not just the ultimate outcome.

For example, consider a bond manager that makes the claim that his or her credit research not only predicts upgrades and downgrades, but makes those predictions before the expectation of a rating change is reflected in the market price. This manager tracks every prediction to see if the market consensus (as reflected by price) and rating agencies come around to his or her view. I get comfort from the facts that (1) such managers know their views only have value if they are not only correct but different than consensus, and (2) they track how prices eventually come to reflect, or not reflect, their views. Similarly, managers that evaluate their own performance with strategy benchmarks designed to replicate their selection universe demonstrate they understand the importance of attempting to differentiate alpha from noise (see Kuenzi [2003]).

2 Managers that recognize that every strategy they come up with is potentially subject to being arbitraged away.

For example, consider a quantitative equity manager that that plays many themes at once. Each theme is viewed as having a finite life, and the performance of each theme is isolated and monitored so as to observe the decay in the value of the theme. The manager considers his or her competitive advantage to be in the identification of new themes, and in the technology for measuring the contribution of each theme to performance. A similar idea is presented in the adaptive market hypothesis of Lo [2004], where the market is always tending toward efficiency, but the types of trades needed to move it towards efficiency rotate and evolve over time.

3 Managers that claim they exploit inefficiencies, and identify the specific inefficiency they are exploiting with every position they take.

Most managers that say they exploit inefficiencies use this claim as a broad justification for their investment process, but are unable to identify the specific inefficiency they are exploiting in any given decision they make. Those that routinely specify how their information or point of point differs from that reflected in price are much more credible.

4 Managers that know their companies so well that they are quicker to interpret change, even though they have no explicit alpha thesis.

There is always an exception to the rule. Sometimes a manager is simply talented and cannot articulate an alpha thesis.

Despite examples such as these, it remains frustratingly difficult to distinguish between true alpha-generators and alpha-pretenders. I believe there is more that alpha-generators can do to distinguish themselves, and that consultants should be more insistent that they do it.

Excerpted from: John R. Minahan, CFA, "The Role of Investment Philosophy in Evaluating Investment Managers: A Consultant's Perspective on Distinguishing Alpha from Noise," *Journal of Investing*, Vol. 15 (2006).

EXAMPLE 7

Investment Philosophy

1 Which of the following is **not** an important consideration when evaluating a manager's investment philosophy?

A What are the compensation arrangements of key employees?

B Are the investment philosophy assumptions credible and consistent?

C Can the manager clearly and consistently articulate their investment philosophy?

2 Generally speaking, inefficiencies can be categorized as:

A large and small.

B internal and external.

C structural and behavioral.

3 Which of the following is **not** an important consideration when evaluating the capacity of an inefficiency?

A Does the strategy rely on unique information?

B Does the inefficiency provide a repeatable source of return?

C Does the inefficiency provide a sufficient frequency of opportunity and level of return to cover transaction costs and fees?

Solution to 1:

A is correct. Employee compensation is a legal and compliance issue considered as part of operational due diligence.

Solution to 2:

C is correct. Behavioral inefficiencies are created by the actions of other participants in the market. These inefficiencies are temporary, lasting long enough for the manager to identify and exploit them before the market price and perceived intrinsic value converge. Structural inefficiencies are created by external or internal rules and regulations. These inefficiencies can be long lived and assume a continuation of the rules and regulations rather than a convergence.

Solution to 3:

A is correct. The uniqueness of information used by the manager is a consideration when evaluating the assumptions of the investment process.

5.2 Investment Personnel

An investment process can only be as good as the people who create and implement it, and even the best process can be compromised by poor execution by the people involved. This view is not a question of liking the manager or team but of trusting that they possess the expertise and experience to effectively implement the strategy.

- Does the investment team have sufficient expertise and experience to effectively execute the investment process? The need for expertise is self-evident. The greater the experience, particularly managing the current strategy across market environments, the greater the confidence in the manager's ability to effectively execute the investment process. As noted with drawdowns, it is especially instructive to see how the manager responded to stressed markets and poor performance.

- Does the investment team have sufficient depth to effectively execute the investment process? A strategy that focuses on a small universe of publicly traded stocks might not require a large investment team. A global macro or multi-strategy fund, which holds positions across numerous global markets, likely requires a large team with expertise and experience supporting the manager.
- What is the level of key person risk? A strategy that is overly dependent on the judgment or particular skills of an individual or small team of people faces **key person risk**, an overreliance on an individual or individuals whose departure would negatively affect the strategy's performance.
- What kinds of agreements (e.g., non-compete) and incentives (ownership, bonus, pay) exist to retain and attract key employees to join and stay at the firm?
- What has been the turnover of firm personnel? High personnel turnover risks the loss of institutional knowledge and experience within the team.

5.3 Investment Decision-Making Process

The investment decision-making process has four elements: signal creation, signal capture, portfolio construction, and portfolio monitoring.

5.3.1 *Signal Creation (Idea Generation)*

An investment signal is a data point or fact that can be observed early enough to implement as an investment position. The basic question is, how are investment ideas generated? The efficient market hypothesis posits that the key to exploiting inefficiencies is to have information that is all of the following:

- **Unique:** Does the strategy rely on unique information? If so, how is this information collected, and how is the manager able to retain an informational edge, particularly in a regulatory environment that seeks to reduce informational symmetries?
- **Timely:** Does the strategy possess an information timing advantage? If so, how is this information collected, and how is the manager able to retain a timing edge, particularly in a regulatory environment that seeks to reduce informational asymmetries?
- **Interpreted differently:** Interpretation is typically how managers seek to differentiate themselves. Does the manager possess a unique way of interpreting information? Or does the manager claim their strategy possesses a "secret sauce" component or that its team is simply smarter than other managers?

5.3.2 *Signal Capture (Idea Implementation)*

The second step is signal capture, translating the generated investment idea into an investment position.

- What is the process for translating investment ideas into investment positions?
- Is this process repeatable and consistent with the strategy assumptions?
- What is the process, and who is ultimately responsible for approving an investment position?

5.3.3 *Portfolio Construction*

The third element is portfolio construction; how investment positions are implemented within the portfolio. This element begins to capture the manager's risk management methodology. Good investment ideas need to be implemented properly to exploit opportunities and capture desired risk premiums. It is also important that portfolio construction is consistent with the investment philosophy and process as well as the expertise of the investment personnel.

- How are portfolio allocations set and adjusted? The allocation process should be consistent with investment philosophy and process. For example, if the portfolio is actively managed, its turnover should agree with the frequency of signals generated and the securities' liquidity. The allocation process should be well-defined and consistently applied, supporting the repeatability of the investment process. For example, are allocations made quantitatively or qualitatively?
- Are portfolio allocations based on the manager's conviction? In other words, do the positions the manager believes will most likely outperform or exhibit the greatest outperformance receive the largest active overweighting, and the securities the manager believes will underperform receive the largest active underweighting?
- How have the portfolio characteristics changed with asset growth? Has the number and/or characteristics of the positions held changed to accommodate a larger amount of AUM?
- Does the portfolio use **stop-losses** to manage risk? If so, are they hard (positions are automatically sold when the loss threshold is reached) or soft (positions are evaluated when the loss threshold is reached)? Although stop-losses represent a clear risk management approach, the goal of protecting against large losses must be balanced with the risk of closing positions too frequently.
- What types of securities are used? Does the manager use derivatives to express investment ideas? What experience does the manager have investing in these securities? The manager should be sufficiently well-versed and experienced with the securities used to understand how they will behave in different market environments.
- How are hedges implemented? What security types are used? How are hedge ratios set? Consider a manager that focuses on stock selection to generate alpha and hedges to reduce or remove market risk. The hedges must be sized correctly, or they can be ineffective (underhedged) or they can overwhelm stock selection (overhedged), with performance driven more by beta than by alpha.
- How are long and short ideas expressed? Are they paired—that is, each long position has a corresponding short position—or are long and short positions established independently? How long and short positions are allocated is important for understanding the portfolio's overall exposure. If long and short positions are paired, with the idea of capturing alpha as prices converge while offsetting market risk, the positions must be well-matched and sized correctly.

An important risk is liquidity. Strategies that are not intending to capture a liquidity risk premium must be aware of portfolio liquidity in terms of adapting to changing information, changing market conditions, and changing investor liquidity demands. An existing portfolio consisting of illiquid securities will be more costly to change, not only to take advantage of new opportunities but also to trade because of higher transaction costs. There is the additional cost of having to sell positions at inopportune times as a result of market events or investor liquidity demands. When assessing security liquidity, it is important to consider all of the assets under management for that particular manager and investment process.

- What percentage of the portfolio can be liquidated in five business days or less? What percentage requires more than 10 business days to liquidate? The less liquid the portfolio, the higher the transaction costs if the manager is forced to sell one or more positions. A more liquid portfolio offers flexibility if the manager faces unexpected investor liquidity demands or rapidly changing market conditions.

- What is the average daily volume weighted by portfolio position size?
- Have any of the portfolio holdings been suspended from trading? If so, what is the name of the company, and what are the circumstances pertaining to the suspension?
- Are there any holdings in which ownership by the firm across all portfolios collectively accounts for more than 5% of the market capitalization or float of the security?
- What is the firm's trading strategy? Does the investment manager tend to provide liquidity or demand it? Has the trading strategy changed in response to asset growth?

5.3.4 *Monitoring the Portfolio*

The investment decision-making process is a feedback loop that consists of ongoing monitoring of the portfolio in light of new information and analysis. This monitoring includes an assessment of both external and internal considerations. External considerations include the economic and financial market environments. Has anything meaningful occurred that might affect the manager's ability to exploit the market inefficiency that is the strategy's focus? Internal considerations include the portfolio's performance, risk profile, and construction. Has anything changed that might signal potential style drift or other deviations from the investment process? Ongoing monitoring and performance attribution help to ensure that the manager remains appropriate for the clients' mandates.

5.4 Operational Due Diligence

Performance appraisal assumes that reported returns are accurate and fully reflect the manager's risk profile. Unfortunately, as we have seen, this assumption is not always true. Although investment due diligence is one step toward understanding these risks, one must remember that investment management firms are *businesses*, and in many cases they are small businesses with a high degree of business risk. Regardless of the strength of the investment process or the historical investment results, investment management firms must be operated as a successful business in order to ensure their sustainability. This requirement creates the potential for a misalignment of interests between the manager and the investor. Operational due diligence analyzes the integrity of the business and seeks to understand and evaluate these risks by examining and evaluating the firm's policies and procedures.

Weaknesses in the firm's infrastructure represent latent risks to the investor. A strong back office (support staff) is critical for safeguarding assets and ensuring that accurate reports are issued in a timely manner. The manager should have a robust trading process that seeks to avoid human error. A repeatable process requires consistent implementation. The allocator needs to understand the following:

- What is the firm's trading policy?
- Does the firm use soft dollar commissions? If so, is there a rigorous process for ensuring compliance?
- What is the process for protecting against unauthorized trading?
- How are fees calculated and collected?

- How are securities allocated across investor accounts, including both pooled and separately managed accounts? The allocation method should be objective (e.g., based on invested capital) to avoid the potential to benefit some investors at the expense of others.
- How many different strategies does the firm manage, and are any new strategies being contemplated? Is the firm's infrastructure capable of efficiently and accurately implementing the different strategies?
- What information technology offsite backup facilities are in place?
- Does the firm have processes, software, and hardware in place to handle cybersecurity issues?

An important constituent of the infrastructure is third-party service providers, including the firm's prime broker, administrator, auditor, and legal counsel. They provide an important independent verification of the firm's performance and reporting.

- Are the firm's third-party service providers known and respected?
- Has there been any change in third-party providers? If so, when and why? This information is particularly important with regard to the firm's auditor. Frequent changes of the auditor is a red flag and may mean the manager is trying to hide something.

The risk management function should be viewed as an integral part of the investment firm and not considered a peripheral function. The extent to which integration exists provides insight into the firm's culture and the alignment of interests between the manager and the investor. The manager should have a risk manual that is readily available for review:

- Does the portfolio have any hard/soft investment guidelines?
- How are these guidelines monitored?
- What is the procedure for curing breaches?
- Who is responsible for risk management?
- Is there an independent risk officer?

5.4.1 *Firm*

An investment management firm must operate as a successful business to ensure sustainability. A manager that goes out of business does not have a repeatable investment process. An important aspect of manager selection is assessing the level of business risk.

- What is the ownership structure of the firm?
- What are the total firm AUM and AUM by investment strategy?
- What is the firm's breakeven AUM (the asset base needed to generate enough fee revenue to cover total firm expenses)?
- Are any of the firm's strategies closed to new capital?
- How much capital would the firm like to raise?

A firm that is independently owned may have greater autonomy and flexibility than a firm owned by a larger organization, but it may have a higher cost structure and lack financial support during market events, raising potential business risks. Outside ownership could create a situation in which the outside owner has objectives that conflict with the investment strategy. For instance, the outside owner might want to increase the asset base to generate higher fee revenue, but this action could prevent the portfolio from holding lower-capitalization stocks. Ideally, ownership should be spread across as many employees as is feasible and practical. A firm managing a smaller asset base may be more nimble and less prone to dilution of returns but will likely have lower revenues to support infrastructure and compensate employees. At a minimum, the asset base needs to be sufficient to support the firm's current expenditures.

Last, and by no means least important, are legal and compliance issues. It is critical that the firm's interests are aligned with those of the investor.

- What are the compensation arrangements for key employees? For example, are any people compensated with stock in the firm, and if so, what happens to this stock when they leave the firm?
- Do employees invest personal assets in the firm's strategies? Investing their own money in the same products in which the firm's clients invest creates an alignment of interests, but too large a proportion of their own assets invested in this one product may create personal/business risk for the manager that overrides the alignment of interests.
- Does the firm foster a culture of compliance?
- What is covered in the compliance manual?
- Has the firm or any of its employees been involved with an investigation by any financial market regulator or self-regulatory organization?
- Has the firm been involved in any lawsuits?
- Are any of the firm's employees involved in legal actions or personal litigation that might affect their ability to continue to fulfill their fiduciary responsibilities?

Hiring a manager requires trust. A firm's culture as expressed by its compliance policies and procedures should provide a level of confidence that the manager's and investor's interests are aligned.

The Investment Process

Bernard "Bernie" L. Madoff ran one of the biggest frauds in Wall Street history. One of the first indications that something was amiss at Bernard L. Madoff Investment Securities arose when Harry Markopolos was unable to reconcile the return track record with the investment process. In addition to observing the unrealistically consistent nature of the claimed returns, Markopolos concluded that there was no way to generate the returns using the claimed investment process. Further analysis convinced him that Madoff's returns resulted not from front running—that is, taking positions to exploit knowledge of investor trade flows—but rather from fraud.

In hindsight, there were many red flags over the years that indicated there was something wrong with Madoff's investment management process. The firm claimed to generate steady returns in every market environment. Mr. Madoff was known to dismiss questions about his strategy, arguing that his business was too complicated for outsiders to understand. He also operated as a broker/dealer with an asset management division, profiting from trading commissions rather than the investment management fees that hedge funds charged. The structure seemed odd to other investment professionals, raising concerns about the firm's legitimacy. Another red flag was raised when it became known that the firm used a small, unknown auditor with only three employees. If, as Mr. Madoff claimed, the strategy was so complex that no one could understand it, a small, three-person audit firm would be unlikely to be able to effectively audit the financial statements (Zuckerman 2008).

Self-Reported Risk Factors

Requesting and obtaining self-reported risk factors not only is important for understanding the manager's investment process but also provides an interesting operational check. A manager should readily comply with all requests for risk reporting. If not, it suggests a lack of transparency that may become challenging for monitoring the manager and strategy in the future. Additionally, it might indicate an inability to generate essential reports, which raises questions about the firm's policies and procedures.

All risk reporting should be meaningful, consistent, accurate, and timely. A lack of meaningful reporting indicates that the reports are not useful in monitoring the manager and that there is a lack of transparency. In the worst case, the manager does not understand the risk exposures or does not want to disclose them.

A lack of consistent reporting also reduces the usefulness of the reporting. Inconsistent reports preclude the ability to track levels and trends of important risk factors. The manager may be choosing to selectively report particular risks that they deem important or interesting. In the worst case, it may mean that the manager is selectively reporting in order to hide risks created by deviations from the stated investment process.

A lack of accuracy suggests that the manager cannot properly measure portfolio risks or is intentionally misreporting results. A lack of timeliness reduces the reports' usefulness and suggests either inefficient procedures or attempts to manipulate the flow of information. In all of these cases, poor risk reporting, at a minimum, suggests a reevaluation of the manager and, if issues are identified, potential termination.

5.4.2 *Investment Vehicle*

There are two broad options for implementing investment strategies: individual separate accounts and pooled (or commingled) vehicles. An additional operational consideration is the evaluation of the investment vehicle—its appropriateness to the investment strategy and its suitability for the investor. Separate accounts offer additional control, customization, tax efficiency, reporting, and transparency advantages, but these come at a higher cost.

In a pooled or commingled vehicle, the money from multiple investors is held as a single portfolio and managed without potential customization for any investor. Such vehicles include open-end funds, closed-end funds, exchange-traded funds, exchange-traded notes, and hedge funds. As the name infers, a separately managed account (SMA) vehicle holds the money in a segregated account in the investor's name. The funds are managed to a particular mandate with the potential to customize the strategy for each investor. The advantages of SMA vehicles include the following:

- **Ownership:** In an SMA, the investor owns the individual securities directly. This approach provides additional safety should a liquidity event occur. Although the manager continues to make investment decisions, these decisions will not be influenced by the redemption or liquidity demand of other investors in the strategy. An SMA also provides clear legal ownership for the recovery of assets resulting from unforeseen events, such as bankruptcy or mismanagement.
- **Customization:** SMAs allow the investor to potentially express individual constraints or preferences within the portfolio. SMAs can thus more closely address the investor's particular investment objectives.

- **Tax efficiency:** SMAs offer potentially improved tax efficiency because the investor pays taxes only on the capital gains realized and allows the implementation of tax-efficient investing and trading strategies.
- **Transparency:** SMAs offer real-time, position-level detail to the investor, providing complete transparency and accurate attribution to the investor. Even if a pooled vehicle provides position-level detail, such information will likely be presented with a delay.

If the SMA is customized, additional investment due diligence may be required to account for differences in security selection or portfolio construction. In addition, there are operational due diligence considerations.

- **Cost:** Separate accounts represent an additional operational burden on the manager, which translates into potentially higher costs for the investor. SMAs do not scale as easily as pooled vehicles. Once a pooled investment is established and the fixed costs paid, the cost of each new investor is largely the incremental costs of custody, trading larger positions, and generating an additional report. With an SMA, a new account must be established for each investor. In addition, SMAs are likely to face higher transaction costs to the degree that trades cannot be aggregated to reduce trade volumes. These costs are a function of the extent to which the strategy is customized or traded differently to accommodate different investor needs.
- **Tracking risk:** Customization of the strategy creates tracking risk relative to the benchmark, which can confuse attribution because performance will reflect investor constraints rather than manager decisions.
- **Investor behavior:** Transparency, combined with control and customization, allows for potential micromanagement by the investor—that is, the investor attempting to manage the portfolio. Such an effort not only negates the benefit of hiring a manager but is particularly problematic if these changes decrease the portfolio's value. Potential investor behaviors include performance chasing, familiarity bias (being overly averse to unfamiliar holdings), and loss aversion (a tendency to disaggregate the portfolio and not appreciate the value of hedging).

The allocator's goal is to evaluate the costs and benefits of the vehicle used and judge its suitability for the IPS:

- Is the vehicle structure consistent with the investment process?
- Does the manager have the operational infrastructure necessary to manage the SMA?
- Is there a benefit to holding the securities in a separate account? If so, are these benefits sufficient to compensate for additional costs?
- Is tax efficiency an important objective of the IPS?
- Are there concerns that the available transparency and ability to customize will result in decisions by the investor that do not add value?

EXAMPLE 8

Pooled Investments and Separate Accounts

Which of the following are advantages of separately managed accounts compared with pooled investments?

A Typically lower cost

B Potential management of the portfolio by the investor

C Ability to take close account of individual client constraints or preferences

Solution:

C is correct. With SMAs, the investor owns the individual securities directly and can potentially express individual constraints or preferences within the portfolio. In particular, SMAs offer potentially improved tax efficiency because the investor pays taxes only on the capital gains realized and allows the implementation of tax-efficient investing and trading strategies.

5.4.3 *Evaluation of the Investment's Terms*

An additional and important aspect of manager selection is understanding the terms of the investment as presented in the prospectus, private placement memorandum, and/or limited partnership agreement. These documents are, in essence, the contract between the investor and the manager, outlining each party's rights and responsibilities. Although these documents cover numerous topics, this section focuses on liquidity and fees. The objective of the decision maker is to determine whether the liquidity and fee structure make the manager suitable for the investor's needs and the "best" manager for expressing a particular portfolio need.

5.4.3.1 Liquidity Different vehicles provide different degrees of liquidity. Liquidity is defined as the timeliness with which a security or asset can be sold at or near the current price. The same criteria can be applied to managers.

The most liquid vehicles are closed-end funds and ETFs. As listed securities, they can be bought and sold intra-day, and the price received will depend on the trading volume and depth of the fund. The obvious advantage of these funds is ease of trading, although there can be some price uncertainty for less liquid funds, particularly when trying to buy or sell a large number of shares. Open-end funds are slightly less liquid, providing daily liquidity but also price certainty; shares are bought and sold at the end-of-day NAV.

Unlike open-end funds, ETFs, or closed-end funds, limited partnerships, such as hedge funds, venture capital funds, and private equity funds, typically require investors to invest their money for longer periods. Hedge fund liquidity has four basic features: redemption frequency, notification period, lockup, and gates. Redemption frequency indicates how often an investor can withdraw capital from the fund, and the notification period indicates how far in advance of the redemption investors must tell the fund of their intention to redeem. A lockup is the initial period, after making an investment, during which investors cannot redeem their holding. Lockups have two types: a hard lock, which allows for no redemptions, and a soft lock, which charges a fee, paid into the fund, for redemptions. A mutual fund redemption fee is equivalent to a hedge fund soft lock. Gates limit the amount of fund assets, or investor assets that can be redeemed at one redemption date.

Private equity and venture capital funds provide the least liquidity. Investors are contractually obligated to contribute specific amounts (capital calls) during the investment phase and then receive distributions and capital as investments are harvested during the remaining term of the fund. A typical investment phase is 5 years. The typical life of a fund is 10 years, with the option to extend the term for 2 1-year periods.

The obvious disadvantage of partnership liquidity terms is the reduced flexibility to adjust portfolio allocations in light of changing market conditions or investor circumstances, as well as the reduced ability to meet unexpected liquidity needs. The advantage of such terms is that they do lock up capital for longer horizons, allowing funds to take long-term views and hold less liquid securities—such as start-up companies, buyouts, turnarounds, real estate, or natural resources—with reduced risk of having to sell portfolio holdings at inopportune times in response to redemption requests. An additional advantage, which was apparent during the 2008 financial crisis, is that limited liquidity imposes this long horizon view on investors, reducing or removing their ability to overreact.

Because SMA assets are held in the investor's name, the securities in the portfolio can be sold at any time. As a result, an SMA's liquidity will depend on the liquidity of the securities held. An SMA holding listed large-cap stocks will likely be highly liquid, whereas an investor in an SMA that holds unlisted or illiquid securities will have to accept a discount when selling.

5.4.3.2 Management Fees[1] Investors seek strong performance net of fees. Managers charge fees to cover operating costs and earn a return on their capital—primarily human capital. A manager's fixed costs are relatively small and primarily cover the costs of technology and the long-term lease of office space. Variable costs, which consist largely of payroll and marketing costs, dominate the income statements of asset management companies. Because a considerable portion of employee compensation comes in the form of bonuses, senior management can reduce bonus payouts as fee revenue declines in order to smooth a company's profitability.

Investors are increasingly sensitive to management fees. Average asset-weighted expense ratios (management fees and fund expenses) incurred by mutual fund investors have fallen substantially. In 2000, equity mutual fund investors incurred expense ratios of 0.99 percent, on average, or 99 cents for every $100 invested. By 2016, that average had fallen to 0.63 percent, a decline of 36 percent. Hybrid and bond mutual fund expense ratios also have declined. The average hybrid mutual fund expense ratio fell from 0.89 percent in 2000 to 0.74 percent in 2016, a reduction of 17 percent. The average bond mutual fund expense ratio fell from 0.76 percent in 2000 to 0.51 percent in 2016, a decline of 33 percent. The decline is a function of several factors: the allocation of the fixed portion of expenses over a larger asset base, increasing investor preference for no-load share classes, and the increasing allocations to lower-cost index funds. Aside from these structural factors lowering average expense ratios, there has been more generalized downward pressure on fees—the average expense ratio of actively managed equity mututal funds has declined from 1.06% in 2000 to 0.82% in 2016. Likewise, the average expense ratio of actively managed bond mutual funds has declined from 0.78% in 2000 to 0.58% in 2016.[2]

Investment firms charge fees in several different ways. In general, mutual funds charge fees based on assets under management in a fund.[3] Some classes of mutual funds, including those with reduced fees, require minimum balances. In contrast, institutional managers frequently offer declining percentage fees on increasing account sizes for separate or commingled pool accounts. Institutional accounts frequently specify minimum account sizes or minimum dollar fees. Fixed-percentage fees are subject to the variability of asset values, whereas dollar fees facilitate managers' and investors' planning for future cash flows.

Fee structures can influence which managers will be willing to accept a particular investment mandate. They can also strongly affect manager behavior. Economic theory suggests that the principal–agent problem is complicated by the fact that an agent's skills and actions are not fully visible to the principal. Although principals control asset availability, agents control both their expenditure of effort and portfolio risk. Moreover, the agent and principal may have different preferences; each might care about different time horizons and agents might not view losses the same way that

1 This section based on Chapter 6 in Essays on Manager Selection, by Scott D. Stewart, PhD, CFA, Research Foundation of CFA Institute. © 2013 CFA Institute. All rights reserved.
2 ICI Investment Company Fact Book, 2017
3 Although mutual funds may offer a declining management fee as fund assets increase, the individual investor does not benefit from investing more money unless the extra money qualifies the investor for a lower-fee fund class.

principals do.[4] Finally, total performance is, to some extent, beyond the control of either party. As a result of these factors, the principal's and agent's interests may not be fully aligned. In reality, managers are motivated to work hard even without incentive fees because they want to retain current clients and expand their client base and pricing power. Incentives are useful, however, to help *ensure* that managers routinely act in their clients' best interest.

Assets under Management Fees Assets under management fees, also called *ad valorem* fees (from the Latin for "according to value"), result from applying stated percentage rates to assets under management. These fees reward managers who attract and retain assets, generate added value, and experience benefits from rising markets. Managers primarily grow their assets through skillful investing, hard work, and effective marketing. A manager's success, however, also results partly from luck, especially in the short term. Managers benefit from rising portfolio values, which are attributable to the combination of alpha and beta decisions, but are also, at least for long-only managers, greatly affected by market cycles beyond the manager's control. A decline in *ad valorem* percentages as assets grow helps reduce the fee impact on investors from rising markets, but does not eliminate it.

Once a manager's assets are large, he might not want to risk losing them. Assets are typically "sticky"—that is, once investors allocate their assets to a manager, the manager often does not need to generate the same level of returns to retain the assets as he did to attract them. Empirical evidence suggests this stickiness is the case, to some extent, for mutual fund assets. To motivate such managers to work harder or discourage them from closet indexing, an incentive fee determined by future performance may be useful.

Performance-Based Fees Performance-based fees are determined by portfolio returns and are designed to reward managers with a share of return for their skill in creating value. Performance can be calculated by using either total or relative return, and the return shared can be a percentage of total performance or performance net of a base or fixed fee. Performance-based fees are structured in one of three basic ways:

1 A symmetrical structure in which the manager is fully exposed to both the downside and upside (Computed fee = Base + Sharing of performance);

2 A bonus structure in which the manager is not fully exposed to the downside but is fully exposed to the upside [Computed fee = Higher of either (1) Base or (2) Base plus sharing of positive performance]; or

3 A bonus structure in which the manager is not fully exposed to either the downside or the upside [Computed fee = Higher of (1) Base or (2) Base plus sharing of performance, to a limit].

Performance fees are paid annually or, in some cases, less frequently. These fees may include maximum and high-water mark (or clawback) features that protect investors from situations such as paying for current positive performance before the negative effects of prior underperformance have been offset. Private equity, hedge fund, and real estate partnerships commonly earn performance fees on total returns and typically do not limit the amount of the performance fee. Hedge funds commonly include high-water mark features.

Consider the example of private equity partnerships, in which base fees are commonly applied to committed (not just invested) capital. Performance fees are earned as profits are realized, and invested capital is returned to investors. A common provision that helps protect private equity limited partners (the investors) is a requirement that the limited partners receive their principal and share of profits before performance fees are distributed to the general partner (the manager).

4 For a summary of theoretical research on investment compensation, see Stracca (2006).

Specific performance-based fee structures are designed by both clients and managers. A formula is agreed upon based on the anticipated distribution of returns and the perceived attractiveness of the investment strategy. Managers who can command attractive terms, such as real estate managers that are in high demand and have limited capacity, have the power to stipulate the highest base fees and profit sharing in their fee agreements. Fee schedules are typically designed by fund managers, included in marketing materials, and set forth in partnership agreements. Large investors may influence the terms of fee schedules or negotiate side letters for special treatment.

A simple performance-based fee, as illustrated in Exhibit 12, specifies a base fee below which the computed fee can never fall. In this case, the manager is protected against sharing for performance below 25 bps. To make the result symmetrical around the commonplace 50 bps fee, the manager does not share in active performance beyond 2.75%.

Exhibit 12 Sample Performance-Based Fee Schedule

Panel A. Sample Fee Structure

Standard fee	0.50%
Base fee	0.25%
Sharing*	20%
Breakeven active return	1.50%
Maximum annual fee	0.75%

Panel B. Numerical Examples for Annual Periods

	Active Return				
	≤ 0.25%	**1.00%**	**1.50%**	**2.00%**	**≥ 2.75%**
Billed fee	0.25%	0.40%	0.50%	0.60%	0.75%
Net active return	≤ 0.00%	0.60%	1.00%	1.40%	≥ 2.00%

* On active return, beyond base fee.

If investment outcomes result from a mix of skill and luck (i.e., a probability distribution around a positive mean alpha), then performance fees constitute risk sharing. Fee structures must be designed carefully to avoid favoring one party over the other. Performance-based fees work to align the interests of managers and investors because both parties share in investment results. Investors benefit by paying performance-based fees, rather than standard fees, when active returns are low. Managers may work harder to earn performance-based fees, inspiring the term "incentive based." Empirical evidence suggests a correlation between performance-based fees and higher alphas (also, lower fees) for mutual funds and higher risk-adjusted returns for hedge funds.[5] Asset managers may consider performance-based fees attractive because such fees provide an opportunity to enhance profits on the upside and ensure guaranteed, although perhaps minimal, streams of revenue from base fees when performance is poor.

Performance-based fees can also create tensions between investors and managers. Investors must pay base fees even when managers underperform. Management firm revenues decline when cash is needed to invest in operations or retain talent. In fact, the failure rate for poor-performing and even zero-alpha managers may tend to be higher when performance-based rather than standard fees are used.[6]

5 See Elton, Gruber, and Blake (2003) and Ackermann, McEnally, and Ravenscraft (1999).
6 See Grinold and Rudd (1987).

Performance-based fee structures may also lead to misestimates of portfolio risk. Such fee structures convert symmetrical gross active return distributions into asymmetrical net active return distributions, reducing variability on the upside but not the downside. As a result, a single standard deviation calculated on a return series that incorporates active returns, above and below the base fee, can lead to the underestimation of downside risk.[7]

Investors and managers may have different incentives when performance-based fees are used. For example, according to a utility maximization model, fully symmetric fees, in which the manager is fully exposed to the downside, tend to yield closer alignment in risk and effort than bonus-style fees.[8] Understandably, symmetrical fee structures are unpopular with managers because of their impact on bankruptcy risk.

Bonus-style fees are the close equivalent of a manager's call option on a share of active return, for which the base fee is the strike price. Consider Exhibit 13, which shows a familiar-looking option payoff pattern using the fee parameters defined in Exhibit 12. In this case, the option payoff is modified by a maximum fee feature. The graph illustrates three fee components: a 25 bps base fee, plus a long call option on active return with a strike price equal to the minimum (base) fee, minus another (less valuable) call option with a strike price equal to the maximum fee.

Exhibit 13 Payoff Line of Sample Performance-Based Fee Schedule

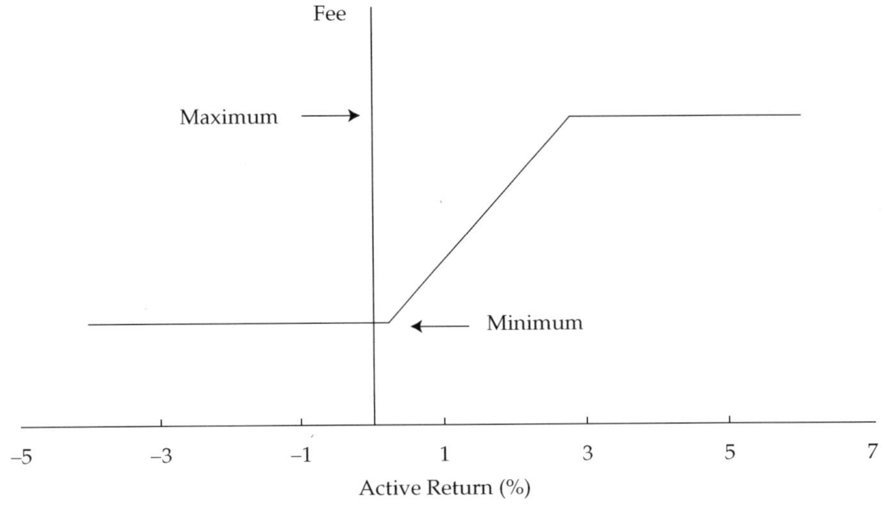

Managers must retain clients year to year, avoid poor performance, and not violate management guidelines. But managers also tend to have an interest in increasing risk, which may conflict with these goals. Based on option pricing theory,[9] higher volatility leads to higher option value, which encourages managers to assume higher portfolio risk. This behavior has been observed in the marketplace.[10] As a result, investors, when possible, should carefully select benchmarks and monitor risk in their portfolios.[11]

7 See Kritzman (2012).
8 See Starks (1987).
9 Margrabe (1978) notes that an incentive fee (without a maximum) consists of a call option on the portfolio and a put on the benchmark. As a result, the value depends on the volatility of the portfolio and the benchmark and the correlation between the two—in other words, the active risk.
10 See Elton et al. (2003).
11 Starks (1987) notes that an investor can simply set a fee schedule incorporating penalties for observed risk to align interests regarding risk levels.

Senior management at investment firms should also ensure that their compensation systems penalize portfolio managers for assuming excessive risk as well as reward them for earning superior returns.[12]

Real Story: The Client's Free Option in a Performance Fee Agreement

Consider the case of an equity manager in the early 1990s offering a performance-based fee that consisted of a 10 bp base fee and a 20% share of active return in excess of the benchmark index (net of the 10 bps). The fee structure also included a maximum annual fee provision that reserved excess fees for subsequent years. Because there was no penalty for cancelling the fee agreement, clients could opt out of the performance-based fee in exchange for a standard flat fee when performance was particularly strong. This arrangement allowed them to avoid paying the manager's accrued, fully earned share, and is precisely what many clients did in the mid-1990s following a period of high active returns.

Other problems exist with performance-based fees. When managers have clients with varying fee structures, it is in their (short-term) interest to favor customers that have performance-based fees. Although doing so may be unethical or potentially illegal, managers can direct trades or deals (including initial public offerings) to performance-fee clients to their benefit and to the detriment of others. It may be difficult for clients to monitor this activity. Fortunately, most managers recognize that such actions, once discovered, could destroy their careers or lead to criminal charges. Here again, due diligence, including the review of internal compliance systems, will help limit an investor's exposure to unscrupulous managers.

When managers can control the timing of profit realization, as is often the case with private equity partnerships, they may have an incentive to hold on to assets until a profit can be realized. Managers may do so even when clients would benefit from selling assets at a loss and investing the proceeds outside of the partnership. In contrast, hedge fund managers have an incentive to return assets in poor-performing partnerships when the high-water mark is substantially above current value (i.e., the performance-fee option is considerably out of the money). This action results in the investor missing the opportunity to recoup previously paid fees based on future strong performance.

Funds of funds (FoFs) commonly charge fees in addition to the fees charged by the underlying funds.[13] These fees pay for the investor's access to the underlying funds and for the FoFs' due diligence, portfolio construction, and monitoring. In addition to these two sets of fees, investors are required to share the profits from well-performing underlying funds but incur the full loss from poorly performing funds.[14] To protect investors from paying overly high fees, hedge fund consortiums have recently begun to offer fee structures based on the total portfolio value of underlying funds, rather than the sum of fees computed at the individual fund level.

12 Although it adds a layer of complexity to the evaluation process, an active-risk-adjusted bonus formula can be specified.

13 When funds of funds were popular in the 2000s, it was common for them to charge a performance-based fee.

14 Kritzman (2012) calls this result an "asymmetry penalty."

The Impact of Fee Structure on Net Returns

Consider four fee structures applied to the same 12-month return series gross of fees:

- 0.50% management fee, 0% performance fee
- 0.50% management fee, 15% performance fee
- 1.50% management fee, 0% performance fee
- 1.50% management fee, 15% performance fee

The fees are accrued at the end of each month. This example is a simplification but illustrates the important effects of fee level and structure on net performance. As Exhibit 14 shows, the average monthly gross return is 0.72% with a 1.37% monthly standard deviation. Not surprisingly, charging a management fee (MF) lowers the level of realized return without affecting the standard deviation of the series. The management fee is a constant shift in the level and thus does not affect volatility. The addition of a performance fee (PF) also lowers the level of realized returns but has the added effect of lowering the realized standard deviation. This dynamic occurs because in up months, the performance fee is accrued, and in down months, it is subtracted from the accrual balance to reflect the appropriate fee for the cumulative performance. This accounting has the effect of adjusting the monthly returns toward zero and lowering the measured volatility. The larger the performance fee, the more pronounced this effect. Exhibit 15 shows a graph of the cumulative returns for each fee structure.

Exhibit 15 Cumulative Return

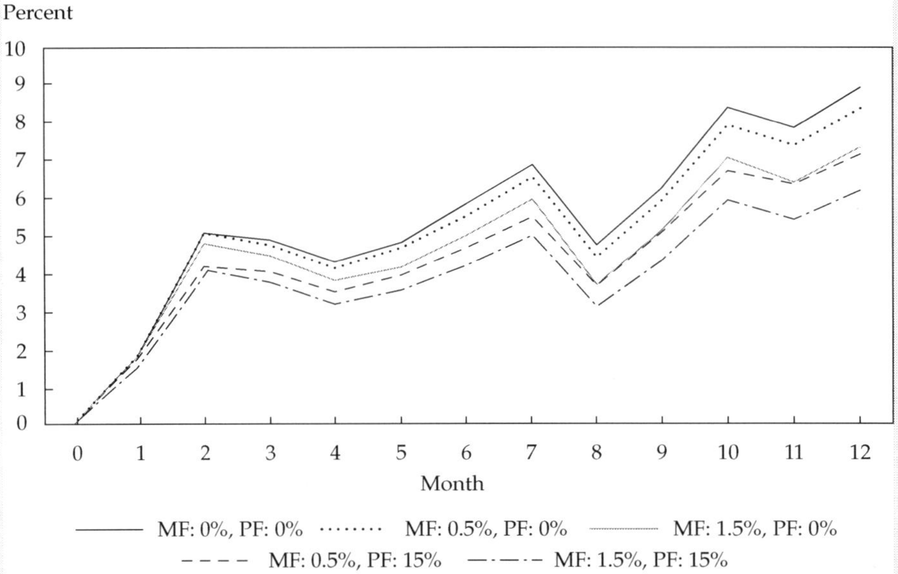

Given the potentially significant effect of expenses, a clear distinction must be drawn between performance analysis based on gross returns and net of expenses returns.

Exhibit 14 Effects of Expense on Portfolio Performance

		Monthly Gross Return													
MF	**PF**	**1**	**2**	**3**	**4**	**5**	**6**	**7**	**8**	**9**	**10**	**11**	**12**	**Avg. Ret.**	**S.D.**
0.0%	0.0%	2.00%	3.00%	−0.20%	−0.50%	0.50%	0.90%	1.00%	−2.00%	1.50%	2.00%	−0.50%	1.00%	0.72%	1.37%
0.5%	0.0%	1.96%	2.96%	−0.24%	−0.54%	0.46%	0.86%	0.96%	−2.04%	1.46%	1.96%	−0.54%	0.96%	0.67%	1.37%
0.5%	15.0%	1.66%	2.51%	−0.21%	−0.46%	0.39%	0.73%	0.81%	−1.74%	1.24%	1.66%	−0.46%	0.81%	0.57%	1.16%
1.5%	0.0%	1.88%	2.88%	−0.32%	−0.62%	0.37%	0.77%	0.88%	−2.12%	1.37%	1.88%	−0.62%	0.88%	0.59%	1.37%
1.5%	15.0%	1.59%	2.44%	−0.28%	−0.53%	0.32%	0.66%	0.74%	−1.81%	1.17%	1.59%	−0.53%	0.74%	0.50%	1.16%

An additional consideration is the different degree of uncertainty between expenses and the potential added value of the active portfolio manager. Expenses are paid for certain, whereas the added value of the active strategy compared with the passive strategy is uncertain. For example, suppose an active strategy is expected to generate a gross return that is 2% greater than the passive strategy, but the cost of the active strategy is 2% greater than the passive strategy. A risk-averse investor would likely prefer the passive strategy; although the expected net return of the strategies is the same, the uncertainty of the outperformance would be unappealing. The riskier the active strategy, the greater the return volatility and the greater the volatility of the added value relative to the passive strategy. The significance is, the added value of the active strategy has to be sufficiently large and certain to justify the higher cost of the strategy.

In sum, the presence of positive significant average excess return is evidence for manager skill. This excess return, however, must be net of fees and expenses for the benefit of this skill to accrue to the investor.[15] The preference is for more linear compensation to the manager to reduce the incentives to change the portfolio's risk profile at inflection points.

SUMMARY

Evaluating an investment manager is a complex and detailed process. It encompasses a great deal more than analyzing investment returns. In conducting investment manager due diligence, the focus is on understanding how the investment results were achieved and assessing the likelihood that the manager will continue to follow the same investment process that generated these returns. This process also entails operational due diligence, including an evaluation of the integrity of the firm, its operations, and personnel, as well as evaluating the vehicle structure and terms. As such, due diligence involves both quantitative and qualitative analysis.

This reading provides a framework that introduces and describes the important elements of the manager selection process:

- Investment manager selection involves a broad set of qualitative and quantitative considerations to determine whether a manager displays skill and the likelihood that the manager will continue to display skill in the future.
- For a manager to be the "best" choice, they must be suitable for the investor. The IPS captures the investor's objectives, constraints, and preferences, thereby providing the criteria for determining suitability.
- The qualitative analysis consists of investment due diligence, which evaluates the manager's investment process, investment personnel, and portfolio construction; and operational due diligence, which evaluates the manager's infrastructure.
- A Type I error is hiring or retaining a manager who subsequently underperforms expectations—that is, rejecting the null hypothesis of no skill when it is correct. A Type II error is not hiring or firing a manager who subsequently outperforms, or performs in line with, expectations—that is, not rejecting the null hypothesis when it is incorrect.

15 Ultimately, the net return to the investor accounts not only for fees and expenses but also for taxes. This more complex issue is beyond the scope of this reading.

- The manager search and selection process has three broad components: the universe, a quantitative analysis of the manager's performance track record, and a qualitative analysis of the manager's investment process. The qualitative analysis includes both investment due diligence and operational due diligence.
- Batting average measures the frequency of positive outcomes that can be used to measure the consistency of performance. The limitation is that batting average does not measure the magnitude of returns. As such, it is best used in combination with other measures.
- Capture ratio measures the asymmetry of returns, and a ratio greater than 1 indicates that the attractive characteristic of greater participation in rising versus falling markets. Drawdown is the loss incurred in any continuous period of negative returns. An asymmetrical return profile or avoiding large drawdowns can result in higher risk-adjusted returns caused by the proportionally larger gain needed to recover from increasingly large losses. In addition, a manager that experiences larger drawdowns may be less suitable for investors closer to the end of their investment horizons.
- The investment philosophy is the foundation of the investment process. The philosophy outlines the set of assumptions about the factors that drive performance and the manager's beliefs about their ability to successfully exploit these sources of return. The investment manager should have a clear and concise investment philosophy. It is important to evaluate these assumptions and the role they play in the investment process to understand how the strategy will behave over time and across market environments. The investment process has to be consistent and appropriate for the philosophy, and the investment personnel need to possess sufficient expertise and experience to effectively execute the investment process.
- Style analysis, understanding the manager's risk exposures relative to the benchmark, is an important component of performance appraisal and manager selection, helping to define the universe of suitable managers.
- Returns-based style analysis is a top-down approach that involves estimating the risk exposures from an actual return series for a given period. Although RBSA adds an additional analytical step, the analysis is straightforward and should identify the important drivers of return and risk factors for the period analyzed. It can be estimated even for complicated strategies and is comparable across managers and through time. The disadvantage is that RBSA is an imprecise tool, attributing performance to an unchanging average portfolio during the period that might not reflect the current or future portfolio exposures.
- Holdings-based style analysis is a bottom-up approach that estimates the risk exposures from the actual securities held in the portfolio at a point in time. HBSA allows for the estimation of current risk factors and should identify all important drivers of return and risk factors, be comparable across managers and through time, and provide an accurate view of the manager's risk exposures. The disadvantages are the additional computational effort, dependence on the degree of transparency provided by the manager, and the possibility that accuracy may be compromised by stale pricing and window dressing.
- The prospectus, private placement memorandum, and/or limited partnership agreement are, in essence, the contract between the investor and the manager, outlining each party's rights and responsibilities. The provisions are liquidity terms and fees. The obvious disadvantages of limited liquidity terms are the reduced flexibility to adjust portfolio allocations in light of changing market conditions or investor circumstances, as well as the reduced ability to meet unexpected liquidity needs. The advantage is that it allows the funds to take long-term views and hold less liquid securities with reduced risk of having

to divest assets at inopportune times in response to redemption requests. A management fee lowers the level of realized return without affecting the standard deviation, whereas a performance fee has the added effect of lowering the realized standard deviation. The preference is for more-linear compensation to reduce the incentives to change the portfolio's risk profile at inflection points.

- The comparison of individual separate accounts relative to pooled (or commingled) vehicles evaluates whether the vehicle is consistent with the investment process, whether it is suitable for the investor IPS, and whether the benefits outweigh the additional costs.
- Investment management fees take one of two forms: a fixed percentage fee based on assets under management or a performance-based fee which charges a percentage of the portfolio's total return or excess return over a benchmark or hurdle rate. Performance-based fees work to align the interests of managers and investors because both parties share in investment results. Most managers that charge a performance fee also charge some level of fixed percentage fee to aid business continuity efforts. Fee structures must be designed carefully to avoid favoring one party over the other.

REFERENCES

Constable, Neil, and Jeremy Armitage. 2006. "Information Ratios and Batting Averages." *Financial Analysts Journal*, vol. 62, no. 3 (May/June):24–31.

DALBAR. 2005. *QAIB 2005: Quantitative Analysis of Investor Behavior*. Boston: DALBAR, Inc.

Khandani, Amir E., and Andrew W. Lo. 2011. "What Happened to the Quants in August 2007? Evidence from Factors and Transactions Data." *Journal of Financial Markets*, vol. 14, no. 1 (February):1–46.

Stewart, Scott D. 1998. "Is Consistency of Performance a Good Measure of Manager Skill?" *Journal of Portfolio Management*, vol. 24, no. 3 (Spring):22–32.

Stewart, Scott D. 2013. "Manager Selection." Charlottesville, VA: Research Foundation of CFA Institute.

Stewart, Scott D., John J. Neumann, Christopher R. Knittel, and Jeffrey Heisler. 2009. "Absence of Value: An Analysis of Investment Allocation Decisions by Institutional Plan Sponsors." *Financial Analysts Journal*, vol. 65, no. 6 (November/December):34–51.

Zuckerman, Gregory. 2008. "Fees, Even Returns and Auditor All Raised Red Flags." *Wall Street Journal* (13 December 2008).

PRACTICE PROBLEMS

1 Which of the following considerations would *most likely* be part of both the manager selection process and the performance appraisal process?

A Verifying risk metrics such as standard deviation

B Determining if the investment process can be consistently applied

C Assessing the likelihood that the investment organization will be a stable on-going firm

2 An investment policy statement that stipulates a need for short-term liquidity *most likely* rules out a manager whose portfolio is largely invested in:

A real estate.

B US short-term securities.

C exchange-traded securities.

3 Which of the following qualitative considerations is *most* associated with determining whether investment manager selection will result in superior repeatable performance?

A Transparency

B Investment process

C Operational process

4 Which of the following is *most likely* a key consideration in investment due diligence?

A Suitability of the investment vehicle

B Back office processes and procedures

C Depth of expertise and experience of investment personnel

5 When manager performance is mean reverting, a Type I error occurs when the investor:

A avoids hiring managers with weak short-term track records.

B does not fire a strong performing manager with a short-term track record.

C fires a poor performing manager and performance improves after the firing.

6 A decision-making investor is *most likely* to worry more about making a Type I error than a Type II error because:

A Type II errors are errors of commission.

B Type I errors are more easily measured.

C Type II errors are more likely to have to be explained as to why a skilled manager was fired.

7 An investor is considering hiring three managers who have the following skill levels:

Manager	Large-cap skill level	Small-cap skill level
1	Skilled	Unskilled
2	Skilled	Skilled
3	Unskilled	Unskilled

Type I and Type II errors both occur when the investor is:

A hiring Manager 1 for large-cap stocks and not hiring Manager 3 for small-cap stocks.

B hiring Manager 3 for large-cap stocks and not hiring Manager 2 for small-cap stocks.

C hiring Manager 3 for large-cap stocks and not hiring Manager 1 for small-cap stocks.

8 Suppose that the results of a style analysis for an investment manager are not consistent with the stated philosophy of the manager and the manager's stated investment process. These facts suggest the:

A absence of style drift.

B investment process may not be repeatable.

C manager should be included in the universe of potential managers.

9 Compared with holdings-based style analysis (HBSA), a returns-based style analysis (RBSA):

A is subject to window dressing.

B requires less effort to acquire data.

C is more accurate when illiquid securities are present.

10 A manager whose relative performance is worse during market downturns *most likely* has a capture ratio that is:

A less than one.

B equal to one.

C greater than one.

11 An investor gathers the following data about an investment manager:

Time	Manager Returns (%)	Benchmark Returns (%)
1	2.0	1.5
2	−1.0	−2.0
3	−0.5	−1.3
4	1.2	0.5
5	1.7	1.2
6	−2.0	−1.1
7	2.5	1.8
8	−0.6	−0.9
9	1.3	1.4
10	3.0	2.5

The downside capture is *closest* to:

A 0.77.

B 0.78.

C 1.31.

12 When an investment strategy generates many small gains with an occasional large loss in a generally rising market, the manager's absolute batting average will *most likely* be:

A less than the relative batting average.

B the same as the relative batting average.

C greater than the relative batting average.

13 Which of the following is consistent with the expectation that exploiting a structural inefficiency is repeatable?

A The inefficiency is a unique event that occurs infrequently.

B The level of gross return is equal to the amount of transaction costs and expenses.

C The aggregate value of all assets affected by the inefficiency is larger than the AUM of the manager and its competitors.

14 Which of the following is **not** a reason that an investor might favor a separately managed account rather than a pooled vehicle? The investor:

A is tax exempt.

B requires real-time details on investment positions.

C has expressed certain constraints and preferences for the portfolio.

15 Which of the following investment vehicles provide investors with the highest degree of liquidity?

A Open-end funds

B Private equity funds

C Limited partnerships

16 Which of the following statements is consistent with the manager adhering to a stated investment philosophy and investment decision-making process?

A Senior investment team members have left to form their own firm.

B A senior employee has been cited by the SEC for violating insider trading regulations.

C A large drawdown occurs because of an unforeseen political event in a foreign country.

17 A manager has a mandate to be fully invested with a benchmark that is a blend of large-cap stocks and investment-grade bonds. Which of the following is **not** an indication that style drift has occurred? The manager:

A initiates an allocation to small-cap stocks.

B decreases investments in investment-grade corporate bonds.

C increases allocation to cash in anticipation of a market decline.

18 Which of the following investment policy statement (IPS) features would *most likely* prevent the investment committee of a socially responsible investment fund from selecting a manager that invests in weapon manufacturers or tobacco companies?

A Risk tolerance

B Return objectives

C Unique circumstances

19 The manager selection process begins by defining the universe of feasible managers. When defining this manager universe, the selection process should avoid:

A excluding managers based on historical risk-adjusted returns.

B identifying the benchmark against which managers will be evaluated.

C using third-party categorizations of managers to find those that might fill the desired role in the portfolio.

20 An investor hires manager A and does not hire manager B. The investor has committed both Type I and Type II errors if:

A both manager A and B are unskillful.

B manager A is skillful and manager B is unskillful.

C manager A is unskillful and manager B is skillful.

21 Which of the following statements with respect to Type I and Type II errors in the manager selection process is correct?

A Type I errors create explicit costs.

B Type I errors are errors of omission.

C Type II errors are errors of commission.

22 A return distribution of skilled managers that is highly distinct from the return distribution of unskilled managers, *most likely* implies a:

A highly efficient market.

B low opportunity cost of not hiring a skilled manager.

C high opportunity cost of not hiring a skilled manager.

23 An advantage of a returns-based style analysis is that such analysis:

A is comparable across managers.

B is suitable for portfolios that contain illiquid securities.

C can effectively profile a manager's risk exposures using a short return series.

24 Which of the following types of style analysis use(s) a bottom-up approach to estimate the risk exposures in a portfolio?

A Returns-based style analysis only

B Holdings-based style analysis only

C Both return-based and holdings-based style analysis

25 In a quarter, an investment manager's upside capture is 75% and downside capture is 125%. We can conclude that the manager underperforms the benchmark:

A only when the benchmark return is positive.

B only when the benchmark return is negative.

C when the benchmark return is either positive or negative.

26 A manager's monthly returns for the second quarter are presented in Exhibit 1.

Exhibit 1

Month	Return
April	0.4%
May	−5.9%
June	−2.7%

The drawdown for the second quarter is *closest* to:

A −8.6%.

B −8.4%.

C −8.2%.

27 Which of the following is an accurate interpretation of a manager's 90% relative batting average?

A The manager had positive returns on 90% of the investment decisions.

B The manager's cumulative return was 90% of the benchmark's return.

C The manager matched or underperformed the benchmark in 10% of the periods.

28 Which of the following fee structures *most likely* decreases the volatility of a portfolio's net returns?

A Incentive fees only

B Management fees only

C Neither incentive fees nor management fees

29 An investor should prefer a pooled investment vehicle to a separately managed account when she:

A is cost sensitive.

B focuses on tax efficiency.

C requires clear legal ownership of assets.

30 Which of the following investment types is the most liquid?

A ETFs

B Hedge funds

C Private equity funds

The following information relates to Questions 31–36

The Tree Fallers Endowment plans to allocate part of its portfolio to alternative investment funds. The endowment has hired Kurt Summer, a consultant at Summer Brothers Consultants, to identify suitable alternative investment funds for its portfolio.

Summer has identified three funds for potential investment and will present the performance of these investments to the endowment's board of directors at their next quarterly meeting.

Summer is reviewing each of the fund's fee schedules and is concerned about the manager's incentive to take on excess risk in an attempt to generate a higher fee. Exhibit 1 presents the fee schedules of the three funds.

Exhibit 1 Fee Schedules

Fund	Computed Fee	Base Fee	Sharing	Maximum Annual Fee
Red Grass Fund	Higher of either (1) base or (2) base plus sharing of positive performance; sharing is based on return net of the base fee.	1.00%	20%	na
Blue Water Fund	Higher of either (1) base or (2) base plus sharing of positive performance, up to a maximum annual fee of 2.50%; sharing is based on active return.	0.50%	20%	2.50%
Yellow Wood Fund	Base plus sharing of both positive and negative performance; sharing is based on return net of the base fee.	1.50%	20%	na

Exhibit 2 presents the annual gross returns for each fund and its respective benchmark for the period of 2013–2015. All funds have an inception date of 1 January 2013. Summer intends to include in his report an explanation of the impact of the fee structures of the three funds on returns.

Exhibit 2 Fund and Benchmark Returns

	2013		2014		2015	
Fund	**Gross Return (%)**	**Benchmark Return (%)**	**Gross Return (%)**	**Benchmark Return (%)**	**Gross Return (%)**	**Benchmark Return (%)**
Red Grass Fund	8.00	8.00	−2.00	−10.00	5.00	4.50
Blue Water Fund	10.00	9.00	−4.00	−1.50	14.00	2.00
Yellow Wood Fund	15.00	14.00	−5.00	−6.50	7.00	9.50

The board of directors of the Tree Fallers Endowment asks Summer to recalculate the fees of the Red Grass Fund assuming a high-water mark feature whereby a sharing percentage could only be charged to the extent any losses had been recouped.

31 Based on Exhibit 1, which fund has a symmetrical fee structure?

A Red Grass

B Blue Water

C Yellow Wood

32 Based on the fee schedules in Exhibit 1, the portfolio manager of which fund has the greatest incentive to assume additional risk to earn a higher investment management fee?

A Red Grass

B Blue Water

C Yellow Wood

33 Based on Exhibit 1 and Exhibit 2, the Yellow Wood Fund's 2013 investment management fee is:

A 3.00%.

B 4.20%.

C 4.50%.

34 Based on Exhibit 1 and Exhibit 2, the Red Grass Fund's 2014 investment management fee is:

A 0.40%.

B 1.00%.

C 2.60%.

35 Based on Exhibit 1 and Exhibit 2, the Blue Water Fund's 2015 investment management fee is:

A 2.40%

B 2.50%.

C 2.90%

36 In which year would the Red Grass Fund's investment management fee be affected by Summer's recalculation using the high-water mark?

A 2013

B 2014

C 2015

The following information relates to questions 37–42

Houston Smith, an analyst at the Argon Foundation, is evaluating the performance of the Tyne US Mid-Cap Growth Fund. Fifteen percent of the foundation's assets are invested in the fund, which has been actively managed on a bottom-up, long-only basis by David Baylor for the last five years. As a charitable organization, the foundation is exempt from income tax.

Smith believes capture ratios help in assessing manager suitability relative to an investor's time horizon and risk tolerance and, therefore, begins his evaluation by calculating the manager's capture ratio. For the most recent five-year period, Baylor achieved an upside capture of 109.8% and a downside capture of 112.3%.

Smith next reviews the fund's performance record for any inconsistency that might indicate a lack of skill on the part of Baylor. Smith calculates a relative batting average of 67% and considers the appropriate interpretation of this value.

Smith asks Baylor to describe his investment philosophy. Baylor replies that he assumes the US mid-cap equity market is sufficiently inefficient that security mispricings can be identified and exploited. In addition, Baylor assumes that these inefficiencies are temporary, with market price and perceived intrinsic value ultimately converging, and that market prices are driven by discernable trends.

Smith also asks Baylor to describe the signal creation aspect of his investment decision-making process. In response, Baylor makes the following statement:

> Profitable investment ideas are generated by identifying trends before other market participants. All of our information sources are in the public domain. Our economists identify nascent trends on a state-by-state basis and forecast their potential to affect national and international consumers, businesses, and governments over time. Our financial analysts research which US mid-cap companies are best situated to take advantage of these trends. And our quantitative analysts continually refine the complex algorithms we use to test investment ideas. We believe our distinctive analysis process allows the firm to consistently add value for our investors.

The foundation is considering moving its assets into a separately managed account vehicle. The account would continue to be managed by Baylor at his firm in its US mid-cap growth strategy. Smith wants to be sure that the benefits are sufficient to compensate for the additional cost of switching from the current vehicle, a commingled fund. Smith is aware that the foundation is also considering adding a new requirement for its asset managers—namely, that they comply with socially responsible investing principles.

To complete his evaluation, Smith reviews the fund's management fees. For separately managed accounts, there are two fee options: (a) the ad valorem fee and (b) the base fee plus a fixed share of any active return above the base fee, up to a maximum. The portfolio manager is not fully exposed to either the downside or the upside under the performance-based fee. See Exhibit 1 for details of the fund's management fees.

Exhibit 1 Tyne US Mid-Cap Growth Fund Annual Management Fee Schedule

Ad valorem fee	0.75%
Base fee	0.50%

(continued)

Exhibit 1 (Continued)

Maximum annual fee	2.00%
Share of active return	10.00%

37 Baylor's five-year capture ratio indicates that the fund *most likely*:

A has a concave return profile.

B exhibits positive asymmetry of return.

C captures larger return increases as benchmark returns increase.

38 The batting average calculated by Smith indicates that Baylor:

A made a profit on 67% of his investment decisions.

B underperformed the benchmark in 33% of the periods.

C underperformed the benchmark by 33% on a cumulative basis.

39 Baylor's investment philosophy can *best* be described as attempting to:

A exploit structural inefficiencies.

B capture alternative risk premiums.

C profit from behavioral inefficiencies.

40 The viability of Baylor's process for generating profitable investment ideas is:

A at risk of being impaired by regulators.

B based on maintaining an information timing edge.

C dependent on interpreting information in a unique way.

41 The *best* reason for the foundation to change to a separately managed account vehicle is to achieve:

A greater tax efficiency.

B lower transaction costs.

C improved transparency.

42 At what level of annual gross-of-fees active return would the foundation be indifferent to the management fee option selected?

A 0.75%

B 3.00%

C 3.25%

The following information relates to questions 43–48

Jennifer Black is a new analyst at an investment advisory firm. The senior analyst on staff, Anne Thornton, is training Black on the firm's manager selection process. Thornton informs Black that an investment policy statement (IPS) determines the universe of funds suitable for a particular investor, and she presents Black with a sample IPS to study (see Exhibit 1).

Exhibit 1 Sample Investment Policy Statement (abridged) Investor in US Equities

Category	Requirement
Return objective	Exceed total return of benchmark by 250 bps per year
Horizon	Intermediate term (more than five years)
Legal and regulatory	Short sales, leverage, and derivatives prohibited; securities must be listed on a major exchange
Liquidity	Infrequent withdrawals
Taxes	Minimize taxes on income and capital gains
Unique circumstances	No weapon manufacturers, tobacco companies, or gambling firms

Thornton tells Black that the qualitative analysis component of the manager selection process consists, in part, of investment due diligence. Thornton remarks that the different aspects of investment due diligence seek to answer the following key questions. First, what market inefficiency does the manager seek to exploit? Second, is the investment process capable of exploiting this inefficiency? And third, do the investment personnel possess the expertise and experience necessary to effectively implement the investment process? Thornton concludes by stating that investment due diligence ultimately attempts to determine which manager best fits the portfolio need.

In Thornton's view, a manager search typically starts with a benchmark that represents the manager's role in the portfolio. There are several approaches to assigning a manager to a benchmark, and Thornton requires a method that is objective, does not depend on timing and the amount of transparency, and defines the universe on the basis of the desired portfolio role.

After discussing hypothesis testing with Thornton, Black inquires about the performance implications of committing Type I and Type II errors when selecting a portfolio manager. Thornton responds with the following two statements:

Statement 1 The smaller the difference in sample size and mean and the narrower the dispersion of the return distributions of the skilled and unskilled managers in the universe, the smaller the expected cost of a Type I or Type II error.

Statement 2 If performance is mean reverting, firing a poor performer (or hiring a strong performer) only to see a reversion in performance results in a Type I error; a Type II error would be not trimming strong performers and avoiding hiring managers with weaker short-term track records.

Thornton informs Black that style analysis is the process of understanding a manager's risk exposures relative to the benchmark. To illustrate, Thornton describes performing a return-based style analysis of a portfolio that invests in large-cap growth stocks in the computer hardware industry. She mentions that in addition to the portfolio's return history, security market indexes representing portfolio concentration, industry, and capitalization risk factors are necessary inputs to the analysis.

Thornton also points out to Black that when performance has been lagging, portfolio managers may sell stocks that have reported substantial losses, replacing them with stocks expected to produce short-term gains to improve the overall performance of the portfolio for the reporting period. This behavior may compromise the usefulness of style analysis and should be considered when choosing which methodology to use.

43 Which of the following investment options *best* satisfies the IPS requirements listed in Exhibit 1?

A An all-capitalization-range index fund tracking the US equity market

B An actively managed microcap commingled fund investing in US stocks

C A tax-efficient US midcap equity portfolio seeking to outperform its benchmark

44 Which key aspect of investment due diligence did Thornton fail to describe when commenting on qualitative analysis in the manager selection process?

A Process

B Portfolio

C Philosophy

45 Which of the following approaches to assigning a manager to a benchmark *best* satisfies Thornton's requirements?

A Third-party categorization

B B. Return-based style analysis

C Holding-based style analysis

46 Which of the following statements by Thornton on Type I and Type II errors is *most* accurate?

A Only Statement 1

B Only Statement 2

C Both Statement 1 and Statement 2

47 Which of the following data items, in addition to those mentioned, is *most likely* to be needed when performing a return-based style analysis on Thornton's computer hardware portfolio?

A A third-party style categorization

B The manager's self-reported risk exposures

C A market index representing the style risk factor

48 Which of the following analysis methods is *most likely* to be compromised by the manager behavior described by Thornton when performance has been lagging?

A Return-based style analysis only

B Holding-based style analysis only

C Both return-based style analysis and holding-based style analysis

SOLUTIONS

1 A is correct. Performance appraisal is primarily a quantitative process that systematically evaluates the investment performance of a fund. This process would include using such risk metrics as standard deviation. In addition to qualitative considerations, manager selection includes assessment of the amount of risk assumed by the manager to generate results.

2 A is correct. An investor with shorter-term liquidity needs should not hold less liquid long-term assets, such as private equity or real estate.

3 B is correct. A critical element of manager selection is to assess if the investment process is superior, repeatable, and can be consistently applied.

4 C is correct. Experienced investment personnel is a key aspect of investment due diligence. A strong back office and suitable investment vehicles are key aspects of operational due diligence.

5 C is correct. A Type I error would be hiring a strong performer or firing a poor performer only to see a reversion in performance. Choices A and B describe Type II errors.

6 B is correct. Type I errors are more easily measured than Type II errors. In addition, Type I errors may be linked to the compensation of the decision maker. Type I errors are errors of commission, whereas Type II are errors in omission. Firing a skilled manager is less transparent to the investor.

7 B is correct. Hiring unskilled Manager 3 for large-cap stocks is an error of commission or Type I error, whereas not hiring skilled Manager 2 for small-cap stocks is an error of omission or Type II error.

8 B is correct. The results of the returns-based style analysis and the holdings-based style analysis should be consistent with the philosophy of the manager and the investment process. If this is not the case, it may suggest that the process is not repeatable or not consistently implemented. For these results the manager should not be included in the universe of potential managers, whereas if the results track over time they may suggest style drift.

9 B is correct. RBSA typically does not require a large amount of additional, or difficult to acquire, data. HBSA requires data on each security in the investment portfolio. HBSA is a snapshot of the portfolio at a single point of time and thus is subject to window dressing. Both HBSA and RBSA are subject to difficulties in interpreting returns when illiquid securities are present.

10 A is correct. A capture ratio less than one indicates the downside capture is greater than upside capture and reflects greater participation in falling markets than in rising markets.

11 A is correct. The downside capture is 0.77. The downside returns are:

Time	R(*m*) (%)	R(*B*) (%)
2	−1.0	−2.0
3	−0.5	−1.3
6	−2.0	−1.1
8	−0.6	−0.9
Geo. Avg.	−1.03	−1.33
Downside Capture = 0.77		

12 C is correct. The absolute batting average includes all positive returns, even those less than the benchmark return, which would not be included when computing the relative batting average.

13 C is correct. Given the amount of inefficient assets compared with the AUM of managers likely to exploit them provides some assurance that the inefficiency is repeatable. It would likely take some time for the inefficiency to converge to efficient valuation. The infrequent nature of the inefficiency and the zero marginal return suggest that the inefficiency is probably not worthwhile to pursue.

14 A is correct. The tax advantages to separately managed accounts do not accrue to a tax exempt investor. Choices B and C are considerations that reflect the investor's preferences and could be better satisfied using a separately managed account.

15 A is correct. Open-end funds provide daily liquidity; shares are bought and sold at the end-of-day NAV. Limited partnerships and private equity funds typically require investors to invest their money for longer periods.

16 C is correct. A large drawdown that results from an unforeseen event is explainable as a single isolated event that does not prohibit the manager from adhering to its investment philosophy and process. The events of senior team members leaving to form their own investment firm and an insider trading investigation by the SEC call into question the ability of the firm to adhere to its philosophy and decision-making process.

17 B is correct. In the normal course of business, the manager conforms to its style by reducing exposure to some class of investment grade bonds. Increasing allocation to cash and small-cap stocks is in violation of the mandate to be fully invested with equity exposure to large-cap stocks.

18 C is correct. An investor's IPS will generally outline any unique circumstances that apply to their assets. Unique circumstances may include such factors as allowable investments and the types of risk exposures permitted. A socially responsible investment policy may prohibit investments in weapon manufacturers or tobacco companies. A and B are incorrect because an investment in weapons manufacturers or tobacco companies does not necessarily present higher risk or higher returns.

19 A is correct. The focus of the initial screening process is on building a universe of managers that could potentially satisfy the identified portfolio need and should not focus on historical performance. Identifying a benchmark is a key component of defining the manager's role in the portfolio, and third-party categorizations are an efficient way to build an initial universe which can then be further refined.

20 C is correct. Hiring an unskillful manager is a Type I error; rejecting a skillful manager is a Type II error. Therefore, both Type I and Type II errors are committed. Hiring a skillful manager and not hiring an unskillful manager are not errors.

21 A is correct. Hiring an underperforming manager (a Type I error—choosing a manager who underperforms expectations) creates an explicit, identifiable cost.

22 C is correct. When the two distributions are highly distinct, the unskilled managers are expected to significantly underperform the skilled managers, implying a high opportunity cost of not hiring the skilled managers. Efficient markets are likely to exhibit smaller differences of returns between skilled and unskilled managers.

23 A is correct. Returns-based style analysis on portfolios of liquid assets is generally able to identify the important drivers of return and the relevant risk factors for the period analyzed, even for complicated strategies. In addition, the process

is comparable across managers and through time. If the portfolio contains illiquid securities, the lack of current prices on those positions may lead to an underestimation of the portfolio's volatility in a returns-based style analysis. Longer return series generally provide a more accurate estimate of the manager's underlying standard deviation of return.

24 B is correct. Holdings-based style analysis estimates the portfolio's risk exposures using the securities held in the portfolio (a bottom-up approach), whereas returns-based style analysis uses portfolio returns to estimate a portfolio's sensitivities to security market indexes (a top-down approach).

25 C is correct. Upside capture of 75% suggests that the manager only gained 75% of benchmark increase when the benchmark return was positive. Downside capture of 125% suggests that the manager lost 125% as much as the benchmark when the benchmark return was negative. Therefore, the manager underperformed the benchmark in both scenarios.

26 B is correct. To calculate drawdown—the cumulative peak-to-trough loss during a particular period—consecutive negative returns are geometrically linked:

$$\begin{aligned}(1 - 0.059) \times (1 - 0.027) - 1 &= (0.941 \times 0.973) - 1\\ &= 0.9137 - 1\\ &= -0.0844 \text{ or } -8.4\%\end{aligned}$$

A is incorrect because the monthly returns must be geometrically linked, not added. C is also incorrect because the positive April return should not be included when calculating the drawdown.

27 C is correct. A 90% relative batting average implies that the manager outperformed the benchmark in 90% of return periods; in other words, the manager matched or underperformed the benchmark in 10% of return periods.

28 A is correct. Because incentive fees are fees charged as a percentage of returns (reducing net gains in positive months and reducing net losses in negative months), its use lowers the standard deviation of realized returns. Charging a management fee (a fixed percentage based on assets) lowers the level of realized return without affecting the standard deviation of the return series.

29 A is correct. Pooled investment vehicles are typically operated at a lower cost than separately managed accounts because operational costs can be spread among multiple investors. An investor who is focused on tax efficiency would prefer a separately managed account because a separate account allows the implementation of tax-efficient investing and trading strategies, and the investor pays taxes only on capital gains realized. If the investor requires clear legal ownership, they would prefer a separately managed account in which the investor owns the individual security directly.

30 A is correct. ETFs, as listed securities that can be bought and sold intra-day, are the most liquid vehicles. Hedge fund liquidity features—such as redemption frequency, notification period, lockup, and gates—limit the liquidity of hedge funds. Private equity funds return capital and make profit distributions to investors only as investments are sold during the life of the fund, which is often 10 years and may be extended.

31 C is correct. A symmetrical fee structure is one in which the fees are affected by both positive and negative performance. Of the three funds in Exhibit 1, only Yellow Wood has a symmetrical structure. Yellow Wood's profit sharing component will be negative if its return is negative and positive if it is positive.

32 A is correct. Red Grass's fee arrangement allows for unlimited performance-based fees on the upside and no negative consequences on the downside.

33 B is correct. The fund's fee schedule includes a base fee of 1.50% and a 20% performance-based fee. The performance-based fee is applied after the base fee is deducted. The total fee is calculated as follows:

$$1.5\% + [20\% \times (15\% - 1.5\%)] = 4.20\%$$

34 B is correct. Red Grass Fund's fee schedule states that the fee will be the higher of either (1) the base fee or (2) the base fee plus the sharing of the positive performance. The 2014 return was negative and only the base fee should be applied.

35 B is correct. The fee schedule states that the fee will be the higher of either (1) the base fee or (2) the base fee plus sharing of the positive performance, with a maximum fee of 2.50%. Furthermore, it states that the performance-based fee is assessed on the active return. Without an upper limit, the fee would be 0.5% + [20% × (14% – 2%)] = 2.90%, which is greater than 2.50%; so, the 2.50% fee is assessed.

36 C is correct. The 2013 fee calculation would not be affected by the high-water mark provision because it is the first year of operation of the fund and the return is positive (no prior losses to be offset). The investment management fee in 2013 is calculated as follows:

$$\text{Investment management fee} = 1.00\% + [20\% \times (8.0\% - 1.00\%)] = 2.4\%.$$

The 2014 fee calculation would also not be affected by the high-water mark provision because the profit sharing component of the fee is zero as a result of a negative return in that year. The investment management fee is calculated as follows:

$$\text{Investment management fee} = 1.00\% + 0.00\% = 1.00\%.$$

The 2015 fee would be affected by the high-water mark provision because the sharing fee percentage would now be part of the 2015 gain and will need to offset the prior year losses, and only the remaining gains will generate a fee. The performance-based fee would be based on only the gains in excess of the high-water mark. The actual investment management fee charged (percentage and dollar value) will depend on the specific feature of the calculation, which is beyond the scope of this reading. Note that the correct answer can be identified by observing that 2015 is the only year in which a positive return follows a negative return in the prior year.

37 A is correct. The capture ratio is the upside capture divided by the downside capture. Baylor's capture ratio is equal to 97.8% (= 109.8%/112.3%). A capture ratio less than 100% indicates a concave return profile.

38 B is correct. The relative batting average measures the number of positive return periods relative to the benchmark (or peers) divided by the total number of periods. A relative batting average of 67% indicates the portfolio underperformed the benchmark in 33% of the periods.

39 C is correct. Behavioral inefficiencies are perceived mispricings created by the actions of other market participants, usually associated with biases, such as trend following or loss aversion. These inefficiencies are temporary, lasting long enough for the manager to identify and exploit before the market price and the perceived intrinsic value converge. Baylor's statements describing his investment philosophy indicate that his strategy is to profit from behavioral inefficiencies.

A is incorrect because structural inefficiencies are perceived mispricings created by external or internal rules and regulations. These inefficiencies can be long lived and assume a continuation of the rules and regulations rather than a convergence to the perceived intrinsic value. This conflicts with Baylor's statements about finding trends to exploit, that these trends are temporary in nature, and that market prices eventually converge to their perceived intrinsic values.

B is incorrect because passive strategies seek to capture return through exposure to systematic risk premiums, such as equity risk, duration risk, or credit risk. These strategies can also look to capture alternative risk premiums, such as liquidity risk, natural disaster risk, volatility risk, or some combination of these premiums. The fund, in contrast, is actively managed on a bottom-up, long-only basis.

40 C is correct. When it comes to signal creation, the typical way mangers try to differentiate themselves is by interpreting public information in a unique way. Baylor believes that "our distinctive analysis process allows the firm to consistently add value for our investors."

A is incorrect because all information sources used by Baylor's team are publicly available. Even in a regulatory environment that seeks to reduce information asymmetries, Baylor's signal creation process is unlikely to face regulatory risks or legal scrutiny.

B is incorrect because Baylor's signal creation process relies not on retaining an information timing edge but on interpreting information in a unique way. All the investment team's information sources are available to the public.

41 C is correct. The change from a commingled fund to a separately managed account (SMA) will have the benefit of greater transparency. SMAs offer real-time, position-level detail to the investor, providing complete transparency and accurate attribution to the investor. Even if a commingled vehicle provides position-level detail, such information will likely be presented with a delay.

A is incorrect because the foundation is exempt from income tax, and therefore, achieving greater tax efficiency is not an objective.

B is incorrect because SMAs are likely to face higher transaction costs than commingled vehicles to the degree that trades cannot be aggregated to reduce trade volumes. These costs are a function of the extent to which the strategy is customized or traded differently to accommodate different investor needs.

42 B is correct. The performance-based fee is equal to the ad valorem fee (0.75%) when the gross-of-fees active return is 3.00%. The performance-based fee is calculated as follows:

$$\text{Base fee} + [\text{Share \%} \times (\text{Annual gross-of-fees active return} - \text{Base fee})] > 0.0$$

$$= \text{Total fee} \le \text{Maximum fee}$$

$$= 0.50\% + 10\%(3.00\% - 0.50\%)$$

$$= 0.75\%.$$

43 C is correct. An actively managed, tax-efficient US midcap equity portfolio satisfies all the requirements listed in the sample IPS. Being actively managed, the portfolio can comply with the prohibitions listed in the unique circumstances category of the IPS.

A is incorrect because the sample IPS states that the return objective is to outperform the benchmark by 250 bps per year, an outperformance unlikely to be achieved by an index-tracking fund. In addition, the fund may not be able to comply with the requirement that all securities be traded on a major exchange, given that it invests in companies of all capitalization ranges.

B is incorrect because many microcap stocks are traded over the counter. The sample IPS includes, under the legal and regulatory category, a requirement that all securities be traded on a major exchange. Also, in contrast to commingled funds, separately managed accounts offer potentially improved tax efficiency because the investor pays taxes only on the capital gains realized and allows the implementation of tax-efficient investing and trading strategies.

44 B is correct. Thornton mentions the key questions related to philosophy and process (and people) but does not touch on the portfolio aspect. This aspect of investment due diligence seeks to answer the following key question: Is portfolio construction consistent with the stated investment philosophy and process?

45 B is correct. Thornton requires a method that is objective, does not depend on timing and the amount of transparency, and defines the universe on the basis of the desired portfolio role. With a return-based style analysis, the risk exposures derived from the manager's actual return series have the advantage of being objective.

A is incorrect because with third-party categorization, database or software providers and consultants typically assign managers to a strategy sector, introducing the risk that the third party's definition may differ from the desired portfolio role.

C is incorrect because, unlike return-based style analysis, a holding-based style analysis depends on timing and the amount of transparency.

46 B is correct. Statement 2 is correct as written. Statement 1 should read, in part, "the *wider* the dispersion of the return distributions of the skilled and unskilled managers within the universe."

47 C is correct. Return-based style analysis is a top-down approach that involves estimating a portfolio's sensitivities to security market indexes representing a range of distinct factors. Thornton's large-cap computer hardware portfolio has a growth-oriented investment style. In addition to the data items mentioned in the vignette, a market index representing the style risk factor is most likely to be needed.

48 B is correct. The behavior described by Thornton is typically labeled "window dressing." Unlike holding-based style analysis, which is potentially subject to window dressing, the use of return data in return-based style analysis provides an objective style check that is not subject to window dressing.

READING

11

Topics in Investment Manager Selection

by Jeffrey C. Heisler, PhD, CFA, Jeffrey R. Nipp, CAIA, CFA, Morgan Webber, Ross Morrison, and Steven G. Bloom, CFA

Jeffrey C. Heisler, PhD, CFA, is at TwinFocus Capital Partners (USA). Jeffrey R. Nipp, CAIA, CFA (USA). Morgan Webber is at Adams Street Partners (USA). Ross Morrison is at Adams Street Partners (United Kingdom). Steven G. Bloom, CFA, is at ARC Fiduciary and Columbia University (USA).

LEARNING OUTCOMES

Mastery	*The candidate should be able to:*
☐	**a.** describe portfolio considerations in selecting investment managers;
☐	**b.** describe points to cover in an investment manager interview and during an on-site visit to the investment manager's firm;
☐	**c.** describe special considerations in the selection of equity portfolio managers;
☐	**d.** describe special considerations in the selection of fixed-income portfolio managers;
☐	**e.** describe special considerations in the selection of passive investment managers;
☐	**f.** describe special considerations in the selection of hedge fund managers;
☐	**g.** describe special considerations in the selection of private equity managers;
☐	**h.** describe special considerations in the selection of real estate managers;
☐	**i.** describe considerations in monitoring investment managers;
☐	**j.** define style drift and judge whether style drift has occurred;
☐	**k.** describe costs and other considerations in terminating and replacing investment managers.

INTRODUCTION

1

The selection of an appropriate investment manager is a challenge with important financial consequences, not only for the investor but for the many investment professionals involved in constructing portfolios of assets. Using the services of an external portfolio manager, whether through a pooled investment vehicle (e.g., mutual fund in the United States, unit trust in the United Kingdom, or SICAV in the European Union) or directly through an individually managed portfolio, introduces a principal–agent relationship in which it becomes critical to understand the incentives of managers and to have confidence that the managers' interests remain aligned with those of the investor (client).[1] In order for the investor to assess the alignment—or possible misalignment—of interests, the manager must be willing to provide some agreed-upon minimum level of transparency. (Transparency is a term that rose to common usage as hedge funds, which have not historically been subject to the disclosure requirements imposed on registered investment vehicles, became more popular. It is used to describe the openness of the manager with respect to discussing details of investment performance, philosophy, process and organization.) Because the level of transparency required by regulators varies considerably across countries and investment vehicles, the investor must build their own understanding of the drivers of the manager's investment success and the likelihood that it will be repeated. Although this reading will focus on investment aspects of manager due diligence, operational characteristics and their adequacy for the strategy and assets under management are also critical to this assessment. Together, investment and operational due diligence allow the investor to evaluate the alignment of interests between the manager and the investor.

The goal of this reading is to integrate the many elements of investment manager due diligence into a hire/fire decision in the context of the investor's overall portfolio.

This reading assumes that the investment policy statement has been drafted, the asset allocation determined, and the decision to use an outside investment manager has been made. The focus is on tools and techniques to use in determining which manager offers the "best" means to implement or express those decisions. The reading is organized as follows:

- Section 2 places investment manager selection in the context of the total portfolio;
- Section 3 builds out the general manager research framework while sections 4 through 9 highlight considerations specific to axtive and passive equity and fixed-income manager selection (including quantitative equity managers), as well as hedge fund, private equity, and real estate manager selection;
- Section 10 discusses monitoring existing managers, including a discussion of the costs and benefits of replacing an investment manager; and
- The final section summarizes selected important points.

2 PORTFOLIO CONSIDERATIONS IN INVESTMENT MANAGER SELECTION

In many cases, investors seeking to construct a well-diversified portfolio employ multiple investment managers and/or implement using multiple investment strategies from a single manager. Accordingly, each individual manager or strategy must be considered not only in isolation, but also in terms of its contribution to the overall

1 We make frequent use of the terms "investor" and "client" throughout the reading. Generally, the term "investor" represents the asset owner who is seeking to hire a manager for a portion of their assets. But at times that entity or individual is a "client" of an investment manager. Furthermore, manager research is often conducted by manager research analysts at an investment consulting firm or a "manager of managers" investment advisory firm. For simplicity, we use the term "investor" to encompass those performing this function whether they are the asset owner or the manager research analyst.

portfolio. The concept is similar to that of building a portfolio of stocks, bonds, or other assets—each individual investment must meet established standards, while also being an appropriate holding in the context of the overall portfolio.

This section introduces and describes general qualitative and quantitative considerations of portfolio fit that arise when an asset owner or adviser is contemplating the addition of an investment manager to an existing portfolio of managers. The terms "investment manager" or "manager" are used to include a broad range of investment vehicles, including pooled vehicles and separate accounts. We discuss how a manager fits into an existing portfolio, evaluating the decision to hire in terms of meeting the return and risk objectives and constraints of the investor as well as the efficiency of the overall portfolio. We will use the term *manager structure* to refer to the characteristics of a portfolio of managers, including such characteristics as the number of managers and the size of the allocation to each, the allocation among active and passive investment strategies, and the allocation of active risk among managers. This section focuses on the portfolio context of manager selection.

2.1 Portfolio Context for Manager Selection

Before hiring a new manager, an investor should evaluate the existing portfolio structure and framework, including asset class representation and weightings, risk factor exposures, and the number and types of managers employed. Risk budgeting and fees are important elements of this evaluation. Risk budgeting—the allocation of the investor's risk tolerance among asset classes, investment strategies, and investment managers—provides a framework for ensuring that the investor's willingness to assume risk is allocated to asset classes and managers where the risk taking is most likely to be rewarded. To build an effective portfolio, the investor should be able to define risk, identify the acceptable level of overall risk, and identify the acceptable sources of that risk. Assessing the fee efficiency of the total portfolio is also an important element of the manager structure; the investor must be cognizant of the consequences of hiring too many managers. Employing multiple managers that provide similar exposures may mean losing the fee breaks that managers often award to larger accounts.

The investor should regularly monitor whether the portfolio is consistent with the structure detailed in the policy document that governs the pool of assets. In the case of a mutual fund, a unit trust, or a SICAV, the policy is governed by the prospectus. In the case of a pension or endowment fund, the policy document is most likely the investment policy statement. That policy document should be aligned with the investor's risk tolerance. Any gaps or biases in the existing portfolio relative to the policy should become evident in the course of this analysis. Although such gaps or biases are not necessarily a problem, they should be intentional and well supported by credible research.

Competing Views of Portfolio Structure

The following chart illustrates how capital allocation does not necessarily equate to risk allocation or return contribution; such factors as the volatility of each asset class, the correlation between asset class returns, and the expected returns of active managers within each asset class affect the components of each allocation–contribution measure. Investors should be aware of, and comfortable with, their allocation–return profile.

Capital Allocation, Risk Allocation, and Return Contribution

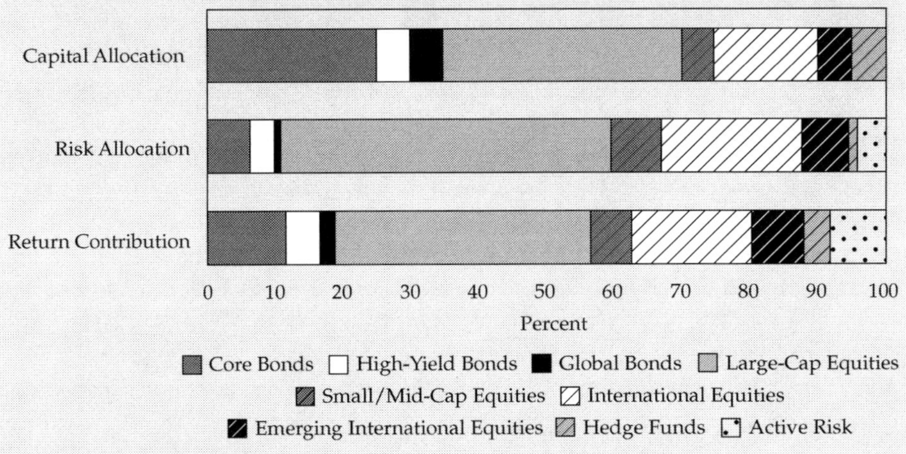

Source: Based on data from NEPC.

The concept of manager structure is often overlooked when evaluating how a manager fits into the overall portfolio; investors should pay close attention to the impact of manager structure on fees, monitoring complexity, reporting, and individual managers' ability to meaningfully contribute to the success of the overall portfolio. The allocation of assets among active and passive portfolio managers is an important part of the manager structure decision. Investors should use active managers only when they believe the market offers sufficient inefficiency, and if the manager demonstrates sufficient insights to exploit that inconsistency, to produce net-of-fee value-added performance. In addition, if electing to pursue active management, investors must ensure that they themselves have the resources and skills necessary to identify successful managers.

Some investors focus more on *manager* risk (often arbitrarily limiting the amount they invest with any one manager or strategy) than on *investment* risk, which results in inefficient portfolios that have too many managers, unnecessarily high fees, and insufficient diversification. Manager risk includes such issues as the percentage of a manager's (or a strategy's) assets under management the investor represents, or simply the amount of assets the investor has with any one manager or strategy. Such issues should be considered, but placing arbitrary limits on allocations without considering the impact on fees, liquidity, monitoring, and other factors can be counterproductive. Instead, such investors would be better served to identify the relevant investment risks, understand their tolerance for those risks, and strive to achieve consistency between the risk contribution made by each manager and the investor's conviction in that manager's ability to achieve the desired performance.

An investor may want to hire a new investment manager to do the following:

- Address gaps or biases in the existing portfolio structure relative to the desired portfolio structure as represented by the **policy portfolio**. (The policy portfolio is a conceptual portfolio allocated among asset classes or risk budgets in a manner the investor believes is most appropriate for his or her long-term risk and return objectives.)
- Reflect changes in the policy portfolio; the investor's objectives, risk tolerance, and/or constraints; or the investor's beliefs regarding the use of active managers.

- Take strategic or tactical advantage of a market opportunity identified by the investor.
- Implement new investment guidelines—for example, the adoption of ESG (environmental, social, governance) or SRI (socially responsible investing) policies or an initiative to allocate assets to managers meeting defined characteristics (e.g., emerging or minority-owned managers).
- Replace a manager that no longer meets the investor's investment or operational due diligence standards.

Any decision to hire a new manager should take into account all of the relevant costs and considerations associated with implementing that decision. It is essential to determine whether the potential improvement associated with adding any new manager(s) is warranted in light of the costs and goals of the investor, be they financial, legal, social, or other.

Once a thoughtful evaluation of the existing portfolio structure has taken place and the investor has determined that the addition of a new manager is justified, the hiring process should begin with the investor clearly defining the role the manager is to play, the source of its funding, the size of the new mandate, and the investment vehicle (e.g., separate account, commingled fund, mutual fund, exchange-traded fund [ETF], or other vehicle) to be used. Care should be applied in determining the appropriate vehicle; mutual fund portfolios, for example, often hold more securities and/or larger cash positions (for liquidity reasons) than separately managed accounts do, so investors need to understand any vehicle-specific portfolio differences and take those into account when structuring the investment.

Importantly, the investor should also specify the type of exposure the new manager is expected to provide; this exposure can be defined in asset class, risk factor, and/or performance terms, and should play a major role in the evaluation of prospective candidates for the assignment.

The universe of prospective manager candidates can be defined through a combination of approaches, such as third-party categorization, returns-based style analysis, holdings-based style analysis, and investor experience. The investor can then conduct qualitative and quantitative investment and operational research on managers of interest to identify those that best fit the defined role. As the investor analyzes candidate managers more closely, recognition of typical biases in each manager's portfolio is a key consideration, as is analysis of each manager's expected performance in various market environments.

By acquiring an accurate understanding of each manager's portfolio risk and return characteristics, investors can tailor the overall portfolio to their outlook, investment policy, and/or risk tolerance. Investors must be self-aware and honest about their ability to withstand deviations, especially downside deviations, from performance targets, and the period of time over which they will tolerate underperformance. Identifying their true risk tolerance will help them to make better and more enduring manager selection decisions. Similarly, investors need to be realistic about a manager's performance potential as well as about their own skills and the resources available to them to aid in the effort to select strong-performing managers. Overly optimistic assumptions often lead to disappointment when those assumptions are not realized.

Quantitative tools and qualitative factors should be used by investors to improve the effectiveness of the manager selection decision. Quantitative tools that can be used to assess the portfolio impact of various manager combinations are discussed in the following sections, and qualitative factors used in researching individual managers are discussed throughout the remainder of the reading.

EXAMPLE 1

The Importance of Portfolio Structure

1 Which gap in an investor's existing portfolio, relative to its policy portfolio, is *least likely* to require the hiring of a new manager?

A An underweighted position in equities as a result of capacity constraints having been reached by the single existing equity manager.

B An underweighted position in equities as a result of the investor's belief that the domestic equity market is currently substantially overvalued.

C An underweighted position in equities as a result of the recent termination of an existing equity manager, with the assets temporarily invested in cash.

2 If manager structure is over diversified, the *most likely* impact on the portfolio is:

A increased fee efficiency.

B decreased monitoring expense.

C decreased fee efficiency and increased monitoring expense.

Solution to 1:

B is correct. In this case, the decision to be underweighted in equities is an intentional one made by the investor for reasons the investor believes are well supported. The other cases reflect situations in which the underweighted position is the result of other factors, which create an unsupported inconsistency with the policy portfolio.

Solution to 2:

C is correct. Fee efficiency is likely to decrease because employing multiple managers with similar exposures could lead to losing fee breaks that are often awarded to larger accounts. Monitoring expense is likely to increase because each additional manager requires a separate vetting process.

2.2 Quantitative Tools

Quantitative tools play an important role in manager selection decisions, but they must be used with care to be effective. Few managers consistently outperform benchmark indexes in every year; most portfolios reflect style, valuation, or capitalization-size biases that may be in or out of favor during certain phases of the economy or the market.

Historical performance track records cannot be relied on to predict future performance, but they can help to identify conditions under which managers are likely to perform well or poorly. By combining the track records of potential new managers with the track records of existing managers in the portfolio, the investor can assess how an overall portfolio that includes a new manager might have performed. Such statistics as alpha, beta, tracking risk (tracking error), volatility, correlations, upside/downside capture, and maximum drawdown can be analyzed to evaluate various manager combinations. Returns-based style analysis can also be applied to potential manager combinations to help judge potential style drift or the impact of varying market environments.

Consider an equity manager focusing on stocks with high growth rates and strong price momentum. In the late 1990s, the manager would have performed well versus a broad-market benchmark but then would have underperformed following the bursting of the "technology bubble" in early 2000. Such a manager might have been an appropriate addition for an investor whose overall portfolio otherwise lacked exposure to these growth and momentum characteristics, but the decision should not have been driven solely by whether the manager was outperforming or underperforming at the time.

Another tool, holdings-based portfolio analytics, can help the investor identify characteristics that are consistently present over time in a prospective manager's portfolio to facilitate the selection of a manager that is likely to be a better "fit" with existing managers. By combining a prospective manager's representative portfolios proportionally with those of existing managers, the investor is able to assess the resulting risk factor exposures for the overall portfolio.

Investors should be cautious of falling into a "buy high, sell low" trap, swapping an underperforming manager in a given asset class for a manager that has historically outperformed. A study by Goyal and Wahal (2008) found that investors tend to hire a manager after that manager has produced large positive excess returns, but this return-chasing behavior rarely delivers positive excess returns thereafter.

Rather than chasing returns, and potentially punishing or rewarding managers for market conditions outside of their control, investors are better served by using historical track records to more fully understand managers and to establish appropriate expectations in various market environments. Analyzing the sources of returns and the reasons why results were good or bad during certain time periods, a key element in the manager evaluation process, will help in the selection of appropriate managers and the ability to use them effectively in a multi-manager structure.

EXAMPLE 2

Why Change Investment Managers?

Which factor is *most likely* to justify changes to an investor's manager lineup/structure?

A Three-year underperformance by an existing manager

B Departure of the portfolio management team from an existing manager

C Deliberate adjustments to an existing manager's portfolio holdings because of security valuations

Solution:

B is correct. The departure of the portfolio management team means that the manager probably no longer meets the investor's due diligence standards, and thus a change is called for. Underperformance, in isolation, does not typically justify a change, particularly when the results have been generated over a relatively short time period that may have been subjected to a particular set of market conditions. Making changes to portfolio holdings/positioning to reflect the impact of price changes is a natural part of active management.

A FRAMEWORK FOR INVESTMENT MANAGER RESEARCH 3

Effective research is the foundation on which successful investment manager selection decisions are made. To be effective, an investor should apply a structured process for evaluating managers, focusing on critical success factors that affect a manager's ability to achieve an investor's goals. Manager interviews are an important part of this process and help the investor understand the manager's culture and investment approach. A key aspect of investing is trust; uncertainty abounds and effective interviews provide a key piece of the puzzle as investors seek to gain comfort that the strategy is correctly understood and the interests of the manager and the investor are aligned. Effective manager interviews contain three components:

- Establishing an appropriate structure for interviews
- Thoughtfully interpreting the results of the interviews
- Recognizing the relevant limitations of the manager research process

This section provides guidance for conducting and assessing the results of manager interviews. Topics include

- interview preparation,
- agenda-setting,
- critical success factors,
- establishing meeting style,
- on-site meetings, and
- assessing the interview and on-site meetings.

This section also discusses issues associated with the consistency and transparency of the manager's communications, addresses the limitations that are inherent in any manager research process, and touches on areas of operational due diligence and organizational strength that are integral to the manager selection decision.

3.1 Interviews and On-site Visits

Manager research is an ongoing process requiring due diligence before, during, and after the selection of a manager. As part of that process, interviews should not be thought of as isolated events but rather as steps in the manager research continuum. By applying techniques that enhance the effectiveness of manager interviews, whether they occur on-site at the manager's office or at another location, the investor can make the most of the opportunity presented.

3.1.1 *Interview Preparation*

Prepare for meetings by gathering information about the manager and the investment strategy in addition to the performance track record.

Sources of information about the manager and the investment strategy include subscription-based manager databases; presentations, due diligence questionnaires, and other materials provided by the manager; publicly available information, such as prospectuses, records of public pension fund investment meetings, press articles, and regulatory filings; references; and background checks on the manager's personnel. These materials will contain a wealth of information regarding the manager's investment philosophy and process, the assets under management, and brief staff biographies.

Information about the performance track record includes an array of returns and statistics that can assist the investor in highlighting important aspects of the manager's performance, which can then be explored further in the face-to-face meeting with the manager. Statistics such as upside/downside capture, alpha, beta, drawdowns, and batting average over various time periods should be analyzed relative to appropriate benchmarks and peer group universes. Exhibit 1 illustrates the return and risk profile of an enhanced index US equity manager. Assessing performance using rolling multi-year periods can help to reduce the sensitivity of the analysis to particular starting points and highlight the impact of differing economic/market environments.

Examining such statistics enables the investor to better understand how consistent the manager's returns are over time, and to "stress test" the returns to understand how well the manager negotiated difficult market environments.

When assessing historical performance, investors should be aware of the nature of the track record and how representative it is of the strategy and vehicle being researched. For example, a fund that has undergone a change in investment approach or in the team managing the fund may have a long track record, but that record would be relevant only for the period in which the current approach and team have been in place. Furthermore, the quality of the performance statistics depends on the accuracy of the underlying performance data. Ideally, a manager's track record has been independently verified through credible audit sources, but such verification is not always available, and investors need to be cautious about over-reliance on historical track records.

Thorough preparation is important in order to make maximum use of the time the manager is allocating to the investor, especially with managers that do not find it necessary to grant many in-person meetings (typically high-performing managers with limited capacity to take on additional clients). Preparation helps the investor build credibility with the manager, which can lead to more useful, free-flowing exchanges that assist the investor in developing an in-depth understanding of the manager.

3.1.2 *Agenda Setting*

After the preparation work, the next step is to establish a defined agenda for each manager meeting by specifying in advance

- the topics to be addressed,
- who should attend from the investment management firm, and
- the best person or people to attend from the interviewing firm.

Recognizing the biases of the people performing the research and conducting the interview is important when making research assignments. Ideally, different people should conduct the initial and, if held, subsequent interviews to get different viewpoints.

Precise time allotments are not necessary when creating the agenda, but topic priorities should be clearly identified and consistent with the amount of time allocated. The agenda will depend in large part on the goals for the meeting and how well the interviewer already knows the manager.

Early in the due diligence process, the focus of the interview should be on building an understanding of the basics of the manager's

- investment philosophy and process;
- organization—the rationale for and impact of the manager's organizational structure, how investment teams function, and the organizational culture; and
- personnel—the firm's approach to recruiting and retaining personnel and reasons for any unusual staff turnover.

Follow-up meetings are more likely to address specific topics, such as

- obtaining an understanding of returns, their attribution;
- a review of current portfolio positions and expected market conditions;
- how and why the investment process has evolved over time; and
- lingering concerns or gaps in the investor's understanding of the manager.

Meetings should be as structured to be as efficient as possible. Basic facts about the manager and the strategy, such as assets under management, ownership structure, and performance records, will have already been gathered through pre-meeting preparation, but asking a few questions about such basic facts during the meeting can help the investor judge the consistency of the manager's message. Ideally, the

Exhibit 1 Quantitative Metrics in Manager Evaluation

Trailing and Calendar Year Returns	1 Year	3 Year	5 Year	7 Year	10 Year	Since Inception	2014	2013	2012	2011	2010	2009	2008	2007	2006	2005
Manager XYZ	14.22	20.73	15.42	7.8	8.81	8.93	14.22	34.37	14.65	4.34	11.54	23.76	−33.24	4.78	21.25	8.26
S&P 500 Index	13.69	20.41	15.45	7.27	7.67	7.99	13.69	32.39	16	2.11	15.06	26.46	−37	5.49	15.79	4.91
Excess Returns	0.53	0.32	−0.04	0.53	1.14	0.95	0.53	1.99	−1.35	2.22	−3.52	−2.71	3.76	−0.72	5.45	3.34

Rolling 3-Year Returns	Dec/14	Jun/14	Dec/13	Jun/13	Dec/12	Jun/12	Dec/11	Jun/11	Dec/10	Jun/10	Dec/09	Jun/09
Manager XYZ	20.73	17.50	17.14	18.81	10.09	15.90	12.93	3.75	−2.68	−8.64	−4.69	−6.31
S&P 500 Index	20.41	16.58	16.18	18.45	10.87	16.40	14.11	3.34	−2.86	−9.81	−5.63	−8.22

Risk and Regression	1 Year	3 Year	5 Year	7 Year	10 Year	SI	2014	2013	2012	2011	2010	2009	2008	2007	2006	2005
Standard deviation	7.82	9.68	13.18	16.55	14.53	14.17	7.82	9.48	11.46	15.72	19.29	21.67	20.74	9.83	6.32	8.25
Correlation coefficient	0.96	0.98	0.99	0.99	0.99	0.99	0.96	0.97	1	1	1	1	0.99	0.99	0.98	0.98
R-squared (R^2)	0.92	0.96	0.98	0.99	0.98	0.98	0.92	0.95	0.99	0.99	1	1	0.99	0.97	0.96	0.96
Annualized alpha	1.65	−0.48	−0.08	0.65	1.2	1.01	1.65	−0.88	−2.37	2.21	−3.09	−1.56	4.8	−0.69	3.3	3.12
Jensen alpha	1.65	−0.47	−0.08	0.64	1.17	0.99	1.65	−0.88	−2.37	2.21	−3.09	−1.56	4.77	−0.67	3.77	3.18
Beta	0.91	1.04	1	0.98	0.98	0.98	0.91	1.09	1.08	0.98	1	0.97	0.98	1	1.1	1.02
Max drawdown	2.6	7.37	15.29	45.31	47.94	47.94	2.6	3.55	7.37	15.29	13.2	18.09	34.67	5.07	2.77	3.26

Efficiency Measures	1 Year	3 Year	5 Year	7 Year	10 Year	SI	2014	2013	2012	2011	2010	2009	2008	2007	2006	2005
Sharpe ratio	1.81	2.14	1.16	0.45	0.51	0.53	1.81	3.62	1.27	0.27	0.59	1.09	−1.69	0	2.61	0.64
Treynor ratio	15.6	19.85	15.28	7.65	7.48	7.61	15.6	31.58	13.44	4.34	11.41	24.3	−35.73	0.04	15.02	5.15
Sortino ratio	4.17	4.17	1.99	0.63	0.71	0.75	4.17	9.14	2.1	0.47	0.97	1.73	−1.57	0.01	5.16	1.23
Calmar ratio	5.47	2.81	1.01	0.17	0.18	0.19	5.47	9.68	1.99	0.28	0.87	1.31	−0.96	0.94	7.67	2.54
Tracking error	2.32	2.01	1.83	1.96	1.89	1.85	2.32	2.33	1.34	1.59	1.12	1.47	2.37	1.64	1.38	1.7
Information ratio	0.23	0.16	−0.02	0.27	0.6	0.51	0.23	0.85	−1.01	1.4	−3.15	−1.84	1.59	−0.44	3.94	1.97
Upside capture	99.32	102.33	100.62	99.6	103.37	102.91	99.32	107.66	97.87	104.7	94.4	94.09	110.14	102.8	128.76	119.39

Exhibit 1 (Continued)

Efficiency Measures	1 Year	3 Year	5 Year	7 Year	10 Year	SI	2014	2013	2012	2011	2010	2009	2008	2007	2006	2005
Upside return	33.55	40.66	47.17	50.75	44.03	42.38	33.55	51.06	36.08	51.68	67.62	78.31	32.15	35.05	27.23	31.25
Batting average	0.42	0.47	0.45	0.46	0.54	0.53	0.42	0.67	0.33	0.67	0.17	0.33	0.67	0.58	0.92	0.67
Downside capture	91.9	103.1	101.17	97.73	98.06	98.39	91.9	110.88	107.01	93.51	104.81	100.35	93.82	107.94	96.76	91.33
Downside return	−16.44	−23.66	−31.69	−41.05	−36.6	−36.24	−16.44	−25.17	−31.42	−28.23	−50.61	−58.63	−52.54	−26.56	−28.6	−17.33

Source: Data from eVestmentAlliance.

majority of the meeting time can be devoted to discussing the rationale for the manager's organizational structure and its influence on the execution of the investment philosophy, the firm's approach to recruiting and retaining personnel, the manner in which investment teams function, the organizational culture, the investment research and decision-making process, and how varying market conditions tend to impact the manager's performance. In short, limit the focus on quantitative facts during the meeting and emphasize exploring the manager's thought processes and outcomes to build evidence of whether the manager has superior investment insight.

3.1.3 *Key Areas of Focus*

An effective framework for evaluating managers includes a qualitative examination of such factors as a manager's organization, personnel, investment philosophy and process, operational process, transparency, and costs. Although there is a great deal of objective information available to investors, and specific metrics can be objectively compared, manager research requires the investor to make subjective judgments about the manager being evaluated. Accordingly, having a well-defined, quantitatively supported framework for making these subjective judgments improves the consistency and effectiveness of the research effort. The people conducting the research should meet as many different managers as possible in order to develop insights into "best practices" and to establish a template of preferred attributes.

3.1.3.1 Alignment of Interests There are a wide variety of manager sizes, organizational structures, teams, and investment processes, and there is no single "right" way to structure a firm or manage portfolios. Nevertheless, knowledgeable manager research practitioners, supported by a variety of academic research studies, have identified a few key characteristics that successful managers tend to exhibit. For the purposes of the discussion below, we have grouped these characteristics into three categories: ownership and business management, personnel and compensation policies, and investment philosophy and process. These characteristics are closely associated with the alignment of interest issues.

Ownership and Business Management Broad-based self-ownership of a manager by its investment professionals (and other key employees) is widely considered to be a positive attribute, in part because resource allocation decisions are then made by people directly involved in portfolio management rather than by some potentially distant parent company with several subsidiaries competing for scarce resources. Investors also tend to perceive a more direct relationship between the success of the manager's business and their satisfaction with the manager's services when the business is employee-owned; they believe that an employee-owned manager will be more willing and able to make long-term decisions. But such self-ownership is not, by itself, enough to demonstrate proper alignment—a manager that uses its revenues to pay its staff as much as possible while not re-investing in the business is not putting the interests of its clients first. Self-ownership can also introduce issues of generational transfer—a manager should have clear plans for addressing the transition of ownership from employees that retire or depart from the firm to those that remain. This issue is particularly important for managers in which a small handful of employees own a majority of the business; investors should ask whether, how, and when ownership will be broadened, and they should evaluate whether the business is being managed for the benefit of investors or for the benefit of the owners.

When researching managers that are publicly owned, investors should ask how the firm balances market pressures for short-term profits with the need to think and operate more strategically. Can the manager demonstrate ways in which it has made long-term investments that provide the foundation for future success, even at the cost of lower near-term profitability? Similarly, investors who are researching a manager owned by a larger, more diversified parent company should explore the parent's financial expectations for the manager—are there specific goals with respect to growth in assets under management, profit margins, or client retention—and how those expectations impact the manager's ability to add people, systems, or other necessary infrastructure.

Capacity management (balancing the amount of assets a manager is willing to manage in a given investment strategy against the liquidity and opportunities available in the relevant markets) is another aspect of a manager's business operations that can directly impact alignment of interests. Controlling capacity is particularly important for managers investing in less-liquid markets or securities, and for those with large asset bases, even if they are investing in liquid markets, such as large-capitalization developed market equities. Investors should ask managers how they determine the capacity of their investment strategies, what those capacity levels are, and whether strategies are closed to new clients when they reach previously defined asset or trading volume levels. Liquidity evolves over time, so it is not unreasonable for a manager to occasionally redefine its capacity levels, but a manager's credibility is certainly enhanced by adhering to pre-established limits.

The evaluation of trading volume and costs is another key component of capacity assessment. Investors should ask managers how their position sizes compare to average daily trading volume (which determines how long it may take the manager to establish or exit positions); investors should also ask how the manager measures trading costs (including market impact) and what steps they take to minimize their impact on investment performance.

Fees are another area in which a manager can demonstrate strong—or weak—alignment of interests. The use of performance-based (rather than asset-based) fees is generally thought to be beneficial to alignment, but if not structured properly, performance fees can actually lead to misalignment. In a publication titled "Are Your Interests Aligned or Misaligned" (Towers Watson 2014), the consulting firm Towers Watson argues for fees that combine fixed and performance components, with the fixed component declining as assets grow (to discourage poor capacity management) and the performance component having a long measurement period, a high-water mark, and a deferred element. They also argue for the manager's fee to represent no more than half (ideally one-third) of the alpha generated and for performance fees to be used only when alpha generation can be clearly defined.

Finally, a manager should be able to demonstrate alignment of interests with a clean regulatory and legal record. This does not mean that any manager that is the subject of a lawsuit is failing to demonstrate alignment, but investors should be fully informed about all relevant issues so that they can make educated decisions about the manager's suitability.

Personnel and Compensation Policies Managers can demonstrate alignment of interests through their personnel and compensation policies, ensuring that they have the right resources in place to effectively execute their investment approach and that those resources have their compensation directly tied to their clients' success. The depth, experience, and stability of the investment team are factors that investors should consider when evaluating a manager, but these need to be evaluated in the context of the manager's investment approach. Team members who have encountered a variety of economic and market environments can provide perspective that less-experienced professionals lack. Stability helps the investor have confidence that the team in place today is responsible for the historical track record and, more importantly, will remain in place going forward, providing a consistent investment approach. It should be noted, however, that zero personnel turnover is not necessarily desired—the manager should demonstrate a willingness to refresh itself through staff changes as necessary.

Other important personnel considerations include the following:

- *Succession.* The manager's plans for team additions and/or the transition of responsibilities (for example, if someone retires).

- *Education.* The quality of team members' education. There is some academic research that supports a belief that portfolio managers who went to "better" colleges produce better investment performance. (Much of this research focuses on managers of US mutual funds, and may not be applicable in other regions or market segments.) This research is summarized in a *Financial Analysts Journal* article by Jones and Wermers (2011); a key point of the authors is that successful managers are better able to process information than their peers—and it is that processing ability that investors should attempt to analyze.
- *Contribution.* Determine the true contributions made by various members of the investment team: Are decisions made by a single person or small group? Or is there more broad-based involvement? There is no "right" way to make investment decisions, but knowing the contributions made by various team members helps the investor evaluate the likely consequences when and if someone leaves the firm.
- *Compensation.* Different pay structures can create different incentives. As such, it is important to understand how employees are compensated and how bonuses are determined and paid. Factors to consider when evaluating compensation arrangements include the following:
  - Are investment personnel compensated based on investment performance relative to a benchmark or relative to a peer group? Or are they compensated on the basis of growth in assets under management?
  - What are the time periods over which performance is assessed?
  - Are bonuses paid as a lump sum or over several periods?

Compensation structures that emphasize investment returns relative to appropriate benchmarks (where available) rather than relative to peer groups are preferred. Additionally, performance-based compensation structures are preferred over those that emphasize growth in assets under management. For truly long-term investors, multi-year (full market cycle) periods for assessing performance are preferred, as are structures that reduce the manager's incentives to inappropriately change the portfolio's risk profile at inflection points. Short-term, lump sum bonus payments can lead to a manager increasing portfolio risk in an attempt to earn an incentive fee or bonus if just shy of the threshold, or reducing risk to lock in the bonus if performance is well above the benchmark. Structures that require portfolio managers to invest at least part of their bonus into their own investment strategies are appealing because they promote the desired alignment of interests between the manager and the investor. Again, both academic research and research practitioners strongly support co-investment as a desired attribute.

Investment Philosophy and Process While assessing alignment of interests is a highly subjective exercise, investors should look for alignment between the manager's rationale for the investment processes it has in place and how the information obtained and insights developed are reflected in portfolios. The investor's evaluation of the manager should thus focus on the degree and consistency of the manager's "informational edge" or the magnitude and sustainability of the behavioral or structural inefficiency being exploited. Managers should be able to articulate what their competitive advantages are and demonstrate how their investment process is designed to best capitalize on those advantages. Investors must then determine whether such claimed advantages and process components make sense given the information obtained through the manager research process.

3.1.3.2 Sources of Information Many managers rely heavily on their own internal security research resources, whereas others rely more on sell-side and other external sources. Research by Busse, Goyal, and Wahal (2010) indicated a negative correlation between alpha and the use of "street" research, so investors should press managers that rely heavily on such research to justify their approach. Similarly, some managers make extensive use of quantitative models to conduct security analysis, whereas others focus on fundamental research gained through discussions with company management teams, suppliers, competitors, and customers.

Whichever approach is used, the manager should be able to demonstrate that it has the appropriate resources to gather and synthesize the research and apply it within the context of its stated approach. Investors should evaluate the depth and experience of the manager's research analysts or quantitative model builders. They should ask analysts about the type and frequency of their contact with company management, inquire about specific holdings, and examine research reports to judge the insight and consistency illustrated. To supplement this analysis, investors might also ask the investor relations staff of publicly traded companies whose securities are held in the portfolio about the quality of research conducted by a fundamental manager.

Many managers focus primarily on "bottom-up," company-specific research, but in recent years, it has become increasingly important for investors to understand how, if at all, managers take into account governmental actions and/or other "macro" factors (such as oil prices) that are not captured in their traditional research approach. Investors should also understand how the manager manages its currency exposure; for example, are equity portfolio managers also deciding whether, and how, to hedge currency risk in their portfolios? What qualifications do they have to make such decisions?

3.1.3.3 Approach to Portfolio Construction To be successful, managers must not only conduct or obtain good research but also appropriately reflect that research in the construction of portfolios. Those researching the manager should focus on the consistency, or lack thereof, between the manager's conviction level regarding individual holdings and the position size and, more importantly, the risk contribution of those holdings. A manager might, for example, have similar expected returns for two securities but hold a larger active position in one because it provides better diversification for the remainder of the portfolio. Investors should evaluate how, and under what circumstances, positions are added to portfolios, and to what extent such factors as valuation, overall market conditions, or liquidity impact the timing of portfolio additions. Country, currency, sector, and security weights, both absolute and benchmark-relative, should also be examined and discussed with the manager.

Questioning should also extend to the overall sell discipline of the manager: Does it make sense? Is it contributing to portfolio performance? Is it consistently executed? Such questions apply to both holdings that have performed well, and thus have become larger contributors to portfolio risk and returns, and to those that have underperformed. For poor performers, investors should ask whether there is a standard process for re-examining such holdings and whether a "stop-loss" limit is applied. The more concentrated the portfolio, the greater the chance that underperformance of a few holdings can significantly affect portfolio returns, so managers need to demonstrate discipline in dealing with underperformers. Again, investors should be looking for consistency between the portfolio's current positioning and the manager's current level of conviction.

Additionally, the manager should be asked about its approach to risk management and the use of risk models: How and when are they used, what biases do they tend to show, and are those biases intentional? For this research, it is helpful for investors to have access to their own quantitative data, such as performance records and portfolio risk analytics. These data do not predict how the manager will perform going forward, but they can provide investors with the basis for questions to ask during manager meetings. Questions derived from risk analytics could focus on the security (and/or macro) research process, portfolio position sizing and adjustments over time, risk definition/monitoring/control (especially how poorly performing holdings are addressed), and portfolio characteristics, particularly if they have changed over time.

Performance records can be used to generate questions regarding the impact of differing market environments, the return contribution attributable to various team members and components of the investment process, and the link between past performance and the manager's business growth (or decline). Managers should be able to clearly articulate why their results were good or bad in the past and what performance expectations are appropriate going forward. Combining holdings-based analysis of the historical portfolio composition with performance results in corresponding periods can help investors develop appropriate expectations.

For taxable investors, the tax implications of a manager's approach should be evaluated. Strategies that have high turnover and short holding periods tend to be less tax efficient than low-turnover, long-term strategies. It is helpful to examine before- and after-tax results and understand how the manager balances tax and investment considerations in constructing portfolios.

EXAMPLE 3

Effective Manager Research

1 Which topic is typically the *most* productive to focus on during a manager research meeting?

   A The professional biographies of investment team members.

   B The rationale for changes to portfolio holdings and positioning.

   C The growth in assets under management in various strategies offered by the manager.

2 Which characteristic *best* demonstrates an alignment of interests between the manager and the client?

   A Basing investment professionals' bonuses on the amount of assets managed.

   B Basing investment professional's bonuses on long-term, benchmark-relative performance.

   C An ownership structure in which 100% of the firm is owned by its founder and her family.

3 Which of the following questions might be asked during an assessment of a manager's investment philosophy and process?

   A One security in the portfolio declined 25% during the period under evaluation. What is the process for reviewing such securities, and what is the current view of that holding?

   B The manager's parent bank recently announced a merger with another bank that also has an asset management subsidiary. Will the two managers be combined into one entity, and which functions may be consolidated?

   C The three most senior members of the investment team are all over age 60. What are their plans for retirement, and who will succeed them when they leave?

Solution to 1:

B is correct. Although all of these topics are important to cover in developing an understanding of the manager and its investment approach, such factual information as professional experience and assets managed can be addressed through pre-meeting research, leaving valuable meeting time for investment team members to explain how the investment process is exemplified by the positions in the portfolio.

Solution to 2:

B is correct. Clients are most likely interested in an active manager's ability to outperform relevant benchmarks (or a passive manager's ability to track benchmark performance), so paying investment professionals on this basis aligns interests. Paying on the basis of assets, rather than performance, could incentivize investment professionals to attempt to manage more assets than the strategy has capacity for, leading to impaired returns in the future. A concentrated ownership structure raises the risk that business management decisions, such as whether to invest in new staff and/or analytical systems, will be made to benefit the majority owner rather than clients and the manager's other personnel.

Solution to 3:

A is correct. Answers B and C are related to the manager's organization and personnel, not its investment philosophy and process. Although important, questions about these issues are not based on the investor's analysis of the manager's performance and/or portfolio compensation, which is what provides the basis for such questions as those in answer A.

3.1.4 *Establishing the Meeting Style*

In all research meetings, those doing the interviewing should try to avoid having the manager simply lecture them or walk page-by-page through a formal presentation. Instead, the meeting should be interactive, with the investor asking open-ended questions of the manager to get the manager's personnel to describe, in their own words, the organization, team, and investment process. Many managers love to talk about individual portfolio holdings, so if the investor comes prepared with informed questions—having done his or her own research on a few holdings—a constructive dialogue can take place.

As with investment management approaches, there is no single "correct" style for manager research meetings, and the meeting style can vary depending on the objective of the meeting and the point at which the meeting occurs in the due diligence process. Nevertheless, the style used should be natural, efficient, and focused (as well as consistent across managers), with the goal of *evaluating,* not just reporting on, the manager. The investor can limit the amount of "selling" that the manager does by specifying the agenda, understanding the roles of the people involved, and controlling the meeting to ensure that the relevant points are properly addressed.

3.1.5 *On-Site Meetings*

There are no substitutes for on-site meetings. Although all of the preceding comments apply to meetings held at any location, on-site meetings at the manager's office provide an opportunity for more in-depth analysis. When visiting a manager's office, the investor should do the following:

- Make an effort to meet people on the manager's staff that would not typically be available for meetings at another location (e.g., research analysts). Meeting with people both individually and in groups can provide useful insights into both the day-to-day activities and the culture of the organization. One particularly useful exercise is to sit in on a manager's internal investment decision-making meetings, which often reveal interesting insights into team dynamics and decision making. Individual meetings with junior team members are also important because the junior members may be more comfortable discussing the firm and their role without their superiors in the room.

- Review written research reports to evaluate the depth of the manager's research and how consistent the information is in reports written by different analysts. Managers may be reluctant to allow such documents to leave their office but should allow them to be viewed on site.
- Request a demonstration of risk systems and other analytical tools used by the manager, and talk to traders about how they communicate with portfolio managers, source inventory, and execute trades, as well as how their performance is measured and what input, if any, they have into investment decisions and capacity considerations.
- Conduct in-depth operational due diligence. Examine and discuss compliance manuals, trade allocation policies, disaster recovery plans, external service provider selection and monitoring, fee calculations, personal trading policies (including whether investment team members invest in their own strategies), error mitigation procedures, and client reporting. There is also a cultural element to on-site operational due diligence because the investor can gauge the importance the manager places on the infrastructure of the firm.

The insights obtained through impressions and anecdotes can be invaluable, particularly if this information is at odds with what the manager claims in presentations or one-on-one. For example, does the firm claim a collegial and team-based approach yet office doors are closed and there is little apparent interaction among personnel? Do portfolio managers sit near analysts and traders?

In short, on-site visits should involve interactive observation as much as possible, not just passive observation. Managers are in "sales mode" when investors visit and often say what they think the investor wants to hear. Accordingly, it is often the "softer" information that is gathered from on-site meetings that is most valuable. Such real-life examples as an investor encountering an employee crying in the bathroom because of fear of an imminent layoff are rare, but any manager's office will contain clues about the firm's culture and priorities. Is there expensive artwork on the walls, or is the design more understated? Do employees defer to the firm's senior leaders, or is there more broad-based, informal interaction? Such information is very useful in helping an investor determine whether they will be comfortable working with the manager.

EXAMPLE 4

The Importance of On-site Visits

1 Which of the following is **not** typically an advantage of conducting research meetings on-site at a manager's office instead of at other locations?

   A Ability to discuss security holdings with portfolio managers

   B Ability to meet a variety of staff members, covering both investments and operations

   C Ability to receive hands-on demonstrations of analytical systems used in the security research and portfolio construction processes

2 Which of the following research techniques would **not** be used by an investor for the purpose of judging the consistency of a manager's message?

   A Conduct on-site research meetings at the manager's office.

B Meet with different members of the manager's staff, both individually and in groups.

C Maintain detailed records of interactions with the manager, and retain documents and materials provided by the manager.

Solution to 1:

A is correct. Simply discussing portfolio holdings or the overall investment process can be done effectively at any location, but gaining access to systems and/or people that are not generally available outside of the manager's office is a primary reason for conducting on-site due diligence.

Solution to 2:

A is correct. Merely conducting on-site meetings still leaves the investor vulnerable to inconsistencies in the manager's message and behavioral biases that can impact the investor's evaluation of the manager. These issues can best be addressed through a disciplined, well-documented, wide-ranging research process that incorporates multiple points of contact with the manager and detailed notes about those discussions.

3.1.6 *Assessing the Interview and On-site Meeting*

As mentioned previously, conducting manager research meetings is not simply a "check the box" exercise, but it should allow the investor to build a better understanding of the manager and its investment process as well as to judge the ability of the manager, the repeatability of the process, and whether the manager's interests are aligned with those of the investor. Three important factors in these judgments are consistency, organizational strength, and transparency.

- *Consistency.* Inconsistencies in a manager's descriptive material or in answers to questions may serve as a warning flag with respect to the manager's investment process. Investors should evaluate whether the manager's statements are consistent with written documents and materials and ask if not, why not? Also, investors should evaluate whether documents or materials have changed over time and ask if so, why? Any restatement of performance or material changes to documents requires an in-depth, credible explanation. Are answers to questions consistent with previous answers? Again, if not, why not? Obviously, keys to judging consistency are to have good records of previous meetings with the manager and good retention of documents and materials—reinforcing the idea that manager research is an ongoing process.
- *Organizational Strength.* A strong organization has the necessary policies and procedures in place to properly support the trading and investment activities of the manager. All managers must have robust trading platforms, strict controls on movements of cash, and well-defined contingency plans to address unforeseen events, including cyber-security threats. In addition, the manager should be focused on building a strong and viable business with proper staffing across investment and non-investment functions. Following the interviews and on-site visits, the investor should be able to answer the following questions:
  - Does the firm have sufficient staffing, of sufficient experience and expertise, to support the continuity and integrity of the business?
  - Have there been any key personnel or compensation changes?
  - Are the firm's hiring plans aligned with the anticipated growth of the business?
  - Is there a clear segregation of duties, with no conflicts of interest?

- *Transparency.* Was the manager forthright in answering questions? An inability or unwillingness to answer questions is a clear red flag. The inability to answer raises questions about the robustness of the investment process. A lack of willingness to answer should make the investor question the alignment of interests. Also, does the manager make the appropriate people available for meetings, particularly those held on site? Although there is a balance between how much time a manager spends on investment decisions versus on business development, the people making the investment decisions are the ones the investor is evaluating. The same holds true for operational due diligence: Are appropriate staff valued and made available? Is the manager willing to demonstrate its operations? Loose operational controls, which are the source of potential errors or fraud, are extremely hazardous to investors and can often be identified through interactive observation of hard evidence, such as a review of the trading process and conducting background checks.

Trade Processing

A review of the trade process typically involves tracking multiple trades through the manager's order management systems and middle office systems, as well as the reconciliation of trades. When evaluating a manager's trade processing function, the investor should look to answer the following questions:

- *Trade processing* translates the investment idea into a market order. How are trades entered into the trade systems? Do the systems mitigate the risk of manual entry? How are trade errors handled? How are trades placed—for example, with multiple brokers, on-line, and so on? Are the internal systems robust enough to handle the volume of trades generated by the manager?
- *Execution* translates the market order into a portfolio position. Which individuals have trading authority? Is there a segregation of execution and trade entry duties? Who has the authority to place trading limits on traders?
- *Reconciliation* confirms the trade among the parties involved. How frequently are trades reconciled? How are discrepancies reconciled? How active is the manager in the process?

The ideal is a trade process that efficiently translates investment ideas into portfolio positions while still providing for sufficient oversight and control, mitigating potential errors, and providing for the correction of any errors.

As with any exercise that contains subjective elements, manager due diligence has inherent limitations that affect its effectiveness. Two primary limitations are behavioral biases on the part of the investor and fraud on the part of the manager.

Behavioral Biases Investors' behavioral biases interfere with effective investment manager due diligence. When making a large purchase such as a house or a car, it's quite logical for people tend to do business with people they like—and trust. It is not surprising, then, that investors tend to invest with people they trust and like. However, charm and good presentation skills do not necessarily equate to investment skill and style does not necessarily equate to substance. This is linked to the representativeness bias in which decisions are made on the basis of stereotypes. To help control this bias, investors should continually review notes to gain insights from general statements, use quantitative analysis to support (and challenge if necessary) the qualitative analysis, and have a systematic process for evaluating managers without taking shortcuts.

Of course, the quantitative analysis itself is also subject to bias. Just because something can be measured does not mean that it is relevant, and investors should resist the temptation to put too much emphasis on performance track records that are of short duration and/or were achieved during market environments that may or may not be repeated. Perhaps the biggest behavioral bias is the tendency to extrapolate, preferring managers with strong recent performance and shunning recent underperformers. The more information an investor has about a manager and the market(s) the manager invests in, the better prepared the investor is to appropriately evaluate the manager and avoid biased decisions.

Fraud If an investment manager is intent on committing fraud, even a thorough interview process and on-site meetings cannot guarantee there will be no unpleasant issues or surprises. It can be difficult to identify a well-crafted and well-executed fraud. For investors, the best defense against fraud is thorough operational due diligence combined with an in-depth understanding of the investment strategy—if investors cannot understand a strategy, they should not invest in it.

Interviews and on-site visits are valuable tools in the manager research process, furthering the understanding of the manager's investment process, skill, and alignment of interests with clients. As with all tools, they have their uses and limitations. This section has described a process for conducting interviews and on-site visits, provided guidance for how to interpret findings, and reviewed potential limitations. Ultimately, manager research and selection involves a combination of art and science, and the decision maker must develop their own philosophy and approach to incorporate information gained from interviews and visits into their research framework.

EXAMPLE 5

Building a Better Understanding through Effective Due Dilligence

1 Which of the following data sets is *most* reliable when building your understanding of a manager's expected performance?

   A A 10-year track record for a non-US developed markets equities manager launching an emerging markets equity product.

   B A five-year track record, established during an equity bull market, for a long–short equity manager.

   C A three-year track record for a leveraged version of the manager's flagship product, which has a 10-year track record.

2 Which of the following is a technique that manager researchers can use to limit the impact of behavioral biases on their evaluation of a manager?

   A Have multiple people research the manager over the course of the research process.

   B Conduct qualitative research only on managers that have ranked in the top quartile of the relevant peer group universe over the past three years.

   C Ask the manager's personnel about their hobbies and interests outside of the office, and spend time in meetings discussing non-investment topics of interest to both the researcher and the manager's personnel.

Solution to 1:

C is correct. Although the track record for the leveraged product is relatively short, the investment processes of the leveraged and unleveraged products should be substantially similar. Experience managing non-US developed market equities does not directly translate to the management of emerging market equity portfolios; it is important to explore what additional skills or resources the manager has acquired to support its emerging markets investment activities. A track record produced during a strongly trending (bull or bear) market will not assist in developing insights into the manager's skill at hedging the portfolio in difficult markets.

Solution to 2:

A is correct. Having more than one person participate in the research on a manager can reduce the impact of personal biases that any one researcher may possess. Although discussing non-investment related issues may help the researcher build rapport with the manager's investment team, such discussions increase the potential for the researcher's judgment to be influenced by a perception that they and the manager's team are "similar," creating a bias that favors the manager. Focusing only on managers that have performed well recently is an example of extrapolation, in which the researcher assumes that historical performance results are, in isolation, an indication of investment skill.

4 CONSIDERATIONS IN THE SELECTION OF ACTIVE EQUITY MANAGERS

Proper benchmarking is particularly important for analyzing the performance of active equity managers. Benchmarks in any asset class should be transparent, investable, and consistently defined, and should appropriately represent the available universe of securities consistent with a manager's approach. Specifically for equity managers, there has been a proliferation of capitalization size, style-specific, and factor-based benchmarks established in recent years, and there has been a corresponding proliferation of investment vehicles (primarily ETFs) designed to track the performance of these benchmarks. So-called "smart beta" strategies contain elements of both active and passive management, often using rules-based portfolio construction techniques to build portfolios with the desired characteristics. With the introduction of these vehicles, investors' ability to efficiently and inexpensively gain exposure to many of the characteristics represented in an active equity manager's portfolio has increased. Properly specified benchmarks help investors determine what a manager's "true" alpha has been and how much apparent alpha has simply been a result of particular biases in favor of certain systematic risk exposures that could be implemented at a much lower fee. For example, it has been well documented that such factors as value and small size have tended to produce excess returns relative to broad market equity indexes over the long term; a manager whose portfolio displays consistent biases to one or both of those factors is not necessarily demonstrating skill. In hiring a particular manager, an investor may be willing to accept certain biases relative to a broad market (not style- or capitalization size-specific) benchmark, but the manager should be measured against a benchmark that takes those biases into account to the extent possible.

Active share is a useful concept in illustrating the extent to which an equity manager's portfolio holdings differ from those of a benchmark index and should be considered in conjunction with the manager's tracking risk (tracking error) and the fee that a manager charges. Investors should also consider the extent to which the manager will hold cash or attempt to time its market exposure; if holding cash positions is part of the investment process, how, and by whom, are such allocation decisions made, and what information is used to make them? The investor should consider a manager's cash positions in the context of the investor's overall portfolio, recognizing how such positions, when combined with those of other managers, may affect the investor's total allocations relative to investment policy.

4.1 Additional Considerations in the Selection of Quantitative Equity Managers

Quantitative equity managers can be broadly defined as those that conduct research and construct portfolios through the systematic application of financial, pricing, and other publicly available information rather than through qualitative evaluation of company management and strategy. For many investors, the evaluation of quantitatively oriented equity managers is difficult, in part because the strategies used by such managers may involve statistical techniques and terminology that are not well understood by the investor. Investors should not hesitate to ask as many questions as are necessary to develop a good understanding of the process. The manager should be able to explain its process in terms that can be understood by the investors and, as discussed in the previous section regarding on-site visits, an in-person demonstration of the modeling and portfolio construction process can be particularly helpful.

Particularly important when researching quantitative equity managers (although not limited to such strategies), investors should investigate whether the manager understands the extent to which other managers are using similar factors in their models, thus creating the potential for "crowded trades" that may limit market liquidity when it is most needed. As an example, in August 2007 managers using similar valuation and momentum factors were negatively affected by a sharp drop in the price of stocks held in common across multiple managers' portfolios. Simultaneous selling of these positions exacerbated the price decline and many quantitative equity strategies significantly underperformed their benchmark indexes despite previously low tracking risk, thus creating the type of unexpected negative surprise that investors thoroughly dislike.

The Impact of Crowded Trades

Quantitative market neutral equity (QMNE) funds and other absolute return-focused strategies, seek to exploit price differences between securities or portfolios with similar risk exposures and benefit as these price difference narrow. The availability of such opportunities tends to decline with volatility. Market volatility declined consistently throughout the early 2000s. In response, many QMNE funds began to increase portfolio leverage to maintain their return and volatility targets. Increasing leverage, however, makes the strategy susceptible to market shocks, particularly if similar positions are held across competing funds. Volatility (measured by the S&P 500 Volatility Index, or VIX) spiked in early August of 2007, causing many of these strategies to experience large drawdowns as the equity markets declined suddenly. Many QMNE funds tend to have rigorous risk management policies that reduce exposure to losing positions in an attempt to limit overall portfolio losses. If too many funds seek to cut exposure in the same securities at the same time, however, (as happened in August 2007) it can result in an unbalanced and illiquid market. The use of leverage in QMNE funds exacerbated the selling pressure and many of the funds experienced redemptions or ended up closing.

Performance attribution is also important in the evaluation of quantitative equity managers because it allows investors to focus on the extent to which results were driven by the investment process factors that the manager claims to be important elements of the investment process (stock selection versus sector allocation, for example). Although batting average can identify whether performance was narrowly driven by a few positions or more broadly by multiple positions across the portfolio, attribution can provide more details into the drivers of performance.

4.2 Operational Considerations for Equity Managers

Investors conducting operational due diligence on equity managers should do the following:

- Inquire about proxy voting policies and processes, which may be particularly important for certain investors and could thus play an important role in determining the suitability of a manager for a particular investor.
- Obtain information regarding a manager's operation of internal crossing networks. Such networks are often used by passive equity managers to limit trading costs—a simple example would be a passive S&P 500 manager with two clients, one of which wants to invest \$100 million and the other of which wants to withdraw \$100 million. The manager would simply transfer ownership of the underlying shares from the departing investor to the incoming one, using the incoming \$100 million to pay the departing investor. By doing so, the manager avoids having to sell and then repurchase the stocks in the portfolio on the open market, incurring commissions and market impact costs. Regulators have strict rules about the operation of such networks to ensure fair treatment of all of a manager's clients, so investors should understand how a manager's network functions and what controls are applied to it.
- Understand the manager's insider trading policies and its policies regarding the use of "expert networks" and other external information sources. Increased regulatory scrutiny of a manager's use of external research resources and its implications for insider trading elevates the operational (and reputational) risk associated with gaining that "research edge."

When Research Crosses the Line to Become Material Nonpublic Information

Two high-profile examples of firms running afoul of insider trading rules involve Galleon Group and SAC Capital Advisors. The head of Galleon, Raj Rajaratram, was convicted of insider trading for using material non-public information to buy stock in Goldman Sachs prior to the announcement that Warren Buffett had agreed to infuse \$5 billion into Goldman Sachs in exchange for preferred shares. He then sold the stock (the next day) once the Buffett infusion was public knowledge. At SAC, portfolio manager Mathew Martoma was convicted of using material non-public information regarding the development of an Alzheimer's drug.

In both instances, the guilty parties were sentenced to prison, and their investment management firms were closed. Both the US Securities and Exchange Commission (SEC) and the European Union have strict regulations against insider trading.

EXAMPLE 6

Equity Manager Evaluation

1 A useful technique that an investor can use to help specifically judge the quality of the insights generated by an active fundamental equity manager's security research is:

  A Evaluate the performance of the strategy over rolling multi-year periods relative to a benchmark index.

  B Analyze portfolio holdings over time to see whether the number of stocks held, and the capitalization size of those stocks, has changed.

  C Use publicly available information to conduct research on a few of the manager's holdings, and then ask the manager to discuss its analysis of those holdings and provide the supporting documentation.

2 Which of the following portfolio changes is *most likely* inconsistent with the manager's articulated investment style?

  A A manager that focuses on stocks with strong price momentum reduces its position in a stock that has outperformed other portfolio holdings.

  B A manager that focuses on stocks with low price-to-earnings ratios adds to its position in a stock after that stock has underperformed other portfolio holdings.

  C A manager that seeks to minimize tracking risk relative to a capitalization-weighted index adds to its position in a stock that has outperformed other portfolio holdings.

Solution to 1:

C is correct. The more information an investor has, the better questions that investor can ask the manager. It is especially helpful for the investor to recognize where a manager's view of a security differs from the consensus view—understanding the rationale for that divergence can provide valuable insight into the manager's approach. The other techniques listed are valuable components of manager research, but do not specifically address the quality of the manager's security-level analysis.

Solution to 2:

A is correct. A momentum-oriented equity manager would be expected to retain or increase its position in stocks that have performed well, not to decrease the position. The other two examples are consistent with the managers' styles—buying more of relatively inexpensive stocks or adding to positions that have grown in capitalization in order to closely track the index. Questioning managers about portfolio positioning, using examples of stocks bought or sold by the manager, is an effective way for an investor to judge the discipline of the manager's investment process.

5 CONSIDERATIONS IN THE SELECTION OF FIXED-INCOME MANAGERS

Fixed-income strategies differ in their focus on country, currency, and market sector exposures, so proper evaluation begins with correctly identifying a manager's strategy in order to make relevant comparisons to benchmarks and peers. Performance track records are typically readily available for fixed-income managers, but fixed-income security pricing is less transparent than equity pricing because the majority of bonds trade in over-the-counter markets, not on exchanges. Additionally, bond prices are frequently derived from pricing models; different pricing services use different models, so there may well be more than one quoted price for a bond, and these prices may not correspond to actual bid or sale prices.

Comparisons among fixed-income managers are also more difficult because of the limited consistency in the risk models and performance attribution systems used. Relative to equity managers, fixed-income managers generally have more decisions to make regarding the elements of portfolio structure. They must not only make decisions with respect to the individual securities and the allocation among industry sectors, countries, and/or currencies, but fixed-income managers are also often called on to determine portfolio duration, rating quality exposure, and market sector (e.g., government, corporate, mortgage) exposure.

As with equity managers, it is helpful to analyze both the fixed-income manager's sources of information and portfolio construction techniques. For security-specific research, many managers rely on their own internal credit research resources. Investors should examine a manager's security-specific research reports for insight and consistency, and if the manager also offers equity strategies, investors should explore how fixed-income and equity research is coordinated and shared. The manager should be able to demonstrate how their research results in better outcomes than simply relying on rating agencies.

For certain fixed-income market sectors, such as mortgage-backed securities, managers need analytical systems for modeling prepayments (the satisfaction of a debt, such as a home mortgage, prior to its official due date); homeowners paying off mortgages early impact the duration and cash flows associated with mortgage-backed securities. Investors should evaluate how, and by whom, those models were developed, how they are maintained and updated, how effective they have been, and how well the manager understands the strengths and weaknesses in the models they have built or chosen. Again, the manager should be able to demonstrate that it has the appropriate resources to apply their investment approach, so investors should evaluate the depth and experience of the manager's research analysts and/or quantitative model builders, and ask how they identify and compensate for known weaknesses in their models.

Fixed-income managers are faced with more top-down allocation decisions based on interest rate and/or credit spread forecasts and, accordingly, place greater emphasis on evaluating central bank policies and market sector valuations than is typical with equity managers. Investors must understand how a fixed-income manager conducts such research and to what extent the manager is willing to take duration or sector weighting positions that differ from the benchmark index. The overabundance of allocation and weighting decisions makes accurately benchmarking many fixed-income strategies difficult, so it is important for investors to understand what exposures they should expect from their managers.

The limited consistency among fixed-income managers in terms of the analytical systems, risk models, and attribution systems used in portfolio management arises because such systems are not easy to build and maintain given the large number of factors that influence bond pricing. Although some managers develop their own systems, others buy systems from external vendors. Managers should be able to explain their rationale for using the systems they do, how they are used, and how they influence portfolio construction. Again, portfolio characteristics consistent with conviction level is important, so country, currency, sector, quality, and bond weights (both absolute and benchmark-relative) as well as duration positioning should be examined and discussed with the manager.

Because of the limited transparency of fixed-income security pricing, managers should have consistent, well-established policies and processes for pricing portfolio positions. Sourcing of prospective securities has become increasingly important as brokerage firms have reduced their market-making activities, so managers should demonstrate strong capabilities in sourcing desired holdings, and they need to be able to address liquidity issues. Key questions the investor might ask: How do you handle significant client outflows resulting from investor concerns about rising interest rates negatively affecting bond prices? What is your policy for allocating a smaller-than-desired position across various clients' portfolios? How would such a smaller-than-desired position impact portfolio construction?

Some fixed-income managers have taken proactive steps to improve portfolio liquidity, such as breaking trades into smaller increments, building positions over longer periods of time, using electronic trading platforms, or using such instruments as credit default swaps and ETFs to gain exposure, especially in the corporate sector of the market. Investors should press managers to explain how they manage counterparty risk if they are using swaps, how their approach to trading and portfolio construction has adapted to the changes in bond market structure, and how they see the market evolving in the future.

5.1 Fixed-Income Manager Performance Analysis

The first step in conducting appropriate fixed-income performance analysis is to determine the goal of the mandate. Some fixed-income portfolios are designed as structured portfolios to produce returns relative to a specific liability profile, whereas others are designed as total return portfolios to outperform a benchmark index. For total return mandates, when analyzing a multi-sector fixed-income manager's performance, it is particularly important for the investor to understand the extent to which the manager's portfolios tend to have permanent biases toward or against certain market sectors—for example, it is very common for managers to persistently underweight the domestic government sector in favor of higher-yielding sectors, such as mortgage-backed securities, foreign bonds, or corporate bonds.

Regardless of sector, fixed-income returns are highly dependent on changes in interest rates and the shape of the yield curve. Potential value added by fixed-income managers is often limited because of the narrow dispersion of returns across bond market sectors and securities, which leads to a narrow dispersion of returns among fixed-income managers. Fees, therefore, are a critical consideration in evaluating fixed-income managers. A manager may have apparent alpha that has simply been a result of particular biases that could be implemented at a lower fee than an active manager typically charges. If such biases are persistently evident in the manager's investment approach, the manager may be delivering beta rather than alpha and may be less skilled than they claim, unable to justify the higher, active management fee they propose to charge.

As mentioned previously, performance attribution is often applied inconsistently among fixed-income managers given the difficulty in disentangling the many factors that influence the performance of fixed-income securities. Investors should ask managers how they conduct performance attribution and should use that attribution to evaluate whether results were driven by the investment process factors that a manager emphasizes. Attribution can also provide more details regarding the biases existing in the manager's portfolios, allowing the investor to inquire whether those biases are based on current market conditions or are more permanent.

5.2 Operational Considerations for Fixed-Income Managers

Given the issues mentioned regarding fixed-income security pricing, investors should inquire about a manager's compliance policies regarding pricing—policies that should be transparent, consistent, and realistic. Complex securities that require sophisticated models for pricing and evaluation can be difficult to value even during "normal" market conditions, and this complexity can create even greater difficulty during periods in which markets are stressed and liquidity is diminished.

EXAMPLE 7

Fixed-Income Manager Evaluation

1 Three fixed-income managers claim to derive the vast majority of their benchmark-relative performance from security and sector (government, corporate, mortgage, etc.) selection. Which performance attribution result would be inconsistent with the manager's professed skillset?

   A Manager A outperforms by 25 bps because of strong results from certain overweighted corporate bond holdings in the portfolio.

   B Manager B outperforms by 50 bps because of overweighting high-quality government bonds during a bear market.

   C Manager C outperforms by 25 bps because of having a significantly shorter-than-benchmark duration during a period in which the central bank raised market interest rates.

2 Which of the following is **not** common to both equity and fixed-income manager evaluation?

   A Security pricing data are readily available and transparent, and can be used by investors to question managers about individual holdings.

   B Performance records can be used by investors to evaluate how managers tend to perform in various market environments and how narrow or broad-based managers' results have been.

   C Investors should focus on both managers' sources of information and portfolio construction techniques.

Solution to 1:

C is correct. A manager (like Manager C) that focuses on security and sector selection to add value would not be expected to have the skill necessary to take significant benchmark-relative duration positions, so Manager C's outperformance is not consistent with its stated approach. Performance attribution can be challenging for fixed-income managers, but investors should be able to question managers about the sources of their returns and evaluate whether those sources are the stated areas of focus in the manager's process.

Solution to 2:

A is correct. Fixed-income security pricing is not transparent or readily available; managers often must determine prices by surveying brokerage firms, and liquidity can be variable.

6 CONSIDERATIONS IN THE SELECTION OF PASSIVE INVESTMENT MANAGERS

Because passive managers seek to closely match the risk and return characteristics of the benchmark rather than to outperform the benchmark, the focus of the manager research will be on the degree to which the manager tracks the index, net of fees, and the methodology for selecting holdings and constructing the portfolio.

6.1 Active vs Passive Manager Decision

A fundamental decision in the manager selection process is whether to use active or passive managers. The choice between active and passive managers is a function of the investor's assumptions about market efficiency, confidence in the ability to identify skilled managers, and the expectation that the manager can add value relative to the benchmark after fees and taxes in taxable portfolios.

Investor beliefs regarding the degree of market efficiency may vary across asset classes, capitalization ranges, and other investment characteristics. When an investor believes that a particular market is highly efficient, the investor would expect no net advantage to attempting to identify mispriced securities. Thus, that investor would likely prefer passive management in that market.

An active manager is expected to deliver positive alpha while still providing sensitivity to systematic risk factors similar to the benchmark. A limit on tracking risk is often specified as a constraint for active managers. Tracking risk (tracking error) is calculated as the standard deviation of the return difference between the manager and the benchmark. In general, as the constraints on tracking risk become tighter, the manager has less opportunity to add alpha. If the investor wants to track the benchmark very closely, a passive manager is more suitable than an active manager.

Rules-Based Active Investing

Rules-based active investing is an active approach that uses a rules-based system to weight each stock in an index. This approach grew out of the anomalies literature, in which early tests of the capital asset pricing model (CAPM) showed the model was insufficient and additional risk factors, such as size and style, also explained returns.

One rules-based approach is to equal-weight the securities in a capitalization-weighted index. This strategy avoids buying more of the stocks that have increased the most in price after the index has risen. Another approach is to assign a greater weight to low-volatility stocks or to weight by financial characteristics, such as sales, dividends, or cash flow.

Rules-based active investing takes on risk exposures that are not present in the index, and thus using this strategy inherently means greater tracking risk and underperformance in times when the risk exposures are not being rewarded. Because risk premiums rather than traditional stock picking drives investment returns, the evaluation of managers is similar to the evaluation of passive managers. The focus is on operational efficiency and the manager's ability to capture the desired risk premiums, in addition to an assessment of the construction of the particular factor.

6.2 Passive Manager Due Diligence

In passive investment manager selection, the manager's ability to capture the risk premiums of the benchmark is of paramount importance. Effective passive managers are expected to have relatively low tracking risk. The selection process seeks to determine whether the manager's investment process is effective and cost efficient in achieving the objectives of passive management. While passive managers typically charge lower fees than active managers within the same investment universe, even low fees constitute a drag on performance.

Sources of tracking risk include imperfect securities weightings (for example, those resulting from delayed adjustment to constituent changes), cash buildup (the portfolio is not 100% invested because of income, corporate actions, contributions, or withdrawals), transaction costs (trading to handle constituent changes and cash flows), and model error (statistical models for building index portfolios that do not own every index constituent and provide imperfect forecasts). Tracking risk may also arise from any premium and/or discount between the fund's NAV and its market price. This risk may arise when investing in a closed-end fund or in an ETF that has suspended the creation and redemption of shares.[2]

Equity managers can choose to construct passive portfolios either by full replication or through a sampling process.

- **Full replication** entails holding all of the constituents in the index at the same weight as the index. This approach is appropriate for large portfolios or indexes with a limited number of constituents. It would work for the FTSE 100 Index or S&P 500 Index but would be difficult for the Russell 2000 Index or bond indexes.
- **Sampling** involves holding a subset of the benchmark universe weighted to replicate the characteristics of the index in terms of factors, such as capitalization size, style, and sector exposure for equity indexes, or term structure and credit risk for bond indexes. Sampling works for even large indexes and can limit the number of portfolio holdings while optimizing to match risk premiums. Sampling has potential basis risk, which is the risk that the realized risk factors of the portfolio do not equal those of the benchmark.

Full replication of broad-market indexes is typically not possible for passive fixed-income managers given the unique characteristics of each bond issued by a government, corporation, or other entity, coupled with the frequent inability to buy the specific underlying issues in the market. Sampling is thus the methodology of choice for the vast majority of passive fixed-income managers. Investors should be aware that, in many cases, passive fixed-income portfolios do not track their benchmark indexes as closely as passive equity portfolios do.

Portfolio management issues to evaluate for passive managers include the following:

- The manager's rationale for their implementation methodology
- Whether ETFs, index futures, or other derivative instruments are used to invest any residual cash positions in portfolios (and thus reduce the tracking risk relative to the benchmark index)
- If derivatives are used, whether credit risk is associated with the instrument(s) used, and how such risk is managed

---

2 Suspending the creation and redemption of shares can result in premiums and discounts because the ability to arbitrage, which works to limit the spread between the market price and NAV, is removed. For example, if an ETF is trading at a premium, an investor could buy the underlying components at roughly the NAV and then exchange the basket for a share of the ETF, which is trading at the higher market price.

- Whether portfolio holdings are used for the manager's securities lending program, and if so, how the proceeds of this program are allocated between the manager and the investor
- How trading costs are managed, including the extent to which internal crossing networks, which match buyers and sellers without going through an exchange, are used to limit market impact.

EXAMPLE 8

Active and Passive Investment Managers

1 The choice between active and passive managers is a function of assumptions about:

 A liquidity needs of the investor.

 B market efficiency and manager skill.

 C manager skill and the investor's investment horizon.

2 If low tracking risk to the benchmark is desired:

 A a passive manager is more suitable than an active manager.

 B an active manager is more suitable than a passive manager.

 C either a passive manager or an active manager is equally suitable.

Solution to 1:

B is correct. Passive managers assume that markets are sufficiently efficient that there is no net advantage in attempting to identify mispriced securities. As such, they seek to replicate, not outperform, the benchmark. Tracking the benchmark is often specified as a constraint for active managers. That is, the manager is expected to deliver positive alpha while still providing systematic risk exposures similar to the benchmark.

Solution to 2:

A is correct. Close tracking of the benchmark is consistent with the assumption of market efficiency, making a passive manager more suitable than an active manager.

EXAMPLE 9

Passive Manager Evaluation

1 Simply selecting the lowest cost passive equity manager, the investor:

 A ignores liquidity.

 B recognizes that differences in performance might be the result of factors other than fees.

 C can be comfortable that the funds under consideration capture the desired risk exposures.

2 Which of the following is **not** an additional potential consideration when selecting a passive emerging market bond manager?

 A Beta risk

 B Country risk

C Currency risk

3 Tracking tolerance is:

A the manager's tracking risk target.

B the difference in return between the manager and the benchmark.

C calculated as the standard deviation of the return difference between the manager and the benchmark.

4 A sampling approach to passive management involves:

A actively selecting securities that are perceived to be mispriced.

B holding all of the constituents within the index at the same weight as the index.

C holding a subset of the benchmark universe weighted so that the portfolio's risk premiums match the benchmark's risk premiums.

5 The quantitative goal of replicating the benchmark does **not** entail:

A low tracking risk.

B high premium/discount.

C replicating the benchmark risk factors.

Solution to 1:

A is correct. A selection based only on fees ignores tracking error and other factors that might affect performance, such as vehicle structure. Furthermore, unlike index funds, which can be purchased and sold at their net asset value, ETFs are traded securities, introducing liquidity risk in the form of the bid/ask spread and market depth.

Solution to 2:

A is correct. Beta exposure is a desired characteristic when implementing a passive exposure. Depending on the underlying index and weighting methodology, selecting a passive emerging market bond fund may have potential currency, country, and credit risk considerations.

Solution to 3:

A is correct. Tracking tolerance is the manager's tracking risk target. Tracking risk is the difference in return between the manager and the benchmark, calculated as the standard deviation of the return difference between the manager and the benchmark.

Solution to 4:

C is correct. Full replication involves holding all of the constituents within the index at the same weight as the index. Active management seeks to select securities that are perceived to be mispriced.

Solution to 5:

B is correct. A quantitative goal of passive management is a low premium/discount to reduce potential tracking risk as the premium/discount changes through time.

CONSIDERATIONS IN THE SELECTION OF HEDGE FUNDS

7

A hedge fund is a privately offered investment vehicle generally available only to wealthy individuals and institutions, and it typically requires a high minimum investment. Similar to mutual funds, hedge funds pool capital from multiple investors and apply an investment strategy toward the goal of producing a desired return and risk profile. But hedge funds are different from mutual funds in several key aspects:

- Hedge funds generally invest in a wider range of securities than do mutual funds; many of those investments may be illiquid or substantially less liquid than the investments held by a mutual fund. Accordingly, most hedge funds have more restrictive redemption rules than a mutual fund.
- Hedge funds often make more extensive use of short positions (selling a borrowed security).
- Hedge funds are not subject to the same liquidity, governance, and reporting requirements as mutual funds are.
- Hedge funds are not subject to the limitations on the use of derivatives and leverage typically imposed on mutual funds.
- Hedge fund managers are usually compensated with a base fee plus a performance fee—a percentage of the returns they earn for investors—whereas mutual funds typically charge a fee based on the assets under management, irrespective of investment performance.

Each of these aspects affects the nature of the due diligence conducted by the investor.

Many investment management firms have recently begun to offer certain hedge fund strategies through mutual fund–like structures, often referred to as "liquid alts" in the United States or "alternative UCITs" in Europe. Despite the mutual fund structure, the evaluation of the liquid alts manager is substantially similar to the evaluation of a hedge fund.

7.1 Hedge Fund Strategies

Strategies used by hedge funds typically fall into one of the buckets defined in Exhibit 2. Any given hedge fund might specialize in a single strategy, whereas another may invest using multiple strategies. Each strategy may use leverage, less liquid or illiquid investments, and short selling in distinct ways that has implications for the due diligence conducted by the investor. Exhibit 2 presents a classification of major hedge fund strategies used by Hedge Fund Research, Inc., a data provider specializing in the hedge fund industry.

Exhibit 2 Hedge Fund Strategy Classifications

Equity Hedge	Event Driven	Macro	Relative Value
Equity Market Neutral	Activist	Active Trading	Fixed Income: Asset Backed
Fundamental Growth	Credit Arbitrage	Commodity Focus	Fixed Income: Convertible Arbitrage
Fundamental Value	Distressed/ Restructuring	Currency Focus: Discretionary	Fixed Income: Corporate

(continued)

Exhibit 2 (Continued)

Equity Hedge	Event Driven	Macro	Relative Value
Quantitative Directional	Merger Arbitrage	Currency Focus: Systematic	Volatility
Short Bias	Special Situations	Discretionary Thematic	Multi-Strategy
		Systematic Diversified	
		Multi-Strategy	

These strategies provide unique opportunities but can represent a steep learning curve for the investor, and each strategy presents unique due diligence challenges. To illustrate some of the potential challenges, a few of the strategies are described in the following.

- *Activist.* Take a large position in a company's shares with the goal of influencing corporate strategy or effecting a major change in the company. The manager seeks to add value largely through advocating financial or operational restructuring.
- *Distressed/Restructuring.* Purchase securities of companies or governments that are experiencing financial or operational distress or default or are in bankruptcy. Managers in this strategy must have a strong understanding of bankruptcy laws, negotiating skills to deal effectively with other stakeholders, and operational skills to be actively involved in company management decisions.
- *Equity Hedge.* Take long positions in stocks that are expected to increase in value and short individual stocks (or indexes) to profit from expected declines in value or to hedge out an undesired risk. Equity hedge strategies may be either fundamental (based on bottom-up security research) or quantitative (using a model to identify securities that are under- or overvalued). The long–short equity manager must have special capabilities to support active management of the net exposure (longs minus shorts) as well as an understanding of the unique risks inherent in shorting stocks.
- *Macro.* Take long and short positions in equity, fixed income, currency, and/or futures markets to express overall economic views across global markets. The information set required to manage a macro portfolio is immense, and managers must have the resources to acquire and analyze the data, as well as a network of contacts or information sources that will allow them to develop accurate expectations regarding economic trends.

7.2 Considerations in Selecting Hedge Funds

A key concept in hedge fund due diligence is transparency. Few hedge funds provide reporting at the level common for mutual fund and traditional investment managers, and they are often keen to protect the proprietary investment processes that they believe give them a competitive edge. But the broad ranging mandates allowed under most hedge fund documents—and the limited ability of investors to move their money if a manager is not executing as the investor expected—heighten the importance of developing a full understanding of a hedge fund manager's organization, investment process, performance, and fees. Although hedge funds do provide a prospectus and will provide monthly performance estimates and audited financial statements, these disclosures are not readily available to the public. Furthermore, an analysis based solely on return-level summary statistics and style analysis, although helpful, may not capture all of the risks that are meaningful to the investor, particularly if the manager pursues a broad mandate spanning multiple markets and multiple strategies. For example, without access to holdings-level information, the investor researcher cannot aggregate the hedge fund's exposures with those of its other managers to understand the risk exposure of the total portfolio.

Thus, thorough up-front due diligence is essential to understand the investment and non-investment risks inherent in an investment with a hedge fund and to establish an appropriate and ongoing level of dialogue with the manager. If the manager demonstrates an unwillingness to provide the types of disclosure required to conduct effective due diligence, the investor should be concerned about the post-investment alignment of interests.

As with other managers, the investor needs to evaluate the investment philosophy, process, people, and portfolio construction. Additional due diligence issues for hedge fund manager evaluation include the following:

7.2.1 *Liquidity*

Whereas the majority of registered vehicles offer daily or weekly liquidity and prompt payment of proceeds from a sale, hedge funds typically take contributions only at month or quarter end and allow withdrawals quarterly or less frequently, sometimes subject to a lock-up period. A typical lock-up period is the first 12 months following the contribution, during which no withdrawals are permitted or, if permitted, are subject to a substantial penalty, similar to a mutual fund redemption penalty. The more limited liquidity of a hedge fund permits the manager to expand the investment universe to less liquid securities or to strategies that may realize returns over extended periods of time. It is important that the manager provide liquidity terms aligned with the liquidity of the underlying assets or strategy. For example, an equity hedge strategy focused on US large-capitalization stocks would be hard-pressed to justify a long lock-up period or infrequent redemptions because the liquidity of the underlying markets reduces the risk of forced selling to meet investor withdrawals. (Pressure to sell portfolio holdings in stressed markets can leave the portfolio unbalanced, to the detriment of other investors.) Less liquid terms would be appropriate for a fund that holds illiquid distressed fixed-income securities for which the manager is involved in the process of modifying repayment terms. Such positions cannot be easily sold and limited liquidity terms are often necessary to successfully implement the strategy.

A related consideration is the impact of the liquidity terms on those investors who choose not to redeem. The investor must assess whether the other investors in the fund, based on their investor profile, are long-term investors or "hot money" (prone to rapidly moving money in and out of a fund). This assessment is done by reviewing the breakdown of investor types—foundations, endowments, pension funds, high-net-worth individuals, or funds of funds—and making some assumptions about the behavior of each investor type. For example, foundations and endowments tend to be long-term investors, whereas high-net-worth individuals and retail funds of funds are generally believed to focus on shorter-term results. A higher concentration of longer-term investors is preferred because a large proportion of hot money investors may leave the long-term investor holding the least liquid positions as others seek to redeem their investments and the manager is forced to sell the more liquid positions. Some funds will impose gates (in addition to lock-up periods) to mitigate this risk. A gate restricts the total amount of withdrawals from the fund during a redemption period. The gate can be applied to total fund assets or to each specific investor account. If possible, the investor should develop an understanding of the nature of the investor base. Some managers will disclose, with permission, the identity of large investors, possibly as references, which allows the investor to better judge the potential behavior of other investors.

7.2.2 *Leverage*

The use of leverage varies greatly among hedge fund managers and the strategy used. Many strategies use leverage to enhance returns, and leverage does allow the hedge fund to potentially add value through strategy diversification. But leverage also introduces another element of risk.

Sources of leverage include prime brokerage margin, short positions, repurchase agreements (repo), secured credit lines, derivatives, and structured financing vehicles. It is incumbent on the investor to understand the sources of leverage and the degree of leverage used as well as to determine whether the manager's use of leverage is appropriate or represents undue risk. This consideration is important because the sudden withdrawal of financing can result in the forced liquidation of positions, generally at inopportune times.

Prime brokerage margin is the simplest and most common form of borrowing. The hedge fund obtains margin financing from the prime broker, either at the position or portfolio level. Although prime brokerage margin is generally easy to obtain, if it is short-duration financing, it can result in a mismatch between the liquidity of the portfolio securities and the financing. If the financing expires or is withdrawn, it could result in the need to sell securities at an inopportune time to the detriment of investors.

When a security is borrowed from a prime broker and sold short (creating a short position), the cash proceeds from the sale, net of the costs of borrowing and holding the short security, can be reinvested to purchase additional securities.

A repo typically involves the delivery of a security that the hedge fund owns to a lender as collateral for a fixed rate loan. Repo transactions are generally short term (overnight to one month), and the fund is obligated to repurchase the collateral at the end of the term.

A secured line of credit is typically structured as a committed revolving line of credit, supported by assets held in the fund. The line of credit is subject to periodic renewal.

Such borrowing arrangements create a potential risk for the portfolio if the financing is withdrawn or unavailable, which may occur during periods of high risk aversion and illiquidity. This loss of financing could result in the forced selling of positions at a loss to the portfolio.

Derivatives contain implicit leverage because a relatively small amount of capital allows for the purchase of notional assets at some multiple of the capital amount. The use of derivatives allows the hedge fund manager to leverage the portfolio without borrowing to finance positions.

Some hedge fund managers create structured vehicles to provide longer-term financing. The hedge fund transfers assets to a structured financing vehicle that then issues debt supported by the cash flows from the underlying assets.

The risks of leverage depend on the degree of leverage used and strategy being implemented. Portfolios with low net exposure or long and short positions in correlated securities are generally considered better able to support leverage. A key assumption is that the level of exposure and correlation between positions will remain stable during periods of market volatility. If the correlation changes, the realized degree of hedging is lower than expected and, therefore, the overall risk exposure level is higher than expected.

There are a number of ways to measure leverage:

- Gross market value/assets under management (AUM): The value of long positions plus the absolute value of short positions divided by the AUM.

- Long market value/assets under management: The market value of long positions divided by the AUM of the portfolio.
- Debt/assets under management: The total value of debt relative to the AUM of the portfolio.

As with other metrics, leverage should be monitored through time to assess the level and its consistency with the manager's strategy.

Investors generally consider multiple measures of leverage. Gross value/AUM measures the total leverage of the portfolio, whereas the long value/AUM takes into consideration the ability of short positions to hedge risk. Debt/AUM provides a direct measure of explicit leverage created using borrowing.

7.2.3 *Short Selling*

The prevalence of shorting as a hedge against portfolio volatility or as an alpha source in its own right raises a distinct set of issues to be evaluated during the course of the manager selection process:

- Does the manager pair short positions with long positions as relative value trades? Or are shorts held as standalone, alpha oriented-trades? Although pair trades can result in low expected net risk exposures, realized risk may be higher than expected if the price spread between the positions widens rather than narrows, as happened with Long-Term Capital Management in the late 1990s.
- Is net exposure managed through security-specific short positions, or does the manager make extensive use of index shorts (short selling broad market indexes)?
- How does the manager approach risk management of short positions? When a long position does not perform as the manager expected, the value of that position is falling and becomes a lower portion of the overall portfolio. When a short position does not perform as expected, it becomes a larger portion of the overall exposure.
- What inputs and processes are used in managing the portfolio's net exposure?
- What is the contribution of long and short positions to portfolio return? Are the contributions consistent with the manager's investment philosophy, process, and expertise? Do the short positions add the value expected and justify the fund's structure and fees?

Long-Term Capital Management (LTCM) implemented a convergence trading strategy seeking to exploit relative value opportunities between fixed-income securities by identifying very similar securities they believed were mispriced relative to each other, buying the less expensive security, shorting the more expensive security, and capturing the spread as the security prices converged. The spreads of such opportunities are typically narrow and the fund used leverage to enhance returns.

The fund was launched in 1994 with $1.25 billion in equity capital. By 1998, equity capital had grown to $4.8 billion and was leveraged 25/1. The balance sheet at that time reflected $125 billion in assets. Incuding off-balance sheet sources of leverage (swaps, options, and other derivatives), the fund's "footprint" (its gross market value—the sum of its notional long and short market value) had ballooned to $1.2 trillion, for a gross market value to AUM ratio of 240×. By one estimate, the fund held positions representing 5% of the total global fixed-income market.

When Russia devalued the ruble on 17 August 1998 and declared a moratorium on 281 billion rubles ($13.5 billion) of its government debt, LTCM was long lower-quality, less-liquid securities and short higher-quality, more-liquid securities, believing the higher quality securities were over-valued and expecting the pricing relationship to converge. Instead, the fund sustained massive losses as spreads widened as other investors sought to reduce risk, bidding up the prices of higher-quality securities and creating pressure on the prices of lower-quality securities.

LTCM's losses were so severe, regulators were concerned that the fund might default on its loans, triggering a global financial crisis. In September 1998, the fund, which had continued to sustain losses, was bailed out with the help of the Federal Reserve and its creditors.

7.2.4 *Fees*

Hedge fund fees usually consist of a fixed management fee and a variable performance fee. The management fee is usually calculated as a percentage of AUM, whereas the performance or incentive fee is charged on returns. In some cases, the performance fee is earned only when returns exceed a pre-specified hurdle rate, and there is typically a high-water mark. The **hurdle rate** is a minimum rate of return below which the fund does not charge an incentive fee. The **high-water mark** is the highest cumulative net asset value attained by the fund, net of fees. Payment of the incentive fee may be contingent on the fund exceeding one or both of these criteria. Note that the management fee is earned even if performance does not exceed the hurdle rate or high-water mark.

The fee structure should support the alignment of interests between the manager and the investor. An incentive fee has characteristics similar to an option—the manager participates in returns (earns a bonus) above the hurdle rate or high-water mark, but no incentive fee is paid for returns below this threshold. As such, there is an incentive to add risk in an effort to avoid a loss or to beat the hurdle rate to earn a bonus. Conversely, there can be an incentive to reduce risk if the manager believes poor performance may result in redemptions. One method to game the incentive fee structure is to close a fund that is well below and unlikely to attain its high-water mark and start another fund with a similar strategy. Current investors, if they choose to invest with the manager under the new fund, should insist that their high-water mark transfer to the new fund.

Shifts in the risk profile of the fund may be motivated by fee, rather than investment, considerations and represent another form of risk to investors. With that in mind, due diligence should incorporate a review of strategies the manager no longer manages, including an analysis of the performance of those strategies and the reason for their closure.

7.2.5 *Key Man Provision*

Given the lock-up period and limited liquidity of many hedge fund offerings, it is important to determine whether investors have accelerated redemption rights should key personnel become disabled or are no longer active in managing the strategy.

7.2.6 *Multiple Funds*

If the manager offers multiple vehicles implementing the same, or nearly the same, investment strategy, the investor should understand the methodology for the allocation of investment opportunities and the manager's time among funds to ensure the allocations are equitable across vehicles. Additionally, the trading of positions between funds should not be permitted. Although it can be argued that such trades reduce transaction costs, the lack of independent, third-party pricing raises the potential to benefit some investors at the expense of others in the allocation of positions.

7.2.7 *Side Pockets*

A side pocket is typically used to hold positions that are less liquid or that have a longer investment horizon inconsistent with the liquidity terms offered by the fund. These side-pocketed investments are not subject to the general redemption privileges outlined in the fund's governing documents. Investors should understand the manager's use of side pockets—what types of investments are allocated to the side pocket and how extensively have side pockets been used.

7.2.8 *Co-investment Opportunities*

At times a manager may have an investment opportunity with more capacity than the fund can absorb. Such co-investment opportunities should be made available to current investors to avoid conflicts of interest.

7.2.9 *Valuation Policy*

Securities should be valued by using market prices or by using indicative quotes from independent parties wherever possible to avoid potential conflicts in portfolio valuation. The process that the manager uses in valuing the portfolio should be clearly outlined.

7.2.10 *Third-Party Service Providers*

Hedge funds make use of a number of third-party service providers—prime brokers, fund administrator, custodians, and auditors are the primary ones—that provide important services and external oversight. The investor should understand the specific services being provided by each third-party provider, the quality of those services, and the manager's process for selecting a provider. Of particular importance is the need to confirm that a clean audit opinion from a reputable auditor has been issued. Although rare, fraudulent audit opinions are possible.

The use of little known or inadequate third-party service providers, as with the Madoff funds, or the frequent and/or unexplained change of providers, as with the Bayou Group, represents potentially serious red flags and should alert investors to the potential for fraudulent statements to hide losses.

7.3 Operational Due Diligence Considerations for Hedge Funds

By one estimate, 50% of hedge fund failures have been the result of operational, not investment, issues. A thorough review of company policies, custodial relationships and client relations is of key importance. Consultants with large research groups often have a separate team dedicated to operational due diligence and smaller groups will often engage outside firms to conduct operational due diligence. Important elements of operational due diligence include a detailed review of the offering documents, a review of any existing side letters (as well as the manager's policies on side letters), and an understanding of the firm's policies with respect to any trading done by its professionals.

The key documents associated with an investment in hedge funds are the private placement or offering memorandum, limited partnership agreement or operating agreement, and subscription documents. The offering memo outlines the objectives, risks, and terms of the investment; the rights and protections offered to the investor; and the restrictions placed on the manager. The limited partnership agreement defines what the partnership can and cannot do. The subscription is the "application" for a limited partnership interest; it is used to assess the eligibility of the investor to participate in a private placement. The investor should read and understand these documents to identify and understand potential conflicts of interest, such as any allowable transactions between the manager and the fund and related parties.

The investor must also be aware of any side letters issued to other investors by the investment manager that may give those investors different or preferential minimum investments, fees, liquidity rights, and/or access to information relative to what is described in the offering documents.

It is also important to understand whether the manager offers a separate investment vehicle for its employees that may invest in strategies that differ from the strategy used by the fund and what policies govern the personal trading of employees. Such internal or private vehicles raise the potential for conflicts of interest with external investors related to the allocation of trades and managerial effort. The personal trading of fund employees can also create conflicts of interest. Sound trading policies typically require pre-approval of all personal trading by employees, and preclude investments within the same opportunity set targeted by the fund.

Although hedge fund investments allow investors access to certain strategies and markets that are not normally available through traditional investment vehicles, such investments come with the costs of a steep learning curve for the investor and due diligence challenges arising from the structure of the investment vehicles and the reduced transparency typically associated with them. As a general guideline, if a hedge fund manager is unwilling or unable to provide sufficient transparency to enable the investor to build confidence in the expected returns of the strategy and that the interests of the manager are aligned with those of the investor, the investor should decline to make the investment.

EXAMPLE 10

Hedge Fund Manager Evaluation

1 An investor needs to investigate the source and degree of leverage because of the risk that leverage can:

   A enhance returns.

   B allow for strategy diversification.

   C result in forced liquidations as a result of the sudden withdrawal of financing.

2 A key man provision:

   A results in lower fees.

   B enhances transparency.

   C allows investors to accelerate redemptions if key personnel are no longer able to manage the fund.

3 Which of the following *most* accurately describes hedge fund fees?

   A The incentive fee is calculated as a percentage of AUM.

   B The high-water mark is the highest cumulative return before fees.

   C A management fee is charged on all assets even if returns are below the hurdle rate.

4 Hedge funds *most likely* restrict redemptions because they:

   A hold illiquid assets.

   B are unregistered vehicles.

   C are not restricted from using derivatives.

Solution to 1:

C is correct. The benefits of leverage include allowing a hedge funds to increase position sizes and boost returns—for example, generate higher returns from narrow spread or increase exposure to different strategies or securities and increase portfolio diversification. A primary risk of leverage is the sudden withdrawal of financing that can result in the forced liquidation of positions, generally at inopportune times.

Solution to 2:

C is correct. Given the limited liquidity of many hedge fund offerings, key man provisions provide for liquidity in the event that the manager is unable to implement the investment process.

Solution to 3:

C is correct. The management fee is charged for all assets under management, including those arising from returns below the hurdle rate. The incentive fee is charged on returns above the hurdle rate, and the high-water mark is the highest cumulative net asset value, net of fees.

Solution to 4:

A is correct. Hedge funds holding illiquid assets restrict redemptions because illiquid assets cannot be quickly sold at fair value. Pressure to sell portfolio holdings in stressed markets can leave the portfolio unbalanced, to the detriment of other investors. As unregistered vehicles, hedge funds may lack transparency, but this fact does not influence whether redemptions are limited. Using derivatives should not restrict investors from redeeming their funds.

CONSIDERATIONS IN THE SELECTION OF PRIVATE EQUITY MANAGERS

8

Private equity is an illiquid, long-term, and inefficient asset class in which performance is predicated on an investor's ability to select managers that have the ability to outperform. The dispersion of investment returns among private equity managers, illustrated in Exhibit 3,[3] is wide, especially when compared with other asset classes.

3 Private equity returns presented in Exhibit 3 are in the form of an internal rate of return (IRR) and include a set of US-based funds that are invested on a primary basis in buyout and venture capital strategies, as noted, in vintage years 1994–2015. Return data are subject to change by Burgiss. Returns are net of fees, carried interest, and expenses charged by the funds' general partners. Public equity returns presented in Exhibit 3 are in the form of a time-weighted return (TWR) and include a set of managers with a US public equity focus and a complete track record from January 1994 to 30 September 2015. The data presented represent the dispersion of TWRs for 10-year periods, measured on a quarterly basis, between 1994 and 2015. Returns are gross of underlying fees charged by managers. Periods of 10-years were used for the purpose of comparison with private equity partnerships, which are characterized by an investment period of approximately 10 years. Differences in the structures of private equity and public equity investment vehicles require the use of IRR and TWR, respectively, as performance metrics. IRR and TWR are different methodologies and should not be compared on an absolute basis.

Exhibit 3 Dispersion of US Public and Private Equity Returns, 1994–2015

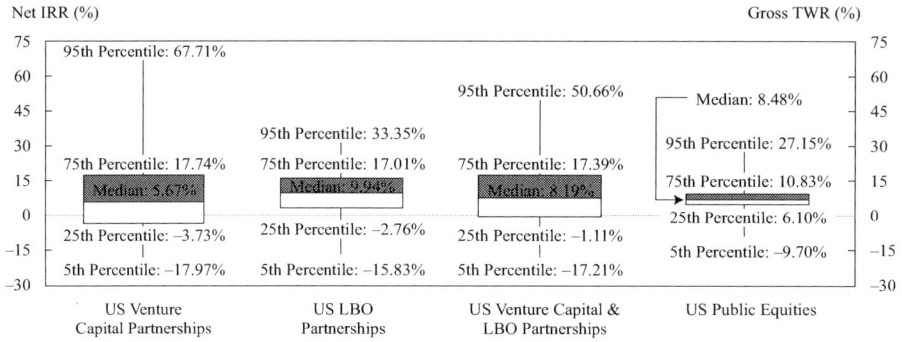

Sources: The private equity data series is from Burgiss. The public equity data series is from eVestment.

The illiquid nature of private equity investments heightens the importance of making the correct manager selection from the outset. Successful private equity manager selection depends on the ability to critically assess the team, strategy, market, and track record of a manager.

Private Equity Basics

There are three main categories, or subclasses, within private equity: venture capital (seed, early stage, and mid/late stage), growth equity, and buyouts. These are shown in Exhibit 4.

Exhibit 4 Private Equity Categories

	Less Mature Company		More Mature Company		
	Seed Venture Capital	Early-Stage Venture Capital	Mid/Late-Stage Venture Capital	Growth Equity	Buyout
Company description	Developing the concept, business plan, and product; building the team.	Developing the technology and testing the product in the market.	Developing new products, expanding into new markets, perfecting the product.	Business model is proven. Further growth into new verticals and markets.	Mature company with proven business model. Revenue growth and margin expansion opportunities.
Revenues	None	Modest, if any	Yes	Yes	Yes
Profitability	No	No	Unlikely	Breakeven; potentially profitable	Yes
Leverage	None	None	None	Modest, if any	Yes

Within each subclass, there are different risks that the investor assumes and various value creation mechanisms for the private equity manager to use in order to generate value for investors. Understanding these risks and value creation mechanisms is important in private equity manager selection.

Private equity investments are typically accomplished via limited partnership structures known as private equity funds. The investor (the limited partner, or LP) commits capital to a fund managed by a general partner (GP), or manager. The GP has full discretion as to the underlying investments. The relationship between the GP and an LP is governed by the limited partnership agreement (LPA). Once an LP commits capital to a private equity fund, the LP may not retract this obligation. A private equity fund usually has a defined strategy related to subclass, size of transaction, and geography. The lifetime of each fund is typically 10 years, with two 1-year extensions. The GP deploys the fund's capital into several companies during the investment period, typically the first five years of the fund's life. The capital committed by the LP is only paid into the fund as requested by the GP. As each investment is identified, the GP issues a capital call.

Private equity fees consist of two components:

- Management fees are charged as a percentage of total committed capital during the investment period, stepping down to a percentage of remaining capital under management after the investment period. Typical fees are 1.5%–2% for buyout funds and 2%–2.5% for venture funds.
- **Carried interest** is a performance-based fee that reflects a share of the profits receivable by the manager, typically once a specific performance hurdle, or "preferred return," has been achieved on overall fund performance. Carried interest typically ranges from 20% to 30%. This structure is intended to create strong alignment between the GP and the LP, with both parties benefiting from high-performing investments.

8.1 Assessing the Team

The strength, stability, and expertise of the investment team are critical to a private equity firm's success. Managers of private equity funds often combine investment acumen with operational and entrepreneurial expertise. There are five key aspects of the team that are important when selecting private equity managers:

- *Investment acumen.* The GP's selection of portfolio companies is the major determinant of an investment outcome, but the outcome can be further enhanced by various value-added efforts of a manager. Investment expertise can only be developed over time. The manager must also display the ability to understand market cycles and to remain disciplined.
- *Domain expertise.* Successful private equity and venture capital investment requires intimate knowledge of sectors, operations, and deal dynamics as well as an ability to assess the risk–reward characteristics of a deal. In venture capital, the best investors are often prior entrepreneurs themselves and intimately understand the needs of the business. The reputation that a venture capital investor gains as an entrepreneur can help drive differentiated deal flow to the venture capital firm. In growth equity and buyouts, an understanding of sector dynamics and capital markets, as well as an ability to identify areas to add value and drive returns to the fund, is crucial. Sector dynamics include aspects of an industry that can be expected to have a meaningful effect on the investment environment, such as the regulatory/reimbursement environment (health care), commodity price volatility (industrials and manufacturing), or innovation (technology). Capital market dynamics include such things as debt availability, debt structures, foreign exchange rates, and the interest rate environment.
- *Resources.* Private equity and venture capital investing are resource intensive and require hands-on involvement by the manager to achieve performance objectives. In venture capital, the manager often helps the company find the right product/market fit, introduces the company to potential customers

within their network, helps hire the most effective management team, and may sit on the board of directors to help guide the strategic vision of the young company. In the buyout space, in which the manager likely has control of the company, the manager sits on the board to help drive the strategic direction of the company and may be involved in key operating decisions. This hands-on involvement requires a significant time commitment from the manager, and it is important to assess the resources and capacity of the manager to monitor an existing portfolio of investments while continuing to assess deal flow and make new investments.

- *Stability and economic sharing agreements.* An important consideration in assessing stability is ensuring that economic sharing arrangements are fair and appropriate to each individual's contribution to the firm. There is no formulaic approach to economic sharing agreements, but an assessment of the structure of the arrangements is essential to understanding individual motivation and team dynamics. If the economics are heavily concentrated among the most senior-level individuals, the next layer of leadership could become frustrated and depart the firm, creating a succession issue. A significant majority of the economics being held by individuals no longer at the firm (the founders, for example) or by senior individuals whose contributions may be declining may also be a trouble spot. Even with an attractive strategy and highly qualified team, if there is internal strife creating instability, returns for investors may be negatively affected.
- *Key person risk.* As noted, private equity is a long-term asset class, with LPs having limited control post-investment. The LPA protects investors in specific situations, including those that include the involvement of key individuals at the GP. It is important to understand the protections the LP has related to the departure (or declining involvement) of any key individuals; ideally, a key departure will cause a suspension of the investment period.

8.2 Assessing the Strategy

The investment strategy defines the profile of companies and the specific approach to a target market in which a manager seeks to invest capital. The prior experience and underlying skills of a manager must match the intended strategy of the firm.

Managers should be able to clearly communicate how their investment approach and competitive advantage will result in attractive and differentiated investment returns. The ability of managers to successfully apply their strategy, within the designated subclass, repeatedly over a prolonged period of time should manifest itself in their track record.

The due diligence skills required of a venture fund manager are materially different from those required of a buyout manager. Because many venture investments are made at the embryonic stage of a company's life cycle, there may be little historical data to analyze. As such, the venture capitalist must have the ability to take a view on the application of a new technology in what may be a new market and to understand the threat of competition. In contrast, buyout managers investing in more mature businesses must be skilled at understanding financial and operational performance. Mature companies have long operating histories, so there are often a lot of data available to analyze and on which to base investment decisions. Careful analysis of past business performance can inform managers about the potential to expand the business or remedy inefficiencies using their corporate finance expertise.

Because buyouts and, to a lesser extent, growth equity investments use both equity and debt, buyout managers must also have the expertise needed to create an appropriate corporate financial structure.

8.2.1 *Understanding a Venture Strategy*

The vast majority of investment capital is deployed in the information technology and life sciences (health care) sectors. The success of venture managers is dependent on their ability to identify which entrepreneurs, products, and market opportunities can converge to create companies of sufficient scale to be exited through mergers and acquisitions (e.g., the sale of the company to another private equity fund or to one of its competitors that may be looking to build scale in the market) or through an initial public offering (IPO). Several variables must align in order to generate an attractive outcome. Venture capitalists tend to make a large number of individual investments to reduce the risk to the portfolio from any one investment and create more opportunities for success. The funding risk of each investment is often shared among venture capital firms as they collaborate by forming funding syndicates to finance each stage of a company's maturity.

Early- and mid/late-stage venture capital managers typically use different strategies (described next), reflecting the difference in risk–return characteristics inherent in the maturity of the companies they are investing in.

- *Early-stage venture capital.* The return to a fund is driven by its share of ownership of each investment at exit. The highest level of ownership is typically obtained in seed or early-stage investments. These stages are characterized by relatively low total company valuations and correspondingly higher risk, given the high degree of unknowns inherent in investing in early ideas or product companies.

  To compensate for the higher incidence of capital loss, early-stage venture capitalists target investments that have the capacity to generate outsized returns, commonly referred to as home runs or hits. These successful individual investments return a high multiple of their invested cost (typically about 25× and higher). A single successful investment often returns the entire committed capital of a fund.
- *Mid- and late-stage venture capital.* In mid- and late-stage investing, financial and operational analysis are of increased importance. Mid- and late-stage venture managers invest larger amounts of capital at higher valuations in more mature companies. They also closely manage their downside loss potential, investment by investment, because there is less opportunity for outsized returns from a single investment that might offset losses on their poorer-performing investments.

8.2.2 *Understanding a Buyout Strategy*

A buyout manager focuses on established, mature companies and seeks to optimize the three main drivers of buyout returns: growth in earnings, valuation multiple arbitrage, and use of debt. Given the tighter band of returns among the underlying investments in a buyout portfolio, there is limited capacity to sustain losses without negatively affecting fund-level returns. Therefore, buyout managers tend to be more cautious in their investment approach in order to minimize capital loss.

- *Growth in earnings.* Buyout managers seek to grow the earnings of a portfolio company during the tenure of their investment by growing organically, growing via acquisitions, or improving the profitability of the company. Given their control of the underlying investment, buyout managers have the ability to directly influence each and all of these earnings levers.
  - *Organic growth.* By making investments that are well positioned in sectors and sub-segments exhibiting higher than average growth characteristics, the buyout portfolio will benefit from fast-growing markets. Buyout managers

may also use capital to enhance a company's team, infrastructure, and R&D investment as well as to open offices in new markets and geographies that can accelerate a company's growth.

- *Growth via acquisition.* The buyout manager may acquire other similar or synergistic companies and merge the new acquisition with the portfolio company. The combination of acquired entities can allow for increased market share and increased earnings.
- *Improved profitability.* Mature companies can become inefficient, and profitability may fall below the average level for its respective industry or market. Through direct intervention, a buyout manager can ensure that companies keep pace with best practices and that profitability is brought up to or above industry norms. Buyout managers may engage executives with operational capability to take an active role in the company to execute needed changes.

- *Valuation multiple arbitrage.* Buyout managers typically quote prices for portfolio companies as a multiple of earnings applied to a designated measure of company earnings. An earnings multiple is comparable to the price-to-earnings multiple used to value companies in the public markets.

  If the buyout manager is able to increase the valuation multiple on a portfolio company over time, it will provide a boost to the return on the investment. There are two principal ways to increase the multiple of earnings during the holding period:

  - *Buying well.* Private markets are inefficient, and the lack of openness along with imperfect competition allow purchasers to acquire assets at discounts to their intrinsic value.
  - *Improving operations.* Improving operations and/or growing the underlying asset such that it commands a higher multiple at exit. By growing an asset and making a company more professional and larger in size, a buyout manager can make it more desirable to potential acquirers.

- *Use of debt.* Debt is commonly used to finance buyout transactions. Adding leverage into the financing mix can enhance the return on the equity put to work in the transaction. Ensuring the appropriate balance of debt and equity in any transaction is critical to avoiding the risk of becoming "over-leveraged" and unable to finance the company's interest payments and repayment of principal, which may ultimately result in failure and liquidation of a company.

As the buyout sector has matured, competitiveness between private equity managers has intensified, bringing increased sophistication and specialization. Value creation has become increasingly operationally focused, requiring managers to have sector expertise and/or a network of experienced operators to help find and assess deals, while also executing operational improvements post-completion. This shift has also led to sector-focused teams within a multi-strategy manager and a proliferation of sector-focused funds.

8.3 Understanding the Market Environment

It is important that a private equity manager's strategy is tailored to the market environment in which it is operating.

Private equity is predominantly a "local" business in which managers must be on the ground to see and discern the best investment opportunities in a particular geographical market. Understanding local culture and business sensitivities and establishing credibility within the local private equity ecosystem are important factors in identifying, accessing, and executing the best deals in a particular region.

An assessment of the target markets considers the volume of high-quality deal opportunities, the regulatory environment, the prevalence of an equity culture, the level of entrepreneurship, the existence of a viable route to exit, and the support of an experienced ecosystem of professionals (such as accountants, lawyers, intermediaries, bankers, and tax experts). In less developed countries, for example, the availability of experienced investors and attractive investment opportunities are more limited compared with developed countries. Additionally, the protections that equity investors receive vary by country, which is an important consideration when assessing the attractiveness of private equity in a region. Exhibit 5 provides one investor's view of the private equity investing environment across various geographical regions.

Exhibit 5 Assessment of Global Private Equtiy Markets

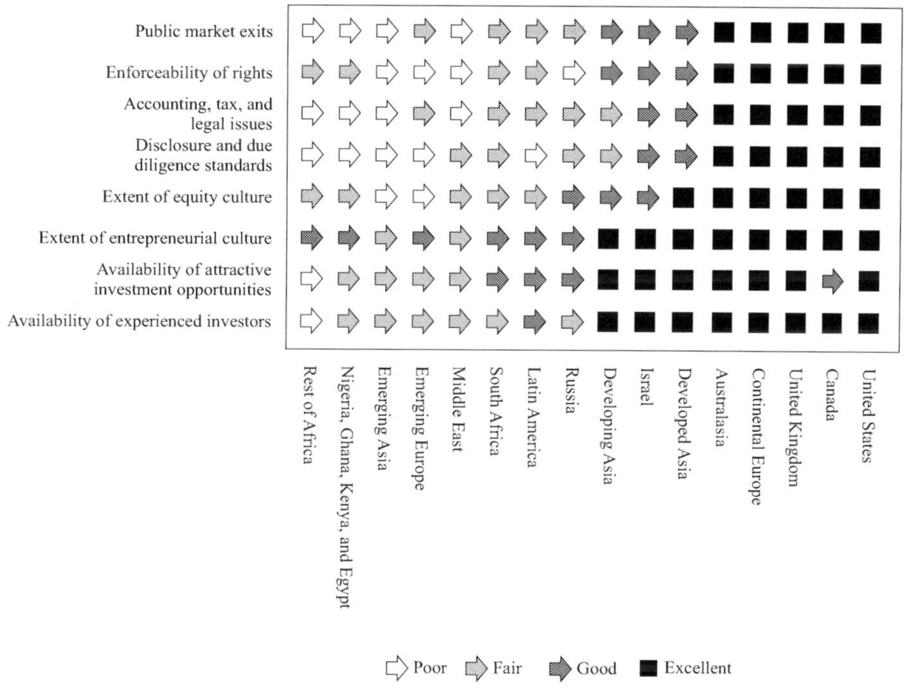

Source: Based on views from Adams Street Partners.

8.4 Assessing the Track Record

Analysis of a manager's track record is a fundamental component of the due diligence process when selecting a private equity manager. Understanding past performance and forming an opinion about the ability of the manager to produce attractive performance in the future require the investor to look at both quantitative and qualitative factors, which are often interconnected. A greater understanding of the manager's capabilities going forward can be developed by looking at firm-level, fund-level, and company-level attributes. Performance evaluation in private equity is materially different from that in other asset classes, and it is important to understand these differences when making relative judgments between asset classes. For example, a private equity internal rate of return cannot be compared with a public equity time-weighted return, and the Sharpe ratio and other measures of risk-adjusted return are less relevant in private equity, for which the volatility of reported returns is muted by the valuation process.

8.4.1 *Performance Measures in Private Equity*

There are both absolute and relative measures of investment performance evaluation in private equity. To facilitate performance comparisons, funds are grouped by vintage year—the year in which the fund makes its initial investment.

Absolute performance evaluation. Whereas public market investments rely on time-weighted returns when assessing investment manager performance, the **internal rate of return** (IRR) and **multiple of invested capital** (MOIC) are the most prevalent measurements of private equity performance. These measures are used largely because, unlike in mutual funds and other public market investment strategies, the manager controls the timing of cash flows into and out of the fund.[4]

- MOIC is the current value of the underlying companies, plus any distributions received, divided by the total invested capital.
- IRR is the rate of return based on the cash flows and the terminal value of the company. It takes into account the time value of money and reflects the private equity manager's control over the timing of cash inflows and outflows. (In contrast, with public market equity and fixed-income managers, the asset owner determines the timing of contributions and withdrawals from the account; thus, the time-weighted return measure is more appropriate.) IRR is a key metric of private equity performance measurement.

An important concept in private equity manager evaluation is the **j-curve**. The j-curve describes the shape of the IRR curve over time. As the private equity fund calls capital early in the fund's life, the IRR dips below zero as fees and expenses erode capital before the manager has had an opportunity to realize returns. As the fund matures and the capital invested starts to create distributions, the IRR turns positive. All things being equal, a private equity manager prefers to shorten the j-curve and demonstrate early positive returns for investors.

Funds and individual investments that exhibit both a high IRR and a high MOIC are generally deemed attractive. There is an implicit relationship among the IRR, MOIC, and holding period. As an investor, it is important to understand this interplay.

Exhibit 6 The Interaction of MOIC and IRR

		IRR given MOIC and Years Invested									
Return Multiple:		**1.5×**	**2.0×**	**3.0×**	**4.0×**	**5.0×**	**6.0×**	**7.0×**	**8.0×**	**9.0×**	**10.0×**
Years Invested	**2**	22%	41%	73%	100%	124%	145%	165%	183%	200%	216%
	3	14%	26%	44%	59%	71%	82%	91%	100%	108%	115%
	4	11%	19%	32%	41%	50%	57%	63%	68%	73%	78%
	5	8%	15%	25%	32%	38%	43%	48%	52%	55%	58%
	6	7%	12%	20%	26%	31%	35%	38%	41%	44%	47%
	7	6%	10%	17%	22%	26%	29%	32%	35%	37%	39%
	8	5%	9%	15%	19%	22%	25%	28%	30%	32%	33%
	9	5%	8%	13%	17%	20%	22%	24%	26%	28%	29%
	10	4%	7%	12%	15%	17%	20%	21%	23%	25%	26%

4 Time-weighted returns are used in the evaluation of public market returns in order to remove the impact of cash inflows and outflows, which are largely outside of the manager's control.

As illustrated in Exhibit 6, any given MOIC can be associated with any number of IRRs, each of which is dependent on the length of time it took to realize that multiple. If a manager realizes a hugely successful investment early in the fund's life, the initial IRR will be artificially inflated and can be expected to come down over time. (Similarly, when comparing funds of different vintage years, it is important to make note of the percentage of fund capital that has been drawn because it will provide the analyst with insights as to the future direction of both the MOIC and the IRR.) As an example, assume a buyout investor invests $1 in a company and realizes an MOIC of 2.0×. If held for two years, this investment equates to an IRR of 41%. However, if it takes 10 years to achieve the 2.0× MOIC, then the IRR is only 7%. Alternatively, an IRR of 26% can be achieved with a 2.0× MOIC over 3 years, a 4.0× MOIC over 6 years, a 5.0× MOIC over 7 years, an 8.0× MOIC over 9 years, or a 10.0× MOIC over 10 years. Which is better? There is no absolute answer. The three-year, 26% IRR gives the manager an opportunity to recycle that capital and generate additional returns over the life of the fund. However, if subsequent investments are less successful than the initial investment, the ultimate return to the LP may be far less than the 26%, three-year IRR. The investor must assess the IRR in the context of the MOIC, and vice versa.

Relative performance evaluation. In addition to analyzing the track record of a private equity manager on an absolute basis, performance can be evaluated relative to a private equity benchmark (composed of similar funds by strategy, geography, and vintage year) or against the performance of public equities.

The CFA Institute Global Investment Performance Standards allow for private equity returns to be presented both gross and net of all taxes, fees, and expenses, including carried interest. The assets in the fund must be valued at least annually using **fair value**.[5]

Private equity benchmarks can be used to compare the managers' individual funds with an appropriate peer group, normally defined by subclass, geography, and vintage year of the underlying fund. Benchmarks commonly used for this purpose include ones prepared by Burgiss, Cambridge Associates, and the Institutional Limited Partners Association (ILPA).

The **public market equivalent** (PME) methodology has been developed to allow comparisons of private equity IRRs with returns of publicly traded equity indexes. The methodology uses cash flow data to replicate the GP's capital calls and distributions, assuming these same cash flows were invested in the chosen equity index. It's then possible to compare the IRR of the fund with the returns available in the public markets to assess the relative performance of the manager. Several PME methodologies exist, the most common being Long–Nickels PME, PME+, Kaplan and Schoar PME, and Direct Alpha PME. It is important to choose the appropriate PME for each private equity fund; a poorly chosen PME raises the risk of leading the investor to an incorrect conclusion.

Although relative performance measures help an investor to understand how a fund performs relative to peers or a relevant public index, there are several limitations to be aware of when comparing returns among managers:

- *Valuation methodology.* The manner in which each manager values its portfolio companies may differ.

5 The amount at which an investment could be exchanged in a current arm's length transaction between willing parties in which the parties each act knowledgeably and prudently. The valuation must be determined using the objective, observable, unadjusted quoted market price for an identical investment in an active market on the measurement date, if available. In the absence of an objective, observable, unadjusted quoted market price for an identical investment in an active market on the measurement date, the valuation must represent the firm's best estimate of the market value. Fair value must include accrued income. (2010 Global Investment Performance Standards)

- *Early losses/early wins.* The IRR of a fund is meaningfully influenced by an early loss or an early win in the portfolio. Although the IRR will normalize over time, an early win or loss may skew the data early in a fund's life.
- *Snapshot in time.* When evaluating the performance of a manager, it is important to recognize that the data are from a specific snapshot in time and the companies in a fund can be at various stages of development.

8.4.2 *Firm-Level Assessment*

At the highest level, an investor is concerned with the ability of the manager to replicate past successes. Key factors to consider in this assessment are fund size, the relevance of the track record to future conditions, the contributions of various team members, and the insight from the management of portfolio companies.

- *Fund size.* Fund size is an important determinant of a manager's ability to repeatedly create strong performance. Demand from LPs who want to invest with specific managers may pressure the manager to raise larger funds in order to accommodate the high level of LP interest. Managing more capital may shift a manager's focus away from its core competitive advantage, stress the manager's fund model, or unfavorably alter the alignment of interests between the GP and the LPs. The confluence of increasing management fee income with increasing fund size can induce managers to raise an amount of capital that exceeds the capabilities and resource capacity of the team. The analyst should seek to determine whether an increase in fund size has caused the manager to invest in too many deals or in deal sizes that do not play to its competitive advantage. The analyst must also assess whether the capacity of the current team is likely to be a constraining factor. Additionally, the larger fund size—and hence increased management fee income—means the carried interest may no longer be the main economic incentive to a manager; it can be dilutive to a manager's risk appetite.
- *Track record relative to future strategy.* As markets, geographies, and teams change, often so do private equity strategies within firms. As an investor, it is important to ensure that the track record being analyzed is relevant to the strategy that the manager will be using in the future. Specifically, an investor should look at the deal size, sector focus, geography focus, and strategy for value creation in assessing the performance of past deals. Is the investment theme repeatable, or has the market opportunity become limited or moved on? How has the competitive environment changed, and does the manager still enjoy the competitive advantage it once had? Are deals being sourced broadly across the firm, and is the approach replicable?
- *General partner attribution.* When analyzing a track record, it is important to understand which individual sourced, completed diligence, and executed the transaction. If there has been turnover on the team, it allows the investor to assess the performance and capabilities of the team going forward. In many instances, the consummation of an investment by a private equity manager is a team-wide effort and understanding individuals' specific roles in a transaction can be difficult.
- *Insight from the management of portfolio companies.* Investments rarely perform consistently well, so a private equity manager's ability to resolve challenges in problem situations is an important insight. The investor can speak to the key executives of a number of portfolio companies to gain insight as to how the private equity manager has contributed to the development of the company. This process can also help to corroborate the expectations a private equity manager has regarding the current and future performance of a company.

8.4.3 *Fund-Level Analysis*

The factors to consider when reviewing fund-level performance include diversification, consistency in returns, realized versus unrealized returns, the loss ratio, and distributions to paid-in capital.

- *Diversification.* Time diversification is the most important consideration in risk mitigation at the fund level. Private equity returns are highly sensitive to vintage year (the calendar year in which the investment is made); therefore, deploying capital evenly over the investment period provides the investor with exposure to multiple valuation and macroeconomic environments. Diversification by industry, geography, and investment team partner are also important characteristics to consider. The assessment of investment performance must consider the prevailing economic environment and the specific time period over which the fund was invested and exited.
- *Consistency in returns.* When assessing a buyout fund, consistency of returns among portfolio holdings is important; overall returns should not be reliant on a small number of deals. Early-stage venture returns, however, can be characterized by a small number of investments with outsized returns driving total fund performance. For mid/late-stage investors, the dispersion in returns among portfolio companies is more muted. An analysis of the manager's track record should indicate the appropriate level of dispersion in performance.
- *Realized versus unrealized performance.* Realized performance refers to companies in the track record that have been sold, or exited, by the manager. **Unrealized performance** refers to the performance of underlying companies that are still managed by the manager. The entirety of a manager's track record can be assessed only with an understanding of the methodology used to value the unrealized companies together with the expected future performance of those companies.
- *Loss ratio.* The **loss ratio** measures the amount of invested capital that is held below cost. It may be measured at the company level or at the portfolio level by using a capital-weighted loss ratio or a percentage of the cost/loss ratio. Loss ratios are calculated on both a realized and unrealized basis and are used to evaluate risk.
- *Distributions to paid-in capital.* The distributions to paid-in capital (DPI) indicates the amount of money that has been returned to investors relative to the amount of capital paid into the fund. A high DPI in the early years of a fund's life indicates that a substantial portion of investors' capital has already been returned in the form of profits, an indication of a successful start.

8.4.4 *Company-Level Analysis*

There are different yardsticks by which venture and buyout managers' portfolio investments are assessed.

- *Buyouts.* The analysis of a buyout manager's track record seeks to discover how the manager has created value in its underlying investments. By disaggregating the returns into the three key drivers—earnings growth, multiple arbitrage, and the use of leverage—the investor can understand how the manager has created value. The results of this analysis should support the stated strategy of the fund. If, for example, a manager's stated strategy is to buy companies for growth but the analysis shows that much of the return has been generated through the use of leverage and debt pay down, the investor should explore this apparent contradiction.

- *Venture*. The investment stage for each of the portfolio companies (early, mid, late) should be consistent with the focus of the manager, and the percentage ownership and valuation multiple paid at purchase should likewise correspond to the stage of investment. For example, an early-stage venture manager should have a portfolio of companies in which investment is made at the entry financing stage and is characterized by a high level of ownership (typically >15%) and low valuations (total company valuation of $15 million or less).

Follow-on financing rounds at increasing total company valuations are indicative of positive developments in underlying companies and can be substantiated by an assessment of the performance milestones a portfolio company has achieved (e.g., revenue growth and profitability). Participation by known and respected venture managers in these subsequent financing rounds is also a positive indicator of a company's development.

EXAMPLE 11

1 Which of the following statements *most* accurately describes an attribute of private equity investing?

A Private equity is an inefficient asset class.

B IRRs are easily compared across managers.

C LPs have the right to veto an investment proposed by the general partner.

2 Which of the following statements *most* accurately describes venture capital manager evaluation?

A IRR is the most important performance measure to consider when comparing managers.

B Assessing financial performance needs to be done with appropriate consideration of the prevailing economic environment.

C The analyst should ensure that the manager's source of value creation at the company level (earnings growth, multiple arbitrage, or the use of leverage) is consistent with the stated strategy of the manager.

Solution to 1:

A is correct. Private equity is an inefficient asset class, and the dispersion of returns between the best and worst private equity managers is typically greater than in any other asset class. B is incorrect because the IRR on a private equity investment is highly subject to the valuation methodology used by the manager, the prevailing economic environment for funds of a given vintage year, and the presence of early wins or losses. C is incorrect because the general partner has full discretion as to the underlying investments.

Solution to 2:

B is correct and is the reason for vintage year comparisons of private equity funds. A is incorrect because, although IRR is a key consideration in private equity manager evaluation, an investor must also assess other metrics, including MOIC, DPI, and loss ratio. C is incorrect because earnings growth, multiple arbitrage, and leverage are methods of value creation used by *buyout* managers and are not key considerations for the evaluation of venture managers.

9 SPECIAL CONSIDERATIONS IN REAL ESTATE MANAGER SELECTION

Most institutional investors achieve their private real estate exposure through commingled funds managed by real estate investment managers.[6] The process of selecting a real estate manager is similar in many ways to the selection of a private equity manager. Investors must evaluate the manager's team, strategy, track record, and fee structures, paying particular attention to performance measures, valuation, benchmarks, governance, and regulations.

Institutional investors typically invest in real estate to benefit from the expected low (observed) volatility and low correlation with other asset classes. Many investors also look to real estate for its inflation-hedging characteristics. High current income is appealing to investors who need a predictable source of income. Taxable investors may appreciate the tax benefits (in the form of depreciation charges and interest expense) inherent in some jurisdictions.

The major property types considered as institutional quality are office buildings, retail shopping centers, industrial warehouses, multifamily residential (apartment) buildings, and, to a lesser extent, hotels. Also included are a number of non-core specialty subsectors, such as hospital and medical office buildings, self-storage centers, data centers, and parking lots. Each property type is unique in the nature of the income flows and sensitivity to the real estate and economic cycles. The new-construction single-family home market is not considered an institutional-quality property sector because returns are driven largely by construction rather than rents.

The Real Estate Cycle Real estate returns are highly sensitive to local business and construction cycles, which are driven in part by the economic cycle but are also subject to significant local influences. Exhibit 7 depicts the different phases of a real estate cycle. Long periods of economic growth that result in net new job creation and increased trade tend to boost demand for space and rents. Construction activity accelerates late in the real estate cycle, when market rents rise high enough to justify the high cost of development. The long lead time required to bring a new property to market means that real estate construction often continues after the economy begins to slow. If the new supply exceeds demand, vacancies are likely to increase and rents to decline, giving rise to a period of retrenchment. Leverage, which is very common in real estate investment, increases both the volatility of earnings and the valuation of the investor's equity ownership.

6 When we use the term "real estate investment managers," we are referring to private real estate managers, not managers of publicly traded real estate securities, such as REITs and REOCs.

Exhibit 7 The Real Estate Cycle

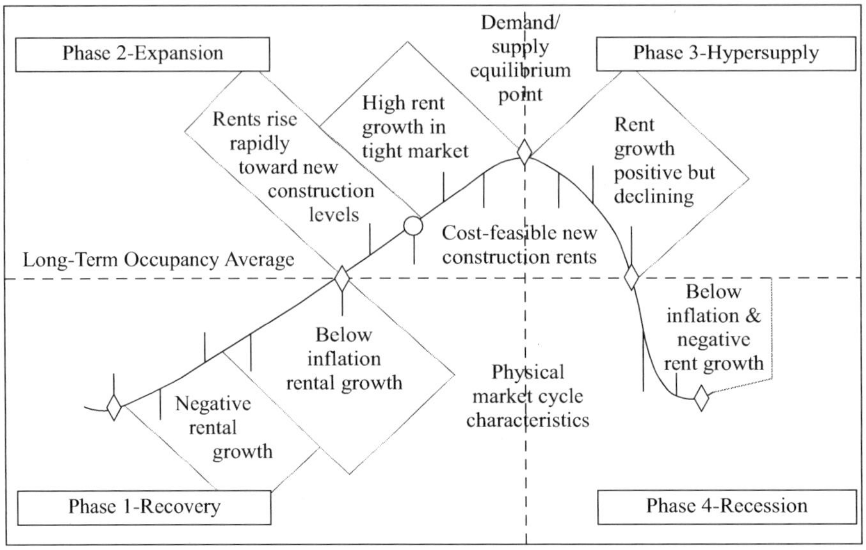

Source: Glenn R. Mueller, PhD, professor, University of Colorado, and Real Estate Investment Strategist, Dividend Capital Research.

While global factors such as interest rates and cross-border capital flows do affect real estate valuations, real estate economics are more heavily influenced by local factors such as regional population and job growth, vacancy rates, and local regulations. In addition to geographic variations, conditions for each property type may differ depending on construction activity, vacancy, and end-user demand.

The sensitivity of a given property type to the economic cycle is directly related to its lease terms. Properties with short-term leases reflect changes in the economic environment more rapidly than properties with long-term leases.With short-term leases, the rental income stream is more quickly "marked to market." Hotels, where rooms are rented on a daily basis, have the shortest leases and are the most sensitive to the economic cycle. Self-storage properties typically use monthly leases; rental apartment leases typically run 6 to 12 months; retail and commercial office leases are typically 5 years (although anchor tenants may have lease terms of 10 years or longer). Major property sale-leaseback transactions (such as when a company sells and then leases its headquarters from the new owner) may have 30-year terms.

Early in a real estate recovery, investors may prefer properties with short-term leases to benefit from rising rents. Prior to a downturn or slowdown, cautious investors may seek out properties with longer-term leases.

Real Estate Investment Styles

Real estate investment funds can generally be categorized into the following investment styles: core, value added, and opportunistic.

Core real estate is defined as high-quality, well-leased properties. Although some core funds concentrate in a specific property type or geographic region, a core portfolio is generally diversified across the largest geographic markets and major product types. Leverage in a core fund is typically less than 30% of asset value, and many core funds employ no leverage at all. (Use of leverage tends to increase the correlation between real estate and financial asset returns.

Investors who are looking for real estate to serve as an inflation hedge may limit the amount of leverage.) Core real estate returns have historically been driven by net rental income, although following the financial crisis of 2007–2009, capital appreciation became a significant return driver as declining interest rates and investors' search for income contributed to rising asset values.

Core investors expect real estate beta to be the primary driver of returns. A core manager is expected to modestly outperform a passive index using skill, knowledge, and insight. Core managers invest primarily in operating, up-to-date, and fully or mostly leased properties, typically avoiding leasing, development, and construction risk.

Value-added strategies are expected to generate higher returns than core investments through greater property-type or geographic concentration and by taking on modest operating risk, such as leasing above-average vacant space, replacing large tenants with expiring leases, and/or modernizing and repositioning properties. Financial leverage is common. When the manager is constrained to take only very modest amounts of risk, the strategy may be referred to as *core-plus* rather than value-added.

Opportunistic investing aims to achieve high returns. These returns are typically derived from successfully timing the real estate cycle, taking on development and redevelopment risk, substantially repositioning properties, taking publicly traded real estate companies private, and employing high financial leverage. The higher return potential may be accompanied by higher volatility and lower correlation with the long-term real estate cycle.

Real Estate Investment Vehicles

Institutional investors in private real estate typically invest via commingled funds. If an investor is deploying large amounts of capital, a separate account may be a viable option.

Separate accounts are managed on behalf of a single investor. A separate account may be attractive to a large investor who desires a high degree of control over the type and timing of investments. Portfolio diversification and asset size will be limited by the size of the investor's capital allocation.

Commingled funds pool investors' capital to purchase real estate assets and provide for future development or redevelopment needs. A commingled fund may be either an infinite-life fund or a finite-life fund. Large funds can achieve broad diversification. Investors have little ability to influence portfolio composition or activity, however.

Infinite-life funds are commingled funds with no mandatory liquidation schedule. With no fixed termination date, the manager can take a long-term view and manage the fund like an operating business rather than as a mere portfolio of properties to be bought, held, and then sold. This structure is commonly used for core strategies.

Finite-life funds are expected to liquidate by a specified date. The liquidation date may be extended for a year or two if market conditions are weak. This structure is commonly used for value-added and opportunistic strategies, although it may be used for core strategies. Investors in finite-life vehicles must be particularly sensitive to their entry and exit points if they are to realize the expected benefits of the real estate allocation.

Commingled funds may be either open-ended or closed-ended and are often structured as limited partnerships.

Open-end funds accept investor capital on an ongoing basis and allow investor redemptions throughout the life of the fund. Fund size will fluctuate with investor activity as well as market conditions. The manager may limit investor subscriptions and redemptions if market conditions warrant. Investors may need to wait in a queue to contribute capital when real estate investment is in high demand or to redeem capital when real estate markets turn down and everyone "heads for the exits." Open-end funds are typically used with core and core-plus strategies.

Closed-end funds accept capital commitments from investors during a one- to two-year marketing period or until the fund reaches a pre-determined maximum size. New investor commitments are not accepted following the final close, and interim redemptions rarely occur. An investor seeking to withdraw from the fund must sell its interest to a third party; the transfer is subject to manager approval. A closed-end finite-life fund typically has a 10-year life, subject to two 1-year extensions. There is an initial two- to four-year investment period during which the manager acquires properties, followed by a five- to seven-year period during which the properties are repositioned and eventually sold. Closed-end funds are often used with value-added and opportunistic strategies. General partners, whose incentive compensation is based on the fund's realized IRR, prefer to realize the bulk of the value quickly, as that action improves the fund's IRR. Similarly, value-added and opportunistic investors do not want ongoing exposure to the lower core-like real estate returns which follow property stabilization. Nor do they want to pay the higher fees charged by value-added and opportunistic managers on these core-like returns.

Limited partnerships are pass-through vehicles for passive investors. There are both private and listed partnerships. Income earned by the partnership is passed through to the limited partners, thus avoiding double taxation. (Double taxation occurs when earnings are taxed at the corporate or entity level, with the residual passed through to investors in the form of dividends, which are then taxed as ordinary income.) Limited partners are not involved in running the business and are not personally liable for the business's activities.

Investors in both public and private partnerships may need to file tax returns to report their share of the fund's income in the country and municipality where the real estate is located. Domestic and foreign tax filings can quickly become complex, not only for individuals but also for institutions, when there are assets held in multiple jurisdictions or countries.

Most private equity real estate funds are formed as private limited partnerships.

A *corporation* is a common structure for real estate investment activity. Shareholders own stock authorized by the corporation and elect the board of directors, which hires the CEO and oversees the business. The corporation pays income taxes on earnings, which may be distributed as dividends to shareholders or reinvested in the business. Tax reporting for the shareholder is vastly simplified compared to tax reporting on partnership income. Shareholder liability is limited to the corporation's net assets.

Real estate investment trusts (REITs) are publicly or privately traded corporations that elect to receive special tax treatment subject to a number of requirements.[7] Provided that REITs adhere to these requirements, their income is not taxed at the corporate level, provided it is distributed as dividends to the shareholders.

---

7 To qualify for REIT status in the United States, the company must derive at least 75% of its gross income from real estate–realted activities (primarily rental and mortgage income), invest at least 75% of all its assets in real estate, and distribute at least 90% of its taxable income. A REIT would owe no income tax if it distrubted 100% of its taxable income. Dividends are taxed as current income to the shareholder. National Association of Real Estate Investment Trusts (NAREIT.com).

REITs can be publicly traded or private, listed or unlisted, finite life or infinite life. Infinite-life REITs are well suited to core investments because there is no time pressure to liquidate holdings. Opportunistic investors may prefer finite-life vehicles, knowing that the manager will be required to liquidate holdings and return the proceeds to the REIT shareholders.

As a means of investing in real estate, the REIT structure has many of the same advantages as the corporate structure: Provided that the qualifications for the preferential tax treatment are not violated, the REIT structure simplifies tax filing and minimizes income taxes.

Core and core-plus private real estate investors typically invest in open-end, infinite-life commingled real estate funds. The long time horizon and the ability to add to or redeem interests in these funds appeal to many core investors. Investors in open-end funds should be aware, however, of two key considerations that may limit their ability to achieve their investment objectives:

- Most managers will impose a limit on how much capital can be contributed or withdrawn at any one time, similar to the "gate" imposed by some hedge fund managers. Commingled funds are, therefore, exposed to potential liquidity mismatch—that is, an investor's ability to withdraw capital may be limited if other investors are also seeking liquidity at the same time. This situation is most likely to occur when it becomes apparent that the real estate market has peaked or has begun to decline.
- Interests in the fund are valued based on property appraisals, which typically lag changes in underlying property fundamentals. If prices are appreciating, subscriptions are likely to be based on net asset values derived from appraisals that reflect the market conditions (lower prices) of the previous 6 to 12 months. If prices are declining, redemptions during weaker markets are likely based on backward-looking appraisals that do not fully reflect the current market conditions. In this case, investors who redeem realize a premium over actual current market value, leaving the remaining investors to absorb all of the price decline as the properties are re-appraised.

9.1 Assessing the Firm

When evaluating a real estate manager, the major areas of focus are:

- overall capabilities—team, experience, market knowledge, and cohesiveness;
- investment evaluation—market assessment, project economics, and scenario analysis;
- sourcing and acquiring of properties;
- asset development, redevelopment, and repositioning;
- property operations—leasing, staffing, maintenance, revenue and expense management, budgeting, and forecasting;
- asset management—development of strategies for each property and buy/sell decisions;
- fund operations—cash management, business continuity, record keeping, and reporting;
- legal processes and compliance—regulatory reporting, property title search, environmental review, lease/contract analysis, and tax planning; and
- risk management culture—robust policies, procedures, and controls to manage investment risk and operating risk, as well as continual improvement in the enforcement of such policies.

9.1.1 *Degree of Integration*

The level of business integration varies significantly among firms. At one extreme, a manager may outsource a range of activities to outside specialists—deal identification and property leasing to brokers; investment due diligence to specialist firms; property management to leading regional organizations; and legal, finance, administration, compliance, IT, and reporting to other third parties. Some managers allocate fund capital among several independent operating partners, each of whom builds, redevelops, and manages properties on behalf of the fund. (This approach is called the *allocator* model.)

At the other extreme are the vertically integrated organizations that can—directly or through affiliates—perform their own development oversight, development, leasing, property management, asset management, financing, and reporting.

In between these two business-model extremes are fund managers that are partially integrated. For example, the manager may have a property management company but outsource construction or leasing to an unaffiliated third party. These managers will oversee the construction and redevelopment firms and the leasing firms before taking over day-to-day property management.

Investors should beware of managers who use their position to collect extra or non-competitive fees. Some GPs receive additional fees for the work the manager and affiliates perform in sourcing, acquiring, financing, developing, leasing, managing, operating, and selling properties. It is important to determine whether the total fees paid to the manager, collected by the GP's affiliates, or charged to the property are appropriate, compare favorably with other managers' fees, and reflect market rates for those services. If the manager charges for other services, the investor should expect the fund management fee to be lower and the fees collected by GP affiliates to be slightly below market.

Exhibit 8 compares the advantages and disadvantages of the different business models.

Exhibit 8 Vertically Integrated GPs Compared to Allocators

	Degree of Integration	
	Fully Integrated	**Allocator**
Services Provided	■ Develop strategy; identify target markets and sectors ■ Source properties, conduct due diligence, and acquire properties ■ Plan and oversee development or redevelopment of properties ■ Handle property leasing and management	■ Develop strategy; identify target markets and sectors ■ Select best operators, leasing organizations, and property managers ■ Conduct due diligence on properties proposed by operating partners
Advantages	■ Control and oversight ■ Broader network to build market intelligence ■ Known service quality ■ Strong network and relationships with buyers, sellers, lenders, tenants, and potential tenants ■ Potential cost savings	■ Partnerships with strong local operators and leasing agents ■ Low fixed overhead costs ■ No need to maintain development organization during downturns or rebuild when conditions firm ■ No legacy commitment to specific property types or geographic markets

Exhibit 8 (Continued)

	Degree of Integration	
	Fully Integrated	**Allocator**
Drawbacks	■ Requires scale to drive economics ■ Difficult and expensive to maintain construction/development team when activity slows ■ Conflicts when manager acquires and manages properties not owned by the fund ■ Affiliate companies become profit centers for GP with no benefit to the fund	■ Extra layers of fees and incentive compensation paid to local operators ■ High expenses when paying market rate to independent service providers ■ Weaker control and oversight ■ Conflicts when independent operators and service providers have other clients ■ Less synergy and market insight when an independent party maintains relationships with brokers, tenants, and buyers/sellers

9.1.2 *Ownership and Capitalization*

In addition to assessing the manager's operating structure, investors should evaluate the GP's ownership and capitalization. Newer real estate managers may sell a stake in the GP to a third party who provides start-up capital. The manager then has dual obligations—to the third-party owner and to the fund investors. It is important to evaluate the potential conflicts of interest in such an arrangement. Questions about the alignment of interests also arise when established managers begin to cash out by selling their GP ownership interests.

Less well-capitalized GPs may take out loans to cover marketing expenses and the GP's capital commitment to the fund. Even successful GPs who are on their third fund may not have realized enough of the prior funds' carried interest to invest their own capital in larger follow-on funds. Prospective investors should review the GP's audited financial statements (including an unqualified audit opinion) to evaluate the firm's financial soundness.

9.1.3 *Governance*

As with private equity funds, investors in commingled real estate funds have limited ability to influence the manager's investment decisions. Long lock-up periods and few redemption options (if redemptions are permitted at all) further restrict the investor's role in guiding or controlling management. While the investor selects the manager because of its skill, value-added, and reputation, the manager's interests may differ from the investor's interests, particularly in weaker markets and when investments are underperforming.

Good governance can help to diminish this agency problem between the manager and the investor. Only prior to committing to a private equity real estate fund does the investor have any significant ability to negotiate the terms governing the fund. The largest fund investors have the greatest strength in negotiations. Smaller investors may request most-favored-nation (MFN) treatment, which gives them the same rights negotiated by other investors whose commitments are the same size or smaller.

Real estate funds with strong governance will create an advisory committee composed of the larger LPs. This advisory committee often has the right to approve the fund auditor, annual report, and valuation. The LPs may be able to replace the manager of the fund (bringing in another firm to oversee the existing portfolio) in the event of an egregious breach of responsibility, such as a key person being convicted of a criminal offense.

LPs in funds with weak governance will have limited ability to prevent managers from making risky investments, expanding into new markets or product types (strategy drift), devoting time to other funds or personal investments, allocating investments to other funds, selling assets from one fund to another, offering co-investment opportunities to friends and family or unrelated fee-paying investors, continuing to call capital and invest following significant team departures, diverting attention from the fund, billing manager expenses to the fund, or taking other actions contrary to the interests of the investors.

9.1.4 *Terms and Conditions*

A term sheet is used to summarize important fund basics. Additional terms and details are spelled out in the offering memorandum, limited partnership agreement, investment management agreement, and other documents. Together, these documents will cover fund life; fund economics; structuring; investment guidelines and restrictions; risk management; reporting and communications; LP and GP rights, responsibilities, and oversight; conflict and conflict-of-interest resolution procedures; key person protections; manager removal; tax allocation; and exit. Thorough due diligence requires a detailed review of these documents, with particular attention to the governance and investor protections.

9.1.5 *Property Tours*

Participating in a tour of properties owned, operated, and/or developed by the manager and its affiliates provides investors with an opportunity to speak with the onsite managers and leasing agents, better understand the management strategy, attain a better grasp of the market, and even compare a given property to assets in the surrounding area. Random checks to confirm that a property is indeed owned by the manager and as well leased as the manager claims are one way to reduce the risk of fraud.

While visiting just one or a few assets pre-selected by the fund manager is of limited value, the onsite visit can still provide a reality check. For example, is the property in the same condition as reported by management, is there substantial deferred maintenance, is the parking lot full, is the property well leased to credit-worthy tenants, and do the onsite leasing agents appear knowledgeable about the property's selling points versus the market and the competition? It is not uncommon for space to be listed as leased even when the rent-paying tenant has chosen to vacate the property. Vacant space generally detracts from a property's appeal, and as in the case of vacated retail space, the property owner will not be able to collect "percentage rents," which are based on a percentage of the tenant's retail sales.

9.1.6 *Third-Party Assessment*

Evaluating the quality of a manager's investment, operating, and risk management capabilities will require an assessment of the service providers that perform key activities for the fund. The manager should hire recognized, reputable, and independent auditors. Beyond hiring an auditor, the use of service providers and the degree of outsourcing will vary according to the manager's strategy and internal capabilities. Most managers use the services of third-party appraisers and administrators; they may also hire real estate developers and operators. The number of firms outsourcing their technology function is likely to increase as cloud computing continues to gain acceptance.

Evaluating managers that outsource key investing and operating activities requires an understanding of how the manager selects and evaluates its partners. This process parallels the due diligence outlined at the beginning of this section. In effect, investors must perform their own due diligence on the manager's due diligence process and even evaluate the manager's partners directly.

Exhibit 9 summarizes the key areas to explore when evaluating the manager's selection of third-party service providers.

Exhibit 9 Third-Party Service Providers

Partner/Service Provider	Topics to Discuss with the Investment Manager	If Speaking Directly to the Third-Party Provider
Real estate operating partner	■ Selection process ■ Due diligence performed ■ Extent of relationship ■ Level of involvement, oversight, and controls ■ Compensation	■ Partner experience ■ Partner skill/value-added ■ Functions handled internally vs. those that are outsourced ■ Market and property due diligence ■ Cash handling ■ Reputation
Property manager	■ Extent of relationship ■ Due diligence performed ■ Level of involvement, oversight, and controls ■ Fees relative to market rates	■ Experience and scale ■ Market knowledge and depth ■ Competitive position ■ Conflicts of interest (services performed for other parties or own portfolio)
Administrator	■ Length of relationship ■ Activities outsourced ■ Communications ■ Cash handling ■ Costs to fund	■ Real estate fund experience ■ Capabilities ■ Level of attention to fund ■ Process audit and error detection results ■ Cash handling ■ Business continuity and disaster recovery ■ Reporting capability, frequency, and timing
Legal counsel	■ Extent of relationship ■ Services performed ■ Costs to fund	■ Experience and specialization ■ Depth of talent
IT	■ Extent of relationship ■ Services performed ■ Due diligence performed ■ Costs to fund	■ Experience and scale ■ Financial stability ■ Security, redundancy, and disaster recovery ■ Data breach detection

EXAMPLE 12

Assessing the Firm

1 Which of the following statements is *most* correct?

A Allocators may pay fees and carried interest to regional developers.

B Regional fund managers outperform national fund managers due to better knowledge of local markets.

C Allocators get better access to deals because they are not tied to a region or product type.

D Vertically integrated managers provide greater property management savings than allocators.

2 Which of the following considerations is *most* important when evaluating real estate managers?

A Fees paid to brokers

B Fees paid to property managers

C Fees paid to management affiliates

D Fees paid to construction managers

Solution to 1:

A is correct. Investors should be aware that the allocator model may result in additional fees and expenses that are not reported to the fund. Like fund-of-funds managers, allocators that receive fees and carried interest may also pay fees and carried interest to their local operating partners. B is not correct because national managers may have local real estate officers who are as knowledgeable as their regional counterparts. C is not correct because either operating model may have local real estate representatives (whether employees of the firm or of an affiliated firm) who would be well positioned to access their respective markets. D is not correct because vertically integrated managers may charge above-market rates for affiliated services, while allocators may be able to negotiate discounts with third-party property managers.

Solution to 2:

C is correct. It is important to understand how all major fees charged to the fund and/or the property affect fund economics and whether the fees charged are fair (at or below market). When a GP derives a significant fee and profit stream from the services its affiliates perform, the GP has greater incentive to extend the property holding period and the fund life. In order to better align the interests of the investors and the GP, investors should ensure that the GP's economics are driven by the fund's performance and not the ancillary revenue derived from related services.

9.2 Assessing the Team

As with other asset classes, investors should seek to meet directly with the staff of the investment manager to evaluate whether the team has the depth and experience required to execute on the strategy. The strongest teams will have a balance between solid real estate operating experience and financial expertise. Staff experience should match the target strategy, sector, and markets. Expanding beyond a core competency or into new markets requires moving up a learning curve and taking time to develop new relationships.

While a manager can generate returns through the acquisition and financing of properties at attractive prices, the team must have adequate property, asset, construction, and risk management capabilities to realize a property's full potential. Strong property managers will appropriately position a property in its market, lease retail properties to tenants that boost customer visits, balance rent levels with occupancy, offer the right blend of lease incentives, determine when a submarket is firming or easing, and maintain an understanding of competing properties to maximize profits. There is an art to knowing when to hold out for higher rents, renew a lease at the existing rent, offer a concession, or upgrade the space to increase, sustain, or defend profits. When space goes unleased, there is no rental income to cover fixed-expense allocations or incremental advertising and leasing costs.

The last major commercial real estate recession, characterized by lower rents and asset values due to overbuilding, concluded in the early 1990s. A number of today's leading real estate investors learned about real estate risk at that time while employed by banks to handle real estate loan default workouts. Many newer managers have not had this experience.

9.3 Assessing the Strategy

LPs need to consider whether the fund strategy can meet their objectives and constraints, whether it is realistic, and whether it can be accomplished by the manager. The investigation will include an analysis of expected returns, return drivers, sector and geographic exposures, diversification, leverage, volatility, and even liquidity. The strategy should target the investor's desired risks, avoid undesired risks, and provide appropriate reward net of fees and expenses. As indicated previously, some strategies target steady, long-term income from numerous holdings in all major markets across most sectors with little leverage, while others may seek shorter-term capital appreciation through concentrated exposure to office property redevelopment in cities with high employment growth driven by high-tech companies, using high leverage. Alternatively, investors whose wealth is derived from specific industries or geographic areas may seek to avoid real estate in the same industries or regions and may even avoid tenants exposed to similar drivers. For example, a foundation funded with stock donated by the founder of an oil exploration company may want to underweight exposure to regions and tenants whose success depends on the oil industry.

The strategy should be appropriate for the point in the real estate cycle. As would be expected, successful and/or popular strategies will attract substantial capital, which increases competition and prices for assets and diminishes expected return. At the height of the cycle, many investors favor well-leased properties with long-term leases, strong tenant credit quality, lower leverage, long-term debt, and staggered lease maturities and may prefer only short-term redevelopments or developments. At the bottom of the cycle, a strategy targeting acquisitions of properties at deep discounts to replacement cost may offer substantial upside. At mid-cycle, exposure to buildings with short-term leases, some vacancy, need for modernization, or leverage could provide attractive upside.

9.4 Assessing the Track Record

Evaluating the performance of a real estate investment manager is a multi-level assessment exercise. The investor should assess the aggregate, firm-level investment performance as well as the performance of specific underlying funds and even individual properties.

9.4.1 *Firm-Level Track Record*

At its simplest, successful real estate investing can be distilled down to (1) buying the right property at the right price; (2) executing operating plans successfully; and (3) leveraging the market cycle in the purchase, sale, and operating decisions. To evaluate a manager's value-added, the investor must assess past performance in the context of the market conditions for each vintage, region, and sector. Large firms with multiple funds, geographic areas, and/or styles can be judged on management's nimbleness in allocating to different strategies as well as its ability to exercise discipline near market peaks.

Consider how the following market drivers influence returns:

- Vintage. Some real estate private equity firms that raised capital in the years preceding the global financial crisis deployed little, if any, of the investors' capital commitments due to the lack of attractive opportunities. Others plowed forward rather than watch fees and assets slip away.
- Sector. Industrial warehouse and distribution properties performed well during the period of rising global trade, while regional shopping centers in weaker secondary cities underperformed as internet shopping gained market share. Multifamily rentals did very well following the subprime mortgage led financial crisis.
- Region. Real estate performed well in gateway cities in many Western countries (e.g., London; New York; San Francisco; Washington, DC) during the decade from 2000 through the financial crisis. From 2012 to 2016, these cities became so expensive that there were few opportunities for continued outperformance. Many value-added and opportunistic funds pursued investments in secondary markets.
- Country and currency risk. Brazil was an investor favorite in the mid-2000s. However, the financial crisis and a change in government were followed by weakening business conditions and large declines in the currency's value from 2010 through the beginning of 2016.

Firms with a long track record should provide evidence of how they have allocated capital and how their investments perform over a cycle. A well-disciplined manager should slow capital deployment when real estate becomes expensive. Such a manager might even recommend selling assets and sending back investor capital when the return outlook has deteriorated—even if it means forgoing fees.

9.4.2 *Fund-Level Track Record.*

Investors pursuing open-end funds or secondary interests in closed-end funds may be able to evaluate the track record of a specific fund they plan to invest in. The manager should be able to describe the investment thesis for each underlying property, its target return, and the property's performance relative to the plan and to the local market. While raising capital for new open- or closed-end funds, the manager should make available performance data on its prior funds.

Even though the GP may be able to point to the performance of prior funds, there may have been too few property sales for the track record to be meaningful. Many managers are quick to harvest successful investments but slow to sell the losers, and this behavior can skew the performance of recent-vintage funds, which carry investments at cost. With some extra local due diligence, investors can independently compare the performance of unrealized investments to the pro forma plan laid out by the manager at the time the property was acquired. For example, managers of competing properties may know the status of local developments, and recently signed tenants can confirm new lease commitments.

Even with these additional insights, performance evaluation in real estate is a complicated endeavor. Finite-life funds may own too few properties for even realized returns to be relevant to future investment activities, especially when the portfolio is diversified across geographic areas and/or sectors rather than concentrated. Open-end funds' subscription and redemption activity are likely to have influenced investment returns, but segregating the impact of those transactions—which were not within the manager's control—is a nearly impossible task.

9.4.3 *Property-Level Performance Assessment.*

Analyzing the performance of individual properties is also challenging. Many idiosyncratic factors affect a property's performance: location, local economic activity, individual tenant activity, new development, changing traffic conditions, weather, etc. Before approving an investment, most firms will produce an internal investment memo describing the property, how it was sourced, the market, the opportunity, the strategy, expected returns (base case, upside, and downside, at a minimum), risks, risk mitigation strategies, due diligence plan or results, and time frame. The potential investment should fit with the fund's strategy in terms of size, geographic area, sector, and style; be consistent with the manager's competencies; and offer upside consistent with the fund's objectives and risk tolerance. The depth and comprehensiveness of the report are important indicators of the strength of the manager's investment process. Even though new managers may not be able to point to a track record, they may have a pipeline of potential investments to evaluate using similar criteria. The ability to source acquisitions through relationships rather than well-publicized auctions provides the manager with additional competitive advantages.

The property-level review should investigate any below-average performers, especially if returns were negative. The manager should be able to address why results differed from the plan. Did the shortfall result from one of the potential risks identified in the firm's underwriting memo or investment committee minutes, or were there other causes? Was it due to exogenous factors, such as a change in market conditions, or could a stronger manager have avoided the problem through better oversight, leasing, or government/community relations? Was the manager capable of adopting a new operating plan once the shortfall became evident?

The property operating performance review should go beyond simple comparisons of rent and occupancy to examine how the manager applies revenue management strategies. Clearly, low rents can boost occupancy while high rents can discourage prospective tenants. Maximizing revenue requires a good understanding of the local market and the ability to convey the strategy to the onsite and leasing personnel. It might mean raising rents when market conditions are firming and increasing occupancy in advance of market weakness, whether that weakness is due to new supply or slowing growth.

A more detailed investigation will examine property operating income. Raising rents too aggressively contributes to higher tenant turnover and longer periods between leases, both of which are expensive. It is common for commercial real estate landlords to provide a variety of incentives for new tenants, such as an improvement allowance to build out and customize the space and/or an initial rent-free period when the tenant's lease commences. Thus, the stated rent may be higher than the effective rent the building owner actually receives over the life of each lease.

Investors with separate accounts, joint ventures, co-investments, and direct investments may receive property-level information that is not generally available to investors in large commingled funds or closed-end funds. A separate account investor may want to review more detailed due diligence material for each property, such as the engineering report, environmental report, marketing package, market study, lease roll, leasing plan, and financial projections.

This "deep dive" provides a better understanding of the main drivers of return and risk (e.g., assumptions about redevelopment costs, rate of lease-up, changes in market or property rents, or exit values). Investors with limited real estate experience may engage an independent consultant to analyze the validity of these assumptions. A specialist can opine on the reasonableness of construction costs and timing, leasing schedules, new tenant build-out expenses, and permitting milestones.

9.4.4 *Real Estate Investment Benchmarks*

As with many alternative investments, benchmarking for performance and risk evaluation in real estate suffers from a number of limitations. Choosing the appropriate real estate benchmark requires careful consideration and an understanding of the limitations of such benchmarks. Some of these limitations are listed below:

- Real estate benchmarks are based on a subset of the real estate opportunity set and therefore are not fully representative of the asset class.
- Index performance is likely to be highly correlated with the returns of the largest fund data contributors.
- Benchmark returns are based on manager-reported performance and may be inherently biased.
- Performance measures based on active managers' results do not represent returns to the unmanaged asset class.
- Benchmarks weighted by fund or asset value may place a disproportionate emphasis on the most expensive cities and asset types.
- Valuations of the underlying properties are typically based on appraisals because there are few transactions to measure. Appraisals are infrequent, smooth changes in property values and can lag underlying property performance; they tend to overstate real estate values after a cycle has peaked and may not reflect distressed sales at the bottom of a cycle.
- Some core benchmark returns are unlevered, complicating the comparison to funds with leverage. Other value-added and opportunistic peer-group benchmarks may include each contributor fund's leverage, making return comparisons difficult.
- Real estate indexes do not reflect the high transaction costs, limited transparency, and lack of liquidity that drive performance for actual real estate investments.
- The indexes are not investable.

A number of private real estate investment benchmarks exist at both the asset (property) level and the fund level.

Industry trade associations—such as the National Council of Real Estate Investment Fiduciaries (NCREIF) in the United States, the European Association for Investors in Non-Listed Real Estate Vehicles (INREV), and the Asian Association for Investors in Non-Listed Real Estate Vehicles (ANREV)—release some of the most widely quoted return series. These organizations collect data by region, sector, and investment style. They prepare their own country/region indexes and contribute to the Global Real Estate Fund Index (GREFI).

Most large and many small pension funds and their managers have agreed to report property and fund performance to these industry trade groups. Nearly all of the contributors are tax-exempt organizations. Although pension funds are among the largest owners of real estate, they do not represent the entire institutional investor universe, and thus their data are not fully representative of the market.

The two most widely used NCREIF indexes in the United States are the NCREIF Property Index (NPI) and the NCREIF Fund Index – Open-End Diversified Core Equity (NFI-ODCE).

The NPI is an unlevered, value-weighted, property-level, time-weighted return index. It breaks out returns from capital appreciation, from income, by region (East, West, South, and Midwest), and by sector (office, retail, industrial, apartment, and hotel). The NPI is the oldest of the NCREIF indexes, with top-level total returns going back to the fourth quarter of 1977. The NPI does not purport to be a core index and may include returns from value-added activities.

The NFI-ODCE is a cap-weighted index of 36 core commingled funds that use not more than 40% leverage. Time-weighted returns are reported gross of fees, although net-of-fee returns are available. These index returns also go back to the end of 1977.

It is important to note that the income component of return in these indexes represents property-level income—rental income minus rental expenses and related costs before financial leverage and taxes—regardless of whether or not the income is distributed to investors. Additionally, asset-level return indexes are usually gross of investment management fees, while the fund returns being compared to the benchmark may be gross *or* net of all fund expenses and manager fees.

Numerous other private data providers publish index returns. Notable among these is MSCI, which publishes an extensive number of listed company and private real estate investment indexes. MSCI's IPD property fund indexes (formerly Investment Property Databank indexes) report returns for unlisted funds and underlying property values based on appraised values, estimated values, and transaction values.

The IPD Global Quarterly Property Fund Index (GPFI) covers 25 countries based on input from 98 core open-end funds with $318 billion of net asset value as of March 2017. Indexes are also available for numerous regions, countries, and property sectors, at the property level and at the fund level, gross and net of fees. The GPFI has come into widespread use for its global coverage.

The following table summarizes high-level characteristics of many of the indexes just described. These indexes represent just a few of the numerous private real estate indexes offered by industry associations, large and small index providers, investment consultants, and others who collect real estate data. There are indexes and sub-indexes for nearly all of the major developed countries, major sectors, investment styles, and structures (open-end and closed-end funds). Transaction-based indexes have become more common, further expanding a universe that initially valued real estate based only on appraisals.

Exhibit 10 Leading Appraisal-Based Private Real Estate Property and Fund Indexes

Index	Provider	Property- or Fund-Level Index	Data Begins	Launched	Region	Universe
Appraisal-Based Indexes						
NCREIF Property Index (NPI)	NCREIF	Property	Q4 1977	1982	US	7,371 properties $515 billion gross assets
INREV Index	INREV	Fund	2001	2005	Europe	497 funds €290 billion net assets
NCREIF Fund Index – Open-End Diversified Core Equity (NFI-ODCE)	NCREIF	Fund	Q1 1978	2005	US	24 active funds $162 billion net assets
ANREV	ANREV	Funds	2006	2011	Asia	94 funds $96 billion gross assets
PREA IPD US Property Fund Index	MSCI, PREA	Fund	Q1 2008	2012	US	36 funds $271 billion gross assets

(continued)

Exhibit 10 (Continued)

Index	Provider	Property- or Fund-Level Index	Data Begins	Launched	Region	Universe
IPD Global Property Fund Index (GPFI)	MSCI	Fund	YE 2007	2013	Global	98 funds $318 billion net assets
Global Real Estate Fund Index (GREFI)	ANREV, INREV, NCREIF	Fund	YE 2009	2014	Global	472 funds $577 billion gross assets

Notes:

NCREIF data as of Q2 2016.

INREV, ANREV, IPD-PREA, MSCI, and NPI and IPD-PREA data as of Q3 2016.

MSCI IPD GPFI data as of March 2017.

GREFI data as of Q1 2016.

Unless specified as core open-end funds, indexes may include closed-end, value-added, and opportunistic funds.

Sources: Pension Real Estate Association, *A Primer on Commercial Real Estate Indices*, PREA Research Report (December 2016). Index provider websites.

Benchmark selection is a subjective exercise. The investor must consider carefully what benchmark is most appropriate and be aware of the limitations inherent in comparing the performance of a property or a fund to the chosen benchmark.

EXAMPLE 13

Real Estate Benchmarks

1 Which of the following statements is *most* correct?

A Fund-level indexes include fees and expenses.

B Property-level indexes exclude transaction costs.

C Transaction-based indexes are better indicators of market performance than appraisal-based indexes.

D A benchmark with frequent appraisals is a good indicator of short-term pricing trends.

2 Which benchmark best represents the returns that investors have received from core US real estate fund investments?

A The IPD GPFI because it contains the largest sampling of funds.

B The NFI-ODCE net of fees and expenses because it measures fund returns.

C The NFI-ODCE gross of fees and expenses because it measures fund returns.

D The NPI because it contains property-level returns from income and capital appreciation.

3 You are attempting to understand the performance of your core real estate investments during the financial crisis of 2007–2009. The NPI declined a relatively modest 6.46% during 2008 as the S&P 500 fell 37% and listed REITs, represented by the FTSE/NAREIT index, dropped 37.73%. (See

accompanying table.) In 2009, the S&P 500 and FTSE/NAREIT indexes each rose by more than 25% while the NPI declined another 16.85%. Which of the following statements is correct?

	2007	2008	2009	2010
NPI	+15.84	−6.46	−16.85	+13.11
S&P 500	+5.49	−37.00	+26.46	+15.06
FTSE/NAREIT	−15.69	−37.73	+27.99	+27.95

A The poor relative performance of private real estate in 2009 is because the NPI represents leveraged real estate returns and leverage magnifies an investor's gains and losses.

B The strong relative performance of the NPI in 2008 is likely because appraisals tend to lag trends in real estate values.

C The performance of the FTSE/NAREIT index better reflects the real-time performance of the real estate asset class and is a more appropriate benchmark to use in evaluating the performance of the fund.

D The strong relative performance of the NPI in 2007 is likely due to real estate's lower sensitivity to the economic cycle.

Solution to 1:

B is correct. A is not correct because some indexes are reported gross of fees and expenses. C is not correct because, although transactions can provide a better picture of real estate and manager performance than appraised values, there may not be enough transactions of similar properties for these indexes to be meaningful in all markets. D is not correct because, while more frequent appraisals do improve index quality, appraisals lag market trends and smooth short-term price movements.

Solution to 2:

B is correct. The NFI-ODCE provides the best indication of the returns investors have received from investing in the major core funds net of fees. It is important to consider returns net of fees rather than gross of fees in measuring returns to the investor because fee loads can vary among funds and managers. A is incorrect because the IPD GPFI is a global index. C is not correct because returns are reported before fees and do not reflect investor-level returns. D is incorrect because the NPI presents property-level returns rather than fund-level returns.

Solution to 3:

B is correct. The NPI is an appraisal-based index. Real estate rents and valuations were negatively affected by the global financial crisis, but because appraisal-based indexes are slow to reflect changes in valuation, the impact of the crisis was not reflected in the index until the public markets (the S&P 500 and the FTSE/NAREIT) had begun to recover. A is incorrect because the NPI is an unlevered index. C is incorrect because the performance of listed REITs, which are levered and subject to swings in investor sentiment, is not directly comparable to the performance of core, unlevered private real estate investments. D is incorrect because real estate rents and valuations were, in fact, negatively affected by the global financial crisis (as reflected in the −15.69% decline in the FTSE/NAREIT Index), but the appraisal process is slow to fully reflect declines in valuations.

9.5 Assessing the Fees and Economics

As mentioned earlier, it is critical to understand what fees the manager collects, which expenses are paid by the fund, and how the **waterfall**—the allocation of distributions between the fund's investors and the GP—works.

Carried interest in private real estate investment ranges from 10% at the low end to 20% for most value-added and opportunistic funds. The manager's carried interest is typically earned on profits in excess of a preferred return. In the early stages of distribution, the cash flows are paid to the LPs until the LPs have earned the specified hurdle rate. Thereafter, profits may be allocated disproportionately to the GP until it has received an amount reflective of the cumulative carried interest. Thereafter, each distribution will be apportioned among the investors and the GP in proportion to the carried interest.

The investor should determine whether management fees are based on committed capital, called capital, or outstanding capital, or on net asset value or gross asset value. (Fees on gross asset value reward the manager for borrowing money—typically not a value-added activity in the same way that asset redevelopment is.) Moreover, when leverage is deployed to lift the fund's return high enough to exceed the preferred return hurdle, the GP may be able to claim its 10% to 20% of the fund's profits for doing nothing other than mortgaging the assets. Nonetheless, some GPs argue that it requires more time and effort to deploy the additional capital and manage a larger portfolio.

An assessment of fees, carried interest, and gross-to-net calculations should be made across sequential fund offerings. As a GP develops a good track record and becomes more successful at raising capital, it may shift fee responsibility (or dilute governance) from one fund to the next. For example, the degree to which the manager and the fund share costs related to the fund offering, property due diligence, and insurance, as well as legal and failed-deal costs, is subject to negotiation.

When evaluating fund economics, it is helpful to conduct a sensitivity and scenario analysis: How do fees and carried interest affect net investor returns under a variety of real estate and capital market scenarios? For example, what would be the downside return in a recession, which might be characterized by higher borrowing costs, lower debt availability, higher vacancy, lower rents, and/or lower real estate valuations? What is the upside? When markets become overheated, with rents, occupancy, and real estate values rising rapidly, construction costs are also likely to rise as developers compete for raw materials and skilled labor. How does the upside compare to the downside? Can the base case or the upside case justify the potential volatility of returns, or are returns skewed to the downside? An established manager should be able to produce this analysis for prospective investors. The investor should check the assumptions for reasonableness.

Once the scenarios have been considered, the investor can use a weighted probability analysis, assigning weights to each scenario based on the likelihood of each occurring, and compare the stated target return to the most likely return.

In addition to a scenario analysis, a sensitivity analysis should also be considered. The sensitivity analysis is straightforward: It measures how much the expected return changes for a given change in interest rates, development costs, expected completions, rents, vacancy, or operating expenses—typically the most important return drivers.

ON-GOING MANAGER MONITORING AND CONTINUANCE

10

After an investment manager has been hired, instituting a defined, consistently applied process for monitoring the manager's activities and performance will enable the investor to better evaluate the manager's investment results, as well as identify potential problem areas before they impact performance. All of the factors considered when hiring the manager should continue to be monitored after hiring. Although "monitoring" is typically thought of as the evaluation of performance results, an appropriate monitoring process will include both qualitative and quantitative components. Monitoring is facilitated by ensuring that the qualities that led to the manager being hired are documented at the time of the investment; those qualities can be subsequently confirmed or questioned through ongoing due diligence.

10.1 Qualitative Manager Monitoring

Scheduling periodic (typically annual) meetings with managers, including some on-site meetings at the manager's office, facilitates a deeper review of investment and operational issues than what can be gleaned through a review of a manager's written reports and quarterly update calls. As in the initial research process, discussions should focus on the manager's organization, personnel, and investment process. Significant changes in any of these areas could serve as "red flags" that may cause the investor to question whether they are still receiving the service they contracted for.

Wherever possible, investors should require managers to promptly inform them about any relevant issues, including the following:

- Alterations to the firm's ownership structure
- Capacity limits
- Business prospects
- Regulatory environment
- Personnel changes, especially in the portfolio manager/analyst team or in top management
- Investment process

Changes in the organization can be positive or may reflect internal turmoil and instability. As such, it is important to understand the context and reason behind personnel changes. All else being equal, personnel continuity is a sign of stability. Unexpected departures or high personnel turnover do not necessarily suggest immediately firing the manager, but continued issues can distract individuals from focusing on the investment process and are likely to negatively affect performance.

- Has there been any loss of key personnel without a clear and credible succession plan? The more senior the people leaving, the more problematic.
- Has there been any turnover among investment or operational staff? An inability to retain staff may signal potential cultural or compensation issues and increases investment and operational risks because of inexperience.
- Have there been new hires, and what are the roles of any new hires? The expertise and experience of an individual must be suitable for the role he or she plays.

- High turnover among sales and investor service may indicate that the firm's future business prospects have dimmed.
- All else being equal, it is of greater concern if the departed personnel take similar positions at competing companies and of less concern if they leave for roles that have greater responsibility. Conversely, it is of even less concern if they leave for a completely different vocation—for instance, running a charitable foundation or opening an art gallery.

Legal and compliance issues should be reviewed to confirm that the firm's interests remain aligned with those of the investor.

- Have there been any changes in third-party service providers? A potential red flag is a change in prime broker, auditor, or administrator. Third-party service providers independently verify manager performance. Changes can signal attempts to reduce transparency or hide potential issues.
- Have there been any changes in the compensation arrangements of key employees?
- Have there been any changes in the way employees invest personal assets in the firm's strategies?
- Have there been any changes in the compliance manual?
- Has the firm or any of its employees been involved in an investigation by any regulator or self-regulatory organization?
- Has the firm been involved in any lawsuits?
- Are any of the firm's employees involved in legal actions or personal litigation that might affect their ability to continue to fulfill their fiduciary responsibilities?

Monitoring growth in AUM is important because a dilution of skill is possible as more capital is directed to a particular opportunity. As noted, one risk is that the manager exhibits style drift in an attempt to maintain performance or implement the strategy with a larger asset base. Ideally, the manager can identify new opportunities. Alternatively, the manager can close the strategy to maintain performance for current investors. Closing a fund or strategy shows desirable discipline and alignment of interests by the manager but raises issues for a decision maker that uses the manager for multiple investors. Preferably, the firm has a clearly stated policy and process for closing funds, but in all cases, such a policy must be applied consistently across strategies and investors.

- **Hard close:** The manager closes to all investors. Although this arrangement protects current investors, it presents a problem to the allocator. If a comparable replacement can be found, there is the added operational cost of maintaining two managers for the same role in the portfolio with higher name count and due diligence costs. If no comparable can be found, there is the problem of basis risk—that is, different investors in the same model realizing different returns. Firing the manager to create a common model, however, penalizes those investors that held the closed manager (opportunity cost of holding a less skillful manager). A hard close can also result in hesitancy to fire the manager for fear of losing access to the manager. For capacity-constrained mandates, it is generally a good practice to negotiate a paid-in-capital capacity amount with the manager before engaging with them.
- **Soft close:** The manager closes to new investors but remains open to current investors. Although this arrangement also protects current investors, it increases the risk that the fund eventually undertakes a hard close.

The decision of whether closure requires terminating a manager requires balancing these issues.

In addition to the level of AUM, it is important to understand the composition of the firm's investor base. A higher concentration in a limited number of investors increases liquidity risk, the potential for redemptions that negatively affect the portfolio's value. A potentially unstable investor base warrants reevaluating the manager.

- What is the investor breakdown (e.g., percentage endowment/foundation, high net worth /family office, pensions, and individuals)? A broader, more diverse investor base is less susceptible to large, concentrated outflows.

Proactively monitoring appropriate news outlets can help investors stay abreast of organizational developments. Once an issue is identified, the investor can evaluate the impact of the change in a timely fashion. If a manager is not forthcoming about such issues, the alignment of interests should be questioned, and regardless of how strong the manager's performance record has been, this concern may be enough to cause the investor to terminate the relationship.

Even if there have not been any significant changes, continued meetings are important so that the investor can remain informed about the manager's views on the market, thoughts on specific holdings, and the overall portfolio positioning. In the early years of a relationship with a manager, when the performance track record is short, the monitoring approach should emphasize such elements as reporting, client service, proxy voting, portfolio characteristics, and process consistency more than performance evaluation. Over time, as the track record lengthens, performance analysis can take on a larger role in the monitoring process, but the qualitative elements should remain in place. These qualitative elements often serve as a leading indicator of potential future performance issues and as a complement to the performance analysis, which considers only historical returns.

One good example of qualitative analysis is studying whether and how the manager's portfolio characteristics change as its asset base grows—an equity manager might buy larger capitalization securities and/or more securities, than it historically did because of liquidity issues caused by asset growth. Such tools as holdings-based risk models, custodial reports, and the manager's own periodic client reports are helpful in highlighting potential issues. This qualitative analysis can be combined with performance-based style analysis to see what impact, if any, the growth in assets is having on characteristics and results.

10.2 Style Drift

An important aspect of selection and manager continuance is determining whether the manager continues to adhere to the stated investment philosophy and decision-making process. Style drift is a deviation from the stated risk factor exposures, identified using RBSA or HBSA, that underpin the investment philosophy and process. For managers whose investment process is expected to consistently adhere to a particular investment style, style drift undermines confidence in the repeatability of the investment process and compromises confidence in the manager's ability to repeat past performance in the future. Style drift may also suggest that the manager is no longer suitable for the investor and continued investment with that manager may cause distort the desired portfolio structure. The manager was hired to fill a particular role within the overall portfolio, and deviations from this role can expose the investor to unwanted risks.

Style drift should be viewed as a relative rather than an absolute concept. Thus, it is important to be clear on how style is measured and what might signal that style drift has occurred.

- *Measurement:* Style is measured as the risk factor exposures that explain the manager's performance. This attribution requires a benchmark, and so style drift is often considered to be deviations from the benchmark. This view has its limitations.
- *Skew versus drift:* Some manager investment processes are broad in nature and will naturally deviate from a stated benchmark. This deviation can be more of a benchmarking issue than a style drift issue and might reflect the lack of a precise benchmark rather than style drift.
- *Cyclical versus structural:* A manager's risk factors will naturally fluctuate through time. The key question is whether these differences represent a short-term deviation of the strategy or a longer-term change in the investment process and/or its implementation.

One method of determining and screening for style drift are snail trail charts.[8] A snail trail chart displays information about the manager's return characteristics through time. Exhibit 11 displays the rolling 36-month returns and standard deviations for an enhanced equity index portfolio relative to the Russell 1000 benchmark. The larger the symbol, the more recent the observation.

Exhibit 11 Manager Risk/Return, January 2001–December 2007

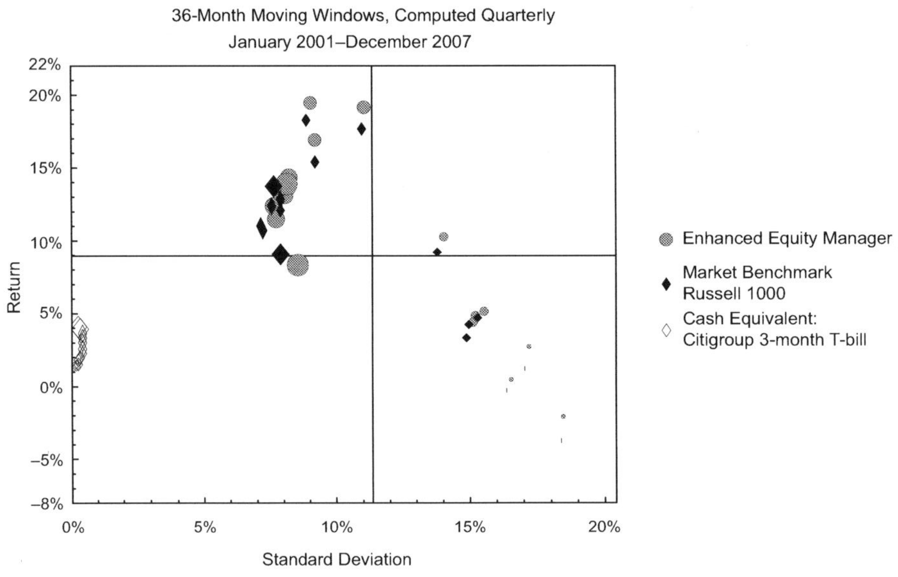

Source: Zephyr Style Advisor

The trail shows that the manager's standard deviation initially declined and has been between 7.5% and 10% for the most recent windows. The manager's return initially increased but has declined through the most recent windows.

Notice that the return and standard deviation of the benchmark follows a similar pattern. To examine the manager's alpha and tracking risk, the graph can be recast to display the rolling 36-month relative returns and relative risk, as shown in Exhibit 12.

8 Examples are from Meier 2009.

Exhibit 12 Manager Risk/Return, January 2001–December 2007

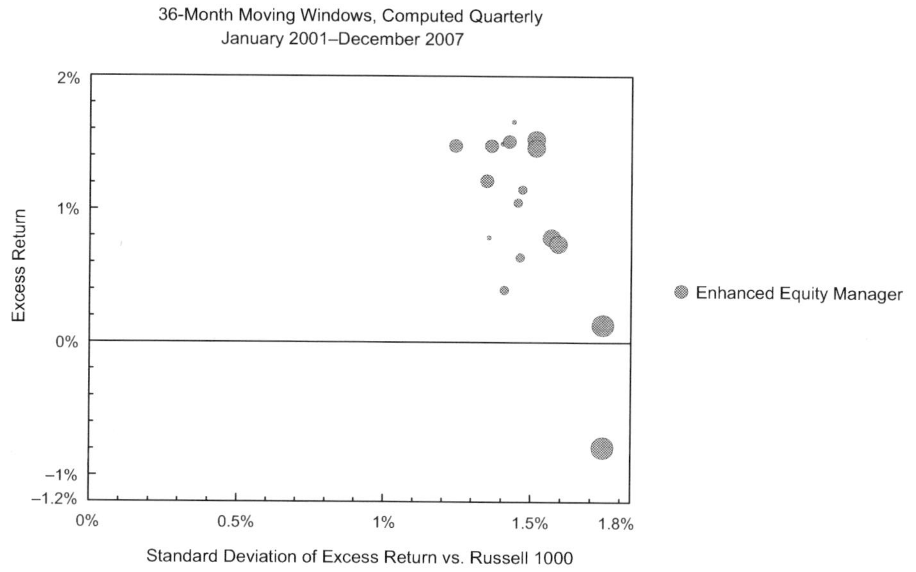

Source: Zephyr Style Advisor

In this case, we are interested in the level and consistency of the realized tracking risk. As an enhanced index strategy, the goal is consistent positive excess return with limited and consistent tracking risk. Consistent performance through time would result in all of the dots falling on top of, or in close proximity to, each other. In this case, the manager has generated consistent tracking, and although there has been a slight increase through time, the overall level of tracking risk has not increased substantially. Excess return, however, has declined noticeably for the most recent windows and is now negative. Such a pattern signals the need for further investigation into the underlying causes of the underperformance.

Snail trail plots can also be used to track the evolution of other portfolio characteristics. For example, we could plot the weighted average market capitalization on the y-axis (small-cap to large-cap) relative to a weighted average style on the x-axis (value to growth) for an equity portfolio manager. A consistent pattern of shifting market capitalization or value/growth tilt would signal potential style drift and the need for further investigation into the portfolio's changing risk exposures.

A consistent deviation, or strong trend away, from the risk factor exposures indicated by the investment philosophy and process is a signal of style drift. Style drift can happen for a variety of reasons. The evaluator must determine whether the deviations represent a long-term change in the manager's investment philosophy and process rather than the result of short-term market movements. An example would be a temporary over-allocation to larger-capitalization stocks because of price appreciation that is subsequently remediated, versus the holding of internet stocks by value funds during the dot-com markets. The allocator needs to understand and evaluate the following:

- Did the manager deviate from their investment process to chase returns in any given quarter or year?
- Did the manager engage in trading that is excessive relative to the investment process?

- Did the manager buy securities that do not fit the parameters of the investment process?
- Does the manager have, and implement, a credible process for remediating breaches of the portfolio investment guidelines?

The allocator also needs to evaluate whether the deviation represents internal issues, such as a potential misalignment of interests.

EXAMPLE 14

Style Analysis in Continuation Decisions

1 Which of the following is **not** a reason why style drift is an important aspect of monitoring?

 A Style drift might signal that the vehicle structure is not consistent with the investment process.

 B Style drift might suggest the manager is no longer suitable for the investor and may be detrimental to portfolio asset allocation.

 C Evidence of style drift undermines confidence in the repeatability of the investment process and compromises confidence is the manager's ability to repeat past performance in the future.

2 Which of the following is a sign of alignment of manager and client interests?

 A The manager closes a strategy to new money.

 B The manager consistently raises or lowers risk exposures toward the end of the year.

 C The manager significantly lowers the portfolio risk exposure in response to a sharp decline in the market.

3 Style analysis does **not** include:

 A understanding how the risk exposures evolve through time.

 B determining whether a manager has lost key personnel.

 C understanding the manager's risk exposures relative to the benchmark.

4 Style analysis that is **not** consistent with the philosophy and investment process can suggest that:

 A the manager has a high batting average.

 B the manager's return profile is asymmetrical.

 C the investment process is not repeatable or is not consistently implemented.

Solution to 1:

A is correct. An important aspect of monitoring is determining whether the manager continues to adhere to the stated investment philosophy and decision-making process. Style drift is the deviation from the stated risk factor exposures that underpin the investment philosophy and process. Style drift may also suggest the manager is no longer suitable for the investor and be detrimental to portfolio asset allocation.

Solution to 2:

A is correct. Consistent year-end changes in risk exposures may be the result of compensation issues. Reducing risk after suffering a large loss may indicate business risk is dominating investment risk and a focus on maintaining AUM at the expense of return. A manager should close a strategy if it believes that adding new capital could dilute returns

Solution to 3:

B is correct. Although a firm can be only as good as the people running it, evaluating personnel turnover is a consideration of operational due diligence, not style analysis.

Solution to 4:

C is correct. Style analysis should be consistent with the manager's philosophy and the investment process. If it is not, the process might be unrepeatable or inconsistently implemented. Or, if the risk exposures deviate through time, such an inconsistency may indicate style drift.

EXAMPLE 15

Manager Continuance

1 Which of the following are considerations in manager continuation?

- **I.** Adherence to the investment philosophy and process
- **II.** Operational due diligence
- **III.** The costs and benefits of replacing the manager

A I and II
B II and III
C I, II, and III

2 Which of the following are considerations in investment manager continuation?

- **I.** Confirming that the manager retains the integrity of their investment process
- **II.** Confirming that the manager remains suitable for their role in the portfolio
- **III.** Confirming the sustainability of the firm

A I and II
B II and III
C I, II, and III

Solution to 1:

C is correct. Monitoring is essentially ongoing investment and operational due diligence. The objective is to confirm that the rationale for selecting a manager remains in place. Even if the manager is no longer the "best," there is a balance between the opportunity cost of not replacing a manager and the actual cost of replacing a manager.

Solution to 2:

C is correct. It is essential that investment managers be monitored on an ongoing basis to confirm that the manager retains the integrity of their investment process and remains suitable for their role in the portfolio. Many changes can take place within the firm that can either erode or enhance the integrity of the investment process and sustainability of the firm.

10.3 Performance Monitoring

When a relationship with a manager is first established, the investor and the manager should agree on an appropriate benchmark, an excess (or absolute) return target, and an active/absolute risk target. The focus should be on net-of-fee returns because those are the results that actually accumulate in the investor's account. In establishing targets, it is important to be realistic about expectations and to link the return/excess return goals to the amount of risk/active risk being taken by the manager (managers with higher active risk targets should be expected to generate higher excess returns). By using databases and other sources of historical returns, investors can see the distribution of returns generated by similar managers over time and can use this information to help determine appropriate targets.

Such targets will be greatly influenced by the investment universe of the manager. Asset classes (such as large-capitalization US equities) that are generally viewed to be fairly efficient provide fewer opportunities for active managers to add significant value than do less-efficient asset classes such as emerging markets equities, and the excess return target for managers operating in efficient markets will be lower than for managers operating in less-efficient markets. The net-of-fee information ratio (active return divided by active risk) is an appropriate measure to use when evaluating relative return strategies in which the manager is expected to outperform a defined market benchmark. The target for the manager should not be so high that only the top 5% of managers in the universe might be expected to achieve it but should be high enough to require the manager to demonstrate skill. The net-of-fee Sharpe ratio (total return in excess of cash divided by total risk) would be an appropriate measure to use in evaluating absolute return strategies in which the manager is expected to outperform cash or an inflation-indexed return.

In evaluating performance, investors should resist the urge to place too much emphasis on short-term results; the investor should expect return targets to be met and measured over full market cycles, which typically encompass several years. Numerous studies show that allocating to managers that have outperformed, and away from managers that have underperformed in the recent past, results in portfolio underperformance over the longer-term.

The primary value derived from evaluating results over longer-term periods is the ability to judge a manager during a variety of market environments. The investor should have a good understanding of the environment(s) represented during the period being evaluated, and how such environments tend to help or hurt the manager's performance.

If the investor has a solid understanding of the weaknesses and strengths of various statistical measures, the inappropriate use of such measures can be minimized and results can be evaluated in the right context. For example, many asset classes, particularly alternative asset classes, feature return patterns that are not normally distributed, so such measures as standard deviation (and measures that rely on standard deviation) that assume a normal distribution are less relevant. Using standard deviation in the assessment of an asset class or investment strategy that displays significantly non-normal return distributions can result in an underestimation of the true variability of returns. An investor making such an underestimation may become unjustly disappointed in (or happy about) a manager's results, leading to the "performance chasing" behavior discussed by Goyal and Wahal (2008).[9]

Even when measures such as standard deviation are relevant, there is still a significant possibility that results, especially short-term results, will fall outside the band of expectations. A manager with an expected active risk of 4% would only be expected to perform within +/− 4% of the benchmark index about two-thirds of the time, leaving plenty of room for results to differ by more without the manager behaving any differently than was expected.

A good framework for evaluating performance connects the time frame and frequency of analysis with the active risk of the investment strategy; the lower the active risk, the more frequently performance monitoring should be conducted. A passively managed equity strategy, for example, that is expected to exactly match the returns of a benchmark index should be monitored frequently (i.e., quarterly reports). But a long-term, low turnover, concentrated equity strategy that is expected to produce returns of 5% above inflation over a 10-year period should not place heavy reliance on quarterly investment results; qualitative factors should play a larger role in the monitoring process.

10.4 Other Monitoring Considerations

Monitoring should also involve evaluating how a manager handles periods of low market volatility and/or high correlations among securities because such environments often restrict the manager's ability to add value. Investors should explore how the manager identifies such periods and how they respond when they occur. For example, if the manager believes that high security correlations are making it difficult to distinguish between attractive and unattractive investments, will the manager lower its active risk temporarily? Investors might also ask whether the manager is open to reducing its fee during such periods, given the lower probability of producing the targeted value added.

The use of peer group universes to evaluate a manager's performance is a widespread but often inappropriate exercise. Issues associated with performance evaluation using peer group universes include the following:

- The identification of true "peers" is difficult because even managers within the same asset class (or sub-asset class) can have substantial differences in their approach to security selection and portfolio construction.
- Managers should be held accountable only for decisions they control, such as how they position their portfolio relative to a defined benchmark index. They should not be penalized for the actions of other managers that might be considered a part of the peer group. (For example, managers that maintain a consistent low risk profile should not be penalized—or rewarded—by comparing them against managers that have deliberately increased the risk profile of their fund.)
- A manager's ranking in a peer universe often depends more on its stated investment philosophy and approach rather than on how well it implements that philosophy and approach.

9 This is not intended to imply that such measures as standard deviation have no relevance, only that such measures should be used with caution and should not be viewed to have precise predictive ability. When possible, supplementing such performance-based measures with holdings-based analysis and/or other statistical measures (beta, upside/downside capture, etc.) can help the investor gain a better understanding of what to expect from a manager.

- Peer group comparisons typically ignore the amount of risk each manager in the universe is taking and, as a result, few sound conclusions can be drawn regarding a given manager's risk–reward profile.
- Known biases in managers' investment approaches will be rewarded at some times and will prove detrimental in others. Having conducted effective due diligence on the manager, the investor should be aware and accepting of such biases and understand that a lower universe ranking when such biases are not rewarded in the markets generally does not necessarily indicate that a manager's skill level has diminished.

In short, peer group universe rankings are generally an ineffective tool for evaluating manager success or failure. However, peer group analysis can provide useful insights when preparing for a discussion with the manager about its process and portfolio positioning. For example, in the late 1980s, when Japan's equity market's performance was exceptionally strong, virtually all global and non-US equity managers were significantly underweight Japan because they viewed that market as overvalued. Any manager that was not significantly underweight Japan likely had very good performance relative to other managers; a logical question would have been why the manager's view of Japan was so different from others' views.

It is possible to incorporate risk into peer-group relative performance by comparing managers' information ratios or Sharpe ratios, both of which provide a risk-adjusted view of returns. Another option for evaluating risk-adjusted returns of a manager relative to its peers is to plot a scatter diagram similar to the one in Exhibit 13 in which each manager in the universe is plotted in risk–return space with performance on one axis and risk on the other. Certain managers may stand out from the crowd and should be questioned regarding their views.

Exhibit 13 Comparing Managers in Risk–Return Space: Small-Cap Global Equity Risk–Return Analysis

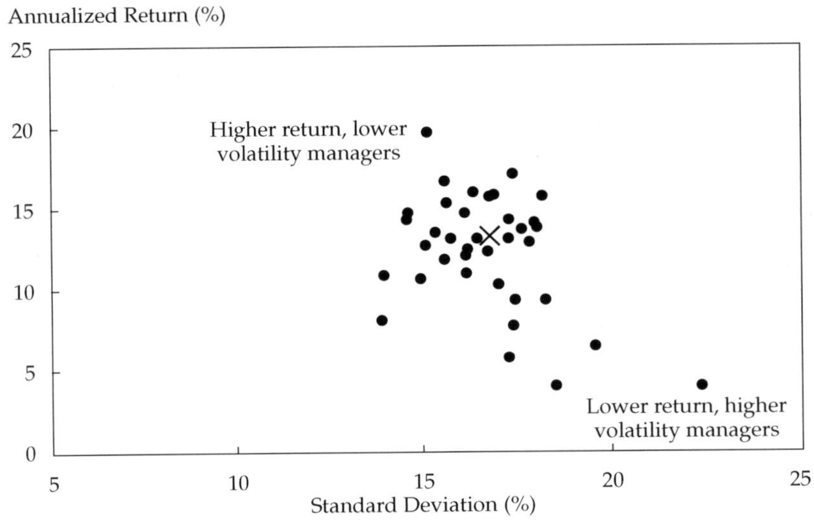

Note: X is the universe median.
Source: Based on data from eVestmentAlliance.

What Makes a Peer Group?

The limitations of peer groups become quite apparent when the dispersion among managers within the group is wide. Consider the case of unconstrained bond funds. Such funds have become popular because of their open-ended, go anywhere mandates in an environment of low interest rates and the expectation of rising rates. According to Lipper, unconstrained bond funds attracted $45.7 billion in 2013 as core bond funds saw $33.4 billion in outflows.

Morningstar places unconstrained bond funds within the non-traditional bond category. The summary statistics for a handful of the largest funds in this category, shown in Exhibits 14 and 15, show considerable differences in such portfolio characteristics as turnover, interest rate, credit, and security type exposures.

Exhibit 14 Non-Traditional Bond Fund Summary Statistics and Exposures as of 31 March 2015

Fund	Turnover Ratio (%)	Modified Duration (years)	Average Coupon (%)	Government (% Net)	Municipal (% Net)	Corporate (% Net)	Securitized (% Net)	Cash (% Net)
Fund 1	1396	2.02	3.3	18.0		12.2	26.6	28.3
Fund 2	157	0.24	3.7	29.7	2.5	22.9	23.5	12.8
Fund 3	728	−0.06	3.8	−1.6	1.1	20.9	8.0	43.0
Fund 4	257	−1.8	4.7	5.1	0.0	33.4	82.6	−25.2
Fund 5	66	1.42	6.4	47.1	0.0	0.3	5.9	24.2

Source: Based on data from Morningstar.

Exhibit 15 Non-Traditional Bond Fund Credit Rating Distribution as of 31 March 2015

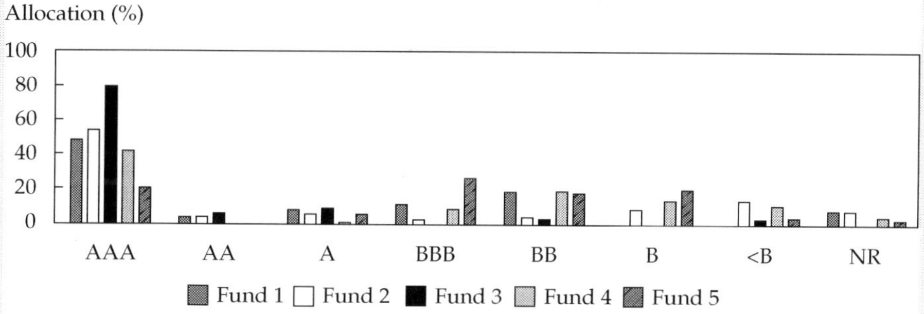

Note: NR is not rated.
Source: Based on data from Morningstar.

Although categorizing managers can be useful, it should not be interpreted to mean that all managers in the category are necessarily peers; for some approaches there is no meaningful or identifiable peer group or holdings-based benchmark.

10.5 Costs and Other Considerations in Replacing Investment Managers

The net expected benefits of replacing an existing manager with a new manager must be greater than the expected costs of terminating the one manager and transitioning to the new manager. Often, the expected total costs of replacing a manager can be greater than the expected total benefits—a negative net benefit. The negative net benefit may be attributable to a relatively small expected improvement in performance, or it may be because the costs of changing managers are certain and realized in the near term, whereas the benefits are less certain and/or realized at some point in the future. In such cases, it may be preferable to retain a seemingly less skillful manager. Exhibit 16 illustrates some common reasons for manager termination and the benefits and costs associated with those decisions.

Exhibit 16 Common Termination Reasons and the Associated Benefits and Costs

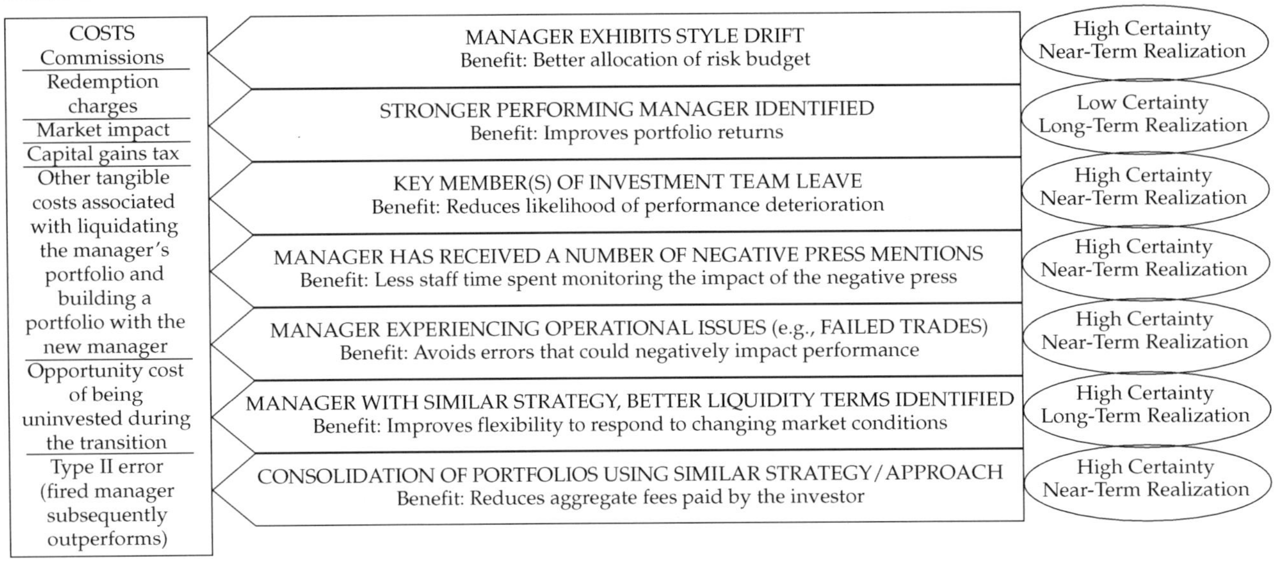

Exhibit 16 highlights a few important points:

- The realized benefits of replacing a manager are largely non-performance related, addressing operational issues linked to red flags, such as elevated business risk or potential misaligned incentives, or shield the investor from negative reputational repercussions.
- Performance benefits are derived largely from resolving a style drift issue when the characteristics of the manager's portfolio are no longer compatible with the mandate for which they were hired. Benefits attributable to "skill" can be long term and very uncertain.
- Costs are largely tangible costs realized in the near term.

Most of the benefits and costs involved in replacing a manager are difficult to quantify, not only in their level but also in their likelihood of realization. This uncertainty means substantial judgment on the part of the decision maker is required, and subjective judgments are subject to behavioral biases and heighten the importance of aligning the advisor's own personal interests with their obligation to act in the client's best interest.

Costs to consider when contemplating the termination of an investment manager include:

- **Transaction costs:** When liquidating a separate account, the investor incurs not only the commissions and fees related to the sale of the assets in that manager's portfolio, but additional commissions and fees on the reinvestment of those assets with another manager. In less-liquid markets, the two-ways costs may be a significant hurdle to replacing a manager. When terminating an investment made through a pooled vehicle, there may be an explicit trading fee, or the manager of the fund may charge any associated liquidation costs to the redeeming investor.
- **Redemption fees:** Many mutual funds charge a fee for exiting a fund within a fixed period after investing to discourage market timers. A typical redemption fee is 2%–3% if the fund is sold within three months of purchase. Hedge funds often impose lockups, particularly strategies that hold less liquid securities, to discourage active trading that may result in having to sell securities at unfavorable times to the detriment of other investors. Typically, lockups either prevent redemption or charge a 2%–3% fee (that is paid to the other investors in the fund) for redeeming the fund within the first year. The lower the redemption fee, the lower the cost of replacing a manager.
- **Holdbacks:** For a full redemption, some hedge funds will retain a portion of assets, typically 5%–10%, until a year-end audit has been completed. This retention provides leeway should the net asset value (NAV) of the portfolio be revised. Depending on when the redemption is placed, the holdback can last more than a year, and the assets do not share in the gains and losses of the strategy and often do not earn interest. The lower the holdback, the lower the cost to replacing the manager.
- **Tax liabilities:** The longer a manager, particularly one that has performed well previously, has been held, the greater the likely tax implication of replacing the manager. The lower the tax liability, the better the investor is able to offset any gains with losses, or the greater the degree of long-term gains, the lower the cost of replacing the manager.

The decision of whether and when to replace a manager depends on whether the expected benefits are sufficient to account for the explicit and implicit costs.

10.6 A Case Study in Manager Retention

A common concern when monitoring managers is return dilution. That is, a strong track record results in growth in assets under management or attracts competition, which results in weaker returns because additional assets cannot be productively invested by the manager. It is often argued that managers or funds with substantial asset bases are unable to generate excess returns because the growth in the size of the fund eventually results in a shift toward larger and more liquid securities and an increased number of holdings. The result can be over-diversification and index-like returns or, at the other extreme, large positions that reduce portfolio liquidity because investment decisions may negatively impact market prices or attract outside attention and scrutiny. This issue can be examined by analyzing the performance of a US large-capitalization growth manager.

A "snail trail" can be used to examine changes in portfolio characteristics through time. Each data marker in Exhibit 17 plots the portfolio's excess return on the y-axis against its tracking error on the x-axis. A larger data marker indicates an observation date closer to the present. The trend of the data markers indicates that the manager's value added has fallen—in many periods, below zero—while the tracking error relative to the benchmark is also drifting lower.

Exhibit 17 Excess Return—and Tracking Error Are Declining, January 2004–March 2015

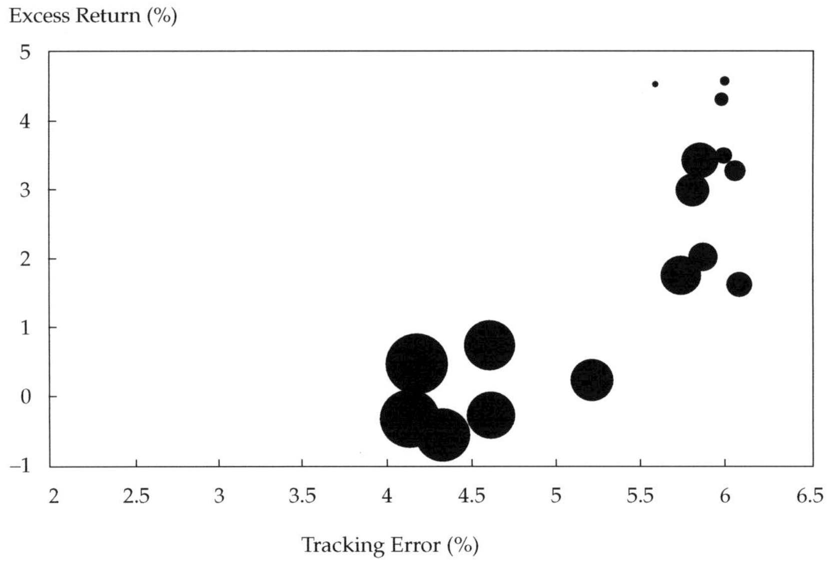

Source: Based on data from Morningstar.

An examination of the size and style (value versus growth) of the underlying portfolio holdings through time, as shown in Exhibit 18, suggests a progression toward larger capitalization and more pronounced growth-oriented equities. The manager is now holding fewer mid- and small-capitalization securities, and the allocations to different capitalization categories are similar to those of the benchmark.

Conversations with the manager indicate that the investment process has been adjusted through time in response to increased fund size. The number of portfolio holdings increased although portfolio concentration also increased recently because the manager has begun to focus the portfolio on best idea stocks.

In addition to holding fewer mid- and small-cap stocks, fund turnover has declined, partly as a result of holding on to successful positions. Although this increases the market capitalization of the portfolio, it is consistent with the goal of focusing on best ideas because it allows the portfolio to retain high conviction ideas rather than sell as a result of capitalization considerations.

Exhibit 18 Holdings-Based Style Analysis Suggests a Shift Toward Higher-Growth and Larger-Capitalization Equities, March 2005–March 2015

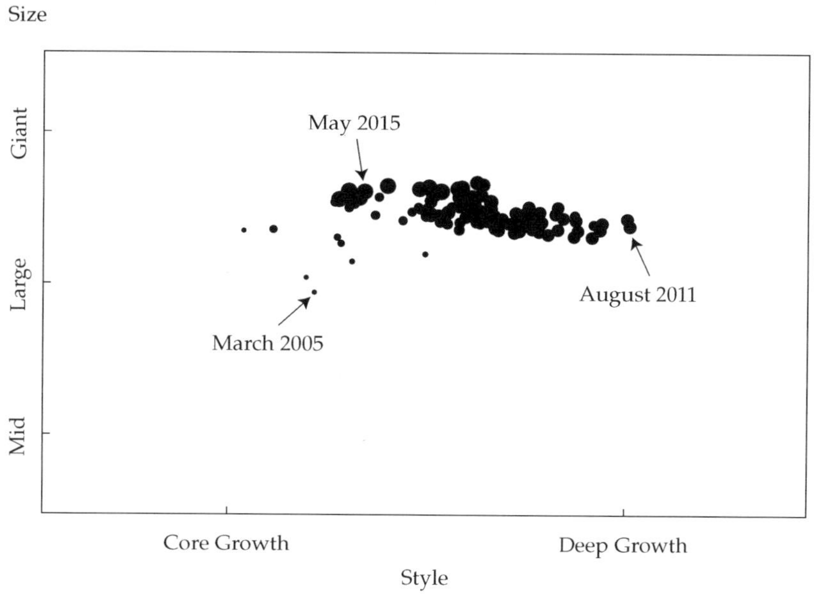

Source: Based on data from Morningstar.

As seen in Exhibit 19, the portfolio has not substantially altered its allocation to stocks, bonds, and cash over the evaluation period.

Exhibit 19 Asset Allocation Is Stable, January 2004–March 2015

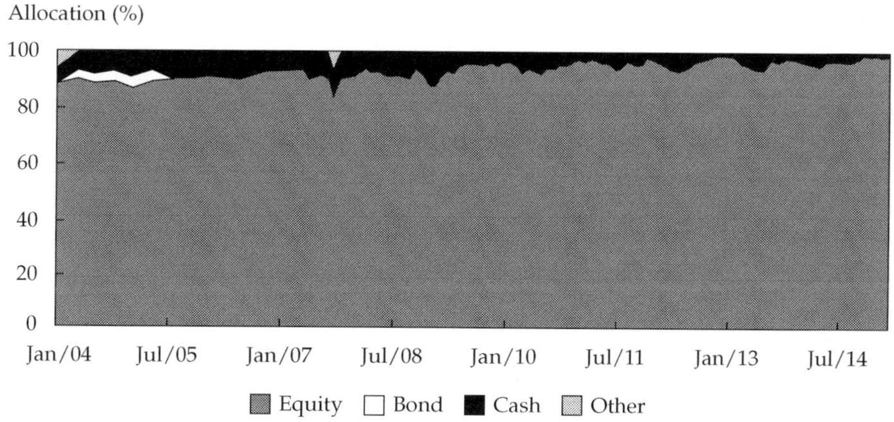

Source: Based on data from Morningstar.

Although the manager has made some adjustments to the investment process in response to large fund size, the key question is whether these changes suggest the manager is no longer a good fit for the portfolio.

Exhibit 20 compares the calendar-year performance of the portfolio with the S&P 500 Index and S&P 500 Growth Index. The results show that

- the portfolio outperformed the benchmark in 6 of the 10 years and year to date in 2015;
- the excess return over the benchmark has diminished since 2008, but that was a period of strong equity market returns when active managers largely trailed the market indexes. In 2013 and 2014, stocks exhibited high intra-stock correlations. As a result, 2014 was a difficult year for most active managers relative to their benchmarks.

Exhibit 20 Benchmark-Relative Performance Is within Expectations, Annual Returns January 2004–March 2015

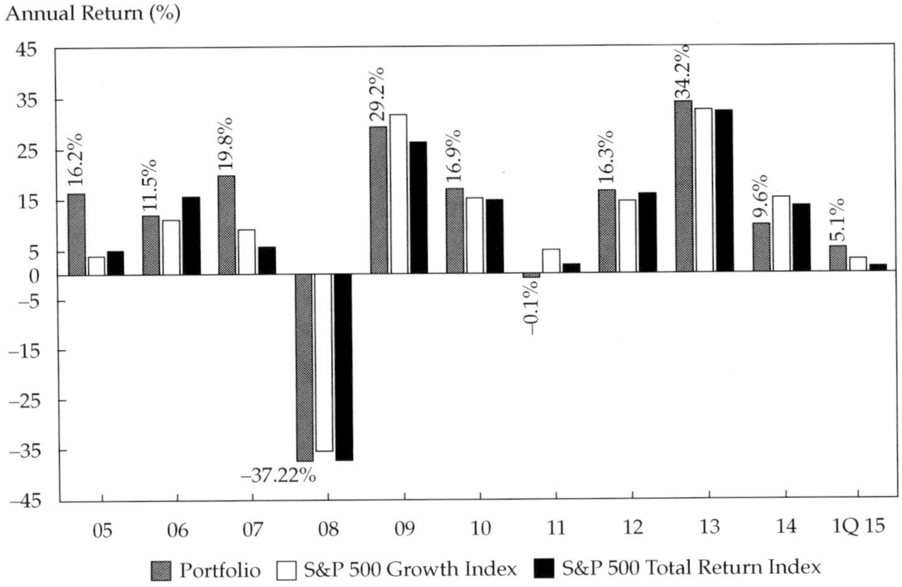

Source: Based on data from Morningstar.

Exhibit 21, which looks at net flows into and out of the funds managed by this manager (all of which use the same strategy), suggests some investors decided to redeem from the manager in 2014. It is not known if these flows were part of a general reduction in investors' exposure to large actively managed growth funds in general or were driven by manager-specific concerns. If the redemptions were driven by manager-specific concerns, only time will tell whether the redeeming investors committed a Type II error—firing a manager that should have been retained. Although the fund has closed in the past to control fund size, the fund is currently open.

Exhibit 21 Sizable Redemptions in 2014

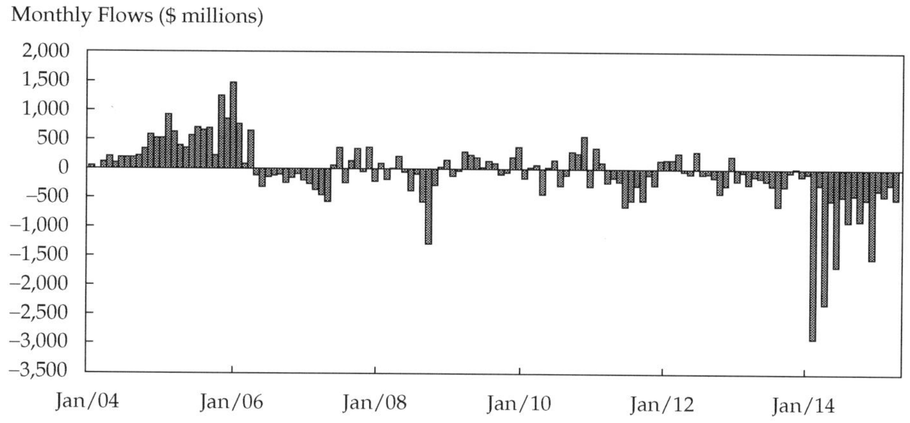

Source: Based on data from Morningstar.

Although asset growth is a concern, the characteristics of the portfolio have shifted, and the manager's AUM in this strategy may limit its flexibility, the fund has had only one manager since inception, and the manager appears to have handled the growth well with minimal evidence of performance dilution.

The narrow dispersion of returns among managers in the large-capitalization growth category also suggests that finding a replacement superior to this manager may be difficult. Taken together, these insights suggest that replacing the manager is not warranted.

As illustrated in this section, the decision to hire or fire a manager is a multi-dimensional process that requires quantitative and qualitative inputs as well as an understanding of the market environment in which the investment returns were generated. On an on-going basis, the investor must review managers that have been hired and determine whether they still represent the best manager for the portfolio and whether the expected costs of replacing the manager are warranted based on the anticipated portfolio impact.

EXAMPLE 16

Evaluating Portfolio Characteristics

1 Which set of factors should be used to evaluate the performance of a manager relative to the chosen benchmark?

   A Fees, active returns, active risk

   B Fees, active returns, peer group ranking

   C Fees, absolute returns, standard deviation

2 Which of the following would be *least* important to an investor monitoring an active manager with a tracking risk of 5%?

   A One-year underperformance of 7%

   B Change in the manager's ownership structure

   C Significant increase in number of securities held in the portfolio

3 Which of the following techniques is *most* appropriate when monitoring manager performance?

   A Using the Sharpe ratio to rank managers of alternative investments

B Evaluating large-capitalization passive US equity managers quarterly

C Ranking managers with a long-term mandate on their most recent 12-month returns

4 Which of the following is likely to receive the *least* emphasis in the monitoring process during the first two years after a manager is hired?

A The investment process used by the manager

B Changes in the portfolio manager/analyst team

C Performance based on historical returns relative to benchmark

Solution to 1:

A is correct. The net-of-fee information ratio (active return divided by active risk) is an effective statistic to use in judging the success of an active manager relative to a defined market benchmark. Absolute return strategies are best evaluated by using absolute returns and risk. Peer group rankings cannot be controlled by the manager—such rankings may depend on how much active risk a certain manager makes use of and what market environment results are being evaluated in.

Solution to 2:

A is correct. Short-term performance differences that are larger than the tracking risk are not at all unusual and should not be a concern as long as the results are consistent with expectations in the prevailing market environment. Significant portfolio or organizational changes, however, do deserve extra focus. A change in the manager's ownership structure may foreshadow changes to the investment process resulting in different style and portfolio risk and return characteristics. A significant increase in the number of securities held may signal potential return dilution because the manager holds a greater number of potentially lower-conviction positions to allocate fund assets.

Solution to 3:

B is correct. A large-cap US equity manager operates in a highly efficient market in which it is difficult to generate excess returns. The decision to use a passive manager is not based on an expectation of generating returns in excess of the benchmark, so more frequent monitoring is appropriate. Some alternative investment returns are not normally distributed and measures, such as the Sharpe ratio, that rely on standard deviation should be used with caution. Long-term investors should place less reliance on short-term 12-month results.

Solution to 4:

C is correct. During the early years of a relationship with a manager, when the performance track record is short, the monitoring approach should emphasize qualitative elements, such as reporting, portfolio characteristics, and process consistency, more than performance evaluation. Monitoring should focus on the manager's organization, personnel, and investment process. Significant changes in any of these areas could serve as "red flags" that may cause investors to question whether they are still receiving the service they contracted for.

SUMMARY

Key points to remember from this reading include the following:

- Manager selection should be made in the context of the planned or existing portfolio structure and framework.
- During on-site visits, meet people on the manager's staff who are not normally available outside of the manager's office, review written research reports, explore the manager's use of risk models and request a demonstration of risk systems and other analytical tools used by the manager, explore the consistency between the manager's conviction level regarding individual holdings and the position size and risk contribution of those holdings, and conduct in-depth operational due diligence.
- Critical success factors that affect a manager's ability to achieve an investor's goals include alignment of the manager's interests with those of the client, a willingness to turn away assets if the effective capacity of the strategy is strained by asset growth, ownership distributed among the key investment professionals, and quality and depth of personnel resources.
- Passive equity managers can implement portfolios using either full-replication or sampling approaches, or derivatives.
- Strategies used by quantitative equity managers managers may involve statistical techniques and terminology that are not well understood by the researcher. It's important to determine if a quantitative equity manager understands their exposure to "crowded trades."
- Performance attribution allows researchers to determine if investment results were driven by the investment factors that the manager claims are important elements of the process.
- Fixed-income managers generally make more top-down allocation decisions (sector, duration, spread) than do equity managers. Fixed-income security pricing is less transparent than equity pricing, and managers should have policies and processes for pricing portfolio holdings.
- Liquidity, leverage, fees, key man provisions, competing funds offered by the same manager, the manager's use of side pockets and co-investment opportunities, valuation policies, and the selection process for third-party service providers are all important elements of the hedge fund selection process.
- Hedge fund, private equity, and real estate manager due diligence requires an extensive review of the offering documents and any existing side letters.
- Five key aspects of evaluating a private equity team are investment acumen, domain expertise, resources, stability and economic sharing agreements, and key person risk.
- Key factors to consider when assessing a private equity manager's ability to replicate past successes are fund size, the relevance to future conditions, the contributions of various team members, and insights from the management of portfolio companies.
- A buyout manager must be skilled at understanding financial and operational performance. The three main drivers of buyout returns are growth in earnings, valuation multiple arbitrage, and use of debt.
- IRR and return on MOIC are the most prevalent measurements of private equity performance.

- The factors to consider when reviewing private equity fund-level performance include diversification, consistency, realized versus unrealized returns, the loss ratio, and distributions to paid-in capital.
- The three primary real estate investment styles are core (and core-plus), value-added, and opportunisitic.
- Evaluating real estate manager, fund, and property performance requires an understanding of the fund style and the underlying property strategy, sector or geographic focus, vintage, and leverage.
- Private real estate benchmarks are limited by the use of infrequent appraisal-based valuations, and results may be skewed toward the largest data contributors.
- Too much emphasis should not be placed on short-term results; performance relative to targets should be measured over full market cycles. A good framework for evaluating performance connects the time frame and frequency of analysis with the active risk of the investment strategy.
- Peer group comparisons are often used inappropriately. The identification of true "peers" is difficult. The returns-only analysis inherent in peer group comparisons ignores the risk profile of the managers.
- The costs of replacing a manager include commissions, redemption charges, market impact, capital gains taxes and other tangible costs of liquidation and reinvestment, the opportunity cost of being uninvested during the transition to a new manager, and Type II errors in which the fired manager subsequently outperforms the newly hired manager.
- An appropriate monitoring process will record the qualities that led to the manager being hired; those qualities can be subsequently confirmed or questioned through ongoing due diligence.
- There is no "perfect" manager; an investor's satisfaction with any manager it selects will depend in large part on the investor's priorities.

REFERENCES

Busse, Jeffrey A., Amit Goyal, and Sunil Wahal. 2010. "Performance and Persistence in Institutional Investment Management." *Journal of Finance*, vol. 65, no. 2 (April): 765–790.

Goyal, Amit, and Sunil Wahal. 2008. "The Selection and Termination of Investment Management Firms by Plan Sponsors." *Journal of Finance*, vol. 63, no. 4 (August): 1805–1847.

Jones, Robert C., and Russ Wermers. 2011. "Active Management in Mostly Efficient Markets." *Financial Analysts Journal*, vol. 67, no. 6 (November/December): 29–45.

Towers Watson. 2014. "Are Your Interests Aligned or Misaligned?" (22 January).

PRACTICE PROBLEMS

The following information relates to Questions 1–5

The White North Corporation (WNC) manages a defined benefit pension plan for its employees. The pension plan currently has 10% of assets invested in a passively managed US small-cap equity exchange-traded fund (ETF). WNC's pension plan investment committee has decided to shift that allocation to an active manager in an attempt to increase returns in that market segment. The committee is considering Manager A, Manager B, and Manager C as possible alternatives. Each of these managers has the same benchmark as the ETF.

To evaluate the managers, the committee compiles the data shown in Exhibits 1, 2, 3, and 4. The committee prioritizes a strong investment organization and high long-term total returns when hiring new managers.

Exhibit 1 Trailing 10-Year Performance Statistics as of 31 December 2015

	Standard Deviation	Tracking Error	Information Ratio	Up Capture	Down Capture
Manager A	20.7%	6.8%	0.2%	97.3%	93.1%
Manager B	17.2%	5.4%	0.0%	82.1%	81.6%
Manager C	21.4%	4.6%	0.3%	108.9%	103.8%
Benchmark index	19.7%	na	na	na	na

Exhibit 2 Portfolio Characteristics as of 31 December 2015

	Expense Ratio	Assets Under Management ($ billions)	Number of Stocks	Active Share	Forward P/E
Manager A	1.15%	1.5	75	89%	20
Manager B	1.40%	9.3	104	71%	19
Manager C	1.11%	8.8	80	77%	18
Benchmark index	na	na	1,988	na	19

Exhibit 3 Annualized Returns as of 31 December 2015

	1 Year	3 Year	5 Year	10 Year
Manager A	–4.3%	14.8%	9.8%	8.0%
Manager B	1.4%	13.3%	8.8%	6.8%
Manager C	–2.6%	13.0%	10.3%	8.2%
Benchmark index	–4.4%	11.7%	9.2%	6.8%

Exhibit 4 Manager Assessment Scores

	Consistency	Organizational Strength	Transparency	Total
Manager A	10	9	9	28
Manager B	8	8	9	25
Manager C	7	4	6	17

Note: Scores range from 1 to 10, with 10 being the best score.

1 Which of the following would *best* justify the shift in the small-cap equity allocation of WNC's benefit plan?

A Decrease tracking error

B Decrease management fees

C Exploit market inefficiencies

2 Based on Exhibit 1, which manager performed *best* in down markets?

A Manager A

B Manager B

C Manager C

3 Based on Exhibit 1, which of the following indicates superior performance for Manager C compared with the other managers?

A Volatility of returns

B Capture of negative market returns

C Active return per unit of active risk

4 Based on Exhibit 2, which manager is *least likely* to face the risk of return dilution?

A Manager A

B Manager B

C Manager C

5 Based on the committee's stated priorities and Exhibits 3 and 4, which manager should the investment committee hire?

A Manager A

B Manager B

C Manager C

The following information relates to Questions 6–10

ABC Corporation is a US-based textile company that provides a defined benefit pension plan for its employees. The pension board hired Jane Smith, senior investment consultant, to conduct due diligence on its current investment in the Credit Opportunities fixed-income hedge fund (CO Fund). ABC has a policy limiting the initial allocation to any single hedge fund to $25 million.

ABC's chief investment officer (CIO) asks Smith to provide suggestions on improving its process for monitoring investment managers and making manager replacement decisions based on the following statements:

Statement 1 The benchmark for investment managers is an investable market index, gross of investment management fees measured across a five-year period.

Statement 2 The costs and the benefits of replacing an investment manager are typically long term in nature, and the benefits are mainly derived from reducing transaction costs.

Smith begins reviewing three passively managed exchange-traded funds (ETFs) as possible replacements for the CO Fund allocation. Smith compiles the information in Exhibit 1 through interviews and on-site visits.

Exhibit 1

	ETF A	ETF B	ETF C
Comparison Index	Global Developed Markets Bond	Global Developed Markets Bond	Global Emerging Markets Bond
Portfolio Construction Method	Full Replication	Sampling	Sampling
Pricing Transparency	High	High	Low
Organizational Strength	High	Average	Low
Expense Ratio	High	Average	Average
Currency Denomination	Local Currency	USD Only	USD Only
Country Allocation (Diversified vs. Concentrated)	Diversified	Concentrated	Concentrated
Length of Track Record	1 year	6 years	8 years

ABC's CIO provides Smith with the following criteria to use in choosing an ETF:

Criteria 1: We prefer to minimize country-specific exposure.

Criteria 2: We prefer investment managers with longer track records and average or below-average fees.

6 ABC's plan policy related to initial hedge fund investment allocations *most likely* indicates a focus on:

A tracking risk.

B manager risk.

C fee efficiency.

7 In response to Statement 1, a suitable recommendation is to change the:

A benchmark to a peer group.

B time period comparison to a one-year period.

C return comparison to net of investment management fees.

8 Statement 2 is correct with reference to the:

A source of the benefits.

B timing of realizing costs.

C timing of realizing benefits.

9 The Organizational Strength rating for ETF A in Exhibit 1 is *consistent* with which of the following?

A Rapid growth in assets with a decline in staffing

B Combined executive investment and compliance roles

C Written operational policies and procedures and robust trading platforms

10 Based on Exhibit 1, ETF B's choice of portfolio construction methodology was *most likely* affected by the:

A objective of generating excess return over the benchmark.

B goal of holding all constituents of the index at their assigned weights.

C inability to buy specific issuances within the benchmark.

The following information relates to Questions 11–17

Kevin Duke is a consultant who provides hedge fund selection and due diligence services. Duke is meeting with a new endowment client that is considering expanding their investments to include hedge funds. Ron Clark, one of the endowment's trustees, expresses two concerns over investing in hedge funds:

> Concern 1: The endowment will be paying a performance fee on gains even if the endowment's overall investment in the fund has lost money.
>
> Concern 2: The endowment's performance will suffer if the fund needs to sell less liquid investments to fulfill redemption requests of other investors.

After addressing Clark's concerns, Duke states that typical long-only equity strategies are limited to investing in a specific style, market capitalization or geographic location. In contrast, he notes that one type of hedge fund strategy takes long and short positions in equity, fixed income, currency, and/or futures markets to express overall economic views across global markets.

Duke presents information on three separate hedge funds to the trustee, as shown in Exhibit 1.

Exhibit 1 Fund Characteristics

Fund	Strategy	Liquidity of Investments	Redemption Gate
A	Macro	Medium	Yes
B	Distressed/Restructuring	Low	No
C	Equity Hedge	High	No

Duke finishes the meeting with a discussion on measuring hedge fund leverage, telling Clark he should calculate a direct measure of explicit leverage created using borrowing.

Clark points out that the degree of leverage used and the strategy being implemented should also be considered. He makes the following statements:

Statement 1	Portfolios with low net exposure can better support leverage.
Statement 2	Portfolios with long and short positions in uncorrelated securities can better support leverage.

11 The use of which hedge fund fee component would *most likely* address Clark's first concern?

A Hurdle rate

B High-water mark

C Fixed management fee

12 Clark's second concern is *best* addressed through the use of:

A side pockets.

B co-investments.

C a key man provision.

13 The hedge fund strategy that Duke contrasts with typical long-only equity strategies is *best* described as:

A macro.

B equity hedge.

C distressed/restructuring.

14 Based on Exhibit 1, a large redemption request would *most likely* have the greatest impact on the remaining investors in:

A Fund A.

B Fund B.

C Fund C.

15 Based on Exhibit 1, which fund is *best* able to mitigate the risk of hot money investors leaving long-term investors holding the least liquid positions?

A Fund A

B Fund B

C Fund C

16 The measure of leverage that Duke advocates is best calculated as:

A debt/assets under management.

B long market value/assets under management.

C gross market value/assets under management.

17 Which of Clark's statements is correct?

A Only Statement 1

B Only Statement 2

C Both Statement 1 and Statement 2

SOLUTIONS

1 C is correct. WNC wants to increase returns in the US small-cap equity segment of its portfolio. It can attempt to do that by moving from a passive to an active manager that will try to outperform the benchmark by exploiting market inefficiencies.

2 B is correct. Manager B's down capture was 81.6%, meaning the manager's returns were less negative than the market returns across periods that the market was down. The down capture was 93.1% for Manager A and was 103.8% for Manager C, both higher than for Manager B.

3 C is correct. Manager C has the highest information ratio (0.3%), which measures active return per unit of active risk.

4 A is correct. The risk of return dilution is defined as the risk that as assets under management grow and more competition enters a manager's space as a result of a good track record, performance may deteriorate because additional assets cannot be productively invested by the manager. Manager A has a significantly smaller amount of assets under management in the strategy than Manager B or Manager C and is less likely to be affected by the growth in the size of the fund.

5 A is correct. The investment committee prioritizes a strong investment organization and high long-term total returns when hiring new managers. Manager A approximately matched the benchmark over the last year (–4.3% for Manager A versus –4.4% for the benchmark) and significantly outperformed the benchmark over the last 3, 5, and 10 years. This performance was substantially better than Manager B's performance, which only matched the benchmark over the last 10 years (6.8% in both cases). Manager C had strong long-term returns, but Manager C's manager assessment score (4) for organizational strength was much lower than Manager A's score (9). Manager A is the most suitable because it has a strong investment organization and a successful long-term performance track record.

6 B is correct because a focus on manager risk may result in policies placing limits on the amount invested with any one manager or strategy, rather than a focus on the investment risk of each strategy and managing those risks through a risk budgeting process.

7 C is correct because the manager should be measured on a net-of-fees basis since those are the results that actually accumulate in the investor's account.

8 C is correct because the benefits from replacing an investment manager are often less certain and/or realized at some point in the future whereas costs are certain and realized in the near term.

9 C is correct because policies and procedures are needed to properly support the trading and investment activities of the manager. Further, managers must have robust trading platforms. These practices are consistent with a "high" Organizational Strength rating.

10 C is correct because ETF B uses a sampling methodology that is common for passive fixed-income strategies due to the unique characteristics of each bond issued and the inability to buy specific issues in the market.

11 B is correct. Clark is concerned that the endowment will have to pay a performance fee on gains of the fund even when the endowment has lost money on its investment. A high-water mark is the highest cumulative net asset value

attained by the fund, net of fees. If the performance fee were subject to a high-water mark, no performance fee would be charged on gains when the fund is below its highest cumulative net asset value, addressing Clark's concern.

12 A is correct. A side pocket is typically used to hold positions that are not liquid enough or that have an investment horizon that is too long to be consistent with the liquidity terms offered by the fund. These side-pocketed investments are not subject to the general redemption privileges outlined in the fund's governing documents. Side pockets would best address Clark's concern about redemption requests negatively affecting the endowment's investment results.

13 A is correct. Macro strategies take long and short positions in equity, fixed income, currency, and/or futures markets to express overall economic views across global markets.

14 B is correct. Fund B has the lowest liquidity of investments and no redemption gates. Redemption gates restrict the total amount of withdrawals from the fund during a redemption period in order to protect the fund and its remaining investors from having a higher percentage of the least liquid positions as other investors seek to redeem their investments and the fund manager is forced to sell the more liquid positions.

15 A is correct. Fund A has a redemption gate to mitigate the risk of hot money investors leaving long-term investors holding the least liquid positions. A redemption gate restricts the total amount of withdrawals from the fund during a redemption period. A gate can be applied to total fund assets or to each specific investor account.

16 A is correct. The debt-to-assets under management ratio is calculated as the total value of debt relative to the assets under management (AUM) of the portfolio. Debt/AUM provides a direct measure of explicit leverage created using borrowing as advocated by Duke.

17 A is correct. Portfolios with low net exposure or long and short positions in correlated securities are generally considered better able to support leverage.

READING

12

Case Studies in Investment Manager Selection

by Jeffrey C. Heisler, PhD, CFA, Jeffrey R. Nipp, CAIA, CFA, Morgan Webber, Ross Morrison, and Steven G. Bloom, CFA

Jeffrey C. Heisler, PhD, CFA, is at TwinFocus Capital Partners (USA). Jeffrey R. Nipp, CAIA, CFA (USA). Morgan Webber is at Adams Street Partners (USA). Ross Morrison is at Adams Street Partners (United Kingdom). Steven Bloom, CFA, is at ARC Fiduciary and Columbia University (USA).

LEARNING OUTCOMES

Mastery	*The candidate should be able to:*
☐	a. recommend and justify the selection of a passive investment manager for a given asset class;
☐	b. recommend and justify the selection of an active investment manager for a given asset class;
☐	c. recommend and justify the selection of a hedge fund manager;
☐	d. recommend and justify the selection of a private equity manager;
☐	e. recommend and justify the selection of a real estate manager;
☐	f. evaluate how an investment manager has been selected;
☐	g. evaluate the selection of a replacement investment manager.

1 INTRODUCTION

The previous reading discussed in detail important elements of the manager due diligence process. This reading presents case studies to illustrate how the manager research analyst might apply the principles and techniques presented in that reading to the manager selection decision. The art of balancing the quantitative and qualitative aspects of manager selection will be demonstrated through these case studies, which highlight the common threads and unique considerations for each asset class. Section 2 illustrates the selection of a passive US large-capitalization equity manager. Section 3 illustrates the selection of a passive emerging market bond manager. Section 4 illustrates the selection of an active global bond manager. Section 5 illustrates the selection of a long–short equity manager. Section 6 illustrates the selection of a private equity manager, and Section 7 illustrates the selection of a real estate manager. The case in Section 8 puts manager selection in a client context, focusing on the replacement of an existing manager. The reading concludes with a summary.

The passive equity and emerging market bond manager cases illustrate the manner in which factors such as benchmark selection, fees, fund structure, tracking error, liquidity, and investment minimums affect the selection decision. The case of the active bond manager highlights the considerations when replacing a passive investment strategy. The selection of the long–short equity manager focuses on the trade-offs that must be made between liquid and non-liquid investment alternatives, while the private equity and real estate selection cases highlight the unique considerations that apply to these illiquid asset classes.

For simplicity, many of the cases use mutual fund vehicles to illustrate key points. Larger investors may often choose separately managed accounts to enhance transparency, to customize the strategy for their particular portfolio requirements or for tax efficiency, or to retain direct ownership of the underlying assets.

2 SELECTION OF A PASSIVE EQUITY INVESTMENT MANAGER

We are assuming, for purposes of this case, that the investor has indicated a preference for passive exposure in large-capitalization US equities and emerging market bonds. This preference may be based on any one or a combination of the following factors:

- The market segment is viewed as relatively efficient, such that the ability of an active manager to add value is limited;
- The investor is highly fee and tax sensitive; or
- Portfolio size limits the investor's ability to diversify given high separate account minimums.

Based on the desire to implement passive exposure, the suitability of various investment options will be evaluated by weighing their relative advantages and disadvantages across such aspects as the following:

- Vehicle structure
- Suitability of the underlying benchmark index for each fund
- Tracking error
- Portfolio construction
- Issuance/redemption risk
- Liquidity
- Fees
- Expenses

In this example, the investor's goal is to capture the S&P 500 Total Return (TR) Index. The assets to be allocated to this manager are $35 million.

Selecting a passive fund is often viewed as a straightforward exercise: (1) Examine the universe of funds seeking to track the performance of the desired target benchmark index, and (2) select the fund with the lowest expense ratio. In general, this simple approach will likely result in the selection of a fund that satisfies the investor's stated selection criteria. But limiting the selection process in this way makes certain assumptions and ignores differences between the funds that may matter in certain cases:

- It assumes that the funds under consideration actually do track the stated benchmark and capture the desired risk exposures;
- It assumes that because the underlying benchmark being tracked is identical, differences in performance are largely attributable to fees, ignoring the fact that different fund structures can impact investment returns; and
- It ignores liquidity. Although index funds can be purchased and sold at their net asset value (NAV), ETFs are traded securities subject to the bid–ask spread that is linked to the liquidity of the ETF and its underlying securities. (To accommodate large trades and manage the bid–ask spread, the market maker can arrange with the management company for the creation and redemption of shares.)

Even assuming the funds track the same benchmark, differences in structure and liquidity can make one preferable to another.

The investor has narrowed the universe of manager candidates to four funds:

- S&P 500 ETF 1
- S&P 500 ETF 2
- S&P 500 ETF 3
- S&P 500 Mutual Fund 1

Fund terms are presented in Exhibit 1. Exhibit 2 provides summary performance statistics. The performance statistics are calculated with a start date of September 2010, the date of the most recently launched fund, which provides the longest common evaluation period.

ETF 3 has the lowest expense ratio and the lowest tracking error. Using the lowest cost manager rule of thumb mentioned earlier, ETF 3 would appear to be the logical choice.

Exhibit 1 Large-Cap Equity Fund Summary Information as of June 2015

Name	Inception	Expense Ratio	Average Daily Volume YTD (million)	AUM ($ billions)	Premium/ Discount	Minimum Investment ($)	Availability
S&P 500 ETF 1	Jan/93	0.09%	111.6	201.7	0.06%	NA	NA
S&P 500 ETF 2	May/00	0.07%	4.3	68.8	0.05%	NA	NA
S&P 500 ETF 3	Sep/10	0.05%	1.3	27.7	−0.01%	NA	NA
S&P 500 Mutual Fund 1	Jan/97	0.14%	NA	1.3	NA	250,000	Limited

Source: Data from Morningstar.

Exhibit 2 Large-Cap Equity Fund Summary Performance Statistics; October 2010–June 2015

Name	One-Year Return	Three-Year Annualized Return	Since Inception Annualized Return	Standard Deviation	Tracking Error	Up Capture	Down Capture	Max Drawdown
S&P 500 ETF 1	7.31%	17.15%	15.56%	11.17%	0.03%	99.53%	100.08%	–16.26%
S&P 500 ETF 2	7.36%	17.24%	15.61%	11.18%	0.02%	99.74%	100.12%	–16.27%
S&P 500 ETF 3	7.39%	17.27%	15.66%	11.19%	0.02%	99.89%	100.05%	–16.26%
S&P 500 Mutual Fund 1	7.27%	17.12%	15.52%	11.20%	0.09%	99.52%	100.48%	–16.43%
S&P 500 TR Index	7.42%	17.31%	15.70%	11.19%	0.00%	100.00%	100.00%	–16.26%

Source: Data from Morningstar.

This superficial comparison of the investment options, however, misses certain facets important to fund (or manager) selection:

- ETF 3 is less liquid, with average daily volume year-to-date of 1.3 million units. For example, at a price of $184.80, if the investor is willing to be, at most, 20% of the average daily volume (in order to not create selling—or buying—pressure that would negatively impact its own position), the liquidity of ETF 3 would support a position size of no more than $48 million (1.3 million × 20% × $184.80/share).
- ETF 3 is a relatively new offering with a limited track record. Although an investor would normally want to examine the historical one-, three-, and five-year performance record of a fund to get a sense of the consistency of returns, that is not possible in this case. Furthermore, ETF 3 has not yet experienced a full market cycle or weathered a serious market dislocation. The investor has determined that this presents an operational risk they are unwilling to assume.

Thus, ETF 3 is removed from the candidate list. The evaluation can now be expanded to include performance history back to July 2005, a 10-year investment horizon. As can be seen in Exhibit 3, all of the funds track well over all of the investment horizons with the difference in return and level of tracking error aligned with the fund expense ratios.

Exhibit 3 Large-Cap Equity Fund Summary Performance Statistics; July 2005–June 2015

Name	One-Year Return	Three-Year Annualized Return	Five-Year Annualized Return	Ten-Year Annualized Return	Standard Deviation	Tracking Error	Up Capture	Down Capture	Max Drawdown
S&P 500 ETF 1	7.31%	17.15%	17.20%	7.80%	14.71%	0.05%	99.57%	99.92%	–50.89%
S&P 500 ETF 2	7.36%	17.24%	17.25%	7.83%	14.72%	0.03%	99.71%	99.93%	–50.89%
S&P 500 Mutual Fund 1	7.27%	17.12%	17.16%	7.79%	14.74%	0.11%	99.74%	100.22%	–50.96%
S&P 500 TR Index	7.42%	17.31%	17.34%	7.89%	14.74%	0.00%	100.00%	100.00%	–50.95%

Source: Data from Morningstar.

All of the funds implement their index exposure using a full replication strategy by holding all constituents in same weight as the index. Each of the funds track the S&P 500 closely and display similar returns, risk, beta, upside and downside capture, and maximum drawdown. Mutual Fund 1 has the lowest return, the highest tracking error, and the highest expense ratio. Although performance and tracking error of passive funds are highly correlated with fees, the difference in expense ratio among these candidates does not fully explain the difference in relative performance.

Exhibit 4 presents additional considerations that factor into the selection process.

Exhibit 4 Large-Cap Equity Fund Summary Evaluation

	Advantages	Disadvantages
ETF 1	■ Low expense ratio ■ Low tracking error ■ Long track record ■ Large asset base ■ Substantial trading volume	■ Unit investment trust; cannot reinvest dividends, lend shares, or use futures.
ETF 2	■ Low expense ratio ■ Low tracking error ■ Long track record ■ Can generate income from security lending and dividend reinvestment	■ Smaller asset base ■ Lower level of trading volume
Mutual Fund 1	■ Mutual fund that redeems at NAV with no premium/discount ■ Can generate income from securities lending and dividend reinvestment	■ Highest expense ratio ■ Highest tracking error ■ Small asset base

As the additional criteria reflected in Exhibit 4 suggest, the selection of a passive manager should consider more than just the expense ratio. The ability of ETFs and mutual funds to reinvest dividends, lend shares, and use futures may be expected to improve performance. Unit investment trusts (UITs) will hold dividends received in cash or cash equivalents until the end of the quarter at which time they are distributed to investors. (Reinvestment of dividends reduces the performance drag of cash balances and can increase returns during periods of rising stock prices. Securities lending generates income that can offset the drag of fees, whereas the use of futures helps reduce cash drag.)

Although most managers tracking the appropriate underlying index are likely to produce reasonable results, the selection process must also consider the size of the expected investment and the anticipated holding period. Mutual Fund 1 appears to be the least attractive choice given its higher tracking error, higher expense ratio, and small asset base, so the investor is left to select either ETF 1 or ETF 2. Although ETF 1 has a slightly greater tracking error, the large asset size and ample trading volume provide good liquidity. These characteristics make it more attractive to investors contemplating a large investment or those that trade actively, for which trading volume and a narrow bid–ask spread are important considerations. ETF 2 provides performance that more closely tracks the desired index but, with average daily trading volume of 4.3 million units and a current price of $25 per unit, the investor would be able to trade just $21 million per day (based on its desire to be less than 20% of the average daily volume). Based on this information, the investor selects ETF 1 to implement its passive large-capitalization US equity exposure.

3 SELECTION OF A PASSIVE EMERGING MARKET BOND MANAGER

Our investor now wants to explore the implications of adding passive exposure to emerging market (EM) bonds as a tactical complement to a longer-term strategic allocation to an actively managed EM bond (EMB) portfolio. The investor is agnostic with respect to the choice of benchmark and will consider local currency-denominated as well as US dollar-denominated funds. The assets to be allocated to this manager are $5 million. In addition to the factors considered in our first case, evaluation of these manager candidates must include an assessment of the index each fund tracks, as well as currency, country, and credit risk.

Using the firm's database that tracks manager performance characteristics and documents the firm's research on investment managers, four ETF candidates have been identified. The ETFs each track different indexes and, as a result, they have different currency and country exposures:

- EMB ETF 1 and EMB ETF 2 each track an index composed of US dollar-denominated debt issued by emerging market entities. EMB ETF 1 includes both sovereign and corporate debt securities while EMB ETF 2 is focused exclusively on sovereign debt securities.
- EMB ETF 3 and EMB ETF 4 also track different indexes, although each index is composed of local currency-denominated debt issued by emerging market sovereign and corporate securities.

Exhibit 5 shows the expense ratio, average daily trading volume, asset base, and premium or discount to NAV of each fund. It also shows the name of the index each fund has adopted as its target benchmark.

Exhibit 5 Emerging Market Fund Summary Information as of May 2015

Name	Inception	Expense Ratio	Average Daily Volume (million)	AUM ($ billions)	Premium/ Discount	Index
EMB ETF 1	Dec/07	0.60%	0.94	4.1	0.66%	JPMorgan EMBI Global Core
EMB ETF 2	Oct/07	0.50%	0.79	2.5	0.98%	DB EM USD Liquid Balanced
EMB ETF 3	Jul/10	0.47%	0.43	1.2	0.75%	JPMorgan GBI-EM Global Core
EMB ETF 4	Oct/11	0.60%	0.04	0.5	−0.31%	Bloomberg Barclays EM Broad Local Currency Bond Index

Source: Data from Morningstar.

With the introduction of competing benchmarks and the added currency exposure, the selection exercise cannot be reduced to simply selecting the cheapest fund.

- EMB ETF 1 and EMB ETF 2 are both US dollar-denominated; they have no foreign currency exposure. EMB ETF 3 and EMB ETF 4 invest in local bonds, which is expected to provide additional diversification but introduces currency exposure. For example, if the US dollar weakens relative to the issuing (local) currencies of the bonds in the index, US dollar returns are enhanced, whereas a strengthening dollar detracts from US dollar returns.

- Emerging market bond indexes use different weighting schemes. Differences in index construction methodology can introduce unwanted country and commodity risk. For example, as shown in Exhibit 6, as of 31 December 2013, the exposure of EMB ETF 4 (benchmarked against the JPMorgan EMBI Global Core Index) to Russia, Brazil, Mexico, Indonesia, Colombia, and Venezuela was nearly 37%. These exposures present possible political or energy risk. In contrast, EMB ETF 2 and EMB ETF 3 have exposure to these countries of 24.6% and 28.6%, respectively.
- Each index also exhibits different allocations across security type (e.g., sovereign and corporate) as well as credit quality, as shown in Exhibit 7.

Exhibit 6 Emerging Market Fund Country Allocations as of 31 December 2013

Name	Mexico	Indonesia	Brazil	South Korea	Turkey	Russia	Hungary	Malaysia	Colombia	Venezuela	Other
EMB ETF 1	5.71%	5.33%	5.28%	0.00%	5.89%	6.93%	3.47%	2.15%	4.51%	4.32%	55.13%
EMB ETF 2	4.29%	3.94%	4.07%	4.59%	3.77%	4.35%	4.78%	0.00%	4.20%	3.78%	62.23%
EMB ETF 3	8.88%	7.60%	6.56%	16.67%	4.95%	4.33%	6.00%	6.70%	1.26%	0.00%	41.37%
EMB ETF 4	6.16%	5.89%	16.16%	0.00%	6.51%	5.28%	4.69%	8.59%	3.35%	0.00%	49.74%

Source: Data from Morningstar.

Exhibit 7 Emerging Market Fund Security Type and Credit Rating Allocations as of 31 December 2013

Name	Government	Corporate	Cash	Investment Grade	High Yield	Not Rated
EMB ETF 1	79%	20%	1%	58%	36%	6%
EMB ETF 2	100%	0%	0%	62%	38%	0%
EMB ETF 3	73%	4%	23%	76%	7%	17%
EMB ETF 4	85%	13%	3%	88%	3%	9%

Source: Data from Morningstar.

As seen in Exhibit 8, the performance differential among these passive emerging market bond alternatives can be quite wide (in this example, the difference in the one-year return is as much as 14.8%). Exhibit 9 shows that much of the divergence in performance arose in the second half of the year, when a strengthening US dollar negatively affected the returns of the two funds with inherent currency exposure (EMB ETF 3 and EMB ETF 4).

Exhibit 8 Emerging Market Fund Summary Performance Statistics; January 2014–December 2014

Name	Annualized Return	Standard Deviation	Tracking Error	Down Capture	Maximum Drawdown
EMB ETF 1	6.69%	6.23%	6.32%	27.29%	−2.72%
EMB ETF 2	9.18%	7.05%	5.82%	28.72%	−2.87%
EMB ETF 3	−5.62%	10.53%	1.89%	92.33%	−10.75%
EMB ETF 4	−4.04%	8.85%	3.40%	79.43%	−9.90%
Benchmark	−4.68%	11.65%	0.00%	100.00%	−11.32%

Source: Data from Morningstar.

Exhibit 9 Emerging Market Fund Cumulative Return; December 2013–December 2014

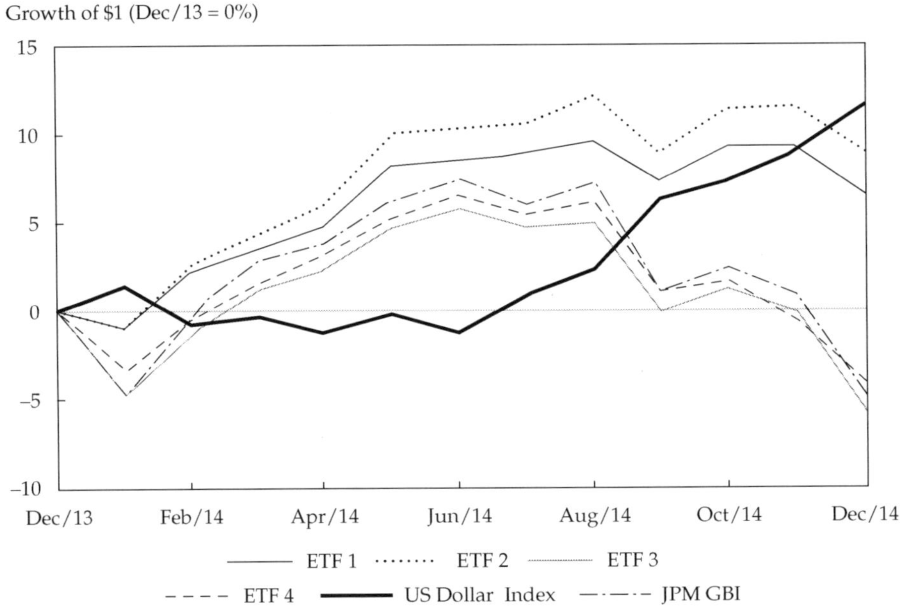

Note: JPM GBI is the JPMorgan Government Bond Index.
Source: Based on data from Morningstar.

This example illustrates the importance of properly specifying the desired exposures, and the benchmark that best captures those exposures, in the selection of a passive manager.

Exhibit 10 presents additional considerations that must be factored into the selection process.

Exhibit 10 Emerging Market Fund Summary Evaluation

	Advantages	Disadvantages	Summary Observations
EMB ETF 1	■ Largest trading volume ■ Largest AUM ■ Long track record	■ High exposure to potential country and commodity risk	■ Holds only US dollar-denominated securities ■ Largest corporate exposure ■ Substantial high-yield and unrated credit exposure ■ Diversified across countries ■ Moderate expense ratio
EMB ETF 2	■ Long track record ■ Reasonable trading volume	■ Small asset base	■ Holds only US dollar-denominated securities ■ Sovereign debt only ■ High allocation to investment grade bonds ■ Highest allocation to high-yield credit ■ Diversified across countries ■ Moderate expense ratio
EMB ETF 3	■ Lowest expense ratio	■ Shorter track record ■ Moderate volume ■ Small asset base	■ Holds local currency-denominated securities ■ Focused on sovereign debt ■ High cash allocation ■ Substantial unrated credit exposure ■ Concentrated country allocations
EMB ETF 4		■ Shorter track record ■ Low volume ■ Small asset base ■ Highest exposure to potential country and commodity risk	■ Holds local currency-denominated securities ■ Balanced security allocations ■ Concentrated country allocations ■ Moderate expense ratio

Based on this assessment, the investor removes the currency component from the allocation, reserving that exposure for the actively managed fund. Thus, EMB ETF 1 and EMB ETF 2 are selected for further consideration.

The investor also determines a preference for a manager with lower exposure to credit risk because of the credit risk exposure of the active manager. EMB ETF 2, with its focus on sovereign debt and a slightly higher allocation to investment grade securities is better aligned with that preference. But the average daily trading volume for EMB ETF 2 is approximately $22 million, based on its current price of $28 per unit and 790,000 average daily unit volume. The investor has previously indicated a desire to limit its position size to not more than 20% of the average daily volume. Therefore, the maximum allocation is $4.4 million. Conversely, the average daily trading volume for EMB ETF 1 is approximately $103 million, based on its current price of \$110 per unit and 940,000 average daily unit volume, implying a maximum allocation of \$20.6 million. As a result, the investor decides to allocate \$3 million to EMB ETF 1 and \$2 million to EMB ETF 2 to achieve its \$5 million target allocation.

4 THE SELECTION OF AN ACTIVE INVESTMENT MANAGER

The selection of an active manager requires the investor to evaluate the suitability of potential managers based on their relative advantages and disadvantages, including the quantitative and qualitative considerations involved in both investment and operational due diligence. In this section we present an exercise in the selection of an active world bond manager.

This investor currently uses a passive fund (World Bond ETF 1) to capture global fixed-income exposure as expressed by the Bloomberg Barclays Global Treasury ex-US Capped Index. This decision was made based on the initial size of the allocation and the desire to minimize fees. The size of the investor's aggregate portfolio has since grown and the investor wants to explore whether an actively managed strategy can provide a global bond exposure which complements the existing position and adds the potential to provide additional return. A screen of the universe identified three candidates with at least 10-year track records that each provide different approaches to investing in global bonds. The research analyst's summaries are presented in Exhibit 11.

Exhibit 11

Active World Bond Manager: Research Analyst's Summaries

World Bond Fund 1

World Bond Fund 1 (WBF 1) seeks current income with capital appreciation and income growth by investing primarily in global government and government agency debt. Research efforts focus on rigorous country/thematic analysis to identify economic imbalances leading to value opportunities in the three Cs—currency, yield curve (interest rates and duration), and sovereign credit—and a continual evaluation of risk to shift portfolio allocations based on relative attractiveness over the course of global economic and credit cycles. WBF 1 takes medium- and long-term approaches to its investment strategy, capitalizing on themes that can take two or three years to play out (sometimes longer). WBF 1 is benchmark insensitive, taking positions wherever the team's research indicates inefficiencies and outsized returns exist. WBF 1 maintains key global allocations throughout Europe and Asia Pacific with a current large cash position in currencies and a tilt toward emerging market debt and currency. High-yield exposure is capped at 25% of total assets. The manager keeps duration under two years. The portfolio is relatively concentrated with around 230 long and 25 short holdings. WBF 1's competitive advantage in this space has been largely a function of the portfolio manager's vast network of contacts with influential policymakers and economic strategists, including central bankers and elected political leaders.

Exhibit 11 (Continued)

World Bond Funds 2 and 3

World Bond Funds 2 (WBF 2) and 3 (WBF 3) are managed by the same investment manager. Each seeks maximum total return and preservation of capital. WBF 3 actively manages currency exposure according to fundamental and technical factors, whereas WBF 2 hedges at least 80% of its exposure to foreign currency. The manager combines a top-down view of the global economy and interest rates, which determines such basic portfolio parameters as duration, region, and credit quality breakdown, with bottom-up fundamental sector and credit research, which determines security selection. At times, positions are expressed using futures rather than bonds. The portfolio is diversified, with at least 80% of assets invested in debt securities issued outside the United States, and can have concentrated geographical exposures. Most bonds are investment grade, but up to 10% of the portfolio can be invested in high-yield securities. Each fund may also invest up to 10% of its total assets in preferred stocks.

World Bond ETF 1

The ETF currently in the portfolio (WB ETF 1) provides passive, diversified exposure to investment-grade foreign-market government bonds. Although a number of strategies are now readily available, at the time this allocation was first made, there were limited options. WB ETF 1 seeks to track the Bloomberg Barclays Global Treasury ex-US Capped Index, which includes fixed-coupon investment-grade government issues denominated in local currency. The bonds must have at least one year until maturity. The portfolio is constructed using a sampling strategy and is rebalanced at the end of each month.

Summary information for each of the investment options is provided in Exhibit 12.

Exhibit 12 World Bond Fund Summary Information as of June 2015

Name	Inception	Duration	Expense Ratio	Average Daily Volume YTD	AUM ($ billions)	Premium/ Discount	Minimum Investment ($)	Availability
World Bond Fund 1	Jan/97	0.15	0.64%	NA	67.9	NA	1,000,000	Open
World Bond Fund 2	Apr/98	7.62	0.50%	NA	8.3	NA	1,000,000	Open
World Bond Fund 3	Apr/04	7.96	0.50%	NA	1.7	NA	1,000,000	Open
World Bond ETF 1	Oct/07	7.74	0.50%	328,000	1.45	−0.27%	NA	NA

Source: Data from Morningstar.

The funds all have minimum investments of $1 million; WBF 1 has a slightly higher expense ratio. The managers are both established firms that, in combination with the substantial asset bases of the funds, reduces potential business risk and provides a strong foundation to support the funds' investment and operational processes. A review of regional exposures, presented in Exhibit 13, highlights the differences between the investment processes and resulting portfolios.

Exhibit 13 World Bond Fund Regional Allocations as of 31 December 2014

Name	United States	Other North America	Latin America	Europe Dev	Europe EM	United Kingdom	Japan	Asia Dev	Asia EM	Other
World Bond Fund 1	0.0%	4.9%	10.9%	0.0%	35.8%	0.0%	0.0%	0.0%	23.7%	24.7%
World Bond Fund 2	−5.0%	1.0%	3.0%	40.0%	3.0%	16.0%	38.0%	2.0%	0.0%	1.0%
World Bond Fund 3	−5.0%	1.0%	3.0%	38.0%	3.0%	16.0%	38.0%	2.0%	0.0%	4.0%
World Bond ETF 1	1.1%	8.6%	0.1%	43.7%	1.5%	10.7%	19.5%	5.3%	2.9%	6.7%

Note: Dev stands for developed.
Source: Data from Morningstar.

The investor makes the following observations:

- WBF 1 has a substantially higher allocation to emerging markets.
- WBF 2 and WBF 3, managed by the same investment manager, display nearly identical regional exposures, with some small variations resulting from the currency hedges.
- The regional allocations of WBF 2 and WBF 3 are more similar to those of the ETF, with larger allocations to developed countries.

Exhibit 14 displays the credit quality distribution of each fund's holdings. The active funds diverge considerably from the benchmark and ETF weightings. WBF 1 takes on considerable credit risk, with nearly 20% of the portfolio invested in high-yield or unrated securities. WBF 2 and WBF 3, although slightly overweight in high-yield and unrated bonds, display credit profiles that are closer to the benchmark.

Exhibit 14 World Bond Fund Security Type and Credit Rating Allocations as of 31 December 2014

Name	Government	Corporate	Securitized	Municipal	Cash	Investment Grade	High Yield	Not Rated
World Bond Fund 1	57.55%	0.56%	0.00%	0.00%	41.90%	80.74%	18.58%	14.96%
World Bond Fund 2	88.40%	1.92%	4.85%	0.66%	4.17%	93.00%	7.00%	4.00%
World Bond Fund 3	86.30%	3.89%	6.21%	1.29%	2.31%	93.00%	7.00%	4.00%
World Bond ETF 1	96.91%	0.26%	0.87%	0.00%	1.96%	100.00%	0.00%	0.00%

Source: Data from Morningstar.

Although the funds display similar allocations among credit rating categories, there are clear differences in the underlying securities held and the degree of credit risk in the portfolios. WBF 1, given its objective of capturing opportunities in the currency markets, has a higher allocation to futures (reflected in a larger cash allocation). WBF 2 and WBF 3 have sector weightings closer to the benchmark, but they are overweighted in corporate bonds as well as securitized instruments and cash (reflecting the expression of some positions using futures contracts).

A quantitative analysis, summarized in Exhibit 15, shows the following:

- WBF 1 has added significant alpha relative to the benchmark over the period, with an attractive downside capture ratio and shallow maximum drawdown. It also currently has significantly lower duration: 0.15 years compared with 7.74 years for the ETF (from Exhibit 12).

- WBF 2 has also added significant alpha relative to the benchmark, with very low downside capture and shallow drawdown.
- WBF 3 has also outperformed the ETF on a relative return basis, although on a much more modest basis and with much more volatility, as evidenced by the downside capture and drawdown statistics.

It is important to note that the investor is evaluating the funds' potential to provide additional return over and above the passive exposure of its current World Bond ETF. Although the benchmark used in the analysis below may not be representative of the managers' active investment strategy, the use of a common benchmark allows the investor to assess the likelihood that a given fund will provide the desired performance enhancement.

Exhibit 15 World Bond Fund Summary Performance Statistics; November 2007–June 2015

Name	Annualized Return	Cumulative Return	Standard Deviation	Annualized Alpha	Up Capture	Down Capture	Maximum Drawdown
World Bond Fund 1	7.03%	68.30%	8.40%	5.76%	90.34%	43.28%	−8.93%
World Bond Fund 3	6.62%	63.51%	4.41%	5.83%	50.82%	1.04%	−9.30%
World Bond Fund 2	4.14%	36.47%	9.93%	2.51%	111.07%	91.42%	−20.98%
World Bond ETF 1	1.71%	13.85%	8.98%	0.00%	100.00%	100.00%	−13.95%

Source: Data from Morningstar.

The plot of the cumulative return for each of the funds in Exhibit 16 shows that the difference in performance between WBF 2 and WBF 3 largely developed from mid-2014 onward—a period when the US dollar largely appreciated relative to global currencies. As you recall from the fund summaries presented earlier, WBF 3 actively manages its currency exposure while WBF 2, managed by the same investment manager, hedges at least 80% of its currency exposure. We might infer from the superior performance of WBF 3 from mid-2014 onward that the active management of currency exposure added to the fund's performance relative to the passive hedging approach taken by WBF 2.

Exhibit 16 World Bond Funds Cumulative Returns; October 2007–April 2015

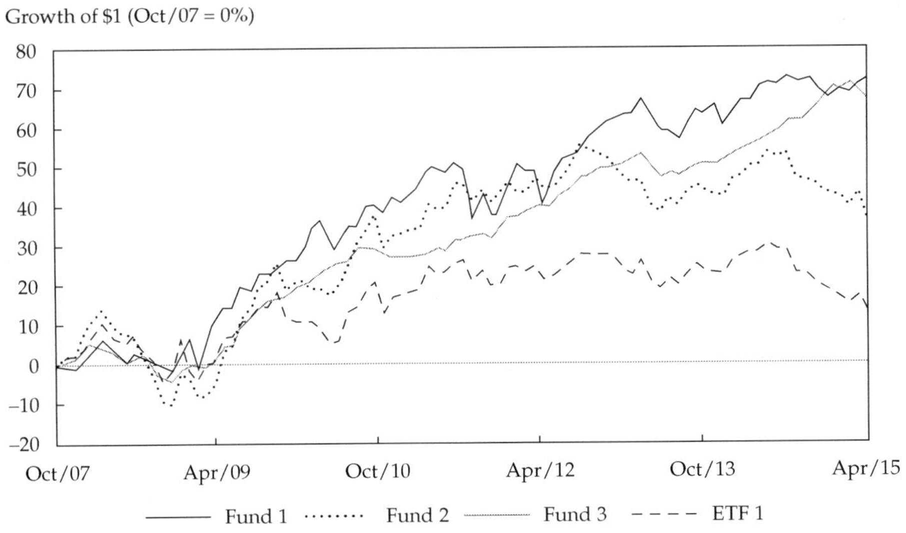

Source: Based on data from Morningstar.

Overall, given the objective of complementing the fixed-income risk exposures captured by the WBF ETF with the potential for generating additional return, an allocation to WBF 1 appears to best meet the investor's goals. WBF 1 diversifies the investor's current exposures with a larger exposure to emerging markets, a different credit risk profile, and active currency risk. Although WBF 2 has exhibited meaningful excess return over the period, the underlying exposures across regions, securities, and credit are closer to the investor's current exposure with WBF ETF.

EXAMPLE 1

Selecting an Active Manager

1 Which of the active world bond managers presented in the preceding discussion *best* meets the needs of an investor that requires alpha and expects interest rates to increase over the next two years? The investor is insensitive to credit risk. Justify your recommendation.

A World Bond Fund 1

B World Bond Fund 2

C World Bond Fund 3

2 An active US-domiciled world bond manager's investment approach emphasizes exploiting anomalies in government yield curves, and its clients require liquidity and accurate pricing. Which of the following is *most likely* to improve the manager's ability to meet client expectations? The manager:

A allocates significant funds to emerging market local currency sovereign bonds.

B allocates funds to developed market sovereign bonds.

C employs a staff of economists to provide interest rate, currency rate, and GDP forecasts.

Solution to 1:

A is correct. Over time, World Bond Fund 1 has experienced meaningful alpha and has gone into markets where returns and credit risk are high, including emerging markets, high yield, and unrated bonds. Its high cash position and low duration provide the flexibility needed to reposition the investor's portfolio to take advantage of a higher interest rate environment. World Bond Funds 2 and 3 are less able to meet the investor's needs.

Solution to 2:

C is correct. Access to accurate economic forecasts that focus on monetary policy, currency movements, and the outlook for the economy are important for an active manager that wants to take advantage of changes in yield curve levels and shapes to generate active returns. Although emerging market bonds can provide high average returns, they are less liquid than developed market bonds, and they add complexity because the manager must now manage currency exposures. Although some developed market sovereign bonds can provide good returns, the strong credit research is essential, and currency exposures must be managed.

SELECTION OF AN ACTIVE LONG–SHORT US EQUITY MANAGER

5

Our investor is a $700 million endowment fund with a long-term investment horizon and sufficient liquid assets that the liquidity of this investment is not a determining factor in the decision. As such, it meets the qualifications to invest in a privately offered hedge fund. The goal is to explore whether investing $15 million with a long–short equity manager can provide alpha relative to the equity markets without increasing portfolio volatility or downside risk.

The investor is presented with three candidates, each of which has at least a 10-year track record. The research analyst's summaries of each candidate are presented in Exhibit 17. Information regarding investment terms is presented in Exhibit 18.

Exhibit 17

Active Long–Short US Equity Manager: Research Analyst's Summaries

LSE Mutual Fund 1

The portfolio manager selects stocks using a disciplined investment process based on valuation, business fundamentals, and whether there is an identifiable catalyst that is expected to result in a revaluation of the stock. For long positions, this translates into companies with good fundamentals and a market price below the manager's estimated intrinsic value. Short positions focus on stocks with unstable business models and excessive valuations. The portfolio is diversified (generally holding 100–150 long positions and 100–300 short positions) and has historically concentrated in small-capitalization value longs and small-capitalization growth shorts in the US market. The manager seeks to time trades using momentum indicators. Because shorting smaller-capitalization names can be difficult and expensive, the manager factors in shorting costs before

(continued)

Exhibit 17 (Continued)

making trades. The manager is supported by two dedicated analysts as well as the other research analysts of the firm. The firm is well known and operational due diligence suggests low business risk and no operational red flags.

LSE Mutual Fund 2

The manager was acquired in late 2007. The investment process was overhauled and the management team was reorganized. Of note, the process was changed to a team approach that implements a fundamental bottom-up long–short process with a focus on US large-capitalization stocks. There are eight senior managers and three analysts. Each of the team members is a generalist and is expected to research and express an opinion on nearly every buy and sell decision. The lead portfolio managers determine position weightings and net exposures. For long positions, the team looks for companies with solid organic growth, experienced management, a positive fundamental outlook, and reasonable valuations. Short positions are often companies originally researched as potential long positions but may be experiencing problems, such as declining margins or struggling product lines. The portfolio is relatively concentrated with 40–50 long holdings and 20–30 short holdings. Portfolio turnover is relatively low because the manager will let appreciating positions run. The manager does not appear to use technical indicators to time trades. The firm is well known and operational due diligence suggests low business risk and no operational red flags.

LSE Hedge Fund 1

The investment process combines a top-down macroeconomic view with bottom-up stock selection. The macroeconomic environment and the current state and positioning of the portfolio factor into overall portfolio exposures and composition. The bottom-up stock selection process combines stock screens that sort the available universe on various fundamental measures. Of the names that make it through this screen, the portfolio managers select their best ideas for additional analysis. The due diligence process includes the creation of individual company earnings projections, industry analysis with comparative statistics across companies, interviews with company management, company and industry news analysis, and market and industry intelligence. From these positions, portfolio managers select the best ideas and size their positions accordingly, with potential short positions exhibiting the inverse characteristics of potential long positions. The fund focuses on large-capitalization companies across various sectors of the US market, typically with market values of more than $10 billion. Portfolio names tend to be some of the most well-known, established corporations in the world. These names are typically very liquid with outsized daily average trading volume, providing an additional measure of liquidity to the fund and investors. The fund is moderately concentrated, with just more than 100 names across both the long and short books. Short positions are traded actively using ETFs, pairs trades, and single-name alpha shorts. The firm is well known and operational due diligence suggests low business risk and no operational red flags.

Exhibit 18 Active Long–Short US Equity Summary Information

Name	Inception	Expense Ratio/ Management Fee	Incentive Fee	Liquidity	AUM ($ billion)	Minimum Investment ($)	Availability
LSE Mutual Fund 1	Nov/98	2.25%	NA	Daily	0.64	100,000	Limited
LSE Mutual Fund 2	Dec/97	1.15%	NA	Daily	0.25	1,000,000	Open
LSE Hedge Fund 1	Jan/95	1.00%	20%	Quarterly	2.40	1,000,000	Limited

Source: Data from Morningstar.

A qualitative assessment of each potential manager reveals the following regarding key aspects of the managers' investment approaches:

- *Philosophy.* The managers all trade publicly listed stocks and seek to exploit behavioral inefficiencies by buying or selling stocks they believe are mispriced relative to their estimates of intrinsic value.
- *Process.* The managers each use fundamental bottom-up research, although LSE Hedge Fund 1 additionally incorporates a top-down macroeconomic view. One potential concern is the generalist, team-based process of LSE Mutual Fund 2. Although a team approach reduces key man risk and provides a forum for considering diverging opinions, it can be less nimble and potentially dilute alpha if a consensus is difficult to reach or the process lacks adequate accountability, which could occur if a given analyst is not consistently monitoring the same set of positions.
- *Personnel.* Although LSE Mutual Fund 1 and LSE Hedge Fund 1 have each had the same managers since fund inception, LSE Mutual Fund 2 has experienced considerable turnover. Although some portfolio managers have been involved in the management of the fund since 2004, eight portfolio managers have departed since the acquisition, raising concerns about the stability of the organization
- *Portfolio.* As shown in Exhibit 19, LSE Mutual Fund 1 has moderate sector over- and underweights relative to the S&P 500 TR Index. LSE Mutual Fund 2, which holds a relatively concentrated portfolio, does not appear to have many large sector bets, whereas LSE Hedge Fund 1 has large relative underweights to a number of sectors.
- *Net Exposure.* LSE Mutual Fund 1 tends to be fully invested on the long side—that is, gross long exposure of 100%, whereas gross short exposure can range between 10% and 90%. Historically, the fund's net exposure has been around 80%, but the fund has increased and decreased exposure based on the ability of their bottom-up research to identify compelling investment ideas. For example, short exposure was only 12.1% during the second quarter of 2009, a factor contributing to the fund's 38.5% return and strong 2009 performance. The fund consequently reduced net exposure starting in 2012 and by October 2014 held a very low net exposure of 26%. The fund has since increased its exposure to 99.25% net long as of 31 March 2015. LSE Mutual Fund 2 has also actively managed its net exposure. Starting from a net exposure of ~40% in 2005, exposure held steady around 70% net long through mid-2009, increased progressively through 2011, and has since been scaled back to around 50%. LSE Hedge Fund 1 sets portfolio net exposure based on its macro view and availability of long and short opportunities. The fund's typical short exposure is 10%–30% but it considered the short opportunity set to be limited in 2013 and 2014 because

of central bank policy, and net portfolio exposure was above average. The fund has been adding short exposure as market volatility has increased and it sees a greater short opportunity set.

Exhibit 19 Active Long–Short Equity Sector Allocations Relative to the S&P 500 TR Index

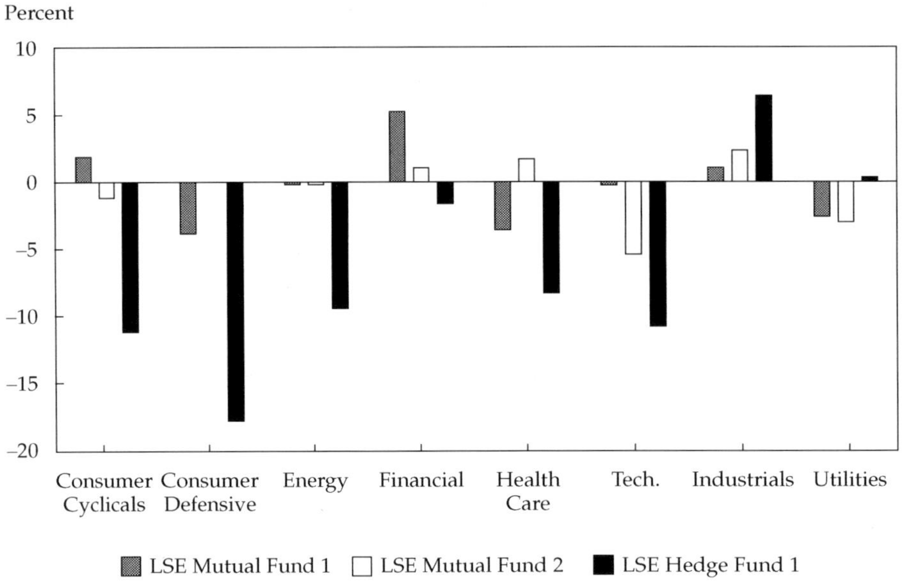

Note: as of January and March 2015.
Source: Based on data from Morningstar.

Examining the performance shown in Exhibits 20 and 21, we find the following:

- Long–short equity hedge funds as group (as measured by the HFRX Equity Hedge Index) underperformed the S&P 500. The period included a significant broad-market correction (down 37.5%) during which the HFRX modestly outperformed the S&P 500. This outperformance was followed by a multi-year period of strong equity market returns during which the HFRX failed to match broad equity market returns.
- LSE Mutual Fund 1 outperformed the HFRX and the S&P 500 over the full 10-year period. The outperformance was particularly notable in the 2009–2011 period when the manager returned 82.37%, 26.44%, and 5.92% sequentially. Conversely, the fund underperformed in 2013, likely a result of the fund's low net exposure during a year in which the S&P 500 returned more than 32%. Over the full period, the fund exhibited a relatively high beta (0.73) relative to the S&P 500, perhaps not surprising given the fund's solid returns during a period of strong equity market performance (2009 onward). The fund had an attractive capture ratio of 1.48, with an upside capture of 80% and downside capture of 54%.
- LSE Mutual Fund 2 outperformed the HFRX over the 10-year period, while underperforming the S&P 500. The fund has generated somewhat modest returns, with just a few years of relative outperformance. In 2007, the fund returned more than 15% compared with 5.5% for the S&P 500, and in 2008 the fund experienced a drawdown of only 13.7%. This pattern is consistent with the

fund's generally conservative low net exposure positioning. This conservative posture is reflected in the fund's low beta of 0.3, modest upside and downside capture ratios, and shallow maximum drawdown (14.8%).

- LSE Hedge Fund 1 outperformed the HFRX and the S&P 500 with relatively low volatility over the period. The fund exhibited more of an absolute return profile with positive returns in every year except 2011 when it was down 3.2%. The fund exhibited a low beta relative to the S&P 500 with an attractive capture ratio of 1.7 (upside capture of 58% and downside capture of 34%) and the shallowest maximum drawdown of 12.6%.

Exhibit 20 Active Long–Short Equity Summary Performance Statistics; June 2005–May 2015

Name	Annualized Return	Cumulative Return	Alpha vs. S&P 500	Correlation with S&P 500	Beta	Up Capture	Down Capture	Max Drawdown
LSE Mutual Fund 1	11.07%	185.78%	4.72%	0.58	0.73	79.82%	53.66%	−34.63%
LSE Mutual Fund 2	3.63%	42.79%	0.07%	0.93	0.30	36.98%	33.66%	−14.80%
LSE Hedge Fund 1	8.93%	135.29%	4.97%	0.88	0.34	58.13%	33.69%	−12.57%
HFRX Equity Hedge Index	0.94%	9.82%	−3.28%	0.83	0.42	37.50%	51.10%	−29.52%
S&P 500 TR Index	8.12%	118.30%	0.00%	1.00	1.00	100.00%	100.00%	−50.95%

Source: Based on data from Morningstar.

Exhibit 21 Active Long–Short Equity Calendar Year Returns; January 2005–December 2014

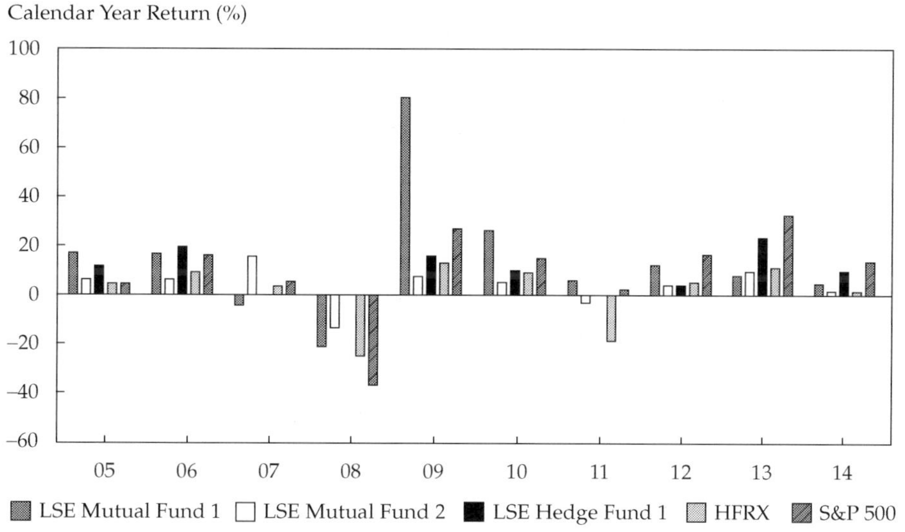

Source: Based on data from Morningstar.

LSE Mutual Fund 2 has the weakest performance record among the candidates but, as noted earlier, the investment process and personnel changed with the acquisition of the manager in late 2007. Isolating the fund's pre-acquisition performance from that of the full period allows us to judge whether the acquisition had a positive or negative impact on the fund.

Examining the June 2005 to December 2007 period, shown in Exhibit 22, we find that LSE Mutual Fund 2 produced the largest alpha with the highest capture ratio and shallowest maximum drawdown. Clearly, the manager's performance post-acquisition deteriorated significantly, dragging LSE Mutual Fund 2 from a top performer to the lowest performer among the funds under consideration. Although additional work may be warranted to better understand the implications of the change in managers and investment process on fund performance, the analysis suggests that the change has not been positive.

Exhibit 22 Active Long–Short Equity Summary Performance Statistics; June 2005–December 2007

Name	Annualized Return	Cumulative Return	Alpha vs. S&P 500	Correlation	Beta	Up Capture	Down Capture	Maximum Drawdown
LSE Mutual Fund 1	7.84%	21.53%	2.17%	0.20	0.20	49.18%	10.35%	–8.36%
LSE Mutual Fund 2	11.30%	31.85%	4.52%	0.52	0.31	66.34%	5.84%	–2.41%
LSE Hedge Fund 1	11.00%	30.94%	1.71%	0.73	0.79	89.06%	66.31%	–5.14%
HFRX Equity Hedge Index	10.49%	29.39%	0.00%	1.00	1.00	100.00%	100.00%	–4.85%
S&P 500 TR Index	7.70%	21.13%	–6.90%	0.80	0.66	71.15%	67.00%	–4.51%

Source: Based on data from Morningstar.

Our analysis then turns to examining the performance differences between LSE Mutual Fund 1 and LSE Hedge Fund 1. An important differentiating factor is that LSE Mutual Fund 1 focuses on small-capitalization stocks (for which the S&P 500 is not an appropriate benchmark), whereas LSE Hedge Fund 1 focuses on large-capitalization stocks. To adjust for this difference, the S&P SmallCap 600 Index, which measures the performance of the small-capitalization segment of the market, is added to the analysis.

As shown in Exhibit 23, small-capitalization stocks outperformed large-capitalization stocks over the June 2008 through May 2015 time frame. Much of the performance differential resulted from the outperformance of small-cap stocks relative to large-cap stocks during the 2010–2013 time period when the S&P 600 posted a cumulative return of 118.5% versus 93.2% for the S&P 500.

Exhibit 23 Cumulative Returns of the S&P 500 and S&P 600; 1 June 2005–31 May 2015

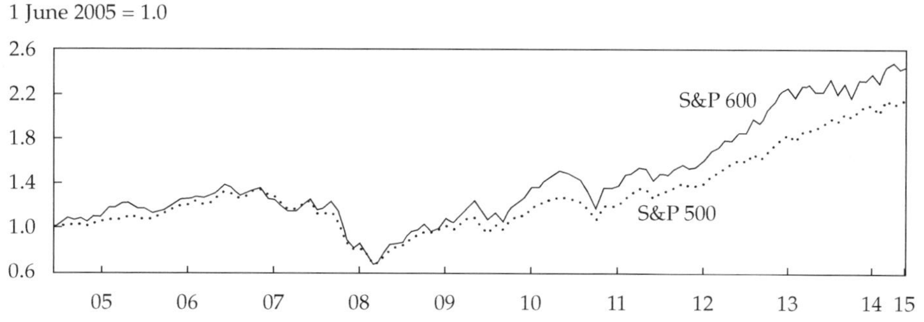

Note: Data are total returns in US dollars.
Source: Based on data from Morningstar.

Exhibit 24 shows that each fund performed well relative to their respective benchmark indexes. LSE Mutual Fund 1 produced positive alpha of 5.0% with a beta of 0.54 relative to the S&P 600, whereas LSE Hedge Fund 1 produced alpha of 5.0% with a beta of 0.34 relative to the S&P 500.

Exhibit 24 Active Long–Short Equity Summary Performance Statistics; June 2005–May 2015

Name	Annualized Return	Cumulative Return	Standard Deviation	Alpha	Beta	Up Capture	Down Capture	Maximum Drawdown
LSE Mutual Fund 1	11.07%	185.78%	14.60%	5.04%	0.54	58.19%	34.50%	−34.63%
S&P 600 TR Index	9.51%	148.13%	18.98%	0.00%	1.00	100.00%	100.00%	−52.15%
LSE Hedge Fund 1	8.93%	135.29%	8.31%	4.97%	0.34	58.13%	33.69%	−12.57%
S&P 500 TR Index	8.12%	118.30%	14.72%	0.00%	1.00	100.00%	100.00%	−50.95%

Source: Data from Morningstar.

Exhibit 25 summarizes the investor's observations regarding each of the investment alternatives.

Exhibit 25 Active Long–Short Equity Summary Evaluation

	Advantages	Disadvantages/Issues
LSE Mutual Fund 1	■ Strong long-term performance ■ Positive alpha ■ Low minimum investment ■ Strong upside/downside profile ■ Daily liquidity	■ Small-capitalization focus introduces an unintentional size bias ■ High expense ratio relative to LSE Mutual Fund 2
LSE Mutual Fund 2	■ Defensive profile limits downside ■ Lower expense ratio	■ Weakest performance ■ Track record prior to 2008 largely irrelevant ■ Defensive profile limits upside ■ High minimum investment

(continued)

Exhibit 25 (Continued)

	Advantages	Disadvantages/Issues
LSE Hedge Fund 1	■ Strong long-term performance ■ Positive alpha ■ Low beta ■ Shallowest drawdown ■ Strong upside/downside profile	■ Potentially highest fees given the 20% performance fee ■ Quarterly liquidity ■ Limited capacity ■ High minimum investment

Overall, both LSE Mutual Fund 1 and LSE Hedge Fund 1 could satisfy the investor's objective of generating positive alpha relative to the equity markets without increasing portfolio volatility and downside risk. Although LSE Hedge Fund 1 has realized lower annualized returns over the period analyzed, it has exhibited a stronger absolute return profile, with a negative return in only one year, a lower market sensitivity, and a lower downside participation. Combined with the analyst's favorable opinion of the manager, LSE Hedge Fund 1 appears to best fit the investor's objective.

When Is a Benchmark Not a Benchmark?

Selecting an appropriate benchmark for a hedge fund can be challenging, even for seemingly straight-forward strategies. Consider long–short equity strategies. Net exposure across such funds can vary considerably; some pair long and short positions as relative value trades, others hold long and short positions with the expectation of profiting from each independently, and still others may achieve their short exposure using derivatives. Market neutral strategies attempt to hold little net exposure to the market and some might argue that the appropriate benchmark for these funds is cash. Benchmarking multi-strategy managers, whose allocations across strategies can differ through time and vary widely among funds, is even more problematic.

Most hedge fund indexes are calculated as weighted averages of a subset of funds that meet certain criteria with respect to length of track record, fund size, or availability requirements. For example, HFRI indexes are calculated as the equally weighted return of voluntarily reporting funds with at least $50 million in assets under management and a minimum one-year track record, without regard to whether the fund is open or closed to investors; the indexes are rebalanced monthly. In contrast, the HFRX indexes (designed to serve as the basis for investable hedge fund products offered by HFR Asset Management, Inc.) are constructed by identifying "similar" funds using cluster analysis, and generally include only funds with at least $50 million in AUM, a minimum two-year track record, and are currently open to investors. The weighting methodology varies by hedge fund strategy, with the HFRX Aggregate Index being an equally weighted composite of strategy-specific indexes. The HFRX indexes are rebalanced quarterly.

Such indexes serve more as a peer group comparison rather than an objective measure of the performance of the opportunity set. These "peer groups" suffer from selection bias (index construction rules exclude smaller and/or newer managers, as well as managers that choose not to report returns to the index provider) and survivor bias (funds can discontinue reporting returns if returns lag). Additionally, the risk characteristics of the index are dampened by the lack of correlation among the constituent funds. Using such an index as the sole arbiter of individual manager performance ignores the wide disparity of underlying investment approaches and manager characteristics.

EXAMPLE 2

Selecting a Long–Short Equity Manager

1 An investor has been presented with three long–short hedge funds with the following characteristics:

Fund	Annual Return	Alpha	Beta	AUM ($ billions)	Maximum Drawdown	Lock-Up Period	Universe
1	8.00%	4.75%	0.50	2.00	18%	12 months	Large cap
2	8.25%	5.00%	0.60	0.10	15%	15 months	Large cap
3	7.75%	5.50%	0.45	1.20	29%	18 months	Small cap

The investor wants to invest $20 million while seeking alpha, risk management, and liquidity. Which fund would *best* satisfy the investor's needs?

A Fund 1

B Fund 2

C Fund 3

2 All else being equal, which of the following characteristics would be *most* desirable in the selection of a long–short equity hedge fund?

A A large drawdown

B A high information ratio

C A high beta and a low alpha

Solution to 1:

A is correct. Fund 1 has return and alpha characteristics that closely match those of Fund 2 but has a lower beta. Fund 1's lock-up period is the shortest of the three funds, and its drawdown is comparable to that of Fund 2 and is much lower than that of Fund 3. Fund 2 is less suitable because of its small size; the $20 million investment is 20% of Fund 2's current AUM. Fund 3's small-cap focus will present difficulties when shorting small-cap stocks. Compared with Fund 1, Fund 3's larger drawdown and longer lock-up period are disadvantage.

Solution to 2:

B is correct. A fund with a high information ratio produces a large amount of active return relative to its unsystematic risk. A fund with a large drawdown gives back a large portion of gains when the market declines. A fund with a high beta and low alpha produces little excess return with high volatility.

6 SELECTION OF A PRIVATE EQUITY MANAGER

An endowment fund has allocated $20 million to be invested in a current vintage year buyout fund in keeping with its longer-term goal of building out its $500 million private equity portfolio across an eight-year window. The endowment is in the middle of that eight-year window. Based on the profile of its existing investments and the anticipated pipeline of funds coming to market in the next few years, the chief investment officer has established the following broad objectives for this investment:

1 An established manager with a track record of investing successfully across multiple business cycles.
2 A stable and cohesive team with operational expertise and a differentiated approach to deal sourcing.
3 A strategy that is able to generate attractive returns and upside for investors, but with a focus on downside protection (low capital loss rates).

The endowment's consultant has proposed two candidates for consideration:

Private Equity (PE) Manager 1 targets middle-market businesses in North America and Europe in four primary sectors: industrial products, chemicals, consumer/retail, and services. The companies are typically fundamentally sound but in need of operational transformation. PE Manager 1 focuses heavily on free cash flow metrics, which helps the manager avoid excess leverage. PE Manager 1 is also careful about maintaining pricing discipline. Historically, the manager has derived the majority of its returns from growth at the company level as well as purchase price multiple expansion on the sale. Debt pay down has been only slightly accretive to returns. The firm was founded 30 years ago and, at the time, invested in both buyout and venture capital deals. Following a long and dramatic succession (with a high level of resulting turnover) from the founders to the next generation of leadership about 15 years ago, the firm now focuses exclusively on buyout transactions. With limited senior-level turnover in the past 10 years and an average tenure of 20 years among the four senior partners, the team has an extensive industry network that enhances both deal flow and due diligence efforts. The manager relies on the operating expertise of this network to add value at the portfolio company level. Although carried interest is concentrated with the senior partners, economics are shared down to the associate level. The manager is now raising its eighth fund, targeting $2 billion (the prior fund was $1 billion) and focused exclusively on buyout transactions.

PE Manager 2 is a US middle-market buyout manager that focuses on investing in profitable companies in the business, consumer, health care, and industrial services, as well as in the manufacturing and distribution sectors. The manager takes a thematic approach to investing, ensuring that it is targeting the most fruitful sectors for investment at any given point in time, and seeks companies with substantial opportunities for earnings growth. To source transactions, the firm uses its junior-level resources to cold call companies that fit certain criteria within its targeted sectors of focus. Two years ago, the firm successfully transitioned from the two founders to the next generation of leadership. The seven senior individuals have an average tenure of about 12 years. Carried interest is equally distributed among the senior-level investment professionals and is shared by every person in the firm. The firm takes an operational approach to adding value, partnering with management teams and using internal operating partners to create value at the portfolio companies. Historical value creation has come primarily from debt pay down and, to a lesser extent, from growth at the company level. The manager is raising its ninth fund, targeting $1.5 billion (the prior fund was $600 million).

Exhibit 26

Private Equity Manager Performance Comparison

PE Manager 1 by Fund ($ millions)												
								Loss Rate				
Fund Name	Vintage Year	Fund Size	No. of Deals	Total Cost	Realized Proceeds	Total (realized + unrealized) Value	MOIC	Deals	Capital	Net IRR	Performance Quartile
PE Manager 1 Fund IV	2001	400	8	380	1,179	1,179	3.1×	0%	0%	20%	2nd
PE Manager 1 Fund V	2005	800	14	712	1,299	1,424	2.0×	17%	4%	15%	1st
PE Manager 1 Fund VI	2009	800	13	766	953	1,993	2.6×	5%	7%	19%	1st
PE Manager 1 Fund VII	2012	1,000	15	787	65	1,417	1.8×	5%	7%	12%	2nd
Total PE Manager 1 since 2000			**50**	**2,646**	**3,497**	**6,013**	**2.3×**	**8%**	**5%**		

PE Manager 2 by Fund ($ millions)											
								Loss Rate			
Fund Name	Vintage Year	Fund Size	No. of Deals	Total Cost	Realized Proceeds	Total Value	MOIC	Deals	Capital	Net IRR	Performance Quartile
PE Manager 2 Fund V	2002	450	9	435	1,293	1,526	3.5×	22%	6%	35%	1st
PE Manager 2 Fund VI	2005	1,000	14	850	870	1,020	1.2×	40%	27%	4%	3rd
PE Manager 2 Fund VII	2008	500	10	486	1,191	1,702	2.5×	10%	3%	18%	1st
PE Manager 2 Fund VIII	2011	600	10	577	503	750	1.3×	0%	0%	15%	2nd
Total PE Manager 2 since 2000			**43**	**2,348**	**3,857**	**4,998**	**2.1×**	**20%**	**11%**		

Note: The returns presented in the tables are hypothetical returns and do not represent the results of an actual manager.

Exhibit 27

Private Equity Manager Summary Evaluation

STRENGTHS	WEAKNESSES
PE Manager 1	
Team/Economics	
■ The team is highly experienced, with senior members having 20 years of experience with the manager. ■ The team is well through its generational transition. ■ The team is well networked. Its extensive industry relationships should help in driving deal flow and conducting diligence prior to investing.	■ Four senior partners is a relatively thin team given the $2 billion target fund size together with the unrealized capital/deals remaining in the portfolios. ■ The next firm succession is an imminent issue and could create internal strife at the manager.
Strategy	
■ The team has the ability to opportunistically allocate capital between North America and Europe. ■ The focus on downside protection with free cash flow metrics is at the forefront of pricing and leverage decisions. ■ The transformational aspect of the strategy provides potential upside.	■ The middle-market environment in both the United States and Europe is highly competitive.
Value Added	
■ Prior returns were generated through organic growth, growth via acquisition, and multiple expansion, which is consistent with the stated and future strategy of the manager.	■ The operating resources are not in-house. The manager relies on its network to help the investment professionals add value at the portfolio company.
PE Manager 2	
STRENGTHS	**WEAKNESSES**
Team/Economics	
■ The team is experienced; the senior members have an average of 12 years' tenure with the manager. ■ Carried interest is shared throughout the firm, aligning the interests of all team members. ■ The large senior investment team (seven individuals) mitigates capacity concerns.	■ The team recently went through a generational transition. Although the senior members have extensive experience with the manager, their leadership capabilities are still unproven.

Exhibit 27 (Continued)

Strategy	
■ The investment themes are constantly updated to find the best opportunities within a space. ■ The cold-calling model is helpful in generating proprietary deal flow.	■ The middle-market environment in the United States is highly competitive.

Value Added	
■ Internal operating partners exclusive to the manager are experienced and able to help execute value maximization plan.	■ Prior returns were driven primarily by the use of debt and, to a lesser extent, growth at the company level, which is inconsistent with the stated strategy of growth.

Exhibit 28

Performance Considerations

Capital Loss Rates

PE Manager 1	PE Manager 2
■ PE Manager 1 had a 4% capital loss rate in the 2005 vintage fund (raised and fully invested right before the 2007-2009 global financial crisis).	■ PE Manager 2 had a 27% capital loss rate in that same vintage year.

The difference in loss rates can be attributed to PE Manager 1's focus on free cash flow metrics, avoidance of excessive leverage, and consistent price discipline. This discipline is consistent with the endowment's goals.

Net IRR

PE Manager 1	PE Manager 2
■ The 2001 fund produced an IRR of 20%. (2nd quartile) ■ The 2005 fund produced a 15% IRR, significantly better than PE Manager 2's 2005 fund. (1st quartile) ■ The 2009 fund displays a 19% IRR, roughly in line with PE Manager 2's 2008 fund. (1st quartile) ■ The most recent fund (2012) displays a 12% IRR. (2nd quartile)	■ The 2002 fund produced an IRR of 35%, significantly outperforming PE Manager 1's 2001 fund. (1st quartile) ■ The 2005 fund produced a 4% IRR. (3rd quartile) ■ The 2008 fund displays an 18% IRR. (1st quartile) ■ The most recent fund (2011) displays a 15% IRR, outperforming PE Manager 1. (2nd quartile)

- In the earliest funds (2001–2002), PE Manager 2 produced an impressive and top-quartile IRR. The private equity industry at that time was a much more nascent industry with limited competition and less efficiency.

(continued)

Exhibit 28 (Continued)

The industry has since become much more efficient and competitive. In today's environment, it is unlikely PE Manager 2 could replicate a 35% IRR executing its buyout strategy.

- PE Manager 1's superior performance in the 2005 vintage fund can be attributed to the firm's focus on free cash flow metrics, avoidance of excessive leverage, and consistent price discipline.
- Despite the poor performance of PE Manager 2's 2005 fund, the two most recent funds are the most relevant funds and should be given greater weight.
- The 2008 and 2009 vintage year funds from each manager produced similar IRRs.
- In the most recent funds, PE Manager 2, with an IRR of 15%, is outperforming PE Manager 1, with an IRR of 12%. Due diligence discussions revealed that PE Manager 2 had a deal that succeeded quickly, resulting in high realizations early in the fund's life.
- Overall, PE Manager 1 lags PE Manager 2 in realized returns. However, PE Manager 1 has substantial remaining value in the 2009 and 2012 funds. The investor must understand the prospects for this remaining value to better assess the ultimate net IRR expectations of the fund.

MOIC

PE Manager 1	PE Manager 2
■ The 2001 fund produced an MOIC of 3.1×.	■ The 2002 fund produced an MOIC of 3.5×.
■ The 2005 fund produced an MOIC of 2.0×.	■ The 2005 fund produced an MOIC of 1.2×.
■ The 2009 fund displays an MOIC of 2.6×.	■ The 2008 fund displays an MOIC of 2.5×.
■ The most recent fund (2012) displays an MOIC of 1.8×.	■ The most recent fund (2011) displays an MOIC of 1.3×.

- On an MOIC basis, PE Manager 2 outperformed PE Manager 1 in the earliest fund, but returns have turned more modest as the industry has become more efficient.
- PE Manager 1 outperformed PE Manager 2 on an MOIC basis with the 2005 vintage funds.
- Comparing the managers' most recent funds, one finds that the rankings based on MOIC are the reverse of what they are on the basis of IRR: PE Manager 2 with an MOIC of 1.3× comes in second to PE Manager 1 with an MOIC of 1.8×.
- The early win in PE Manager 2's portfolio inflated the IRR, whereas the 1.3× gross MOIC suggests an expectation of mediocre future performance from the portfolio of companies.
- Although PE Manager 1's most recent fund lags PE Manager 2's on an IRR basis because of the lack of an early winner, PE Manager 1's gross MOIC of 1.8× suggests a higher-quality portfolio than that of PE Manager 2. Ultimately, we would expect PE Manager 1 to outperform PE Manager 2 upon the fund's eventual liquidation.

Conclusion

The endowment chose PE Manager 1 based on its focus on low capital loss rates, its proven discipline, its demonstrated ability to invest successfully across multiple business cycles, and its experienced and cohesive team. Although the overall performance for PE Manager 2 is compelling, its larger downside losses—in particular, the apparent lack of discipline shown during the financial crisis—is inconsistent with the endowment's desire for downside protection.

EXAMPLE 3

Selecting a Private Equity Manager

In writing a research report, you state that PE Manager 1's Fund VII (Fund 7) has had stronger performance than PE Manager 2's Fund VIII (Fund 8). Which of the following statements would *most likely* be used to support your belief?

A Fund 7 has substantial unrealized gains.

B Fund 7 has substantial unused capital to use for additional investments.

C Fund 8's 15% IRR is subject to downward adjustment as the fund approaches liquidation.

Solution:

C is correct. While Fund 8 has a higher IRR, substantially all of its capital has been deployed. Unless there is significant appreciation potential in the one-third of capital not yet realized, the IRR can be expected to erode with the passage of time. A is not correct because Fund 7's unrealized gains are merely paper gains and may or may not be realized. B is not correct because Fund 7's investment period has likely expired and the unused capital would not be available for additional investments.

SELECTION OF A REAL ESTATE PRIVATE EQUITY MANAGER

7

The Investment Committee of ABC Corporation has allocated 10%, or $5 million, of its pension portfolio to real estate. Of the real estate allocation, 80% ($4 million) is invested in a commingled open-end core real estate fund. The pension fund portfolio manager intends to invest the remaining 20% of the real estate allocation ($1 million) in a value-added real estate fund.

The portfolio manager is searching for a fund that can generate a higher return than core real estate through manager skill with only incrementally higher risk or valuation volatility. Income is not a primary objective. A modest amount of leverage is acceptable. The portfolio manager does not have a favored sector, but he wants to avoid exposure to hotels, and no more than half the assets can be invested in rental housing. The portfolio manager is concerned about the prospects for retail properties, given slow retail sales and market share lost to internet retailers, but retail is not excluded from the list of permissible assets. The portfolio manager is not allowed to invest in first-time funds.

Real estate fundamentals are expected to hold firm as supply and demand are in balance nationwide. Increases in new construction are not likely to disrupt rent growth. Further capital appreciation is unlikely if interest rates increase. Retail sales are expected to advance 3% per year during the next few years, real economic growth is forecast to increase at a 2.0% to 2.5% rate, and inflation should remain at the 2.0% to 2.5% level.

The portfolio manager has asked the pension fund's consultant to provide two funds for his consideration. He recognizes that there are numerous trade-offs in selecting managers. For example, the best-known managers often charge above-average fees, which can offset strong performance; even though emerging managers can outperform some of the larger, better-established fund companies, they typically entail more operating risk; and investment returns are highly influenced by vintage, sector, and capital markets.

The information provided by the pension fund's investment consultant is summarized below.

RE Manager X has $6 billion in assets under management and is raising capital for its fifth value-added fund with a $1 billion commitment target. The fund purchases and renovates older properties in most major sectors with the expectation that higher rents will support higher valuations. The manager may engage in development of supermarkets, strip retail, and big-box shopping centers only if strong credit tenants commit to long-term leases before construction has begun. The organization has a nationwide footprint. Property leasing and management are handled internally, while local construction companies are hired for development work. Local contractors are used for redevelopment. All the construction activity is supervised by the manager.

The firm's two co-founders worked together for 15 years at a large construction company before leaving to start their own investment business. Each founder has a 30% stake in the firm, and the construction company owner holds the remaining 40%. The co-founders invested the capital of friends, family, and the construction company owner for five years before launching the first fund. The fund manager hires their former employer, the construction company, for most redevelopment projects.

RE Manager Y has $1.2 billion in assets under management and is marketing a fifth value-added fund with a capital-raising target of $500 million. The founder developed a wide network of real estate contacts while working as an investment banker, providing strategic advice and capital market solutions to regional developers, listed real estate companies, and other private equity real estate firms. The founder is good at marketing and well known in the industry, which facilitated capital raising for the first fund. The founder owns 100% of the firm.

The manager is sector and region agnostic and instead scours the country for the best deals. The firm likes to partner with regional operators who have solid projects but lack access to capital. If the local operating partner does not have a strong leasing and property management team, those functions will be outsourced.

Each acquisition has its own story. Past investments have included taking over a multifamily development from a builder who ran out of money; buying a warehouse distribution portfolio from a large struggling retailer, subdividing the space, and leasing it to smaller, rapidly growing tenants; and renovating an older office property for a tenant that owned the property but wanted to downsize and sell the building. In each case, the manager was able to purchase the property at an attractive valuation and generate substantial capital gains.

Exhibit 29 shows certain highlights of each firm's track record.[1]

1 Note that the performance data presented in these tables are not GIPS compliant and represent only highlights for the purposes of the case study.

Exhibit 29 Manager Track Records through 31 December 2016

RE Manager X

Value-Added Funds	Vintage	Size	No. of Inv.	Capital Called	Realizations	Gross IRR	Net IRR	Gross ROI	Net ROI
Fund I	2000	250	8	200	350	15.0%	12.0%	1.8×	1.6×
Fund II	2003	500	12	405	650	12.5%	9.7%	1.6×	1.5×
Fund III	2006	1,000	15	560	620	4.6%	3.0%	1.3×	1.2×
Fund IV	2012	1,000	18	855	525	8.8%	6.6%	1.4×	1.3×
Total		2,750	53	2,020	2,145	8.9%	7.0%	1.4×	1.3×

Notes: Returns based on realized and unrealized gains. Realizations are gross of fees and carry.
Fund III has one property that has not been liquidated.
Fund IV has 10 properties that have not been liquidated.
Figures are rounded.

RE Manager Y

Value-Added Funds	Vintage	Size	No. of Inv.	Capital Called	Realizations	Gross IRR	Net IRR	Gross ROI	Net ROI
Fund I	1999	50	6	43	70	12.5%	9.7%	1.6×	1.5×
Fund II	2004	125	11	110	155	8.8%	6.8%	1.4×	1.3×
Fund III	2008	200	12	180	235	21.1%	17.0%	2.0×	1.8×
Fund IV	2012	350	15	312	170	7.5%	5.8%	1.3×	1.2×
Total		725	44	645	630	12.2%	9.5%	1.5×	1.4×

Notes: Returns based on realized and unrealized gains. Distributions are gross of fees and carry.
Fund IV has six properties that have not been liquidated.
Figures are rounded.

The investment consultant provided the following additional commentary:

RE Manager X	RE Manager Y
Strengths	
■ RE Manager X has a large, well-established organization that manages core, value-added, and opportunistic strategies. The firm has a deep team, a national footprint, and a good reputation. ■ The investment committee consists of the two founding partners, the CIO, the head of asset management, and the head of risk management. Four of the five have been with the firm since its founding. ■ The members of the senior management team each have at least 15 years of real estate experience, and all but one has been with the firm at least 5 years. ■ The nationwide exposure allows the company to pursue the most attractive opportunities. The manager has regional offices in Atlanta, Boston, Charlotte, Chicago, Dallas, Los Angeles, New York, Phoenix, Seattle, St. Louis, and Washington, DC. Nine of the 11 regional real estate officers have been with the company at least five years. ■ The firm has invested in office, retail, multifamily, industrial, and long-term sale-leaseback transactions. No single sector accounts for more than 40% of any fund. Ground-up development is limited to 15% of fund capital. ■ The track record is attractive despite the disappointing return of Fund III, which was invested in the years leading up to the global financial crisis. Note, however, that the GP called less than 60% of Fund III's commitments due to high pre-crisis real estate prices. ■ Managing core assets in many major markets provides additional market insight when evaluating transactions for the value-added fund. ■ Several investors from Funds III and IV have already committed to Fund V. A first close of $275 million took place on 30 July.	■ RE Manager Y has a strong track record, and senior management has worked together for at least eight years. ■ Each member of the senior management team has at least 14 years of real estate experience. ■ Although the founder owns 100% of the company, senior executives are allocated a portion of the carry, which allows them to share in the success of the firm. ■ The founder is well regarded, and all of the Fund IV LPs plan to commit to Fund V. ■ Fund V has already identified a pipeline of six assets it will bid on following the first close. ■ The manager has strong relationships with several local operators who have worked on multiple projects for the company and continue to present new transactions. ■ The firm has experience across several asset classes. In addition to multifamily, office, industrial, and retail, it has also invested in health care facilities and medical office buildings. ■ The funds have been able to move opportunistically from one sector or geographic area to another because the manager is not tied to maintaining a construction or property management organization in each city in which it invests. ■ Fund III was able to invest quickly and aggressively following the financial crisis, when asset values were depressed, without taking on additional real estate risk. ■ A simple majority of investors can vote to replace the manager.
Weaknesses	
■ The 40% owner of RE Manager X heads the construction company that performs most of the value-added funds' redevelopment. Although the GP assures investors that the funds never pay more than the market average for construction, there is little transparency, and it is difficult to know whether the fund is getting the best deal. ■ Fund III sold two completed assets to the manager's core real estate fund when the acquisition market shut down following the financial crisis. Two independent appraisers provided fair market value estimates, and the limited partner advisory board approved the transaction. ■ Fund III may extend the fund life while waiting to dispose of the remaining asset. ■ The manager may be removed subject to a 67% majority vote of LPs. Securing a majority of votes may be difficult because the construction company owner, who has 40% share of the manager, has subscribed to 10% of Fund V.	■ The allocator model results in an extra level of fees. ■ The company has been able to generate high cash flow yields by investing in secondary and tertiary cities and specialized real estate, such as health care properties, which carry higher risk. These properties could be more difficult to sell during market pullbacks. ■ Some investments have a more opportunistic than value-added return and risk profile. For example, prior funds have invested in a joint venture to redevelop a poorly performing enclosed mall into an open-air street-retail/lifestyle shopping center. ■ Key man risk is high owing to the founder's large role in managing relationships and sourcing fund deals. ■ Fund II co-invested in a transaction led by another real estate private equity fund. Despite the deal's success, the other fund received a 10% carried interest on co-investment capital.

Fund Economics	
■ Fund V has a 10% gross IRR target. ■ RE Manager X charges a management fee of 1.25% on committed capital during the investment period and 1.25% on outstanding equity after the investment period. ■ Fund V will have a preferred return hurdle of 6%, down from 7% for Fund IV. ■ The manager receives a 15% carry. Cash flow is split 85% to the GP, 15% to the LPs, once the preferred return has been distributed to the LPs. The cash flow split changes to 15%/85% once the GP has caught up to 15% of total profits. ■ Leverage is limited to 60% based on cost.	■ Fund V has a 11% gross IRR target. ■ RE Manager Y charges a management fee of 1.5% on committed capital during the investment period and 1.25% on outstanding equity after the investment period. ■ Fund V will have a preferred return hurdle of 7%, down from 8% for Fund IV. ■ The manager receives a 20% carry with a 100% catch-up. ■ Leverage is limited to 65% based on cost.

Additional Commentary

Track Record	
■ Fund III invested just before the financial crisis at high real estate prices, which hurt performance. Other funds performed well.	■ RE Manager Y has a stronger track record due to the success of Fund III, which invested after the financial crisis at bargain prices. The track record is not as strong for the other funds.
Return Target and Risk Profile	
■ Appropriate for style.	■ Higher return achieved by investing in higher-yield, higher-risk secondary and tertiary cities and specialty properties.
Economics	
■ Slightly lower management fee and slower catch-up favor LPs; lower hurdle favors GP.	■ Slightly higher management fee and faster catch-up favor GP; higher hurdle benefits investor and reflects slightly higher risk profile.
Alignment of Interests	
■ GP commitment will be funded up front.	■ GP commitment will be funded by forgiving first-year management fee, which means the GP does not need to fund commitment up front.
Manager Removal Powers	
■ Weak manager removal powers.	■ Stronger manager removal clause.
Conflicts of Interest	
■ Construction contracts awarded to financial partner, properties sold to manager's core funds.	■ Lower
Key Man Risk	
■ Medium	■ High
Leverage	
■ Medium to high	■ Higher leverage permitted

Which manager is a better fit for the real estate allocation of ABC's pension fund?

Conclusion

Both managers have been successful, are disciplined investors, and take different approaches to creating value. Both have been able to source attractive deals. RE Manager X offers a larger organization and a better track record, after adjusting for the timing of RE Manager X's pre–financial crisis investing versus RE Manager Y's post–financial crisis investing. One important distinction is that RE Manager Y appears to take on slightly higher risk to achieve its return. LPs will likely be disappointed that RE Manager X sold properties from one of its funds to another and that RE Manager Y paid a carry to invest alongside another real estate manager.

RE Manager X appears better suited for this particular investor because of its larger organization, presence in most major markets, strong track record, and slightly slower catch-up provision. RE Manager Y takes on slightly more risk, investing in smaller markets and specialty sectors, and uses slightly higher leverage. Although RE Manager Y has a higher preferred return hurdle, it does not appear to generate better returns across all funds. In addition, RE Manager Y has been more active in discretionary retail, which the ABC portfolio manager prefers to avoid.

8 A CASE STUDY IN MANAGER RETENTION

This case study is designed to synthesize the teaching from both the Principles and Expert level readings that address the manager due diligence process, both qualitative and quantitative, as well as the issue of portfolio fit.

Our investor is a Netherlands-based corporate defined benefit pension fund using a combination of passive and active investment managers. The pension fund employs an investment staff that is responsible for manager selection and monitoring; strategic asset allocation and other policies are set by the fund's board of trustees. In recent years, the board of trustees has increasingly emphasized environmental, social, and governance (ESG) issues as part of the fund's operations.

This case study will focus on the pension fund's global equity managers. As of January 2015, the fund employs three global equity (GE) managers, each managing €200 million in separate account portfolios benchmarked to the same global developed markets equity index. Each of the three managers has a different investment approach, as described in the following:

- *GE Manager A* is a passive manager using a sampling approach to track the performance of the index. The manager has been employed by the fund for 10 years and has produced annualized net-of-fee performance within 15 bps of the index.
- *GE Manager B* is an active manager using a fundamental research-based process to produce a concentrated 30/40 stock portfolio with active share of more than 80%. The manager has been employed by the fund for seven years and has produced annualized net-of-fee performance 250 bps above that of the index since inception, with tracking risk of 8%. The manager's approach favors growth-oriented stocks, leading to typically good index-relative performance in strong bull markets and poor relative performance in declining markets.
- *GE Manager C* is also an active manager using a fundamental research-based process, but unlike GE Manager B, GE Manager C holds a diversified (90/100 stock) portfolio with active share of about 50%. This manager has also been employed by the fund for seven years but has produced annualized net-of-fee performance 1% below that of the index since inception, with tracking risk of

4%. This manager's approach favors more defensive value-oriented stocks, leading to typically good index-relative performance in down markets and index-like, or slightly lower, results in strong bull markets.

The pension fund also employs a single dedicated global emerging markets equity manager and has allocated assets to this manager in line with the emerging markets weighting in an all-inclusive (developed and emerging markets) global equity index, which serves as the pension fund's overall equity benchmark. The investment guidelines for the two active global equity managers allow them to hold up to 10% in emerging market equities although emerging market exposure is not included in their benchmark index. GE Manager B has at times held a couple of emerging market stocks in its portfolio, but the overall weighting has rarely exceeded 6%. GE Manager C has had more consistent, and higher, exposure to emerging markets stocks, with its allocation averaging about 8%.

Through its ongoing manager due diligence process, the pension fund's investment staff has raised concerns regarding GE Manager C. The manager performed well during the early years of its relationship with the pension fund because its defensive approach provided some downside protection during the 2007–2009 global financial crisis. Following this period of strong relative results, the manager gained many new clients and saw its asset base nearly double. Results have lagged the benchmark in the past five years, and the manager has seen several large institutional clients terminate their relationship, leading to the loss of about one-third of the manager's AUM.

Although the pension fund's staff is certainly aware of GE Manager C's since-inception underperformance, it is most concerned about changes it has noticed in the manager's portfolio characteristics. In the course of staff's monitoring of this manager, they have noticed that the number of stocks held in the portfolio has increased to about 120 and that the active share and tracking risk have decreased. Additionally, risk factor analysis shows that the manager's portfolio has become less value-oriented.

Accordingly, the pension fund's staff is considering replacing GE Manager C. Through database screenings, conversations with other institutional investors, internet-based information gathering, consultant recommendations, and meetings with managers, the staff has identified three potential replacements for GE Manager C:

- *GE Manager 1* uses a quantitative approach to construct global equity portfolios with most characteristics similar to those that GE Manager C exhibited when it was first hired—a diversified portfolio of 90/110 stocks, with moderate active share (50–60%) and tracking risk of about 4%. But unlike GE Manager C, this manager's portfolios do not include emerging market exposure. GE Manager 1 has €10 billion in global equity AUM, plus another €40 billion in various regional/single country equity strategies. The firm is 100% owned by its employees. Performance has been slightly ahead of the global equity index over the past five to seven years.
- *GE Manager 2* is a relatively small firm, with €2 billion in AUM, all in their global equity strategy. This manager was established at the beginning of 2010 when five of the senior investment professionals at a large investment manager left to found their own firm, in which they have majority ownership stake (a private equity firm provided financing and holds 25% of the equity). GE Manager 2's approach is based on fundamental research, producing concentrated (40/50 stock) portfolios with high active share (>80%), 8% tracking risk, and a strong value orientation; emerging market exposure is typically around 10%, and

turnover is low (around 20% per year). The manager specifically evaluates and documents ESG issues as part of their company research process. Performance has lagged that of the index since the firm's inception in 2010.

- *GE Manager 3* is a bank-owned investment management firm with a large team of portfolio managers and research analysts; there has been some personnel turnover in the team over the past several years. It manages €20 billion in global equities, and another €200 billion in a wide variety of other equity, fixed-income, and alternative strategies. This manager's 70/80 stock portfolios have active share of 60–70%, with 5–6% tracking risk; emerging market exposure is typically less than 5%. The manager describes its investment style as "quality-oriented and pragmatic," with portfolios generally having a moderate value orientation but with the risk factor characteristics varying somewhat over time. When asked, the manager explains that it considers ESG issues in its security research but does not specifically document its findings regarding such issues. The performance track record is long (>10 years), and index-relative results have generally been good, especially in recent years.

Exhibits 30 through 33 provide more details regarding the performance, portfolio characteristics, and fees for each of the three potential replacement managers, as well as for existing GE Manager C.

Exhibit 30 Net Performance Results as of 31 December 2014

Manager Name	1 Year	3 Years	5 Years	7 Years	10 Years
GE Manager C	6.5%	11.0%	10.0%	3.0%	na
GE Manager 1	7.5%	12.9%	15.8%	4.5%	9.0%
GE Manager 2	6.9%	11.8%	13.0%	na	na
GE Manager 3	8.2%	13.8%	16.5%	5.2%	9.9%
Index	7.0%	12.0%	15.0%	4.0%	10.0%

Source: Data from eVestmentAlliance.

Exhibit 31 Trailing Five-Year Performance Statistics as of 31 December 2014

Manager	Tracking Risk	Up Capture	Down Capture	Batting Average	Correlation with GE Manager B
GE Manager C	3.7%	90%	87%	0.42	0.80
GE Manager 1	4.1%	102%	96%	0.57	0.85
GE Manager 2	7.9%	92%	82%	0.52	0.75
GE Manager 3	5.5%	110%	102%	0.55	0.90

Source: Data from eVestmentAlliance.

Exhibit 32 Current Portfolio Characteristics

Manager	Average Emerging Market Weight	Active Share	Number of Stocks	Fee (on €200 Million)
GE Manager C	8%	50%	120	60 bp
GE Manager 1	0%	55%	100	50 bp
GE Manager 2	10%	85%	45	70 bp
GE Manager 3	4%	65%	75	60 bp

Source: Data from eVestmentAlliance.

Exhibit 33 Global Equity Assets and Stated Capacity

Manager	Assets Year-End 2010	Assets Year-End 2014	Capacity
GE Manager C	€29 billion	€19 billion	€30 billion
GE Manager 1	€8 billion	€10 billion	€25 billion
GE Manager 2	€1 billion	€2 billion	€10 billion
GE Manager 3	€15 billion	€20 billion	€30 billion

Source: Data from eVestmentAlliance.

The staff recognizes that the market environment of the past few years has not been favorable for GE Manager C's defensive investment style and that replacing GE Manager C would involve costs associated with transitioning GE Manager C's portfolio to the new manager, as well as administrative and other costs and demands on the staff's time. These costs, however, were deemed to be acceptable because of the staff's concerns regarding the changes in GE Manager C's portfolio characteristics and the stability of GE Manager C's business. In short, the staff believed that GE Manager C was no longer fulfilling the role it had been hired to perform, and they no longer had sufficient conviction in GE Manager C to justify retaining the firm.

Although the staff reached consensus regarding GE Manager C, they had a more difficult time deciding which manager to hire as a replacement. The various staff members applied differing priorities to arrive at their preferred choices. Among the factors considered were the managers'

- business stability,
- ownership structure,
- capacity management,
- operational infrastructure,
- personnel depth and experience,
- investment processes,
- portfolio characteristics,
- performance results, and
- fees.

The perceived advantages and disadvantages of each potential new manager are outlined in Exhibit 34.

Exhibit 34 Global Equity Structure Summary Evaluation

	Advantages	Disadvantages
GE Manager 1	■ 100% employee ownership ■ Demonstrated capacity management on other strategies ■ Lowest fee ■ Most consistent index-relative performance	■ Quantitative process difficult to understand ■ Relatively low active share ■ High correlation with existing GE Manager B ■ Lack of ESG factors in quantitative model
GE Manager 2	■ Lowest correlation with existing GE Manager B ■ Highest active share ■ Explicitly stated, and relatively low, capacity limit ■ Specific ESG focus ■ Majority ownership by employees	■ Small, single-product firm with the lightest operational infrastructure ■ Highest fee ■ Small team ■ Relatively short track record ■ Since-inception underperformance
GE Manager 3	■ Large firm with diversified product line and client base ■ Strong operational infrastructure provided by parent bank ■ Flexible investment approach more adaptable to market conditions ■ Best performance track record	■ Highest correlation with existing GE Manager B ■ Lack of employee ownership ■ Concerns about capacity management ■ Some personnel turnover ■ Lack of specific ESG documentation

Those who favored GE Manager 1 liked that the firm's investment professionals own 100% of the firm, the performance results were not particularly volatile relative to the index, the firm's fee was the lowest of the candidates, and the portfolio held only developed market stocks. But others were not comfortable with the firm's quantitative process, which they found difficult to understand and believed that in the three-manager global equity structure used by the pension fund, a more concentrated, higher active share portfolio with the potential for opportunistic emerging market exposure was more appropriate. Also, some staff members would have preferred that the manager's quantitative process explicitly include ESG factors given the board of trustees' focus on such issues.

Those who favored GE Manager 2 liked the firm's defensive portfolio characteristics, which they believed provided the best complement to the more growth-oriented GE Manager B, as well as the high active share, which complemented the very broadly diversified passive GE Manager A. They appreciated GE Manager 2's explicitly stated capacity limit, which they believed was especially important for a firm that is managing concentrated portfolios, and the manager's specific focus on ESG factors. Others, however, were less comfortable with GE Manager 2's operational infrastructure, small asset base, single-product focus, and higher fees. Additionally, they were concerned that the pension fund's 10% limit on emerging market exposure might restrict GE Manager 2's ability to add value. They also found it difficult to recommend hiring a manager that had underperformed since its inception five years ago.

Those who favored GE Manager 3 liked the pragmatic nature of the firm's investment process, which they believed allowed it to be more adaptable to changing market conditions. In addition, they preferred the stability provided by a large and diversified asset base, as well as the operational infrastructure provided by the parent bank. Those who did not favor GE Manager 3 were concerned about the reduced alignment of interest created by the lack of ownership on the part of the investment professionals, thinking that some team members might be tempted to follow the example of the team at GE Manager 2 and leave to establish their own firm. They also believed that the other managers provided better diversification for the overall global equity portfolio and were concerned about GE Manager 3's capacity management given its large and growing global equity asset base. ESG issues got a mixed reaction—some staff members believed that GE Manager 3 merely needed to better communicate their research on such issues, whereas others believed that the lack of specific documentation meant that the manager did not actually consider ESG in their investment process.

This case illustrates the issues involved with researching and selecting investment managers. There is no single right solution, and an investor's satisfaction with any manager will depend in large part on the investor's priorities. Throughout the research and selection process, the investor should focus clearly on those priorities, evaluate managers in the context of those priorities, and build as compete a picture as possible of each manager's organization, personnel, investment approach, portfolio characteristics, and performance tendencies. In situations when more than one manager is used, the investor should also consider each individual manager in the context of the overall portfolio structure. Ongoing monitoring is important in helping the investor determine whether a manager is continuing to provide the service it was hired to perform.

EXAMPLE 4

Replacing an Existing Investment Manager

1 Which of the following is of *lesser* concern to a researcher when evaluating the impact of GE Manager C's loss of one-third of its assets between 2010 and 2014?

   A The associated reduction in revenue impairs the manager's ability to offer competitive pay to its investment staff and to make necessary investments in its business.

   B The manager appears to be placing more emphasis on managing business risk than investment risk, with the number of portfolio holdings increasing and active share and tracking risk decreasing.

   C After having been near its stated capacity in 2010, the manager now has significantly more capacity available.

2 Portfolio "fit" is the most important criteria staff will use in selecting a replacement manager, and they have determined that GE Manager 3 is the least attractive candidate. Which of the following factors is *least likely* to influence the staff's decision?

   A Fees

   B Upside/downside capture

   C Correlation with existing GE Manager B

Solution to 1:

C is correct. The fact that GE Manager C now has additional capacity available is, if anything, a positive factor. But the reason that capacity is available is that significant assets have been lost, which creates issues with compensation and business investments and puts pressure on the firm to stem the outflows. The resulting lowering of active risk in portfolios is not unusual for a firm that is more concerned with keeping the clients it has than taking appropriate investment risk to generate attractive returns and the expected portfolio characteristics for those clients and potential new ones.

Solution to 2:

A is correct. The upside/downside capture information, as well as the correlation information, point to the fact that GE Manager 3 tends to perform most similarly to existing GE Manager B, doing well in bull markets but poorly in down markets. The fees charged by the various managers are similar enough to not have a major impact on the overall portfolio construction.

PRACTICE PROBLEMS

The following information relates to Questions 1–7

ABC is an Irish wealth management firm looking to replace its active small-cap equity manager because of high manager turnover and underperformance. When investing in new funds, ABC values management longevity, the capability of providing positive absolute returns across market environments, and managers willing to take risks with concentrated positions.

ABC forecasts that, over the next several years, Ireland's capital gains tax will increase significantly while its tax rates on dividends and investment income will remain unchanged. ABC also forecasts that the firm's base currency, the euro, will appreciate relative to other currencies.

ABC has narrowed its search down to three funds, each having a five-year (or longer) track record. Information pertaining to each fund is summarized in Exhibit 1.

Exhibit 1 Fund Summaries

Fund 1	The long-only fund seeks long-term capital appreciation and invests primarily in common stocks that pay little or no dividends. Eighty percent of the assets are invested in euro-denominated small-cap equities with the remainder invested in non-euro small-cap stocks. The fund typically holds 30 to 40 stocks but can hold as few as 20 and as many as 50. A new portfolio manager was retained in the past year owing to the retirement of the previous manager.
Fund 2	The long-only fund seeks both capital appreciation and income by investing in a broadly diversified portfolio of euro-denominated small-cap stocks with high dividend yields. The fund has a requirement to diversify to at least 100 different companies. The portfolio management team has been in place for the past 10 years.
Fund 3	The fund seeks to provide positive alpha by investing long and short in small- to mid-cap common stocks. Long positions are selected on the basis of their expected appreciation in most market environments and short positions are selected on the basis of perceived excess valuations. Short positions typically represent 30% of the long positions value but can increase depending on market conditions. The fund is mandated to invest 40% of its long holdings in non-euro-denominated stocks. The fund typically holds 15 to 25 names representing the portfolio manager's best ideas. The current portfolio manager has been in place for eight years.

ABC hires an investment consultant to provide advice on the selection of the new small cap manager. The consultant prepares Exhibit 2 which displays key statistics for each fund.

Exhibit 2 Fund Summary Statistics December 31, 20XX

Fund	Alpha	Beta	Information Ratio	Minimum Investment (€)	Liquidity	Downside Capture	Upside Capture
1	3.25%	1.30	0.15	1,000,000	Daily	115%	170%
2	2.75%	1.20	0.40	10,000	Daily	100%	130%
3	3.40%	0.70	0.80	100,000	Monthly	20%	70%

The investment consultant recommends that ABC select a fund with high active returns relative to active risk and with low systematic risk.

ABC's typical client has €10 million to €15 million in invested assets (of which only a portion would be invested in this fund) and regularly makes cash withdrawals throughout the month from their portfolio. ABC's investment policy is to limit its clients' small-cap allocation to not more than 5% of the clients' invested assets

The head of ABC's marketing department believes its clients cannot tolerate underperforming during bear markets.

ABC wants to expand its client base by offering a new investment product called ABC Aggressive. The product is for tax-exempt entities with a higher risk tolerance, a longer time horizon, and more investable assets than the firm's typical client has. ABC plans to target those domestic investors seeking small-cap exposure with over €25 million available to invest.

1 Based on what ABC values in its fund managers, which of the following would be the *most likely* replacement fund?

A Fund 1

B Fund 2

C Fund 3

2 Based on Exhibit 1, which of the three funds is *most likely* to benefit from ABC's tax and currency forecasts?

A Fund 1

B Fund 2

C Fund 3

3 Based on the information provided in Exhibit 2, which fund *best* satisfies the consultant's recommendation?

A Fund 1

B Fund 2

C Fund 3

4 Which of the three funds would *best* meet the needs of a typical ABC client?

A Fund 1

B Fund 2

C Fund 3

5 Based on the head of marketing's belief about clients' tolerance, which of the following fund metrics should ABC be *most* concerned about?

A Beta

B Upside capture

C Downside capture

6 Based on Exhibit 1, selecting an appropriate benchmark would be *most* difficult for which fund?

A Fund 1

B Fund 2

C Fund 3

7 Which fund would the firm *most likely* select for its new ABC Aggressive product?

A Fund 1

B Fund 2

C Fund 3

SOLUTIONS

1 C is correct. ABC values management longevity, the capability of providing positive absolute returns across market environments and managers willing to take risks with concentrated positions. Fund 3 is the only fund that meets all three of these criteria with a long/short strategy capable of generating positive absolute returns across all market environments, a manager that has been in place for 8 years and concentrated positions with 15 to 25 holdings. A is incorrect because the current management team has been in place for only a year. B is incorrect because the fund is broadly diversified with 100 different stocks.

2 B is correct. Fund 2 invests in a broadly diversified portfolio of euro-denominated common stocks with high dividend yields. ABC believes that the tax treatment on income (which includes dividends) will be more favorable than that on capital gains. Additionally, ABC believes that the euro will strengthen relative to other currencies and as a result it would be advantageous to have investments locally. A is incorrect because Fund 1's strategy is to primarily invest in companies that do not pay a dividend and as a result will experience most of their gains in capital growth. This is inconsistent with ABC's forecast that taxes on capital gains will increase significantly over the next several years. C is incorrect because Fund 3 mandates that 40% of its long-only holdings are in non-euro currencies, which ABC believes will weaken relative to the euro.

3 C is correct. Fund 3 is the only fund that meets both criteria in the recommendation of the consultant. The high information ratio (0.80) supports the preference for high active returns relative to active risk and the low beta (0.70) supports the desire for low systematic risk.

A is incorrect because of the low information ratio which indicates that the fund has a small amount of active return relative to its active risk. B is incorrect because of the high beta which reflects that the fund has high systematic risk. The consultant recommends that ABC select a fund with both high active returns relative to active risk and low systematic risk.

4 B is correct. Based on the fact that the clients request cash from ABC throughout the month, they are going to need to invest in a fund with daily liquidity. This would exclude Fund 3. Fund 1's minimum investment (€1,000,000) would violate the firm's policy to invest no more than 5% of the client's assets in small-cap funds (€15,000,000 × 5% = €750,000). Fund 2 is the only fund that meets the needs of a typical ABC client.

5 C is correct. Clients want to see their investment beat the benchmark during down markets. Downside capture measures how well the fund did in down markets relative to the benchmark.

6 C is correct. Fund 3 follows a long/short equity strategy. Net exposure to the market across such funds can vary considerably. Most hedge fund indexes are calculated as weighted averages of a subset of funds that meet certain criteria with respect to length of track record, fund size or availability requirements. Such indexes serve more as a peer group comparison than an objective measure of the performance of the opportunity set. These peer groups suffer from both selection bias and survivor bias.

A is incorrect because Fund 1 follows a small-cap growth strategy for which third-party benchmarks are readily available. Benchmarks for long-only funds like Fund 1 would not be as difficult to find as they would be for Fund 3. B is incorrect because Fund 2 follows a small-cap growth-and-income strategy for which third-party benchmarks are readily available. Benchmarks for long-only funds like Fund 2 would not be as difficult to find as they would be for Fund 3.

7 A is correct. Investors in the fund will be domestic, tax-exempt entities, so changing tax rates in the future are not an issue. Liquidity needs also are not an issue since the fund allows daily withdrawals. With 80% of its portfolio in euro-denominated equities, Fund 1 is positioned to benefit should ABC's currency forecast come to fruition. Fund 1 has the largest upside capture ratio and the largest market beta compared with the other options and may generate superior returns in advancing markets. Fund 1's alpha is higher than Fund 2's and is only slightly lower than that of Fund 3. For clients with higher risk tolerances, Fund 1 would be the appropriate selection for ABC.

READING

13

Setting Weights for Active and Index Managers

by Scott D. Stewart, PhD, CFA

Scott D. Stewart, PhD, CFA, is at Cornell University (USA).

LEARNING OUTCOMES

Mastery	The candidate should be able to:
☐	a. describe the components of the investor's utility function for manager selection;
☐	b. explain why the investor's utility function for manager selection uses active return instead of total return;
☐	c. describe approaches to incorporating risk into the manager selection process;
☐	d. describe the optimal mix of managers;
☐	e. describe how search and monitoring costs affect the manager selection process.

REVIEWING THE MANAGER SELECTION PROCESS 1

The manager selection process involves identifying skillful managers, conducting due diligence on the most appealing ones, and determining the proportion of assets each manager should control. Investors set manager weights to meet strategic asset allocation goals, capture active managers' alpha potential, and access index managers' tracking abilities.

IMPLEMENTING STRATEGIC ASSET ALLOCATION 2

Once an investor's asset allocation has been set, the next step is to hire and fund portfolio managers to establish the target allocations. The optimal mix of portfolio managers depends on an investor's expectations for alpha, his or her attitude toward active risk, and the manager's risk exposures. Investors may seek optimal trade-offs

Based on Chapter 5 in *Essays on Manager Selection*, by Scott D. Stewart, PhD, CFA, Research Foundation of CFA Institute.

between active return and active risk or, alternatively, may seek to maximize active return while holding active risk to an acceptable level. This reading reviews both of these techniques.

The optimal trade-off problem can be expressed as a mathematical model. The model's complexity depends on what assumptions are made regarding the number of market factors, correlations between factor returns and active returns, and correlations among managers' active returns. In practice, volatility, correlations, and means vary through time, which further complicates the problem.

A simplified version of this problem—assuming a single-factor return model with zero correlations between alpha, the market return, and the error term—appears in Appendix A of this reading. Investors can use this model to choose a group of managers and determine appropriate weights so (1) that their portfolio's beta equals 1, (2) the portfolio provides attractive exposure to alpha, or (3) active risk is acceptable.

3 UTILITY FUNCTION OF MANAGER SELECTION

Assuming an investor's utility function[1] can be expressed in common quadratic form, one can convey the problem of setting manager weights by defining the expected utility of active returns as follows:

$$E[U] = E[rs - rb] - \lambda\sigma^2(rs - rb)$$

where

$E[U]$ = expected investor utility,

$E[rs - rb]$ = expected active return defined as strategic portfolio return, rs, minus benchmark return, rb,

λ = a constant measure of active return risk aversion, and

$\sigma^2(rs - rb)$ = the variance of the difference in returns.

An optimal level of utility can be determined (the objective function will be maximized) by selecting portfolio weights that result in the highest level of $E[U]$ while satisfying portfolio weight constraints (typically, weights are non-negative and sum to 1) as follows:

$$\text{Subject to } \Sigma_j ws_j = 1.0,$$

$$ws_j \geq 0.0,$$

where

ws_j = the weight of each manager j within the strategic allocation.

The expressions raise two questions: Why active return instead of total return? and total portfolio or single asset class?

Why Active Return Instead of Total Return? In theory, investors that are maximizing expected utility should determine asset allocation and select investment managers simultaneously. But in practice, institutional investors rarely choose manager and asset class weights concurrently. They typically select managers only after setting their asset allocation strategy. Investors write an investment policy statement (IPS) to define their strategic allocation and subsequently set guidelines for manager selection. This practice may result from a lack of confidence regarding alpha forecasts over long horizons. Or it might stem from a desire to simplify the solution by breaking down the problem

1 A full discussion of investor utility of return, including Excel applications, appears in Stewart, Heisler, and Piros (2011).

into pieces that are easier to solve (although the solution will be less comprehensive). Institutional investors may be comfortable accepting market risk but do not want their strategic allocation efforts to be overwhelmed by the manager decision.

Although strategic asset allocation is set for the long term, based on long-term views, manager selection, especially for active managers, is made based on short-term views. Asset classes have existed for centuries, but a portfolio manager's career is relatively short and can end on short notice. Grinold and Kahn (2000) proposed that this two-step approach occurs because investors (principal asset owners) and managers (agents) have different preferences. Investors accept beta risk, whereas managers carry residual risk. Investors worry about total returns and returns relative to liabilities. Managers are concerned about their returns versus their benchmarks and peer groups. Deriving optimal solutions using quadratic functions can be difficult. Optimal asset weights can vary substantially even when expected returns change only slightly. As a result, changes in expected manager alphas could lead to large changes in proposed asset allocations, creating a cumbersome solution that would be difficult to implement.

Total Portfolio or Single Asset Class? Benchmarks are strategic allocation targets that can be set across multiple asset classes or for single asset classes. The utility optimization approach is best used for setting manager weights for a single asset class or sub-asset class. Running an optimization to assess manager weights for these classes is consistent with standard theory if the benchmark is an efficient asset—sitting on the efficient frontier using consensus estimates. This approach may result in some loss in optimization efficiency because correlation of active returns across markets (for example, exposure to the business cycle of both equities and credit markets) is not considered. As previously mentioned, however, optimal solutions using total risk models across asset classes are not stable, and single-factor models are not ideal for multiple asset classes.

The aforementioned utility expression includes the following variables, which are explored in greater detail in Appendix A.

- Risk aversion is commonly defined as a constant incorporating the investor's change in marginal utility with a change in cumulative return. Investors prefer gains over losses and typically dislike losses more than they like gains. In the expression shown earlier, a higher risk aversion parameter (λ) reflects a higher degree of risk aversion (dislike of risk). A higher λ will lead to a lower-risk portfolio (and as a result, lower expected active return) for given alpha assumptions.
- In a single-factor or beta world, active beta will influence both expected active returns and portfolio risk. Optimal solutions will favor betas close to 1.0; however, a formal constraint is required to guarantee this result, as long as the problem is feasible.
- In the objective function, risk is described as active return variance. Assuming normality, the probability of outperforming or underperforming by a given amount is a residual effect of optimizing the objective function, unless additional constraints are specified.

Risk can also be described in terms other than active return variance. For example, the optimization model can incorporate downside risk, or the probability of underperforming by a certain percentage, by limiting probability. A portfolio can be designed in which the probability of underperforming by 1% or more in a given 12-month period is no more than 10%.

Standard deviation or downside risk can also be targets in a modified optimization model. For example, a term to represent a risk budget can be incorporated using active return standard deviation or downside probability in the model. It can be defined within a constraint, and expected active return can be the model's objective function. The optimization problem can be expressed as follows:

Maximize $E[rs - rb]$

$$\text{Subject to } \Sigma_j ws_j = 1.0$$
$$ws_j \geq 0.0$$
$$\text{Risk level} \leq B$$

where risk can be defined either as beta, active return standard deviation, the probability of active return falling below a target, or value at risk (VaR).

Another approach for incorporating risk into the manager selection process uses mean-lower partial moments (LPMs).[2] LPMs define risk as the sum of squared differences below a target mean. It can be computed by using an assumed probability distribution or a historical return series that does not require the specification of a return distribution. The optimal solution yields a portfolio with a low level of volatility below a given threshold, such as 0% or −1%.

Active managers can have management styles that are not well represented by published indexes. In these cases, a "normal" portfolio can be constructed as a custom benchmark. Custom benchmarks do not line up with investors' benchmarks. The delta between investor benchmarks and normal portfolios, namely "misfit" risk, can be incorporated into the optimization model by modifying the utility function as follows (alpha is assumed constant for this expression), where *rn* is the strategic portfolio incorporating normal benchmarks in place of manager portfolios.[3] Alpha must be listed separately because normal portfolios are indexes.

$$E[U'] = E\left[rn - rb + \Sigma_j ws_j \alpha_j\right] - \lambda' \sigma^2 (rn - rb)$$

As illustrated with an example later, a standard optimization tool, such as Solver in Microsoft Excel, can be used to maximize the objective function. Investors must specify risk aversion parameters and provide expected active returns as well as active return variance/covariance matrices to solve the problem. Alpha and risk parameters can be computed using historical returns. But care should be taken to avoid selecting periods of unusually strong performance or low correlations that will tend not to repeat. It is advisable to practice running optimizations using different utility functions and parameter values to gain a feel for the influence of different assumptions on optimal portfolios.

Investors should carefully study historical returns and not simply rely on summary statistics of optimal portfolios. Much can be learned from computing the frequency of active returns within particular ranges, the size and length of periods of poor performance (commonly referred to as drawdown), the timing and size of subsequent performance, and patterns of cyclicality. A case study presented later in this reading illustrates this point.

Each of these techniques assumes that manager selection decisions occur within a single period. In other words, preferences, expected returns, and risks are all assumed to be constant. As a result, these techniques might not provide flawless guidance for managing allocations through time because key variables will undoubtedly change. But dynamic programming techniques, which are commonly used by researchers, can be used to set asset class allocations over time. Although not yet applied in the manager selection process, they could provide new insight to investors.[4]

2 Appendix B provides the formula for LPM, and Stewart et al. (2011) provide a detailed summary and sample applications of the approach.

3 See Waring, Whitney, Pirone, and Castille (2000).

4 For example, as an investment horizon draws closer, risk aversion may increase, leading investors to favor managers who offer more attractive downside protection.

4 WHAT TYPES OF PORTFOLIOS ARE CONSIDERED ATTRACTIVE?

Utility maximization, risk budget management, and targeting probability distribution are all useful techniques for exploring optimal manager weights. In general, an optimal mix will be achieved when the most heavily weighted portfolios are those that offer the highest alpha and the lowest combination of alpha risk and risk resulting from factor mismatch. Assuming a single-factor model and defining alpha as a variable rather than a constant, expected return and risk can be defined as follows (see Appendix A for the mathematical expressions):

$E[rs - rb]$ = weighted average alpha, plus weighted average difference in beta exposure multiplied by expected excess return

$\sigma^2(rs - rb)$ = weighted average alpha risk, plus weighted difference in beta exposure multiplied by market risk, plus weighted average residual risk

Unsurprisingly, investors prefer high-alpha managers over low-alpha managers with identical risk profiles. Investors can reduce risk by hiring more managers (via diversification) or by hiring managers with low alpha and residual risk. To limit active risk, ideal total beta should equal 1, but achieving this beta will likely require sacrificing alpha. Therefore, managers with unit betas or combinations of managers with offsetting betas will be attractive.

5 CASE STUDY

To illustrate how these tools work in practice, a sample of four funds has been chosen from which to build a strategic portfolio designed to outperform a small-cap US equity index with limited risk of underperformance. The manager portfolios include an index fund, a growth-style portfolio, a value-style fund, and a style-neutral core active portfolio. Performance statistics for the four funds and four mixes of them, calculated from 10 years of monthly returns, are provided in Exhibit 1. The index fund (Column 1) displays the lowest active risk and closest beta match relative to the index. The value fund (Column 2) displays the lowest beta, and the growth fund (Column 3) displays the highest beta. The index earned 7.6% a year during the period, so a high beta would benefit a portfolio's performance for the period.

Various techniques are used to construct different types of fund mixes. Exhibit 1, for example, illustrates mixes created in the following ways:

- by equal-weighting the funds,
- by setting weights to provide minimum active risk (defined as the standard deviation of $rs - rb$),
- by setting weights to provide maximum expected utility $[E(rs - rb) - \lambda\sigma^2(rs - rb)]$, and
- by setting weights to provide maximum utility with beta controlled to equal 1.

Portfolios are created "in sample" using a full series of historical returns. Although no return distributions are assumed, the return history is assumed to be known in advance. As a result, the goal of this exercise is simply to illustrate, not back-test, these techniques. See directions in the Excel sidebar for creating a spreadsheet to run the analysis.

The equal-weighted portfolio (Column 5) yields a standard deviation of active returns of 3.69%. This value is lower than the average fund's standard deviation (5.65%) because of diversification benefits. The average correlation between active fund returns is only 15.8%. Because of this correlation, and despite the value and growth funds' high active risk, the minimum risk portfolio (Column 6) includes positions in these two funds and also delivers less active risk than the index fund itself.

Exhibit 1 Alternative Mixes of Funds Using Various Optimization Techniques with In-Sample Data and a Small-Cap US Equity Mandate

	Individual Funds			
Descriptive Statistics	**1 Index Fund**	**2 Value**	**3 Growth**	**4 Core**
Beta	0.99	0.84	1.04	0.91
Annual active return	−0.33%	1.00%	−0.23%	1.13%
Annual active standard deviation	1.68%	6.98%	7.79%	6.13%
Percent annual active < 0%	52.3%	50.5%	47.7%	51.4%

	Fund Combinations			
Descriptive Statistics	**5 Equal Weighted**	**6 Minimum Risk**	**7 Maximum Utility***	**8 Maximum Utility* Beta = 1.0**
Beta	0.94	0.99	0.88	1.00
Annual active return	0.52%	−0.25%	1.17%	0.00%
Annual active standard deviation	3.69%	1.63%	5.12%	3.36%
Percent annual active < 0%	50.5%	51.4%	50.5%	45.9%
Weights				
Index fund	25%	93%	0%	50%
Value	25%	4%	40%	0%
Growth	25%	3%	0%	37%
Core	25%	0%	60%	13%

* $\lambda = 2.0$

Notes: Portfolio built using S&P 600 small-cap index and four live portfolios. Monthly net returns are from 30 September 2001–30 September 2011.

Sources: Based on data from Capital IQ and Stewart (2012).

The two maximum utility portfolios seek to optimize trade-offs between risk and return but differ in their beta exposures. The value of the risk aversion parameter, λ, affects the optimal portfolios: A higher value will penalize risk and lead to a lower active return portfolio but will not necessarily lead to a unit-beta portfolio. Setting λ at 2.0 results in an unconstrained portfolio that is heavily weighted in the two highest active-return value and core funds. The optimal portfolio's beta, however, is only 0.88, which is biased to underperform in up markets. Restricting the beta to equal 1.0 in the optimization process yields a unit-beta portfolio. Despite their negative active returns, the optimization system replaces the value fund, which has higher returns, with the index and growth funds because they allow the beta to increase (to 1.0). The growth fund acts like a "completeness fund," neutralizing the misfit of a non-unit beta, even though the fund does not add to the return. As a result of eliminating the bias, the proportion of active returns less than 0% drops from 50.5% to 45.9% of 12-month periods.

Many investors who use active managers have limited tolerance for risk, regardless of alpha. The maximum target value for active risk is called the risk budget. Utility can be maximized subject to an active risk constraint (such as an active standard deviation not to exceed 3%) or a probability-of-active-loss constraint (such as no more than a 10% probability of an active return below –5%). Investors can benefit from diversifying active risk across all managers, not simply within a given asset class; therefore, it makes sense to implement a risk budget at the total portfolio level, including all managers. Maximizing total portfolio utility, with constraints to match strategic asset allocations and betas, is a way to meet those objectives; but, as stated earlier in this reading, it is a challenge to implement.

Standard quadratic optimizers, such as the one offered within Excel's Solver tool, can be used to manage active standard deviations using historical time series or estimated probability distributions. However, either an integer-style optimizer or the assumption of a particular probability distribution must be adopted to control downside protection. In practice, many distributions, including the normal, have smaller tails than are seen in the markets, so assuming a normal distribution for downside risk management can lead to problems. Some practitioners suggest using rules of thumb to address this shortcoming—for example, assuming the probability of a downside event to be two or three times the level indicated by the normal distribution.[5]

One of the key issues in building a portfolio of managers using mathematical techniques, whether it is within one or across multiple asset classes, is the lack of stability in statistical relationships. Investors are wise to closely examine past periods of market stress, not simply average periods, for clues to potential strategy failure. The 2008–2009 financial crisis followed a pattern set by many past crises—correlations between risky assets increased in times of stress as investors sought relative safety. Correlations between active risks may increase because of factor and residual exposures. As an example, consider the portfolios described in Exhibit 1. Although the correlations between active returns averaged 16% for the full period, the level of correlation increased substantially in 2008 and 2009 to 31%. Residual return correlation also increased, from 15% to 24%.

Excel

OPTIONAL SEGMENT

The following screenshot shows a template used to compute optimal mixes of funds. These data are the source of the information displayed in Exhibit 1. The template is divided into two sections: inputs (TOTAL RETURNS) and outputs (ACTIVE RETURNS). Cells C5 through F5 include weights of individual funds, and G5 is the total [=SUM(C5:F5)]. Cells in Columns C to I (from C7 to I7) are populated with 10 years of monthly returns beginning in October 2001 (shown as 200110). Cell I7 includes a formula to calculate the weighted average of fund returns, +$C$5*C7+$D$5*D7+$E$5*E7+$F$5*F7, which is copied through Row 126.

5 See Coleman (2011) for a discussion of this approach.

	A	B	C	D	E	F	G	H	I
1		TOTAL RETURNS							
2			Index Fund	Value Fund	Growth Fund	Core Fund	Index	1 month Risk Free	Combined Portfolio of Funds
3									
4							TOTAL		
5	WEIGHTS		0	0	0	1	1		
6		Month							
7		200110	0.057364	0.0415	0.10707	0.060631	0.063643	0.0022	0.060631
8		200111	0.065899	0.0635	0.071325	0.100724	0.070591	0.0017	0.100724
9		200112	0.066613	0.0534	0.057247	0.088763	0.062348	0.0015	0.088763

Cell J7 (the first row of numbers in the section ACTIVE RETURNS) includes a formula to calculate active return (+I7–G7), and cell L3 provides the standard deviation of monthly active returns [(=STDEV(J7:J126)]. Cell L4 is the mean return [=AVERAGE(J7:J126)], and Cell L5 is the annualized standard deviation [=({[L3^2+(1+L4)^2]}^12–(1+L4)^24)^0.5]. Excess returns of the portfolio and of the benchmark index, above the risk-free rate, are needed to calculate beta. These returns begin in Row 7 of Columns N (beginning with the formula +I7–H7 and copied down) and O (beginning formula +G7–H7). The formula for a single-factor beta is in Cell O3 [=SLOPE(N7:N126,O7:O126)]. Cumulative returns are in Columns P (beginning with =(1+I7)*P6 in Row 7 with Row 6 value of 1.0 and copied down) and Q (beginning with =(1+G7)*Q6). The active 12-month return is computed in Column R (not shown in the screenshot above). It begins in Row 18 with the formula (+P18/P6)–(Q18/Q6) and is copied down to Row 126.

J	K	L	M	N	O	P	Q	R	S	T
ACTIVE RETURNS					COMPUTATIONS					
Active Return vs. Index		Active Return Descriptive Statistics			Beta	Ann. Comb. Port. Return	Ann. Index Return	Ann. Active Return	Frequency ≤ Downside	Utility
	std dev	0.017547			0.906	0.087	0.076	0.011	51.4%	0.00375
	mean	0.00071						12 Month		
	ann sd	0.06131		rp - rf	rm - rf	Cum Ret	Cum Idx	Active	Downside	
						1	1		0	
-0.003012				0.058431	0.061443	1.060631	1.063643			
0.030134				0.099024	0.068891	1.167462	1.138726			
0.026414				0.087263	0.060848	1.271089	1.209724			

Utility is defined as expected active return (the historical mean in this example) minus risk (historical variance) multiplied by a risk aversion parameter. It is provided in Cell T3 with the formula =+R3–2*L5^2 (risk aversion is assumed to be 2 in this example but may easily be changed). The frequency of annual active returns below a target value is generated in cell S3 with the formula =SUM(S18:S126)/COUNT(S18:S126). Column S includes an "if" statement =IF(R18<$S$6,1,0) in Rows 18 through 126 that returns the value 1 if the active return is less than the parameter set in S6 under the heading "Downside" and 0 otherwise.

Once the data and formulas are entered, the spreadsheet can be used to compute optimal portfolios of funds based on expected active return, risk, and utility. The spreadsheet uses historical data to estimate expected return (based on the mean historical return) and risk (based on historical standard deviation). In practice, the spreadsheet can be customized to incorporate exogenous active return and risk estimates.

As an example, consider a portfolio that offers the maximum level of utility. Open the "Solver" feature in Excel, set the target cell to T3, and click on "Max" to set up the objective function. Be sure to include the weights C5:F5 as the cells to change in order to find the optimal value of the objective function. To ensure weights are all greater than zero and sum to 100%, add two constraints: "C5:F5 >= 0" and "G5 = 1". Click "Solve" for the solution. The optimizer will yield the "Maximum Utility" portfolio summarized in Column 7 of Exhibit 1.

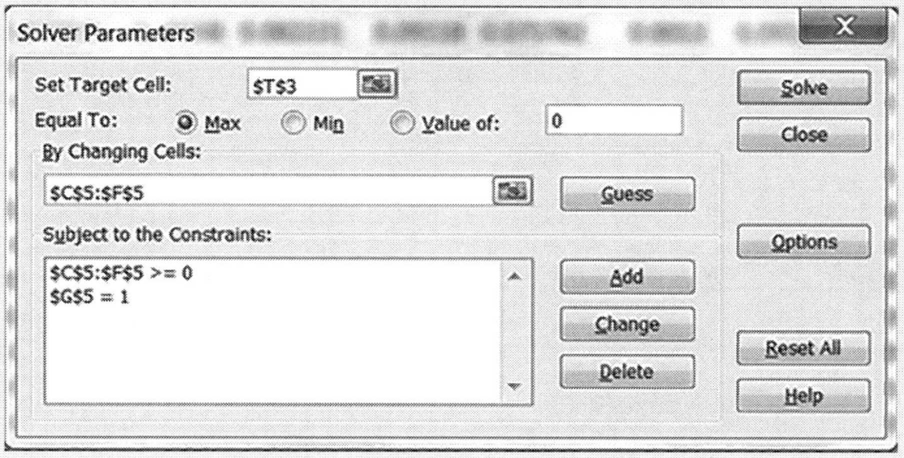

The solution will look like the following:

	A	B	C	D	E	F	G	H	I
1		TOTAL RETURNS							
2			Index Fund	Value Fund	Growth Fund	Core Fund	Index	1 month Risk Free	Combined Portfolio of Funds
3									
4							TOTAL		
5	WEIGHTS		0	0.396733	0	0.603267	1		

J	K	L	M	N	O	P	Q	R	S	T
ACTIVE RETURNS					COMPUTATIONS					
Active Return vs. Index		Active Return Descriptive Statistics			Beta	Ann. Comb. Port. Return	Ann. Index Return	Ann. Active Return	Frequency ≤ Downside	Utility
	std dev	0.014664			0.878	0.088	0.076	0.012	50.5%	0.00642
	mean	0.00060						12 Month		
	ann sd	0.05117		rp - rf	rm - rf	Cum Ret	Cum Idx	Active	Downside	
						1	1		0	

Note that beta does not equal 1, so the solution will be biased to underperform in up markets. To address this bias, an additional constraint requiring beta (provided in Cell O3) to equal 1 may be added to the solver setup.

It may be tempting to control the frequency of underperformance. Because the cells computing frequency in this spreadsheet include an "if" statement, the optimization problem will require an "integer" solution that cannot be accessed in standard Excel. One way to address this issue is to assume a probability distribution (such as normal) and calculate the downside probability (or partial moments) by using the assumed distribution instead of the realized series of active returns displayed in the spreadsheet.

END OPTIONAL SEGMENT

COSTS

6

The performance analysis of the portfolio mixes summarized in Exhibit 1 includes returns net of management and other expenses allocated to the funds. Costs associated with searching for and monitoring managers were not included in the optimization process. Institutional investors commonly hire pension consultants to help with manager selection, and high-net-worth individual investors often hire financial advisers.

Pension consultants may charge one-time fees for a single- or multiple-mandate search. Depending on the mandate criteria, the search may be expensive. Search costs can be amortized over the term of the mandate, deducted from future returns, and added to a utility function via a separate term. In the optimization, portfolios would have unique search and monitoring costs, and the weighted average cost would be subtracted from expected return. Index funds, which are associated with lower costs, would be favored in the optimization. Including search costs in the optimization process influences the dynamics of manager selection. Investors are less inclined to change managers when searches create new costs.

Consider the financial adviser business model. Financial advisers typically include the cost of manager searches and monitoring in their percentage-of-assets fee, which also covers data collection, reporting, and asset allocation monitoring. Exhibit 2 illustrates that total fees can be substantial.

Exhibit 2 Average Annual Financial Adviser Fees by Asset Size, 2010

Asset Size ($ millions)	Percentage Fee
$1 – $2	1.17%
$2 – $3	1.07%
$3 – $4	0.98%
$4 – $5	0.93%
More than $5	0.63%

Source: From PriceMetrix (2011).

Quarterly or annual reviews of managers generate ongoing costs. The use of active managers requires more monitoring on the investor's part than would be required for indexed managers. This higher monitoring requirement stems, in part, from the number of managers, increased complexity, and reduced transparency of actively managed funds. Many active managers, such as hedge fund managers, are uncomfortable sharing information regarding trades and holdings.

Investors who require this information to estimate risk in their portfolios will need managers who are comfortable sharing it. It is important for investors to consider all types of costs when formulating investment plans.

APPENDIX A

The Mathematics of Optimal Manager Allocation

The problem of setting the optimal allocation of investment managers is straightforward when one assumes a single-factor risk model with independently distributed alpha and error terms. Recall the following equation that decomposes the total return on a given portfolio. A portfolio's total return is defined by rp, its beta by β_p, and its error term by ep. The t (time) subscripts have been omitted. Note that the alpha term may be zero (index fund) or non-zero (active fund). We can make the model more interesting by assuming that alpha (α) is a random variable with non-zero mean, independent of the market and error term (which has zero mean).

$$rp = \alpha_P + R_f + \beta_P\left(R_M - R_f\right) + ep$$

Define rs as the return on the investor's total strategic portfolio implemented with a combination of individual portfolios. It is the return on the weighted sum of the underlying portfolios, each weighted by ws_j, and may be expressed as

$$rs = \Sigma_j ws_j rp_j = \Sigma_j ws_j\left[\alpha_{Pj} + R_f + \beta_{Pj}\left(R_M - R_f\right) + ep_j\right]$$

The total portfolio's benchmark's return, rb, is shown below. Note that alphas are omitted because the benchmark is composed of indexes, not live portfolios. The benchmark beta does not necessarily equal 1—the investor may seek different weights than those represented by market capitalizations.[6] Each live portfolio j has its own benchmark index j, but benchmark (wb) and live total portfolio (<u>ws</u>) weights do not necessarily match.

$$rb = \Sigma_j wb_j ri_j = \Sigma_j wb_j\left[R_f + \beta_{Ij}\left(R_M - R_f\right) + ei_j\right]$$

The goal of the investor is to set the weights, ws_j, of the individual live portfolios to yield the optimal implementation of the total benchmark portfolio. As a result, the focus is on active return as listed in the following equation:

$$\begin{aligned} rs - rb &= \Sigma_j ws_j rp_j - \Sigma_j wb_j ri_j \\ &= \Sigma_j ws_j \alpha_{Pj} + \Sigma_j\left[ws_j\beta_{Pj} - wb_j\beta_{IJ}\right]\left(R_M - R_f\right) \\ &\quad + \Sigma_j\left[ws_j ep_j - wb_j ei_j\right] \end{aligned}$$

Assuming the weights sum to 1 and the residual return components are uncorrelated, the expected return and variance of active return for the overall live portfolio may be expressed as

$$E[rs - rb] = \Sigma_j ws_j E\left[\alpha_{Pj}\right] + \Sigma_j\left[ws_j\beta_{Pj} - wb_j\beta_{Ij}\right]\left[E\left(R_M\right) - R_f\right],$$

$$\begin{aligned} \sigma^2(rs - rb) &= \Sigma_j ws_j^2\sigma^2\left(\alpha_{Pj}\right) + \Sigma_j\left(ws_j\beta_{Pj} - wb_j\beta_{IJ}\right)^2\sigma^2\left(R_M\right) \\ &\quad + \Sigma_j\left(ws - wb_j\right)^2\sigma^2\left(ep_j - ei_j\right) \end{aligned}$$

The expected active return on the live portfolio includes two terms: (1) the weighted average expected alpha, and (2) the expected market excess return over the risk free rate multiplied by the difference in weighted beta exposures. Stated differently, active return equals alpha plus the return from beta misfit. The active return variance term

6 Note that the total market, including non-tradable assets, might not be investable in any case.

includes three components: (1) the weighted (by the sum of weights squared) variance of alpha, (2) the weighted beta (by the sum of active weights and squared) exposures multiplied by the market return variance, and (3) the weighted (by the sum of squared active weights) variance of the difference in error terms.[7] Risk depends on alpha exposure weighted by alpha volatility, beta mismatch weighted by market volatility, and a measure of weighted active residual risk.

As introduced in the body of this reading, assuming the investor's utility function is of common quadratic form, we can specify expected utility of active return as follows:

$$E[U] = E[rs - rb] - \lambda\sigma^2(rs - rb)$$

where λ is a constant measure of active return risk aversion.

The investor's utility is determined by expected active return minus risk aversion multiplied by risk, where risk is defined as active return variance. The risk aversion parameter (λ) expresses the relative importance of active return and risk to a particular investor. A higher value of λ means that the investor dislikes risk to a greater extent.

To solve the investor's manager selection problem, identify the manager weights that provide the highest utility. A requirement that weights are positive and sum to 100% is a common constraint. Other options include constraining the probability of a given level of underperformance (downside constraint).

Alternatively, an investor may be comfortable accepting a given level of risk defined in terms of standard deviation (B_S), downside risk (percentage loss of D_P or more at percentage probability P_P), or value at risk (a form of downside risk but valued in dollars D_V at percentage probability P_V). These different approaches may be specified mathematically as follows:

1 Maximize utility

$$\text{Maximize } E[rs - rb] - \lambda\sigma^2(rs - rb)$$

$$\text{Subject to } \Sigma_j ws_j = 1.0,$$

$$ws \geq 0.0$$

2 Risk budget controlling active return standard deviation

$$\text{Maximize } E[rs - rb],$$

$$\text{Subject to } \Sigma_j ws_j = 1.0,$$

$$ws_j \geq 0.0,$$

$$\sigma(rs - rb) \leq B_S$$

Risk constraints for optimizing with respect to a risk budget may be specified differently than standard deviation by replacing the last term σ, with

1 downside risk of losing D_P or more in percentage, referred to as probability P_P:

$$\text{probability}(rs - rb \leq D_P) \leq P_P$$

2 value-at-risk (VaR)[8] dollar target D_V at tail probability P_V at dollar value \$:

$$\left[\text{VaR}(rs - rb) / \$, P_V\right] \leq D_V$$

7 Note that the three risk terms can be separated because of the assumption of independence among the return components.

8 Defined in Appendix B.

An investor may also choose to control the portfolio's beta to match the benchmark's beta by adding a further constraint as follows:

$$\Sigma_j\left[ws_j\beta_{Pj} - wb_j\beta_{Ij}\right] = 0$$

An investor can choose to minimize active risk altogether and focus solely on selecting the lowest-risk mix of portfolios. In that case, there will be no maximization, only minimization of active risk:

$$\text{Minimize } \sigma^2(rs - rb)$$

$$\text{Subject to } \Sigma_j ws_j = 1.0$$

$$ws_j \geq 0.0$$

In practice, one can use a standard optimization tool, such as Solver in Microsoft Excel to solve this problem, as illustrated in this reading's Excel sidebar. Of course, the investor needs to specify a risk aversion parameter and provide expected total returns and alphas, as well as provide a variance/covariance matrix of total returns, alphas, and residual returns for the problem. In practice, one may wish to run several scenarios using different formulations and assumed values to develop a feel for the influence of different assumptions on the optimal solution.

It is also recommended that investors study historical return patterns. Doing so may include computing the frequency of active returns within particular ranges, the size and length of periods of poor performance, the timing and size of performance subsequent to unusually strong or weak performance, and general patterns of cyclicality.

As discussed in this reading, investors tend to select strategic asset class and manager weights in two separate steps: first setting strategic asset allocation, and then setting manager allocation. There is another way to build a portfolio of managers: selecting weights for alphas without being constrained by strategic allocation. Investors can select the best managers regardless of asset class and use derivatives to adjust the asset allocation to match the strategic allocation. Piros (1998)[9] proposes this approach and notes that "as the relative attractiveness of various asset classes changes over time, there is no need to forgo the value-added generated by the most skilled managers just because their asset class is out of favor." One key caveat: Derivatives—including swaps, warrants, and futures—all involve fees and transaction costs, so the alpha calculations must be computed net of hedging expenses.

Allocation optimization can be conducted assuming single or multiple periods. The expressions listed in this appendix reflect a single-period world where optimal allocations are fixed for the entire horizon and are realistic only if market parameters and investor preferences are fixed. Dynamic optimization (namely, dynamic programming or optimal control) techniques also exist and can be used as an alternative to the single-period method described here.

9 See also Clarke, de Silva, and Thorley (2009).

APPENDIX B

Definitions of Potential Optimization Parameters

These definitions are presented in Stewart, Heisler, and Piros (2011). Define θ as the return level R that the investor seeks to avoid falling below and P as the probability that the realized return will equal that level or less. If returns are arranged in ascending order (the i associated with the lowest possible value is 1), we can define K to denote the largest integer such that $R(K) \leq \theta$. Downside probability is given by

$$\text{Downside probability} = \sum_{1}^{K} P(i)$$

A downside probability of 5% may be interpreted as a 5% chance that returns will equal θ or less. A value of 0 for θ is commonly used.

Lower partial moment (LPM) is the sum of squared deviations of returns below a threshold level. The LPM of degree "2" with threshold return θ and probability P is

$$\text{LPM} = \sum_{1}^{N} P(i)\left\{\max\left[0, \theta - R(i)\right]\right\}^2 = \sum_{1}^{K} P(i)\left[\theta - R(i)\right]^2$$

If θ is set equal to the expected return, the LPM is also known as the semi-variance.

Value at risk (VaR) is a measure of risk expressed in currency value (such as the number of dollars at risk), not return percentage. Both the size of the exposure and the probability of a given loss must be computed to determine VaR. The common interpretation is a given dollar loss (the value that is at risk) or lower that has a stated chance of occurring.[10] Let $CP(k) = \sum_{1}^{k} P(i)$ be the cumulative probability for the k lowest return values; R is return. Let L be the *largest* value of k such that $CP(L) \leq TP$, a target probability of loss. As a result, $R(L)$ is the (highest) return at the top of the outcomes in the distribution's left-side tail. For an investment of \$X and tail probability of TP, the VaR equals $X \times R(L)$. That is,

$$\text{VaR}(X, TP) = X \times R(L),\ L \text{ such that } CP(L) \leq TP$$

Note that VaR is only meaningful if TP is chosen so that $R(L) < 0$—that is, a loss. Typically, $TP = 0.05$, implying that a loss of VaR *or more* occurs 5% of the time. As a result, the actual loss may be (or perhaps probably will be) worse than VaR.

10 VaR is frequently understood to be the amount that can be lost. This interpretation is flawed; as mentioned in the text, VaR is that amount or more, *not* that amount or less.

REFERENCES

Clarke, Roger, Harindra de Silva, and Steven Thorley. 2009. *Investing Separately in Alpha and Beta*. Charlottesville, VA: Research Foundation of CFA Institute (April).

Coleman, Thomas. 2011. *A Practical Guide to Risk Management*. Charlottesville, VA: Research Foundation of CFA Institute (July).

Grinold, Richard, and Ronald Kahn. 2000. *Active Portfolio Management*. 2nd ed. New York: McGraw-Hill.

Piros, Christopher. 1998. "Asset Allocation: Separating Alphas and Asset Classes." Working paper, Massachusetts Financial Services (March).

PriceMetrix. 2011. "Fee and Managed Asset Pricing." *Insights*, vol. 3 (March).

Stewart, Scott. 2012. "Training Student Equity Analysts and Utilizing their Recommendations in Active Portfolio Management." Research Series Paper No. 2012–17, Boston University (May).

Stewart, S., J. Heisler, and C. Piros. 2011. *Running Money: Professional Portfolio Management*. New York: McGraw-Hill.

Waring, Barton, Duane Whitney, John Pirone, and Charles Castille. 2000. "Optimizing Manager Structure and Budgeting Manager Risk." *Journal of Portfolio Management*, vol. 26, no. 3 (Spring):90–104.

PRACTICE PROBLEMS

The following information relates to Questions 1–4

Frank Augusta, a high net worth individual investor, recently attended his only child's graduation from a private university. As a result, Augusta informs Mary West, his financial advisor, that his investment planning needs have changed and he would now like to focus on long term retirement planning. After reviewing Augusta's investment policy statement (IPS), West recommends revising Augusta's strategic asset allocation and increasing the weight of equity and lowering fixed income. They agree on the new target allocation, which also includes adding exposure to emerging markets.

West indicates that her first decision in the manager selection process will be to choose the most appropriate type of return in the utility function.

West selects a published emerging markets index in calculating the active return and the active return variance to optimize Augusta's expected utility. Augusta reminds West of the following IPS constraint: No money shall be invested in the country that has the highest market capitalization in the published market index.

Augusta invests in global timber and uses this asset class as an inflationary hedge. He believes that with increasing environmental pressures the return from global timber will underperform the broader market over the next five years; however, he desires to remain invested in this asset class.

Augusta is also seeking advice on his real estate holding, which currently consists of a real estate exchange traded fund. He would like to hire active managers and is considering an active manager for his real estate investments. He asks West how costs affect the optimization in the manager selection process.

1 West's first decision in the manager selection process should be to choose:

- **A** total return.
- **B** active return.
- **C** passive return.

2 In order to comply with Augusta's IPS constraint, West should adjust the manager selection process for:

- **A** misfit risk.
- **B** downside risk.
- **C** mean-lower partial moments risk (LPM).

3 In order to satisfy Augusta's desire to remain invested in global timber, West should set manager weights in the utility function to provide maximum:

- **A** active risk with beta controlled to equal one.
- **B** active return with beta controlled to greater than one.
- **C** expected utility with beta controlled to less than one.

4 With respect to Augusta's question regarding the selection of a real estate manager, West's *best* response should be that in the optimization process:

- **A** active management funds are favored over passively managed funds.

B manager search costs discourage the investors from changing managers.

C unique manager monitoring costs are added to the expected active return.

The following information relates to Questions 5–9

Randy Garrity, the trustee of the Forever Young endowment, has engaged investment consultant Jeff Weller to assist in the manager selection process for the endowment's US large-cap equity portfolio.

Weller suggests using a quadratic utility function to determine the optimal mix of managers. He makes the following comments regarding the utility function for manager selection:

Comment 1 An investor's expected utility for manager selection can be analyzed as expected active return adjusted for the investor's risk aversion and the level of active return variance.

Comment 2 An investor with higher risk aversion will select a portfolio with higher active return variance, all else being equal.

Concerning risk in optimization models, Weller makes the following statements:

Statement 1 Beta, active return standard deviation, downside risk, and value at risk are acceptable measures of risk.

Statement 2 Risk can be incorporated into expected utility optimization in the form of a constraint.

Garrity notes that the endowment has been instructed to use the S&P 500 Index instead of an internally developed custom benchmark to benchmark its active investments in US large-cap equities. Garrity adjusts Weller's optimization model to address this situation.

Weller tells Garrity about a relatively new manager selection technique using mean-lower partial moments (LPMs) to define risk. Weller notes that the LPM technique has some useful features that might improve Forever Young's manager selection.

When working on the final report for Forever Young, Weller makes the following observations on the treatment of search and monitoring costs in the optimization:

Observation 1 Search costs can be incorporated into the utility function via a separate term.

Observation 2 Search costs do not influence the process of optimally selecting managers.

Observation 3 Using active managers rather than index managers reduces ongoing monitoring costs.

5 Which of Weller's comments regarding expected utility is correct?

A Comment 1 only

B Comment 2 only

C Both Comment 1 and Comment 2

6 Which of Weller's statements regarding risk is correct?

A Statement 1 only

B Statement 2 only

C Both Statement 1 and Statement 2

7 In Garrity's adjustment to Weller's optimization model, misfit risk is represented as the:

A variance of the overall portfolio return relative to the S&P 500 return.

B variance of the custom benchmark return relative to the S&P 500 return.

C difference between the probability of loss of the custom benchmark and the S&P 500 with respect to a target level of return.

8 Which of the following is a feature of the relatively new manager selection technique Weller talks about with Garrity?

A Risk is defined as the sum of differences below a target mean.

B An assumed probability distribution of active returns is required to compute risk.

C The technique yields a portfolio that is optimal with respect to volatility below a given threshold level.

9 Which observation about search and monitoring costs is *most* accurate?

A Observation 1

B Observation 2

C Observation 3

SOLUTIONS

1 B is correct. Investors may seek optimal tradeoffs between active return and active risk or, alternatively, maximize active return while holding active risk to an acceptable level. The two-step approach used by Augusta (asset allocation first, manager selection second) is also logical, considering that investors carry beta risk whereas managers carry residual risk. So, investors worry about total returns, and managers are concerned about their returns versus their benchmarks.

A is incorrect because total return would be used in the utility function if asset allocation and manager selection were set simultaneously; here, asset allocation has been set first. C is incorrect because passive return and passive risk is the benchmark return and risk.

2 A is correct. When active managers need to have management styles that are not well represented by published indexes (here, the exclusion of the most important country in the index), a "normal" portfolio can be constructed as a custom benchmark. The delta between investor benchmarks and normal portfolios, namely "misfit" risk, can be incorporated in the optimization model by modifying the utility function.

B is incorrect because although a term to represent a risk budget could be incorporated using active return downside probability in the model, this does not address the country exclusion here. C is incorrect because LPM defines risk as the sum of squared differences below a target mean, but it does not address the country exclusion here.

3 C is correct. The maximum expected utility portfolio seeks to optimize tradeoffs between risk and return; keeping the beta less than one will lead to outperformance of the benchmark in the down market of the timber class. A is incorrect because maximizing active risk will produce a riskier portfolio but will match the market return. B is incorrect because maximizing active return will produce the greatest return ignoring risk and underperform the index in the forecasted down market.

4 B is correct. Investors are less inclined to change managers when searches create new costs. A is incorrect because index funds, which are associated with lower costs, would be favored within the optimization. C is incorrect because portfolios would have unique search and monitoring costs and the weighted average cost would be subtracted from expected return, not added.

5 A is correct. Comment 1 is correct because expected utility is given by the following:

$$E[U] = E[r_s - r_b] - \lambda\sigma^2(r_s - r_b),$$

Where $r_s - r_b$ is the active return. The active return variance, $\sigma^2(r_s - r_b)$, is a measure of active return risk, and λ is a constant measure of active return risk aversion. Comment 2 reverses the relationship between risk aversion and active return variance.

6 C is correct. Statement 1 is correct because risk can be defined as either beta, active return standard deviation, the probability of active return falling below a target, or value at risk. Statement 2 is correct because risk concerns can be incorporated in a modified optimization model in the form of a constraint.

7 B is correct. Misfit risk in the adjusted optimization model is represented by $\sigma^2(r_n - r_b)$, which is the variance of the custom benchmark relative to the benchmark return (the S&P 500 return).

8 C is correct. The conclusion follows from the fact that an LPM, used in the technique, defines risk with respect to deviations below a threshold level.

9 A is correct. Search costs can indeed be incorporated into the utility function via a separate term.

READING

14

The Dimensions of Active Management
Why Alpha and Active Risk Are the Only Things That Matter

by M. Barton Waring and Laurence B. Siegel

M. Barton Waring is at Barclays Global Investors, Retired (USA). Laurence B. Siegel is at the CFA Institute Research Foundation (USA).

LEARNING OUTCOME STATEMENTS

Mastery	*The candidate should be able to:*
☐	**a.** describe the components of total risk (market risk and pure active risk) and explain how these components are related to strategic asset allocation;
☐	**b.** explain misfit risk (i) for a single active manager and (ii) for a portfolio of active managers chosen by an investor (*net* misfit risk);
☐	**c.** explain the calculation of the pure information ratio (i) for a single active manager and (ii) for a portfolio of active managers;
☐	**d.** distinguish between active investment results that are under an investment manager's control and those that are under an investor's control;
☐	**e.** explain the limitations of historical alphas, style boxes, and traditional active risk concepts for building a portfolio of managers;
☐	**f.** describe how to estimate the inputs needed in the optimization process that leads to the efficient frontier of active managers;
☐	**g.** explain why the manager optimization process favors lower active-risk managers.

The authors gratefully acknowledge the assistance provided by Peter Bernstein, Bruce Goddard, Blake Grossman, Ronald Kahn, Kenneth Kroner, Gerry Rocchi, Clinton Stevenson, and Linda Strumpf. Many other colleagues, who are too numerous to thank, also provided helpful comments.

Every reader of this article likely either employs active managers or is one. But what exactly are active managers? What role do they play with regard to the investor's portfolio? What should their role be? What are the real dimensions in which active managers vary? Are current practices for building portfolios of managers the best that can be designed, or is there a better way?

Most investors know something about the answers to the questions we pose, as common sense goes a long way here. Active managers select securities. They invest the portfolio, and it is hoped that they will add alpha, an incremental return over their benchmark. Investors, for their part, work hard to hire the best managers they can identify. Our ambition here is to support that effort.

To that end, we hope to convey two fundamental insights. The first is that one hires active managers to generate what we'll call pure active return, or pure alpha, knowing that in their efforts to do so they will generate pure active risk. (We use the unconventional modifier "pure" for reasons discussed below).

We also note that building a portfolio of managers is like building a portfolio of anything; it's an optimization problem. And if pure active return and risk are the key dimensions describing active managers, then building a portfolio of managers involves optimizing the trade-off between these two dimensions.[1]

Second, pure active return, subject to a penalty for pure active risk, is what managers should be hired to deliver. And it is what investors should pay active fees for. Current practice, to the contrary, typically draws only a fuzzy distinction between a manager's pure alpha and the market exposures (including style and other systematic risk factor exposures) delivered by that manager. By making this distinction clear, and by quantifying it, one can greatly improve the payoff to the decision to hire active managers.

Holding active managers, then, is like any other proposition in finance: balancing the hope for gain against concern about risk. The current state of practice does not do a good job of managing that tension, and doesn't even explicitly focus on it, but there are new technologies and ways of thinking that do.

WHAT IS ACTIVE MANAGEMENT?

You already know that active managers try to beat an asset class or style benchmark, using securities held in other than benchmark weights. Can this be successful on average? What can such managers do for your portfolio? How should you choose them? How should you weight them in your portfolio? Does more active risk mean more active return? If so, under what circumstances?

Active managers are *forecasters*. They use the information available to them, and whatever their native talents are, to make stock-by-stock (or factor-by-factor, or market-by-market) forecasts of pure active return based on information that they believe is not yet impounded in the price, and then they translate these forecasts into portfolios.[2]

1 While there hasn't been much academic research focused on managing active decisions, an authoritative, general, and up-to-date example is Grinold and Kahn [2000a]. The technology they describe can be recast in a form that applies not just to the security selection problem, where their work is focused, but also to the manager selection and structuring problem (see Waring et al. [2000]). Both these works provide a bibliography of the research in this area.

2 We'll often refer to securities as stocks, although our comments apply to securities in any asset class or across any group of asset classes. Also, while we set this discussion on the familiar turf of security selection, the observations apply equally to the alpha-generating efforts of tactical asset allocation, market timing, sector rotation, and other methods of actively managing across groups of securities.

Well, not exactly. The traditional manager typically doesn't make explicit forecasts of stock-specific returns, or optimize those forecasts to construct portfolios (although these practices are followed by the best of the risk-controlled active managers). Instead, traditional managers may establish price targets or express forecasts in some other forecasting space that does not translate directly to expected alphas. At the end of the day, they do hold a portfolio of securities, often more or less equal-weighted, that they hope will beat their benchmark. This portfolio is informed more by traditional research, intuition, and experience than by optimization and risk control considerations.

Whether the manager knows it or not, however, stock-specific alpha forecasts are always there, implied by the bets in the portfolio. They can be backed out of the portfolio holdings, using reverse optimization.[3]

If you can't forecast better than the average market participant, you shouldn't be an active manager. And if you can make superior forecasts, but don't agree with the forecasts implied by your holdings, then you should have different holdings, consistent with forecasts you do agree with.

Likewise, investors make alpha forecasts for the managers they hold. These forecasts are rarely explicit in current practice, but they are also always implicitly there. They also can be backed out through reverse optimization—and they can be embarrassingly high.[4]

Investors should hire active managers only if they have skillfully formed positive alpha forecasts for the managers. And if they have these forecasts they should use them (more detail later).

Superior forecasting, then, is what generates the positive expected alpha that we hope to earn from hiring active managers. Forecasting is important at two levels: for managers looking at stocks, and for investors looking at managers.

Market Risk and Active Risk, Rewarded and Unrewarded Risk

To begin to identify the dimensions of active management, we must first break total risk into its component parts. Following Sharpe [1964], the total risk of any investment can be broken into: 1) *market risk,* also called policy, systematic, undiversifiable, or beta risk; and 2) *pure active risk,* also called specific, unsystematic, idiosyncratic, diversifiable, or alpha risk.

Policy risk is usually managed by investors through their adoption of a strategic asset allocation (SAA) policy, with its attendant asset class benchmarks, all fully diversified and therefore subject only to market risk by definition. Active risk comes into the investor portfolio through the use of active managers who, while holding some components of the policy benchmarks, try to beat them.

Academicians have focused much of their finance research in the last few decades on market risk, observing that if markets are efficient, then we can't beat the market. In practice, however, investors don't seem to completely believe this. Investors still routinely hire active managers, whose returns can differ widely from benchmark returns. In fact, the all-passive institutional portfolio is a rarity. So active risk is in fact taken in the search for pure active return, and this trade-off needs to be managed too, besides the trade-off between market return and risk that is at the heart of asset allocation policy.

---

3 In addition to the weights of the securities held, for reverse optimization one needs a reference portfolio (the benchmark); estimates of the pure active risk (standard deviation) of each stock; the correlation of each stock with every other; and the expected alpha for one of the stocks (to get the scale right). For a general discussion, see Sharpe [1974].

4 A very simple case: If three active managers hold half the portfolio (the other half in index and enhanced index), an 8% expected alpha may be implied for them.

Capital markets must function so that the expected return on the overall equity market must be higher than that on fixed-income investments.[5] As a result, fully diversified market risk (such as one takes by buying an index fund) must be rewarded. Pure active risk, in contrast, cannot be rewarded *on average*, since active managers are betting against each other in a zero-sum game.[6]

Particular active managers, of course, will beat the market by a large margin—but they are doing so at the expense of the others, either through luck or through special skill. Active managers (and other market participants) in aggregate *are* the market, however, so they must again in the aggregate earn the return on the market—minus fees, transaction costs, and other expenses, which can be substantial.[7]

Where's the Expected Alpha?

Does this mean that investors should just index, shunning active managers entirely? Not necessarily, although it may mean that for some. The market efficiency story is incomplete. Under a couple of fairly easily satisfied conditions, you can beat the market.

As long as a market is not completely efficient (and we believe that none are), and as long as there are native differences in human intelligence and skill levels, some managers will outperform through real skill, not just by virtue of random variation. Under these conditions, the notion that there can be an expected alpha or pure active return makes perfect sense. It is important to notice that while inefficiency is a necessary condition for good active managers to exist, it is not a sufficient condition—skill is also required.

But no manager will ever have so much skill as to be able to manage the portfolio without adding some active risk. We measure skill with an information coefficient (IC), a correlation coefficient of forecasts with realizations. Forecasting skill will

5 While the difference in returns between equity and fixed-income markets (the equity risk premium) may vary in size over time, logic largely dictates that it must always be positive for markets to clear. See Grinold and Kroner [2002] and Leibowitz et al. [2001].

6 The Evans-Archer diagram [1968] is the classic tool used to introduce this point, showing that risk declines asymptotically to some irreducible amount as the portfolio becomes more and more diversified. Although Evans and Archer contrast only policy and active risk, without saying what risks are rewarded, one can deduce that diversifiable risk need not be rewarded since investors can avoid it, almost for free, by indexing; but the undiversifiable risk does need to be rewarded.

Sharpe [1964] shows that, under the stringent assumptions of the capital asset pricing model, policy risk is associated with an expected reward while active risk is not. Many subsequent observers have criticized the CAPM as relying on unrealistic assumptions or as empirically unsupported. Ross [1976] demonstrates in developing his arbitrage pricing theory that, even if the CAPM conditions do not hold, policy risk is still rewarded while active risk is not. Thus, while acknowledging the limitations of the CAPM, we can proceed with confidence in dividing investment risk into rewarded and unrewarded components.

7 This version of the argument is developed most eloquently in Sharpe [1991]. Managers sometimes argue that they are not on a par with non-professionals, that as professionals they can take advantage of other market participants even if the return across all participants must be a zero-sum game—and that therefore it makes sense to hire them. Given that professionals represent a large portion of the total market, it is difficult to imagine that this could be a large factor; their own substantial activities will discipline prices for themselves as well as for others.

We can find a little evidence to support the claim, but not sufficient to make their case usefully persuasive. Brinson, Hood, and Beebower [1986] and Brinson, Singer, and Beebower [1991] conduct a series of empirical studies of the returns achieved by professional investors (that is, pension plans and other institutions and their managers, and mutual funds). The data are slightly different in each study, but it isn't unfair to summarize the results as saying that active management underperforms its passive benchmark, after costs, by about 0.5 percentage point per year. Sharpe [1991] would justify a prediction that in the absence of a professional effect the average loss would be well over 1 percentage point per year, which is the estimated sum of manager fees, explicit trading costs, and market impact trading costs.

So, given this empirical difference, there is an implication that the professionals did in fact beat the other market participants over the time periods studied, on average—but not by enough to cover fees and costs or to give the professionals a return higher than that of their passive benchmark. For similar results and an updated interpretation, see Ibbotson and Kaplan [2000] and Surz, Stevens, and Wimer [1999].

seldom carry a very high information coefficient, so there will always be risk left over, the chance of underperformance even in the hands of the quite good manager. This risk represents variability in active returns not explained by skill but rather by luck.

The luck component of risk, period-by-period, is nearly as large for the skillful as for the unskillful manager. Over long time spans, of course, positive alpha is much more likely to accumulate for the skillful.[8]

The bad news is that active management overall is in fact a zero-sum game—but the good news is that, for the skillful investor, there is an opportunity to add value to the portfolio over and above market returns. This really is good news, especially if you contrast it with the returns to be expected from your benchmark and strategic asset allocation decisions. You can't influence or control the return of your SAA policy; the market is going to do what the market is going to do. Other than making a risk-level decision—to be more or less aggressive in your SAA policy—you're just a passenger.

But if you have skill at security selection (or market timing or sector rotation, any active process), you have some control over returns, and this will add value, pure alpha, over and above the return of the SAA policy. The search for such alpha is, arguably, the investor's highest calling.

Remember, we're not saying it is easy. It's not—but it can be done.

DEFINING PURE ACTIVE RETURN AND RISK

We agree on the separation of market or policy risk and pure active risk, in principle. Let's go one step further and apply that in practice, separating these gross components of market risk (and return), and pure active risk (and return) in a real-world context.

The returns that usually pass for alphas—the simple differences between the benchmark return and the manager's return—are properly known just as active returns (not pure active returns). But these simple active returns might have more or less exposure to market risk than the amount implicit in the investor's benchmark.

Market risk can be measured by a capital asset pricing model single-factor beta, or, more usefully, in a multifactor manner. The most intuitive of these multifactor approaches measures market risk in terms of *style factors*: the familiar large-capitalization, small-capitalization, value, and growth categories.[9] Other, often more complex, factor models have been identified that more completely explain market risks, but some of these are hard to describe in plain English, so we'll stick with style factors in this discussion. Style factors also have the benefit of convenient investibility through low-cost style index funds.

---

8 The proportion of variance that is explained by luck rather than skill is surprisingly high. Since the IC is just a correlation coefficient, for a process with correlated signals we can convert it to an R^2 by just squaring it (Grinold and Kahn [2000, p. 292]). A manager with a very respectable IC of 0.10 would have an R^2 of 0.01, meaning that just 1% of active variance is explainable by the manager's skill, the remaining 99% of active variance being just random luck. Small wonder that it is so difficult to separate skill from luck over short time periods.

9 We aren't sure who was first to classify investments or managers on the basis of regression factors, but certainly Barr Rosenberg and his successors at BARRA have been the most complete at making this practice into a science. See www.barra.com/research/barrapub/risk_models.asp for a good introductory-level description. Sharpe [1988, 1992] saw that style and size factors could be productively and intuitively used in such regressions (called return-based style analysis), and developed special types of regressions designed to make the output more intuitive to lay audiences. Sharpe's approach is certainly the most commonly used in practice.

For determining which styles or common risk factors are most relevant for use in return-based style analysis, one authoritative source is Fama and French [1993], drawing on earlier observation by Banz [1981] and Reinganum [1981] that small-cap stocks had historically outperformed larger-cap stocks and by Basu [1977, 1983] that value stocks (with low price/book, price/earnings, or other valuation ratios suggesting that the stocks were cheap) had outperformed growth stocks (with high valuations).

The manager's returns, then, can be explained in terms of the exposures, or betas, to an intuitive series of style factors that express the manager's return from market risks, plus a pure alpha, or the return generated over and above market returns. Simple active return and pure active return are the same only if the manager's factor exposures are weighted the same as they are in the benchmark. Since the benchmarks flow from the SAA decision, managers can and should be chosen with factor weights so that, at least in sum across the managers, they are consistent with the benchmark's factor weights.

Once a set of market factor weights—a custom benchmark such as large-cap growth or 80% large-cap value and 20% large-cap growth—is established for a given manager, the proper objective of the manager is simply to beat that customized benchmark. That's why you hire active managers. You hire them to give you the levels of market risk exposure that you expect from them and that you assign to them through their customized benchmark, and to beat that benchmark.

If a manager does anything else, with or without the knowledge of the investor, it is changing an important aspect of the investor's SAA policy. The common term for this is *misfit risk*, but it's really the risk that the particular mix of benchmarks representing one's SAA policy is not being delivered.

In other words, the valuable and important return added by a manager isn't the total return that it delivers, but only that part of the return that is beyond what could be delivered through a set of index funds reflecting the manager's persistent style biases, its market risk exposures. This unique contribution of the manager to the return is what we're calling pure active return, or pure alpha.

We know it is redundant to say pure alpha, but we're trying to call attention to this precise definition, one that doesn't entail a market (or style) risk component. It is also what Sharpe means by the term *selection return* in his work on style analysis, and what those familiar with the very detailed factor models of BARRA know as *specific return*.

Realized pure alpha is easily separated from market risk factors and measured by regression analysis.[10] The regression determines the effective style weights of the manager, or the mix of style benchmarks that has the best fit to the manager's actual returns. The pure alpha is then the residual: the manager's actual return in excess of the return on this amount of market risk.

On a forward-looking basis, we assign to a manager the customized benchmark or normal portfolio, capturing the style and other market risk exposures that will best describe that manager's neutral or home position. It's easy for index funds or risk-controlled active managers. For others, this customized benchmark might be informed by the historic regression or by any other information that is useful to characterize the normal style biases of the manager. Even a tactical asset allocation manager or a style rotator has such a home position.

10 Realized pure alpha may be determined by an actual multivariate regression or by a constrained optimization technique that mimics a regression such as Sharpe's style analysis method. The purpose of the optimization technique is to allow for a no-shorting constraint; that is, to require all factor exposures to be between zero and one. We generally prefer ordinary regression, because it can more accurately describe deep value and growth managers.

Pure active return, of course, is properly thought of after fees. One should also incorporate manager transition costs into the pure active return; these must be amortized over the time period for which the manager is likely to be held, so that the cost (which is paid only when the manager is hired or fired) is properly converted into annualized return form.

The view of market risk that that we've been describing, by the way, is continuous and scalar; that is, a manager can have any amount of exposure to a single benchmark or to multiple style (or any other factor) benchmarks. The market exposure or style weight, at its essence, is just a beta, after all. And betas are a good way to determine or describe the level of exposure to any market risk.[11]

The investor may or may not be able to collect a portfolio of managers whose normal portfolios, in the aggregate, look like the benchmark. The misfit risk of a single manager goes away if it is cancelled by misfit risk of an opposing character from another manager (e.g., a growth manager is offset by a value manager, a large-cap manager with some small-cap exposure is offset by a small-cap manager with some large exposure). But such perfect offsets of style and other factors are not often the case.

So when we're optimizing a manager structure, as we do below, we'll be optimizing pure active return against *total* active risk, and on the risk side we'll control not only the pure active risk added up from each manager, but also the *net* misfit risk taken across all managers, calculated properly using scalar values for the managers' exposures to all the market risk factors we are tracking. This net misfit risk is a part of the active risk investors actually face.

The Information Ratio

The information ratio summarizes the key dimensions of active management. The standard deviation of the period-by-period pure alphas may be thought of as the pure active risk, representing the tracking error to the manager's customized benchmark. These two parameters, pure active return or pure alpha, α, and pure active risk or omega, ω, can be combined to arrive at a single measure of manager achievement (either historical or expected), the pure information ratio: $IR = \alpha/\omega$.

The IR represents the amount of pure active return delivered (or expected) per unit of pure active risk taken (or expected) by an individual manager, relative to its customized benchmark.[12]

Across the portfolio of managers held by the investor, the denominator would be the aggregation of the ω terms plus any net misfit risk remaining across the group of managers. We indicate this denominator, which is simple active risk, as σ_A. One would wish for the misfit component to be zero across all managers, but in practice it is difficult to make every last bit of misfit risk go away.

Level Playing Field for Evaluating Managers

Now that we have defined pure active return and risk, we can use these measures (and particularly the ratio of return to risk, the pure information ratio) as well as misfit risk, to compare any manager with any other, across asset classes, styles, and risk levels, creating a level playing field for all managers.

Even more important, we can use these measures to properly separate investment results that are the investor's responsibility from those that are created by the manager. The returns delivered by the capital markets on the particular mix of styles that

---

11 The CAPM uses just a single factor to capture the market. We are simply trying to control risk relative to the asset allocation policy better, by dividing market risk into more granular subcomponents. Either way, regression is a useful model for sorting out the market and idiosyncratic components of risk and return.

12 In our experience, some investors don't find that the term information ratio conveys much about its meaning. Observing that IR measures the consistency with which the active return is delivered, perhaps consistency ratio would be a better term and more likely to be understood. IR is a key measure of historic goodness for a manager, and on a forward-looking basis is a key input into the manager's role in the portfolio. It is very useful—it incorporates the two key dimensions of active management into one measure.

constitute the manager's custom benchmark are the responsibility of the investor who selected the manager, if only because the investor is the only party in a position to control the market risk exposures across the whole portfolio of managers.

Too often, performance evaluation practices confuse the benchmark return and the pure alpha, apportioning credit and blame incorrectly. Even the smartest and most well-intentioned investors are tempted to blame the active manager, rather than themselves, when the manager's asset class delivers a poor policy return (no matter what pure alpha the manager achieves). With the pure active return and risk clearly defined and calculated, these errors need no longer occur.

As a common example, think of the value manager that boasts of beating the S&P even when it fails to beat the value benchmark. Which one should the manager really be held against? If a manager persistently chooses to exercise its expertise in one domain of market risk such as deep value, isn't that the domain against which its value-added should be measured?

WHAT ARE ACTIVE MANAGERS FOR?

So why hire active managers? They provide the possibility of adding pure active return, of course, but they also add active risk.

The risk added by active management is in and of itself undesirable, so a manager has to do more than just have an expected alpha that is positive. It must add enough to more than compensate for the added risk. Active managers are there to add utility, not just expected return.

The methodology for determining the utility of active decisions is parallel to that for strategic asset allocation decisions. In general, the expected active utility (or usefulness, or desirability) of a portfolio of active managers is equal to its expected alpha, minus a risk penalty for active risk:

$$E(U_{\alpha}) = E(\alpha_p) - \lambda_{\alpha} \cdot E(\sigma_A^2) \quad (1)$$

where

$E(U_{\alpha})$ = the expected utility of active management in the portfolio;

$E(\alpha_p)$ = the expected alpha on portfolio p;

λ_{α} = the active risk aversion parameter for the investor (or the rate at which risk is translated into a negative return, or disutility); and

$E(\sigma_A^2)$ = the simple active risk (expected variance) of portfolio p (including both ω risk from each manager and the net misfit risk across the managers).

How do we figure out whether a portfolio that includes active managers provides incremental utility over the benchmark—that is, whether the combination of managers selected adds enough expected alpha to justify the extra risk? How, taking this one step farther, does one maximize expected utility? Through optimization.

Harry Markowitz [1952, 1991] developed this tool a half century ago. Although it's the dominant practice for building efficient portfolios of asset classes and, increasingly over the last 15 years, of securities within an asset class, optimization has just begun to be used for building efficient portfolios of *managers* within the investor's portfolio over the last 6 or 7 years.

But why? Building a portfolio of managers is like building a portfolio of anything. It's all about balancing risk and return, trying to find the best trade-off. Optimization is the technology that explicitly calculates these trade-offs in search of the highest-utility portfolio (of anything) for a given investor.

Increasingly, if they think about how managers interrelate in the total portfolio's utility function through optimization, investors are beginning to see their task as one of building *portfolios* of managers, rather than looking at each manager in isolation. To accomplish this task, investors hiring managers are increasingly using optimization as a portfolio-building tool.

Specifically, one must optimize on the managers' pure active return and risk—the real dimensions of active management—while dealing with the other (policy and misfit) return and risk components in a sensible way such as we describe.

BUILDING PORTFOLIOS OF MANAGERS

Let's first hold up to the mirror some of the chief features of current practice for building portfolios of managers. These features represent a good portion of the common sense that guides us in manager structure today. Albert Einstein said, "Common sense is the collection of prejudices acquired by age eighteen" (quoted in Bell [1952]). But is this good enough?

Mining the Historical Data

The most widespread current practice for building portfolios of managers is to assume, tacitly if not explicitly, that managers will continue to earn whatever alpha they've been earning in the past. Great effort is put into identifying and sorting candidate managers depending on their historic active returns, despite massive evidence that past performance is at the very best a weak predictor of future results, and despite the muddling of these returns with market components.[13]

That's probably because analysis of past performance is something that investors can do with a sense of objectivity and confidence. It's hard to argue with actual historical returns. They provide a feeling that one is dealing with something real and concrete.

Except when making forecasts.

While past performance should not be ignored—it is one of many factors that should be considered when evaluating a manager—the investor should remember that performance track records do not by themselves distinguish between luck and skill. Two managers, one lucky (but producing random variation around the properly style-adjusted benchmark) and the other truly skillful, can have the same track record. This can be true even over fairly long time horizons.

We'd like to give credence only to statistically significant performance data, right? Statisticians use the t-statistic to test whether data are statistically significant, or, more precisely, to test whether one can conclude with reasonable confidence that any given alpha, positive or negative, has been achieved through skill rather than luck.

There is general agreement (with only minor dissent) that if a manager's alpha over the period studied is more than two standard deviations away from that of the benchmark (that is, if its t-statistic is greater than two), we can say the manager has

13 See, for example, Kahn and Rudd [1995], who provide an extensive review of the literature to that time, which happens to include most of the relevant literature even today. Further work on the topic is in Wermers [2000] and Carhart [1997], and their results do not differ much from those summarized in Kahn and Rudd [1995]. Most of these performance studies cover mutual funds because of easy data availability, but the findings are likely to apply in roughly the same way to institutional funds, which are largely managed by the same managers.

a statistically significant alpha. This simply means that there is a very high probability (roughly 95% if alphas are normally distributed) that the manager's alpha really is different from zero. It is evidence of skill rather than luck.[14]

Here is why we digress on statistics. If a manager's historical alpha is not statistically significant in this way, it makes no sense to even consider whether the manager's historical alpha will repeat going forward. Since a lack of statistical significance says that we don't even understand whether the underlying non-random component of the alpha was different from zero or not, the data are meaningless noise and should not be used.

That's what not statistically significant means. The investor will have to make the alpha forecast for that manager according to a more qualitative or fundamental type of analysis, which of course can be done—it is just hard.

If a performance history does display statistical significance, it is fair to include it among one's other inputs when evaluating a manager. Yet one still doesn't just extrapolate it into the future without thought. A high t-statistic doesn't by itself prove skill, but a low t-stat should be interpreted as meaning that the performance record, at least, shows no evidence of skill.

If we cannot usually rely on past performance to select active managers, then how can we select them at all? We don't have a recipe, and we know that there aren't any recipes. If there were, everyone would be following it, and of course then it wouldn't work.

Each investor will have to develop his or her own methodology for forecasting manager alphas. The key ingredient is the tough one—one has to have great insight and ability. This is no different from how excellent active managers pick stocks; they use a tremendous amount of research into fundamentals, and at the end of the day they make a judgment call informed by their trained instincts.

Unfortunately, significant t-statistics on managers are quite rare—and this is exactly what theory predicts. We almost never see t-statistics used, because using them would require the investor to throw out and not use the historic alphas in most all cases.

Ignoring historical returns seems at first blush like a peculiar practice, but isn't it right to reject historical data when they provide no useful information?

Style Boxes and Style Maps

A practice developed over the past couple of decades or so is to divide the equity universe into *style boxes* (such as large value, large growth, small value, small growth, and perhaps mid-cap or core categories) and then to staff each style box with managers. This practice seems useful for breaking the arduous manager selection task into manageable pieces. The idea is to assign managers to each of these buckets, and that once the buckets are all staffed, the plan is well structured.

Since a cap-weighted combination of all the style boxes gives you back the market portfolio, it might appear there's nothing really wrong with style boxes per se. Unfortunately, value managers, growth managers, large-cap managers, and small-cap managers don't all come prepackaged neatly in these boxes. Some are stronger (deep value) or weaker (growth at a reasonable price) than others. The amount of "valueness" or "growthiness" does not always come in units of one.

14 To calculate a manager's alpha t-statistic, divide the realized historic monthly, quarterly, or annualized arithmetic alpha (regression or pure alpha) by the standard deviation of that alpha (expressed at the same frequency), and multiply the result by the square root of the number of periods represented in the data. Note that if the data are expressed in annualized terms, this result is just the information ratio times the square root of the number of years of data. Every regression software package, including Microsoft Excel™, provides this t-statistic automatically whenever a regression is conducted.

By using a regression alpha, we eliminate any accidental market return effects that might otherwise distort the manager's actual non-market-related returns. It is pure active return, or alpha.

Most large-capitalization active managers are equal-weighted, and as a result end up having some amount of small-cap exposure and less than full large-cap exposure (and vice versa for most small-cap managers, who seem to hedge a bit toward large stocks). Anyone who has conducted style analysis on managers knows that it is common for, say, a growth manager to be characterized as 70% in large growth, 15% in large value, 10% in small growth, and 5% in large value.[15]

Particularly for traditional active managers, style exposures usually do come from a continuous spectrum, not from an all-or-nothing bucket. (The percentage weights, by the way, are just a convenient way to express the betas of the manager relative to the style factors.)

Rather than simply using boxes to represent styles, some investors plot their managers and their total portfolio of managers on a style map. Managers who don't fit neatly into a style box can be hired in such an improved framework, as it is usually calculated in a manner that accommodates continuous scalar values. The investor's total portfolio style map displays the net misfit of the portfolio. One can also use it to simulate changes in managers, or in manager weights, to see the effect on misfit risk and other portfolio characteristics.

Style maps are much better than style boxes, since they recognize the continuous nature of styles and the importance of managing *net* misfit risk across all managers. If we aren't going to formally optimize as we suggest in this article, style maps and tables of the effective asset mix are the next best thing.

But the fundamental problem with using either style boxes or style maps to organize the manager structure effort is that neither one requires the investor to deal face to face with the managers' expected alphas. Used in the conventional way, style boxes and maps can subtly invite investors to just fill them up, without critically examining their own skill in assessing expected manager alpha or the relative expected alphas of the candidate managers. For investors who aren't strongly disciplined, style boxes and maps invite taking on active risk without a real expectation of pure active return.

Reliance on Traditional Active Management

As we've already noted, many investors who rely heavily on recent past performance and on style boxes as aids in selecting managers are also strongly biased toward traditional active management, with its high degree of active risk. They equate greater active risk with higher active return. Such investors often express disdain for risk-controlled active strategies and a preference for concentrated high-risk active strategies.

These investors make two mistakes. First, having learned that risk is related to return, they fail to distinguish between policy risk (which is in fact associated with a higher expected return) and active risk, which is rewarded only conditionally, depending on skill.

Second, such investors don't realize that their optimal portfolio of managers, at whatever active risk level they are comfortable with, will be constructed from good low-risk active managers in preference to higher-risk managers, for two reasons. The first is that the mathematics of optimization dictate that an investor's manager allocation should be dominated by managers with a combination of the highest forecast information ratios and the lowest levels of active risk.

Next, due to the no-short-selling constraint, high active risk portfolios tend to have lower information ratios than low active risk portfolios at the same level of manager skill. Feed this lower information ratio back into the first reason, and you see a loop that requires unimaginably high skill levels to justify giving large allocations to concentrated managers.

---

15 One can use either return-based or holdings-based style analysis, or both, to calculate these weights. There is no clearly best single method.

We conclude that sophisticated investors don't really want more risk-laden ventures. What they really want, or should want, is higher alphas, and less risk.

Current Practices Overall

Although in practice they are informed by the best efforts of investors, the conventional dimensions within which active manager decisions are framed—historical alphas, style boxes, the search for active risk to produce higher returns—do not generally support the investor's goal to add value, or utility, to the portfolio. Practices for building portfolios of managers could be better attuned to the real dimensions of active management, maximizing expected alpha while controlling active risk.

Can we suggest practices that point in that direction?

BUILDING PORTFOLIOS OF MANAGERS USING OPTIMIZATION

Tomorrow's best practices have a lot to do with portfolio theory.

Treat Each Manager Like a Stock

Active return/active risk optimization may not be what investors first think of when they set out to build a portfolio of managers, but it has been growing in use for building active portfolios of stocks for well over 15 years. It is becoming common practice in that context, with many advantages over traditional methods of constructing active stock portfolios.

We suggest treating each manager as one would a stock, giving investors the same powerful tools for managing their portfolios of managers that the best managers have for managing their portfolios of stocks. Specifically, one must optimize on the managers' pure active return and risk—the real dimensions of active management—while dealing with the other (policy and misfit) return and risk components in a sensible way.

We set up the utility function for this optimization earlier. Now, let's implement it using managers as the securities or stocks across which we will optimize. From this, we can construct an active efficient frontier across managers. An example is shown in Exhibit 1.

Exhibit 1 Efficient Frontier of Active Managers

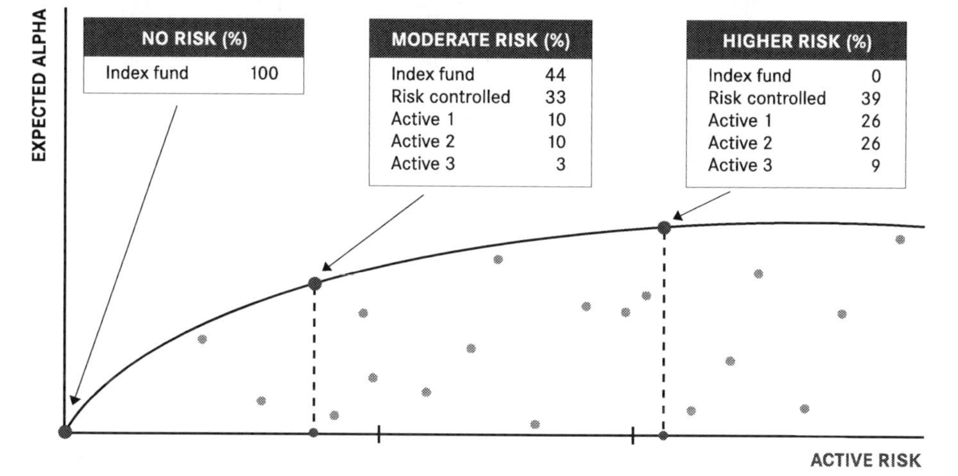

Thus, following Waring et al. [2000], who call their method manager structure optimization (MSO) to echo Markowitz's MVO, or mean-variance optimization, we can implement this utility function on a practical basis.[16]

We need only to form the investor's estimate of:

1 The expected pure alpha and pure active risk of every manager.
2 The expected correlation of every manager's alpha with that of every other manager.
3 The market factor betas that fairly characterize each manager's normal portfolio.
4 The expected return and risk of each market factor used, and the expected correlation of each factor with every other factor.

This may look more daunting than the usual list of MVO inputs, but it is easier than it looks. The correlations of the pure alphas are often simply estimated as zeros for two reasons.

First, we have eliminated the market-related risk factors by calculating a regression alpha, the pure active return that is uncorrelated with the market factors. While this does not necessarily mean that all common factors have been removed so that the alphas are necessarily uncorrelated with each other, the alphas by virtue of the process will tend to have low correlations.

Second, we observe in alpha histories that the correlations are in fact low, generally running between −0.2 and +0.2. Given the sample error in these observations, one fair solution is to regard all the alpha correlations as zero on a forward-looking basis unless there is a specific reason to expect some pair to be different.[17]

---

16 To correct an error in the optimization formula (Equation (2) in Waring et al. [2000]), the first term, representing misfit return, should include a beta, as follows:

$$\left(h^T X - \beta h_b^T\right) r_k$$

If the return and risk assumptions are all estimated so that they fall on a common security market line, this is a zero term. In this case, the whole term can be dropped.

17 At least for US equity managers. For international equity managers and for fixed-income managers, correlations between pure alphas are empirically non-zero (because these asset classes have fewer degrees of freedom; in fixed-income, there are only a few major bets to be made, and for international equity managers, there appears to be more emphasis on regions and industries than on individual security selection). Thus one might wish to make specific estimates of manager cross-correlations in these asset classes.

The third and fourth items are the descriptions of the managers' customized benchmarks, expressed in terms of the market risk factors that are relevant to the manager structure question at hand, and the capital market assumptions related to those market risk factors. Analysts are accustomed to providing capital market assumptions for SAA work; the assumptions used for manager structure optimization should be consistent with the SAA assumptions (but may need to be more detailed).[18]

The difficult item is the first, and in particular the return component of it, expected alpha. We'll come back to this.

Notice in Exhibit 1 that at zero active risk only an index fund is held, but that as risk tolerance increases (going to the right on the efficient frontier), the proportions held in risk-controlled active and traditional active increase. A more detailed example is in the appendix.

Expected Alphas

In our experience, practically everyone sees our point that the key dimensions of active management are expected alpha and active risk, that these need to be balanced, and that building portfolios of managers should be an optimization problem. In theory. They follow along and nod their heads in agreement at each step in the progression of the discussion.

But, also in our experience, as soon as it sinks in that they will need to form specific numerical estimates of the expected alpha of their candidate managers, the mood changes. The efficient market and zero-sum game alarm lights go on in their heads. They can't see themselves estimating alphas so that they can solve the optimization problem for managers in practice, and they mentally start moving back to their comfort zone—filling out style boxes.

But the same investors who quail at the task of forming expected alphas on efficient market and zero-sum game grounds almost always do in fact hire active managers. The resulting portfolios incorporate *implied* alpha forecasts, which, as we have pointed out, can be calculated through reverse optimization. Thus, investors are forecasting expected alphas whether they resist the notion or not. Worse yet, they don't know what alphas they have implicitly forecast, and if they did know they would quite likely reject many of them as unreasonable.

How can one reconcile these conflicting impulses? If you don't think you can forecast alphas, expressing a quantified degree of confidence in a given manager, maybe you shouldn't hire active managers. You should index instead. If you are going to hire active managers, you might as well make alpha forecasts explicitly, rather than implicitly. This is more honest and productive than simply selecting some active managers and hoping that the alpha forecasts implied by the holding weights turn out to be accurate.

Having done this, run an optimizer to select the portfolio. If the prospect of specific numerical alpha forecasts for managers is too daunting, then at the very least *think about* manager selection as an optimization problem. Your goal, as in any problem in portfolio construction, is to control risk while maximizing expected return.[19]

18 There are few factors if one uses style analysis, but not necessarily so few if one uses a more detailed factor model such as BARRA's. The good news is that the highly detailed factor models are commercially developed and conveniently come with capital market assumptions for each factor.

19 As Michaud [1989, 1998] has pointed out, optimization outputs are no better and may in fact be worse than the quality of the inputs, which are statistical estimates and thus subject to natural estimation error. Kritzman [2003] responds by noting that, for any given set of inputs, optimization is still the tool that gives the best outputs. He also makes many valuable suggestions about forming good forward-looking optimizer inputs.

You don't have to be a prophet, just a good forecaster. In other words, you don't have to be right about every forecast, just a little bit more right than wrong across all forecasts to add value over time.[20]

Why Low Active Risk Managers Are Preferred

All these prescriptions embed the idea that active risk is in and of itself bad—that of two equally skillful managers (managers with the same information ratio), the lower active risk manager is to be preferred. But why? Grinold [1990] and Kahn [2000] analyze the utility function for active management and get the result:

$$h_{mgr} \sim E\left(IR_{mgr} \cdot \frac{1}{\omega_{mgr}}\right) \tag{2}$$

where:

h_{mgr} = the holdings weight of portfolio or manager (its percentage allocation);
IR_{mgr} = the expected information ratio of the manager; and
ω_{mgr} = the expected volatility of the manager's pure alpha around a properly established benchmark.

Expressed in words, the size of a manager's allocation is directly proportional to the expected information ratio and inversely proportional to a lower level of active risk. If this seems to punish for risk twice (because active risk is also in the denominator of the information ratio), it does. Risk squared, or variance, is the real operator.

Another way to state this result is that a manager's allocation will be higher in direct proportion to a higher expected *alpha* and in inverse proportion to active *variance*. You want managers with more alpha, and a lot less risk.

There is another effect to consider as well. It tends to diminish the extent of allocations to managers that have greater active risk.

Most managers are prohibited by their mandates from taking short positions, and thus hold long-only portfolios. This limits a manager's ability to make bets on its insights, and the limitation is exacerbated as active risk is ratcheted up and requires larger and larger active positions.

As a result, even with skill levels held constant, the information ratio that can be achieved is reduced as a manager constructs a portfolio with greater concentration and active risk (see Grinold and Kahn [2000b]). Exhibit 2 illustrates this concept.

---

20 To get started in forecasting alphas, investors might consider using the forecasting relation:

Alpha = IC(Volatility)Score

where IC (information coefficient) is a measure of your manager selection skill, the expected correlation between one's forecasts and the subsequent realizations of those forecasts; volatility is the standard deviation of the return forecasted (volatility of the pure alpha); and score is the strength of the manager under evaluation, expressed in standard deviations above or below zero (a score of +2 or −2 would be considered very strong, and a score near zero would be weak). This formula is further elucidated, in a security selection context, in Grinold and Kahn [2000a]. Additional improvements to recognize that most managers are subject to the long-only constraint, and to include the effect of fees, can be incorporated.

The score is the key input variable. A two-standard deviation manager, with a score of 2, is the type of unusually skillful manager one might hope to find, but of course is quite rare. For IC, if you have no skill at manager evaluation, put in a zero (you're right about managers only half the time) and quit. Those truly blessed with selection skill might try a 0.3 (you're right about managers 65% of the time) or if you're rakishly overconfident, a 0.5 (you're right about managers 75% of the time).

Exhibit 2 Impact of Long-Only Constraint on Portfolio Efficiency (Assuming Equal Skill Levels)

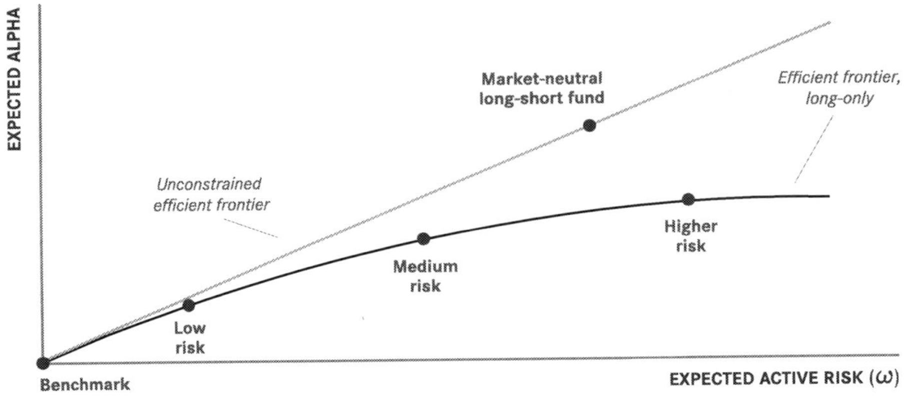

What are these limitations? A skillful alpha forecasting process is equally at home generating sell signals (negative expected alphas) as buy signals (positive expected alphas). But few of the negative alphas can be acted on in a constrained, long-only portfolio. A given security can be sold down from the benchmark weight to only a zero weight, and not below, no matter how strong the negative signal. The manager's insights are wasted, and the effect is greater as greater risk is taken on (larger negative positions are indicated but can't be achieved without violating the constraint).

The amount of alpha per unit of active risk thus goes down as the active risk level goes up, generating a declining information ratio for a constant level of skill. This effect is remarkably powerful. At a given skill level, enhanced index funds and market-neutral long-short funds are shown in Kahn [2000] to have roughly twice as high an expected information ratio as their long-only, traditional active counterparts that have moderate risk.

How Much Active Risk is Enough?

Since pure active risk is uncorrelated with policy risk, the relationship is Pythagorean, and total risk is less than the ordinary sum of policy and active risk and typically only slightly greater than policy risk alone. For example, if policy risk is 9% and the active risk is 3%, the total risk will be

$$\sqrt{9\%^2 + 3\%^2} = \sqrt{0.009} = 9.5\%$$

So total risk goes up only by half a percentage point as a result of adding 3% risk from active management. Does this relatively small increment to total risk suggest that investors should take more active risk, choosing a more aggressive position on the active efficient frontier?

Good question. Theory doesn't give us much help in the practical domain of putting a value on the risk aversion term in any optimization. This term, called λ, determines how much risk an investor will take in search of the available expected return. We have to look at sources other than theory to get a proper sense for the appropriate ranges of active λ for investors.

One source to look at is our own behavior. According to Brinson, Hood, and Beebower [1986], Brinson, Singer, and Beebower [1991], and related studies, about 90% of the variance of a typical portfolio's returns is attributable to strategic asset allocation decisions (market risk); only about 10% is attributable to active decisions (security selection and tactical asset allocation). What does this mean?

Let's translate numbers that we know from the familiar turf of standard deviation into variance, to get a hint. An investor who takes policy risk with a 9% standard deviation (about mid-range) has a policy variance of 9% squared or 0.0081; if this same investor's active risk (standard deviation) is 3%, the investor has a 0.0009 active variance, lower than the policy variance in a ratio of 90 to 10. Thus Brinson's observed variance ratios (90% to 10%) are consistent with more or less ordinary standard deviation numbers (9% and 3%) for policy and active risk, respectively. In other words, investors, voting with their feet, reveal a preference for taking far less active risk than market risk.

If "risk is risk," why don't investors choose to take on the same amount of variance with respect to active bets as they do with market risk bets? The answer goes back to our motivating theme: Policy bets are expected to be rewarded, unconditionally, and proportionally to risk taken. Active bets are rewarded only conditionally on skill, and in a declining proportion to risk taken at that; they aren't rewarded at all on average.

Thus, one kind of risk is more worth taking than the other. Putting it this way, it makes sense that investors would give a higher risk budget to unconditionally expected market returns than to highly conditional and proportionally declining expected alphas.

We should almost certainly implement this observation by using a λ risk aversion term that is higher when we are optimizing in the active risk dimension than when we are optimizing in the policy or SAA dimension. Thus, in Equation (1), we indicate with the subscript α that the λ is specifically an active risk λ, different from the λ expressing aversion to policy risk.

At the end of the day, the specific λ used sets the active risk budget, and the active risk budget has to be a comfortable one to the investor, given that investor's perception of the alpha expected in return for taking on that risk.

Core–Satellite?

In the late 1980s many investors started using the *core–satellite* concept as a way to temper the risk of an all-active portfolio. An indexed core was added to moderate the overall active risk of the portfolio. The concept was used by some even to justify holding extremely high-risk, concentrated managers as the satellites. This made some sense at the time, and represented a first stab at controlling active risk.

With today's technology, particularly the ability to manage and optimize active risks and returns, we can reject the notion of the core–satellite portfolio as too rigid. For the same reasons that we reject style buckets as not reflective enough of the continuous and scalar nature of managers' actual market exposures, we can also set aside the two buckets of core and satellite.

An optimally constructed portfolio of active managers is likely to also hold index funds. But as any active risk is contemplated, and if good low-risk active funds are available, the proportion held in index funds will rapidly shift to low-risk active funds. This shift will happen smoothly, not abruptly, with increasing risk, not in a discrete way. Further, the other active managers held will be more likely to have moderate risk levels than high risk levels. And, absent extraordinary skill levels, not really imaginable, the concentrated portfolio of just 20 good stocks is a dinosaur. The core–satellite idea is no longer useful when one conceives of manager selection as an optimization problem.

To illustrate this smooth shift among types of managers, examine the allocations at different risk levels in the example case in the appendix. It shows the allocations across a set of candidate managers including an equity index fund, a risk-controlled active manager, two traditional active managers, and a concentrated manager.

WHAT DOES A PORTFOLIO THAT REFLECTS THESE PRINCIPLES LOOK LIKE?

Having built the case for regarding manager structure and selection as an optimization problem, reflecting the reality of pure active return and risk as the real dimensions of active management, we can state what a portfolio reflecting these principles might look like. Moreover, a portfolio reflecting the principles we've advanced should have much the same characteristics whether one formally optimizes or not. Not everyone has the time, focus, or patience to run an optimizer, and we're all equipped with rather good fuzzy optimizers above our shoulders.

For investors who use an actual optimizer and for those who don't, our basic points can inform one's intuition, providing common sense that is directed by the nature of the underlying optimization problem:

1. Be disciplined in forming expected alphas, and in giving the greater weights to managers with higher ratios of expected alpha over active risk squared. Be rigorous when examining *historical* alphas, looking for clues to the future. If a manager's alpha is not statistically significant, why are you looking at it? Your final estimate of expected alpha should be strongly supported by fundamental analysis of the manager and its process.
2. The best portfolio is one that balances the two key dimensions of active management—maximizing pure active return and controlling the total active risk, summed across managers.
   - The portion of the portfolio that moderates its overall risk will consist of some combination of good risk-controlled active funds (sometimes called enhanced index funds) and traditional index funds, which together will likely represent roughly one-third to two-thirds of the total fund. If an investor has little tolerance for active risk, this portion will lean more toward index funds. If there is more tolerance for active risk, it will lean toward risk-controlled active funds.
   - Risk-controlled active funds will be more heavily weighted than equally skillful traditional active funds at most risk levels chosen by institutional investors.
   - Among traditional active managers, prefer skillful lower active risk managers over higher-risk, concentrated managers. Bias toward diversified portfolios, away from concentration (unless completely carried away by the concentrated manager's extraordinary forecasting skill).
   - Good market-neutral long-short funds will receive a substantial weight for investors not limited to long-only managers.[21]
3. Set the overall active risk at a comfortable level, your risk budget. For US equities, a typical investor seems to be most comfortable (in our experience) at an overall active risk level of 1.5% to 2.0%, and the very largest investors prefer even less active risk (between 0.75% and 1.25%).
4. Keep a careful eye on misfit risk, trying to minimize it while still maximizing expected alpha. If you don't use an optimizer designed especially for this purpose, you'll have to use a style map or effective asset mix table as a supporting tool.

21 And alphas delivered by high information ratio managers sourced in one asset class can, at least theoretically, be ported to another asset class (where, perhaps, high information ratio managers are scarce) by the use of futures or other derivatives. Such a portable alpha strategy is most frequently used to add alpha, generated in hedge fund programs, to an equity or fixed-income account.

CONCLUSION: MANAGING IN THE RIGHT DIMENSIONS

Two first principles emerged decades ago from the basic academic work in finance. The first is Harry Markowitz's observation that investors should be concerned about risk as well as return, which he shaped into the mandate that investors build mean-variance efficient portfolios using an optimizer. The second is William Sharpe's demonstration that the total risk of an investment can be broken into policy risk, which is rewarded by an equity risk premium, and active risk, which is a zero-sum game when summed across managers and thus not rewarded on average.

We have added the observation that manager skill levels really do differ. In addition, capital markets aren't completely efficient. As a result, someone is going to win the active game due to real skill—not just luck or random variation—even while someone else is losing. It pays for the skillful investor to try to discern who will be the winners, giving active management a vital role in the portfolio.

We note that while the payoff to market-related (policy) risk is linearly related to the amount of policy risk taken, this is not true of pure active risk, even conditional on the manager having real skill. Without skill, there is no payoff for pure active risk. In the presence of skill, there is a payoff, declining as a proportion of pure active risk as the amount of risk taken increases (it does not decline for unconstrained, long-short strategies).

There are some logical consequences of this view of the world. First, investors should build efficient, or optimized, portfolios of managers just as they should of asset classes (or securities within an asset class). Market or policy risk and return are commonly managed through the strategic asset allocation process. We are suggesting that the active risk decision across the portfolio of managers, as uncorrelated with policy, can and should be managed through its own separate optimization process.

To do so, investors must estimate the expected alpha for each manager. Let's spend a moment recalling the importance of this step.

An investor must meet two conditions if he or she is to hire active managers (see Waring, Harbert, and Siegel [2001] and Waring et al. [2000]). First, one must believe that superior managers really do exist. This is easy, if one accepts that managers differ in their skill levels. Second, but harder, investors must believe that they can identify which ones will be the winners. To accomplish this, you need to be able to make specific alpha forecasts for managers, forecasts that are somewhat more right than wrong. If you can't do that, you should just index.

At ordinary risk levels, and with manager skill levels generally equal, the optimization will give us a mix of index funds, risk-controlled active managers, equity market-neutral long-short funds, and moderate-risk traditional active managers. Most likely, it won't give us more than light allocations to concentrated managers. At typical risk levels, it will favor lower active risk managers over higher-risk managers.

Second, investors should disentangle pure alpha, the part of the active return that is the unique creation of the manager, from the various market factors that are in the manager's customized benchmark or normal portfolio. The manager's job is to beat this customized benchmark, not the naive asset class return. Moreover, when investors make alpha forecasts for managers, it is this pure alpha that they should be forecasting.

We can let the optimization process reduce the net misfit risk across all managers, balancing value managers appropriately against growth, and large-cap managers against small, so that the portfolio of managers looks as much like the investor's benchmark as is sensible. This is important. If the collection of the managers' market-related risks doesn't look like the benchmark, the investor's strategic asset allocation policy has been changed.

Managing active managers in these dimensions is simpler than in conventional practice—we are dealing with risk and return, the basic building blocks of finance. Yet it is at the same time more complex; the difficult task of specifying scalar values for pure alpha and for misfit risk replaces the easier task of just filling out discrete style boxes. But the scalar approach is the only one that reflects reality. We don't want to pretend that the world is simple when it is complex and there are fine gradations. As Einstein is reported to have said, "Everything should be made as simple as possible but no simpler."[22]

Active management offers the skillful an opportunity to influence the portfolio meaningfully, by adding pure alpha. For those confident of their skill, the question is not whether to use active management, but how. Hard-working people have entrusted us, the community of investors and asset managers, with trillions of dollars. We owe them nothing less than the best application of sound financial knowledge that we can deliver.

We know that the first principles synthesized here are valid, to the extent that today's understanding of economic science allows us to make such a claim. Let's apply these principles the best that we realistically can.

22 Although there is no written record of this statement, Peter Neumann, a former Stanford University professor who knew Einstein personally, writes, "I was probably just one of many people who heard him say something like [this]" (see www.csl.sri.com/users/neumann/neumann.html).

APPENDIX: MANAGER STRUCTURE OPTIMIZATION EXAMPLE

Our example below shows a stylized manager structure optimization case. The alpha assumption is entirely artificial, assuming a constant pure information ratio of 0.05.

At a typical 2% active risk level, the optimal portfolio would be about half traditional active and half risk-controlled active, with no index fund. The declining holdings of index funds and their replacement by risk-controlled active funds demonstrate the point made in our discussion of core-satellite investing. The concentrated manager receives only a small allocation, contrary to some core-satellite interpretations.

To make the best possible case for choosing concentrated managers, we use the same information ratio of pure alpha to active risk for the concentrated manager as for the others. In the real world, and assuming equal skill, the long-only constraint would cause the concentrated manager's information ratio to be much lower than the others, so these small allocations are in reality much overstated.

Manager Assumptions

Manager	Expected Alpha	Expected Active Risk
Index Fund (Russell 3000)	0.00%	0.00%
Risk-Controlled Active Mgr (Russell 3000)	0.75%	1.50%
Growth Fund (80% R3 Growth 20% R3 Value)	2.50%	5.00%
Value Fund (20% R3 Growth 80% R3 Value)	2.50%	5.00%
Concentrated Fund (Russell 3000)	9.00%	18.00%

Capital Market Assumptions *

Style Index	Expected Total Risk	Correlations			
		R1 G	R1 V	R2 G	R2 V
Russell 1000 Growth	19.39%	1.00			
Russell 1000 Value	14.11%	0.70	1.00		
Russell 2000 Growth	25.44%	0.78	0.49	1.00	
Russell 2000 Value	14.24%	0.55	0.70	0.76	1.00
Equity Benchmark (Russell 3000)		46.6%	46.6%	3.4%	3.4%

* Based on 10 years of data (11/92–11/02)

Optimal Manager Allocations

	Active Risk Budget (%)						
	0.0	**0.5**	**1.0**	**1.5**	**2.0**	**2.5**	**3.0**
Index Fund	100.0	72.2	44.4	15.8	0.0	0.0	0.0
Risk-Controlled Active Mgr	0.0	16.5	33.0	50.0	52.5	38.7	17.2
Traditional Active: Total	0.0	11.3	22.6	34.2	47.5	61.3	82.8
Growth Fund	0.0	5.0	9.9	15.0	20.7	26.4	35.2
Value Fund	0.0	5.0	9.9	15.0	20.7	26.4	35.2
Concentrated Fund	0.0	1.4	2.8	4.2	6.2	8.6	12.4

Sponsor benchmark: Russell 3000 broad capitalization US equity.

REFERENCES

Banz, Rolf W. 1981. "The Relationship Between Return and Market Value of Common Stocks." *Journal of Financial Economics*, March:3–18.

Basu, Sanjoy. 1977. "Investment Performance of Common Stocks in Relation to their Price–Earnings Ratios: A Test of the Efficient Market Hypothesis." *Journal of Finance*, June:663–681.

Basu, Sanjoy. 1983. "The Relationship Between [Earnings] Yield, Market Value, and Return for NYSE Common Stocks." *Journal of Financial Economics*, June:129–156.

Bell, Eric Temple. 1987. *Mathematics, Queen and Servant of the Sciences*. Mathematical Association of America reprint edition (December). See www.history.mcs.st-andrews.ac.uk/history/index.html.

Brinson, Gary P., L. Randolph Hood, Jr., and Gilbert L. Beebower. 1986. "Determinants of Portfolio Performance." *Financial Analysts Journal*, July/August: 39–44.

Brinson, Gary P., Brian D. Singer, and Gilbert L. Beebower. 1991. "Determinants of Portfolio Performance II: An Update." *Financial Analysts Journal*, May/June.

Carhart, Mark M. 1997. "On Persistence in Mutual Fund Performance." *Journal of Finance*, March.

Evans, L. John, and N. Stephen Archer. 1968. "Diversification and the Reduction of Dispersion: An Empirical Analysis." *Journal of Finance*, December: 761–767.

Fama, Eugene F., and Kenneth R. French. 1993. "Common Risk Factors in the Returns on Stocks and Bonds." *Journal of Financial Economics*, February: 3–56.

Grinold, Richard C. 1990. "The Sponsor's View of Risk." In Frank J. Fabozzi, ed., *Pension Fund Investment Management: A Handbook for Investors and Their Advisors*. Chicago: Probus.

Grinold, Richard C., and Ronald N. Kahn. 2000a. *Active Portfolio Management*, 2nd ed. New York: McGraw-Hill.

Grinold, Richard C., and Ronald N. Kahn. 2000b. "The Surprisingly Large Impact of the Long-Only Constraint." *Investment Insights*, Barclays Global Investors, May.

Grinold, Richard C., and Kenneth F. Kroner. 2002. "The Equity Risk Premium." *Investment Insights*, Barclays Global Investors, San Francisco, July.

Ibbotson, Roger G., and Paul D. Kaplan. 2000. "Does Asset Allocation Policy Explain 40%, 90% or 100% of Performance?" *Financial Analysts Journal*, January/February.

Kahn, Ronald N. 2000. "Most Pension Plans Need More Enhanced Indexing." In Brian R. Bruce, ed., *Enhanced Indexing: New Strategies and Techniques for Investors*. New York: Institutional Investor, Inc. Investment Guides.

Kahn, Ronald N., and Andrew Rudd. 1995. "Does Historical Performance Predict Future Performance?" *BARRA Newsletter* (Spring). Available online at www.barra.com/research/BarraPub/hpp-n.asp.

Kritzman, Mark P. 2003. "Value In – Garbage Out." *Economics and Portfolio Strategy*, Peter L. Bernstein, Inc. (January 15).

Leibowitz, Martin L. et al. 2001. *Equity Risk Premium Forum*. Sponsored by the Association for Investment Management and Research (November 8). Available at www.cfapubs.org/toc/cp.1/2002/2002/7.

Markowitz, Harry M. 1952. "Portfolio Selection." *Journal of Finance*, (March).

Markowitz, Harry M. 1991. *Portfolio Selection: Efficient Diversification of Investments*, 2nd ed. Oxford: Basil Blackwell.

Michaud, Richard O. 1998. *Efficient Asset Management*. Boston: Harvard Business School Press.

Michaud, Richard O. 1989. "The Markowitz Optimization Enigma: Is 'Optimized' Optimal?" *Financial Analysts Journal*, January/February.

Reinganum, Marc R. 1981. "Misspecification of Capital Asset Pricing: Empirical Anomalies Based on Earnings Yields and Market Values." *Journal of Financial Economics*, March:19–46.

Ross, Stephen A. 1976. "The Arbitrage Theory of Capital Asset Pricing." *Journal of Economic Theory* (December), 341–360.

Sharpe, William F. 1991. "The Arithmetic of Active Management." *Financial Analysts Journal*, (January/February).

Sharpe, William F. 1992. "Asset Allocation: Management Style and Performance Measurement." *Journal of Portfolio Management*, Winter: 7–19.

Sharpe, William F. 1964. "Capital Asset Prices: A Theory of Market Equilibrium under Conditions of Risk." *Journal of Finance*, September:425–442.

Sharpe, William F. 1988. "Determining a Fund's Effective Asset Mix" (corrected version). *Investment Management Review*, November/December: 59–69.

Sharpe, William F. 1974. "Imputing Expected Security Returns from Portfolio Composition." *Journal of Financial and Quantitative Analysis*, June: 463–472.

Surz, Ronald J., Dale Stevens, and Mark Wimer. 1999. "The Importance of Investment Policy." *Journal of Investing*, (Winter).

Waring, M. Barton, Duane Whitney, John Pirone, and Charles Castille. 2000. "Optimizing Manager Structure and Budgeting Manager Risk." *Journal of Portfolio Management*, (Spring).

Waring, M. Barton, Lee D. Harbert, and Laurence B. Siegel. 2001. "It's 11 p. m.—Do You Know Where Your Employees' Assets Are?" *Investment Insights*, Barclays Global Investors (October).

Wermers, Russ. 2000. "Mutual Fund Performance: An Empirical Decomposition into Stock-Picking Talent, Style, Transaction Costs, and Expenses." *Journal of Finance*, (August).

PRACTICE PROBLEMS

The following information relates to Questions 1–5

John Lamari is an investment consultant who specializes in assisting pension plan sponsors with investment manager searches. Lamari is meeting the investment committee of the Yaba Corporation pension plan to discuss its search for an emerging market equities manager. The plan is based in the United States and currently employs three active managers: a manager of global fixed income, a manager of large-cap US equities, and a manager of large-cap equities in developed market countries.

Marcia Pedden, chairperson of the investment committee, tells Lamari that one of the primary objectives for adding an emerging markets manager is to increase returns while reducing risk in the plan. Pedden asks Lamari if this objective can be achieved given the higher risk typically involved with investing in emerging markets. Lamari responds with the following statement:

> Yes, it is possible to earn higher expected returns while lowering the expected total risk of the portfolio. Total risk has two components: 1) market risk and 2) pure active risk.

Pedden observes that the large-cap developed global equity manager currently employed by the plan has always held a small allocation in emerging market equities. Lamari states that a manager's failure to deliver the expected exposure represents misfit risk, which the investment committee should consider when selecting the new manager.

Pedden asks Lamari what metric the committee should use to compare the risk and return profiles of the active managers under consideration. Lamari explains that his preferred metric is the pure information ratio.

Pedden tells Lamari that she has used style maps in the past to compare managers and asks Lamari about the limitations of that approach. Lamari replies with the following three statements:

Statement 1	Style maps do not reflect the continuous or scalar nature of manager style.
Statement 2	Style maps do not recognize the importance of managing misfit risk.
Statement 3	Style maps may result in investors taking on more active risk without a real expectation of pure active return.

Lamari explains to the committee that he conducts an optimization process to find the efficient frontier of managers. In Exhibit 1, Lamari presents the investment committee with active return and active risk data for three manager candidates for the emerging market equities mandate.

Exhibit 1 Active Return and Risk Data for Manager Candidates

	Active Return (%)	Active Risk (%)	Information Ratio
Manager A	6	8	0.75
Manager B	9	12	0.75
Manager C	8	11	0.73

1 According to William Sharpe, investors are rewarded, on average, for which component(s) of total risk as described by Lamari?

A Market risk

B Pure active risk

C Both market risk and pure active risk

2 To offset the misfit risk identified by Lamari, the committee should select an emerging market manager with a portfolio consisting of:

A emerging market equities only.

B emerging market equities and a small allocation to small-cap equities in developed market countries.

C emerging market equities and a small allocation to large-cap equities in developed market countries.

3 Which of the following *best* describes the denominator in Lamari's preferred metric for evaluating the risk and reward profile of a portfolio of active managers? The sum of the pure active:

A risk of all managers.

B return of all managers.

C risk of all managers plus net misfit risk.

4 Which of the statements made by Lamari regarding style maps is correct?

A Statement 1

B Statement 2

C Statement 3

5 Based on Exhibit 1, the optimization process will *most likely* favor:

A Manager A.

B Manager B.

C Manager C.

The following information relates to Questions 6–17

The New Star Fund (the Fund) is a large cap fund benchmarked to the S&P 500 Index. The Fund's investment policy statement specifies that the Fund may only employ active managers who invest in long positions in large cap stocks. The Fund currently employs three managers who use style indexes as their benchmarks, presented in Exhibit 1.

Exhibit 1 Benchmarks and Tracking Errors of the Fund's Active Managers (2013–2017)

Manager	Benchmark	Tracking Error
A	S&P 500 Growth Index	2.1%
B	S&P 500 Value Index	2.5%
C	60% S&P 500 Value Index/40% S&P 500 Growth Index	4.7%

Kevin Hurley, the performance analyst of the Fund, and Eric Tai, the risk manager of the Fund, review the managers' performance records over the past five years (2013–2017). Tai is concerned with Manager C's tracking error and discusses that risk with Hurley.

Later, Hurley suggests that the Fund can manage its risks by adopting a strategic asset allocation policy. Tai replies that the Fund can only manage some risks in this manner.

Manager B achieved the highest active return among the three managers. Hurley is very impressed and suggests investing more with Manager B. Following a review of Manager B's holdings, Tai notes that Manager B invests a substantial amount in growth stocks. Tai says these holdings are a risk to the Fund and suggests replacing the manager.

Hurley questions Tai's suggestion to terminate Manager B and makes the following two statements regarding the risk introduced by Manager B's holdings.

- Statement 1: "This type of risk can probably be cancelled by the allocations made to other managers used by the Fund."
- Statement 2: "This type of risk does not contribute to the total active risk of the Fund and, therefore, has no impact on manager structure optimization."

Tai wants to calculate the pure information ratios for Manager B and for the Fund. He asks his three interns what the denominator of the equation should be in these two cases. Their answers are presented in Exhibit 2.

Exhibit 2 Suggested Denominators of the Pure Information Ratio

Intern	For Manager B	For the Fund
X	Pure active risk	The aggregation of pure active risks from individual managers
Y	Total risk	The aggregation of pure active risks from individual managers plus any net misfit risk remaining across the group of managers
Z	Pure active risk minus misfit risk	The aggregation of pure active risks from individual managers minus any net misfit risk remaining across the group of managers

Hurley and Tai review Manager A's return and benchmark return, along with the Fund's benchmark return, as shown in Exhibit 3. They discuss how to apportion the credit for Manager A's positive return.

Exhibit 3	Returns of Manager A and Benchmarks (2013–2017, annualized)
	Return
Manager A	14.25%
S&P 500 Index	12.18%
S&P 500 Growth Index	13.23%

Both Hurley and Tai agree to optimize the Fund's manager structure further by adding new active managers. Tai asks his interns to study two popular methods: mining historical data of active managers and manager structure optimization (MSO).

While reviewing the practice of mining historical data, the interns find three related comments on an online forum:

- Comment 1: "Evidence shows that past performance is a strong predictor of future results."
- Comment 2: "When a manager has a statistically significant positive alpha, there is a very high probability that the manager's alpha is actually different from zero."
- Comment 3: "When a manager's historical alpha is not statistically significant, we can conclude that the manager has no skill."

They also learn that the MSO method would require the Fund to estimate the expected alphas of each manager and the expected correlation of every manager's alpha with that of every other manager. The interns have different ideas about how to estimate the expected alphas. Intern X suggests making the estimates by filling out style boxes. Intern Y suggests giving explicit numeric estimates to all managers. Intern Z suggests selecting active managers first and then calculating their implied alpha forecasts through reverse optimization. The interns all agree to simply estimate each alpha correlation as zero.

After running the optimization, two new active managers are added to the Fund. The managers' expected active returns and information ratios are listed in Exhibit 4. Hurley and Tai discuss the asset allocations of both managers.

Exhibit 4 Active Returns and Information Ratios of New Active Managers

Manager	Expected Pure Active Return	Expected Information Ratio
D	2.0%	0.5
E	6.0%	0.5

6 The risk that Tai discusses with Hurley related to Manager C *most likely* results from:

A asset class returns.

B financial market volatility.

C the manager's stock picks within the asset class.

7 Which of the following risks can be managed by the Fund using Hurley's suggested approach?

A Misfit risk
B Policy risk
C Active risk

8 What risk does Manager B introduce to the Fund by investing in growth stocks?
A Misfit risk
B Active risk
C Market risk

9 Which statement made by Hurley, regarding Manager B's risk, is correct?
A Only Statement 1
B Only Statement 2
C Both Statement 1 and Statement 2

10 Which intern's choice of denominator for calculating Manager B's pure information ratio, as presented in Exhibit 2, is correct?
A Intern X
B Intern Y
C Intern Z

11 Which intern's choice of denominator for calculating the pure information ratio for the Fund, as presented in Exhibit 2, is correct?
A Intern X
B Intern Y
C Intern Z

12 Based on Exhibit 3, the return credited to Manager A's active management is *closest* to:
A 1.02%.
B 1.05%.
C 2.07%.

13 Based on Exhibit 3, how much of Manager A's return should be credited to the Fund's policy decisions?
A 12.18%
B 13.23%
C 14.25%

14 Which comment from the online forum is correct?
A Comment 1
B Comment 2
C Comment 3

15 Which intern's suggested methodology to estimate the managers' expected alphas is *most* appropriate?
A Intern X
B Intern Y
C Intern Z

16 Which of the following *best* supports the interns' choice of correlation estimate for every manager's alpha with that of every other manager?
A Alpha histories always show zero correlations
B The chosen method requires active manager returns with low correlations
C Managers' pure alphas tend to have low correlations because market-related risk factors are removed from pure alphas

17 Based on Exhibit 4, when compared with Manager E, Manager D's holdings weight is *most likely*:

A smaller.

B the same.

C larger.

SOLUTIONS

1 A is correct. Only market risk, also known as policy, systematic, undiversifiable, or beta risk, is rewarded. Pure active risk, in contrast, cannot be rewarded, on average, because active managers are betting against each other in a zero-sum game.

2 C is correct. The existing manager of large-cap equities in developed markets has created misfit risk by holding emerging market equities (even as a small allocation). By adding an emerging market equities manager that does just the opposite (that is, hold emerging market equities with a small allocation to large-cap equities in developed market countries), the misfit risk of the plan is reduced.

3 C is correct. The denominator of the pure information ratio for a portfolio of active managers would be the aggregation of the pure active risk of each manager plus any net misfit risk remaining across the group of managers.

4 C is correct. Style maps do not require investors to estimate the expected alpha of a manager. The result is that investors may take on more active risk without a real expectation of pure active return.

5 A is correct. The optimization process will most likely favor managers with low active risk. In this case, Manager A and Manager B have identical information ratios, but Manager A has lower active risk and is thus more likely to be favored by the optimization process.

6 C is correct. Tai discusses tracking error risk with Hurley. The standard deviation of the period-by-period pure alphas may be thought of as the pure active risk, representing the tracking error to the manager's customized benchmark. Active risk comes into the investor portfolio through the use of active managers who, while holding some components of the policy benchmarks, try to beat them by picking stocks within the asset class.

7 B is correct. Hurley suggests managing the Fund's risk by adopting a strategic asset allocation policy. Policy risk is usually managed by investors through their adoption of a strategic asset allocation (SAA) policy, with its attendant asset class benchmarks, all fully diversified and therefore subject only to market risk by definition.

8 A is correct. Manager B has a large-cap value benchmark. Manager B's investment in growth stocks is inconsistent with the benchmark, leading to misfit risk.

9 A is correct. The misfit risk of a single manager goes away if it is canceled by the misfit risk of an opposing character from another manager.

10 A is correct. The information ratio represents the amount of pure active return (pure alpha) delivered (or expected) per unit of pure active risk taken (or expected) by an individual manager, relative to its customized benchmark.

11 B is correct. Across the portfolio of managers held by the investor, the denominator would be the aggregation of the ω (pure active risk) terms plus any net misfit risk remaining across the group of managers.

12 A is correct. Manager A achieves a return of 14.25%, while his benchmark returns 13.23%. The Fund chooses Manager A's benchmark. So only the surplus return of 14.25% – 13.23% = 1.02% is attributed to Manager A's active management.

13 B is correct. The Fund chooses Manager A's benchmark, which has a return of 13.23%. Manager A can achieve this return, before fees, simply by investing in an index fund. Therefore, this strategy benchmark index return should be credited to the Fund's decision.

14 B is correct. A statistically significant positive alpha means that there is a very high probability (roughly 95% if alphas are normally distributed) that the manager's alpha really is different from zero. It is evidence of skill rather than luck.

15 B is correct. As the Fund hires active managers, it should make alpha forecasts explicitly, expressing a quantified degree of confidence in a given manager.

16 C is correct. The correlations of the pure alphas are often simply estimated as zero. Because the market-related risk factors have been eliminated by calculating a regression alpha, the pure active return is uncorrelated with the market factors.

17 C is correct. Based on the utility function for active management, the size of a manager's percentage allocation is directly proportional to the expected information ratio and inversely proportional to a lower level of active risk:

$$h_{mgr} \sim E\left(IR_{mgr} \times \frac{1}{\omega_{mgr}}\right)$$

Given the same information ratio, the holdings weight will be higher for the manager with a lower active risk. The information ratio for an individual manager is calculated as the pure active return divided by the pure active risk (IR = α/ω). Thus, the manager's active risk is the pure active return divided by the information ratio: $\omega = \alpha/\text{IR}$.

Manager D's expected active risk (ω) = 2.0%/0.5 = 4%

Manager E's expected active risk (ω) = 6.0%/0.5 = 12%

Manager D has a lower expected active risk (4%) than Manager E (12%), so Manager D will get a larger asset allocation.

Investment Performance Presentation

STUDY SESSION

Study Session 6	Investment Performance Presentation

TOPIC LEVEL LEARNING OUTCOME

The candidate should be able to assess claims of compliance with the GIPS standards, recommend corrective actions in the event of non-compliance, and evaluate verification procedures.

INVESTMENT PERFORMANCE PRESENTATION

STUDY SESSION

6

Investment Performance Presentation

At Level II, you will learn about the required and recommended provisions of the GIPS standards and how to apply them in practice. This study session presents and illustrates the application of the Standards.

READING ASSIGNMENTS

READING

15

Global Investment Performance Standards

by Carl Bacon, CIPM

Carl Bacon, CIPM, is in the United Kingdom.

LEARNING OUTCOMES

Mastery	*The candidate should be able to:*
☐	a. explain the fundamentals of compliance with the GIPS standards, including the definition of the firm, calculating total firm assets, and the conditions under which an investment management firm can claim compliance;
☐	b. evaluate the classification of portfolios as discretionary or non-discretionary in accordance with the GIPS standards;
☐	c. evaluate the appropriateness of composite construction according to the GIPS standards, including (i) inclusion of new portfolios and termination and switching of portfolios, (ii) treatment of portfolios with external cash flows, and (iii) linked performance of model or simulated portfolios;
☐	d. state the requirements and recommendations of the GIPS standards with respect to presentation and reporting;
☐	e. state the requirements of the GIPS standards with respect to disclosures;
☐	f. determine the portability of performance track records from a past firm or affiliation in accordance with the GIPS standards;
☐	g. explain benefits of verification.

INTRODUCTION

1

The Global Investment Performance Standards (the GIPS® standards) fulfill an essential role in asset management around the world. They meet the need for globally accepted standards for investment management firms (asset managers) and asset owners in calculating and presenting their results to prospective clients, prospective investors, and those who have direct oversight responsibility for asset owner assets, such as a board of pension fund trustees.

To appreciate the value of industry-wide performance presentation standards, consider some of the many ways in which unscrupulous firms or individual employees might attempt to gather and retain assets by misrepresenting a firm's historical record. In communicating with a prospective client, they could

- present returns only for the best-performing portfolios as though those returns were fully representative of the firm's expertise in a given strategy or style;
- base portfolio values on their own unsubstantiated estimates of asset prices;
- inflate returns by annualizing partial-period results;
- select the most favorable measurement period, calculating returns from a low point to a high point;
- present simulated returns as though they had actually been earned;
- choose a benchmark that casts the selected portfolios in the most favorable light during the measurement period;
- self-select return methodologies to ensure the most favorable return;
- include or exclude portfolios in composites according to their performance rather than objective strategy criteria;
- portray the growth of assets in the style or strategy of interest so as to mask the difference between investment returns and client contributions; or
- use the marketing department's expertise in graphic design to underplay unfavorable performance data and direct the prospect's attention to the most persuasive elements of the sales presentation.

Without established, well-formulated standards for investment performance measurement and presentation, the ability of a prospective client or a prospective investor to make sound decisions in selecting investment managers would be impaired. Individual investors and their advisers, as well as pension plan sponsors, foundation trustees, and other institutional investors with fiduciary responsibility for asset pools, need reliable information. The GIPS standards give them greater confidence that the returns they are shown fairly represent an investment firm's historical record. The GIPS standards also enable them to make reasonable comparisons among different investment management firms before hiring one of them. Evaluating past returns is only one dimension of the manager selection process, but it is an important one, and the due diligence legally and ethically expected of fiduciaries cannot be satisfied without it.

Global standards for performance presentation, including the requirement that a firm show each composite's investment returns alongside the returns of an appropriate benchmark, can lead to an informed discussion about the firm's investment decision-making process. The prospective client might ask, for instance, why the composite outperformed the benchmark in some periods and not in others, inviting the firm's spokespersons to explain past returns and to describe how the investment product is positioned for the future.

Although the GIPS standards can facilitate the comparison of investment managers through the use of properly calculated, fully disclosed historical results, they do not exempt the prospective client from a thorough investigation of the candidate firm's background, resources, and capabilities for the mandate under consideration. Due diligence in selecting an investment manager includes, among many other important elements, examining a firm's regulatory history, the experience and professional credentials of its decision makers, the soundness of its investment philosophy, the nature of its investment and operational risk controls, and the independence of its service providers.

The GIPS standards are ethical standards for investment performance presentation to ensure fair representation and full disclosure of investment performance. Firms that claim compliance with the GIPS standards must adhere to rules governing not only rate-of-return calculations but also the way in which returns are displayed in a performance presentation. They are required to make certain disclosures in a performance presentation; these disclosures assist prospective investors in interpreting and evaluating the reported returns. Prospective and existing clients and investors can have confidence that the information shown in a GIPS Report reflects the results of the presenting firm's past investment decisions. They are also assured that the returns are calculated and presented on a consistent basis and that they are objectively comparable for a given strategy to those reported by other firms claiming compliance with the GIPS standards.

The 2020 Edition of the GIPS Standards has three chapters:

GIPS Standards for Firms

GIPS Standards for Asset Owners

GIPS Standards for Verifiers

Organizations that compete for investment management business must comply with the GIPS Standards for Firms, which is divided into the following eight sections:

1 Fundamentals of Compliance
2 Input Data and Calculation Methodology
3 Composite and Pooled Fund Maintenance
4 Composite Time-Weighted Return Report
5 Composite Money-Weighted Return Report
6 Pooled Fund Time-Weighted Return Report
7 Pooled Fund Money-Weighted Return Report
8 GIPS Advertising Guidelines

There is also an essential glossary of defined terms as well as four useful appendices including samples of GIPS Reports, lists of composites and pooled fund descriptions, and GIPS advertisements. A **GIPS Report** is defined in the GIPS Glossary as either a GIPS Composite Report or a GIPS Pooled Fund Report.

Candidates are responsible for reading the Global Investment Performance Standards (GIPS®) for Firms 2020 in their entirety. The full text of the GIPS for Firms 2020 can be found at https://www.cfainstitute.org/-/media/documents/code/gips/2020-gips-standards-firms.ashx.

This reading supplements the GIPS standards themselves. This reading focuses on the fundamentals of compliance with the GIPS standards; composite construction, including the classification of portfolios as discretionary or non-discretionary; the requirements and recommendations of the GIPS standards with respect to presentation and reporting as well as disclosure; portability of investment results; and the benefits of independent verification.

MANAGEMENT COMMITMENT

Senior management's stated commitment to the spirit and objectives of the GIPS standards and steadfast willingness to invest the necessary time and resources are essential for a firm to achieve compliance with the GIPS standards. The implementation effort is most likely to succeed if senior management makes achieving compliance a high priority, clearly communicates the importance of the initiative throughout the firm, oversees the preparation of a comprehensive project plan, and establishes an adequate budget, with particular attention to consulting and information system requirements.

Some firms may wrongly assume that implementation of the GIPS standards involves "re-crunching" a few numbers and reformatting performance presentation tables. In fact, achieving compliance can be a complex, challenging, and potentially expensive undertaking. Simply adopting the GIPS standards as a means of passing the initial screening in request for proposal (RFP) competitions without addressing their underlying substance may lead to shortcuts that ultimately compromise the firm's application of the GIPS standards, deprive it of valuable internal benefits, and needlessly expose it to reputational and regulatory risk.

A firm must also have a high level of commitment from its compliance, investment management, operating, and marketing staff. Achieving and maintaining compliance with the GIPS standards typically involve an investment firm's portfolio accounting, market data services, information technology, portfolio management, risk-control, marketing, and compliance groups, as well as the performance measurement team. It is a complex process for investment management organizations to define and document policies, gather and validate input data, calculate rates of return, construct and maintain meaningful composites, and present investment results in accordance with the GIPS standards. Careful planning with the active participation of diverse organizational units is a critical element of the implementation project.

The GIPS standards consist of **GIPS Requirements** which *must* be followed in order for a firm to claim compliance, and **GIPS Recommendations**, which are optional but *should* be followed because they represent best practice in performance presentation. Firms must comply with all applicable requirements of the GIPS standards, including any Guidance Statements, interpretations, and Questions & Answers (Q&As) published by CFA Institute and the GIPS standards governing bodies.

2 FUNDAMENTALS OF COMPLIANCE

Section 1 of the GIPS Standards for Firms outlines the fundamentals of compliance with the GIPS standards. There are 39 required provisions in Section 1 covering issues including the following:

1 Properly defining the firm
2 Providing GIPS Reports to all prospective clients and prospective pooled fund investors
3 Correcting errors in GIPS Reports
4 Use of time-weighted and money-weighted rates of return in GIPS Reports
5 Creating and maintaining policies and procedures to support the firm's claim of compliance
6 Adhering to applicable laws and regulations
7 Ensuring that information presented is not false or misleading
8 Benchmark selection
9 Linking of theoretical and actual performance
10 Portability of returns from one firm to another

The GIPS standards are the authoritative source for candidates and provide official explanations for each section. Several of these provisions are elaborated on in the following sections.

2.1 Defining the Firm and Calculating Total Firm Assets

The definition of the firm is the foundation for firm-wide compliance and creates defined boundaries whereby total firm assets can be determined. The GIPS standards must be applied on a firm-wide basis; firms cannot claim to be in compliance with the GIPS standards with regard to only certain asset classes, investment strategies, products, or pooled funds that they manage. A firm cannot claim compliance with the GIPS standards until it meets the applicable requirements of the GIPS standards for a least a five-year period or since inception of the firm if the firm has been in existence for less than five years.

To comply with the GIPS standards, a firm must be an investment firm, subsidiary, or division *held out to clients or potential clients as a distinct business entity.* The GIPS Glossary defines a **distinct business entity** as a "unit, division, department, or office that is organizationally and functionally segregated from other units, divisions, departments, or offices and that retains discretion over the assets it manages and that should have autonomy over the investment decision-making process." Possible criteria for identifying a distinct business entity are the organization being a legal entity, having a distinct market or client type, or using a separate and distinct investment process.

An investment organization might include multiple GIPS-defined firms if these defined firms are genuinely distinct business entities, such as a private client unit and a hedge fund division of a larger firm. Even two entities within the same parent company offering substantially similar investment products but in separate geographic jurisdictions might be considered distinct business entities. The GIPS standards encourage the broadest, most meaningful definition of the firm. The scope of this meaningful definition should include all geographical (country, regional, etc.) offices operating under the same brand name, regardless of the actual name of the investment management firm.

The way in which the investment management organization is held out to the public is a key factor in defining the firm. For example, if a unit of a larger company specializes in providing investment management services to private clients and is marketed as a specialist in meeting the investment needs of high-net-worth individuals and family offices, then that organizational unit might qualify as a "firm" for the purpose of compliance with the GIPS standards. The unit's entitlement to be considered a firm under the GIPS standards could be further justified if it additionally were incorporated as a subsidiary and had its own dedicated financial analysts, portfolio managers, and traders located in a separate building or area of the company and reporting through a separate chain of command to the parent organization's senior management.

DEFINING THE FIRM

For small investment management boutiques, defining the firm may be a relatively easy task, but it can prove challenging for large firms or subsidiary companies.

Consider the case of a regional bank whose asset management department consists of two separate and distinct divisions, the private client division and the institutional division. The private client division, called Eastern National Bank Private Client Services, offers investment management to private individuals and families. The institutional division, called Eastern Institutional Asset Advisers, serves tax-exempt non-profit organizations, including pension funds and charitable foundations; it does not solicit or handle non-institutional business. Each division has its own investment management team, traders, marketing department, administrative personnel, and accounting department. After a few years of operating in this manner, the institutional division decides to achieve compliance with the GIPS standards, but the private client division makes a business decision not to implement the GIPS standards. The institutional division may nonetheless be in position to become GIPS compliant because it holds itself out to customers as a distinct business unit, with its own autonomous investment management, research, trading, and administrative team.

Based on the information provided, the institutional division appears to satisfy the conditions for defining itself as a firm for the purpose of compliance with the GIPS standards. Sample language might be, "The firm is defined as Eastern Institutional Asset Advisers, the institutional asset management division of Eastern National Bank."

However, if both divisions were to use the same investment process, approved security list, style models, and so on, were not held out to the public as separate business entities, and merely divided assets between private and institutional portfolios, then neither division alone could compellingly claim compliance. If the senior investment personnel of the private client division had authority to dictate the institutional division's investment strategy or tactical asset allocations or to mandate the investment of institutional clients' funds in specific securities, then the institutional division would likely not qualify as a distinct business unit having autonomy over the investment decision-making process and discretion over the assets it manages. If the two divisions were organizationally segregated but shared the same trading desk, the institutional division would have to determine whether its decision-making autonomy is compromised by the trading arrangement; if the traders merely fill the portfolio manager's orders, then the institutional division arguably remains autonomous, but if the traders actively participate in the identification of misvalued securities, a greater impediment to the autonomy argument would exist.

Defining the firm in such a situation calls for the scrupulous exercise of professional judgment, with due attention to the ethical objectives of the Global Investment Performance Standards.

In view of the complexity of modern organizational structures, it may require judgment to determine whether a given unit properly meets the definition of a firm. This decision has immediate and lasting practical consequences. Because the GIPS standards apply firm-wide, the definition of the firm will determine the extent of the initial implementation and ongoing compliance activities. It also establishes the boundaries for determining total firm assets. The phrase **total firm assets** refers to the aggregate fair value of all assets (whether or not discretionary or fee-paying) for which a defined firm has investment management responsibility. Firms must be sure that assets are not double-counted (e.g., for a portfolio that is attached to more than one composite) because counting assets more than once would not fairly represent total firm assets. Total firm assets include assets managed by subadvisers that the firm has authority to select but must not include **advisory-only assets**, uncalled **committed capital**, or overlay exposure.

The GIPS Glossary defines advisory-only assets as assets for which the firm provides investment recommendations but has no control over implementation of investment decisions and no trading authority. There is an important distinction between advisory-only assets, which are excluded from total firm assets, and non-discretionary portfolio assets, which are included. In the case of advisory-only assets, the firm has no direct authority to manage or trade the account. In the case of non-discretionary assets, firms are unable to fully implement the intended investment strategy.

If a firm wishes to report firm-wide advisory-only assets, it may present a separate value or, in addition to total firm assets, a combination of total firm assets and firm-wide advisory-only assets.

Committed capital is defined in the GIPS Glossary as pledges of capital to an investment vehicle by investors (limited partners and the general partner) or the firm. Committed capital is typically drawn down over a period of time. Uncalled committed capital is the amount of committed capital that has yet to be drawn into the investment vehicle.

If a firm wishes to report firm-wide uncalled committed capital, it may present it as a separate value or present a combination of total firm assets and firm-wide uncalled committed capital as a supplement to the required disclosure of total firm assets.

Firms may wish to provide firm-wide overlay exposure, and for overlay strategy composites, the firm is not required to report total firm assets and may instead report firm-wide overlay exposure.

2.2 Providing a GIPS Report to Prospective Clients and Investors

Firms must "make every reasonable effort" to provide a GIPS Report to all prospective clients and to all *limited distribution* pooled fund prospective investors. The GIPS Glossary defines a **prospective client** as any person or entity that has expressed interest in one of the firm's composite strategies and qualifies to invest in the composite. The GIPS Glossary defines a **prospective investor** as any person or entity that has expressed interest in one of the firm's pooled funds and qualifies to invest in the pooled fund. Existing clients and investors may also qualify as prospective clients and investors for any strategy that is different from their current investment strategy or pooled fund. Investment consultants and other third parties are included as prospective clients and investors if they represent individuals or entities that qualify as prospective clients or investors.

A GIPS Report is either a GIPS Pooled Fund Report or a GIPS Composite Report. A GIPS Composite Report may be provided to the prospective investor if the pooled fund is included in the composite. The requirement to make every reasonable effort to provide a GIPS Report is met if a prospective client or investor has received a GIPS Report within the previous 12 months. The GIPS standards differentiate between broad distribution and limited distribution pooled funds. The GIPS Glossary defines a **broad distribution pooled fund** as a pooled fund that is regulated under a framework that would permit the general public to purchase or hold the pooled fund's shares and is not exclusively offered in one-on-one presentations. In most jurisdictions, broad distribution pooled funds are well regulated. Because of both the complexity and diversity of laws and regulations applying to broad distribution pooled funds, which typically specify what must be included in the materials for these funds, as well as what must not be included, it is not required that a GIPS Report be provided to broad distribution prospective investors. If a firm wishes to provide a GIPS Pooled Fund Report or GIPS Composite Report that includes the broad distribution pooled fund to a broad distribution pooled fund prospective investor, however, it may do so.

The GIPS standards consider any pooled fund that is not a broad distribution pooled fund to be a **limited distribution pooled fund**.

The GIPS standards require that firms comply with all applicable laws and regulations regarding the calculation and presentation of performance, irrespective of whether the performance is presented in a GIPS Report or a report mandated by the laws of the jurisdiction. In the rare cases when laws and regulations conflict with the GIPS standards, firms are required to comply with the laws and regulations and disclose the manner in which the laws or regulations conflict with the GIPS standards. The GIPS standards also require firms to create policies and procedures to monitor and identify changes in and additions to laws and regulations regarding the calculation and presentation of performance.

Firms must also provide a list of composite descriptions to any prospective client asking for such information, and they must provide upon request a compliant presentation for any composite listed. Discontinued composites must remain on the list for at least five years after their termination date. Firms must also provide a complete list of pooled fund descriptions for limited distribution funds to any limited distribution pooled fund prospective investor that makes such a request, although the list need only include funds for which the prospective investor is eligible. The availability of these lists is intended to discourage firms from cherry-picking strategies to present to prospective clients and investors. Firms must also provide a complete list of broad distribution pooled fund names to any prospective investor upon request. Although this list is not required to include broad distribution pooled fund descriptions, a firm must provide a description of a specific broad distribution pooled fund to any broad distribution pooled fund investor who makes such a request.

2.3 Correcting Errors in GIPS Reports

Firms must correct material errors in GIPS Reports and provide the corrected GIPS Report to the current verifier, any former verifier, and current clients and investors that received the erroneous GIPS Report and make every reasonable effort to provide the corrected GIPS Report to all current prospective clients and investors that received the erroneous GIPS Report. The firm is not required to provide the corrected GIPS Report to former clients, former investors, former prospective clients, or former prospective investors. Material errors may also apply to benchmarks (whether or not the error was caused by the firm), incorrect or missing disclosures, and other requirements.

A firm that has been defined for the purposes of the GIPS standards may very well undergo subsequent changes in its corporate structure or organizational design. However, changes in a firm's organization are not permitted to lead to alteration of historical composite results. In fact, apart from correcting errors, historical composite results may not be altered.

2.4 Use of Time-Weighted and Money-Weighted Returns

Firms must present **time-weighted returns** unless certain criteria are met, in which case the firm may present **money-weighted returns**. The GIPS Glossary defines a time-weighted return as a method of calculating period-by-period returns that reflects the change in value and negates the effects of external cash flows. The GIPS Glossary defines a money-weighted return as the return for a period that reflects the change in value and the timing and size of external cash flows. Firms may present money-weighted returns only if (1) the firm has control over the external cash flows of the portfolios in the composite or the pooled fund *and* either (2a) the portfolio is a closed-end, fixed-life, or fixed-commitment portfolio *or* (2b) illiquid investments are a significant part of the investment strategy.

Time-weighted returns are intended to neutralize the timing impact of external cash flows and allow fair comparison of performance track records of managers with different cash flow experience. Fair comparison of investment management performance is the core of the GIPS standards; however, the GIPS standards recognize that time-weighted returns are not appropriate for all circumstances, in particular for illiquid assets, such as private equity, infrastructure, and real estate, and for specific fund structures, such as closed-end, fixed-life, and fixed-commitment funds for which the presentation of money-weighted returns remains dominant. It should be noted that control of external cash flows is a necessary condition to use money-weighed rates of return, but this alone is not sufficient; the portfolio must also meet one of the other requirements specified by the GIPS standards. Slightly different reporting requirements apply to GIPS Reports using money-weighted returns.

2.5 Maintaining Policies and Procedures

Firms must document the policies and procedures used in establishing and maintaining compliance with the GIPS standards. Those policies and procedures must be applied consistently. Completing and updating the firm's documentation of performance-related policies and procedures may prove to be one of the biggest contributions the GIPS implementation effort makes to effective operations management. Because preparing proper documentation is typically treated as less urgent than other business matters, it is not uncommon for refinements in policies and processes to be documented only in emails and memoranda. If these changes are not integrated into manuals or handbooks, over time, the existing documentation can become inadequate or inaccurate. Implementing the GIPS standards may help managers assemble resources and allocate time to upgrading their existing documentation. Often the effort to document longstanding policies and procedures leads to actions taken that improve internal controls and achieve operational efficiencies.

2.6 False or Misleading Performance Information

Firms must not present performance or performance-related information that is false or misleading. Showing a return calculation with a known uncorrected, material error is an example of providing false performance information, as is a presentation that implies that theoretical returns are based on actual asset performance. Showing total return portfolio performance against a price-only benchmark would be misleading. The "false or misleading" requirement is not limited to materials that reference the GIPS standards. However, the GIPS standards do allow a firm to provide any performance information specifically requested by an existing or prospective client or investor, even if the presentation of that information may be in conflict with the GIPS standards. Such information may be provided only in a one-on-one presentation to the prospective client or investor who made the request.

2.7 Claiming Compliance with the GIPS Standards

A firm cannot represent that it is in compliance with the GIPS standards using "except for" or other such language or make any other statements that might indicate partial compliance: No exceptions to the GIPS standards are permitted. Moreover, statements characterizing the calculation methodology used in a composite presentation as being in accordance with, in compliance with, or consistent with the GIPS standards or similar statements are prohibited.

Statements referring to the performance of a current portfolio as being "calculated in accordance with the Global Investment Performance Standards" are also prohibited except when a GIPS-compliant firm reports the performance of a segregated account to current clients or a pooled fund to current investors.

The GIPS standards represent more than just return calculations. They are ethical standards designed to ensure fair representation and full disclosure, and they rely on the integrity of input data; correctly developed, consistently applied policies and procedures; and appropriate presentation of performance.

A firm must notify CFA Institute of its claim of compliance by submitting the **GIPS Compliance Notification Form**. This form must be filed when the firm initially claims compliance with the GIPS standards, must be updated annually with information as of the most recent 31 December, and must be filed annually by 30 June.

2.8 Recommendations vs. Requirements

Recall that the GIPS standards consist of requirements, which must be followed without exception in order for a firm to claim compliance, and recommendations, which are optional but represent best practice in performance presentation. Firms should comply with the recommendations of the GIPS standards through such actions as updating GIPS Reports quarterly, being verified, and providing a GIPS Report to each current client on an annual basis. The GIPS Glossary uses the word "must" to describe a provision, task, or action that is mandatory or required to be followed or performed. The GIPS Glossary uses the word "should" to describe a provision, task, or action that is recommended to be followed or performed and is considered best practice but is not required.

EXAMPLE 1

Fundamentals of Compliance

1 With regard to the definition of the firm, the GIPS standards:
   - **A** recommend the broadest, most meaningful definition of the firm.
   - **B** require each regional office making investment decisions to be separately defined.
   - **C** do not allow multiple firm definitions within a single investment organization.

2 The GIPS standards:
   - **A** do not allow GIPS-compliant firms to state that any return calculation is in accordance with the GIPS standards.
   - **B** allow GIPS-compliant firms to state that the composite calculation methodology of any composite is in accordance with the GIPS standards.
   - **C** allow GIPS-compliant firms to state that any return calculation of a segregated account presented to a current client is calculated in accordance with the GIPS standards.

3 According to the GIPS standards, firms may present money-weighted returns if:
   - **A** the manager has control of external cash flows.
   - **B** illiquid investments represent a significant part of the investment strategy.
   - **C** the manager has control of external cash flows and illiquid investments represent a significant part of the investment strategy.

Solution to 1

A is correct. The GIPS standards encourage the broadest, most meaningful definition of the firm.

B is incorrect. The GIPS standards encourage the broadest, most meaningful definition of the firm and do not *require* each regional office making investment decisions to be separately defined.

C is incorrect. The GIPS standards do allow multiple GIPS firms within a single investment organization if they are distinct business entities.

Solution to 2:

C is correct. The GIPS standards allow firms to state that the performance of a current client or pooled fund investor is in accordance with the GIPS standards when presented to that current client.

A is incorrect because firms are allowed to state that the performance is in accordance with GIPS when reporting performance of a segregated account to current clients.

B is incorrect because GIPS-compliant firms are not allowed to say the composite calculation methodology of any composite is in accordance with the GIPS standards. Statements that indicate partial compliance are not allowed.

Solution to 3:

C is correct. Firms may present money-weighted returns if they have control of external cash flows and have at least one of four characteristics, one of which is that the fund includes illiquid investments as a significant part of the investment strategy.

A is incorrect. Control of external cash flows is necessary but not sufficient on its own to justify the use of money-weighted returns.

B is incorrect. Firms must have control of external cash flows; illiquid assets alone are not sufficient to justify the use of money-weighted returns.

3 DISCRETION

The firm's definition of discretion is based on its freedom to implement its investment strategies. A portfolio is discretionary if the firm is able to implement the intended investment strategy. For example, the manager of a fully discretionary domestic mid-cap value portfolio is free to purchase any stock issued in the investor's home country that meets the pertinent market capitalization and style criteria. The firm might define mid-cap stocks as those whose market capitalization falls within a certain range. Similarly, the firm might define value stocks in terms of their price-to-earnings multiple, price-to-book ratio, or dividend yield or other characteristics intended to distinguish them from growth stocks. In line with best practice, the firm and the client will agree in advance that the portfolio's investment objective is to outperform a specified benchmark that is an appropriate measure of success in the domestic mid-cap market. For instance, the firm might construct a custom benchmark that is acceptable to the client, or the firm and the client might agree to use a commercially available index that mirrors the domestic mid-cap market.

If the client imposes restrictions on the firm's freedom to make investment decisions to buy, hold, and sell securities or requires approval to be sought before initiating a transaction in the course of implementing the investment strategy, then the firm must consider whether the portfolio is, in fact, discretionary. In general, restrictions that impede the investment process to such an extent that the strategy cannot be implemented as intended may be presumed to render the portfolio non-discretionary.

Investors commonly set forth investment restrictions in investment policy statements (IPSs). In addition to articulating the investor's overall financial objectives, an IPS normally expresses a number of constraints intended to limit the investment risks to which the assets are exposed. For example, the IPS may limit an individual equity portfolio's economic sector exposure to a certain percentage of portfolio assets or a certain relationship to the comparable benchmark weight: "No portfolio shall hold more than 15% of assets or 125% of the corresponding benchmark weight, whichever is greater, in any given sector, such as consumer discretionary stocks or information technology stocks." A fixed-income portfolio may be constrained to hold no securities rated below investment grade and to maintain the portfolio's weighted-average duration within a specified range, such as 75%–125% of the benchmark duration.

These client-mandated restrictions are generally intended to shield the portfolio from losses that might arise from inadequate sector diversification, excessive credit quality risk, or unacceptable levels of interest rate risk. Investors must be careful to formulate constraints that achieve their intended risk-control objectives without unduly impairing the portfolio managers' ability to act on their professional judgment regarding the relative attractiveness of sectors and securities. In other words, a well-written IPS meets the client's need for risk mitigation while respecting the portfolio manager's discretion. The firm should discuss with the client any restrictions that are incompatible with the intended investment strategy. Upon accepting the investment management assignment, however, the portfolio manager is ethically (and perhaps legally) bound by the client's stated policies.

In some cases, the client's investment constraints may inhibit the portfolio manager's flexibility. A personal investor might prohibit investment in securities issued by companies operating in industries he or she considers socially unacceptable, such as alcohol, tobacco, or gaming. A corporate client might prohibit the sale of company stock, or a foundation might similarly ban the sale of "sentimental holdings," securities issued by the company in which its founder made a fortune. Additionally, legal restrictions may apply. For instance, a public fund might be statutorily precluded from investing in non-domestic securities. None of these constraints automatically renders a portfolio non-discretionary. Rather, in these and other cases, the portfolio managers must determine whether these restrictions materially affect the manager's ability to execute the composite strategy. In some cases where there are multiple portfolios with similar constraints (such as the prohibition of alcohol, tobacco, or gaming stocks cited previously), it may be appropriate to classify a portfolio as discretionary and include it in a composite with other, similarly constrained portfolios.

Recognizing that degrees of discretion exist, the firm must consider the interactions among client-directed constraints, the portfolio's strategy or style, and the investment process, notably including the financial instruments used. For example, a client's investment policy might prohibit the use of derivative securities, such as futures, swaps, and options. In this case, the firm must consider whether the restriction is pertinent. To take up the example of the domestic mid-cap stock portfolio again, the fact that the client prohibits the use of derivatives may be irrelevant if the manager simply buys, holds, and sells common stocks. If the use of derivative securities is central to the firm's implementation of the investment mandate, however, then the client's policy may render the portfolio non-discretionary.

In some cases, the pattern of external cash flows might make a portfolio non-discretionary. For example, if a client frequently makes large withdrawals, perhaps on a regular schedule, the portfolio managers might have to maintain such a high level of liquidity that they cannot truly implement the investment strategy as they do for other portfolios with a similar stated investment mandate, objective, or strategy.

The firm's definition of discretion establishes criteria by which the firm determines which portfolios must be included in a composite. If an actual, fee-paying segregated account is discretionary, it must be included in at least one composite; if it is not discretionary, it must not be included in any composite. What is discretionary to one firm might be non-discretionary to another. Likewise, what is considered discretionary to the client might be considered non-discretionary to the firm and vice versa. The firm must make the determination of discretionary status consistent with its definition of discretion. This determination must be documented and consistently applied over time.

EXAMPLE 2 DISCRETION

1 According to the GIPS standards, discretion is determined by the:

A firm.

B client.

C GIPS standards.

2 A firm defines discretion as the ability to implement its investment strategy for each portfolio in full. According to the GIPS standards, which of the following situations is *most likely* to be considered non-discretionary for this firm?

A Client A disallows the use of derivatives in its portfolios.

B Client B does not allow investment in "sin" stocks, such as alcohol, gambling, and armament companies.

C For Client C, the firm must request and receive approval for each trade in the portfolio (no request has been declined within the last year).

Solution to 1

A is correct. Discretion is defined and determined by the firm; the firm must have a clear written definition of discretion.

B is incorrect. Discretion is defined and determined by the firm. On the one hand, the client might consider a heavily restricted strategy as discretionary, whereas the firm might determine that the restrictions are so severe that, in effect, the strategy is non-discretionary. On the other hand, legally, a relationship might technically be non-discretionary; however, the firm might determine that it has sufficient flexibility to implement its investment strategy to classify it as discretionary.

C is incorrect. There is no universal definition of discretion; each firm must establish its own definition of discretion. What is discretionary to one firm may not be to another.

Solution to 2

C is correct. Requiring approval for each trade is *most likely* to be considered non-discretionary. The firm cannot implement its investment strategy in full if approval for certain trades are declined. The fact that no approval has been declined in the last year does not necessarily result in discretion unless the firm can demonstrate that the approval is simply a technical process in which approval is automatically given.

A is incorrect. Disallowing the use of derivatives is not *most likely* to cause a loss of discretion in situations where an asset manager does not use derivatives or there exists composite definitions that reflect this restriction on derivative instruments.

B is incorrect. Restrictions on holding certain types or classes of stocks do not normally indicate a lack of discretion, particularly if the composite strategy reflects this restriction or the asset manager's benchmark also reflects this restriction.

4 COMPOSITE CONSTRUCTION

A composite is an aggregation of one or more **portfolios** managed according to a similar investment mandate, objective, or strategy. The GIPS Glossary defines a portfolio as an individually managed group of investments. A portfolio may be a **segregated account** or a **pooled fund**. The GIPS Glossary defines a segregated account as a portfolio owned by a single client and a pooled fund as a fund whose ownership interests may be held by more than one investor. The composite return is the asset-weighted average of the performance of all portfolios in the composite. Creating meaningful composites is essential to the fair representation, consistency, and comparability of performance over time and among firms. Pooled funds must be included in composites if they meet a composite definition.

In order to promote fair representations of performance, the GIPS standards require firms to create and maintain composites for all strategies for which the firm manages segregated accounts or markets as a segregated account. Firms must include *all* actual fee-paying, discretionary, segregated accounts in at least one composite defined by investment mandate, objective, or strategy. Firms must maintain and make available information about all the strategies they manage using composites or pooled funds.

4.1 Creating Composites

The firm must create composites for the firm's strategies that are managed for or offered as a segregated account. The firm is not required to create a composite that includes only one or more pooled funds unless the firm offers the strategy as a segregated account. In order to prevent firms from presenting only their best-performing portfolios to prospective clients, the GIPS standards require firms to include all segregated accounts that meet certain criteria in at least one composite. The first requirement for composite construction reads, "All actual, fee-paying, discretionary segregated accounts must be included in at least one composite." It goes on to clarify that non-fee-paying portfolios may be included in a composite provided that they are discretionary and subject to the same policies and procedures as fee-paying portfolios, but non-discretionary portfolios must not be included in a firm's composites.

COMPOSITE CONSTRUCTION: PORTFOLIO DOCUMENTATION

The GIPS standards require that all data and information necessary to support all items included in a compliant presentation must be captured and maintained. At the outset of the implementation project, it is useful to develop a complete list of the firm's portfolios. The list can then be used to check that all documentation, such as investment management contracts, custody agreements, investment policy statements (IPSs), and compliance documents, are available and up to date. This exercise creates a good opportunity for managers and administrative staff to confirm that portfolios are discretionary and to verify target asset mixes, acceptable asset ranges, portfolio size, tax status, investment restrictions, and other characteristics pertinent to the portfolios' assignment to composites. It is also advisable to conduct a formal review and update of the master portfolio list annually. Doing so will help ensure that documentation is kept current and that portfolios are assigned to the correct composites, particularly if clients have modified portfolio mandates and constraints during the year. The review will also point out the need for the creation of new composites if a significant number of portfolios no longer fit the definition of existing composites or if a new investment strategy is launched.

Defining and constructing meaningful composites is a vital step toward achieving the ideal of fair representation and the goal of providing prospective clients with useful comparative information. Under the GIPS standards, composites must be defined according to investment mandate, objective, or strategy; composites must include all segregated accounts that meet the composite definition as documented in the firm's policies and procedures; and the composite description, including detailed criteria that determine the assignment of portfolios to the composite, must be made available upon request. The firm must not exclude portfolios from composites based solely on legal structure differences. Well-defined composites will be objectively representative of the firm's products and consistent with the firm's marketing strategy. It is a guiding principle of composite definition that firms are not permitted to include portfolios with different investment mandates, objectives, or strategies in the same composite.

The GIPS Glossary defines **composite definition** as detailed criteria that determine the assignment of portfolios to composites. Criteria may include but are not limited to investment mandate, style or strategy, asset class, the use of derivatives, leverage or hedging, targeted risk metrics, investment constraints or restrictions, and portfolio type (e.g., segregated account or pooled fund, taxable versus exempt).

The GIPS Glossary defines **composite description** as general information regarding the investment mandate, objective, or strategy of the composite. The composite description may be more abbreviated than the composite definition but must include all key features of the composite and must include enough information to allow a prospective client to understand the key characteristics of the composite's investment mandate, objective, or strategy, including the following:

- The material risks of the composite's strategy
- How leverage, derivatives, and short positions may be used, if they are a material part of the strategy
- If illiquid investments are a material part of the strategy

To differentiate between a composite definition and a composite description, it might be helpful to think of a composite description as focused on the description of the strategy represented by the composite. In contrast, a composite definition includes not only the composite description but also the detailed criteria that determine whether and when a portfolio is included in a composite.

Composite descriptions are disclosed in GIPS Composite Reports and on the list of composite descriptions. Composite definitions must be documented in the firm's policies and procedures.

EXAMPLE OF A COMPOSITE DESCRIPTION

Environmental, Social, and Governance (ESG) European Equity Composite

The Environment, Social, and Governance (ESG) European Equity Composite includes all segregated accounts and pooled funds that invest in European equity securities issued by companies that make a positive contribution to the environment and society through sustainable and socially responsible practices. Only securities of companies that meet our proprietary ESG score threshold are allowed. The strategy aims to provide long-term capital appreciation together with a growing income stream through investment in a portfolio of core equity holdings diversified by economic sector, industry group, and geography. Direct investments in illiquid, environmentally beneficial infrastructure projects are allowed to a maximum exposure of 10%. The strategy cannot use leverage or derivative instruments of any type. The ESG process may result in a more concentrated strategy than a fully diversified strategy. The benchmark is the XYZ European ESG Index in euros.

Further sample composite descriptions can be found in Appendix D in the GIPS Standards for Firms.

DEFINING COMPOSITES

One of the greatest challenges in implementing the GIPS standards is devising the set of composites that will most meaningfully represent the firm's products. The GIPS standards require each actual, fee-paying, discretionary segregated account to be included in at least one composite. What appears to be a straightforward exercise—defining composites and assigning portfolios to them—may prove rather difficult in practice.

A useful guideline is to build a set of composites that will accurately represent the firm's distinct investment strategies. With too few composites, a firm risks grouping diverse portfolios together into a single, overly broad composite subject to a wide dispersion of portfolio returns. With too many composites, in addition to incurring unnecessary costs, the firm runs the risk of creating narrowly defined composites that are too similar to other composites, contain too few portfolios or assets to be useful, or compromise client confidentiality.

Assuming that the implementation team has already defined the "firm" and "discretion" and compiled a master list of portfolios, the following is a common-sense strategy for reaching agreement on composite definitions.

1 Review the firm's organizational structure and investment process to see whether distinctive strategies can be readily identified. For instance, an equity adviser might have units specializing in one or more active management strategies as well as index fund construction and quantitatively driven enhanced indexing.

2 Review the firm's existing marketing materials, including, if possible, marketing materials from competitors and recently received requests for proposals (RFPs). The objective is to determine how the industry defines products similar to those the firm offers.

3 Construct a provisional framework using descriptive captions to identify possible composites.

4 Taking into consideration clients' investment policies, test how well the firm's actual, fee-paying, discretionary portfolios would fit the provisional framework. The inevitable identification of exceptions—that is, the discovery that portfolios that must be included in some composite do not really fit any composite—will lead to the redefinition of proposed composites or the creation of new composites. Several iterations may be needed.

5 Review the proposed set of composites for compliance with the GIPS standards.

6 Document the composite definitions in detail, and circulate the definitions for final review by all affected parties in the firm.

Of course, the most effective process for defining composites may differ from one firm to another in view of such variables as organizational structure, culture, and investment strategies. Nonetheless, composite definitions have lasting consequences, and it is highly desirable to have a plan for reaching consensus.

Firms may define composites on the basis of the portfolios' benchmarks, as long as the benchmarks reflect the investment strategy and the firm has no other composites with the same characteristics. This approach is particularly appropriate if the portfolios are limited to holding stocks that are held in the index.

If a firm manages portfolios with **Overlay Strategy**, the firm is required to create an overlay composite for an overlay strategy when the overlay strategy is managed separately from the underlying portfolio and the firm offers the overlay strategy as a segregated account. Firms are not required to create an overlay strategy composite when the overlay strategy is implemented as part of a broader strategy but may do so. The GIPS Glossary defines an overlay strategy as a strategy in which the management of a certain aspect of an investment strategy is carried out separately from the underlying portfolio. Overlay strategies are typically designed either to limit or maintain a specific risk exposure that is present in the underlying portfolio or to profit from a tactical view on the market by changing a portfolio's specified risk exposure.

Reporting currency must not be used as a criterion for composite definition unless it affects the investment strategy. Portfolios with different base currencies may be included in the same composite, but their assets and returns must be expressed in the same currency as the composite. A hedging strategy will most likely require establishing additional composites; for example, global equities 100% hedged to the US dollar will most likely create a return profile very different from that of global equities 100% hedged to the Swiss franc.

Finally, portfolios sharing distinctive risk–return profiles may reasonably be grouped together. For example, enhanced index funds with similar benchmark-specific targeted excess returns and tracking error tolerances might naturally be clustered in a single composite.

Fixed-income composites can likewise be meaningfully and usefully defined in many dimensions. For example, composites might conform to (1) asset classes or market segments, such as government debt, mortgage-backed securities, convertible bonds, or high-yield bonds; (2) investment strategies, such as fundamental credit analysis, sector rotation, or interest rate anticipation; or (3) investment styles, such as indexing or core-plus. In whatever way a firm chooses to define the composites representing its investment products, they must be composed of portfolios managed in accordance with similar investment strategies or objectives.

4.2 Inclusion of New and Terminating Portfolios in Composites

The GIPS standards governing composite construction require all actual portfolios that are fee-paying and discretionary to be included in at least one composite. New portfolios must be included in a composite on a timely and consistent basis after the portfolio comes under management. Firms are required to establish, document, and consistently apply a policy of including new portfolios in the appropriate composites on a timely basis. Preferably, new portfolios should be included as of the beginning of the next full performance measurement period after the firm receives the funds. For example, if a portfolio is funded on 20 May, the composite should include the new portfolio as of the beginning of June. It may take time, however, to invest the assets of a new portfolio in accordance with the desired investment strategy, particularly when the portfolio is funded in kind (that is, with securities other than cash and cash equivalents) and the portfolio has to be repositioned to align with the firm's strategy or when the securities to be purchased are relatively illiquid (e.g., in emerging markets). Accordingly, the GIPS standards give firms some discretion to determine when to add the new portfolio to a composite. In such cases, the firm must establish a policy on a composite-by-composite basis and apply it consistently to all new portfolios.

In addition to winning new business, firms routinely close portfolios for a variety of reasons, including the loss of a client relationship. Under the GIPS standards, a firm must include a terminated portfolio in the historical performance of the appropriate composite through the last full measurement period that the portfolio was under management. In many cases, the firm loses its discretion over the portfolio upon being notified of a pending termination. The client may instruct the firm to stop buying securities immediately and to commence the liquidation of holdings in preparation for an outbound cash transfer on a specified date. Alternately, the client may halt trading and transfer control of the portfolio to a transition management organization to facilitate the transfer of assets to a new firm. When the firm being terminated thus loses its discretion over the portfolio, it should include the portfolio in the composite through the last full measurement period prior to notification of termination. For example, if a firm is informed on 20 May that its management contract is being terminated effective 31 May and is instructed to stop trading immediately, then the firm should include the portfolio in its composite through 30 April. It is incumbent upon the GIPS-compliant firm to have defined and documented its policies governing the removal of terminated portfolios from composites and, of course, to apply those policies consistently.

The GIPS provisions for composite construction additionally address the issue of minimum asset levels. A firm might decide that a particular composite will not include any portfolios whose value is below a specified level because the investment strategy can be fully implemented only for portfolios above a certain size. The GIPS standards indicate that if a firm sets a minimum asset level for portfolios to be included in a composite, the firm must not include portfolios below that asset level in that composite. The same provision further states that any changes to a composite-specific minimum asset level must not be applied retroactively.

The GIPS standards also recommend that firms should not present a composite presentation to a prospective client who is known not to meet the composite's minimum asset level. It is to be presumed that the firm has sound reasons for establishing a minimum asset level for a given strategy. Accordingly, it would not be in the prospective client's best interest to be shown a compliant presentation of a composite that does not represent a strategy available to that prospective client.

4.3 Switching Portfolios between Composites

The GIPS standards also stipulate that portfolios cannot be switched from one composite to another unless documented changes in the portfolio's investment mandate, objective, or strategy or the redefinition of the composite make it appropriate. The historical performance of the portfolio must remain with the original composite. This provision is important; if the GIPS standards permitted firms to transfer portfolios from one composite to another at will, an unethical firm might identify and exploit opportunities to improve the reported performance of selected composites by re-populating them with the portfolios whose investment results were most advantageous during the measurement period.

A portfolio can be switched from one composite to another if the client revises the mandate, objective, or strategy governing the investment of portfolio assets and the guideline changes are documented. For instance, a client might decide to modify the portfolio mandate from mid-cap value to large-cap value or from domestic equity to global equity with a corresponding change in the benchmark while retaining the same investment adviser to restructure and manage the "same" portfolio in accordance with the new strategy. Or perhaps a client might decide to allow the use of previously prohibited derivative securities, triggering a change in the investment strategy and making it suitable to assign the portfolio to a composite made up of portfolios that use derivatives.

Alternatively, a portfolio can be reassigned to another composite if the original composite is redefined in such a way that the portfolio no longer fits it. For example, a composite might initially be defined broadly to cover emerging market equities, and at a later date, the strategy may be explicitly broadened to include frontier market equities. A current portfolio whose mandate prohibits investments in frontier markets would no longer be eligible for inclusion in the redefined composite. This portfolio would be eligible to be transferred to a newly created composite that specifically excludes frontier markets. The entire performance history of the portfolio may be reflected in the new composite, although its past performance must also remain with the original composite. The GIPS standards are clear that changes to a composite definition must not be applied retroactively.

4.4 Treatment of Portfolios with External Cash Flows

The GIPS standards allow firms to temporarily remove a portfolio from a composite because of a **significant cash flow**, provided a policy to do so is established in advance. The GIPS Glossary defines a significant cash flow as the level at which the firm determines that one or more client-directed external cash flows may temporarily prevent the firm from implementing the composite strategy. Basically, a significant cash flow means that for a short period, the portfolio cannot follow the composite strategy while the cash flow (in or out) is being absorbed or processed; therefore, any performance during this period is not representative of the composite strategy. However, firms should be careful: If they have a single-portfolio composite and that portfolio experiences a significant cash flow, temporarily removing that portfolio from the composite will create a hiatus or gap in the track record. Alternatively, firms may use temporary new accounts to remove the effect of a significant cash flow—again provided that an appropriate policy is established in advance. The GIPS standards recommend that temporary new accounts be used to remove the effects of a significant cash flow, but because of the technical difficulties involved in implementing temporary new accounts, in practice it is more common to temporarily remove portfolios that are affected by significant cash flows from the composite.

ADDING, REMOVING, AND SWITCHING PORTFOLIOS

GIPS-compliant firms must have written policies setting forth when portfolios may be added to or removed from composites. These policies should be composite specific. A policy statement might read as follows:All new portfolios funded with cash or securities on or before the 15th day of the month shall be added to the appropriate composite at the beginning of the following month. All new portfolios funded with cash or securities after the 15th day of the month shall be added to the appropriate composite at the beginning of the second month after funding. All portfolios shall be deemed "non-discretionary" on the date notice of termination is received and removed from the composite at the end of the month prior to notification. The historical performance of terminated portfolios shall remain in the appropriate composite.

Policies similar to the previous example allow firms a reasonable amount of time to implement the strategy without delaying inclusion of the portfolio in the appropriate composite. Each firm should develop a policy that conforms to its own investment process while meeting the GIPS standards' requirement to include portfolios in composites on a timely basis. The firm's policy for adding or removing portfolios should also include language strictly limiting the switching of portfolios from one composite to another. The following is a sample statement for a policy:Portfolios shall not be moved from one composite to another unless the composite is redefined or documented changes in the client's guidelines require restructuring the portfolio in such a way that another composite becomes more appropriate. The portfolio shall be removed from the original composite at the end of the last calendar month before the event causing the removal occurred and shall be added to the appropriate new composite at the beginning of the calendar month following the date on which the portfolio is substantially invested. The historical performance of the portfolio shall remain in the appropriate composite.

4.5 Carve-Outs

The GIPS standards describe the proper treatment of asset class segments "carved out" of multiple-strategy portfolios. The GIPS Glossary defines a **carve-out** as a portion of a portfolio that is by itself representative of a distinct investment strategy. It may be used to create a track record for a narrower mandate from a multiple-strategy portfolio managed to a broader mandate. Typically, carve-outs are used by asset managers to demonstrate a competency to manage a strategy where standalone portfolios do not exist or are low in number with a short track record but for which portions of larger portfolios do exist. An example might be German equities within a European equity mandate.

The GIPS standards state that any carve-out included in a composite must include cash and any related income. Cash may be accounted for separately (often these are described as sub-portfolios) or allocated synthetically to the carve-out on a timely and consistent basis. Carve-outs that are managed including their own cash allocation within a broader portfolio are considered to be portfolios in their own right in the context of the GIPS standards.

Crucially, the GIPS standards require that any carve-out included in a composite must be representative of a standalone portfolio managed according to that strategy. Standalone portfolios typically include some degree of cash, which is, in effect, an overweight allocation to a non-correlated asset. This allocation can have a significant impact over time. If the carve-out does not include cash, it will not suffer the "cash-drag" effect that surfaces for typical portfolios over long periods of time given generally rising markets. This is why the GIPS standards are so explicit about including cash.

There are other potential issues associated with carve-outs: It can be difficult to allocate currency hedges appropriately, allocation decisions in a broader portfolio are made in the context of a broader benchmark rather than the narrower benchmark of the carve-out, and carve-outs tend to be more concentrated with greater specific risk than standalone portfolios.

If the firm chooses to create a composite based on a carve-out from an existing strategy, the GIPS standards require the firm to consistently carve out that segment, including allocated cash, from all portfolios managed to that strategy and include those carve-outs in the composite. This can be very difficult to accomplish.

When the firm obtains standalone portfolios managed in the same strategy as the carve-outs with allocated cash, the firm must create a separate composite for the standalone portfolios that gives any prospective client access to the "true" performance of the strategy and the ability to compare the performance of the composite based on carve-outs with the performance of the composite based on standalone portfolios managed to the same strategy.

If carve-outs with allocated cash are included in the composite, the firm must include the carve-out in the composite name, disclose that the composite includes carve-outs with allocated cash, disclose the policy to allocate cash to carve-outs, present the percentage of composite assets represented by carve-outs with allocated cash as of each annual period end, and disclose that the GIPS Composite Report for the composite of standalone portfolios is available upon request if it exists. In addition, the composite returns for each annual period and the composite assets as of each annual period end for which the composite of standalone portfolio exists must be included in the GIPS Composite Report of the composite that includes carve-outs with allocated cash. Collectively, these onerous requirements and disclosures are designed to discourage the misleading use of carve-outs with allocated cash where more appropriate standalone composites are available.

4.6 Model or Simulated Performance

Firms must not link **theoretical performance** with actual performance. The GIPS Glossary defines theoretical performance as performance that is not derived from a portfolio or composite with actual assets invested in the strategy presented. In the process of developing, testing, and refining new investment strategies, firms frequently construct model portfolios and use historical security prices to simulate theoretical performance in past measurement periods. Composites cannot include simulated, backtested, hypothetical, indicative, *ex ante*, forward-looking, or model portfolios. The firm must not combine different composites, pooled funds, or carve-outs to create a simulated strategy and present it as a composite.

EXAMPLE 3 COMPOSITE CONSTRUCTION

1 According to the GIPS standards, if a pooled fund qualifies to be included in a composite of segregated accounts:

- **A** it may be included in the composite.
- **B** it must be included in the composite.
- **C** it must not be included in the composite.

2 According to the GIPS standards, carve-outs:

- **A** must be included in composites that consist only of carve-outs.
- **B** can be included in composites only if they manage their own actual cash allocation.
- **C** can be included in composites if they manage their own cash allocation or if cash is allocated synthetically on a timely and consistent basis.

3 According to the GIPS standards, can firms link theoretical performance with actual performance?

- **A** No
- **B** Yes, provided that performance consists of model portfolios using historical security prices
- **C** Yes, provided that the theorical performance is based on the combined performance of actual composites

Solution to 1

B is correct. Pooled funds must be included in composites if they meet a composite definition.

A is incorrect. Pooled funds must be included if they meet a composite definition. Note the firm is not required to create a composite that includes only pooled funds unless the firm wishes to offer the strategy as a segregated account. In this question, segregated accounts exist; therefore, the pooled fund must be included in the composite.

C is incorrect. Pooled funds must be included if they meet a composite definition.

Solution to 2

C is correct. Carve-outs can be included in composites if cash is accounted for separately or allocated synthetically to the carve-out on a timely and consistent basis.

A is incorrect. The GIPS standards require that composites of standalone-only composites be created but do not require the creation of carve-out-only composites.

B is incorrect. Carve-outs with synthetically allocated cash are allowed.

Solution to 3

A is correct. Firms must not link theoretical performance with actual performance.

B is incorrect. Firms must not link model portfolios (theoretical performance) with actual performance.

C is incorrect. The firm must not combine different composites to create a simulated strategy. Such performance would be regarded as theoretical, which cannot be linked with actual performance.

5 PRESENTATION AND REPORTING

There are four reporting sections in the GIPS standards that detail the requirements and recommendations for reporting using the following types of returns:

- Composite time-weighted return
- Composite money-weighted return
- Pooled fund time-weighted return
- Pooled fund money-weighted return

Each of the four reporting sections is self-contained and includes requirements and recommendations relevant to that particular report. For the most part, the requirements for composite and pooled fund time-weighted returns are replicated, as are the requirements for composite and pooled fund money-weighted returns. With a few notable differences, disclosures are consistent across all four reports. Firms must include the information from the respective section depending on whether they are preparing a Composite Time-Weighted Return Report, a Composite Money-Weighted Return Report, a Pooled Fund Time-Weighted Return Report, or a Pooled Fund Money-Weighted Return Report.

After constructing the composites, gathering the input data, and calculating returns, the firm must incorporate this information along with the required disclosures in GIPS Reports based on the requirements in the GIPS standards for presenting investment performance. No finite set of requirements can cover all potential situations or anticipate future developments in industry structure, technology, products, or practices. The GIPS standards rely on the ethics and integrity of GIPS-compliant firms to determine when additional information and disclosures are called for.

5.1 Elements of the GIPS Standards Related to Presentation and Reporting

The GIPS standards contain numerous provisions for required and recommended elements of GIPS Reports. The provisions related to presentation and reporting can be found in the following sections of the GIPS standards:

- For GIPS Composite Reports that present time-weighted returns: Sections 4A and 4B
- For GIPS Composite Reports that present money-weighted returns: Sections 5A and 5B
- For GIPS Pooled Fund Reports that present time-weighted returns: Sections 6A and 6B
- For GIPS Pooled Fund Reports that present money-weighted returns: Sections 7A and 7B

The most broadly applicable provisions are discussed in the following subsections. Unless a provision is explicitly referenced as applicable to a specific GIPS Report (e.g., Composite Time-Weighted Return Report or Composite Money-Weighted Return Report), candidates can reasonably assume that the provision is applicable to all reports.

Returns

Requirements For GIPS Composite Reports presenting time-weighted returns, the firm must present at least five years of performance (or performance since the inception date of the composite if it is less than five years old). The firm must present an additional year of performance each year building up to a minimum of 10 years of GIPS-compliant performance. An appropriate total return benchmark return for each period must be included.

Returns must be clearly labeled as gross-of-fee or net-of fee returns.

For money-weighted reports, the firm must present the annualized composite since-inception money-weighted return for the composite and for the benchmark (unless the firm determines there is no appropriate benchmark) through the most recent annual period end.

For money-weighted reports, if a **subscription line of credit** is used, the firm must present the composite since-inception money-weighted return both with and without the subscription line of credit through the most recent annual period end. The firm is not required to present returns without the subscription line of credit when the principal was repaid within 120 days using committed capital drawn down through a capital call and no principal was used to fund distributions. The GIPS Glossary defines a subscription line of credit as a loan facility that is put in place to facilitate administration when the firm is calling for funds from investors. Alternatively, it can be used in lieu of calling funds from investors. These requirements are in place to clarify any impact of leverage caused by subscription lines of credit.

Recommendations The GIPS Standards recommend that the firm should present both gross-of-fee and net-of fee returns.

For time-weighted reports, the GIPS standards recommend that firms present cumulative returns for composite or pooled funds and the benchmark for all periods, equal-weighted composite returns, quarterly and monthly returns, annualized returns for periods greater than 1 year, and more than 10 years of performance.

It is recommended that for money-weighted reports, the firm present annualized since-inception money-weighted returns as of each annual period end.

Number of portfolios, measure of dispersion and risk

Requirements For each annual period, firms must present the number of portfolios in the composite at period end provided the composite had six or more portfolios at period end. Additionally, firms must present for each annual period a measure of the **internal dispersion** of the returns of the individual portfolio within a composite if the composite contains six or more portfolios for the entire period. Because there are different ways to convey dispersion, the GIPS standards require firms to disclose which measure of internal dispersion they present. This important requirement is intended to allow prospective clients and their advisers to see how consistently the firm implemented its strategy across individual portfolios. A wide range of results should prompt the recipient of the performance presentation to inquire about possible causes of the variability of returns to portfolios that are purportedly managed in accordance with the same strategy. It may suggest, among many other possibilities, that the composite is defined too broadly to provide meaningful information. The dispersion of the annual returns of individual portfolios within a composite can be measured in various ways; measures include but are not limited to high/low, interquartile range, and the standard deviation of returns (equal or asset weighted). The GIPS Glossary defines internal dispersion as a measure of the spread of the annual returns of individual portfolios within a composite.

For time-weighted reports where monthly returns are available, the firm must present the three-year annualized *ex post* standard deviation (using monthly returns) of the composite or pooled fund and of the benchmark as of each annual period end. The rationale is to give prospective clients an indication of the risk of an investment strategy as executed by the firms under consideration. Because all GIPS-compliant performance presentations include the same risk measure and that measure is based on historical experience rather than subjective inputs, the GIPS standards allow for some degree of comparability among firms that claim compliance.

Recommendations For all periods for which an annualized *ex post* standard deviation of the composite and the benchmark are presented, the GIPS standards recommend that firms present the annualized returns of the composite and the benchmark for the same periods. If additional *ex post* risk measures are relevant, the GIPS standards recommend that these also be included.

Assets and asset valuation

Requirements The firm must present the value of total firm assets and assets in the composite as of each annual period end.

If the composite presents net-of-fees returns calculated using actual investment management fees, the percentage of composite assets as of each annual period end held by non-fee-paying portfolios must also be presented.

The firm must also present the percentage of the total fair value of composite or pooled fund assets that were valued using subjective unobservable inputs as of the most recent annual period end, if material.

Recommendations The firm should present the percentage of composite assets consisting of proprietary assets.

The firm should present the percentage of assets in the composite that were valued using preliminary, estimated values as of each annual period end.

Currency

Requirements All required and recommended information in the GIPS Report must be presented in the same currency.

Expense ratio

Requirements For pooled fund reports, the firm must present the pooled fund expense ratio appropriate to prospective investors.

Committed capital

Requirements If the firm has committed capital, the firm must not include uncalled committed capital when calculating total firm assets.

If the portfolios in the composite have committed capital, the firm must present the following as of the most recent annual period end:

- Since-inception paid-in capital
- Since-inception distributions
- Cumulative committed capital
- Total value to since-inception paid-in capital (investment multiple or TVPI)
- Since-inception distributions to since-inception paid-in capital (realization multiple or DPI)
- Since-inception paid-in capital to cumulative committed capital (PIC multiple)
- Residual value to since-inception paid-in capital (unrealized multiple or RVPI)

If the firm chooses to present the amount of uncalled committed capital (separately from the calculation of total firm assets), the firm must also present committed capital for the same periods and clearly label uncalled committed capital as such.

Recommendations If the portfolios in the composite have committed capital, the firm should present as of each annual period end the same items listed previously as required for the most recent annual period end.

Supplemental information

Requirements Any **supplemental information** included in the GIPS Report must relate directly to the composite or pooled fund, must not contradict or conflict with the required or recommended information in the GIPS Report, and must be clearly labeled as supplemental information. Supplemental information is defined in the GIPS Glossary as any performance-related information included as part of a GIPS Report that supplements or enhances the requirements and/or recommendations of the GIPS standards. Meeting the intent of the GIPS standards may necessitate including information in GIPS Reports beyond existing requirements and recommendations. Supplemental information should provide prospective clients and investors with the proper context to fully understand the performance presentation. Supplemental information does not include information that is already required or recommended or non-performance-related information that is essentially narrative describing the firm's investment process, economic conditions, and general information about the firm.

Typical supplemental information includes the following:

- Attribution analysis for the composite and portfolios within the composite
- Segment returns
- Composite or portfolio-level holdings, country weightings, and sector weightings
- Peer group rankings

5.2 Disclosures

Disclosures allow firms to elaborate on the data provided in the presentation and give the reader the proper context in which to understand the performance. To comply with the GIPS standards, firms must disclose certain information in all GIPS Reports regarding their performance and the policies adopted by the firm. Although some disclosures are required for all firms, others are specific to certain circumstances and may not be applicable in all situations. This section discusses certain major disclosures, but it is not meant to be an exhaustive description of all disclosures that may be required to comply with the GIPS standards. Firms are not required to make negative assurance disclosures.

Once a firm meets all the applicable requirements of the GIPS standards, it must appropriately use the claim of compliance to indicate compliance with the GIPS standards. The GIPS standards specify the precise wording of the claim of compliance to be used only in a GIPS Report. The wording differs depending on whether a firm has been verified and additionally examined.

The compliance statement in a GIPS Report for a firm that has been verified is as follows:

> [Insert name of firm] claims compliance with the Global Investment Performance Standards (GIPS®) and has prepared and presented this report in compliance with the GIPS standards. [Insert name of firm] has been independently verified for the periods [insert dates]. The verification report(s) is (are) available upon request.

A firm that claims compliance with the GIPS standards must establish policies and procedures for complying with all the applicable requirements of the GIPS standards. Verification provides assurance on whether the firm's policies and procedures related to composite and pooled fund maintenance, as well as the calculation, presentation, and distribution of performance, have been designed in compliance with the GIPS standards and have been implemented on a firm-wide basis. Verification does not provide assurance on the accuracy of any specific performance report.

The compliance statement in a GIPS Report for a firm that has not been verified is as follows:

> [Insert name of firm] claims compliance with the Global Investment Performance Standards (GIPS®) and has prepared and presented this report in compliance with the GIPS standards. [Insert name of firm] has not been independently verified.

The firm must not exclude any portion of the compliance statement.

The firm must also disclose the following: "GIPS is a registered trademark of CFA Institute. CFA Institute does not endorse or promote this organization, nor does it warrant the accuracy or quality of the content contained herein."

Definition of the firm

The definition of the "firm" used to determine the firm's total assets and firm-wide compliance is a required disclosure. A clear explanation of the way in which the firm is defined enables the prospective client to understand precisely which investment organization (or unit of a larger entity) is presenting results, is claiming compliance, and will be responsible for managing the client's assets if hired. If a firm is redefined, it must disclose the date and describe the redefinition. If a parent company contains multiple firms, the GIPS standards recommend that each firm within the parent company disclose a list of the other firms contained within the parent company.

Composite and pooled fund information

Firms must disclose the composite or pooled fund description and must indicate the availability, upon request, of the firm's complete list of composite descriptions, limited pooled fund descriptions, and broad distribution pooled funds. This information enables prospective clients to determine whether the GIPS Report they have been shown is the most appropriate for their needs and to request GIPS Reports of any other composites or pooled funds of interest. Recall that the list must include not only all of the firm's current composites but also any that have been discontinued within the last five years; thus, poor performance in terminated composites or unsuccessful strategy launches cannot be hidden. Discontinued pooled funds are not available for investment and do not have to be shown.

Firms must also disclose the **composite creation date**, the date on which the firm first grouped one or more portfolios to form the composite. This is not necessarily the earliest date for which composite performance is reported. This information allows the prospective client to determine whether this is a long-established strategy or perhaps one that was created recently, perhaps for the purposes of the current presentation. Firms must also disclose the **composite inception date**, which is the initial date of the composite's track record, a quite different concept from that of the composite creation date. If a firm has redefined a composite, the firm must disclose the date and description of the redefinition. Similarly, firms must disclose any changes to a composite's name.

Further requirements apply in certain cases:

- If the firm imposes a minimum asset level for a portfolio to be included in the composite, this minimum asset level must be disclosed. This information alerts prospective clients to the investment manager's assumption that the strategy cannot be implemented in smaller portfolios.
- If the firm has adopted a significant cash flow policy for a specific composite, then the firm must disclose how it defines significant cash flows for that composite and the periods to which the significant cash flow policy applies.

Valuation policy

Firms must disclose if the composite's or pooled fund's valuation hierarchy materially differs from the valuation hierarchy recommended in the GIPS standards and must present the percentage of the total fair value of composite assets that were valued using subjective unobservable inputs as of the most recent annual period end, if material. Firms must also disclose that policies for valuing portfolios, calculating returns, and preparing GIPS Reports are available upon request. To cite obvious examples, GIPS-compliant firms should be prepared to respond to prospective clients' questions about their valuation methods and sources, return calculation methodology, or treatment of large external cash flows. The GIPS standards recommend but do not require that firms disclose material changes to calculation policies and/or methodologies.

If the firm adheres to any industry valuation guidelines in addition to the GIPS valuation requirements, the firm should disclose which guidelines have been applied.

Currency

Firms must disclose the currency used to express performance.

Benchmark description

In view of their importance for evaluating performance, it is not surprising that benchmarks are subject to disclosure requirements. The GIPS Glossary defines the **benchmark description** as general information regarding the investments, structure, and characteristics of the benchmark. In a GIPS Report, firms must disclose the benchmark description, which must include the key features of the benchmark or the name of the benchmark for a readily recognized index. If returns are calculated less frequently than monthly, firms must disclose the periodicity of the benchmark. If a custom benchmark or a combination of multiple benchmarks is used, the firm must disclose the benchmark components, weights, rebalancing process, and calculation methodology and clearly label the benchmark to indicate that it is a custom benchmark. For example, a firm might construct a custom security-based benchmark composed of securities that conform to the firm's investment process and the composite's strategy. Or, as another example, a firm's balanced composite might have a blended benchmark reflecting the strategic asset mix with reference to which the portfolios are managed. The benchmark in this case might be constructed by weighting capital market indexes with desirable characteristics, such as asset class representativeness and investability.

BENCHMARK PRESENTATION

Eastern Institutional Asset Advisers presents the performance of its Global Balanced Composite. The strategic asset mix of the portfolios in the composite is 50% global equity and 50% global bonds. The composite has a blended benchmark composed of capital market indexes weighted in accordance with the strategic asset allocation. Eastern Institutional Asset Advisers includes the following disclosure in the Global Balanced Composite's performance presentation:

> The benchmark for the Global Balanced Composite is composed of 50% XYZ World Index and 50% ABC Government Bond Index. The benchmark is rebalanced monthly.

If the firm determines that no appropriate benchmark for the composite exists, the firm must disclose why no benchmark is presented. If the firm changes the benchmark, the firm must disclose the date and description of the change. The GIPS standards recommend that firms disclose material differences between the composite investment mandate, objective, or strategy and the strategy represented by the benchmark. If the firm includes more than one benchmark, the firm must present and disclose all required information for all benchmarks presented. The firm must disclose if benchmark returns are net of withholding tax if this information is available. When using benchmarks that have limitations, such as peer groups, the firm should disclose these limitations. The firm must not use a price-only benchmark; it is clearly misleading to present composite and pooled fund returns against a benchmark that excludes income.

It is permissible to have more than one benchmark in a GIPS Report, but all benchmarks in the GIPS Report must adhere to the requirements applicable to benchmarks.

Fees

Numerous provisions address the topic of fees. The GIPS Glossary defines the **gross-of-fees return** as the return on investments reduced by any transaction costs and the **net-of-fees return** as the gross-of-fees return reduced by the investment management fees (including performance-based fees and carried interest).[1] Transaction costs are the costs of buying or selling investments. These costs typically take the form of brokerage commissions, exchange fees and taxes, and bid–offer spreads from either internal or external brokers. Custodial fees charged per transaction should be considered custody fees and not transaction costs. For real estate, private equity, and other private market

1 Performance-based investment management fees are typically contingent on the portfolio's exceeding a specified level of return, either an absolute return or a return relative to a benchmark. Carried interest, commonly used in private equity and real estate investing, refers to the profits allocated to general partners from the profits made by the investment vehicle.

investments, transaction costs include all legal, financial, advisory, and investment banking fees related to buying, selling, restructuring, and recapitalizing investments but do not include dead deal costs. Gross-of-fees returns, net-of-fees returns, or both may be presented. When presenting gross-of-fees returns, firms must disclose if they deduct any other fees in addition to transaction costs. Similarly, when presenting net-of-fees returns, firms must disclose if any other fees are deducted in addition to the transaction costs and the investment management fee and if the net-of-fees returns are net of any performance-based fees or carried interest. Also, if presenting net-of-fees returns, the firm must disclose if model or actual investment management fees are used. If model fees are used and gross-of-fees returns are not presented, the model fees used and the methodology used to calculate the model fees must be disclosed.

The firm must disclose the **fee schedule** appropriate to the prospective clients or prospective investors. As explained in the GIPS Glossary, the term "fee schedule" refers to the firm's current schedule of investment management fees or bundled fees appropriate to prospective clients or prospective investors. If the fee schedule includes performance-based fees or carried interest, the firm must disclose the performance-based fee description or carried interest description. If estimated transaction costs are used, the firm must disclose that fact, the estimated costs, and how they were determined. The firm must disclose if gross-of-fees or net-of-fees returns are used to calculate presented risk measures. If the composite contains portfolios with bundled fees, the firm should disclose the type of fees included in the bundled fee.

Leverage and derivatives

It is an important, albeit challenging, provision that firms must disclose the presence, use, and extent of leverage, derivatives, and short positions, if material. The disclosure must include a description of the frequency of use and characteristics of the instruments sufficient to identify risks. As a practical matter, it is admittedly difficult to explain in writing the use of leverage or derivative securities and the risks of their use, especially for the benefit of prospective clients or prospective investors who may not have been exposed previously to complex investment strategies. A clear explanation, however, will help prospective clients or prospective investors interpret the historical performance and evaluate the additional risk resulting from the use of leverage or derivatives.

For example, a fixed-income manager might use interest rate futures contracts as an efficient and economical means of adjusting the sensitivity of corporate bond portfolios to anticipated changes in interest rates. The firm might provide the following description of its use of derivatives: "Crystal Capital routinely uses US Treasury bond futures contracts to change the portfolios' modified duration. Because of their call features and credit risk, the corporate bonds held in the portfolio may experience price changes that do not closely match movements in the US Treasury bond futures contracts, resulting in portfolio valuations that differ from the targeted outcome."

Conflicts between the GIPS standards and laws and regulations

Firms must disclose if the presentation conforms with laws and/or regulations that conflict with the requirements of the GIPS standards. The manner in which any laws or regulations conflict with the GIPS standards must also be disclosed

Material changes

Firms are recommended to disclose material changes to valuation and calculation policies and methodologies, as well as the key assumptions used to value investments.

Significant events

Firms are required to disclose all significant events that would help a prospective client or prospective investor interpret the GIPS Report. For example, a firm must advise the prospective client or prospective investor if past results in a given strategy were achieved substantially by a portfolio manager who has since left the firm or if all key members of the research team supporting the strategy have resigned. This disclosure must be included for a minimum of one year and for as long as it is relevant to interpreting the track record.

Miscellaneous

For any performance presented for periods prior to the minimum effective compliance date that does not comply with the GIPS standards, firms must disclose the periods of non-compliance.

If the firm changes the type of return presented for the composite (e.g., changes from money-weighted returns to time-weighted returns), the firm must disclose the change and the date of change.

Firms must disclose the use of a subadviser and the periods a subadviser was used.

The firm should disclose how research costs are reflected in returns.

If a parent company contains multiple firms, each firm within the parent company should disclose a list of the other firms contained within the parent company.

Certain disclosures must be included for a minimum of one year and may subsequently be removed if the firm determines that the disclosure is no longer relevant to interpreting the track record, including the following:

- Changes to the name of the composite/pooled fund
- Retroactive benchmark change
- Correction of a material error
- Change in the type of return
- Significant events that would help a prospective client/investor interpret the GIPS report

Meeting the objectives of fair representation and full disclosure may call for providing more information than the GIPS standards minimally require. Practitioners are well advised to prepare compliance checklists to ensure that the disclosure requirements and, where feasible, the recommendations of the GIPS standards are met for the firm as a whole and for each composite or pooled fund presented.

EXAMPLE 4 DISCLOSURE, PRESENTATION, AND REPORTING.

1 According to the GIPS standards for money-weighted reports, firms must present:

A the annualized since-inception money-weighted return as of the most recent period end.

B the annualized money-weighted return for the five years as of the most recent period end.

C the annualized since-inception money-weighted return as of each annual period end.

2 The agreed benchmark for a particular composite strategy is price only. Can the firm include the price-only benchmark in the GIPS Report?

A No

B Yes, provided there is no total return alternative

C Yes, provided the benchmark is clearly labeled as price only

Solution to 1

A is correct. The GIPS standards require that firms present the annualized since-inception money-weighted return as of the most recent period end.

B is incorrect. The GIPS standards require at least five years of performance for time-weighted reports, not money-weighted reports.

C is incorrect. The GIPS standards recommend but do not require the annualized since-inception money-weighted return as of each annual period end.

Solution to 2

A is correct. The firm cannot present a price-only benchmark in a GIPS Report unless it is presented as supplemental information and in addition to a total return benchmark.

B is incorrect. The fact that there is no total return alternative does not alter the fact that total return performance compared with a price-only benchmark is misleading.

C. is incorrect. Clearly labeling the price-only benchmark does not solve the problem of providing only a price-only benchmark.

PORTABILITY 6

The "portability" of past performance is a complex and sometimes contentious subject, but the GIPS standards allow performance from a past firm to represent the historical performance of the new or acquiring firm and for that performance to be linked to the performance of the new or acquiring firm, on a specific composite or pooled fund basis, if the following requirements are met:

- substantially all the investment decision makers are employed by the new or acquiring firm;
- the decision-making process remains substantially intact and independent within the new or acquiring firm;
- the new or acquiring firm has records that document and support the reported performance; and
- there is no break in the track record.

A break may occur in a track record if an investment team transfers from one firm to another and for a period of time was not able or did not have discretion to make investment decisions. The track record of the past firm may be available with the records to support the performance—thus, it is *portable*—but the performance of the managers while at the first firm may not be linked to their performance at the new firm because of the gap or break in the track record. The performance prior to the break must be presented separately.

If a GIPS-compliant firm acquires another firm or affiliation, the firm is given one year to bring any non-compliant assets into compliance. One year might appear to be a long grace period, but portability is a complex area that frequently requires an entire year to resolve adequately.

EXAMPLE 5 PORTABILITY

1 The requirements for portability from a past firm to represent the historical performance of a new firm have been met on some but not all firm composites. The historical performance for the qualifying composites:

A may be linked to the performance of the new firm.

B must be linked to the performance of the new firm.

C must not be linked to the performance of the new firm.

2 In a friendly "lift-out" of an equity management team from one asset management firm (Silver Management, Inc.) to another (Gold Managers, Ltd.), the equity team wants to link its old track record to the new firm for specific composites only. All the investment decision makers from Silver Management, Inc., transferred, and the decision-making process remains intact and independent. The records supporting the old track record are complete and available to Gold Managers, Ltd. For a period of one month during the transfer from Silver Management, Inc., to Gold Managers, Ltd., trading was suspended and effectively non-discretionary. Can the team's old track record be linked to the new track record as desired?

A Yes

B No, because all composites managed by the equity team must be linked, not just specific composites

C No, because there must not be a break in the track record and the suspension of trading would cause a break

Solution to 1

A is correct. The GIPS standards allow linking on a qualifying composite-by-composite or qualifying pooled-fund-by-pooled-fund basis.

B is incorrect. The GIPS standards do not require linking if the portability conditions are met.

C is incorrect. The GIPS standards allow linking on a qualifying composite-by-composite or qualifying pooled-fund-by-pooled-fund basis; it does not matter that the entire past firm did not meet the conditions of portability.

Solution to 2

C is correct. The break in the track record is an issue; in all other respects, the track record is portable.

A is incorrect. The track record cannot be linked across a break in performance.

B is incorrect. The track record of specific composites can be linked, but there is no requirement to link all composite strategies of the team.

7 VERIFICATION

The GIPS standards include a separate chapter for verifiers. This chapter includes guidance that verifiers must follow when conducting verifications and performance examinations. The GIPS Glossary defines **verification** as a process by which an independent verifier conducts testing of a firm on a firm-wide basis, in accordance with the required verification procedures of the GIPS standards, and defines a **performance examination** as a process by which an independent verifier conducts testing of a specific composite or pooled fund in accordance with the required performance examination procedures of the GIPS standards. Verification and performance examinations must be performed by a qualified independent third party. Firms must understand the verifier's policies for maintaining independence and must consider the verifier's assessment of independence. Verification tests whether a firm's policies and procedures for complying with the GIPS standards related to composite and pooled fund maintenance, as well as calculation, presentation, and distribution of performance, have been, in all material respects, designed in compliance with the GIPS standards and implemented on a firm-wide basis. The minimum period for which verification can be performed is one year or since the firm's inception if less than one year.

Firms may choose to have a performance examination of a composite or pooled fund to provide additional assurance. A performance examination tests, for a specific composite, whether the firm has constructed the composite and calculated the composite performance in compliance with the GIPS standards and whether the firm has prepared and presented the GIPS Composite Report in compliance with the GIPS standards. A performance examination tests, for a specific pooled fund, whether the firm has calculated the pooled fund performance in compliance with the GIPS standards and whether the firm has prepared and presented the GIPS Pooled Fund Report in compliance with the GIPS standards. A performance examination may be performed only either concurrently with or subsequent to the completion of a verification.

Verification is intended to provide the firm and its prospective and current clients and pooled fund investors additional confidence in its claim of compliance with the GIPS standards. Verification does not ensure the accuracy of any particular composite presentation. However, in addition to making the claim of compliance on a firm-wide basis more credible, the verification process may benefit the firm in other ways: increased knowledge and expertise among the performance measurement team, consistently higher quality of performance presentations to current and prospective clients and investors, improved internal processes and procedures, improved and complete documentation, and greater confidence on the part of senior management that the firm is actually compliant. Of course, there are also the potential marketing advantages because many requests for proposals ask whether the performance presented complies with the GIPS standards and whether the firm has been independently verified. Above all, verification supports the guiding principles of fair representation and full disclosure of investment performance.

At the completion of the verification process, the firm must provide a management representation letter to the verifier confirming compliance with the GIPS standards. Based on the procedures performed, the verifier will express an opinion on whether the firm's policies and procedures for complying with the GIPS standards related to composite and pooled fund maintenance, as well as calculation, presentation, and distribution of performance, have been, in all material respects, designed in compliance with the GIPS standards and implemented on a firm-wide basis. If the verifier concludes that the firm is not in compliance, it must not issue a verification report. The firm must not state that it has been verified unless a verification report has been issued. After the verification is complete, the verifier should issue a recommendation letter to the firm describing specific findings, recommendations, and other areas for improvement arising from the verification.

The GIPS standards recommend firms undergo verification, but performance examinations are neither required nor recommended as part of the GIPS standards. Although voluntary, a majority of firms choose to be independently verified. Performance examinations, however, are less common and extremely rare outside the United States.

EXAMPLE 6 VERIFICATION

1 Independent verification:

A ensures the returns of a specific composite are accurate.

B tests, for a specific composite, whether the firm has constructed the composite and calculated the composite performance in compliance with the GIPS standards and whether the firm has prepared and presented the GIPS Composite Report in compliance with the GIPS standards.

C tests whether a firm's policies and procedures for complying with the GIPS standards related to composite and pooled fund maintenance, as well as calculation, presentation, and distribution of performance, have been, in all material respects, designed in compliance with the GIPS standards and implemented on a firm-wide basis.

Solution

C is correct. Verification tests whether a firm's policies and procedures for complying with the GIPS standards related to composite and pooled fund maintenance, as well as calculation, presentation, and distribution of performance, have been, in all material respects, designed in compliance with the GIPS standards and implemented on a firm-wide basis.

A is incorrect. Independent verification does not ensure the returns of a specific composite are accurate.

B is incorrect. This answer describes a performance examination, not a verification.

SUMMARY

The Global Investment Performance Standards meet the need for globally accepted standards for investment management firms (asset managers) and asset owners in calculating and presenting their results to prospective clients, prospective investors, and oversight bodies. This reading has made the following points:

- The GIPS standards are ethical standards that promote fair representation and full disclosure of an investment firm's performance history.
- The GIPS standards include provisions for fundamentals of compliance, input data, calculation methodology, composite construction, reporting, presentation and disclosure, advertising guidelines, and verification requirements.
- The GIPS standards must be applied on a firm-wide basis, and a firm may claim compliance only when it has satisfied all the requirements of the GIPS standards.
- Total firm assets include discretionary and non-discretionary assets, fee-paying and non-fee-paying assets, and assets managed by sub-advisers that the firm has authority to select but must exclude advisory-only assets, uncalled committed capital, and overlay exposure.
- Firms must make every reasonable effort to provide a GIPS Report to all prospective clients and to all limited distribution pooled funds' prospective investors.
- Firms must notify CFA Institute of its claim of compliance by submitting the GIPS Compliance Notification Form.
- Firms must present time-weighted returns unless certain criteria are met, in which case the firm may present money-weighted returns. Firms may present money-weighted returns only if the firm has control over the external cash

flows of the portfolios in the composite or the pooled fund and the composite or the pooled fund has at least one of the following characteristics: closed-end, fixed-life, fixed-commitment, or illiquid investments are a significant part of the investment strategy.

- The firm's definition of discretion establishes criteria to judge which portfolios must be included in a composite and is based on the firm's ability to implement its investment strategies. There is no universal definition of discretion; each firm must document its own definition of discretion.
- A composite is an aggregation of one or more portfolios managed according to a similar investment mandate, objective, or strategy. Creating meaningful composites is essential to the fair representation, consistency, and comparability of performance over time and among firms.
- A composite or pooled fund description is general information regarding the investment mandate, objective, or strategy of the composite or pooled fund strategy.
- Composite definition includes the composite description and detailed criteria that determine whether and when a portfolio is included in a composite.
- All actual, fee-paying, discretionary portfolios must be included in at least one composite. Portfolios are discretionary if client-imposed restrictions do not prevent the firm from implementing the intended investment strategy. Pooled funds must be included in a composite if they meet a composite definition.
- Firms must include new portfolios in composites on a timely and consistent basis. Terminated portfolios must be included in the historical performance of the appropriate composite up to the last full measurement period they were under management. A firm cannot switch portfolios from one composite to another unless documented changes to a portfolio's investment mandate, objective, or strategy or the redefinition of a composite makes it appropriate.
- The GIPS standards allow firms to remove portfolios from composites owing to a minimum asset level policy or significant cash flow policy, providing the policy was established *ex ante.*
- The GIPS standards state that any carve-out included in a composite must include cash and any related income. Cash may be accounted for separately (often these are described as sub-portfolios) or allocated synthetically to the carve-out on a timely and consistent basis.
- When a firm obtains standalone portfolios managed using the same strategy as a carve-out with allocated cash, the firm must create a separate composite for the standalone portfolios.
- If carve-outs with allocated cash are included in a composite, the firm must include the carve-outs in the composite name, disclose that the composite includes carve-outs with allocated cash, disclose the policy to allocate cash to carve-outs, present the percentage of composite assets represented by carve-outs with allocated cash as of each annual period end, and disclose that the GIPS Composite Report for the composite of standalone portfolios is available upon request if it exists. In addition, the composite returns for each annual period and the composite assets as of each annual period end for which the composite of standalone portfolios exists must be included in the GIPS Composite Report of the composite that includes carve-outs with allocated cash.
- Firms must not link theoretical performance with actual performance.
- The GIPS standards for composite presentation and reporting require for time-weighted returns that at least five years of annual compliant performance (or since-inception performance if the firm or composite has been in existence for

a shorter period) must initially be shown. The compliant performance record must then be extended each year until at least 10 years of results are presented. When money-weighted returns are presented, the annualized since-inception money-weighted return through the most recent annual period end is required.

- The GIPS standards include detailed disclosure requirements related to the firm, performance calculations, benchmarks, fees, composites, composite and pooled fund performance presentations, and other items. Additional disclosures are also recommended.
- The GIPS standards specify required items to be included in a GIPS Report presenting time-weighted returns, including composite or pooled fund and benchmark total returns for each annual period presented, the number of portfolios in the composite (if more than five) at annual period end, the amount of assets in the composite at annual period end, the amount of total firm assets at the end of each annual period, a measure of dispersion of individual portfolio returns within the composite, and the three-year annualized *ex post* standard deviation of composite and benchmark returns. Other items may be required in certain cases, and additional items are recommended.
- The GIPS standards specify required items to be included in a GIPS Report presenting money-weighted returns, including annualized composite since-inception money-weighted returns for the composite and for the benchmark (unless the firm determines there is no appropriate benchmark) through the most recent annual period end, the number of portfolios in the composite (if more than five) at annual period end, the amount of assets in the composite at annual period end, and the amount of total firm assets at the end of each annual period, and if a subscription line of credit is used, the firm must present the composite since-inception money-weighted returns both with and without the subscription line of credit through the most recent annual period end. Other items may be required in certain cases, and additional items are recommended.
- Acceptable measures of internal dispersion for composites include but are not limited to high/low, interquartile range, and standard deviation.
- If a firm uses a custom benchmark or a combination of multiple benchmarks, it must disclose the benchmark components, weights, and rebalancing process. The frequency of rebalancing can affect the reported benchmark return. Firms are not allowed to present only price-only benchmarks.
- Performance of a past firm or affiliation may be linked to or used to represent the historical performance of a new or acquiring firm if all the following requirements are met on a composite- or pooled-fund-specific basis: Substantially all the investment decision makers are employed by the new or acquiring firm, the decision-making process remains substantially intact and independent within the new or acquiring firm, the new or acquiring firm has records that document and support the performance, and there is no break in the track record.
- If a GIPS-compliant firm acquires another firm or affiliation, the firm is given one year to bring any non-compliant assets into compliance.
- Verification is a process by which an independent verifier assesses whether a firm's policies and procedures for complying with the GIPS standards related to composite and pooled fund maintenance, as well as calculation, presentation, and distribution of performance, have been, in all material respects, designed in compliance with the GIPS standards and implemented on a firm-wide basis.
- If a verifier concludes that a firm is not in compliance, it must not issue a verification report.

- The verification process may benefit a firm in terms of increased knowledge and expertise for the performance measurement team, consistently higher quality of performance presentations, improved internal processes and procedures, improved and complete documentation, greater confidence for senior management that the firm is actually compliant, and potential marketing advantages.
- Firms may choose to have a performance examination of a composite or pooled fund to provide additional assurance, provided a firm verification has also been conducted.

PRACTICE PROBLEMS

1 Which of the following firms may claim compliance with the GIPS standards?

A A two-year-old investment firm that has met all applicable requirements since its inception

B An investment firm that has met all applicable requirements for the most recent two years of its five-year existence

C A firm that presents itself publicly as a distinct business entity that provides investment recommendations to clients

2 To be in compliance with the GIPS standards, total firm assets *must* include:

A advisory-only assets.

B committed capital yet to be called.

C assets managed by sub-advisers hired by the firm.

3 Which of the following types of accounts is *most likely* to be prohibited from composite inclusion under the GIPS standards?

A Fee-paying, non-discretionary segregated accounts

B Discretionary, and non-fee-paying segregated accounts

C Pooled funds for strategies not marketed for segregated accounts

4 An existing client has requested, in writing, that her fully discretionary account be moved to a different, more aggressive strategy offered by a GIPS-compliant firm. In this case, the account:

A and its historical performance must be moved from the original strategy's composite to the new strategy's composite.

B must be moved from the original strategy's composite to the new strategy's composite, retain the historical performance in the original composite.

C must remain a constituent of the original strategy's composite, since the account is fully discretionary with an exemplary performance record.

5 In the event a discretionary portfolio experiences a cash flow deemed "significant" under the firm's significant cash flow policy, a GIPS-compliant firm:

A must use a temporary new account to remove the effect of the significant cash flow.

B must follow its existing policy and, if required, temporarily remove the portfolio from the composite.

C can suspend temporarily the significant cash flow policy and leave the portfolio in the composite if it is the composite's only constituent and where the removal of the portfolio would cause a gap in the performance record.

6 Under the GIPS standards, any client-directed restrictions on the management of a portfolio:

A must lead to a consistent discretionary versus non-discretionary classification for all of a firm's strategies.

B should cause a portfolio to be classified as non-discretionary, even if the constraint has minimal impact on the implementation of the intended strategy.

C could be material to the implementation of some strategies and immaterial to others, leading to different discretionary versus non-discretionary classifications for a firm's strategies.

7 A firm has a micro-cap equity strategy that has included only one portfolio since its inception five years ago. A new client interested in the same micro-cap strategy has a number of restrictions in his investment policy statement that the portfolio manager has determined will materially affect the manager's ability to execute the composite strategy. A GIPS-compliant firm must classify the new portfolio as:

A discretionary and include it in the existing composite.

B non-discretionary and exclude it from all firm composites.

C as either non-discretionary or discretionary and include it in a new micro-cap equity composite that reflect the client's restrictions.

8 Which of the following composite returns *must* be presented in a Composite Time-Weighted Return Report?

A Annual returns

B Net-of-fee returns

C Gross-of-fee returns

9 Which of the following items *may* be presented on a Pooled Fund Money-Weighted Return Report and labeled as supplemental information?

A Fund expense ratio

B Peer group rankings

C Proprietary assets as a percentage of fund assets

10 The compliance statement in a GIPS Composite Report:

A can be condensed at the discretion of the firm.

B indicates whether the firm has been independently verified or not.

C gives a report recipient assurance that the performance report is accurate.

11 In a GIPS Composite Report, firms *must* disclose:

A the historical fee schedules used to calculate net-of-fees returns.

B whether net-of-fees returns reflect the deduction of transaction costs.

C whether net-of-fees returns are based on model or actual management fees.

12 In a GIPS Report, firms *must* disclose the presence, use, and extent of any:

A significant use of leverage in the investment strategy.

B futures, options, or swaps, along with their characteristics.

C speculative short positions, excluding any hedges of long positions.

13 Which of the following is a GIPS requirement addressing the portability of an acquired firm's historical performance record to a new or acquiring firm?

A At least one of the investment decision makers is employed by the new or acquiring firm.

B The investment decision-making process remains substantially intact and independent within the new or acquiring firm.

C The new or acquiring firm has records that document and support at least 80% of the historical performance record of the acquired firm.

14 GIPS-compliant firms may have a performance examination conducted:

A on a specific pooled fund.

B in lieu of a firm-wide verification.

C by the firm's compliance department.

15 According to the GIPS standards, a firm-wide verification:

A must be performed every five years, at a minimum.

B can be performed for quarterly periods selected by the manager.

C benefits the firm by making its claim of GIPS compliance more credible.

The following information relates to Questions 16–19

Grey, Bank, & Turner (GBT) began as a multinational financial company focused on retail and commercial lending and personal investment management services for private individuals. Ten years ago, the firm created an investment management subsidiary called Palace Institutional Advisers (PIA) to provide investment management services to institutional investors. Gary Black is the director of performance at PIA and leads the project to bring PIA into compliance with the Global Investment Performance Standards (GIPS).

Black's first objective is to determine whether PIA can qualify as its own firm to comply with GIPS requirements for the definition of a firm. PIA shares an office location with GBT, offers similar investment strategies as GBT, and has a client type distinct from GBT. Frank Smith, the CEO of GBT, asks Black to include some composites managed by GBT within the PIA firm definition in order to increase the overall reported assets under management.

Next, Black identifies the accounts to include in PIA's High-Yield Bond Composite. The composite will include a qualifying account at the beginning of the first full month under management and exclude an account at the end of the last full month under management. Black identifies the accounts that meet the composite definition in Exhibit 1. The date that discretion was gained or lost is represented by the open and close dates.

Exhibit 1 High-Yield Bond Composite Account Activity

Account	Open Date	Close Date
1	18 March 2016	Still open
2	25 July 2016	13 December 2022
3	15 September 2016	Still open
4	5 December 2022	Still open

The High-Yield Bond Composite team's lead portfolio manager left the firm in June 2020. The departure of the lead portfolio manager was considered a significant event and remains relevant to the track record. The position was quickly filled with another senior member of the team.

16 Which of the following *best* supports defining PIA as a separate firm for GIPS purposes?

A Client type

B Office location

C Investment strategies

17 Implementing Smith's request to include GBT composites violates the GIPS requirements applicable to:

A PIA's proposed firm definition.

B GBT's partial claim of compliance.

C PIA's adoption of the broadest, most meaningful definition of the firm.

18 Based on Exhibit 1 and the High-Yield Bond Composite inclusion and exclusion rules, the accounts included in the December 2022 composite return are:

A Accounts 1 and 3.

B Accounts 1, 2, and 3.

C Accounts 1, 3, and 4.

19 Is PIA required to disclose the departure of the lead portfolio manager in the High-Yield Bond Composite disclosures?

A Yes

B No, because the lead portfolio manager departed over one year ago

C No, because disclosure for significant events is recommended, not required

The following information relates to Questions 20–23

Radford Street Capital is an investment management firm specializing in equity investments. The firm has one strategy, the US All-Cap Equity Strategy. Radford Street Capital has been in operation and serving retail clients for five years as of 31 December 2022 and is composed of an investment team that previously managed the same strategy at another firm, Delta One Capital.

The team has managed the strategy for a combined total of 9.5 years. All staff involved in managing the strategy at the prior firm moved to Radford Street Capital at its inception and took, with the permission of Delta One Capital, all records that document and support the performance. The decision-making process has remained intact from inception, and there was no break in performance.

In December 2021, Radford Street Capital created an institutional division to offer the same US All-Cap Equity Strategy managed by the investment team. The retail and the institutional divisions are together held out to the public as a single business entity. The institutional composite is made up of a single non-fee-paying account fully funded with the firm's own capital. A material portion of the composite assets at period end are valued using subjective, unobservable inputs. Because of different client characteristics, Radford Street Capital decided to publish two separate composites: a retail composite and an institutional composite.

Radford Street Capital's marketing department asked for a GIPS Composite Report based on the retail composite's performance presentation. The marketing department also asked the senior analyst to link the investment team's prior performance record at Delta One Capital. The senior analyst agreed and, in addition, proposed that the GIPS Composite Report be verified.

20 To comply with the GIPS standards, Radford Street Capital's current firm definition *must* include the:

A retail division only.

B institutional division only.

C retail and institutional divisions.

21 For a GIPS-compliant performance presentation, the institutional composite *must* provide:

A a measure of internal dispersion.

B returns clearly identified as gross of fees for each annual period.

C a benchmark that reflects the investment mandate, objective, or strategy of the composite.

22 For a GIPS-compliant performance presentation, Radford Street Capital's institutional composite *must* present the:

A three-year annualized *ex post* standard deviation.

B number of portfolios in the composite for all periods.

C percentage of composite assets valued by subjective, unobservable inputs.

23 Is Radford Street Capital required to link the performance record of its US All-Cap Equity Strategy from Delta One Capital to its retail composite?

A Yes

B No, because Radford Street Capital must not link these performance records

C No, because Radford Street Capital is not required but may choose to link these performance records

SOLUTIONS

1 A is correct. A firm that has met the applicable requirements since the inception of the firm may claim compliance with the GIPS standards, even if the period of compliance is shorter than five years.

B is incorrect because a firm cannot claim compliance with the GIPS standards until it meets the applicable requirements of the GIPS standards for at least a five-year period (if it has been in existence for five years).

C is incorrect because a firm claiming compliance with the GIPS standards must retain discretion over the assets it manages and should have autonomy over the investment decision-making process. In this case, the firm provides only investment recommendations.

2 C is correct. Total firm assets must include assets managed by sub-advisers selected by the firm. The total firm assets value is the aggregate fair value of all assets (whether or not discretionary or fee paying) for which a defined firm has investment management responsibility. By selecting a sub-adviser, the firm is demonstrating investment management responsibility.

A is incorrect because total firm assets must not include "advisory-only" assets. The GIPS Glossary defines advisory-only assets as assets for which the firm provides investment recommendations but has no control over implementation of investment decisions and has no trading authority.

B is incorrect because total firm assets must not include uncalled committed capital. Committed capital is defined as pledges of capital to an investment vehicle by investors (limited partners and the general partner) or the firm. Committed capital is typically drawn down over a period of time. Uncalled committed capital is the amount of committed capital that has yet to be drawn into the investment vehicle.

3 A is correct. Non-discretionary segregated accounts must not be included in a firm's composites, regardless of whether the account is fee paying.

B is incorrect because non-fee-paying portfolios may be included in a composite provided that they are discretionary and subject to the same policies and procedures as fee-paying portfolios. However, composite inclusion for non-fee-paying portfolios is not required.

C is incorrect because pooled funds must be included in a composite if the firm offers the strategy in question as a segregated account and may be included in a composite if the firm does not offer the strategy as a segregated account.

4 B is correct. The GIPS standards stipulate that portfolios cannot be switched from one composite to another unless documented changes in the portfolio's investment mandate, objective, or strategy or the redefinition of the composite makes it appropriate. The historical performance of the portfolio must remain with the original composite.

A is incorrect because the historical performance of the portfolio must remain with the original composite after the strategy change.

C is incorrect because if the portfolio's investment strategy has changed, it would be inappropriate to leave it in the composite for the original strategy when there is a composite for the new strategy.

5 B is correct. Under the GIPS standards, firms can temporarily remove a portfolio from a composite owing to a significant cash flow, provided a policy to do so has been established in advance.

A is incorrect because the use of temporary new accounts to remove the effect of significant cash flows is an optional alternative to a significant cash flow policy that temporarily removes portfolios from composites.

C is incorrect because a firm must follow any existing significant cash flow policy each and every time it is called for. If the only portfolio in a composite experiences a significant cash flow and must be removed under the policy, the composite's performance record will have a gap.

6 C is correct. A portfolio is discretionary if the firm is able to implement the intended investment strategy. A specific client-directed constraint may be very impactful to the implementation of some strategies and irrelevant to others. The constraint should lead to a portfolio being classified as non-discretionary only if it materially affects the manager's ability to implement the intended strategy.

A is incorrect because a constraint should lead to a portfolio being classified as non-discretionary only if it materially affects the manager's ability to implement her intended strategy, which could vary for different strategies.

B is incorrect because a constraint should lead to a portfolio being classified as non-discretionary only if it materially affects the manager's ability to implement her intended strategy.

7 C is correct. Client restrictions do not automatically render a portfolio non-discretionary. The firm must determine if the restrictions materially affect the manager's ability to execute the composite strategy. A new composite could be created that reflects the client's restrictions.

A is incorrect because client restrictions significantly inhibit the manager's ability to implement the micro-cap equity strategy, so the new portfolio cannot be included in the existing composite.

B is incorrect because client restrictions do not automatically render a portfolio non-discretionary. The firm must determine if the restrictions materially affect the manager's ability to execute the composite strategy and may create a new composite that reflects the client's restrictions.

8 A is correct. For Composite Time-Weighted Return Reports, the firm must present at least five years of annual performance (or performance since the inception date of the composite if it is less than five years old). The firm must present an additional year of performance each year, building up to a minimum of 10 years of GIPS-compliant performance.

B is incorrect because net-of-fee returns may be presented but must be clearly labeled. The GIPS standards recommend that the firms present both gross-of-fee and net-of fee returns.

C is incorrect because gross-of-fee returns may be presented but must be clearly labeled. The GIPS standards recommend that the firms present both gross-of-fee and net-of fee returns.

9 B is correct. Supplemental information is performance-related information included as part of a GIPS Report that supplements or enhances the requirements or recommendations of the GIPS standards. Required or recommended information is not supplemental information. Peer group rankings are an example of typical supplemental information.

A is incorrect because presenting the pooled fund expense ratio that is appropriate to prospective investors is a GIPS requirement, so it is not supplemental information.

C is incorrect because presenting proprietary assets as a percentage of fund assets is a GIPS recommendation, so it is not supplemental information.

10 B is correct. There are two different compliance statements: one that must be used by verified firms and one that must be used by firms that have not been verified.

A is incorrect because a firm must not exclude any portion of the GIPS compliance statement.

C is incorrect because verification does not provide assurance on the accuracy of any specific performance report, and this is included in the GIPS compliance statement.

11 C is correct. If presenting net-of-fees returns, the firm must disclose whether model or actual investment management fees are used.

A is incorrect because only the firm's current fee schedule must be disclosed.

B is incorrect because all returns must reflect the deduction of transaction costs, so that does not need to be disclosed. When presenting net-of-fees returns, firms must disclose if any other fees are deducted in addition to transaction costs and the investment management fee and if the net-of-fees returns are net of any performance-based fees or carried interest.

12 A is correct. Firms must disclose the presence, use, and extent of leverage, if material. The disclosure must include a description of the frequency of use and characteristics of the instruments sufficient to identify risks.

B is incorrect because the presence, use, and extent of derivatives must be disclosed only if material.

C is incorrect because the presence, use, and extent of short positions must be disclosed only if material. The GIPS standards do not provide any specific measures for determining whether a short position is "material."

13 B is correct. The investment decision-making process must remain substantially intact and independent within the new or acquiring firm in order to meet the portability requirements. If the process is substantially changed at the new firm, then the performance from the past firm will not be representative of the ongoing strategy.

A is incorrect because substantially all the investment decision makers must be employed by the new or acquiring firm in order to meet the portability requirements.

C is incorrect because the new or acquiring firm must have records that document and support all the reported performance in order to meet the portability requirements.

14 A is correct. A performance examination is a process by which an independent verifier conducts testing of a specific composite or pooled fund in accordance with the required performance examination procedures of the GIPS standards.

B is incorrect because a performance examination may be performed only concurrently with or subsequent to the completion of a firm-wide verification.

C is incorrect because verification and performance examinations must be performed by a qualified independent third party. The firm's compliance department is not an independent third party.

15 C is correct. Verification is intended to provide the firm and its prospective and current clients and pooled fund investors additional confidence in the firm's claim of compliance with the GIPS standards.

A is incorrect because firm-wide verification is recommended but not required by the standards.

B is incorrect because the minimum period for which a verification can be performed is one year or since the firm's inception if less than a year.

16 A is correct: To comply with the GIPS standards, a firm must be an investment firm, subsidiary, or division held out to clients or potential clients as a distinct business entity. Possible criteria for identifying a distinct business entity are the organization being a legal entity, having a distinct market or client type, or using a separate and distinct investment process. The fact that PIA specializes in investment management for institutional investors whereas GBT provides retail and commercial lending, as well as investment management to private individuals, gives PIA a distinct client type relative to GBT, providing support that PIA qualifies as a distinct business entity.

B is incorrect. PIA's sharing an office location with GBT does not support treating PIA as organizationally and functionally segregated from GBT. If PIA were in a separate building, operating from a different office location would further support that it qualifies as a distinct business entity.

C is incorrect. PIA implements strategies similar to those of GBT. This fact could call into question whether PIA retains autonomy over the investment management decisions of its strategies, potentially preventing PIA from qualifying as a distinct business entity.

17 A is correct. Smith asks Black to include certain composites managed by GBT into PIA's proposed firm definition. Doing so would violate PIA's proposed firm definition, which is based on PIA being a distinct business entity that provides investment management to institutional investors.

B is incorrect. PIA, not GBT, is the firm intending to claim compliance. If Smith were to request that only certain composites of GBT were to claim compliance, it would result in a partial claim of compliance, which is prohibited. In this case, however, Smith is asking Black to include certain GBT composites within PIA's firm definition.

C is incorrect. PIA is not *required* to adopt the broadest, most meaningful definition of the firm. This standard is a recommendation, not a requirement.

18 A is correct. The High-Yield Bond Composite's inclusion and exclusion rules are as follows: The composite will include qualifying portfolios at the beginning of the first full month under management and exclude accounts at the end of the last full month under management. Based on these rules, Accounts 1 and 3 will be included in the December 2022 composite return. See the table below for details.

Account	Open Date	Close Date	Include/Exclude?
1	18 March 2016	Still open	Include
2	25 July 2016	13 December 2022	Exclude, closed
3	15 September 2016	Still open	Include
4	5 December 2022	Still open	Exclude, not open for full month

B is incorrect. Account 2 was not under management for the entire month of December 2022 and, therefore, is not eligible for inclusion in the composite under the High-Yield Bond Composite's inclusion and exclusion rules.

C is incorrect. Account 4 opened on 5 December 2022 and, being not open for the first month under management, is not eligible for inclusion in the composite under the High-Yield Bond Composite's inclusion and exclusion rules.

19 A is correct. PIA must disclose all significant events that would help a prospective client interpret the GIPS report and that are still relevant. In this case, the departure of the lead portfolio manager is a significant event, and it is still relevant to interpreting the track record.

B is incorrect. The disclosure must be included for a minimum of one year and for as long as it is relevant to interpreting the track record. Although the lead portfolio manager departed over a year ago, this information is still relevant to understand the longer-term track record.

C is incorrect. Significant event disclosure is required, not recommended.

20 C is correct. To comply with the GIPS standards, the firm must be an investment firm, subsidiary, or division held out to clients or potential clients as a distinct business entity. The retail and the institutional divisions are held out together to the public as Radford Street Capital and, therefore, must be included in Radford Street Capital's firm definition.

A is incorrect. Radford Street Capital cannot be just the retail division, because the retail and institutional divisions are held out together to the public.

B is incorrect. Radford Street Capital cannot be just the institutional division, because the retail and institutional divisions are held out together to the public.

21 C is correct. If provided, a composite or pooled fund benchmark must reflect the investment mandate, objective, or strategy of the composite. The firm may determine that no appropriate benchmark exists and, if so, must disclose why no benchmark is presented.

A is incorrect. A measure of internal dispersion is not required if the composite contains five or fewer portfolios. The institutional composite contains only one portfolio and, therefore, is not required to present a measure of internal dispersion. However, the firm is required to disclose that the internal dispersion measure is not applicable.

B is incorrect. There is no requirement to present gross returns.

22 C is correct. The firm is required to present the percentage of composite assets at period end valued by subjective, unobservable inputs, if material.

A is incorrect. The three-year *ex post* standard deviation is not required, because there is only one year of performance for the institutional composite.

B is incorrect. The GIPS standards do not require the number of portfolios to be disclosed if the composite contains five or fewer portfolios at period end. The institutional composite has only one account for all periods. However, the firm is required to disclose that the composite contains five or fewer portfolios

23 C is correct. Radford Street Capital meets all portability requirements and, therefore, may (but is not required to) link the performance of the two firms: (1) All staff involved in managing the strategy at Delta One Capital moved to Radford Street Capital at its inception, (2) the decision-making process remains intact, (3) Radford Street Capital has the necessary records that document and support the Delta One Capital performance, and (4) there is no break in performance.

A is incorrect. Radford Street Capital is not required to link performance even if all portability requirements are met.

B is incorrect. Radford Street Capital may link performance if all portability requirements are met, and in this case, they are.

Glossary

Accounting Book of Record (ABOR) It is the official fund accounting record, produced by custodians or administrators. The data contained in the ABOR are used to value portfolios and to generate NAVs and NAV-based performance metrics.

Active share A measure, ranging from 0% to 100%, of how similar a portfolio is to its benchmark. The measure is based on the differences in a portfolio's holdings and weights relative to its benchmark's holdings and their weights. A manager who precisely replicates the benchmark will have an active share of zero; a manager with no holdings in common with the benchmark will have an active share of one.

Advisory-Only Assets Assets for which the firm provides investment recommendations but has no control over implementation of investment decisions and no trading authority.

Amortized price The historical cost (initially recognized cost) of an asset, adjusted for the allocation of a premium (amortization) or discount (accretion) until the asset's maturity.

Autocorrelation When regression errors are correlated across observations; see serial correlation.

Base currency See *domestic currency.*

Batting average A measure of investment performance consistency that reports (a) the percentage of investment decisions that result in a profit divided by the total number of investment decisions, or (b) the percentage of positive return periods relative to the benchmark or peers divided by the total number of return periods.

Benchmark Description Must include the key features of the benchmark or the name of the benchmark for a readily recognized index.

Benefit of hedging In the case of currency forward contracts, the condition where using the forward rate results in a higher return than the current spot rate.

Broad Distribution Pooled Fund A pooled fund that is regulated under a framework that would permit the general public to purchase or hold the pooled fund's shares and is not exclusively offered in one-on-one presentations.

Capture ratio A measure of the manager's gain or loss relative to the gain or loss of the benchmark.

Carried interest A performance-based fee that reflects a share of the profits receivable by the manager.

Carve-Out Defined in the GIPS Glossary as a portion of a portfolio that is by itself representative of a distinct investment strategy.

Committed Capital Defined in the GIPS Glossary as pledges of capital to an investment vehicle by investors (limited partners and the general partner) or the firm.

Composite Aggregation of one or more portfolios that a firm manages according to a similar investment mandate, objective, or strategy.

Composite Creation Date The date on which the firm first grouped one or more portfolios to form the composite.

Composite Definition Detailed criteria that determine the assignment of portfolios to composites.

Composite Description General information regarding the investment mandate, objective, or strategy of the composite.

Composite Inception Date The initial date of the composite's track record.

Composite System The set of processes, tools, and equipment used to maintain and manage the composites.

Confidence interval The expected range of a statistic's value.

Conventional bond See *plain vanilla bond.*

Cost of carry The net of the costs and benefits of holding, storing, or "carrying" an asset.

Cost of hedging In the case of currency forward contracts, the condition where using the forward rate results in a lower return than the current spot rate.

Covered interest rate parity Relationship which states that the forward rate will be a function of the spot rate and relative interest rates in the two countries.

CTD bond The bond which, based on the then-prevailing price, financing rates, and conversion factor, is the lowest cost to deliver upon expiry of a futures contract.

Currency overlay The case where a portfolio's currency exposures are managed separately from the management of the portfolio itself.

Currency spot return The percent change in an exchange rate over a specified time period.

Discretion The ability of a firm to implement its intended strategy.

Distinct Business Entity A unit, division, department, or office that is organizationally and functionally segregated from other units, divisions, departments, or offices and that retains discretion over the assets it manages and that should have autonomy over the investment decision-making process.

Domestic currency The currency an investor uses for consumption purposes (e.g., Canadian dollars are the domestic currency for a Canadian investor). Also called *base currency* or *home currency.*

Downside capture ratio A measure of capture when the benchmark return is negative in a given period; downside capture less (greater) than 100% generally suggests out (under) performance relative to the benchmark.

Due diligence Investigation and analysis in support of an investment action, decision, or recommendation.

Economic exposure The risk of loss from a position in an asset class.

Fair value The amount at which an investment could be exchanged in a current arm's length transaction between willing parties in which the parties each act knowledgeably and prudently. The valuation must be determined using the objective, observable, unadjusted quoted market price for an identical investment in an active market on the measurement date. Fair value must include accrued income.

Fee rebate In a short sale, the portion of the income earned on the invested collateral that is returned to the borrower of shares.

Fee Schedule Refers to the firm's current schedule of investment management fees or bundled fees appropriate to prospective clients or prospective investors.

Forward A non-standardized and non-exchange traded contract between two parties to buy or sell an asset at a specified future time at a price agreed upon today.

Forward currency contracts Contracts between two parties for the exchange of a specified amount of currency at a fixed exchange rate at a future date.

GIPS Compliance Notification Form The form that must be filed when the firm initially claims compliance with the GIPS standards and must be updated annually.

GIPS Recommendations Are optional but *should* be followed because they represent best practice in performance presentation.

GIPS Report A presentation for a composite or pooled fund that contains all the information required by the GIPS standards and may also include recommended information or supplemental information.

GIPS Requirements *Must* be followed in order for a firm to claim compliance.

Gross-of-Fees Return The return on investments reduced by any transaction costs.

Hedged return When using currency forward contracts, the return that reflects the foreign asset return in local currency terms and the forward discount or premium.

High-water mark the highest cumulative net asset value attained by the fund, net of fees.

Holdings-based style analysis A bottom-up style analysis that estimates the risk exposures from the actual securities held in the portfolio at a point in time.

Hurdle rate a minimum rate of return below which the fund does not charge an incentive fee.

Independent and identically distributed (IID) When the residuals from a given statistical analysis are independent and identically distributed, the data is said to be IID. Independence means that the data in any one period are not influenced by the data in any other period. If the sample statistics (e.g., mean and standard deviation) from a particular subperiod of the data series being evaluated is the same statistics drawn from another subperiod of the entire data series.

Internal Dispersion Internal dispersion of annual returns of individual portfolios within a composite can be measured in various ways, including but not limited to high/low, interquartile range, and the standard deviation of returns (equal or asset weighted).

Internal rate of return The rate of return based on the cash flows and the terminal value of the company. It takes into account the time value of money and reflects the private equity manager's control over the timing of cash inflows and outflows.

Investment Book of Record (IBOR) It is a set of fund data for trading and portfolio-management purposes.

Investment policy statement A written investment planning document that includes statements of a client's investment objectives and investment constraints.

J-curve The shape of the IRR curve over time. As the private equity fund calls capital early in the fund's life, the IRR dips below zero because fees and expenses erode capital before the manager has had an opportunity to realize returns. As the fund matures and the capital invested starts to create distributions, the IRR turns positive.

Key person risk The risk that results from over-reliance on an individual or individuals whose departure would negatively affect an investment manager.

Limited Distribution Pooled Fund Any pooled fund that is not a broad distribution pooled fund.

Long–short portfolio A portfolio that contains both long positions in assets expected to rise in value and short positions in assets expected to fall in value.

Loss ratio In private equity, the amount of invested capital that is held below cost.

Margin calls A request for the short seller to deposit additional funds to bring their balance up to the initial margin.

Market-neutral strategies Long/short strategies that match long and short risk exposures and are intended to eliminate market exposure.

Modified duration A measure of a bond's price sensitivity to interest rate movements.

Money-Weighted Returns The returns for a period that reflect the change in value and the timing and size of external cash flows.

Moneyness The relationship between the option exercise price and the underlying price.

Multiple of invested capital The current value of the underlying private equity portfolio companies, plus any distributions received, divided by the total invested capital.

Net-of-Fees Return The gross-of-fees return reduced by the investment management fees (including performance-based fees and carried interest).

Notional exposure See *notional market value*.

Notional market value The amount of an underlying security that would cause approximately the same change in value for a given change in the price of the underlying security as the change in the futures and associated cash position. Also called *notional exposure*.

Option delta The change in call option value relative to a change in the value of the underlying.

Overlay Strategy A strategy in which the management of a certain aspect of an investment strategy is carried out separately from the underlying portfolio.

Partially hedged A position in an asset that is not fully hedged.

Performance Examination The process by which an independent verifier conducts testing of a specific composite or pooled fund in accordance with the required performance examination procedures of the GIPS standards.

Plain vanilla bond An option-free bond that makes periodic, fixed coupon payments during the bond's life and a lump-sum payment of principal at maturity. Also called *conventional bond*.

Policy portfolio A conceptual portfolio allocated among asset classes or risk budgets in a manner the investor believes is most appropriate for his or her long-term risk and return objectives.

Pooled Fund A fund whose ownership interests may be held by more than one investor.

Portfolio An individually managed group of investments.

Prospective Client Any person or entity that has expressed interest in one of the firm's composite strategies and qualifies to invest in the composite.

Prospective Investor Any person or entity that has expressed interest in one of the firm's pooled funds and qualifies to invest in the pooled fund.

Public market equivalent The use of cash flow data to replicate the private equity GP's capital calls and distributions to allow comparisons of private equity IRRs with returns of publicly traded equity indexes.

Returns-based style analysis A top-down style analysis that involves estimating the sensitivities of a portfolio to security market indexes.

Risk premium An extra return expected by investors for bearing some specified risk.

Segments Groups of securities within a portfolio, e.g., countries, sectors, or industries.

Segregated Account A portfolio owned by a single client.

Serial correlation When regression errors are correlated across observations; see autocorrelation.

Short extension A portfolio consisting of a long position of 100 plus *x* percent and a short position of *x* percent.

Short sale The sale of borrowed securities with the intention to repurchase them later at a lower price and return them to the lender.

Short selling Asset positions designed to profit from negative views on the asset.

Significant Cash Flow The level at which the firm determines that one or more client-directed external cash flows may temporarily prevent the firm from implementing the composite strategy.

Spot curve The yield curve that shows the discount rates for various bond maturities that apply to bonds with a single cash flow.

Spot exchange rate The rate at which one currency can be exchanged for immediate delivery of another currency.

Stop-losses A trading order that sets a selling price below the current market price with a goal of protecting profits or preventing further losses.

Subscription Line of Credit A loan facility that is put in place to facilitate administration when the firm is calling for funds from investors.

Supplemental Information Any performance-related information included as part of a GIPS Report that supplements or enhances the requirements and/or recommendations of the GIPS standards.

Swap An instrument in which the counterparties agree to exchange a series of future cash flows.

Theoretical Performance Performance that is not derived from a portfolio or composite with actual assets invested in the strategy presented.

Time-Weighted Returns A method of calculating period-by-period returns that reflects the change in value and negates the effects of external cash flows.

Total Firm Assets The aggregate fair value of all assets (whether or not discretionary or fee-paying) for which a defined firm has investment management responsibility.

Unrealized performance The performance of underlying companies that are still managed by the private equity manager.

Upside capture ratio A measure of capture when the benchmark return is positive in a given period; upside capture greater (less) than 100% generally suggests out (under) performance relative to the benchmark.

Verification The process by which an independent verifier conducts testing of a firm on a firm-wide basis, in accordance with the required verification procedures of the GIPS standards.

Waterfall The allocation of distributions between the fund's investors and the GP.

Yield to maturity The discount rate that equates the present value of the bond's expected cash flows until maturity with the bond's price.

Made in United States
Orlando, FL
05 November 2026

90295296R10238